Strangers in the South Seas

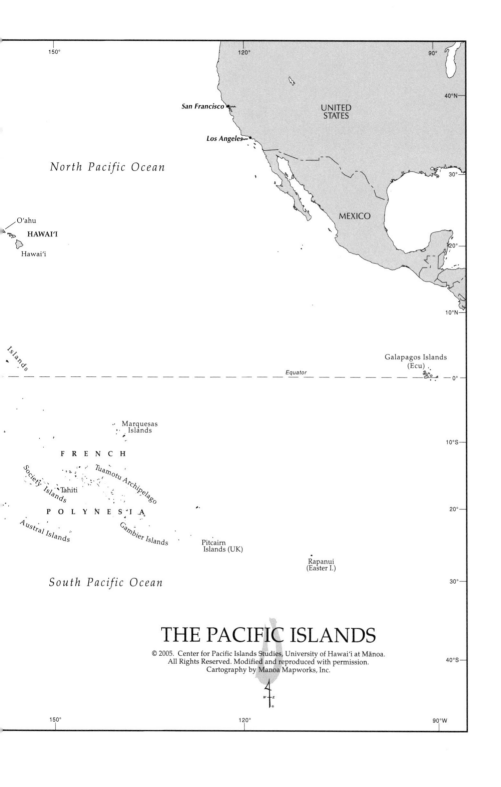

North Pacific Ocean

San Francisco

Los Angeles

UNITED STATES

MEXICO

O'ahu
HAWAI'I

Hawai'i

Galapagos Islands
(Ecu)

Islands

Equator

Marquesas
Islands

FRENCH

Tuamotu Archipelago

Society Islands

Tahiti

POLYNESIA

Austral Islands

Gambier Islands

Pitcairn
Islands (UK)

Rapanui
(Easter I.)

South Pacific Ocean

THE PACIFIC ISLANDS

CONTENTS

5. *"How Many Adams Must We Admit?"*
The Varieties of Man

6. THE ISLAND AS COLONY
From Backwater to "Ocean of the Future"

ACKNOWLEDGMENTS

First, last, and at all stages in between comes my family, who have had to put up once again with the apparently endless business of a book coming about. Thank you Angela, Sam, and Holly for your patience, love, and support; at least the books were better to look at and more interesting than last time.

Professors Dan Jacobson and Peter Pierce, of University College London and James Cook University, respectively, kept a tutelary watch on this project throughout, making countless suggestions and corrections to the materials I drafted. (I was a very young man when I first saw the two pictures of the missionary John Williams, described in Chapter 3, on the wall of Dan's office at UCL. Then they seemed to me graphically to embody his unsentimental sense of humor and his deeply felt sense of historical retribution. How strange that I should write about them now, so many years later!) My colleague Paul Turnbull also made many excellent suggestions, not all of which could be carried out. The readers at the University of Hawai'i Press were extraordinarily patient, positive, and constructive, and guided an amateur emigrant to Pacific shores with great tact and enthusiasm. One was kind enough to step outside the veil of anonymity, so a special thanks is due to Jane Samson of the University of Alberta. A few texts here—by Commerson, Cuvier, and Dumont d'Urville—have been translated from the French. Rae and Catherine Pierce came stoutly to my aid on those occasions, and when we all got stuck (especially with Commerson's diabolical syntax), my colleague Chris Mann baled us out. The library at James Cook University is wonderfully well served where the Pacific is concerned, and I am profoundly grateful to the librarians who so often dug up books as fragile and sometimes as smelly as could be. The (then) Faculty of Arts and Business at James Cook University found money in the early days for an exploratory trip to London; since then I have been the recipient of a University Special Studies Program leave of absence and a Teaching Relief Award, both of which gave me valuable time at important stages.

Publication of this book was made possible by the generosity of a number of institutions: the Foundation for Australian Literary Studies, the Australian Academy of the Humanities, the School of Hawaiian, Asian, and Pacific Studies at the University of Hawai'i, the Faculty of Arts, Education, and Social Science at James Cook University, and the School of Humanities within that Faculty. I am very grateful for their help.

A number of publishers, agents, libraries, and art galleries were kind enough to reduce or to waive permission fees for materials and images held in their trust, and so to reduce the author's financial exposure: Yale University Press (Pigafetta's *Magellan*), the Australian National Library (Cook's journal, 1769), the Bibliothèque Centrale of the Muséum National d'Histoire Naturelle, Paris (Commerson's "Postscript"), the British Library (Cook's journal, 1773), Victoria University Press (Dumont d'Urville's *New Zealanders*), the Council for World Mission (Puckey, Hassall, and Harris documents at the School of Oriental and African Studies, London), the State Library of New South Wales (the Missionaries' journal, Wilks' letter to Mrs. Cover, and Paula David's photographs of Samoa), the Sutro Library at the State Library of California (Haweis' letter to Joseph Banks), HarperCollins Pty Ltd. (Banks' journal), the Blubber Head Press, Hobart (Péron's Maria Island observations), the Library at the London School of Economics (Malinowski's tent and sketch map), John Murray Publishers (Grimble's *A Pattern of Islands*), Norman Mailer and the Wylie Agency *(The Naked and the Dead),* and the University of Queensland Press (Peter Medcalf and Nancy Phelan). Despite my best efforts, I could not find the copyright holders of two texts: the late Vern Haugland's *Letter from New Guinea* (1943) and the late Jonathan Griffin's translation of Gauguin's *Noa Noa* (1961, reprinted under license in 1985). The author and publisher would gladly hear from copyright claimants on those materials.

Jane Eckelman, at Manoa Mapworks, Honolulu, drew the map, then gallantly added fiddly territories at my insistence. The Captain Cook Backpackers Resort in Cairns, Far North Queensland, allowed me to photograph their concrete mascot for my cover. The reproductions staff at the National Library of Australia pictures, maps, and books departments produced the lion's share of the illustrations here: their standard of service is a model. Last but not least, Susan Stone undertook the copyediting task with huge professionalism and an eagle eye, Wendy Bolton handled the proofs, and Ann Ludeman was managing editor for the project. My thanks go to all these people for making the book look good and make sense.

The extent to which I have depended on other scholars will be evident to any reader, and I encourage him or her to consult the Works Cited section and the guides to further reading added to each chapter. But some writers have been at particular times of peculiar importance to the ideas I have tried to develop: Stephen Eisenman, Margaret Hodgen, Arthur O. Lovejoy, William Manchester,

Dean MacCannell, the sextet of Melbourne historians who wrote *Mission to the South Seas: The Voyage of the* Duff, *1796–1799* (Michael Cathcart, Tom Griffiths, Lee Watts, Vivian Anceschi, Greg Houghton, and David Goodman), Nigel Plomley, Neil Rennie, Bernard Smith, Frans Stafleu, William Stearn, Nancy Stepan, and George Stocking.

Finally, my profound thanks to the editorial board at the University of Hawai'i Press, who supported this project. I have been blessed with great commissioning editors throughout my career: primus inter pares, Pamela Kelley.

NOTE ON TEXTS

Many texts printed below come either directly or indirectly from manuscript sources; others from the sixteenth, seventeenth, and eighteenth centuries, when spelling, punctuation, syntax, and typesetting varied widely from modern norms. Generally speaking the texts are reproduced as they originally appeared; on a very few occasions—among the missionaries and in Captain Cook's journals, for example—I have silently corrected some spelling or supplied a letter passed over in the writer's haste. Sources for each text are given at the end of each chapter.

Almost every text below is an extract, or this book could never have been contemplated. Frequently, too, the reader will find cuts *within* extracts: these are marked by ellipsis within square brackets: [. . .]. Ellipses without square brackets are the authors' own, except in quotations in introductory material that I have written. Simple terms are glossed within the text in square brackets; longer glosses and explanations appear as footnotes. When necessary, I have occasionally added linking passages, in italics in square brackets, for narrative consistency.

*I*NTRODUCTION

Diaspora, Discovery, and Settlement

Exactly how long ago *Homo sapiens* entered northwestern Australia and the colossal island of New Guinea to its north we do not know. (The major constraint on knowledge here is the fact that radio-carbon dating is unreliable for objects older than about 40,000 years.) Suffice it to say that 40,000 years ago humanity had settled both Australia and coastal New Guinea, and had evolved cultures of great diversity in response to the diversity of environments it discovered. Then, 10,000 years ago, the Ice Age receded, water locked in glaciers escaped, and sea levels began to rise. The land bridge between northern Australia and New Guinea sank beneath the waves, and ocean-going trips between the Indonesian archipelago and both Australia and New Guinea began to lengthen. The Australians were left alone, as were the New Guineans; contact between them was limited to the islands now formed in the Torres Strait; and humanity in the region evolved along different trajectories as its experience dictated. The New Guinean population was in the process of adhering itself to either one or the other of two relatively fixed forms of life: agriculture in the interior highlands, fishing by the sea. The Australians were adapting to a more diverse habitat, from grasslands and deserts to eucalyptus woods and rainforests. All the Australians were settled—all knew their environment as intimately as any people on earth has ever done—but most of them moved, over distances long or short as need be, in search of resources. Settled agriculture was not practiced, simply because conditions made it relatively inefficient as a food source.

What happened next is so hard to establish that even the word "next" may be inappropriate. Two theories are currently available. The first has its intellectual origins in the work—sampled in Chapter 5—of late-eighteenth- and early-nineteenth-century explorers like Johann Reinhold Forster and Jules Sébastian César Dumont d'Urville. The second, which is essentially a revision of the first, is in the process of emerging as a result of modern archaeological and linguistic discoveries in the region.

New Guinea became more isolated as the Ice Age waned. But it appears— and this is theory number one—that around four thousand years ago people began arriving in northwestern New Guinea from Asia. The evidence for this is bound up less with archaeological remains than with the languages these people spoke: "Austronesian" languages, as distinct from the "Papuan" group of languages that continue to be spoken by the majority of mainland New Guineans. Papuan languages are overwhelmingly based in New Guinea (though some are found elsewhere); Austronesian languages are found in Malaysia, Indonesia, Vietnam, Cambodia, and Taiwan. They are also found throughout Polynesia, in the island communities of Melanesia, and in coastal communities of New Guinea itself. The explanation appears to be that certain peoples, ultimately originating in continental Asia, spread into the Asian archipelagos and from there through coastal New Guinea to find their way out to island Melanesia and then to Polynesia beyond. It is as if the bucket of humankind had tipped over once more and sent a further flood of individuals out among the original inhabitants. But this second flood was not flowing unaltered over a solid surface: the dispersal took hundreds of years, and it took place at all times through the coastal New Guinean people, involving a constant mingling with them, making new peoples as the dispersal took place. The nineteenth-century missionary-anthropologist Robert Codrington found an appropriate analogy for this process: "We may conceive of the peopling of Melanesia and the settlement of its languages," he wrote,

> as the filling with the rising tide of one of the island reefs. It is not a single simultaneous advance of the flowing tide upon an open beach, but it comes in gradually and circuitously by sinuous channels and unseen passages among the coral, filling up one pool while another neighbouring one is dry, apparently running out and ebbing here and there while generally rising, often catching the unwary by an unobserved approach, sometimes deceiving by the appearance of a fresh-water stream on its way to the sea, crossing, intermixing, running contrary ways, but flowing all the while and all one tide till the reef is covered and the lagoon is full. (Codrington 1885: 33)

The Austronesian speakers were accomplished sailors, as their origins in archipelagical Asia dictated. They were the inventors of the double-hulled oceangoing canoe, which aided their movement through island Melanesia and beyond. Another thing it seems they developed was pottery, and the spread of "Lapita ware" (named after the site in New Caledonia where it was first excavated) has been used by theory number one to chart what happened "next": the movement of the always-evolving Austronesian speakers out beyond the Papuan linguistic sphere. The first Lapita items appear to be about three thousand years old; 1,500 years later Lapita ware had traveled so far and so widely as essentially to lose its cultural distinctness as it was copied and traded. But during that period it helps trace the movement of the Austronesian-speaking New Guineans out to the Fijian, Tongan, and Samoan island groups where settlement paused.

By tracking the Austronesian group of languages back we can—the theory proposes—see a series of linguistic offshoots that accompanied the movement of populations: from China to the Philippines and Sulawesi; from Sulawesi to northern Maluku; and from Maluku to modern-day Irian Jaya (about four thousand years ago); from there along coastal New Guinea to the Bismarck Archipelago; thence to the Solomon Islands, Vanuatu, and New Caledonia (about 3,200 years ago); and from Vanuatu to Fiji, Tonga, and Samoa (about three thousand years ago). From the Bismarck islands in the north to New Caledonia in the south, the interisland distances are often short and never truly long—for navigators as talented as the Austronesian speakers at any rate. But the jump between Vanuatu and Fiji is 700 miles. So it was that while the Austronesian New Guineans were great sailors, the amount of interchange that could take place between the Vanuatu region and the Fijian one was limited, whereas the amount of interchange that went on within those two regions was large. Inevitably the two areas grew apart, and Fiji, Tonga, and Samoa began to develop in a degree of isolation. Five hundred years after arriving in Fiji, these people had begun to evolve a culture sufficiently distinct from their western Austronesian cousins to require a different name. This culture was the antique form of Polynesia.

Fiji, Samoa, and Tonga are among the largest of the Pacific island groups, and the Polynesians took time to establish themselves among them. But some eight hundred years after their arrival and two hundred years BC, the Polynesians began the series of voyages that took them over stretches of open sea previously unexperienced by humankind: 1,700 miles to Tahiti (by AD 800), and 2,400 miles to the Marquesas (by AD 500). They also began to filter back toward Melanesia, and in so doing they made settlements anomalous to Western eyes, like Bellona in the Solomon Islands or Tikopia to the north of Vanuatu. Nor did the Polynesians rest on these tiny islands (gigantic though they may be compared to the minuscule atolls of Kiribati and the Marshall Islands of Micronesia, which they settled between AD 1 and 500) but by AD 600 had completed the 2,600 mile voyage north to Hawai'i, and by AD 1000 the 2,800 mile one south to New Zealand.

Theory number two proposes that there is no need to look for a new people coming into New Guinea from the archipelagos of Asia—and perhaps less evidence for such a development than was at first thought. First, the linguistic evidence is less clear-cut than it has seemed. Second, the makers of Lapita ware might have had their origins not in Asia but in western Melanesia itself: probably in the Bismarck Archipelago (where the oldest such pottery has been found), from whence their manufactures spread far out across the islands to the south and east. That is to say, the movement of pottery may simply reflect the movement of pottery by trade and exchange, rather than the movement of some particular ethnic group. The theories concur that the Polynesians had their origin in the Fiji-Tonga-Samoa triangle and that eastern Polynesia and Micronesia have been settled very recently. It is the "previous step" that remains subject to dispute.

The story of indigenous humanity in the Pacific is a long one; the story of Western humanity there is correspondingly short. (It takes up more room here only because this is a book about Western attitudes to the region as opposed to indigenous ones.) In 1473 Portuguese explorers reached the equator by traveling down the West African coast; in 1492 Christopher Columbus (an Italian working for the Spanish court) discovered America. As a result of such developments, the Portuguese and the Spaniards entered into the Treaty of Tordesillas of 1494, whereby a line was drawn down the middle of the Atlantic Ocean: the "West Indies" (America, north and south) would belong to Spain, the "East Indies" (whatever they should prove to be) would belong to Portugal. No one knew where these two hemispheres would meet, but the treaty did set further developments in train. In 1497 Vasco da Gama (Portugal) rounded the Cape of Good Hope and reached India; in 1511 Antonió de Abrea (Portugal) sighted New Guinea; and in 1513 Vasco Núñez de Balboa (Spain) crossed the Isthmus of Panama, sighted the "Mar del Sud"— the South Sea—and claimed it for Spain.

So at the beginning of the sixteenth century the Pacific lay between the jaws of two great Catholic imperial enterprises bent on gold, spices, and heathen souls. Yet there were good reasons why those jaws failed to snap shut immediately. First and foremost, the two powers concerned had plenty to be getting on with in South America, India, and the Spice Islands of Indonesia. But the Pacific was also protected by natural barriers that made further penetration difficult. In the east, the South American coastline stretched fifty degrees south below the equator. Further north, the continent was very broad. So the Spaniards faced either a long voyage round Cape Horn or the establishment of a settlement on the western shores of South America. The Portuguese in Indonesia were much closer to the insular Pacific, but they, too, faced barriers. Travel south of the equator came up against the remote and inhospitable shores of Australia and New Guinea, and the only keyhole providing entry to the ocean beyond was the treacherous Torres Strait. Travel eastward on or just north of the equator meant confronting prevailing winds and currents blowing and flowing full in the face of any exploratory voyage.

So the Portuguese and the Spaniards paused before capitalizing on their discoveries. But in time the inevitable happened. In 1520 Ferdinand Magellan (a Portuguese captain of a Spanish fleet of five vessels) entered the Pacific through the strait that bears his name, above Tierra del Fuego. Then he was swept up the western coast of South America and crossed the breadth of the Pacific Ocean, initially a little to the south and then a little to the north of the equator, seeing land only once before making landfall at Guam, 1,200 miles

FIGURE 1. "Isles des larrons" [Island of Thieves: Guam] from Antonio Pigafetta, *Navigation et Descouvrement de la Inde Superieure et Isles de Malucque . . .* (1525). The Beinecke Rare Book and Manuscript Library.

east of the Philippines (see Figure 1). Magellan himself was killed by Islanders in the Philippines, and in September 1522, three years after setting out from Spain, one ship limped home, the vast majority of the crew having died of starvation on the endless trip across the great South Sea: the first circumnavigation of the globe. Magellan had sailed over 12,000 miles, from Cape Horn to Guam—the sixteenth-century equivalent of flying to the moon—*and seen only one coral atoll along the way.* The Pacific had begun to reveal its first and most overwhelming mystery: its gigantic size and desolation.

Small wonder the Spaniards waited some time before making a similar attempt; but in the second half of the sixteenth century they would make three voyages, each with the aim of founding colonies somewhere in the void Magellan had discovered. In 1567 Álvaro de Mendaña de Neira sailed due west from the Peruvian coast until he reached the Solomon Islands—which he named as such because he believed he had found the islands from which the biblical king Solomon reputedly drew his gold. After a six-month stay Mendaña recrossed the ocean to the north until he returned to Peru. He was given permission for another voyage in 1595. This time he found the Marquesas Islands in easternmost Polynesia. (It gives us some idea of the state of European navigation at this time, where longitudinal travel (west to east) as opposed to latitudinal (north to south) was concerned, that Mendaña thought he had rediscovered the Solomon Islands, lying in fact about 4,000 miles to the east.) From the Marquesas he sailed west again and started a colony on the Santa Cruz Islands (between the Solomon Islands and Vanuatu), where he died before the pilot of the expedition, Pedro Fernández de Quirós, took the remaining ship on to Manila, which had been colonized by the Spanish in 1569.

Now it was Quirós' turn, and in 1605 he set out from Peru once more. Because he sailed south of the lines followed by Magellan and Mendaña, he encountered islands in significant numbers and eventually landed at what we call Vanuatu, which he called La Australia de Espiritu Santo (The South Land of the Holy Ghost). The colonists soon gave up here, too, and sailed home; but two of Quirós' ships, under Luís Vaéz de Torres, carried on west from Espiritu Santo and, finding themselves trapped beneath the southern coast of New Guinea, made a painstaking passage through the strait that bears Torres' name before finding their way to Manila. No European would pass that strait again until James Cook in 1770.

After Torres the Spaniards made no more colonial attempts in the central Pacific and confined themselves to South America, the Philippines, and the galleon trade that plied between them: South American silver for Chinese goods. But the Spanish voyages illustrate a vital fact about the early European exploration of the Pacific. From the poles winds travel toward the equator and are diverted in a westerly direction by the earth's rotation; the currents follow a similar pattern. A ship rounding Cape Horn will be swept up along the South American coast before finding westerly sailing directly along the equator—as Magellan did. Conversely, to cross the Pacific from west to east, you must head north from the Philippines or south from Indonesia. Nobody at this stage went south from Indonesia; European shipping, therefore, normally went west along the equator and east to the north of Hawai'i. On both routes there is practically no land at all. It is no suprise, therefore, that Spanish discoveries in the Pacific were close to the equator. Only as explorers began to go south from Indonesia would Australasia begin to be revealed, and only as navigators rounding the Horn sailed below the equator would the island groups of Tahiti, Fiji, Tonga, Samoa, and the rest be discovered by Europeans.

If the sixteenth century had been the Spanish century in the Pacific, then the seventeenth would belong to the Dutch. In 1606, 1616, and 1627, respectively, Willem Jansz, Dirk Hartog, and Pieter Nuyts had close encounters with the northern, western, and southern coasts of Australia. In 1642 Abel Tasman sailed way down to the south from Java before heading east and hitting the southern coast of Tasmania. He went on to find New Zealand, Tonga, Fiji, and the New Britain Archipelago off New Guinea before returning to Batavia (modern-day Jakarta): yet Tasman landed hardly anywhere, presumably because he could see no opportunities for trade or settlement. Finally, in 1721 Jacob Roggeveen came around the Horn and, keeping well to the south of the equator, encountered Easter Island (sighted at Easter 1722), Bora Bora (near Tahiti), and Samoa. But the Dutch East India Company that stimulated exploration also eventually stifled it. Like the Portuguese they had displaced in the East Indies, the Dutch were more concerned with holding on to the Spice Islands, where ready profits were to be made, than with finding new worlds in the south.

The British and French between them undertook in the eighteenth century the roles previously carried out by the Iberians and the Dutch, though a series of wars kept their attention nearer home until 1763. The Spaniards had been interested in founding colonies and converting the heathen but were half-hearted explorers nonetheless; the Dutch were positively reluctant to undertake such voyages. The British and the French were ready, willing, and financially able to muster expedition after expedition, with the stated aim of rolling back the frontiers of European ignorance—and the unstated one of empire-building.

The English captains Samuel Wallis and Philip Carteret circled the Horn together in 1767, only to split up thereafter. Their discoveries were small but out of all proportion to their physical size. Carteret found tiny Pitcairn Island, and the discovery was duly recorded in a compendium of English Pacific voyages that Captain Bligh took aboard the *Bounty* in 1787. When the famous mutiny took place two years later and the chief mutineer, Fletcher Christian, was looking for a bolthole in the ocean, he found the record from Carteret's log and promptly set sail. But Carteret had misrecorded the location of Pitcairn by three degrees of longitude, and the compendium had compounded the error by five degrees of latitude, so Christian's escape hatch was itself an invisible one. It was 1790 when the mutineers landed on Pitcairn

Island and 1808 before they were found, by accident, by an American whaler. Carteret did well enough, then, in terms of South Sea legend; but Wallis did even better. On 23 June 1767 he found Tahiti: the pearl, navel, and epicenter of the oceanic myth and the focus for fifty years thereafter of European imaginative constructions of the Pacific. Within ten months the Frenchman Louis Antoine de Bougainville had also paid a call. But Bougainville's voyage was important in another respect, too. Sailing due west from Vanuatu after his visit to Tahiti, he ran up against the Great Barrier Reef, off Australia's east coast, and was convinced that a major landmass must lie behind it.

By the time Wallis and Bougainville got back to Europe, the island groups and landmasses of the Pacific were beginning to emerge from obscurity. The really important areas of European ignorance were Antarctica, the east coast of Australia, New Zealand, Hawai'i, and New Caledonia. These matters would be settled by James Cook's three voyages of 1768–1779. In his first voyage Cook rounded the Horn to Tahiti, where he was under orders to observe the transit of Venus across the sun (an experiment that would help establish the distance of the sun from the earth by measuring how long it took for Venus to make its eclipse); but from there he entered upon the more secret phase of his expedition, discovering the eastern coast of New Zealand in October 1769 and completing the six-month task of circumnavigating and charting the coastline of both North and South Island. Leaving New Zealand, he headed west and found the great south land at last, turning into Botany Bay on 29 April 1770, before sailing up the entire east coast, passing through the Torres Strait and turning for home—having stopped off at what he named Possession Island to claim the continent in the name of His Britannic Majesty George III. (This was not the arbitrary process it might appear: Cook had strict definitional instructions about those lands he might claim and those he must leave to their indigenous inhabitants. Because Australian Aborigines seemed not to farm, practice religion, build permanent homes, or gather in social groups larger than the family, they seemed to meet those requirements, and his legal (or legalistic) view of the continent subsisted until an Australian High Court decision of the mid-1990s; because New Zealanders did not meet the requirements, the British entered into the Treaty of Waitangi with the Maoris in 1840.)

Cook's second trip was hardly less revelatory. He visited New Zealand again in March 1773, was in Tahiti in August, traveled west to Tonga in October, and turned to New Zealand once more before heading south in the polar summer to visit Antarctica, whose waters no one had entered before. He sailed south until ice blocked his path. Coming up below Cape Horn in Feburary 1774, he then visited Easter Island, the Marquesas (not seen since Mendaña in 1595), and Tahiti once more, made a thorough circumnavigation of the New Hebrides, discovered New Caledonia in September 1774, Norfolk Island in October, and visited New Zealand again before an easterly passage round Cape Horn to home.

It is hardly surprising that Cook was fending off ill health by the time he set out for the third time in July 1776. It had been Terra Australis the first time and Antarctica the second; on the third occasion it would be the legendary Northwest Passage that would absorb his massive sense of purpose. Sailing north from Tahiti, he discovered Hawai'i in January 1778. Pressing far to the north, he sailed into the Bering Sea before ice made progress impossible and he turned south again, this time finding Hawai'i's eastern islands in November 1778. What happened next is subject to historical dispute. It appears that his slow clockwise circumnavigation of Hawai'i, combined with the fact that his masts and sails bore a resemblance to certain seasonal votive symbols, may have convinced the Islanders that Cook was a god, Lono, making his annual progress. Or it may be that no one thought of him as a god but only as a great visitor. In any event, his departure coincided with the end of one religious season and the beginning of another. Eight days later he returned with a broken mast, and this time there was no welcome. A series of violent incidents followed, and when on 14 February Cook attempted to take a local chief hostage to ensure the return of a stolen boat, he was surrounded by an angry crowd on the beach. Cook fired a pistol and killed a man; then he was stabbed and clubbed to death. His body was taken by the Islanders and divided among the chiefs; in due course some bones were returned to the English commanders. Then the ships sailed away.

On his first voyage Cook had secret instructions to watch for opportunities favorable to the British government. Little came of this aspect of the expedition until the loss of the American War of Independence in 1783 brought the practice of exporting British criminals to Maryland to a halt. It was then that the government was reminded of Botany Bay by Cook's "scientific gentleman" and fellow traveler Joseph Banks. So it was that the first real colony in the South Seas was a penal one—appropriately enough, given Australia's reputation as a nightmarish antipodean other world. In January 1788 the First Fleet arrived in Australia, carrying 750 convicts and 250 officers, marines, and sailors. They swapped Botany Bay for Port Jackson and made their landfall alongside the point where Sydney's Opera House now stands.

It was the beginning of a new era. Now the white man was no longer passing through as a bird of passage, explorer, or buccaneer: he was here to stay. Now he had his own settlement in a land he had decided was empty and thus belonged to him outright. From this settlement others would follow. Until now, although Europeans had discovered many foreign shores, the actual extent of contact was highly restricted. Even Tahiti had no settled European population in 1788: when missionaries came to stay in 1797, they found only a few beachcombers. After Sydney, the second biggest European settlement in the Pacific in 1788 was the unknown one of Pitcairn—also populated by criminals, nine in number. The overwhelming majority of Islanders had never seen the white man, and those who had might have seen a ship pass, call for water, or briefly land a boat and fire a gun: no more. But the founding of Sydney was an event of a different order.

The Island Imagined

The discussion so far constitutes a necessary introduction but an outsider's perspective: quintessentially, some might argue, a Westerner's perspective, implying a particular view of history. Those periods of time in which nothing is believed to have happened shrink almost to nothing; those periods of time packed with "events" (the period since Magellan entered the Pacific, say) enlarge in corresponding fashion. The summary offered also displays the Western fascination with "discovery," whether by indigenous peoples or by Europeans. Not only is the emphasis on what happened "next"; it is also only on what happened next at the pioneering fringe. Indeed, it is assumed that nothing happened in the lands safely gathered in behind the advance parties of humanity.

Where the human story in the Pacific is concerned, distance makes these patterns of historical attention highly persuasive—to Westerners. That is one of the things this anthology seeks to record: not only the European story of the Pacific and its peoples but the story *of* the story. Why did Europeans come to look for certain things in the Pacific and therefore come to see those things even if they were not there? Why should it be that two thousand years or so of Polynesian culture should absorb more of the Europeans' imaginative attention than forty thousand years of Melanesian culture? How, indeed, did those adjectives ever get coined? Conventionally, the Pacific peoples are parceled out into three regions: Polynesia, Melanesia, and Micronesia. But these words do not describe the same thing. Polynesia (Greek: *polys,* "many"; *nisos,* "island") and Micronesia (Greek: *mikros,* "little") are linguistic and cultural entities with genuine structural integrity because their settlement has been so recent. Melanesia, by contrast, is useful only as a geographic category since the peoples of that region are more culturally diverse than any other human group. In fact, the word has its roots in early-nineteenth-century European ignorance (Greek: *melas,* "black"). It is not the contrast between Polynesia and Melanesia that modern authorities reject, therefore, but the suggestion implicit in such terms that the latter has a culture as uniform as the former. "Polynesian," in short, is a legitimate adjective to use in describing a culture; "Melanesian" is not.

Long before the British started their penal colony on the shores of Sydney Harbour, Europeans had entertained notions of seas, islands, and settlements at the opposite end of the earth. "Consider the Island," a recent historian of the region writes: "the *idea* of the island" (Scarr, 1). Unless we follow his advice, the actions and attitudes of those Westerners who came to the Pacific are only half explicable. The idea of insularity, for example, is itself a European fixation projected onto the Pacific: that in that ocean there were an almost infinite number of tiny communities, utterly isolated from each other, whose shores never saw a stranger, and so on. What Westerners brought with them governed what they saw, and the ideas they brought with them were deeply entrenched. Myths of the "Islands of the Blest," the Hesperides, the islands where King Solomon found or kept his gold, the Garden of Eden as an island, Atlantis, sunken kingdoms, and ideal states are old enough and common enough to be mocked by Lucian in *The True History* of AD 150:

> Instead of wheat, their eares beare them loaves of bread ready baked, like unto mushrummes: about the citie are three hundred threescore and five wells of water, and as many of honey, and five hundred of sweet ointment, for they are lesse than the other: they have seven rivers of milke and eight of wine: they keepe their feast without the citie, in a field called *Elysium,* which is a most pleasant medow invironed with woods of all sorts, so thicke that they serve for a shade to all that are invited, who sit upon beds of flowres, and are waited upon, and have every thing brought unto them by the windes, unlesse it be to have the wine filled . . . (Lucian, 29)

Again and again the island has figured in the European mind as a place where human potential would emerge unhampered by the conventional life, where a passage over the sea would involve leaving behind items of cultural, moral, social, psychological, or historical baggage and allow a new experiment in living. On islands, too, the strange and unfamiliar—be it within the voyager's mind or outside it, animate or inanimate, human or natural— would and could be confronted.

"Those of us involved in Pacific studies," writes another historian, "have been too impressed with the apparent novelty of the eighteenth-century Pacific dream island. But that Tahitian mirage was at the end of a very long imaginative tradition, one that long predated the Enlightenment, and even the Renaissance. Indeed it goes back to the very beginnings of Western civilization" (Howe 2000: 14). Nor was the dream island the only such mirage Westerners saw; there were nightmare islands, too. Imaginative visions of these kinds were connected to similar ideas about ideally good or ideally bad places: utopias or dystopias. ("Utopia" is a term invented by the sixteenth-century English humanist Thomas More and derived from Greek *topos,* "place," and the prefix *eu,* "good," but also the prefix *ou,* "not" or "none." So it is a good place that does not exist.) "Basically, utopia is a place where one is *not* at the moment; therefore its qualities are naturally the opposite of current, unpleasant conditions," J. W. Johnson advises. "Northern climates tend to cause physical discomfort; mammals need warmth, and icy winds result in more than mere bodily discomfort. Food supplies grow scarce and require great exertion to obtain. Hunger and disease become further burdens. Death intervenes and grief accompanies it. This was the reality of cold climates, as prehistoric European man . . . knew it." Johnson goes on: "In contrast, the south was the Land of the Sun, the kingdom of the immortal gods." "It is strikingly apparent," therefore, "that from Homer on, writers most often turned toward the south to seek the sweet golden climes where the traveller's journey was done" (Johnson, 43).

Among classical writers like Lucian, therefore, the utopian island in the south is commonly a dream of physical sufficiency or an agricultural land of plenty (whereas Renaissance writers like Thomas More stress social innovations like egalitarianism and primitive communism). In 20 BC the Latin poet Horace, for example, wrote of leaving a homeland wracked by civil war for an ideal island away to the south:

> The girdling sea calls us; lets seek out strait
> Those fields bleste fields and islands fortunate,
> Where the earth untilld each year her fruit doth give,
> And vineyard never prund doth ever live;
> And the nere-failing olives branch doth sprout,
> And the ripe fig her native tree sets out.
> From hollow oaks drops honey, from high hills
> The nimble spring with ratling feet distills
> There goats uncalld unto the milk pailes come,
> And the faire flock their full swoln bag brings home . . .   (HORACE, 134)

One element of physical sufficiency remained to be supplied on such destinations: free love; and that was delivered in bulk in the epic celebration of Vasco da Gama's discoveries, *The Lusiads,* published by Luis de Camoëns in 1572. Here Venus provides the homesick and exhausted Portuguese mariners with "an *Isle* divine": a hyperfeminine landscape copiously stocked with willing sea nymphs:

> The *second* Argonauts now disembarke
> From the tall *ships* into an Eden green.
> *There,* in this *Isle,* this *Forest,* or this *Parke,*
> The fair *Nymphs* hide, with purpose to be seen.
> Some touch the grave *Theorba* in shades darke,
> *Some* the sweet *Lute,* and gentle *Violeen:*
> *Others* with golden *Cross-bows* make a show
> To *hunt* the *Bruits,* but do not *hunt* them though.
>
> Thus counsell'd them *their Mistress,* and her *Arts:*
> That so, the more their own desires they Master,
> And seem a *flying prey* to their *sweethearts,*
> It might make *them* to follow on the faster.
> *Some* (who are *Conscious* that their *skins* have *darts,*
> And put their trust in *naked Alabaster*)
> Bathe in *Diaphane* streams, their *Roabs* by-thrown,
> And ask no *Ornament* but what's their own.   (CAMOËNS, 290)

This is a dream from which Westerners will perhaps never wake up.

"There is a conviction, subliminal in most of us," writes William Peck, "that a few primal instincts determine the course of events on an island and that by immersing ourselves in simple island ways we can avoid the complications, the stresses and agonies of an over-wrought civilization and thus benevolently renew our lives. By this interpretation an island is a refuge and a beatitude." "But the reverse is true," Peck continues. "An island is a miniature universe, complete unto itself. It is a compressed universe with all the complexities of our disordered world: its treacheries, its conflicting ambitions, its dishonesties, its follies, as well as its kindnesses and pleasures, all brought unrelentlingly into one's daily life" (Peck, 1). The idea of the island and the idea of the utopia or dystopia have often overlapped. "The first common feature of utopias is natural isolation. Utopias are by nature, if not always nowhere, at least far away, separated. They have a particular affinity with islands" (Garagnon, 93). The number of utopian or dystopian fictions that are set on islands is correspondingly large—some well-known examples in English being *Utopia* itself (1516), *The Tempest* (1611), *Robinson Crusoe* (1719), *Gulliver's Travels* (1726), *The Swiss Family Robinson* (1812), *The Coral Island* (1857), *Erewhon* (1872), *The Island of Dr. Moreau* (1896), and *Lord of the Flies* (1954).

A pattern emerges from stories such as these whereby storm, shipwreck, and landfall lead to eventual transformation:

> During the storm the sailors do not know where their ship is going and lose all sense of direction; during the shipwreck they nearly drown and lose consciousness; and then they are thrown into a new world. Storm and shipwreck can therefore be described as the equivalent of a temporary nowhere, followed by the arrival to an elsewhere; temporary disorder followed by the emergence of a perfect order; a temporary death followed by the rebirth to a new life; a kind of no man's land where a rite of purification is performed (the travellers are "washed" ashore), before the higher truths can be revealed. (Garagnon, 94)

More's Utopia was once a peninsula, turned into an island by its first king, Utopos. It is shaped "like to the new moon" with arms of land enclosing a lagoon behind rocks that are "very jeopardous and dangerous." In social terms it goes beyond egalitarianism toward homogeneity: "As for their cities, whoso knoweth one of them knoweth them all." In personal terms it goes beyond a lack of private property to a lack of privacy: "there is nothing within the houses that is private, or any man's own"; "all the void time that is between the hours of work, sleep, and meat, that they be suffered to bestow, every man as he liketh best himself; not to the intent that they should misspend this time in riot or slothfulness, but being then licensed from the labour of their own occupations, to bestow the time well and thriftily upon some other science, as shall please them" (More, 65, 69, 71, 75).

Like More's Utopia some of these "elsewheres" or "miniature universes" can produce feelings of ambivalence; others can be highly remote, bleak, or forbidding. During his circumnavigation of Australia between 1801 and 1803, Matthew Flinders entered shallow Nepean Bay on Kangaroo Island, off present-day South Australia—a massive roost for pelicans:

> Flocks of old birds were sitting upon the beaches of the lagoon, and it appeared that the islands were their breeding places; not only so, but from the number of skeletons and bones there scattered, it should seem that they had

for ages been selected for the closing scene of their existence. Certainly none more likely to be free from disturbance of every kind could have been chosen, than these islets in a hidden lagoon of an uninhabited island, situate upon an unknown coast near the antipodes of Europe; nor can any thing be more consonant to the feelings, if pelicans have any, than quickly to resign their breath, whilst surrounded by their progeny, and in the same spot where they first drew it. (Flinders, 1:183)

What Flinders saw to be sentimentally appropriate in isolation others might see as a nightmare of centrifugalism. Rufus Dawes, the convict hero of Marcus Clarke's Australian classic *For the Term of his Natural Life* (1874), is at one point in the novel left in chains on Grummet Rock, off Sarah Island, off Tasmania, off Australia, at the very end of the world. (This pattern in dystopian literature is inverted in utopian fiction, which often emphasizes centripetalism: perhaps having, as in Denis Veiras' 1677 South Seas utopia *L'Histoire des Séverambes,* a jet of water in the middle of a basin, in the middle of a yard, in the middle of a palace, in the middle of a capital, in the middle of an island, in the middle of a lake, in the middle of a continent, and so on. A similar pattern is to be found in Plato's Atlantis utopia, the *Critias,* from the fourth century BC.) Being at the other end of the world can seem like an opportunity, a freedom, and a release, or like a punishment, a rejection, and an excommunication.

"In imagining the Pacific Europeans imagined from a reality that they had to come to terms with, not a fancy or a fantasy that might eventually disappear" (Smith, 1992: ix); and this is true even though Westerners' idea of the Pacific was for a long time extremely vague. (The "South Seas" have at times encompassed two oceans [the Pacific and the south Atlantic] and sometimes a third [the Indian], stretching from the Brazilian coast of South America to the Malay Archipelago and the shores of Western Australia, and from Hawai'i, twenty degrees above the equator, to the tip of the South Island of New Zealand, forty-seven degrees below it.) The islands were real places, composed of real rock and soil, flora and fauna, men and women. Even Westerners grow tired of fantasies if such fantasies never encounter reality, and the overwhelming majority of the texts collected here are concerned with that encounter. One of the most important such encounters was the scientific one. Whatever dreams were entertained by the men who sailed with James Cook, the ships under his command charted coastlines, established the whereabouts of terra firma in a waste of water, collected botanical and zoological samples by the thousand, drew pictures of many thousands more, and observed stars and planets from previously inaccessible platforms. Into the late-eighteenth- and early-nineteenth-century intellectual perplexity concerning the origins and variety of species, the South Seas flung a cornucopia of bewildering variety: animals and plants that seemed to come from a different world, and people of apparently limitless diversity. Protoevolutionary and protoanthropological disciplines cut their teeth on this explosion of data. It was a "South Sea" set of islands—the Galapagos—that gave Charles Darwin a crucial set of stimuli toward a theory that would explain biological diversity in the context of time. Thus the South Seas have contributed not only imaginative stories to Westerners but also hard facts.

The first influential attempt to impose reality on the idea of the southern hemisphere was that of the second-century Greek geographer Ptolemy, who believed that a large landmass must exist in the earth's south to balance the north, or else the planet would roll over like a top-heavy ball. Accordingly, Ptolemy is the origin of the myth of the Antipodes, or the Great South Land (Terra Australis). "From the Tropick to 50° North latitude," as an eighteenth-century exploration lobbyist put it, "the proportion of land and water is nearly equal; but in South latitude, the land, hitherto known, is not ⅛ of the space supposed to be water. This is a strong presumption, that there are in the southern hemisphere, hitherto totally undiscovered, valuable and extensive countries, in that climate best adapted for the conveniency of man, and where, in the northern hemisphere, we find the best peopled countries" (Dalrymple, 91). It followed that "the space unknown in the Pacifick Ocean, from the Tropick to 50° S. must be nearly all land" (Dalrymple, 94). In fact hardly any of it is.

The antipodes (Greek: *anti,* opposite; *pous,* foot) were inevitably opposite to the European world. In Richard Brome's comedy *The Antipodes* (1623) they are simply a place where women dominate men, servants rule households, lawyers refuse to charge a fee, and old men go to school, leaving children in parliament. In Amerigo Vespucci's *Mundus Novus* (1503) they presented much more of a challenge, particularly in theological terms:

> I found myself in the region of the Antipodes. . . . This land is very agreeable, full of tall trees which never lose their leaves and give off the sweetest odours. . . . Often I believed myself to be in Paradise. . . . This land is populated by people who are entirely nude, both men and women. . . . They have no law, nor any religion, they live according to nature and without any knowledge of the immortality of the soul. They have no private property, everything is owned communally; they have no borders between provinces and countries, they have no king and are subject to no one. (quoted in Eisler, 16)

Vespucci's remarks—about windy and treeless Patagonia, at the tip of South America—are in marked contrast to the English buccaneer William Dampier's reports from the coast of western Australia, published in 1697. "The Land," he wrote, "is of a dry sandy Soil, destitute of Water . . . yet producing divers sorts of Trees; but the woods are not thick, nor the Trees very big. . . . There was pretty long Grass growing under the Trees; but it was very thin. We saw no Trees that bore Fruit or Berries." If the environment is disappointing, compare Dampier's inhabitants with Vespucci's:

> The Inhabitants of this Country are the miserablest People in the World. The *Hodmadods* [Hottentots] of *Monomatapa* [a mythic kingdom of central Africa], though a nasty People, yet for Wealth are Gentlemen to these; who

have no Houses, and skin Garments, Sheep, Poultry, and Fruits of the Earth, Ostrich Eggs, &c. as the *Hodmadods* have: and setting aside their Humane Shape, they differ but little from Brutes. They are tall, strait-bodied, and thin, with small long Limbs. They have great Heads, round Foreheads, and great Brows. Their Eyelids are always half closed, to keep the Flies out of their Eyes. (Dampier, 312)

So the idea of the antipodes greatly exaggerated the utopian/dystopian pattern. The result was "a bipolar vision of Terra Australis prior to the great Pacific voyages of the late eighteenth century: on the one hand, that of a generally barren region inhabited by brute savages; on the other, a more beautiful, plentiful land with a far more attractive and hospitable population" (Eisler, 2).

This bipolar vision is much the most influential intellectual inheritance Westerners brought to the Pacific. A later and more sophisticated form of the antipodean myth was the belief frequently voiced by European travelers of the eighteenth and nineteenth centuries that to travel in space was to travel in time. Vespucci and Dampier had different views of the indigenes they found, but both felt they had traveled *back*: either to the Garden of Eden or to humanity's primitive early condition. Antipodeanism exaggerated such sensations: it made Vespucci's forest dwellers greatly more fortunate than Europeans who no longer lived "according to nature" and made Dampier's Australians greatly less fortunate than "civilized" people. Had humankind fallen away from what Vespucci saw in Patagonia, or had it risen up from what Dampier saw in New Holland? For centuries the "bipolar vision" forced peoples apart: the European from the inhabitant of the South Seas but also certain Pacific peoples from certain others (the Polynesians from the Melanesians, for example).

"The Pacific did not provide an answer to the problems that faced Western man":

Rather, it raised questions about himself that he had never asked before. Travelers went to the Pacific with varying assumptions and values, and returned with new questions which demanded new answers. Some found a golden age in which the laws of nature pointed to the proper rules of life. Some found a brutal land in which man had to improve upon nature to be human. Sometimes the same areas and the same peoples evoked two contrary sentiments. (Washburn, 334)

Entertaining "two contrary sentiments" about the same people is one thing. To expand a bipolar vision to bear on compatriots and foreigners alike is quite another. One of the first people to do it consistently was the Frenchman Michel de Montaigne in his essay "On the Cannibals" (1580). Montaigne was not discussing what we would call the Pacific at all, but the indigenous inhabitants of a colony on the Atlantic coast of South America—"Antarctic France," as he called it. But so vague was the European sense of "the South Seas" at that time that (like Vespucci's) his comments can find a place here. "Now . . . I find," Montaigne wrote, that there is nothing savage or barbarous about those peoples, but that every man calls barbarous anything he is not accustomed to; it is indeed the case that we have no other criterion of truth or right-reason than the example and form of the opinions and customs of our own country. There we always find the perfect religion, the perfect polity, the most developed and perfect way of doing anything! Those "savages" are only wild in the sense that we call fruits wild when they are produced by Nature in her ordinary course: whereas it is fruit which we have artificially perverted and misled from the common order which we ought to call savage. It is in the first kind that we find their true, vigorous, living, most natural and most useful properties and virtues, which we have bastardized in the other kind by merely adapting them to our corrupt tastes. (Montaigne, 231–232)

"So we can indeed call those folk barbarians by the rules of reason," Montaigne concluded, "but not in comparison with ourselves, who surpass them in every kind of barbarism" (Montaigne, 236). Antipodeanism can be confronted only by an act of responsible cultural relativism of this kind (that inverts the binary opposition) or by the historical process that transforms intellectual superstition into a discipline like anthropology (so dissolving the opposition). And that process of confrontation is not over yet. "At the very heart of all Pacific history, whether imperial or postcolonial," as Kerry Howe argues, "lies a morality tale. It is about the meeting of two perceived entities—the West and Pacific peoples. . . . Pacific history is fundamentally about the idea of Western civilization, its perceived rise and fall, its fears and triumphs, and its creation of a Pacific Other onto which are projected and tested its various priorities and expectations" (Howe 2000: 85).

This anthology is not a revisionary one. It does not attempt to reduce the imaginative distortions Western people have visited upon the Pacific region but to record those imaginative fabulations so that we can more easily recognize them for what they are and more easily understand the intellectual and imaginative origins of European and American interventions in the insular Pacific. In such a project "imaginative," "literary" sources are as useful as "factual" or "historical" ones, as I hope readers will discover for themselves.

Contact

So it was that when the Pacific islands were discovered by Europeans, an abundance of ideas existed by means of which to comprehend them. No stranger in the South Seas could ever see only what was in front of him: he (it mostly was a "he" at this stage) also saw what it was he had inherited from his cultural tradition. Some blinded themselves to anything else. (There are some important exceptions to this rule, needless to say. Robert Louis Stevenson's Pacific writings and Paul Gauguin's Pacific paintings remain vital treatments of Pacific colonialism because they frequently go against the grain of Western habits of thought and representation.) So it was, too, that Pacific islands, which proved themselves negligible in resource terms for Westerners, had on a number of occasions an intellectual influence out of all proportion to their physical size. When Tahiti was discovered in the 1760s, for example, the Europeans encountered for the first and only time in their experience a group of people whom they were forced to concede—albeit only for a matter of years—might be living a life better than their own. Some American settlers had admired the American Indians they saw, and the myth of the Noble Savage is older than the discovery of Tahiti. But Tahiti seemed to prove that this was no myth or that the myth had been proved true. Nothing Europeans had seen in Asia, Africa, and America had a remotely similar intellectual effect.

The noble savage soon found its opposite incarnation: the ignoble savage. What unites those ideas, and is a core principle of primitivism in any guise, is the Western belief (mentioned at the beginning of the previous section) that for certain peoples of the earth progress had come to a stop or never started. This was not true. When humanity made its way to Australia and New Guinea so many thousands of years ago, time did not stand still. As Austronesian-speaking New Guineans (ultimately of either local or Asian origin) spread down the Melanesian archipelagos to the doorway of what would become Polynesia, time did not stop behind them; nor did it for the Polynesians themselves as they fanned out across the ocean. Visitors came and went; trading patterns evolved and mutated; natural resources blossomed and withered; populations grew and left their mark on the environment; technological changes were introduced, refined, and finally superseded; political structures grew up; infractions, wars, and truces followed in turn: in short a historical sequence was laid down, just as detailed and just as momentous for those caught up in it as anything Europeans had experienced. Yet when the Europeans arrived, they often jumped to the conclusion either that these were peoples who had no history or society, or that the history and society they possessed could be explained only in European terms. Thus Australia was decided by James Cook to meet the definitional requirements of *terra nullius* (an "empty land"), whereas Tahiti was the most civilized nation of the South Seas not only because the people's physical appearance coincided with European taste, but precisely because it seemed to *be* a nation, apparently governed by dynastic kings and queens, possessing both a priestly class and an aristocratic one, and having a history of civil war and an architectural record of religious buildings to match. Pacific peoples were sometimes regarded in the eighteenth and nineteenth centuries as living beyond the touch of time; just as often Westerners strove to design histories for them, out of the Bible or from secular sociohistoric theories of their own devising, like "degeneration" or "evolution."

What would happen, then, when the white man's great canoes burst the bubble? Nothing less than catastrophe, many white men predicted. The childlike natives, absolutely defenseless in the face of the Europeans' guns, diseases, religion, and alcohol, would reach the end of history in another sense:

they would be annihilated even if no one meant them any harm. This is the essence of another great myth about the people of the South Seas, nearly as widespread as the Noble Savage one it complements: "Fatal Impact." Here the story goes that a timeless yet fragile way of life, wholly unprepared by past experience for any form of change more rapid than the passage of the seasons, would literally disappear in the face of the brutal and technologically superior European. As Alan Moorehead put it in the book that gave the idea its name: "All these visitors—perhaps intruders is a better word—were going to make their separate contributions to the transformation of the Tahitians, whether by firearms, disease or alcohol, or by imposing an alien code of laws and morals that had nothing to do with the slow, natural rhythm of life on the island as it had been lived up till then" (Moorehead, 3).

Historians nowadays tend to be critical of the attitude represented by Moorehead. "To see Islanders as passive, helpless, and always persecuted and suffering at the hands of Europeans . . . denies the Islanders their humanity" (Howe 1984: 351–352). It is becoming clearer now that the Islanders did not live a life of primeval innocence, that their cultures did not simply crumble away, and that they accepted Western ideology to an important extent on their own terms. In short, Pacific Islanders were and are human beings like the rest of us, met the challenge the white man presented, and in doing so mitigated and altered it. The peoples of the Pacific had had a history before white intervention and had always had one. Thus the admittedly dramatic and momentous arrival of the European was not a wholly unprecedented and apocalyptic catastrophe; it was an event different in degree, rather than in kind, to their experience up to that time.

Still, even as we must see the justice of this argument, we should not run to the opposite extreme from Alan Moorehead—especially as doing so could be interpreted as a revisionary move in the other sense, amounting to an exculpatory palliation of European activity in the Pacific. The Islanders' ability to absorb and divert the impact of European interference was not the same everywhere. From the imperialist period on, in particular, Islander peoples found it progressively more difficult to cope with cultural and political forces beyond their control. They never stopped trying; they have not stopped now. But "an indigenous cultural logic" (Thomas 1989: 114) has become increasingly difficult to sustain since the middle of the nineteenth century.

Moreover, there have been occasions when the impact of strangers has been fatal indeed. One hundred fifty years after first settlement in Australia, the Aboriginal population had fallen by 90 percent (Denoon, 244). According to Donald Denoon, the population of Vanuatu was halved in the nineteth century (Denoon, 114); according to Malama Meleisa and Penelope Schoeffel, the population of Yap fell from between 30,000 and 50,000 to 7,500 in approximately the same period (Denoon, 127). The Marquesas experienced 90 percent depopulation in the hundred years after 1798; the Tahitian population fell by three-quarters between 1767, when Tahiti was first discovered, and 1797, when missionaries arrived (Scarr, 144, 114). Three thousand people lived on Kosrae in Micronesia in the 1820s but only three hundred or so sixty years later (Denoon, 244). In 1837 every male Islander on Ngatik, near Pohnpei, was killed by the crew of a Sydney ship seeking tortoiseshell (Scarr, 139). "Aneityum, the southernmost of the New Hebrides . . . had about 4000 people in 1848, collapsing by two-thirds in a generation, then to 680 in 1895 and 186 in 1940" (Denoon, 244). The indigenous population of Hawai'i fell from 50,000 in 1872 to 35,000 twenty years later (Scarr, 135). Measles arrived in Fiji in 1875, and 40,000 from a population of 150,000 succumbed (Denoon, 245). Easter Island experienced a population crisis before strangers arrived, caused by the locals deforesting the land. But that crisis was intensifed by the introduction of foreign diseases, and the remnants of the population were carried away to Peru holus-bolus in a slave raid of 1862 (Scarr, 173). The Chamorro people of Guam, in the Mariana Islands, met a similar holocaust at the hands of the Spanish, who reduced their numbers from 50,000 to 5,000 between 1676 and 1695 (Howe 1984: 77). On tiny Banaba in the Gilbert Islands (Kiribati) in August 1945, Stewart Firth recounts, the invading Japanese gathered the population together, told them the war was over, and shot the entire population of one hundred, bar one (Denoon, 299). These are only the disasters we know about.

Nor is a body count all there is to fatal impact. European technology, morality, foods, and firearms also had far-reaching effects on Islanders' work patterns, diets, and social organizations. In the nineteenth century tobacco rapidly overtook trade goods, guns, and alcohol as the major currency of the Pacific, for the simple reason that it is far more addictive than those other mediums of exchange. "The whole population of Pohnpei were addicted smokers by the 1840s" (Denoon, 158), and what was true of them was true of many other island communities. The indigenous Hawaiians suffered appallingly in terms not only of population loss but of alienation from their land, their customs, and (ultimately) their language: a pattern repeated in Australia and New Zealand. According to Jocelyn Linnekin, "Christianity and capitalism almost succeeded in reducing Islanders in the eastern Pacific to caricatures of the colonizers" (Denoon, 430)—which was essentially Alan Moorehead's point in the first place. This process was resisted where possible and always subject to negotiation, but its destructive force was often very great.

The significance of this argument about fatal impact is greater than any conceivable resolution of it because the discussion suggests that there are European ideas, on the one hand, and the pressure those ideas come under by contact with Islanders, on the other. As the age of eighteenth-century exploration reached its end, contact between Pacific Islanders and European navigators was under way, and contact would thereafter become a fact of life for all concerned: a different matter from disputes in far-off Europe about utopias and antipodes.

The difference contact can make to Western thinking is illustrated by William Dampier's description of the indigenous inhabitants of Western

Australia quoted earlier: "The Inhabitants of this Country are the miserablest People in the World. . . . Setting aside their Humane Shape, they differ but little from Brutes." So the Aborigines appeared in Dampier's best-selling book of 1697, *A New Voyage round the World;* but that is not how they appeared in the original entry in his ship's journal: "They are people of good stature but very thin and leane I judge for want of foode[;] they are black yett I believe their haires would be long if it was comed out, but for want of combs it is matted up like negroes haire" (quoted in Williams and Frost, 124). The journal account is balanced by contrast with the published one: the Aborigines are people of good stature but lean; and they are lean from lack of food, not deformity. They are black, but their hair is "like negroes haire" only for want of combing. The movement from Dampier's journal to his book suggests the power of the "bipolar vision," which emphasizes the contrast between Europeans and Antipodeans. But it also suggests that bipolarity is culturally conditioned: it asserts itself at home but is less confident abroad. Reading back, from the published account to the journal, we find the antipodean vision losing focus and the rhetoric giving way to an objective impression; reading forward, from the journal to *A New Voyage round the World,* we find bipolarity coming to the fore and the complexities of contact giving way to racism.

The power of the "them-and-us" bipolar vision is such that Western writers rarely deviate from it. Islanders appear as travesties of themselves by virtue either of their winsome childishness or their barbaric degradation; the possibility of their being normal moral agents "like us" was normally the last thing admitted or even speculated about. So we have to look very carefully to see Pacific people actually behaving *as* people rather than being forced into preconceived roles and preconceived positions. The event most bitterly fought over by historians in this regard is the labor trade that brought Melanesians to work in sugar plantations in Fiji and Queensland, north Australia. Nineteenth-century missionaries called this trade "blackbirding," and it may be that by doing so they sought to bring into disrepute a mutually beneficial practice in which sugar farmers got labor and Melanesian Islanders got money and a chance to see the world. Here is a case in point: if you find it hard to accept that such a trade was a positive development, what are the reasons for your skepticism? Surely that power corrupts, that white traders were unlikely to have put industrial best practice before the chance of making a profit, and that the Islanders—ignorant of the value of money, the distances concerned, and the lengths of time at issue—were unlikely fully to understand the nature of the contracts they were entering into. This is a "fatal impact" point of view insofar as it involves a pair of stereotypes: the unscrupulous trader and the ignorant Islander. It could be argued that such a view depends more on modern guilt by association with colonialism than on real knowledge and that it represents colonial influence as monolithically consistent and prepotent, and Islanders as universally weak and passive.

But the side of the coin that stresses Islander initiative has problems, too. The very facts we most need to know—the attitudes of Western and

Islander actors on the scene—are the ones most deeply in dispute. "While plantation life in Queensland and Fiji might appear harsh by our standards, with its long hours and hard physical labour, and while the incidence of ill health and mortality may seem high, the Islanders themselves appeared relatively unconcerned about these matters" (Howe 1984: 339). To what moral position exactly does an appeal like this—"might *appear* harsh"; "may *seem* high"—take us? With whose eyes is the historian asking us to see these events? Moreover, whereas Islanders' willingness to become involved in labor schemes is an important factor in our evaluation of those schemes, it can hardly be the deciding one. Fully conscious moral agents do many things we cannot approve of. Thus the assertion of indigenous agency in the face of "fatal impact" can tilt the balance too far the other way.

Readers might be asking themselves whether we are bound to choose "between only two [Islander] archetypes: either 'happy campers' who manipulated the foreign guests until they moved on, or helpless prey for brutal aliens and germs" (Chappell, 316). The argument about contact presents a pair of interpretive alternatives vital to this anthology and our response to its contents: what Bronwen Douglas calls an anticolonialist position (stressing foreign impact) and a postcolonialist one (stressing indigenous agency). "From the venerable anticolonial perspective which represents the colonised as powerless victims of irresistible structural forces," she writes,

> arguments in favour of indigenous agency seem naïvely utopian. . . . A postcolonial rejoinder would decry this classic position as ethnocentric, essentialist, hierarchical and teleological, pointing out that hindsight is the luxury . . . of those who think they know the outcome, including historians, but that it was unavailable to actors, who had only culturally and strategically conceived experience to go on. Outcomes, anyway, like all discursive constructs, are always contested and unstable.

Not if you're dead, perhaps. But Douglas goes on:

> On the other hand, arguments in favour of indigenous agency can be insidious when the concept is appropriated by reactionaries to deflect the shame of colonialism ["blackbirding," for example] by invoking the responsibility of the colonised for their own oppression. This same motivation is sometimes imputed to postcolonialist advocates of the concept of agency by anticolonial sceptics. A further postcolonialist riposte would insist that postcolonial positions do not discount the always humiliating, sometimes tragic fact of colonialism, or the immorality of its drive for domination, but seek *as well* to contest the *a priori* assumption that colonialism always operated and signified locally in the ways its proponents intended. (Douglas, 186–187)

We cannot resolve the argument between anti- and postcolonialists here, but we can acknowledge that writers like Douglas are trying to achieve a way of looking at contact that makes room for the complexities involved: "social actions," as she calls them, "observed in particular situations and in terms of actors as subjects, enacting culturally conceived roles and manipulating ritual, political and ideological elements for personal and group advantage" (Douglas, 72). In such situations the Islander may confound our expectations by "appropriating" the Westerner's plan of action, and the Westerner may confound us by failing to play his or her role according to the script. By breaking the identification of victimhood with passivity and the identification of colonialism with some uniformly operative system, historians may be able to break the double bind of Western historical perceptions.

This intellectual project also has difficulties to overcome, however. First, as Douglas herself says, "my interest is the existential one of what people did and what it meant, rather than the teleology of causes or wider functional relationships" (Douglas, 124). But causes and relationships of this kind surely help constitute the "particular situations" in which the actors engage, and such causes and relationships in turn are illuminated by what people did. If that is not so, then the expression "what it meant" has little meaning. Second, Douglas has to proceed by what she calls "textual archaeology" or "against-the-grain critique and exploitation of colonial texts" (Douglas, 120, 159). The "history," after all, is in the hands of the colonial powers, whereas the colonized were generally illiterate at the time of contact and arguably "contaminated" by Western education thereafter. Indigenous oral history aside, therefore, Douglas and historians like her have only two sources where contact is concerned, both basically in Western hands: anthropology (which seeks to reconstruct the "particular situation" as Islanders might have seen it) and the accounts produced by Westerners themselves.

The first of these problems—the "existential situation" versus the "bigger picture"—would be a serious one if Douglas took herself at her own word and restricted her attention to existential situations alone (which no historian has ever done). The second—the "Westernization" of the Pacific record—is less a problem than an opportunity, and a crucial one for this anthology. Indigenous histories of contact are rare, Douglas points out, but they do exist:

> Together with ethnographies, they provide vital clues for identifying and systematising ethnohistorical inscriptions in contemporary colonial texts—the inadvertent, partial, shadowy traces of local agency, relationships and settings. Such textual traces are keys to exploring the preliterate worlds and colonial engagements with which they were contemporaneous: colonial tropes and classifications at once "invented" *and were partly shaped by* particular indigenous actions, desires and contexts which, filtered through screens of colonial prejudices, fantasies and phobias, dialectically helped constitute the very images in which they were themselves constituted historically. (Douglas, 162)

This is a vital statement, for generally speaking the only indication we are likely to get of local agency from "contemporary colonial texts" (everything, that is, from Magellan onward) is precisely that which Douglas describes:

something won against the grain, something noted inadvertently, something "shadowy." It follows that the tools of literary criticism are as useful in such an enterprise as those of history and anthropology: "the idea of the island" (including the island's inhabitants) is part of the textual archaeology we must uncover.

In thinking broadly about Euro-American attitudes to the other cultures and peoples the West has encountered, we might come to feel that such peoples were always ingested, assimilated, or incorporated in some way, as circumstances permitted. In America, North and South, this process was carried on by the horse, the cutlass, and the gun, with catastrophic effects. Many people died at the hands of Westerners in the Pacific, too; but the process of ingestion has been more peaceable and prolonged in this case. And it has mostly been an ideological and intellectual process, which permits a degree of negotiation and exchange rather than the mere exercise of brute force. This anthology attempts to show how Western attitudes to the Pacific have changed in the five hundred years since Magellan entered the Mar del Sud. It is important that the contents suggest the importance of local dramas to the big picture: "colonial tropes and classifications at once 'invented' *and were partly shaped by* particular indigenous actions, desires and contexts" on particular occasions, as Bronwen Douglas suggests.

Among the earliest stories of which we have a written record is an ancient Egyptian one called "The Shipwrecked Sailor," dating from nineteen centuries before the birth of Christ. In it the hero lands on a deserted island and meets an "indigenous" snake, thirty cubits long, who surprises him by saying: "What has brought thee, what has brought thee, little one, what has brought thee? If thou sayest not speedily what has brought thee to this isle, I will make thee know thyself; as a flame thou shalt vanish, if thou tellest me not something I have not heard, or which I knew not, before thee" (Petrie, 84). The snake goes on to make the fisherman's fortune: it is a contact narrative. As we shall see in Chapter 1, Antonio Pigafetta's account of the Magellan circumnavigation contains another contact narrative, mostly involving ethnocentric arrogance. But it also contains abject superstition ("several of our sick men had begged us, if we killed man or woman, to bring them their entrails. For immediately they would be healed") and a kind of reluctant, almost wistful recognition of a common humanity ("And we saw some of those women weeping and tearing their hair, and I believe it was for love of those whom we had killed"). Many other writings excerpted here can be subjected to "textual archaeology" in the same way, to reveal unexpected consequences of contact.

FURTHER READING

There are two excellent encyclopedias of the Pacific: Richard Nile and Christian Clerk's *Cultural Atlas of Australia, New Zealand and the South Pacific* (New York: Facts on

File, 1996); and Brij Lal and Kate Fortune, eds., *The Pacific Islands: An Encyclopedia* (Honolulu: University of Hawai'i Press, 2000). Colin McEvedy's *Penguin Historical Atlas of the Pacific* (London: Penguin, 1998) packs a great deal of information into a small space and involves the entire Pacific rim.

Further detail is provided by six modern histories: Kerry Howe, *Where the Waves Fall: A New South Sea Islands History from First Settlement to Colonial Rule* (Honolulu: University of Hawai'i Press, 1984), supplemented by Kerry Howe, Robert C. Kiste, and Brij Lal, eds., *Tides of History: The Pacific Islands in the Twentieth Century* (Honolulu: University of Hawai'i Press, 1992); I. C. Campbell, *A History of the Pacific Islands* (Berkeley: University of California Press, 1990); Deryck Scarr, *The History of the Pacific Islands: Kingdoms of the Reefs* (London: Macmillan, 1990); Donald Denoon et al., eds., *The Cambridge History of the Pacific Islanders* (Cambridge: Cambridge University Press, 1997); and Steven Roger Fischer, *A History of the Pacific Islands* (London: Palgrave, 2002).

The issue of prehistoric settlement of the Pacific is contextualized in Brian M. Fagan, *People of the Earth: An Introduction to World Prehistory,* 10th edn. (Upper Saddle River: Prentice-Hall, 2001). The theory of movement through New Guinea by an ethnic group out of Asia is summarized in the histories listed above but also by O. H. K. Spate in *The Pacific since Magellan*, volume 3: *Paradise Found and Lost* (Canberra: Australian National University Press, 1988), chapter 1, and by Patrick V. Kirch in Alan Howard and Robert Borofsky, eds., *Developments in Polynesian Ethnology* (Honolulu: University of Hawai'i Press, 1989). See also Peter Bellwood, *Man's Conquest of the Pacific* (New York: Oxford University Press, 1979), and *The Polynesians: Prehistory of an Island People* (London: Thames and Hudson, 1987). Alternative arguments are mounted by John Terrell, in *Prehistory in the Pacific Islands: A Study of Variation in Language, Customs, and Human Biology* (Cambridge: Cambridge University Press, 1986), and a neutral eye is cast by Philip Houghton, *People of the Great Ocean: Aspects of Human Biology in the Pacific* (Cambridge: Cambridge University Press, 1996).

For Western attitudes to other peoples encountered since the classical era, see Mary B. Campbell, *The Witness and the Other World: Exotic European Travel Writing, 400–1600* (Ithaca: Cornell University Press, 1988); David Hadfield, ed., *Amazons, Savages, and Machiavels: Travel and Colonial Writing in English, 1550–1630. An Anthology* (Oxford: Oxford University Press, 2001); and Stuart B. Schwartz, ed., *Implicit Understandings: Observing, Reporting, and Reflecting on the Encounters between Europeans and Other Peoples in the Early Modern Era* (Cambridge: Cambridge University Press, 1994).

The literature on utopias is huge, but see John Ferguson, *Utopias of the Classical World* (London: Thames and Hudson, 1975); David Fausett, *Writing the New World: Imaginary Voyages and Utopias of the Great Southern Land* (Syracuse: Syracuse University Press, 1993); Gregory Claes, ed., *Utopias of the British Enlightenment* (Cambridge: Cambridge University Press, 1994); and (particularly good) Helen Wallis et al., *Australia and the European Imagination* (Canberra: Humanities Research Centre, 1982).

Many books deal with the European exploration of the Pacific. See George H. T. Kimble, *Geography in the Middle Ages* (New York: Russell and Russell, 1968); Geoffrey Badger, *The Explorers of the Pacific* (Sydney: Kangaroo Press, 1988), which makes an excellent introduction; J. C. Beaglehole, *The Exploration of the Pacific* (Stanford: Stanford University Press, 1966); John Dunmore, *French Voyagers in the Pacific,* 2 vols. (Oxford: Oxford University Press, 1965); Philip Edwards, *The Story of the Voyage: Sea*

Narratives in Eighteenth-Century England (Cambridge: Cambridge University Press, 1998); Miriam Estensen, *Discovery: The Quest for the Great South Land* (London: Palgrave, 1999); Herman R. Friis, ed., *The Pacific Basin: A History of its Geographical Exploration* (New York: American Geographical Society, 1967); Andrew Sharp, *The Discovery of Australia* (Oxford: Oxford University Press, 1963); O. H. K. Spate's monumental *The Pacific since Magellan*, 3 vols. (Canberra: Australian National University Press, 1979–1988); and Glyndwr Williams and Alan Frost, eds., *Terra Australis to Australia* (Melbourne: Oxford University Press, 1988). Three valuable works of reference are John Dunmore, *Who's Who of Pacific Navigation* (Honolulu: University of Hawai'i Press, 1991); Peter Kemp, *Oxford Companion to Ships and the Sea* (Oxford: Oxford University Press, 1988); and Raymond John Howgego, *Encyclopedia of Exploration to 1800* (Potts Point, NSW: Hordern House, 2003).

Intellectual and imaginative responses to the Pacific are discussed in Bernard Smith's *European Vision and the South Pacific*, 2nd edn. (New Haven: Yale University Press, 1985); Neil Rennie's *Far-Fetched Facts: The Literature of Travel and the Idea of the South Seas* (Oxford: Oxford University Press, 1995); Kerry Howe's *Nature, Culture, and History: The "Knowing" of Oceania* (Honolulu: University of Hawai'i Press, 2000); and Jonathan Lamb's *Preserving the Self in the South Seas, 1680–1840* (Chicago: University of Chicago Press, 2001). On "the idea of the island" see the stimulating set of essays edited by Rod Edmond and Vanessa Smith, *Islands in History and Representation* (New York: Routledge, 2003).

For contemporary approaches to Pacific historiography, see two essays in the first volume of the *Journal of Pacific History* (1966): J. W. Davidson's "Problems of Pacific History" (which turned historians' attention to "island-centered" history, as opposed to seeing the region as a theater for Western interests), and Greg Dening's "Ethnohistory in Polynesia: The Value of Ethnohistorical Evidence" (which inaugurated the convergence of historical and anthropological perspectives on the Pacific, represented by Marshall Sahlins, *Islands of History* [Chicago: University of Chicago Press, 1985]). A group of historians' reflections chart developments from that date: H. E. Maude, "Pacific History—Past, Present, and Future," *Journal of Pacific History* 6 (1971); Kerry R. Howe, "Pacific Island History in the 1980s: New Directions or Monograph Myopia?" *Pacific Studies* 3:1 (Fall 1979); and the essays collected in Brij Lal, ed., *Pacific Islands History: Journeys and Transformations* (Canberra: Journal of Pacific History, 1992), and Brij Lal and Peter Hempenstall, eds., *Pacific Lives, Pacific Places: Bursting Boundaries in Pacific History* (Canberra: Journal of Pacific History, 2001). Doug Munro has edited a special issue of the *Journal of Pacific Studies* 20 (1996): *Reflections on Pacific Historiography*. Finally, see the essays collected in Aletta Biersack, ed., *Clio in Oceania: Toward a Historical Anthropology* (Washington, D.C.: Smithsonian Institution Press, 1991); Alex Calder, Jonathan Lamb, and Bridget Orr, eds., *Voyages and Beaches: Pacific Encounters, 1769–1840* (Honolulu: University of Hawai'i Press, 1999); and Robert Borofsky, ed., *Remembrance of Pacific Pasts: An Invitation to Remake History* (Honolulu: University of Hawai'i Press, 2000).

The discussion of Pacific contact is now very lively. Apart from works cited above, compare W. H. Pearson, "The Reception of European Voyagers on Polynesian Islands 1568–1797," *Journal de la Société des Océanistes* 26 (1970), with I. C. Campbell, "European-Polynesian Encounters: A Critique of the Pearson Thesis," *Journal of Pacific History* 29:2 (Dec. 1994); and see Jonathan Lamb, Vanessa Smith, and Nicholas Thomas, eds., *Exploration and Exchange: A South Seas Anthology, 1680–1900* (Chicago: University of Chicago Press, 2000); Klaus Neumann, " 'In Order to Win

Their Friendship': Renegotiating First Contact," *Contemporary Pacific* 6:1 (Spring 1994); Edward L. Schieffelin and Robert Crittenden, *Like People You See in a Dream: First Contact in Six Papuan Societies* (Stanford: Stanford University Press, 1991); and two items by Nicholas Thomas: "Partial Texts: Representation, Colonialism and Agency in Pacific History," *Journal of Pacific History* 25:2 (Dec. 1990), and *Entangled Objects: Exchange, Material Culture, and Colonialism in the Pacific* (Cambridge, MA: Harvard University Press, 1991). On "blackbirding," see Peter Corris, *Passage, Port and Plantation: A History of Solomon Islands Labour Migration, 1870–1914* (Melbourne: Melbourne University Press, 1973); and Kerry R. Howe, "The Fate of the 'Savage' in Pacific Historiography," *New Zealand Journal of History* 11:2 (Oct. 1977).

1

THE ISLAND AS ELDORADO AND THE SOUTH SEA BUBBLE

In 1883 Walter Coote suggested that the South Seas had become an object of Western fascination on three occasions in particular. The first "was doubtless when the intrepid Spanish navigators returned home after the discovery of the Solomon Islands, and the second when that extraordinary phenomenon, the South Sea Bubble, was exciting the imagination of all classes of the community" (Coote, viii). The third such occasion, Coote believed, was that of Australia's request that Britain annex New Guinea and thus establish a protective ring of colonies around the island continent: the issue Coote was himself addressing.

Few nowadays would see things as Coote did in 1883. The Australian request for annexation was a minor episode indeed in Britain's late-nineteenth-century colonial history, and though the Spanish navigators were intrepid, their voyages and discoveries were kept secret by the Spanish bureaucracy for decades and sometimes hundreds of years, so the discovery of the Solomons could hardly be called a matter of public note. Moreover, Coote passes over eras like the 1770s, when—as we shall see in the next chapter—French and British explorers began decisively and systematically to reveal the South Seas to European eyes and to electrify European intellectual circles in the process.

Still, the Spanish navigators and the financial catastrophe known as the South Sea Bubble demand consideration because they shed light on European expectations in an era—between the Magellan circumnavigation of 1520 and the time of Cook and Bougainville in the 1770s—when the Pacific was almost completely misconceived: a blank zone on the world's maps, but a teeming one in Westerners' minds. "It is necessary, of course," writes a modern geographer, "to define what we mean by the Pacific Ocean. Today there can be no doubt that we mean the physical reality of the Pacific lands, waters, and peoples whose description and measurement . . . have now been accurately charted. But so long as the element of the unknown, the unexplored, and the uninvestigated remained, so long did imagination, ignorance, prejudice, and uncertainty influence the decision" (Washburn, 321).

The Spanish explorers' activities involved real discovery and real loss of life; the English stock exchange scandal involved nothing actually happening in the Pacific at all (that is what made it scandalous). The Spaniards were intent on a repetition of their monumental American adventure, the British on much less exalted varieties of speculation. Yet both produced real disaster and real humiliation, and both had their origins in the misty shape that the Pacific was before the middle of the eighteenth century.

Between 1689 and 1748 Britain was at war with France for twenty-nine years; between 1756 and 1763 it was at war with France again; the same struggle was taken up between 1793 and 1815, when nearly 130 years of conflict was ended with the defeat of Napoleon at the battle of Waterloo. Britain won in the end, despite its smaller physical resources, not because of "the roast beef of old England" (as contemporary cartoonists often claimed) but for two reasons of far greater practical significance: the employment of a good system of continental alliances and an effective system of state credit and taxation. This system allowed Britain to throw more resources than it actually had into the struggle with France. In 1689 Britain spent 1.2 million pounds on the navy, for example; in 1812 it spent 20 million pounds. Its loans and subsidies to foreign states in the period from 1783 to 1814 alone amounted to 46 million pounds (Gregory and Stevenson, 199–204). To allow the state to make use of credit required a complex range of financial instruments and institutions that kept money fluid yet secure so that loans could be given with confidence and the government could offer bonds beyond its nominal capacity to repay, repaying only some of the debts maturing at any given moment and extending others, without plunging the entire system into crisis. A government bureaucracy, a central bank, a stock exchange, and an insurance industry were the most visible elements in such an array, but the groundwork for them had been laid some time earlier.

Two developments in late-seventeenth-century Britain helped produce this financial transformation: a reliable system of land tenure and survey made mortgages less risky and easier to come by (at a lower rate of interest), encouraging long-term credit and investment; and the regularization of the joint-stock company as an ongoing form of commercial structure allowed easier disinvestment in the form of shares, so more people *did* invest, instead of leaving their money under the bed. By these two means, Britain's financial system became at once more stable and more flexible. The British government also recognized the role of the Amsterdam Bank in the Dutch economic miracle of the seventeenth century and founded the Bank of England in 1694. The bank was a manifestation of the new economic thinking associated with the political group in power at the time, the Whigs, associated with "new money," mercantilism, anti-Catholicism, and centralized government institutions, as opposed to the Tories, associated with the court, the country, and conservative features in British political life.

The Whig government's support for such economic developments and its dependence on state debt to finance war were regarded with suspicion by the Tories. Politically, they distrusted the centralization of funds and the growing independence of Parliament from both the monarch and landed interests; economically, they feared money was being diverted from land, trade, or the colonies to financial speculation and that taxes raised to service government debt would drive prices and wages up, increasing costs and reducing trade; socially, they disliked the class of individuals that emerged alongside these changes: nouveaux riches, whose social mobility challenged the aristocratic class structure. Add the eighteenth-century addiction to gambling, and the stock exchange came to be seen as the most diabolical of these developments. For Daniel Defoe, stockbrokers were "more dangerous than a whole nation of enemies abroad, an evil more formidable than the pestilence, and in their practice more fatal to the public than an invasion of Spaniards" (Defoe, 269). Like many commentators, Defoe had no objection to credit, trade, colonial expansion, and commercial enterprise. It was the paper speculation on stocks and shares in Exchange Alley that he regarded with suspicion. Most such fears proved unfounded, but the South Sea Bubble of 1720 nearly did bring the entire system into crisis.

In a time of war, the British government of the early eighteenth century found it hard to meet the interest payments on the national debt. The suggestion was made—by the Tories on this occasion, such was their loathing of the Bank of England—that a commercial company might take over the debt, that state creditors might be induced to swap their government bonds and annuities for shares in that company, and thus the debt would gradually get parceled out as shares. For the scheme to be attractive—especially if, as a state creditor, you had a government annuity paying a fixed sum per annum—creditors must be tempted by a high return. The government could not offer such a prospect, but capital appreciation in the financial market could. So the South Sea Company took over much of the national debt in three phases between 1711 and 1720. But on what commercial basis? What was the business that would provide returns substantial enough to persuade the government's creditors to swap their bills and annuities for risk-laden shares?

When the War of the Spanish Succession came to an end in Britain's favor in 1713, Britain acquired from the French what was known as the *asiento:* the permission to monopolize the slave trade between Africa and the South American colonies. This went to the South Sea Company along with a monopoly over British trade in the region as a whole. Schemes were floated of ports up and down the Atlantic and Pacific shores of America, sending goods hither and yon between China, America, and Europe—but nothing in fact eventuated. "In the year 1711," James Burney recorded, "was erected in *England*, a *South Sea* Company, concerning which it is sufficient in this place to observe, that its formation had no relation to any scheme or plan for establishing a commercial intercourse between the British Nation and the Countries bordering on the *South Sea*, or to any maritime enterprise then carrying on, or in contemplation" (Burney, 4:486).

The entire confection illustrated conservative anxiety about financial markets. Indeed, as there was by 1720 no real capital and no real business, everything had to center on the stocks and shares the South Sea Company issued; everything depended on a permanent bull market in South Sea stock. It had to keep rising because exchange of stock was not in this case a reflection of the value of the business: it *was* the business and the only source of profit it possessed. (The stock was in competition, after all, with the rate of interest achievable on government bonds.) Company "profits," creditors' willingness to convert government bonds to shares, and the government's ability to shed debt all depended on the price rising. In particular, the company had to offer dividends or the investors would leave the scheme; and if there was no profit, dividends had to come from somewhere else. At first the company paid dividends in government bonds, but that simply created debt the entire project was designed to reduce; it soon occurred to the directors that they could pay dividends with more stock. And then that stock must pay a dividend. . . .

To modern eyes the situation seems as implausible as could be, but four things allowed it to come about: the novelty of the entire financial arrangement and its institutional organization (especially the stock exchange, which remains a mystery to many even today); the lack of any regulatory bodies in the system; the support for the scheme coming from government and senior establishment figures, including the royal family itself; and, last but by no means least, credulity about "the South Seas" as a source of wealth and even as a geographic entity. (The *asiento* covered the slave trade across the South Atlantic, after all, and there was practically no prospect of Pacific trade at all; yet the entire region was "the South Seas," and as South America had proved a silver mine to the Spaniards, so "the South Seas" had to be a source of limitless wealth taking other forms; nothing else was conceivable.) Everything depended on a grasp of marketing combined with a permanently skewed stock market. If ever the market looked like it was collapsing, the directors would heap on more coals: lend people money to buy stock or sell stock on a part-payment scheme so that subscription receipts (or "scrip") themselves became a speculative holding to be bought and sold.

Widespread credulity of this nature was abetted by an almost identical scheme in operation in Paris: the Mississippi Company headed by the Scottish financier John Law. Again there was a monopoly exchanged for the national debt; again an almost complete lack of capital or business; again a remote region promising more than it could fulfill. In France, however, the national bank and the Mississippi Company were the same; so when the bubble burst and investors deserted the company stock in favor of gold, Law simply made gold illegal as a medium of exchange; and when more money was needed to advance to investors to buy stock, Law simply had it printed. (Paper money was another of his innovations.) Thus the entire financial system of France was involved, whereas in England at least the Bank of England stood outside the vortex.

For a while all went well in London:

> With down-payment requirements so small, everyone could have a gamble and plenty of fortunes were made in the lower echelons. An Exchange Alley porter, who immediately became known as "the Duke," made £2,000 and bought himself a splendid carriage. "Our South Sea Equipages increase every day," wrote *Applebee's Journal*, "the City ladies buy South Sea jewels, hire South Sea maids, and take new country South Sea Houses; the gentlemen set up South Sea coaches and buy South Sea estates." (Cowles, 137)

The ongoing social effects of this were enough for some to raise the alarm:

> it has a natural Tendency to debauch the Morals of the Nation, and may, in Time, endanger the *British* Constitution. . . . What can be the Consequence of carrying Gaming to the present prodigious Heighth, so as to become the universal Employment of all Orders and Degrees of Men? Is there not, therefore, Reason to dread, That, in Time, Gain may be declared Godliness, and Fraud and Deceit the laudable Arts by which Wise Men ought to aspire to Wealth and Power? That the Love of one's Country, and Care for innocent Posterity, and every other Concern, except the Gratification of our present Lusts, will be thought ridiculous Amusements, and fit only for Lunaticks and Madmen? And, in fine, That all Distinctions between Virtue and Vice, Right and Wrong, will be intirely abolished? (Hutcheson 1720c: 66)

In the end, however, the South Sea Company was a victim of its own success. Hundreds of companies sprang up in imitation of it: dealing in American fisheries, in African trade, in the Bay of Campeachy, in Russian trade, in importing jackasses from Spain, in building pirate-proof ships, in insuring marriage against divorce, in perpetual motion machines, in breeding silkworms in Hyde Park, in a prototype machine gun, and—best of all— "a company for carrying out an undertaking of great advantage, but no one to know what it is" (see Anon. 1720a). (Parallels with the dot-com bubble of 1999–2000 present themselves here, in which certain companies were World Wide Web "domain names" and nothing more.) There were good schemes, too, but many were as fanciful as the South Sea scheme itself, and all diverted funds from the great conglomerate. So in June 1720 the company acted in Parliament to close down unchartered companies and to get the stream of capital back on tap.

This proved a disaster. The pricking of smaller bubbles pricked the South

Sea Company's own because, like most investors today, investors of 1720 had diversified their portfolios. They had stock in the South Sea Company but also in Welsh copper and perpetual motion. And when those companies began to collapse, investors needed ready money to cover their subscriptions (many of which were on tick), and so they began to call in South Sea stock, too, in need of cash. (Some also needed cash to meet scheduled payments on South Sea subscriptions.) In effect, the company's action turned the first bull market in history into the first bear market. At the end of June 1720, South Sea stock stood at £1,000; by the end of September it had fallen to £135.

"Most people thought the time wou'd come," wrote the poet Alexander Pope, "but no man prepar'd for it; no man consider'd it would come like a *Thief in the night,* exactly as happens in the case of our deaths" (Pope 2000: 139). The financial system was saved by prompt government action, led by a Whig MP, Robert Walpole, who went on to become in effect Britain's first prime minister and to hold the office for no less than twenty years (Walpole earned the nickname "Screen-Master General" by saving establishment figures from scandal and financial liability). For some, however, the financial recovery was one thing; a moral recovery was something else. "I am really of the Opinion," wrote Archibald Hutcheson,

> that the Execution of the *South Sea* Scheme, and the late Phrenzy which has reigned amongst us, is a Pestilential Infection from our Neighbour Nation [i.e., France]; And I beseech God, That the Bodily Plague, which now rages in some Part of that Kingdom, may not reach us. And, I am persuaded, we cannot more effectually prevail with Providence to interpose in our Favour, than by a sincere Repentance for the late Inundation of Corruption, and by a General Reformation of our Lives. And I hope the Humour of *Free-Thinking,* as 'tis usually called, has not yet so far prevailed, as to render the Doctrine which I advance Ridiculous in the Christian Nation. (Hutcheson 1720a: 118)

The financial system had proved itself sufficiently diversified (the Bank of England separate from the South Sea Company, the government under scrutiny in Parliament) to take the strain, yet many individuals "who have adventured into this unhappy Ocean" (Hutcheson 1720b: 90) came to grief:

> The Ruin is general, and every Man has the miserable Consolation to see his Neighbour undone; for as to the *Class of Ravens,* whose Wealth has cost this Nation its *All,* as they are *manifest Enemies* to *God* and *Man,* no Man can call *them his Neighbours;* they are *Rogues of Prey,* they are *Stock-Jobbers,* they are a Conspiracy of *Stock-Jobbers:* A Name which carries along with it such a detestable deadly Image, that it exceeds all humane Invention to aggravate it; nor can Nature, with all her Variety and Stores, furnish out any Thing to illustrate its Deformities by; nay, it gains visible Advantage by the worst Comparisons you can make: Your terrour lessens, when you liken them to *Crocodiles* and *Cannibals,* who feed, for *Hunger,* on humane Bodies. (Gordon and Trenchard, 30)

The South Seas in the seventeenth and early eighteenth centuries held out to some that limitless kind of expectation that only a blank on the map can provide, combined with a belief inherited from the Renaissance that Europeans were obliged by God and their own sense of destiny to discover and to civilize. By the time Mendaña discovered the Solomon Islands in 1568, the belief in a great southern continent—Terra Australis—was very strong. "Natural and Moral History," the British philosopher John Locke wrote in 1704,

> is embellish'd with the most beneficial Increase of so many thousands of Plants it had never before receiv'd, so many Drugs and Spices, such variety of Beasts, Birds and Fishes, such rareties of Minerals, Mountains and Waters, such unaccountable diversity of Climates and Men, and in them of Complexions, Tempers, Habits, Politicks and Religions. . . . To conclude, the Empire of Europe is now extended to the utmost Bounds of the Earth, where several of its Nations have Conquests and Colonies. These and many more are the Advantages drawn from the Labours of those, who expose themselves to the Dangers of the vast Ocean, and of unknown Nations. (Churchill and Churchill, 1:lxxiii)

But what if what came back from the "vast Ocean" were "*Crocodiles* and *Cannibals,* who feed, for *Hunger,* on humane Bodies" or if the "Advantages" drawn from such extravaganzas were only *"Rogues of Prey"*? The South Seas might as easily send back monsters as "beneficial Increase" or might produce anarchy at home by a variety of antipodean inversion. They might encourage *"Free-Thinking"* for which "General Repentance" was the only remedy. A contemporary farce has the young Englishwoman Miranda (whose name is borrowed from the heroine of Shakespeare's *The Tempest*) being offered by her father, Mississippi ("A Merchant dealing in Stocks"), to Africanus ("A new created Gentleman"), "drest in the Skin of a Boar, upon all four, and a large Sword tied to his Waste." "Pray," Miranda asks her father, "what Shape am I to assume to be fit to pair with such a Savage Brute?" "I am no Brute," Africanus replies, "but a Gentleman, Madam; I bear for my Arms an Ass Rampant—I am worth One Hundred Thousand Pounds, and keep a Coach and Six" (Anon. 1720b: 32). This was a world turned upside down.

As far as the British were concerned, a good deal separated them and their interest in the Pacific from that of the Spanish explorers of the sixteenth century. "In the latter part of the 15th, during the 16th, and beginning of the 17th centuries," Alexander Dalrymple suggested,

> a spirit of enterprize, inflamed perhaps by avarice and enthusiasm, laid open the East-Indies, America, and other remote regions of the globe: this spirit of enterprize ceased to actuate . . . before the compleat examination of the world was effected: hence the southern regions remain still indeterminate, and we continue ignorant, so far as absolute experience, whether the southern hemisphere be an immense mass of water, or whether it contains another continent, and countries worthy of our search. (Dalrymple, 88–89)

That spirit of Spanish (and Catholic) enterprise the British tended to decry: "The example of the Spaniards," John Callander wrote, "will prove a useful lesson, and teach us to avoid avarice and cruelty" (Callander, 1:11). The passage of time allows us to see what the two forms of enterprise had in common as well as what separated them. There was plenty of avarice among the Londoners of 1720, for example, and little evidence of cold-blooded cruelty in Quirós. "They err who believe the Conquistadores were incited by love of gold and religious fanaticism alone," the nineteenth-century traveler and scientist Alexander von Humboldt wrote:

> Perils always exalt the poetry of life; and, moreover, the remarkable age whose influence on the development of cosmical ideas we are now depicting, gave to all enterprises, and to the natural impressions awakened by distant travels, the charm of novelty and surprise, which is beginning to fail us in the present well-instructed age, when so many portions of the earth are opened to us. Not only one hemisphere, but almost two-thirds of the earth, were then a new and unexplored world,—as unseen as that portion of the moon's surface which the law of gravitation constantly averts from the glance of the inhabitants of the earth. (Humboldt, 648)

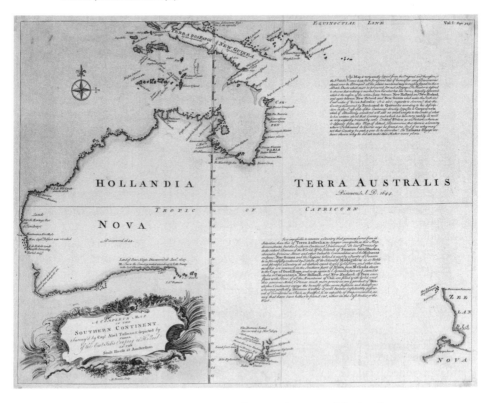

FIGURE 2. Emanuel Bowen (1714–1767), "A Complete Map of the Southern Continent" (1744). By permission of the National Library of Australia.

"The charm of novelty and surprise" that makes Quirós' account of the New Hebrides nearly as ecstatic as Bougainville's later one of Tahiti gripped those duped by the Bubble in much the same way. Of Magellan's, Mendaña's, and Quirós' sufferings and disappointments below the equator the British in 1720 knew almost nothing: "As one Spanish official complained, Mendaña found 'no specimens of spices, nor of gold and silver, nor of merchandise, nor of any other source of profit, and all the people were naked savages' " (quoted in Williams and Frost, 9). But even the unremunerative voyages of men like Tasman and Dampier failed to "destroy the shining image of Terra Australis" (Eisler, 142).

Indeed, not even the South Sea Bubble itself could do it, as the case of Daniel Defoe, the poet and prophet of English mercantilism, proves. In 1730 he was still dismayed by British inactivity in this wonderland of possibility. "As for new Colonies and Conquests," he wrote, "how do we seem entirely to give over, even the Thoughts of them . . . as if we had done our utmost, were fully satisfied with what we have, that the enterprising Genius was buried with the old Discoverers, and there was neither Room in the World nor Inclination in our People to look any farther" (quoted in Williams and Frost, 137). In 1744 the cartographer Emanuel Bowen was still enthusing about the empty spaces of the Pacific:

> It is impossible to conceive of a Country that promises fairer from its Situation, than this of Terra Australis; no longer incognita, as this Map demonstrates, but the Southern Continent Discovered. It lies precisely in the richest Climates of the World . . . and therefore whoever perfectly discovers & settles it will become infallibly possessed of Territories as Rich, as fruitful, & as capable of Improvement, as any that have hitherto been found out, either in the East Indies, or the West. (quoted in Williams and Frost, 26; see Figure 2)

For Callander, "experience has taught us, that a solid and well-regulated commerce should form our principal object in those distant climes, and not the conquest of large kingdoms beyond the Line" (Callander, 1:12). But it was a new and unexplored world, and solid and well-regulated commerce was as hard to sustain in it as the kingdoms beyond the equator dreamed of by Mendaña and Quirós.

from Antonio Pigafetta, *Magellan's Voyage* (1525)

The best-known account of Magellan's circumnavigation of the globe (which Magellan himself did not complete, as he was killed in the Philippines) is that provided by his fellow traveler Pigafetta (c. 1491–c. 1534) a learned member of the Italian nobility. We join the fleet as they emerge from the Straits of Magellan, their fleet of five ships already reduced to three. Within a month of the passage, the expedition would be facing starvation.

On Wednesday the twenty-eighth of November, one thousand five hundred and twenty, we issued forth from the said strait and entered the Pacific Sea, where we remained three months and twenty days without taking on board provisions or any other refreshments, and we ate only old biscuit turned to powder, all full of worms and stinking of the urine which the rats had made on it, having eaten the good. And we drank water impure and yellow. We ate also ox hides which were very hard because of the sun, rain, and wind. And we left them four or five days in the sea, then laid them for a short time on embers, and so we ate them. And of the rats, which were sold for half an écu[1] apiece, some of us could not get enough.

Besides the aforesaid troubles, this malady was the worst, namely the gums of most part of our men swelled above and below so that they could not eat.[2] And in this way they died, inasmuch as twenty-nine of us died, and the other giant died, and an Indian of the said country of Verzin.[3] But besides those who died, twenty-five or thirty fell sick of divers maladies, whether of the arms or of the legs and other parts of the body, so that there remained very few healthy men. Yet by the grace of our Lord I had no illness. During these three months and twenty days, we sailed in a gulf where we made a good four thousand leagues across the Pacific Sea, which was rightly so named. For during this time we had no storm, and we saw no land except two small uninhabited islands, where we found only birds and trees. Wherefore we called them the Isles of Misfortune.[4] And they are two hundred leagues distant one from another. And there is no place for anchoring for no bottom can be found. And we saw there a very large kind of fish which they call *Tiburoni*.

The first island is in fifteen degrees of latitude going by the south wind, and the other island is in nine degrees. By this wind we made each day fifty or sixty leagues or more, sometimes at the stern, at others at the windward side, or otherwise. And if our Lord and the Virgin Mother had not aided us by giving good weather to refresh ourselves with provisions and other things we had died in this very great sea. And I believe that nevermore will any man undertake to make such a voyage.[. . .]

During this time of two months and twelve days, we sailed between west and northwest, and northwest by west, until we came to the equinoctial line at one hundred and twenty-two degrees from the line of demarcation. Which

---

1. Type of Spanish currency; see the modern *escudo*.

2. This is scurvy, a problem for long-distance voyagers until the late eighteenth century, when its origin was traced to deficiencies in sailors' diets.

3. Magellan kidnapped two inhabitants from Patagonia, and Pigafetta is the origin of the myth that Patagonians were "giants." Verzin is an antique name for Brazil.

4. The first island is likely to have been been Pukapuka in the Tuamotu group; the second, named the Island of Sharks (Portuguese: tiburones), may have been Flint Island or Vostok in the Line Island group of Kiribati: considerably farther than 200 leagues apart.

ISLAND AS ELDORADO

line of demarcation is thirty degrees from the meridian, and the meridian is three degrees east of Cape Verde.[5]

And on this course we passed near two very rich islands. One is twenty degrees of latitude toward the Antarctic Pole, and is called Cipanghu. The other is fifteen degrees toward the said pole and is named Sumbdit Pradit.[6]

After we had passed the equinoctial line, we sailed between west and northwest, and west by north, and then we made two hundred leagues towards the west, and changed course to west by south as far as thirteen degrees toward the Arctic Pole in order to approach the land of Cape Gaticara.[7] Which cape (under correction of those who practiced cosmography, for they have not seen it) does not lie where they think, but is to the north in twelve degrees or thereabout.

After sailing sixty leagues on the aforesaid course, and being in twelve degrees of latitude and one hundred and forty-six degrees of longitude, on Wednesday the sixth of March we discovered a small island to the northwest, and two others towards the southwest.[8]

One of these islands was larger and higher than the other two. And the captain-general wished to approach the largest of these three islands to replenish his provisions. But it was not possible, for the people of those islands entered the ships and robbed us so that we could not protect ourselves from them. And when we wished to strike and take in the sails so as to land, they stole very quickly the small boat called the skiff which was fastened to the poop of the captain's ship. At which he, being very angry, went ashore with forty armed men. And burning some forty or fifty houses with several boats and killing seven men of the said island, they recovered their skiff.

Soon after, we left, taking the same course. And before we landed several of our sick men had begged us, if we killed man or woman, to bring them their entrails. For immediately they would be healed. And know that whenever we wounded any of these people with a shaft which entered their body, they loooked at it and then marvelously drew it out, and so died forthwith.

Soon we left the said island going on our way. And when those people saw that we were departing they followed us for a league in one hundred boats or more and came near our ships, showing us fish and making signs that they wished to give it to us. But they threw stones, then fled away, and

---

5. This "line of demarcation" down the Atlantic is the one established under the Treaty of Tordesillas (1494) to separate the Spanish from the Portuguese realms: the "West Indies" from the "East Indies." The Cape Verde Islands are off the coast of West Africa.

6. Cipanghu is an antique name for Japan; Sumbdit Pradit is conceivably a mistake for "Septem Cidades," a mythical island of seven cities recorded on some maps. Magellan's ships cannot have seen these places; Pigafetta assumes (on current geographic knowledge) that they passed by them.

7. Another mythic place, Cape Cattigara, which the second-century geographer Ptolemy included as part of the "Golden Chersonese": his imagined version of the Far East.

8. The Mariana Islands; Rota and Guam are the most likely candidates.

in their flight they passed between the boat towed astern and the ship in full sail. But this was done so nimbly and with so much skill that it was a marvel. And we saw some of those women weeping and tearing their hair, and I believe it was for love of those whom we had killed.

Those people live in freedom and as they will, for they have no lord or superior,[9] and they go quite naked and some of them wear a beard. They have long hair down to their waist, and wear small hats after the manner of the Albanians, and these hats are made of palm.

These people are as tall as we, and well built. They worship nothing. And when they are born they are white, then they become tawny, and they have black and red teeth.[10] The women also go naked, but that they cover their nature with a bark as thin and supple as paper, which grows between the wood and the bark of the palm tree. They are handsome and delicate, and whiter than the men, and they have disheveled hair, very black and hanging down to the ground. They do not go to work in the fields, but do not leave their house, where they make cloth and boxes from palm leaves.[11] Their food is certain fruit called *Cochi* [and] *Battate*.[12] They have birds, figs a palm in length, sugarcanes, and flying fish.

Those women anoint their body and their hair with coconut and beneseed oil.[13] And their houses are made of wood covered with planks or boards with fig leaves, which leaves are very large, and the houses are six fathoms wide and have only one story. Their rooms and beds are furnished with mats made of palms and very beautiful, and they lie on palm straw, which is very soft and fine.

Those people have no weapons but they use sticks with a fishbone at the tip. They are poor but ingenious, and great thieves. And on this account we called those three islands the Islands of the Thieves.[14]

The pastime of the men and women of that country and their sport, is to

---

9. This "negative utopia" would be a perennial fascination with Western writers. In "Of the Cannibals" Montaigne discussed a people that "have no trade of any kind, no acquaintance with writing, no knowledge of numbers, no terms for governor or political superior, no practice of subordination or of riches or poverty, no contracts, no inheritances," and so forth (Montaigne, 233).

10. It was a belief commonly held among Westerners into the nineteenth century that people whose color was other than white were born pale and became darker by degrees. The state of the Guamians' teeth was brought about by chewing the mildly intoxicating fruit of the betel-nut palm.

11. This is a vital matter: as men are physically stronger than women, they are in a position to enslave women in the tasks of food gathering. Thus the treatment of women can be interpreted as an index of civilization.

12. That is, coconuts and (sweet) potatoes.

13. An oil derived from seeds of the bean family of plants.

14. The Mariana Islands, of which Guam is one of the largest, were known as the Ladrones (Portuguese: thieves) until far into the nineteenth century. As we shall see in Chapter 2, Westerners consistently recorded a lax attitude to personal property among Pacific Islanders: evidence of natural simplicity and innocence according to some; for others evidence of the reverse.

ISLAND AS ELDORADO

go in their boats to catch those flying fish with hooks made of fishbones. And the form of their boats is painted hereafter, and they are like *fuseleres*,[15] but narrower. Some are black and white, and others red. And on the other side of the sail they have a large spar painted at the top. Their sails are of palm leaf sewn together like a lateen sail to the right of the tiller. And they have for steering oars certain blades like a shovel. And there is no difference between the stern and the bow of the said boats, which are like dolphins jumping from wave to wave. Those thieves thought (by the signs which they made) that there were no other men in the world but themselves.

Pedro Fernández de Quirós, "Relation of a Memorial Presented to His Majesty, About the Settling and Discovery of the Fourth Part of the World, *Australia Incognita*" (1608)

The Portuguese Pedro Fernández de Quirós (1565–1615) commanded a Spanish expedition the major discovery of which was the New Hebrides (now Vanuatu). Quirós christened his discovery La Tierra Australia del Espíritu Santo (South Land of the Holy Ghost), thinking he had found the coast of a great southern continent. He took possession in the name of the King of Spain, and designed a city, Nova Jerusalem, as its capital. This grandiose settlement lasted for thirty-five days, after which the Islanders' hostility drove the Europeans away. Quirós sailed east for Acapulco, where he arrived in November 1606. He was back in Madrid by October 1607 and immediately began showering the king and his ministers with a series of *memoriales,* of which the most famous is reproduced here. In late 1614 royal support was at last forthcoming, but Quirós died on his way to Peru to initiate his dreamed-of voyage. (Note: As a Portuguese, the author should be referred to as Fernandes de Queirós, but he is generally called by the Spanish version of his name, as here.)

Sir,

I Captain Pedro Fernandez de Quiros say, That with this I have presented to your Majesty eight Memorials, relative to the settlement, which ought to be made in the country which your Majesty commanded to be discovered in *Australia Incognita,* without, to this time, any resolution being taken with me, nor any reply made to me, nor hope given to assure me, that I shall be dispatched; having now been fourteen months in this court, and having been fourteen years engaged in this cause, without pay, or any advantage in view, but the success of it alone; wherewith, and through infinite contradictions, I have gone by land and sea some 20,000 leagues, spending all my estate, and incommoding my person, suffering so many, and such terrible things, that even to myself they appear incredible: and all this has come to pass, that this

---

15. *Fisolere*: a small, oared Venetian fishing vessel.

work of so much goodness and benevolence should not be abandoned. In whose name, and all for the love of God, I most humbly supplicate your Majesty, that you will be pleased not to permit, of so many and such continual labours and watchings, and of so noble and determinate a perseverance, that I should fail to reap those fruits which I so much desire and solicit, being, as it is, so much to the honour and glory of God, and to the service of your Majesty, and productive of innumerable benefits, which shall last as long as the world subsists, and then be eternal.

1. The magnitude of these countries newly discovered, is judged of, by what I saw, and by what Captain *Baez* my admiral,[16] informed your Majesty on good grounds: its longitude is as much as that of all *Europe, Asia-Minor,* and to the *Caspian Sea,* and *Persia,* with all the islands of the *Mediterranean* and *Ocean,* which are in its limits embraced, including *England* and *Ireland.* That unknown part is a quarter of the whole globe, and so capacious, that it may contain in it double the kingdoms and provinces of all those your Majesty is at present Lord: and that without adjoining the Turks, or Moors, or others of the nations which are accustomed to disquiet and disturb their neighbours.[17] All the countries seen fall within the torrid zone, and there is part of them which toucheth the equinoctial, whose latitude may, perhaps, be of 90 deg[rees] and others of somewhat less, and if it comes to pass as it promises, there will be countries, which will be antipodes to the better part of *Africa,* and all *Europe,* and the rest of all *Asia Major* and will not be inferior to them.

It is to be observed, that since the countries which I saw in 15 deg[rees] S[outh] are better than *Spain,* as presently will be seen; that opposed to it in latitude, ought to be in itself quite a terrestrial paradise.

[2.] The people of these countries are many; their colours white, negroes, mulattoes, Indians, and mixed of one and the other. The hair of some is black, long, and lank, the others curled and woolly, and of others very red and fine, which variety is an indication of great commerce and intercourse. For which reason, and for the goodness of the countries, and because they have no artillery, or other fire arms for destruction, and because they do not work mines of silver, and for many other reasons, it is to be believed, these people are extremely numerous. They have not the arts, great or small, walls or forts, king nor law, nor are they but the most simple gentiles,[18] divided into clans, and are little friends among themselves. Their arms are lances and darts of wood, clubs and bows and arrows without poison. They cover

---

16. This is Luis Váez de Torres, who became parted from Quirós after the Nova Jerusalem debacle. Torres continued sailing west, passing between Australia and New Guinea in the strait that bears his name before reaching safe harbor in Manila, where he passed the remainder of his days.

17. Historically, the Spaniards had experienced a good deal of disquiet from the Islamic peoples of North Africa ("the Moors"); from the ninth century to 1492 they fought to evict the infidel occupiers.

18. "Gentile" here does not mean pagan but rather member of a clan-based, or small-tribal society.

their obscene parts.[19] They are clean, chearful, sensible, and very grateful, as I have experienced. For all which it ought to be expected, with the assistance of Divine Providence, and gentle means, that it will be extremely easy to settle, instruct, and satisfy them; which are three things very necessary in the beginning, that afterwards all may be led to such holy ends.

Their houses are of wood, covered with palm-leaves; they use earthern pots: have looms, and other nets; they work stones, marble, flutes, drums, and spoons of wood varnished: they have oratories and burying places, and plantations very well laid out in divisions, and pallisaded. They benefit much by the mother-of-pearl shells, of which they make gouges, chizels, formers, saws, hooks, hatchets, and plates, large and small, which they hang in strings about their necks. The islanders have their embarkation well wrought, and sufficient to navigate them from one country to another, all which is a certain indication of their vicinity to people more civilized, and it is no small confirmation of this, that they castrate their hogs, and make capons.

3. The bread they have is of three different kinds of roots, of which there is vast plenty; and they prepare them without trouble, nothing more being required, than to roast and boil them: they are savoury, wholsome, and nourishing, and keep long, and there are some a yard long, and half that in thickness. The fruits are many, and very good, plantans of six kinds, almonds four kinds. Large *obos,* which is a fruit like quinces, many nuts of the country, and oranges and lemons, which the Indians do not eat, and another excellent and large fruit, and others not less good, which were seen and eaten, with many and large sugar-canes, and intimation of apples. There are palms without number, of which may hereafter be had *tuba* [toddy], of which is made spirits, vinegar, honey and *whey,* and the palm cabbage is very fine. These same palms, the fruit they yield are coconuts; when green, they serve instead of artichokes; and the kernel like cream, when ripe, they serve for meat and drink at sea and land; when old, they yield oil for lamps, and wax also like balsam, and good to eat when new. Their shells are cups and bottles. The coire serves for oakum to caulk ships, and for making all their cables, hausers, and common cordage, and is the best match;[20] of the leaves they make sails for small embarkations, and fine mats, and mats wherewith they line and cover houses, which they frame of their trunks, which are streight and tall, and of them they make targets and lances, and other kinds of arms, with other things, good for common use; and it is to be noted that these coconut topes [groves] are vineyards, which all the year round yield fruit and wine, and that they do not require any culture; and thus neither expend money nor time. The garden-stuffs which were seen were pumkins, large blites [beets], and much purslain [salad herb], and they had intimation of beans. The flesh

---

19. An issue of great religious significance: if the Islanders cover their loins, as Adam and Eve did after eating from the Tree of Knowledge, they evidently are "fallen" humans like the Europeans. Pigafetta noted that Guamanian women also "cover their nature."

20. That is, fuse for the visitors' muskets.

are many hogs, tame like ours, and fowls, capons, country partridges, geese, turtles [turtle doves], ringdoves, and goats, which the other captain saw, and the Indians gave us intimation of cows or buffaloes. The fish are many *pargos* [bream], *reyes* [king fish], skait, soals, mullets, whitings, shads, *macabos,* skuttlefish, *pampanos* [pompanos], *sardinas,* thornback, *palometas* [variety of pompano], *chitas viejas* [puffer fish], eels, *peezes puercos* [pigfish], shellfish, gurnets, muscles, prawns, and other kinds, of which I do not remember the name, and there ought to be many more, for all the above-mentioned were fished close to the ships. And if it be well considered, it must certainly be found, that besides so many and so good [things], presently may be obtained great, and many dainties, reckoning amongst them sweetmeats and preserves of many kinds, and that without requiring any thing from abroad; and for sea provisions, besides the above-mentioned, there will be no want of plenty of large gammons of bacon, nor of jars of lard, and what else is to be had from large hogs, nor want of pickles, or spices. It is to be observed, that many of the above-mentioned things are like ours, and that much more may be had; and by this the country appears to be very fit to produce all the other things Europe produces.

4. The riches are silver and pearls, which I saw, and gold, which the other captain saw, as he mentions in his relation, which are the three species most rich which nature brings forth. There is vast plenty of nutmegs, mace, pepper, and ginger, which we both have seen. There is intimation of cinnamon, and perhaps there may be cloves, since there are the other spices, and the rather, because these countries are almost parallel with *Ternate* and *Bachian.*[21] There is beside conveniency to grow and make pita [aloes] , sugar, indigo. There is good ebony, infinite woods for building any number of ships, with all their sails, and cordage of three kinds, one resembling our hemp; and with the oil of the coconut may be made galgala,[22] which serves instead of pitch, and there was seen a certain resin, which the Indians use for paying their piraguas [canoes]; and since there are goats, and intimation of cattle, there will be cardobanes [fleeces], corambre [skins], tallow and flesh in plenty; and from the bees, which were also seen, there will be honey and wax. And besides all these riches, the situation and disposition of the country assures many others, which joined with the many things which industry will afford, having, as there is so much similarity, besides its own things, conveniency to grow ours, which I intend to carry, together with all the better and more beneficial, which are produced in *Peru* and *New-Spain* [Spanish South America]. It appears, that all together will make the country so rich, that it will alone be able to support itself, and also *America,* and will aggrandize and enrich *Spain* in such a manner, as I will shew, if I am assisted by others in the execution. In regard to what I have seen, since it was the sea-shore, I say,

---

21. Ternate and Bacan are "Spice Islands" in the Moluccas group, west of New Guinea.

22. "Galagal is the plaister-sheathing used in India and China for all their shipping," according to Quirós' anonymous eighteenth-century English translator.

we ought with good ground to hope of the country so many and such great things, riches, and good things as are got from ours.

It is to be observed, that my chief intent was only to seek out so large a country as I have found, and on account of my infirmities, and other things which dispirited me, I could not see so much as I wished; nor can all that is desirable be seen in one month, the year having twelve, wherein are shewn the qualities and the fruits, which all cultivated countries produce; and that the Indians must not be judged of by our necessities, taste, wants, and estimation of things, but as men who intend to pass life with the least trouble, without vexing themselves with those things, in the pursuit whereof we fatigue ourselves.

The conveniency, and pleasures of life will be as great as can be found in a cultivated, pleasant, and delightful country, black and fat, and of great [missing word] for making hereafter bricks, tiles, and the other things made thereof, and near at hand many quarries of marble, and other stones, for building sumptuous and curious edifices, and many woods, well adapted for all uses. There are plains, valleys, and high double lands, and in them rivers, brooks, and fountains, whence, with all conveniency, may be had plenty of water-mills, sugar-mills, and other water-engines; and in the salt marshes, and in the places where canes grow, testimonies of the fertility of the country, whose joints are of five and six palms [hand-widths apart], and less, and the fruit in proportion. The stone fine and hard, and fine grained, and as good flints as in *Madrid*.

[5.] The bay of *St. Philip* and *St. Jago* has twenty leagues of sea-shore; it is all clear, and free for entrance by day and night; it has around it many towns; in them, and very distant, were seen by day many smoaks, and by night many fires. Its port of *Vera-Cruz* ["True Cross"] is so capacious, that it will contain in it above 1000 ships: its soundings clear, and of black sand; worms [sea worms attacking ships' timbers] were not seen: one may anchor in any depth from 40 to ½ fathom, between two rivers, the one as large as *Guadalquivir,* at *Seville,* with a bar of more than two fathom, by which good frigates and small ships may enter. At the other our boats went in freely, and from it was taken water, which is extremely fine. The landing-place is a beach of three leagues, and the greatest part of it a pebble bank, black, small, and heavy, excellent for ballasting ships. The shore, as it has not gaps, nor breaks, and the verdure on its edge, was understood not to be beaten by the waves. And because the trees are all streight, and without azotes,[23] or broken limbs, it was judged from thence not to have great storms. This port, besides being so airy, has another great excellence in what concerns recreation; that from the breaking of the dawn is heard through all the neighbouring wood, a very great harmony of thousands of different birds, some to appearance nightingales, black-birds, larks, and gold-finches, and infinite numbers of swallows, and besides them

---

23. In Spanish *azote* is a lash or a whip: perhaps spindly branches produced when tree limbs are lost in storms and high wind.

many other kinds of birds, and even to the chirping of grasshoppers and crickets.

Every morning and evening were enjoyed sweet scents, wafted from all kinds of flowers, amongst them that of orange-flowers and sweet basil. And for all these, and other good effects, it is judged the climate there is temperate, and that nature maintains her order.

This port and bay are rendered more excellent by the neighbourhood of so many and so good islands, especially of seven, which are 200 leagues in circuit, one of them is 50, and is distant 12, it is very fertile and populous.

And, in short, I say, Sir, that in this bay and port of 15 deg[rees] 20 min[utes] S[outh] lat[itude] may presently be built a very large and populous city, and that the people which will inhabit it, will enjoy all riches and conveniences pointed out, and what my small capacity cannot explain, and what time will shew, and that there may be a communication with the provinces of *Chili, Peru, Panama, Nicaragua, Guatimala, New-Spain, Ternate,* and the *Philipinas,* of all which lands your Majesty is Lord.

And if your Majesty will be of these others which I offer; I hold them to be of so much importance, that besides being as keys of all the above-mentioned places, I apprehend they will become such for the commerce of curious and valuable commodities, besides other great things from *China, Japan,* and the other provinces of the coast of *Asia,* with its islands, and shortly, according to my opinion. And I can shew this in a committee of mathematicians: nor shall I make many words in saying, that it will presently accommodate and sustain 200,000 Spaniards. In short, that this is the globe whereof *Spain* will be the centre, and where there is a body there is a nail; and this point is to be well considered.

[6.] The temperature and goodness of the air, is, Sir, as fine as any in the whole world, and in so much as our people, being all strangers, none fell sick with such continual labour, sweating, and getting wet, without avoiding to drink water fasting, nor to eat every thing the country yielded, nor to keep out of the dews, moon or sun, which was not very hot in the day, and towards midnight woollen cloths were desired, and could well be borne. And whereas the natives in common are corpulent, and very strong, and some of them very old; and as they live in houses with ground floors, which is a great indication of much healthiness, for if the country was unhealthy, they would be raised from the ground, as is done in the *Philipinas,* and in other parts which I have seen. And whereas fish and flesh keep sound to salt [without being salted] two or more days, and whereas, the fruit brought from thence (as may be seen in two I have here) are perfectly good, though taken from the trees out of season; and as I have not seen any barren sandy grounds, nor any kind of thistles, nor prickly trees, nor such as have roots above ground, nor mangrovy swamps, nor morasses, nor snow on the high mountains, nor crocodiles in the rivers, nor in the mountains any venomous insects, nor ants, which commonly are very destructive in the houses and to the fruits, nor niguas [sandflies], nor ticks, nor mosquitoes, which is an excellence above all excellencies for our advantage, and so worthy of estimation, that there are countries in the *Indies* which for these plagues alone are uninhabitable, and others where they suffer very much from them; as I can well bear testimony.

7. These, Sir, are the greatness and goodness of the countries which I have discovered, and of which I took possession in your Majesty's name, under your royal standard, and so the acts declare which I have here, &c. [. . .] All this, and more I have done as a loyal vassal to your Majesty, and that your Majesty may soon add, for the greatness of it sounds well, the title Of *The Australia del Espiritu Santo,* for the greater glory of the same Divinity, who carried me, and who pointed it out to me, and who has brought me to the presence of your Majesty, where I *am,* with the same willingness which I have always had for this cause, to which I gave birth, and for its nobleness do love it, and long after it with infinite solicitude.

8. I am very well convinced from the wise councils, magnanimous disposition, and christian piety of your Majesty, of the great care which will be taken, when further knowledge is had, towards the peopling of these countries now discovered; the chief reason for not leaving them deserted, being, that this will be the means that in all of them the true *God* be known, believed, and adored, the Devil having there so much influence. And further still, for it will be the gate by which to so many nations under the jurisdiction of your Majesty, will be diffused all good and relief, and the many more cares which will arise, if to them the enemies of the church of *Rome* should go to sow their false doctrines, and turn the benefits I have represented to worse evils, and would stile themselves Lords of the *Indies.* I also trust, that your Majesty will well consider, that the doubtful remedy of an evil so pernicious as has been predicted, or of what other disaster, which may be expected now or hereafter, would cost millions of gold, and thousands of men. Acquire, Sir, since you can, with a little money, which will be required but once, acquire *Heaven,* eternal fame, and that New World, with all its promises. And since there is none who solicit of your Majesty the rewards for the *glad tidings* of so great and signal a blessing of *God,* reserved for your happy time, I, Sir, supplicate *them,* and as such my *dispatch,* for the galleons are ready, and I have many places to go to, and much to provide, and to do, and much spiritual and temporal loss attends every hour's delay, which can never be recovered.

9. If *Christoval Colon's*[24] conjectures did make him pertinacious, what I have seen, what I have felt, and what I offer must make me so importunate: wherefore, let your Majesty order, that of the many means which there are, some one be adopted adequate to what is proposed, and let it be observed, that in all I shall be found very submissive to reason, and will give satisfaction in every thing.

---

24. Christopher Columbus, who discovered America in 1492.

from Daniel Defoe, *An Essay on the South-Sea Trade.*
With an Enquiry into the Grounds and Reasons of the
Present Dislike and Complaint against the Settlement
of a South-Sea Company (1711)

The founding father of the English novel and author of a canonical "South Seas" text, *Robinson Crusoe*, Daniel Defoe (1660–1731) was also a tireless pamphleteer, journalist, and political agitator for the Tory party, employed by Lord Harley. Here we see him seeking to influence British colonial policy at a complex moment. The War of the Spanish Succession would actually end with the Treaty of Utrecht of 1713, but its outcome was not in doubt: the Spanish empire was weakened substantially and other European powers could finally become involved in South America. "During this period he had been an enthusiastic proponent of Harley's South Sea Company Scheme," Defoe's biographer writes. "There were actually two schemes in one package presented to Parliament in May 1711. The first was a holding company for consolidating government debts under a single roof. . . . The second involved the creation of a new company to trade to the South Seas" (Novak, 400–401). Defoe's preference is clearly for the second proposal, which he understands in militant terms.

> And thus I am brought to enquire, as *in the Title,* Whether this Trade is to be carried on, 𝔜𝔢𝔞 or 𝔑𝔬? Whether in Reality such a trade is Probable or Feasible? Or, Whether it is Impracticable, and not to be attempted but with a Folly next to Lunacy, which is suggested.
>
> To come at this Question in a Posture that may render the Answer intelligible it seems necessary to state the Thing itself question'd about, and to lay down in as clear Terms as possible what this Thing call'd the *South-Sea* Trade is; what it means as it is now vulgarly accepted; and what we are to understand by it.
>
> By the Trade to the *South Seas* we are to understand One of these Three Things.
>
> 1. An Open, Free Commerce of the *British* Nation to and in the several Ports and Places of *America,* possess'd by the *Spaniards,* either such as are, or shall be, Reduced by us, or by King *Charles* III,[25] with Liberty to carry our Manufactures and Merchandizes, Ships and Factors, thither directly, without Stop in *Old Spain,* and to lade, return and bring back from thence such Goods as shall be purchased there; and in short, to Trade thither as the *French* do now with the *Spaniards* under King *Philip,* or as we do to the *East-Indies.*—And this Sense I think it can be no Offence to say this Trade can never be carried on.
>
> 2. Or, *we are to understand* a Settling in some Part of the *Spanish* Do-

---

25. Charles VI of Austria was also Charles III of Hungary; as such he had a claim on the Spanish throne, the exercising of which was a cause of the War of the Spanish Succession (1701–1713), fought between a coalition of European states and France.

minions in *America,* whether by Way of Conquest, Factory, or otherwise, as by the 6th Article of the Grand Alliance[26] (quoted before) we are allowed to do; and keeping the said Settlement as our own, erect there a Free Market for our *European* Goods; the *Spaniards* having Free Access to come thither to Buy, and we having Liberty from thence to trade to their Dominions above.—And in this Sense it is as Impracticable to carry on this Trade as in the other.

3. Or, by a Trade to the *South-Seas,* we are to understand our Seizing some such Part or Place in *America* whether already possess'd, or not possess'd, as we shall think proper, and taking it as our own, by Virtue of the Treaty above noted, to settle, plant and inhabit the same as a Colony, erecting there such Trade with the Adjacent Countries, whether *Spaniards* or others, and improving the Native Fruitfulness of the Place as much as possible, taking at the same Time all Opportunities to open a Trade with the *Spaniards* as much as Circumstances will admit, and which there is no Question will be considerable.—And this is the Way a Trade may be carried on.—This I am of the Opinion is the Way of Trade the Government proposes, and what they mean by a Trade to the *South-Seas;* and this is so far from being little or inconsiderable, however it may be less than the Golden Mountains some People have form'd Notions of in their Imagination, that this Trade is not only probable to be Great, but capable of being the Greatest, most Valuable, most Profitable, and most Encreasing Branch of Trade in whole *British* Commerce, well worth all the Hazard, Adventure, Expence, and Pains of the Undertaking; sufficient to encourage us in the Prospect, and reward us in the Execution; a Trade, which had it been offered to the Merchandizing Part of Mankind who understood Trade, who were employ'd in Commerce, and accustom'd to Adventures, and not unhappily join'd in and tied down to a Rabble of casual Subscribers, neither inclin'd to, capable of, or in the least having a Genius to trade, it would no doubt have met with another kind of Reception than now it has.

It were to be wisht that in order to set Things right among us, People would give themselves leave to distinguish a little between what **is,** and **is not,** the Design in this Thing, called the *South-Sea* Trade, and between what *may be done,* and *may not be done,* that we may not presently argue ourselves out of all the Trade because we have not the Gates of *Mexico* opened to us. This is no Part of the Thing, the very Word *South-Seas* in the Act of Parliament denotes otherwise, the Words *find out* and *discover* mention'd in the Act tell us otherwise.

We are to find or discover some Place or Places in *America,* where we may fix and settle a *British* Colony, which by the Treaty is to be our own; and is this not enough? Will not Trade fall in? Will not the Country produce to

---

26. In general, a political understanding reached between Austria, England, Spain, and Holland to counter French dominance of continental Europe at the end of the seventeenth century; in particular, the treaty binding these nations together in opposition to France in the War of the Grand Alliance (1689–1697).

us as well as to the *Spaniards*? Are we less industrious than they; if we fix in a barren Spot that's our Fault, but why not somewhere among the Gold, the Silver, the Drugs, the Indico, Cocoa, Cocheneal, and the like, as well as they; and being situated here, fixt, and settled, can we want a Trade? Did any Man think all we were to do was only to carry Goods to *Cartagena* and *Panama* and bring home Money? This bears no Proportion to our Design, nor is of a Duration worth our depending upon; for it would be every Day in the Power of the *Spaniards* to put an end to it, and prohibit it again. But our Business is to seize and possess, *mark the word in the Article of the Grand Alliance,* and to keep it for our own.

This is then what we are to understand by a Trade to the *South-Seas, (viz.)* that we shall, under the Protection, in the Name, and by the Power of Her Majesty, *Seize, Take,* and *Possess,* such Part or Place, or Places, Land, Territory, Country, or Dominion, *call it what you please,* as we see fit in *America,* and *Keep it for our own,* 𝕶𝖊𝖊𝖕𝖎𝖓𝖌 𝖎𝖙 implies Planting, Settling, Inhabiting, Spreading, and all that is usual in such Cases: And *when this is done,* what are we to do with it? *Why,* we are to Trade *to* it, and *from* it; *Whither?* Where ever we can with *Spaniards,* or any Body that will Trade with us; and it is not saying we shall have no Trade with the *Spaniards,* when we say they will not suffer their People freely to Trade with us; but let the *English* get a good Footing on the *South-Sea* Coast of *America,* and let them and the *Spaniards* alone for Trading with one another, let the King of *Spain* prevent it if he can.

This is what I am willing to have called the True Design of this *South-Sea* Company; and I am the rather so, because I have seen no Scheme, nor can I form any Scheme in my Thoughts upon any other Foundation that is Feasible in its Nature, or Practicable in any of its Parts.

The Contrivers of this Undertaking know too well the Temper, Constitution, and State of Affairs, of the *Spaniards* in *America,* to have promis'd to themselves, that by any Treaty, Capitulation, or Stipulation, either in *New Spain* or *Old,* they will ever be brought to lay open the Trade of their *Indies* to the *English,* or indeed to any Nation of the World.

Perhaps they might be brought to admit a Trade to particular Places for Provisions, Fish, Corn, or such Things as they may more particularly want in those Places for the Subsistence of their People: Or, they may be brought to treat with you for an Assento or Permission to bring Negroes to them; a Thing more proper for the *African* Company than any other; and the Reason for that may be only because they know not where else to have them. But that they will permit you to a Free Importation among them of your *European* Manufactures, and Exportation of Bullion from them, is so contrary to the Nature of their Trade, so destructive to their own Interest, and would be so fatal to the very Life and Being of the *Spanish* Dominions in *Europe,* I mean as to Commerce, that unless the *Spaniards* are to be divested of their common Sense, Infatuate, and given up, abandoning their own Commerce, throwing away the only Valuable Stake they have left in the World, and in short, bent to their own Ruin, we cannot suggest that they will ever on any Consideration, or for any Equivalent, part with so Valuable, indeed so Inestimable a Jewel, as the Exclusive Power of Trade to their own Plantations in *America.*

The Mistaking of this I believe to be another Reason, and perhaps One of the Chief too, of the pretended Dislike and Complaint against this Undertaking.

It is always a Disadvantage to any Undertaking to have it represented in Unintelligible Terms, and to have it make high Pretensions, even to Things Impracticable in their own Nature; and nothing has been more the Misfortune of this Affair before us.

from William Bond, *An Epistle to His Royal Highness the Prince of Wales; Occasion'd by the State of the Nation. Presented on his Birth-Day by Mr Stanhope* (1720)

William Bond (d. 1735) was a dramatist of no particular distinction and evidently a confirmed snob. But his poem has a force typical of early-eighteenth-century satiric verse: a force less to do with reforming zeal and self-assurance than with a deep-seated anxiety about (and fascination with) social change. The Prince of Wales was the future King George II, whose birthday was 10 November, suggesting this poem was written in the aftermath of the collapse of the Bubble. Charles Stanhope, secretary of the Treasury, was much involved with the South Sea scheme and with profiteering from it: perhaps by November he was already coming under suspicion. (In February he was tried in the House of Commons but acquitted on a vote of 180 to 177.)

When *Stocks* ran high, and Wit's Productions fell,
Wit grew a Stock, which *Wits* began to sell.
These taught the *Cits* their Birth-right was to Cheat,[27]
That Fortune could ligitimate Deceit;
On glitt'ring Ruins it was brave to rise,
No Fault they knew but unsuccessful Vice:
To prove each Paradox they understood,
For *Vile* and *Rich* with them was *Great* and *Good.*
Proud of this flatter'd infamous Desert,
Cits grew the Patrons of perverted Art;
Then Poets first turn'd Usurers of Sense,
And lent out Scraps of Brains for Heaps of Pence.
Exchange of *Paper* made their Verse renoun'd,
Half Twelve-score Lines subscrib'd a thousand Pound;
Buoy'd up with Flatt'ry, what can't Flatt'ry do!
The Tricksters, all, that Av'rice prompts, pursue:
Grown weary of defrauding by Retale,
Towns, Provinces, and Kingdoms, set to Sale.

---

27. "Cits": City folk, those working in "the City," the financial district of London.

Here, those, that on his Menials joy'd to wait,
With *South-Sea* Squibs, besiege a Duke's Estate;
For *Cypher Scrolls* his *Rent-Rolls* they command,[28]
He gets their *Paper,* and they get his *Land.*
His Titles thus are sold to foul Disgrace,
And *Angel-Ladies* made a Beggar'd Race.
Too late he tells his Daughters of their Fate,
They wring their snowy Hands, and pray *too late:*
While in his spacious Palace proudly sits
A clumsy, couzening Tribe of *South-Sea Cits,*
Blessing the *Harpy*-Master of the Seat,
Whom nought but Fortune's Blindness could make Great.[29]

Next after him, they Hail his ill-bred Wife,
A Lump of Savage Mould, the Seed of Strife;
Who by her very Nature seems to be
Form'd for the lowest Acts of Drudgery:
To tend in daily Labours of the Loom,
Or fit to deck a Bed, or cleanse a Room.
Her aukward rustick Body, rudely spread,
With Giant-Limbs prophanes th' embroider'd Bed;
Banishing Beauties, that, when there they lay,
Waking, gave Lustre to the opening Day.

See here Two ruin'd Countesses in Tears;
While there a *South-Sea* upstart's Strumpet wears
Two *Pendants,* worth two *Mannors,* in her Ears.

There a *Militia*-Warrior ne'er renown'd,
For aught but Sieges in th' *Artill'ry-Ground,*
More Skill'd in the contentious Frauds of Trade,
Than Souldiers to Repel, or to invade,
Undoes some Gallant Heroe, that abroad
Fought, and led Armies like a *Homer*'s God;[30]
Who, prodigal of Life, did shed his Blood,
Guarding, in *Martial* Fields, his Country's Good:
'Till spent with Age, and wearied out with Toils,
He lives but on the Gains of Hostile Spoils.
These Spoils a *Broker*'s single Contract gains,
And mocks the valiant Toils of ten Campaigns.

There's One, whose utmost Promise of his Birth,
Was in his Shop, that narrow Spot of Earth,

---

28. A rent roll is a register of land and rent owed on it: a summary of assets and income.

29. The Roman goddess Fortuna was often depicted as blind; to cozen is to cheat; a harpy is a legendarily rapacious bird-monster.

30. In the early eighteenth century Britain was involved in extensive European wars, most famously under the command of John Churchill, First Duke of Marlborough. His victories at Blenheim (1704), Ramillies (1706), Oudenaarde (1708), and Malplaquet (1709) are alluded to here.

31. This is a tailor holding his yardstick, used for measuring fabric.

To wave a *Yard-Wand* in his servile Hand,[31]
Hoards Wealth, that might a Scepter'd Power command:
Yet from that narrow Spot of Earth can buy
A more than Petty Principality.
So Rich! such Subjects would be dang'rous grown,
To any other Monarch, but our own.
    Now count the *Treach'ries,* number all the *Snares;*
Each Knave to rob the Innocent prepares.
See by what *Lies,* what *Perjuries,* what *Deceit,*
Each makes Tribes fall, to make him singly great.
How many Families, nay Towns, undone,
To make one *Monster's* Fortune over-grown!
For half a Hundred *Knaves,* half *London* fails,
And *South-Sea* shuts more Houses than *Marseilles.*[32]
    Around the spacious City cast your Eyes,
Where Wealth did late, like *Thames's* River, rise;
Which from the Sea she rolls her swelling Tide,
Surveys Ten Thousand Turrets on each Side,
And on her Surface shews their Tow'ring Pride:
To her fair Waters draws the floating Town,
And paints *Augusta* with her Mural Crown.[33]
But Now——
As dry its Channel leaves the Ebbing *Thames,*
So our Wealth leaves Us with departing Streams:
With mighty Streams, but not too Great to be
Quite lost, and swallow'd in th' *unbottom'd Sea.*
Gone is our glitt'ring Tide, by which we shin'd,
Left, *Poverty,* and *Dirt,* and Naked Shores behind.

from Anonymous, *A Poem Occasion'd by the Rise and Fall of South-Sea Stock. Humbly Dedicated to the Merchant-Adventurers Trading in the South-Seas* (1720)

This author is a good deal less paranoid than Edward Bond; in fact the social eruptions and irruptions of the Bubble provide more amusement than

---

32. French Mediterranean port associated in English folklore with the plague. At times of plague individuals shut their houses for fear of infection.

33. An elliptical and allusive paragraph. London's wealth, the source of which lies in trade across the seas, is imaginatively embodied in tidal flows up the River Thames and actually embodied in the buildings along its banks, reflected on the river's surface. A mural crown taking the shape of a battlement was given by Roman generals to the soldier who first mounted the wall of a besieged city. So the image on the water is that of Augusta (a personification of London and the feminine version of the great Roman emperor Augustus, with whose reign early-eighteenth-century English culture has frequently been associated) "crowned" with the buildings along the Thames. But now the tide is ebbing . . .

outrage for him. But at the end of his piece he, too, comes to an apocalyptic climax: comparing South Sea speculators with the devils Christ cast out of a madman named Legion and transferred into the "Gadarene Swine" (see Mark 5:1–13). Also strongly present here is the idea of "woman" as a place in which nature and culture blend, in some proportion or other.

> But still fresh Objects our Amazement claim,
> Sights ne'er recorded in the Books of Fame;
> Strange as the Phantoms that are seen on high,
> When glaring Meteors rack the groaning Sky;
> When armed Legions in the Heavens appear,
> And shining Squadrons combat in the Air.
> Neglected now the darling Mirror lies,
> Nor more reflects the Rays from *Cælia*'s Eyes;
> The widow'd Toilet mourns the absent Fair,
> And *Shock* forsaken,[34] to the Couch repairs;
> Admires the Cause why *Cælia*, so unkind,
> Could leave her lov'd Companion thus behind:
> But little does the pretty Fondler know,
> 'Tis out of Kindness that she serves him so,
> Lest the dull Crowd, either thro' Chance or Spight,
> Should shroud his Beauties in eternal Night;
> For Mobs, like *Æsop*'s Dunghil-cock, despise
> The brightest Gem, thro' Ignorance of its Price:[35]
> Ev'n *Abigail*, before the circling Sun
> Has half his Race thro' Heav'n's bright Regions run,
> Now unemploy'd, reclines her drowsy Head
> On downy Truckle negligently laid,
> Dreams o'er the weighty Business which so oft
> Has been the Subject of her waking Thought,
> Dresses with nicest Art the lovely Fair;
> In graceful Order lays each stragling Hair:
> With jetty Spots then skilfully does grace
> The native Beauties of the Charmer's Face;[36]
> (So sable Clouds make *Sol* appear more bright,[37]
> And Day fresh Lustre takes from the black Shades of Night.)
> With strictest Care the azure Sleeve is rowl'd,
> And due proportion kept in ev'ry Fold;

---

34. In eighteenth-century satiric verse "Shock" is a generic name for a lady's lapdog, just as Cælia is a generic name for an aristocratic lady, and Abigail is a generic name for a lady's maid, one of whose functions is to dress her mistress' hair each morning.

35. In the first book of Aesop's famous *Fables*, there appears the story of "The Cock and the Precious Stone," an allegory about the uselessness of wisdom to the foolish.

36. An allusion to the eighteenth-century women's fashion of wearing cosmetic "beauty spots" in imitation of real ones.

37. *Sol*: "sun" (Latin).

The slender Pin with nicest Art's conceal'd.
Not the least glittering Particle reveal'd,
Till straight a visionary sudden Frown
From *Cælia's* angry Brow shoots awful down;
Frighted, she starts, and rubs her drowsy Eyes,
Trembling with Fear, and in a wild Surprize,
Scarce if she dreamt, or if awake believes,
And hardly credit to her Senses gives.
Mean while, in Disabilee,[38] the muffled Fair
Of Projects full, to the *Exchange* repairs;
Whilst the rude Crowd officious round her press,
And their fond Eyes with heav'nly Beauties bless;
Upon each Charm with Admiration gaze,
Ravish'd with Extasy and sweet Amaze;
Those Limbs, which Monarchs would be proud to clasp,
And pawn their Kingdoms for a single Grasp,
Now tustling Throngs of Lovers close surround,
Whilst killing Glances each Beholder wound:
Happy the Man that can approach so near
To touch the yielding Garments of the Fair;[39]
But ev'n thus blest, he secret fears, that soon
His Happiness will with her Sight be gone.
Thus Dread of loosing what he ne'er enjoys,
Ruins the Miser's Peace, and all his Ease destroys.
Mean while, regardless no Concern she feels,
Nor mourns the numerous Victims which she kills;
Unknowing, certain Deaths does round dispence,
And murders with her very Innocence,
Still different Passions take up all her Thought,
When best to sell, when safest to be bought;
What Prospect of an advantageous Rise
To enhance the Value, and encrease the Price;
Or if a sudden Fall may likely blast
Her Hopes, and ruin all her Projects past.
Ah! cease, fair Maid, this greedy Passion curb,
Nor let one single Care thy Peace disturb;
To Misers the mean Thought of Gain resign
Nor give it Harbour in a Breast like Thine,
Too foul a Vot'ry at so fair a Shrine.
No added Store thy Value can enhance,

---

38. Properly, *déshabillée:* "not fully dressed" (French).

39. A blasphemous allusion to another of Christ's miracles, in Matthew 9:20–21: "And, behold, a woman, which was diseased with an issue of blood twelve years, came behind him, and touched the hem of his garment. For she said within herself, If I may but touch his garment, I shall be whole."

Or new-gain'd Grandeur can thy Worth advance,
Already all we can desire, you boast,
And new Additions were on you but lost;
Gems would but borrow Brightness from your Eye,
And their faint Luster in your Presence dye;
Such blooming Beauty needs no help of Art,
To captivate the most obdurate Heart;
Why should the Silk your softer Skin conceal,
And hide more Charms than e'er it can reveal?
Roses might borrow Sweetness when you breathe,
And from your Lips a brighter Red receive.
Let antiquated Dames with Jewels grace,
The Wrinkles of a Monumental Face,
Moil to get Stock to set their Furrows off,
And make themselves each empty Templer's Scoff;[40]
Awkwardly Gay and Antick-like appear,
And scandalize the very Cloaths they wear;
In your own nat'ral Charms you brightest shine,
Each feature God-like, and each Look Divine.
Not *Cytherea*, the fair Queen of Love,[41]
E'er with more Beauty grac'd the Court of *Jove*,
When pleading at the mighty Thundrer's Throne,
She puts her softest winning Graces on.
Numbers of those who want for Charms attend,
In hopes their Stocks may their stale Wares commend
To the brisk Arms of some young vig'rous Friend.
The wither'd Maid lets loose th' imprison'd Gold,
In Stocking long immur'd in secret Hold;
Gold, which for Ages past has Captive been,
Nor Sun, nor Moon, for num'rous Years has seen,
Now Travels thro' the winding Alleys free,
Rejoicing in the new-gain'd Liberty;
Whilst with the glitt'ring Store, she seeks to Bribe
Some needy Fop to warm her frozen Side.[42]
The greasy Cook, with brawny Fist, unlocks

---

40. A "Templer" is a student of law at one of two London inns of court, the Inner or Middle Temple; "antiquated dames" strive ("Moil") to come by South Sea shares ("Stock") to make their elderly complexions ("Furrows") less repellent to superficial or impecunious young men of that kind.

41. *"Cytherea"*: like Venus, an alternative name for Aphrodite, the goddess of love. Cythera was the Mediterranean island where Aphrodite landed after being born at sea. (Nouvelle Cythère [New Cythera] was the name the French explorer Bougainville gave to Tahiti on his visit there in 1769.) Aphrodite's extramarital affair with Ares (Latin: Mars) caused her much embarrassment before the gods and especially before Zeus, who punished offenders by striking them with thunder.

42. Fop: dandy, man-about-town.

ISLAND AS ELDORADO

The pond'rous Lid of Grandame's Money-Box,
And puts the hoarded Treasure in the Stocks.
　　From *Betty*'s Magazine the cast-off Robes
Releas'd, in *Drury* Hundreds seek Abodes;[43]
The sable Velvet Scarf does Quarters take
Upon the Ridge of Mother *T*——'s Back,
The spreading Petticoat at once does grace,
And cools the Heat of *Daphne*'s postern Face;
Whilst seeming careless, all she strives to show,
And wounds us with the Charms lay hid below;
Th' embroider'd Apron slovenly is plac'd
Around the greasy *Mopsa*'s bulky Waste,[44]
Scarcely can half her Porpoise-Belly hide,
Nor cover her great Paunch from Side to Side;
The silver Trimming is to Ashes burn'd,
And tarnish'd Orices to Rhino turn'd;[45]
Reverted Smocks, by Transformation strange,
To round ear'd Night-Caps, on a sudden change;
The curious Wardrobe is compleatly sold,
And in the Stocks she sinks the glitt'ring Gold.
　　All Ages and all Qualities repair,
And seek to make, or mend their Fortunes here;
In all Degrees the wild Contagion reigns,
And in each Breast a sov'raign Rule maintains:
With furious Haste all frantick hither run,
Some to undo, but More to be undone;
Alike all flounder in this boundless Sea,
Nor can from the bewitching Ruin flee;
So once deep down the craggy Precipice,
The Herd possess'd, ran headlong to the Seas.

from Daniel Defoe, *A New Voyage round the World, by a Course Never Sailed Before* (1724)

So convinced was Defoe of the need to get the English nation involved in South Sea colonialism that, when prospects for South American development came to nothing, he invented a wholly fictional voyage under a wholly

---

43. Magazine: storehouse, wardrobe (here a maidservant, "Betty," has inherited her mistress' secondhand clothes); Hundreds: an ancient division of an English county, containing a hundred families (used ironically here, since London's Drury Lane and its famous theater were places of ill repute).

44. "Mopsus" is a standard name for a shepherd in Latin literature; hence "Mopsa" is a working-class female.

45. Orices (or "orris"): gold or silver lace; Rhino: obsolete slang for "money."

nonfictional title, suggesting that virgin lands of conquest, settlement, and trade only awaited discovery in the Pacific. Here his narrating captain records the desertion of some of his crew on the shores of a fabulous southern continent.

Our men were so fond of this place and so pleased with the temper of the people, the fruitfulness of the soil and agreeableness of the climate, that about twenty of them offered me, if I would give them my word to come again, or send to them to relieve and supply them with necessaries, they would go on shore and begin a colony and live all their days there. Nay, after this, their number came up to three-and-thirty; or they offered, that if I would give them the sloop, and leave them a quantity of goods, especially such toys as they knew would oblige the people to use them well, they would stay at all hazards, not doubting, as they told me, but that they should come to England again at last with the sloop full of gold.

I was not very willing to encourage either of these proposals because, as I told them, I might perhaps find a place as fit to settle a colony in before we came home, which was not at such an excessive distance from England, so that it was scarce possible ever to relieve them. This satisifed them pretty well, and they were content to give over the project; and yet at last, which was more preposterous than all the rest, five of our men and a boy ran away from us and went on shore; and what sort of life they led or how they manage, we are scarce ever likely to know, for they are too far off us to enquire after them again. They took a small yawl with them, and it seems had furnished themselves privately with some necessary things, especially tools, a grindstone, a barrel of powder, some peas, some wheat, and some barley; so that it seems they are resolved to plant there.[46] I confess I pitied them, and when I had searched for them and could not find them, I caused a letter to be written to them, and fixed it upon a post at the place where our ship careened, and another on the south side, to tell them that in such a certain place I had left other necessaries for them, which I did, made up in a large case of boards or planks, and covered with boards like a shed.

Here I left them hammocks for lodging, all sorts of tools for building them a house, spades, shovels, pickaxes, an axe, two saws, with clothes, shoes, stockings, hats, shirts, and, in a word, everything that I could think of for their use; and a large box of toys, beads, &c., to oblige the trade with the natives.

One of our men, whom they had made privy to their design, but made him promise not to reveal it till they were gone, had told them that he would persuade me if he could to leave them a further supply; and bid them come to the place after the ships were gone, and that they should find directions left for them on a piece of a board, or a letter from him, set up upon a post. Thus they were well furnished with all things for immediate living.

I make no doubt but they came to find these things; and since they had

46. In this context "plant" means to settle or colonize, not grow crops.

ISLAND AS ELDORADO

a mind to make trial of a wild retired life, they might shift very well; nor would they want anything but Englishwomen to raise a new nation of English people in a part of the world that belongs neither to Europe, Asia, Africa, or America. I also left them every man another gun, a cutlass, and a horn for powder, and I left two barrels of fine powder, and two pigs of lead for shot, in another chest by itself.

I doubt not but the natives will bestow wives upon them, but what sort of posterity they will make I cannot foresee. For I do not find by inquiry that the fellows had any great store of knowledge or religion in them, being all Madagascar men, as we called them—that is to say, pirates and rogues; so that for aught I know there may be a generation of English heathens in an age or two more, though I left them five Bibles and six or seven prayer-books, and good books of several sorts, that they might not want instruction if they thought fit to make use of it for themselves or their progeny.

It is true this is a country that is most remote from us of any in the yet discovered world, and consequently it would be suggested as unprofitable in our commerce; but I have something to allege in its defence which will prove it to be infinitely more advantageous to England than any of our East India trade can be, or that can be pretended for it. The reason is plain in a few words: our East India trade is all carried on, or most of it, by an exportation of bullion in specie and a return of foreign manufactures or produce, and most of these manufactures also, either trifling and unnecessary in themselves or such as are injurious to our own manufactures. The solid goods brought from India which may be said to be necessary to us, and worth sending our money for, are but few; for example:—

1. The returns which I reckon trifling and unnecessary are such as china ware, coffee, tea, japan works,[47] pictures, fans, screens, &c.

2. The returns that are injurious to our manufactures, or growth of our own country, are printed calicoes, chintz, wrought silks, stuffs of herbs and barks, block tin, cotton, arrack,[48] copper, indigo.

3. The necessary or useful things are pepper, saltpetre, dyeing-woods and dyeing-earths, drugs, lacs, such as shellac, stick-lac, &c.,[49] diamonds, and some pearl, and raw silk.

For all these we carry nothing or very little but money, the innumerable nations of the Indies, China, &c., despising our manufactures and filling us with their own.

On the contrary, the people in the southern unknown countries, being first of all very numerous, and living in a temperate climate which requires clothing, having no manufactures or materials for manufactures of their own, would consequently take off a very great quantity of English woollen

---

47. Japan works are small wooden items decorated or varnished in Japanese style.

48. Distilled spirit obtained from fermented palm toddy.

49. Lac is a transparent resin left by certain insects on Eastern trees: shellac is used as a glue to this day.

manufactures, especially when civilised by our dwelling among them and taught the manner of clothing themselves for their ease and convenience; and in return for these manufactures, it is evident we should have gold in specie, and perhaps spices, the best merchandise and return in the world.

I need say no more to excite adventurous heads to search out a country by which such an improvement might be made, and which would be such an increase of, or addition to, the wealth and commerce of our country.

Nor can it be objected here that this nook of the country may not easily be found by any one but us that have been there before, and perhaps not by us again exactly; for not to enter into our journal of observations for their direction, I lay it down as a foundation, that whosoever, sailing over the South Seas, keeps a stated distance from the tropic to the latitude of fity-six to sixty degrees, and steers eastward towards the Straits of Magellan, shall never fail to discover new worlds, new nations, and new inexhaustible funds of wealth and commerce, such as never were yet known to the merchants of Europe.

This is the true ocean called the South Sea; that part we corruptly call so can be in no geographical account, or by any rule, but by the mere imposition of custom, it being only originally called so because they that sailed to it were obliged to go round the southernmost part of America to come into it;[50] whereas it ought indeed to be called the West Sea, as it lies on the west side of America, and washes the western shore of that great continent, for near eight thousand miles in length, to wit, from fifty-six degrees south of the line to seventy degrees north, and how much farther we know not. On this account I think it ought to be called the American Ocean, rather than with such impropriety the South Sea.

But this part of the world where we were may rightly be called the South Sea by way of distinction, as it extends from India round the globe to India again, and lies all south of the line (even for aught we know to the very South Pole), and which, except some interpositions of land, whether islands or continent, really surrounds the South Pole.

We were now in the very centre or middle of the South Sea, being, as I have said, in the latitude of thirty-four degrees twenty minutes; but having had such good success in our inquiry or search after new continents, I resolved to steer to the S. and S.E. as far as till we should be interrupted by land or ice, determining to search this unknown part of the globe as far as nature would permit, that I might be able to give some account to my employers, and some light to other people that might come that way, whether by accident or by design.

---

50. In fact the South Seas were so named because the first European to see the Pacific, the Spanish explorer Vasco Nuñez de Balboa (in 1513), had crossed the peninsula of Panama, where the land lies east to west: thus Balboa was looking south, not west, when he made his discovery.

ISLAND AS ELDORADO

Antonio Pigafetta, *Magellan's Voyage: A Narrative Account of the First Circumnavigation,* trans. R. A. Skelton (New Haven: Yale University Press, 1969). Reproduced by permission of Yale University Press.

Pedro Fernández de Quirós, "Relation of a Memorial Presented by Captain Pedro Fernandez de Quiros to His Majesty, About the Settling and Discovery of the Fourth Part of the World, *Australia Incognita.* Its great Riches and Fertility discovered by the said Captain," in Alexander Dalrymple, *An Historical Collection of the Several Voyages and Discoveries in the South Pacific Ocean* (London, 1770–1771).

Daniel Defoe, *An Essay on the South-Sea Trade, With an Enquiry into the Grounds and Reasons of the Present Dislike and Complaint against the Settlement of a South-Sea Company* (London, 1711).

William Bond, *An Epistle to His Royal Highness the Prince of Wales; Occasion'd by the State of the Nation. Presented on his Birth-Day by Mr Stanhope* (London, 1720).

Anonymous, *A Poem Occasion'd by the Rise and Fall of South-Sea Stock. Humbly Dedicated to the Merchant-Adventurers Trading in the South-Seas* (London, 1720).

Daniel Defoe, *A New Voyage round the World, by a Course Never Sailed Before* (London, 1724).

FURTHER READING

On seventeenth- and eighteenth-century Pacific exploration, see William Eisler, *The Furthest Shore: Images of Terra Australis from the Middle Ages to Captain Cook* (Cambridge: Cambridge University Press, 1995), an excellent and well-illlustrated survey; Derek Howse, ed., *Background to Discovery: Pacific Exploration from Dampier to Cook* (Berkeley: University of California Press, 1990), especially contributions by Charles L. Batten Jr. ("Literary Responses to the Eighteenth-Century Voyages") and Daniel S. Baugh ("Seapower and Science: The Motives for Pacific Exploration"); H. E. Maude, *Of Islands and Men: Studies in Pacific History* (Melbourne: Oxford University Press, 1968), chaps. 2 and 3, on Spanish exploration; O. H. K. Spate, *The Pacific since Magellan,* vol. 1: *The Spanish Lake* (Canberra: Australian National University Press, 1979) and vol. 2: *Monopolists and Freebooters* (London: Croom Helm, 1983); and Glyndwr Williams and Alan Frost, eds., *"Terra Australis" to Australia* (Melbourne: Oxford University Press, 1988), an illustrated survey covering Spanish, Dutch, and British explorations. For Magellan, see Charles McKew Parr, *So Noble a Captain: The Life and Times of Ferdinand Magellan* (New York: Crowell, 1953).

On "perceptions," see two books by Percy G. Adams: *Travellers and Travel Liars, 1660–1800* (Berkeley: University of California Press, 1962), and *Travel Literature and the Evolution of the Novel* (Lexington: University of Kentucky Press, 1983); David Fausett, *Images of the Antipodes in the Eighteenth Century: A Study in Stereotyping* (Amsterdam: Rodopi, 1994); Jonathan Lamb, "Re-Imagining Juan Fernandez: Probability, Possibility and Pretence in the South Seas," in Nicholas Thomas and Diana Losche, eds., *Double Vision: Art Histories and Colonial Histories in the Pacific* (Cambridge: Cambridge University Press, 1999), and *Preserving the Self in the South Seas, 1680–1840* (Chicago: University of Chicago Press, 2001), chap. 2, "The Romance of

Navigation"; and Helen Wallis et al., *Australia and the European Imagination* (Canberra: Humanities Research Centre, 1982).

On empire, see the seventeenth- and eighteenth-century British plans and proposals from 1625 to 1788 reprinted in George Mackaness, ed., *Some Proposals for Establishing Colonies in the South Seas* (Sydney: Australian Historical Monographs, 1943); and two books by J. H. Parry: *The European Reconnaissance: Selected Documents* (London: Macmillan, 1968), and *Trade and Dominion: The European Overseas Empires in the Eighteenth Century* (New York: Praeger, 1971), section III, "The Second Age of Discovery." The doyen of the field is Glyndwr Williams: see his *The Expansion of Europe in the Eighteenth Century: Overseas Rivalry, Discovery and Exploitation* (London: Blandford, 1966), " 'The Inexhaustible Fountain of Gold': English Projects and Ventures in the South Seas, 1670–1750," in John E. Flint and Glyndwr Williams, eds., *Perspectives of Empire: Essays Presented to Gerald S. Graham* (London: Longman, 1973); "Buccaneers, Castaways and Satirists: The South Seas in the English Consciousness Before 1750," *Eighteenth-Century Life* 18:3 (Nov. 1994); *The Great South Sea: English Voyages and Encounters, 1570–1750* (New Haven: Yale University Press, 1997); and *The Prize of All the Oceans: The Triumph and Tragedy of Anson's Voyage round the World* (London: HarperCollins, 1999).

There are three monumental studies of English finance in the period: John Brewer, *The Sinews of Power: War, Money and the English State, 1688–1783* (New York: Knopf, 1989); P. G. M. Dickson, *The Financial Revolution in England: A Study in the Development of Public Credit, 1688–1756* (London: Macmillan, 1967); and Larry Neal, *The Rise of Financial Capitalism: International Capital Markets in the Age of Reason* (Cambridge: Cambridge University Press, 1990). For the Bubble itself, see John Carswell's excellent *The South Sea Bubble* (London: Alan Sutton, 1983). In addition to Bubble literature extracted or cited above, see W. R. Chetwood's *South Sea; or, the Biters Bit. A Tragi-Comi-Pastoral Farce,* and his *The Stock-Jobbers; or, the Humours of Exchange Alley;* Jonathan Swift's "The Bubble" and John Gay's "A Panegyrical Epistle to Mr. Thomas Snow"; and (from 1823) Charles Lamb's "The South-Sea House" in his *Essays of Elia.*

On Daniel Defoe, see Robert Markley, " 'So Inexhaustible a Treasure of Gold': Defoe, Capitalism, and the Romance of the South Seas," *Eighteenth-Century Life* 18:3 (Nov. 1994); Maximilian E. Novak, *Daniel Defoe: Master of Fictions* (Oxford: Oxford University Press, 2001); Daniel Defoe, *The Anatomy of Exchange Alley* (1719), and *Robinson Crusoe,* best read in Michael Shinagel's edition, which reproduces material from the landing and survival of Alexander Selkirk on Juan Fernández (New York: Norton, 1994). *Robinson Crusoe* has spawned an immense progeny, most notably Johann Wyss, *The Swiss Family Robinson* (1812), Jean Giradoux's *Suzanne and the Pacific* (1923), Michel Tournier's *Friday, Or the Other Island* (1969), and J. M. Coetzee's *Foe* (1986), not to mention Defoe's own *Farther Adventures of Robinson Crusoe* (1719), in which Robinson returns to his island via Canada to found a Christian colony before coming home via China and Russia.

For travel compendia of the era with a Pacific focus, see John Callander, ed., *Terra Australis Cognita: Or, Voyages to the Terra Australis, or Southern Hemisphere, during the Sixteenth, Seventeenth, and Eighteenth Centuries* (Edinburgh, 1766), an anglicization and plagiarism of Charles de Brosses, *Histoire de navigation aux terres australes* (Paris, 1756); A. and J. Churchill, *A Collection of Voyages and Travels* (London, 1704); and Alexander Dalrymple, *An Account of the Discoveries Made in the South Pacifick Ocean Previous to 1764* (London, 1767).

For Quirós see *The Voyages of Pedro Fernandez de Quirós, 1595 to 1608,* trans. Clements R. Markham (London: Hakluyt Society, 1904). His career has inspired three remarkable reimaginings: Tom Harrisson's chapter "The Last Conquistador," in *Savage Civilization* (New York: Knopf, 1937); James Macauley's poem sequence *Captain Quiros* (Sydney: Angus and Robertson, 1964); and John Toohey's novel *Quiros* (Sydney: Duffy and Snellgrove, 2002). For Mendaña, similarly, see Robert Graves, *The Isles of Unwisdom* (1950).

2
THE NOBLE SAVAGE

A geologist approaches the issue of Pacific island discovery in a revealing way. There are thousands of islands in the Pacific, but H. W. Menard decides there are 267 islands or island groups significant enough to have attracted the attention of visiting Westerners. The first was discovered by Magellan in 1521; the last, by Captain N. C. Brooks in 1859. Therefore, "the whole period of discovery lasted 338 years. If we divide it into 50-year intervals, it is evident that there were two major phases of discovery. The first began with 32 discoveries before 1550 and tapered off to the interval 1651–1700, when only three islands were discovered. The second and greater phase began with 12 discoveries in 1701–1750 and peaked at 113 in 1751–1800. Two-thirds of all the islands were discovered in the century beginning with 1751" (Menard, 9).

Historians agree that there was a lapse in Pacific discovery during the seventeenth century. "The religious and political problems of Europe in the mid and late seventeenth century left little time for exploration, and between the voyage of Tasman [1642] and the end of the seventeenth century there was a hiatus, a hiatus reflected in the dearth of travel literature between the publication of *Purchas His Pilgrimes* in 1625 and the appearance of the 'Buccaneer' literature of Queen Anne's reign" (Jack-Hinton, 233). This hiatus coincided with a period of intense intellectual reflection in early modern Europe on religious and political matters. This was an era when ideas that were both cause and effect of the Renaissance and the Reformation were still being fought over and when feudal relations were the subject of discussion and bloody strife. That the name and nature of humankind should come into question at such a time is hardly surprising.

Seventeenth-century Europeans had been aware of the Africans and the Chinese for many centuries and had come to regard the former as godless, anarchic, and unregenerate, and the latter as godless, mysterious, yet to be envied for their technological achievements. The discovery of America during the sixteenth century and Magellan's circumnavigation of the globe in 1519–1522 added two further immense unknowns, and for the first time Christian Europe began to confront the possibility that it occupied a relatively small region of the globe, that it itself suffered from a form of isolation, and that God had left huge areas and populations to languish in heathenism. How could all this be understood? "Since all men are Descendants of Adam, and consequently of Noah and his Posterity," Bernard Mandeville asked in his *Fable of the Bees* (1714), "how came savages into the world?" (quoted in Hodgen, 380). "Were these naked savages, who had grown up outside the framework of the Judeo-Christian ethic, moral beings? Were they capable of practicing the Christian virtues?" (Hodgen, 359).

Europeans' responses to what Margaret Hodgen calls "the problem of savagery" were essentially threefold:

> Since the sentiments which inspired comment were predominantly religious or ethical, they were generally explored in relation to current European standards of the good life. By some inquirers attempts were made to measure savage morality by the touchstone of European conscience; by others, moral criteria were abandoned in favor of an easy-going relativism; while still others, moved by the force of popular theological pessimism, made all members of the human family, including the savage, the tragic remainders of a process of corruption and degeneration. (Hodgen, 359–360)

Montaigne's essay "On the Cannibals" (quoted in the Introduction) adopts a culturally relativist position by arguing that if savages are savage, so are Europeans. The measurement of savage morality by European standards, in contrast, is represented by the political theorist Thomas Hobbes in a famous passage comparing savagery to war:

> In such condition, there is no place for Industry; because the fruit thereof is uncertain: and consequently no Culture of the Earth; no Navigation, nor use of the commodities that may be imported by Sea; no commodious Building . . . no Knowledge of the face of the Earth; no account of Time; no Arts; no Letters; no Society; and which is worst of all, continuall feare, and danger of violent death; And the life of man, solitary, poore, nasty, brutish, and short. (Hobbes, 186)

As for theological pessimism, it is crisply summed up by the American divine Cotton Mather. The American Indians, he concluded, were simply "the veriest ruines of mankind" (quoted in Hodgen, 380).

That which divided Montaigne from Hobbes was the choice between "chronological" and "cultural" primitivism. For Hobbes the savage was backward in time: a crude ancestor to be repudiated. "Cultural primitivism," however, "is the discontent of the civilized with civilization": "It is the belief of men living in a relatively highly evolved and complex cultural condition that a life far simpler and less sophisticated in some or in all respects is a more desirable life" (Lovejoy and Boas, 7). "A culture wishing to be free of itself," as Henri Baudet puts it (Baudet, 38–39), "experiences a perpetual longing for the uncivilized." "But above all,"

> the cultural primitivist's model of human excellence and happiness is sought in the present, in the mode of life of existing primitive, or so-called "savage" peoples. These contemporary embodiments of this idea have usually been found among races not intimately known to, and existing at some considerable distance from, the people to whom the preacher of primitivism commends them as examples to be followed, or exhibits them as more fortunate branches of our species whose state is to be envied. (Lovejoy and Boas, 8)

When European exploration of the Pacific went into hibernation after Tasman, the problem of savagery was already being articulated. When it came out of hibernation in the 1760s, intellectual means lay at hand to provide a new answer to that problem: a synthesis still based on "European standards of the good life" and still involved with issues of conscience, relativism, and pessimism but in which these standards and issues were radically reinterpreted in the light of Reason.

It is in the eighteenth century that the idea of the Pacific island comes into its own, and that idea was for a short but momentous period almost completely bound up with the discovery of Tahiti by Wallis, Bougainville, and Cook between 1767 and 1769. "Unlike the sixteenth century, which was obsessed with the finding of new continents," Barbara Maria Stafford suggests, "the eighteenth century was fascinated by the apparition of islands" (Stafford, 129), and that fascination was triggered by accounts like Bougainville's dreamlike landfall at Nouvelle Cythère. But the discovery of Tahiti also took place after the intellectual sea change described above. "When Wallis and Bougainville came across this island, they came as Columbus did—as discoverers; but the times had changed; and the meeting with a new race in this island of Tahiti . . . affected European minds very differently from the manner of three centuries before, when the Spaniards went for the first time through a like experience." John Lafarge concluded, "It is this new introduction of *modern* and *changed* Europe to another fresh knowledge of the savage world that makes the solemnity of the discovery" (Lafarge, 291–292). Above all, the discovery of Tahiti coincided with the flood tide of the intellectual movement known as the Enlightenment, the great decade of which had been the 1750s, when Montesquieu's *Spirit of the Laws*, Diderot and d'Alembert's *Encyclopaedia*, Condillac's *Essay on the Origin of Human Knowledge*, Voltaire's *Candide* and his *Essai sur les moeurs*, and Rousseau's discourses *On the Sciences and the Arts* and *On the Origin of Inequality* were all either published or gathering acclaim, and Buffon's multivolume *Histoire naturelle* began. English sailors like Wallis and Cook had not read such books, but Louis Antoine de Bougainville was a horse of a very different color. "Aristocrat, soldier, diplomat, he was truly a man of the Enlightenment . . . well-read in Montesquieu, Voltaire, Rousseau, and Buffon" (Marshall and Williams, 264–265).

The Enlightenment is a movement hard to define in positive terms. First and foremost, it opposed feudalism, so Enlightenment thinkers were bent on exposing injustice, illuminating government inefficiency, and rectifying administrative abuses. Furthermore, the movement hoped to free humankind from superstition and religious dogma, and it believed that scientific knowledge and education could do this—which explains why the publication of what is nowadays a universally accepted intellectual tool like an encyclopedia could have played so vital and so controversial a role in their intellectual campaign. Positively speaking, the *philosophes* favored religious tolerance and intellectual freedom, but two particular themes stand out. First, a critical attitude toward the religious institutions that had grown up to serve Christianity (particularly the Catholic Church and the Bible) led them to propose a science of man. Whereas the Renaissance still considered humanity a divinely created overlord separate from nature and with a separate destiny accordingly, the Enlightenment began to take issue with the biblical account of creation. Writers like Buffon became convinced that the earth was a good deal older than the six thousand years accorded to it by the church and that both the earth and the people inhabiting it had a history. A second theme uniting many Enlightenment thinkers, therefore, was the conviction that humanity could change and had changed in time and in space according to the conditions in which it found itself.

So the Enlightenment encouraged the rise of a secular intelligentsia devoted to a science of human beings that was independent from the Church and the Bible. Humanity had its origins not in the hands of God but in an older form of society. What remained to be established was whether that society was a golden age or a Hobbesian nightmare. In considering this question, the Enlightenment adopted a historical and anthropological approach to humankind's variety and variableness. As we shall see in Chapter 4, what Aristotle had called "the great chain of being" (from God to human beings, human beings to beasts, and beasts to rocks and stones) began to be replaced by what Buffon called "époques de la nature": *eras* of nature. The discovery of "new worlds" in the sixteenth century played a vital role in this development. As the philosopher John Locke had remarked, once upon a time "all the world was America"; such places marked the youth of nature and humankind, and studying them "might be a way of catching live, as it were, aspects of Europe's own prehistory" (Howe 1993: 247). At present, humanity was everywhere *different,* as nature, civilization, and history dictated. But the very extent of this variety suggested to some that it must be the outcome of a historical process and that humanity must therefore have had a prehistory when it was everywhere the *same* and when humankind was in a "state of nature" before civilization had diversified it: "when," as John Dunmore Lang put it, "the earth was still wet . . . with the waters of the deluge" (quoted in Howe 1993: 251).

No writer was more interested in this possibility than Jean-Jacques Rousseau (1712–1778), with whom the expression "noble savage" has become inextricably entwined. (In fact he never used it. It comes from the English poet John Dryden's play *The Conquest of Granada* (1672)—

> I am as free as nature first made man,
> Ere the base laws of servitude began,
> When wild in the woods the noble savage ran.

—though Dryden's emphasis on nature and the "base laws of servitude" is itself proleptically Rousseauistic.) The extent to which Rousseau actually believed that what Dryden described was ever true in reality remains subject to debate. On the one hand, he did describe Native Americans (or "Caribs") as folk "who of all existing peoples have up to now least strayed from the state of nature" (Rousseau 1996: 50). On the other hand, he certainly did not believe that modern humans could go back to that state; nor did he believe the savage could live among Europeans. A natural person raised amidst civilized circumstances, he believed, "would be like a shrub that chance had caused to be born into the middle of a path and that the passers-by soon cause to perish by bumping into it from all sides and bending it in every direction" (Rousseau 1979: 37). However, as the first great thoroughgoing cultural primitivist in the modern Western tradition, Rousseau added to the Enlightenment program described above an element that in time drew him away from the *philosophes* and made him the first great philosopher of Romanticism: his abiding belief that humankind possessed an unconscious, innate, or "natural" morality, superior to received religious ethics and absolute where religion was subject to historical change: "the natural excellence of the human heart," as George Forster calls it below. Far from science, education, and knowledge rolling back the frontiers of ignorance, such things progressively cut humanity off from innate morality. So Rousseau became a pessimist and an antiprogressivist: a kind of disenchanted inversion of Enlightened belief.

In other respects, however, Rousseau's beliefs (as stated in the *Discourse on Inequality*) are clear. He "saw man evolving through a series of stages,"

> beginning with "des hommes seuls errants dans les bois" [solitaries wandering in the woods] and going on to embryonic forms of society, forced upon man by the need to survive through co-operation . . . until their dependence on "fer et blé" [iron and corn] leads to division of labour and to the ownership of private property, with the consequent need to institute laws to protect the owning classes and regulate a society thenceforth corrupted. (Dunmore, 160)

Rousseau's depiction of outright savage life is by no means attractive:

> His imagination portrays nothing; his heart yearns for nothing; his modest needs are easily within reach; and he is so far from having sufficient knowledge to wish to acquire even more that he can have neither foresight nor curiosity.

Nature's spectacle becomes so familiar that it leaves him indifferent. . . . His soul, perturbed by nothing, is concerned only with the sense of his current existence, with no idea of the future, however near, and his plans, as limited as his horizon, barely extend to the end of the day. Even today, such is the foresight of a Caribbean Indian: in the morning he sells his cotton bed and returns weeping to buy it back in the evening, having failed to foresee he would need it for the coming night. (Rousseau 1996: 35–36)

Outright savages are not so much happy as fortunate, and nowhere is the absence of the debased moral sense of modern self-consciousness more conducive to fortune than in sexual relations:

Confined solely to the physical side of love and fortunate enough to be unacquainted with those preferences that inflame the urge for it and increase the difficulties of satisfying it, men must experience the ardours of their sexual nature less often and less keenly, and consequently must have fewer and less violent disputes among themselves. Imagination, which wreaks much havoc among us, never speaks to the savage's heart; each one calmly awaits the urge of nature, responds to it automatically, with more pleasure than frenzy, and once the need is satisfied, all desire is extinguished. (Rousseau 1996: 49)

As we shall see, Enlightenment voyagers looked at Islander women and their relations with Islander men and European sailors with deeply enquiring eyes, whether "anthropological" or speculative. Such relations raised questions of nature (sexual instinct) versus repression (morality) and of the treatment of women ("the weaker vessel") as an index of cultural sophistication. They also—as the *philosophe* Diderot's work suggests—raised questions of a more searching kind about European society, such as the purposes that institutions like marriage and the nuclear family were designed to serve: the retention and transmission of property, requiring the patriarchal control of women's fertility. Many writers reproduced below discuss sex and theft, and that area where they overlap: property.

Ultimately, Rousseau converts the dystopia described by Hobbes, in which the lack of civilized amenities produces a life "solitary, poore, nasty, brutish, and short," into one that was at least undisturbed by the kinds of insatiable longings that condemned Western life to the miseries of inauthenticity:

Savage man wandering in the forests, without work, without speech, without a dwelling, without war, and without ties, with no need of his fellow men and no desire to harm them, perhaps not even recognizing any one of them individually, subject to few passions and subject unto himself, had only such sentiments and knowledge as were suited to his condition; he felt only his true needs, saw only what he thought it was in his interest to see, and his understanding made no more progress than his vanity. If he happened to make some discovery, he was unable to communicate it to others, for he did not even recognize his own children. Every art perished with its inventor. There was no education or progress; the generations multiplied unproductively, and because each began anew from the same point, centuries passed by in all the crudeness of the earliest ages; the species was already old, and man remained ever a child. (Rousseau 1996: 51)

The depth of Rousseau's ambivalence is clear. In so far as savages are frozen in this way, they are released from the burdens of education, progress, and the anguish consequent on sexual fetishization, and are therefore privileged to live in a world of complete moral authenticity; but this produces a ghastly paradox, in which species become immeasurably old while individuals die in prolonged childhood. It may have taken untold millennia, but change and development were bound to arise:

> As long as men were content with their rustic huts, as long they confined themselves to stitching their garments of hides with thorns or fishbones, and adorning themselves with feathers or shells, to painting their bodies with various colours, to improving or decorating their bows and arrows, and to carving fishing-boats or a few crude musical instruments; in short, as long as they applied themselves only to work that one person alone could accomplish and to arts that did not require the collaboration of several hands, they lived as free, healthy, good, and happy lives as their nature permitted. . . . But from the moment one man needed help from another, and as soon as they found it useful for one man to have provisions enough for two, equality evaporated, property was introduced, and work became mandatory; vast forests were transformed into sunny open country that had to be watered with the sweat of man, and where slavery and adversity were soon seen to germinate and ripen with the crops. (Rousseau 1996: 62)

Rousseau was well aware that outright savagery had disappeared from the earth. At the beginning of the second part of the *Discourse,* he described an intermediate stage between savagery and civilization:

> Men who had once roamed the woods . . . slowly came together, gathered in various clusters, and in each region eventually formed a particular nation, united by customs and character—not by rules and laws, but through having a common way of living and eating and through the common influence of the same climate. . . . As ideas and feelings succeeded one another, and hearts and minds were cultivated, the human race became more sociable, contacts increased, and bonds grew tighter. People developed the habit of gathering together in front of their huts or around a large tree; song and dance, true children of love and leisure, became the entertainment, or rather the occupation, of the idle men and women thus flocked together. (Rousseau 1996: 60)

"This," he suggested, "is precisely the stage reached by most of the savage peoples known to us . . . *placed by nature midway between the stupidity of brutes and the fatal enlightenment of civilized man*" (Rousseau 1996: 61; italics added), and this was the picture of tribal life reported by mid-eighteenth-century voyagers with a philosophical turn of mind. Such reports were doubly effective coming from islands because of their quality of isolation:

> For students of primitive peoples the Pacific held advantages over North America and West Africa, ravaged and contaminated as they were by centuries of European exploitation. In the South Seas there had no been such contact, no slave trade, no frontier wars. Here in unspoilt surroundings would surely be found evidence to prove or disprove the presumptions of the "noble savagery" school of thought, and indicate more reliably the relationship between western and primitive man. (Marshall and Williams, 259)

Rousseau's ideas about man in his natural state were based on what he knew of America, but the discovery of Tahiti set light to them in a way nothing in the history of American culture contact could have done; some have argued that this intellectual crystallization had momentous implications indeed, playing a preparatory role in the French Revolution itself. "The discovery of Tahiti," the historian Henry Brooks Adams believed, "was the strongest possible proof that Rousseau was right. The society of Tahiti showed that European society had no real support in reason or experience, but should be abolished, with its absurd conventions, contrary to the natural rights and innate virtue of man" (Adams, 55).

"In many respects," Richard Grove suggests, "the isolated oceanic island . . . directly stimulated the emergence of a detached self-consciousness and a critical view of European origins and behaviour, of the kind dramatically prefigured by Daniel Defoe in *Robinson Crusoe*" (Grove, 8). (In his educational treatise *Émile*, Rousseau named *Robinson Crusoe* as the first book a child should read because in it the hero puts aside Western self-consciousness in favor of strategies for survival on a South Sea island.) However, "Tahiti proved that there was once a Golden Age; Tahiti also proved that it had long passed away. The island entered into the more serious and reflective levels of European art and thought not as a symbol of the normality of human happiness but as a symbol of its transience" (Smith 1985: 44). Because Tahiti was an island, it followed the noble savages it contained would be far more pure than their African or American cousins; it also followed that they would fall into corruption all the more rapidly and all the more completely. They had nowhere to go but down. So the noble savage became a moral antipode of himself: from being infinitely better than Europeans he became infinitely worse; he became ignoble and debased, or simply sad, threatened, and helpless. And when this intellectual change of attitude took place, Europeans began to apply to people like the Tahitians all the qualities Rousseau had originally ascribed to out-and-out savages: mindlessness, crudity, childishness, and so on.

Many of the explorers were themselves the first to voice anxiety regarding the Islanders they had encountered. "If the knowledge of a few individuals can only be acquired at such a price as the happiness of nations," George Forster wrote, "it were better for the discoverers, and the discovered, that the

South Sea had still remained unknown to Europe and its restless inhabitants" (quoted in Finney, 34). James Cook was even more graphic:

> What is still more to our shame as civilised Christians, we debauch their [Islanders'] morals already too prone to vice, and we introduce among them wants and perhaps disease which they never before knew, and which serve only to disturb that happy tranquillity which they and their forefathers enjoyed. If anyone denies the truth of this assertion let him tell me what the natives of the whole extent of America have gained by the commerce they have had with Europeans. (Cook 1955–1967, 2:175)

Thus the fatal impact grew up alongside the noble savage; both ideas voiced "the discontent of the civilized with civilization," as Lovejoy and Boas suggested. In the writings of a nineteenth-century missionary, discontent could easily take the form of repudiatory self-disgust:

> Is some race of merciless savages about to burst in upon these interesting people and destroy them? Yes, the same "irreclaimable and indomitable savages" that have ravaged every nation which they have conquered, "from China to Peru." . . . The savages of Europe, the most heartless and merciless race that ever inhabited the earth—a race, for the range and continuance of its atrocities, without a parallel in this world, and, it may be, in any other, are busy in the South Sea Islands. (Howitt, 484–485)

from James Cook, "Journal of the HMS *Endeavour*" (1769)

It has been suggested (see Further Reading, below) that the greatest discovery of James Cook (1728–1779) was not the east coast of Australia, or Antarctica, or Hawai'i, but Polynesia itself, which he triangulated in the course of his three voyages of discovery (1769–1771, 1772–1775, and 1776–1779). Cook was in a unique position to note cultural and linguistic similarities in populations as far apart as New Zealand, Easter Island, and Hawai'i, and—in that geographic sense at least—came to know more about the Polynesians than they knew themselves. On 13 April 1769 he made his first Polynesian landfall, at Tahiti.

> FRIDAY Apl. 14th. This morning we had a great many Canoes about the Ship, the Most of them came from the westward but brought nothing with them but a few Cocoa-nuts &ca. Two that appear'd to be Chiefs we had on board together with several others for it was a hard matter to keep them out of the Ship as they clime like Munkeys, but it was still harder to keep them from Stealing but every thing that came within their reach, in this they are prodiges expert. I made each of the two Chiefs a present of a Hatchet things

that they seem'd mostly to Value. As soon as we had partly got clear of these people, I took two Boats and went to the Westward all the Gentlemen[1] being along with me, my design was to see if there was not a more commodious Harbour and to try the disposission of the Natives having along with us the two Chiefs above mentioned: the first place we landed at was in Great Canoe Harbour (so call'd by Capt Wallis) here the Natives Flock'd about us in great Numbers and in as friendly a Manner as we could wish, only that they shew'd a great inclination to pick our pockets. We were conducted to a Chief who for distinction sake we call'd Hercules, after staying a Short time with him and distributing a few presents about us, we proceeded further and came to a Chief who I shall call Lysurgus,[2] this Man entertain'd us with Broil'd fish Bread fruit Cocoa-nuts &ca with great hospitality, and all the time took great care to tell us to take care of our pockets, as a great number of people had crowded about us. Notwithstanding the care we took Dr Solander and Dr Munkhouse[3] had each of them their pockets pick'd the one of his spy glass and the other of his snuff Box, as soon as Lycurgus was made acquainted with the theift he disperse'd the people in a Moment and the method he made use of was to lay hold of the first thing that came in his way and throw it at them and happy was he or she that could get first out of his way; he seem'd very much concern'd for what had happend and by way of recompence offer'd us but every thing that was in his House, but we refuse'd to except of any thing and made signs to him that we only wanted the things again. He had already sent people out after them and it was not long before they were return'd. We found the Natives very Numerous where ever we came and from what we could judge seem'd very peaceably inclin'd. About 6 oClock in the evening we return'd on board very well satisfied with our little excursion.

[. . .]

TUESDAY 9th, WEDNESDAY 10th and THURSDAY 11th [May]. Nothing remarkable happen'd for the three days. Obarea, the Dolphins Queen,[4] made us a Visit for the first time sence the Quadrant was Stolen,[5] she introduce'd her self with a small Pigg for which she had a Hatchet and as soon as She got it she lugg'd out a Broken Ax and several peices of Old Iron, these I believe she must have had from the Dolphin, the Ax she wanted to be mended and Axes made of the Old Iron. I obliged her in the first but excuse'd my self from the

---

1. That is, the nonsailors on board the *Endeavour:* accompanying scientists, artists, and so forth.

2. It was the university-educated expedition scientist, Joseph Banks, who awarded these classical names to two Islanders. Hercules is a hero of Greek myth; Lycurgus, a legendarily wise ruler of Athens.

3. Daniel Solander, expedition naturalist; William Monkhouse, naval surgeon.

4. "Obarea" (Purea) was a local leader who engaged in negotiations with Captain Wallis of HMS *Dolphin* during his visit of 1767.

5. On 2 May a quadrant had been stolen from the tent where scientific observations were to be made of the transit of Venus across the sun, one of the main objects of the first Cook voyage. It was returned later the same day.

latter. Sence the Natives have Seen the Forge at work they have frequently brought pieces of Iron to be made into one sort of Tools or other, which hath generally been done when ever it did not hinder our own work, being willing to oblige them in every thing in my power; these peices of Old Iron the natives must have got from the Dolphin, as we know of no other Ship being here and very probably some from us; for there is no species of theft they will not commit to get this Article and I may say the same of the common seamen when in these parts.

FRIDAY 12th. Clowdy weather with Showers of Rain. This Morning a Man and two young women with some others came to the Fort whome we had not seen before: and as their manner of introduceing themselves was a little uncommon I shall insert it: Mr Banks was as usual at the gate of the Fort trading with the people, when he was told that some Strangers were coming and therefore stood to receive them, the compney had with them about a Dozn young Plantains Trees and some other small Plants, these they laid down about 20 feet from Mr Banks, the People then made a lane between him and them, when this was done the Man (who appear'd to be only a Servant to the 2 Women) brought the young Plantains Singley, together with some of the other Plants and gave them to Mr Banks, and at the delivery of each pronounce'd a Short sentence, which we understood not, after he had thus dispose'd of all his Plantain trees he took several peices of Cloth and spread them on the ground, one of the Young Women then step'd upon the Cloth and with as much Innocency as one could possibly conceve, expose'd herself intirely naked from the waist downwards, in this manner she turn'd her Self once or twice round, I am not certain which, then step'd of the Cloth and drop'd down her clothes, more Cloth was then spread upon the Former and she again perform'd the same ceremony; the Cloth was then rowled up and given to Mr Banks and the two young women went and embraced him which ended the Ceremoney.[6]

SATURDAY 13th. Nothing worthy of note happen'd dureing the day, in the night one of the Natives attempted to get into the Fort by climing over the Walls but being discover'd by the Centinals he made off; the Iron and Iron tools daily in use at the Armourers Forge are temptations that these people cannot possibly withstand.

SUNDAY 14th. This day we perform'd divine Service in one of the Tents in the Fort where several of the Natives attended and behaved with great decency the whole time: this day closed with an odd Scene at the Gate of the Fort where a young fellow above 6 feet high lay with a little Girl about 10 or 12 years of age publickly before several of our people and a number of the Natives. What makes me mention this, is because, it appear'd to be done more from Custom than Lewdness, for there were several women present particu-

---

6. The significance of this "Ceremoney" remains unclear: a sexual invitation to Banks, a fertility ritual, or perhaps simply a stylized welcoming party.

THE NOBLE SAVAGE

larly Obarea and several others of the better sort and these were so far from shewing the least disaprobation that they instructed the girl how she should act her part, who young as she was, did not seem to want it.[7]

[. . .]

SUNDAY 4th [June]. Punished Arch[ibal]d Wolf with two Dozn Lashes for theft, having broken into one of the Store rooms and stolen from thence a large quantity of spike Nails, some few of them were found upon him.[8] This evening the gentlemen that were sent to observe the Transit of Venus returnd with success. [. . .]

MONDAY 5th. Got some of the Bread a Shore out of the Bread room to dry and clean. Yesterday being His Majestys Birth Day we kept it to day, and had several of the Chiefs to dine with us.

TUESDAY 6th. This day and for some days past we have been inform'd by several of the Natives that about 10 or 15 Months ago, Two Ships touched at this Island and stay'd 10 days in a Harbour to the Eastward call'd Ohidea, that the Commanders name was Toottera so at least they call'd him and that one of the Natives call'd Orette Brother to the Chief of Ohidea went away with him;[9] they likewise say that these Ships brought the Venerial distemper to this Island where it is now as common as in any part of the world and which the people bear with as little concern as if they had been accustomed to it for ages past. We had not been many days before some of our people got this disease and as no such thing happen'd to any of the Dophins people while she was here that I ever heard off, I had reason (notwithstanding the impossibility of the thing) to think that we had brought it along with us which gave me no small uneasiness and did all in my power to prevent its progress, but all I could do was to little purpose for I may safely say that I was not assisted by any one person on ye Ship, and was oblige'd to have most part of the Ships Compney a Shore every day to work upon the Fort and a Strong guard every night and the Women were so very liberal with their favours, or else Nails, Shirts &ca were temptations that they could not withstand, that this distemper very soon spread it self over the greatest part of the Ships Compney but now I have the satisfaction to find that the Natives all agree that we did not bring it here. However this is little satisfaction to them who must suffer by it in a very great degree and may in time spread it self over all the Islands in the South Seas, to the eternal reproach of those who first brought it among them. I had taken the greatest pains to discover if any of the Ships Company had the disorder upon him for above a month before our arrival here and ordered

---

7. Again the significance of the event is unclear, though it seems ceremonial. Cook's syntax is also ambiguous: does "want it" refer to instruction or the act itself?

8. Sailors on board the *Endeavour* were stealing nails to pay for sex with Islander women.

9. The commander of *La Boudeuse* and *L'Etoile* was Bougainville, who stayed at Tahiti between 6 and 16 April 1768 and who took a young chief, Aotourou, back to France. Aotourou died of smallpox on his journey home.

the Surgeon to examine every man the least suspected who declar'd to me that only one man in the Ship was the least affected with it and his complaint was a carious shin bone; this man has not had connection with one woman in the Island. We have several time seen Iron tools and other articles with these people that we suspected came not from the Dolphin and these they now say came from these two Ships.

from Louis Antoine de Bougainville, *A Voyage round the World* (1771)

Louis Antoine de Bougainville (1729–1811) had already had a distinguished career as scientist, diplomat, and soldier before being chosen to lead France's major eighteenth-century voyage of Pacific exploration (1767–1768), a voyage that came within a whisker of discovering the east coast of Australia. He was a far more educated, literary, and "philosophical" man than Cook, but however rapturous his account of Tahiti, he was no unreflective primitivist and in his voyage found plenty of evidence to refute sentimental notions of the "natural man."

As we ran along the coast, our eyes were struck with the sight of a beautiful cascade, which came from the tops of the mountains, and poured its foaming waters into the sea. A village was situated at the foot of this cascade, and there appeared to be no breakers in this part of the coast. We all wished to be able to anchor within reach of this beautiful spot; we were constantly sounding aboard the ships, and our boats took soundings close under the shore; but we found a bottom of nothing but rocks in this port, and were forced to go in search of another anchorage. [. . .]

As we came nearer the shore, the number of islanders surrounding our ships increased. The periaguas were so numerous all about the ships, that we had much to do to warp in amidst the crowd of boats and the noise. All these people came crying out *tayo,* which means friend, and gave a thousand signs of friendship;[10] they all asked nails and ear-rings of us. The periaguas were full of females; who, for agreeable features, are not inferior to most European women; and who in point of beauty of the body might, with much reason, vie with them all. Most of these fair females were naked; for the men and the old women that accompanied them, had stripped them of the garments which they generally dress themselves in. The glances which they gave us from their periaguas, seemed to discover some degree of uneasiness, notwithstanding the innocent manner in which they were given; perhaps, because nature has

---

10. Bougainville was not to know, but the Tahitians' behavior, which seemed to him so spontaneous, was in fact learned from their bruising encounter with the *Dolphin,* commanded by Captain Wallis, in 1767. The most important account of their coming to terms with their first European visitors is given in George Robertson, *A Journal of the Second Voyage of HMS* Dolphin *around the World* (London: Hakluyt Society, 1948).

THE NOBLE SAVAGE

every where embellished their sex with a natural timidity; or because even in those countries, where the ease of the golden age is still in use, women seem least to desire what they most wish for. The men, who were more plain, or rather more free, soon explained their meaning very clearly. They pressed us to choose a woman, and to come on shore with her; and their gestures, which were nothing less than equivocal, denoted in what manner we should form an acquaintance with her. It was very difficult, amidst such a sight, to keep at their work four hundred young French sailors, who had seen no women for six months. In spite of all our precautions, a young girl came on board, and placed herself upon the quarter-deck, near one of the hatch-ways, which was open, in order to give air to those who were heaving at the capstern below it. The girl carelessly dropt a cloth, which covered her, and appeared to the eyes of all beholders, such as Venus shewed herself to the Phrygian shepherd,[11] having, indeed, the celestial form of that goddess. Both sailors and soldiers endeavoured to come to the hatch-way; and the capstern was never hove with more alacrity than on this occasion.

At last our cares succeeded in keeping these bewitched fellows in order, though it was no less difficult to keep the command of ourselves. One single Frenchman, who was my cook, having found means to escape against my orders, soon returned more dead than alive. He had hardly set his feet on shore, with the fair whom he had chosen, when he was immediately surrounded by a croud of Indians, who undressed him from head to feet. He thought he was utterly lost, not knowing where the exclamations of those people would end, who were tumultuously examining every part of his body. After having considered him well, they returned him his clothes, put into his pockets whatever they had taken out of them, and brought the girl to him, desiring him to content those desires which had brought him on shore with her. All their persuasive arguments had no effect; they were obliged to bring the poor cook on board, who told me, that I might reprimand him as much as I pleased, but that I could never frighten him so much, as he had just now been frightened on shore.

[. . .]

The climate upon the whole is so healthy, that notwithstanding the hard work we have done in this island, though our men were continually in the water, and exposed to the meridian sun, though they slept upon the bare soil and in the open air, none of them fell sick there. Those of our men who were sent on shore because they were afflicted with the scurvy, have not passed one night there quietly, yet they regained their strength, and were so far recovered in the short space of time they staid on shore, that some of them were afterwards perfectly cured on board. In short, what better proofs can we desire of

---

11. This is Paris, prince of ancient Troy, who was raised as a shepherd in Phrygia and as an adult took part in the "judgment of Paris," when he decided which of three goddesses should be awarded a fabulous golden apple. He chose Venus, and as a reward she helped him abduct Helen of Troy from Greece.

the salubrity of the air, and the good regimen which the inhabitants observe, than the health and strength of these same islanders, who inhabit huts exposed to all the winds, and hardly cover the earth which serves them as a bed with a few leaves; the happy old age to which they attain without feeling any of its inconveniences; the acuteness of all their senses; and lastly, the singular beauty of their teeth, which they keep even in the most advanced age?

Vegetables and fish are their principal food; they seldom eat flesh, their children and young girls never eat any; and this doubtless serves to keep them free from almost all our diseases. I must say the same of their drink; they know of no other beverage than water. The very smell of wine or brandy disgusted them; they likewise shewed their aversion to tobacco, spices, and in general to every thing strong.

The inhabitants of Taiti consist of two races of men, very different from each other, but speaking the same language, having the same customs, and seemingly mixing without distinction. The first, which is the most numerous one, produces men of the greatest size; it is very common to see them measure six (Paris) feet[12] and upwards in height. I never saw men better made, and whose limbs were more proportionate: in order to paint a Hercules or a Mars, one could no where find such beautiful models. Nothing distinguishes their features from those of the Europeans: and if they were cloathed; if they lived less in the open air, and were less exposed to the sun at noon, they would be as white as ourselves: their hair in general is black. The second race are of a middle size, have frizzled hair as hard as bristles, and both in colour and features they differ but little from mulattoes.[13] The Taiti man who embarked with us, is of this second race, though his father is chief of a district: but he possesses in understanding what he wants in beauty. [. . .]

The inhabitants of Taiti are often seen quite naked, having no other clothes than a sash, which covers their natural parts. However, the chief people among them generally wrap themselves in a great piece of cloth, which hangs down to their knees. This is likewise the only dress of the women; and they know how to place it so artfully, as to make this simple dress susceptible of coquetry. As the women of Taiti never go out into the sun, without being covered, and always have a little hat, made of canes, and adorned with flowers, to defend their faces against its rays; their complexions are, of course, much fairer than those of the men. Their features are very delicate; but what distinguishes them, is the beauty of their bodies, of which the *contour* has not been disfigured by a torture of fifteen years duration.[14]

Whilst the women in Europe paint their cheeks red, those of Taiti dye their loins and buttocks of a deep blue. This is an ornament, and at the same

---

12. A unit of length current in France as opposed, say, to England. (Before the introduction of the metric system, measurement varied widely in Europe.)

13. The offspring of black and white parents. Bougainville's is one of the first European attempts to quantify physical differences among Pacific populations, in particular whether such differences were racial (and therefore permanent), social, or climatic.

14. The corset, universally endured by aristocratic women of Bougainville's time.

time a mark of distinction. The men are subject to the same fashion. I cannot say how they do to impress these indelible marks, unless it is by puncturing the skin, and pouring the juice of certain herbs upon it, as I have seen it practised by the natives of Canada. It is remarkable, that this custom of painting has always been found to be received among nations who bordered upon a state of nature. When Cæsar made his first descent upon England, he found this fashion established there; *omnes vero Britanni se vitro inficiunt, quod cæruleum efficit Colorem.*[15] The learned and ingenious author of the *Recherches philosophiques sur les Americains,*[16] thinks this general custom owes its rise to the necessity of defending the body from the puncture of insects, multiplying beyond conception in uncultivated countries. This cause, however, does not exist at Taiti, since, as we have already said above, the people there are not troubled with such insupportable insects. The custom of painting is accordingly a mere fashion, the same as at Paris. Another custom at Taiti, common to men and women, is, to pierce their ears, and to wear in them pearls or flowers of all sorts. The greatest degree of cleanliness further adorns this amiable nation; they constantly bathe, and never eat nor drink without washing before and after it.

The character of the nation has appeared mild and beneficent to us. Though the isle is divided into many little districts, each of which has its own master, yet there does not seem to be any civil war, or any private hatred in the isle. It is probable, that the people of Taiti deal amongst each other with unquestioned sincerity. Whether they be at home or no, by day or by night, their houses are always open. Every one gathers fruits from the first tree he meets with, or takes some in any house into which he enters. It should seem as if, in regard to things absolutely necessary for the maintainance of life, there was no personal property amongst them, and that they all had an equal right to those articles.[17] In regard to us, they were expert thieves; but so fearful, as to run away at the least menace. [. . .]

We have asked Aotourou many questions concerning his religion; and believe, we understood that, in general his countrymen are very superstitious; that the priests have the highest authority amongst them; that besides a superior being, named *Eri-t-Era,* king of the sun or of light, and whom they do not represent by any material image, they have several divinities; some beneficent, others mischievous; that the name of these divinities or genii is *Eatoua;* that they suppose, that at each important action of human life, there presides a good and an evil genius; and that they decide its good or bad success. What we understand with certainty is, that when the moon

---

15. Quotation from Roman emperor Julius Caesar's account of his Gallic wars: "All true Britons dye themselves with woad, which produces a blue color."

16. *Recherches philosophiques sur les Americains, ou Memoirs intéressants pour servir à l'histoire de l'espèce humaine* (1771), by Cornelius de Pauw.

17. Bougainville's account here is strikingly similar to Thomas More's imaginary island *Utopia* (1516), where houses have no locks, property is held in common, and intercommunal rivalry is unknown.

has a certain aspect, which they call *Malama Tamai*, or moon in state of war, (an aspect in which we have not been able to distinguish any characteristic mark, by which it could be defined) they sacrifice human victims. Of all their customs, one which most surprised me, is that of saluting those who sneeze by saying, *Evaroua-t-eatoua*, that the good *eatoua* may awaken thee, or that the evil *eatoua* may not lull thee asleep. These are marks which prove, that they have the same origin with the people of the old continent.[18] Upon the whole, scepticism is reasonable, especially when we treat of the religion of different nations; as there is no subject in which it is more easy to be deceived by appearances.

Polygamy seems established amongst them; at least it is so amongst the chief people. As love is their only passion, the great number of women is the only luxury of the opulent. Their children are taken care of, both by their fathers and their mothers. It is not the custom at Taiti, that the men occupied only with their fishery and their wars, leave to the weaker sex the toilsome works of husbandry and agriculture. Here a gentle indolence falls to the share of the women; and the endeavours to please, are their most serious occupation. I cannot say whether their marriage is a civil contract, or whether it is consecrated by religion; whether it is indissoluble, or subject to the laws of divorce. Be this as it will, the wives owe their husbands a blind submission; they would wash with their blood any infidelity committed without their husbands' consent. That, it is true, is easily obtained; and jealousy is so unknown a passion here, that the husband is commonly the first who persuades his wife to yield to another. An unmarried woman suffers no constraint on that account; every thing invites her to follow the inclination of her heart, or the instinct of her sensuality; and public applause honours her defeat: nor does it appear, that how great soever the number of her previous lovers may have been, it should prove an obstacle to her meeting with a husband afterwards. Then wherefore should she resist the influence of the climate,[19] or the seduction of examples. The very air which the people breathe, their songs, their dances, almost constantly attended with indecent postures, all conspire to call to mind the sweets of love, all engage to give themselves up to them. They dance to the sound of a kind of drum, and when they sing they accompany their voices with a very soft kind of flute, with three or four holes, which, as I have observed above, they blow with their nose. They likewise practice a kind of wrestling; which, at the same time, is both exercise and play to them.

Thus accustomed to live continually immersed in pleasure, the people

---

18. That is, the Tahitians appear to say "God bless you" when one sneezes, as some Westerners do.

19. Bougainville reveals his intellectual debt to the French thinker Montesquieu and his *De l'esprit des lois* [The spirit of the laws, 1748] here, which first systematically asserted the correlation between climate and morality—summarized and satirized fifty years after Bougainville's visit by the Romantic poet Lord Byron: "What men call gallantry and the gods adultery, / Is much more common where the climate's sultry."

of Taiti have acquired a witty and humorous temper, which is the offspring of ease and of joy. They likewise contracted from the same source a character of fickleness, which constantly amazed us. Every thing strikes them, yet nothing fixes their attention: amidst all the new objects, which we presented to them, we could never succeed in making them attend for two minutes together to any one. It seems as if the least reflection is a toilsome labour for them, and that they are still more averse to the exercises of the mind, than to those of the body.

I shall not, however, accuse them of want of understanding. Their skill and ingenuity in the few necessary instances of industry, which notwithstanding the abundance of the country, and the temperature of the climate they cannot dispense with, would be sufficient to destroy such assertion. It is amazing with how much art their fishing tackle is contrived; their hooks are made of mother-of-pearl, as neatly wrought as if they were made by the help of our tools; their nets are exactly like ours; and knit with threads, taken from the great American *Aloes*. We admired the construction of their extensive houses, and the disposition of the leaves of the *Thatch-palm*, with which they are covered.

Philibert Commerson, "Postscript: On the Island of New Cythera or Tahiti" (1769)

Philibert Commerson (1727–1773) was "Royal Botanist and Naturalist" attached to the Bougainville voyage. A prickly character who found the expedition unconducive to his studies, he still made a significant collection of botanical specimens, which remained unsorted when he left the expedition at Mauritius on its way home. As a consequence his scientific work received less recognition than it deserved. His "Postscript," however, was a key document of "noble savage" speculation in mid-eighteenth-century France. His final claim to fame lies in the fact that he smuggled his mistress, Jeanne Baret, aboard the voyage disguised as his valet: she would become the first woman to circumnavigate the globe.

> I retrace my steps to give you a brief sketch of this happy island, to which I made only a passing reference in the enumeration of the new lands we saw in circumnavigating the globe. I had given it the name, *Utopia*, that Thomas More awarded to his ideal republic (deriving it from the Greek roots *ou* and *topos*: a sort of *felix locus*).[20] I did not know then that M. Bougainville had called it New Cythera; and it was only much later that a prince of that nation who had been brought to Europe told us it was called Tahiti by its own inhabitants. Its position in longitude and latitude is a government secret, and I impose silence on myself accordingly. But I can tell you it is the only comer

20. *Felix locus* (Latin): happy place.

of the earth where men live without vices, prejudices, needs, or disagreements. Born under the finest sky, fed on the fruit of a soil fecund without tillage, ruled by heads of the family rather than by kings, they recognize no other god but love. Every day is consecrated to Him, the entire island is His temple, every woman His altar, and every man His celebrant. And women of what kind, I hear you ask? The rivals of the Georgians in beauty and sisters of the utterly naked Graces.[21] There neither shame nor modesty exercise their tyranny at all, and the lightest of gauzes always wafts where winds or desires direct it. The act of creating a fellow human being is a religious one, the preludes to which are encouraged by the vows and the songs of all the assembled people, and the climax celebrated by universal applause. Every stranger is admitted to share these delightful mysteries: it is even a duty of hospitality to invite them to do so. So the good Utopian ceaselessly thrills at either the sensations of his own pleasures or the spectacle of those of others. A double-banded faultfinder[22] would find nothing in all this but a breaking down of public standards, a foul prostitution, the most shameless cynicism: but he grossly deludes himself in misunderstanding the condition of natural man, born essentially good, exempt from all preconceptions, and following without suspicion as without remorse the sweet impulses of an instinct always sure, because it has still not degenerated into reason.

A language most sonorous and most harmonious, made up of about four or five hundred indeclinable and unconjugable words—that is, without any syntax—suffices them to convey all their ideas and to express all their needs. A noble simplicity excluding neither the modifications of tone nor the mime of passions keeps them free of that pompous vulgarity[23] that we call the richness of languages and that makes us lose in the labyrinth of words our clarity of perception and alacrity of discrimination. The Utopian, by contrast, gives a name immediately to each object that he sees, the tone in which he pronounces the name of that object having already expressed the way in which he is affected by it. Few words makes for rapid conversation; the workings of the soul and the movements of the heart are synchronous with the stirring of the lips; he who speaks and he who listens are always in unison. Our Tahitian prince, who in the seven or eight months he has been among us has still not learned ten of our expressions, as often as not dazed by their volubility, has no other resource but to block his ears and laugh in our faces.

---

21. In Greek myth, three sisters who bestowed beauty and charm; the women of Georgia (southern Russia) are legendarily attractive.

22. In the original, "censeur à deux rabats." *Rabat:* band or turned down piece of fabric; *rabat-joie:* killjoy. Commerson may simply mean a double-bound faultfinder, or he may have in mind the folded collar, sometimes with two ribbons, associated with the European clergy of his day.

23. In the orginal, "cette superbe buttologie." *Buttologie* appears to be a coinage of Commerson's, with several possible implications. *Butor:* oaf, vulgar person; *buter:* to prop or shore up; *buttage:* earthwork or rampart. Thus European intellectual and linguistic habits are either vulgar, laborious, or defensive—or all three.

We should guard against the suspicion that the issue here concerns only a mob of coarse and stupid savages. Everything among them bears the stamp of the most perfect intelligence: the canoes constructed along previously unknown lines, their navigation guided by study of the stars; the immense native buildings of an elegant, practical, and regular shape; the art not of weaving thread by thread but of making fabric come out suddenly altogether under the beater;[24] the coloring of that fabric with purple drops so that women's monthly secret is never betrayed; the fruit trees carefully spaced in their fields just as our orchards are but without the boring symmetry; the reefs of their coasts marked and lit at night to aid those at sea; the plants known and distinguished by names that go as far as to indicate their affinities; the tools of their crafts though made of primitive materials yet still worthy of being compared with ours by the choice of shapes and the certainty of their operation: such are the reasons that bring these people into our esteem despite the short time we have known them.

With what industry did they not already deal with iron—this metal so precious to this people who know only how to turn it to useful ends, so vile for us who have made it into instruments of death and despair. With what horror did they not reject the knives and scissors we offered them because they seemed to guess the abuse they could be put to. With what readiness, in contrast, did they not take the measure of our dinghies, our longboats, our sails, our tents, our barrels, or (in a word) anything they believed could be copied to advantage.

Regarding the simplicity of their customs, the fairness of their dealings with their women in particular (who are by no means subjugated by them as happens with savages), their brotherly love to all, their recoiling from the spilling of human blood, their idolatrous respect for their dead (whom they regard as only sleeping), and finally their hospitality to strangers: the merit of speaking at length on these things as our admiration and our gratitude requires must be left to the ship's journals.

When invited to our meal, everything that appeared on the table excited their chiefs' curiosity. They wished us to give an account of every dish; if a vegetable seemed good to them, they immediately asked for its seed, receiving which they informed themselves where and how to plant it, and when it would bear fruit.

Our bread appeared excellent to them, but we needed to show them the grain from which it was made, the means of grinding it, the way of making flour into dough, of making it rise, and baking it. All these processes were followed and noted in detail. Often enough, however, it sufficed to explain half the thing: the other was already anticipated and divined. Their aversion to wine and spirits was invincible. Wise in everything, they faithfully

---

24. This is *tapa* (Polynesian): cloth of the Pacific region made from beating out the bark of the paper-mulberry tree. Bougainville had noted classically simple clothes made from this material: like those worn by the ancient Greeks and Romans, perhaps.

received their food and drink from the hands of nature; there was neither fermented liquor nor cooking pots among them, so one never saw anything but the finest teeth and the most beautiful complexions. It is a shame that the only man that we can exhibit from that nation [Aotourou] is perhaps the most unprepossessing. We should guard against judging it from this sample; but if I am obliged to disparage him in this respect, I must do him the justice he deserves of being studied and known by all others, a truly interesting individual, worthy of all the ministry's attentions[25] and of any compensation that is also due in the name of justice for all the voluntary sacrifices he made in the enthusiasm of his attachment to us.

I have often heard the question: from what continent, from what race, do these Islanders come? As if it was only from emigration upon emigration that continents and islands must have been populated. As if we cannot (even admitting the hypothesis that from time to time migrations have occurred) imagine on all distant lands and continents a primitive people that received and incorporated the emigrant people or who were driven away or destroyed.[26] For me—considering this question simply as a naturalist—I willingly accept the existence of these protoplastic peoples [ces peuples protoplastes] of whom, whatever physical changes may have ever occurred in certain parts of the globe, there has always been preserved at least a couple on each of those parts that remained inhabited; only from the perspective of a historian of human upheavals would I take all the emigrations into account, real or imagined. I see very distinct races of men, moreover: these mixed races have certainly been able to produce slight variations, but only a mythologist can explain how the whole lot would have come from a common stock.

So I do not see why our good Tahitians should not be the genuine sons of their soil: I mean descending from wholly Tahitian ancestry and going back as far as a race most jealous of its ancestry. I see even less to which other people we should give the credit for the peopling of a Tahiti that has always remained within the limits of nature, pure and simple. A society of humans once corrupted can never entirely regenerate itself; colonies carry everywhere with them the vices of their metropolis. If one were to find for me similarities in the language, customs, and habits of other people near to or far from Tahiti, I would admit defeat—though even then the question would only be thrown back and never resolved. I can only form a conjecture that I submit happily to those who like discussing subjects of this kind. I find in the Tahitian language four or five words derived from Spanish: among others that of *haouri,* which evidently comes from *hierro* (iron), and *matao mate,* which means "killing" or "killed." Might it be some Spaniards ship-

25. Commerson's article was written for the French Academy of Sciences and published in the *Mercure de France* in November 1769.

26. Commerson takes Bougainville's speculations on color, race, and ethnicity a stage further: what evidence might the Tahitians provide for the peopling of the earth?

wrecked during the first navigations of the South Sea who furnished them with the word in giving them their first knowledge of the thing? What a new subject for reflection! Would the Tahitian language then be as glorious in not having until then a word suitable for expressing the act of killing as the ancient laws of Sparta are for not having pronounced any penalty at all for patricide, having never imagined its possibility? If one were to accord me the accuracy of this supposition—with which, however, I would not wish to denigrate a nation [Spain] I respect, given the lack of evidence—I would before long draw from it the explanation of some habits and the origin of some animals that seem to me borrowed from Europeans. [. . .]

I will not leave these dear Tahitians without having cleared them of an insult done to them in considering them as thieves. It is true that they took many things from us and that too with a dexterity that would do credit to the most skillful pickpocket of Paris, but do they deserve for this the name of thieves? Let us see: what exactly is theft? It is the taking of something that rightfully belongs to another. For anyone to complain with justice of having been stolen from, it must be proven to be a thing their ownership of which is preestablished. But is the right of ownership a natural one? No; it is purely a convention. One must needs say then that no convention dictates that it be known or accepted, and the Tahitian who has nothing of his own and who offers and gives generously all that he sees is wished for has never known this right of exclusivity. Then the act of his taking something from you that excites his curiosity is, according to him, only an act of natural justice by which he makes you do what he would do himself. It is an inverse of the law of an eye for an eye by which one applies to oneself all the good that one would have done to others. I do not see the shadow of theft in it. Our Tahitian prince was an agreeable thief: he took with one hand a thing or a glass or a biscuit, but it was to give them with the other to the first of his own people he met, while at the same time taking their bananas, chickens, and pigs—which he brought to us. I have seen the cane of an officer raised over him as if he had been caught in this kind of swindle, the generous motive of which was ignored. I put myself with indignation between the two at risk of receiving the blow myself. Such is the soul of the sailors, on which Jean-Jacques Rousseau so judiciously places a question mark!

from James Cook, "Account of His Second Voyage round the World" (1773)

The prime scientific objective of Cook's first voyage had been the observation of the transit of Venus across the sun. The second voyage entered Antarctic waters for the first time, but it also occupied itself a great deal with ethnography and ethnology: how the indigenous peoples it encountered behaved and how such behavior might be explained in terms of knowledge of humanity at large. In this passage of his journal (written in September 1773), Cook takes issue with some of the observations he found in Bougainville's account.

> I shall not in this Journal take any notice of the general produce of these isles [Tahiti], the manners and Customs of the Natives &ca as these subjects have been treated at large in the Published account of my former Voyage. But as M de Bougainville in his Voyage round the world has mentioned some customs being amongst them not taken notice of by me in the said published account, and as they were to me rather doubtfull they became the object of my enquirey. He mentions, page 268, human sacrifices; in order to satisfie my self in this point, I went one day to a marai in Matavai[27] in company with Captain Furneaux, having a long with us, as I had upon every other occasion a marine who was with me last voyage and who spoke the language tolerable well. Several of the Natives were with us one of whome appeared to be an intelligent sencible man. In the marai laid a Corps upon a Watarau,[28] some viands &ca so that every thing promised success to my inquireys. I began with asking questons relating to the several objects before us: if the Plantans &ca were for the Eatua; if they sacrificed to the Eatua Hogs, Dogs Fowles &ca to all of which he answered in the afformative. I then asked if they sacrificed men to the Eatua, he answered Taata eno they did, that is bad men, first Teparrahy or beating them till they were dead; I then asked him if good men were put to death in this manner, he answer'd no Taata eno, I asked if any Aree's[29] he said no and said these had Hogs &ca to give to the Eatua and again repeated Taata eno. I next asked him if Towtows, that is servants or slaves, who had nither Hogs, Dogs or fruit, but yet good men if they were sacrificed to the Eatua, his answer was no only bad men. I asked him several more questions, and all his answers seemed to tend to this one point that men for certain crimes were condemn'd to be sacrificed to the gods provided they have not wherewithall to redeem themselves which I think implies that on certain occasions human sacrifices are necessary, when they take such men as have committed crimes worthy of death and such will generally be found amongest the lower class of people. The man of whom I made these inquiries as well as some others took some pains to explain the whole of this Custom to us but we were not masters enough of their language to understand them. [. . .]
>
> He [Bougainville] is again very much misstaken when he says, p. 25, that "every one gathers fruit from the first tree he meets with or takes some in any house on which he enters"; he likewise seems to think there is no personal property among them. So far from it being so, that I much doubt if their is a fruit tree on the whole island that is not the property of some individual in it. We are even told that who ever takes fruit &ca the property of any other

---

27. *Marae* (Tahitian): sacred open space. Matavai is a bay in northwest Tahiti frequently used by Western visitors and now the site of the capital, Papeete.

28. *Fatarau* (Tahitian): altar.

29. The *arii* were the chiefly, "aristocratic" caste of Tahiti, as far as the Westerners understood.

THE NOBLE SAVAGE

person is punished with death or a good beating. Indeed it is highly obsurd to suppose every thing in Common in a Country where almost every article is raised by cultivation, it is true some things require but little labour, but others again require a good deal, such as roots of every kind and Bananas and Plantains will not grow spontaneously but by proper cultivation, nor will the Bread and Cocoa nutt trees come to perfection without. These are not the only Mistakes M. Bougainville has committed in his account of the Customs of these people nor can I See how it could be otherwise, a stay of ten days was by no means sufficient for such a task. The love of truth alone obliges me to mention these things and not with a view of finding fault with Mr Bougainville's Book, on the Contrary I think it the most usefull as well as entertaining Voyage through these Seas yet published. When I was at Ulietea [Raiatea] in 1769, we thought the people but little addicted to thieving, probably they were at that time restrain'd by their countryman Tupia, for we now found them as expert thieves as the Otaheitians; the temptations were indeed now far greater and occured oftener, as being more of us and less upon our guard, though very little attention would have been sufficient as my self and some few others experienced while others less on their guard had their Pockets Picked every day. A forced restitution is all that can be expected, but unless this can be done immidiately or what you have lost be of some Value or concequence, it will be better to put up with the loss, for one no sooner attempts to force a restitution than the whole country is alarmed and a total stop put to all manner of supplies till all matters reconciled. One ought not to be too severe upon these people when they do commit a thieft sence we can hardly charge them with any other Vice, Incontency in the unmarried people can hardly be call'd a Vice sence neither the state or Individuals are the least injured by it. Maried Women are perhaps as faithfull to their husbands as any others whatever, at least I have not seen an instance to the contrary; upon the whole I think the women in general were less free of their favours now than formerly, none but common women would yeild to the embraces of our people; not one of the gentlemen were able to obtain such favours from any women of distinction, though several attempts were made, but they were always jilted in the end. In short the more one is acquainted with these people the better one likes them, to give them their due I must say they are the most obligeing and benevolent people I ever met with. [. . .]

Sence we can hardly charge them with any other vice great Injustice has been done the Women of Otaheite and the Society Isles, by those who have represented them without exception as ready to grant the last favour to any man who will come up to their price. But this is by no means the case; the favours of Maried women and also the unmarried of the better sort, are as difficult to obtain here as in any other Country whatever. Neither can the charge be understood indiscrimenately of the unmaried of the lower class. Much the greater part of these admit of no such familiarities. That there are Prostitutes here as well as in other Countrys is very true, perhaps more in proportion and such were those who came on board the Ship to our people and frequented the Post we had on shore. By seeing these mix indiscrimi-

nately with those of a different turn, even of the first rank, one is at first inclined to think that they are all disposed the same way & that the only difference is in their price. But the truth is, the Women who becomes a Prostitute,
do not seem on thier opinion to have committed a crime of so deep a die as
to exclude her from the Esteem and Society of the Community in general.
On the whole a stranger who visits England might with equal justice draw
the Characters of the women there, from those which he might meet with
on board the Ships in one of the Naval Ports, or in the Purlieus of Covent
Garden & Drury lane.[30]

from Denis Diderot, "Supplement to Bougainville's *Voyage*" (1772)

Though he has never had the same profile as Rousseau and Voltaire, Denis
Diderot (1713–1784) was a key intellectual of the Enlightenment, and a highly
radical one, whose work would be an important influence on Karl Marx. All
the writers so far represented have discussed the status of women in Tahitian
society; in his "Supplement" Diderot—who left his native France only to visit
Catherine the Great in Russia—uses Bougainville as the springboard for a
profound analysis of the European cult of chastity, relating it to patriarchal
anxieties about fatherhood and inheritance.

from section III. Conversation between the Almoner and Orou

B. When Bougainville and his crew landed among the Tahitians, the Almoner[31] fell to the lot of Orou. The Tahitian and the Almoner were about the
same age, thirty-five or thirty-six years old. At that time Orou had but his
wife and three daughters, named Asto, Palli, and Thia. They undressed him,
washed his face and hands and feet, and served him with a wholesome and
frugal meal. When he was on the point of retiring, Orou, who had meanwhile absented himself with his family, reappeared, presented his wife and
his three daughters, all unveiled, saying:

"You have supped, you are young, you are in good health; if you sleep
alone you will sleep badly: man needs a companion by his side at night. Here
is my wife, here are my daughters: choose the one that pleases you most, but
if you would oblige me you will give the preference to the youngest of my
daughters, who has not yet borne a child."

The mother added: "Alas! I have nothing to complain about; poor Thia,
it is not her fault!"

---

30. The great London theaters of Covent Garden and Drury Lane were notorious for
prostitutes.

31. A better translation of *aumonier* would be "chaplain." The chaplain on Bougainville's
expedition was called Jean-Baptiste Lavaisse, a Franciscan monk from Paris who (like
Commerson) left the voyage at Mauritius on the journey back to France. Hardly anything more
is known of him or whether Diderot's fable has any basis in truth.

THE NOBLE SAVAGE

The Almoner replied that his religion, his vocation, his morals, and decency did not permit him to accept their offer.

Orou replied: "I do not know what this thing is that you call religion; but I cannot but think ill of it, since it prevents the enjoyment of an innocent pleasure, to which Nature, that sovereign mistress, invites us all: prevents you from calling into being one of your fellow creatures; from rendering a service that the father, the mother, and the children ask of you; of discharging a debt to your host who has made you welcome; and from enriching a nation by thus giving it another subject. I do not know what this thing is that you call vocation, but your first duty is to be a man and to be grateful. I do not suggest that you should carry back the customs of Orou to your own land; but Orou, your host and your friend, beseeches you to lend yourself to the custom of Tahiti. Are the customs in Tahiti better or worse than yours? It is a question that is easily decided. Has the land where you were born more men than it can feed? If so, then your customs are neither better nor worse than ours. Can it feed more than it has? Then our customs are better than yours. As to the sense of decency you plead, I understand you: I confess I am wrong, and I ask your pardon for it. I do not demand that you should injure your health, and should you be tired, you must rest; but I hope you will not continue to sadden us. Look at the shadow you have spread over all their faces: they fear lest you have remarked blemishes in them which have roused your disdain. Even were it so, would not the pleasure of doing honour to one of my daughters, chosen from her sisters and companions, and thus of doing a good action, suffice you? Be generous!"

ALMONER: "It is not that: they are all four equally beautiful, but my religion! but my vocation!"

OROU: "I offer them to you; they belong to themselves, and they give themselves to you. Whatever purity of conscience this thing *religion* and the thing *vocation* impose on you, you may accept them without thought. I am not abusing my authority, and you may be certain that I know and respect the rights of others."

Here the truthful Almoner acknowledged that never had Providence exposed him to such violent temptation. He was young; he was disturbed; he was in torment; he turned away his gaze from the charming suppliants; he let it fall on them again, he raised his hands and his eyes to Heaven. Thia, the youngest, embraced his knees, and said to him: "Stranger, do not distress my father, do not distress my mother, do not distress us! Honour me in my hut and among my own people; raise me to the rank of my sisters who mock at me. Asto, the eldest, has already three children, Palli, the second, has two, and Thia has none! Stranger, good stranger, do not rebuff me: make me a mother; make me a child that I can lead by the hand one day in Tahiti; that I can see in nine months' time at my breast, of whom I shall be proud, and who will become part of my marriage-portion when I go from my father's hut to another's. I may perchance be more lucky with you than with our young Tahitians. Should you grant me this favour, I will not forget you, I will bless you all my life; I will write your name on my arm and on that of thy son; we will pronounce it continually with joy, and when you leave this shore my good wishes will follow you on the seas until you have reached your own land!"

The simple Almoner said that she pressed his hands, that she gazed into his eyes, and with such a touching expression; that she wept, that her father, her mother and her sisters withdrew, that he remained alone with her, and even while saying, "But my religion, but my vocation," he found himself the next morning lying by the side of this young girl, who showered caresses on him; and she invited her father, her mother, and her sisters, when they drew near, to join their gratitude to hers.

Asto and Palli, who had retired, re-entered with native dishes, liquors, and fruits. They embraced their sister and wished her joy. They made their repast together; thereafter Orou, left alone with the Almoner, said to him:

"I see that my daughter is content with you, and I thank you. But can you let me know what is meant by this word *religion,* which you have so often repeated, and with such sorrow?"

The Almoner, after a moment's reflection, replied: "Who was it made your hut and the utensils which furnish it ?"

orou: "It was I."

almoner: "Very well. We believe that the world and all it contains is the work of a Maker."

orou: "Has he a head, hands, and feet?"

almoner: "No."

orou: "Where is his dwelling place?"

almoner: "Everywhere."

orou: "Even here?"

almoner: "Here."

orou: "We have never seen him."

almoner: "He is not seen."

orou: "A very indifferent Father! He must be old: he must at least be as old as his work."

almoner: "He does not grow old. He spoke with our ancestors, he gave them laws. He prescribed for them the manner of their worship. He ordained certain actions as good; He forbade others as being bad."

orou: "I understand; and one of the actions he forbade as bad was to lie with a woman or young girl. Why then did he make two sexes?"

almoner: "For their union; but on certain requisite conditions, after certain preliminary ceremonies, whereby a man belongs to one woman, and to her alone; and a woman belongs to one man, and to him alone."

orou: "For all their life?"

almoner: "For all their life."

orou: "So that if a woman lay with another than her husband, or a husband with other than his wife . . . but it cannot happen. For since he is there, and it displeases him, he would prevent it."

ALMONER: "No, He leaves them to their devices, and they sin against the Law of God (for so we name the Great Maker), against the law of the land; and they commit a crime."

OROU: "I should be sorry to give you offence by any word of mine, but grant me permission and I will tell you my thought."

ALMONER: "Speak."

OROU: "These strange precepts seem to me to be opposed to nature and contrary to reason: made to multiply crime, and to irritate at every moment the Ancient Maker, he who made all things without hands, or feet, or head, who is everywhere, and seen nowhere; who lives to-day and to-morrow, and is not a day the older for it; who commands and is not obeyed; who can prevent, but does not prevent. Contrary to nature, for they suppose that a thinking, sentient, free being can be the property of another like himself. On what is this right founded? Do you not see that, in your country, they have confounded what has neither consciousness, nor thought, nor desire, nor will; what one picks up, puts down, keeps, or exchanges without injury to it or complaint on its part, with what cannot be exchanged or acquired, which has liberty, will, and desire; which can give or refuse itself for a moment, or altogether; which makes complaint and suffers; which cannot become an article of commerce unless one forget its character, and do violence to its nature; contrary to the general law of being? Does anything seem to you more contrary to sense than a precept which forbids the change which is in all nature; which orders a constancy which cannot be found in it, and which violates the liberty of the male and of the female by tying them to one another for ever; a fidelity confining the most capricious of pleasures to one and the same individual; a vow of immutability between two creatures of flesh and blood, and that under a sky which is never for two minutes the same, in grottos which threaten ruin, at the base of crumbling rocks, beneath falling trees, on the unstable stones? Believe me, you render man's state worse than that of the animals. I know not what your Great Maker may be; but I rejoice that he did not speak with our fathers, and I desire that he may not speak with our children; for he might communicate to them the same follies, and they might commit the folly of believing them. Yesterday, while we supped, you talked to us of magistrates and priests: I know not what these personages may be whom you named *magistrates* and *priests,* whose authority regulates your conduct; but, tell me, are they masters of good and evil? Can they make what is just unjust, and the unjust just? Is it for them to label bad actions as good, and innocent and useful actions as evil? You cannot think so, for at that rate there would be neither true nor false, nor good nor bad, nor beautiful nor ugly—at least, only what it should please your Great Maker, your magistrates, and your priests so to call; and from one moment to another you would be forced to change both notions and conduct. One day one of your three masters would say to you *kill,* and you would, in consequence, be obliged to kill; another day *steal,* and you would have to steal; or *eat not of this fruit,* and none dares eat it; or *I forbid you this vegetable, this animal,* and all must avoid it. Nothing good but it might be forbidden you; nothing wicked but it might be ordained you. And where would you be if your three masters, not agreeing among themselves, bethought themselves of permitting, enjoining, and forbidding the same thing, as I imagine must often happen? Then, to placate the priest, you must fall out with the magistrate, and to satisfy the magistrate, displease the Master Maker; and to render yourself agreeable to his sight, renounce your nature. And do you know what would come to pass? You would neglect all three, and be neither man nor citizen, nor reverence your Maker. You would be nothing; you would be at war with authority of every kind; at war even with yourself; embittered, and tormented by your own heart, persecuted by witless masters, and unhappy even as I saw you but last night when I brought you my wife and daughters, and wrung from you the cry, "But my religion! But my vocation!" Would you know once and for all, and everywhere, what is good and bad? Hold fast to the nature of things and of actions; to your relations with others of your kind, to the influence of your conduct on your particular utility, and in the general welfare. You are mad, if you are persuaded that there is anything in the universe, either up above or down below, which can add to or retrench on the laws of Nature. Her will is eternally that good should be preferred to ill, and the general good to the particular. You may ordain the contrary, but you will not be obeyed. You will multiply by fear, punishment, and remorse, the evil-doers and the wretched; you will deprave consciences; you will corrupt minds; they will know no more what to do and what to avoid. Troubled in innocence, untroubled in crime, they will have lost the pole-star of their path."

from George Forster, *A Journey round the World* (1777)

Joseph Banks had been the chief scientist aboard Cook's first voyage and was to accompany the second, but his grandiose ideas for his retinue and accommodation on board made his inclusion impossible, and the Admiralty replaced him with the Prussian polymath Johann Reinhold Forster and his son George (1754–1794). We join George Forster in August 1774 at Tanna, one of the southern islands of the New Hebrides (Vanuatu), a Melanesian island group often noted by eighteenth- and nineteenth-century visitors for the savagery of its people by contrast with Polynesian islands like Tahiti. (See Figures 3 and 4.)

FIGURE 3. William Hodges (1744–1797), "Man of Tanna" (1774). By permission of the National Library of Australia.

FIGURE 4. William Hodges (1744–1797), "Woman and Child of Tanna" (1774). By permission of the National Library of Australia.

We passed the day before and after noon, in the plain behind the watering-place, and collected the flowers of an unknown sort of tree, which we could obtain no other way, than by shooting at them. In the evening the seine was hauled, and we caught about two hundred weight of fish, which afforded another, though rather scanty fresh meal to the whole ship's company. Dr. Sparrman[32] went up the flat hill with me, where we passed about half an hour very agreeably with our friends the natives, who made us a present of fruit at parting. We amused them as usual by singing to them, and they became so familiar at last as to point out some girls to us, whom from an excess of hospitality not uncommon with uncivilized nations, they offered to their friends with gestures not in the least equivocal. The women, at the first hint of the civility which the men intended to confer upon us, ran off a great distance seemingly much frightened, and shocked at their indelicacy. Our Indians, and particularly the young people, were very desirous that we should pursue the girls, whether only to frighten them or not, we could not ascertain. However, they seemed to be very well pleased, that we did not take the hint; and we parted from them, after distributing several presents, and especially some mother of pearl hooks with tortoise-shell barbs.

The next morning we were ready for sailing, having taken in a sufficient quantity of ballast, wood, and fresh water; only the wind, which blew right into the harbour, prevented our putting to sea. We went on shore after breakfast, with the captain, and a party of people; and he continued to trade with the natives, whilst we went into the country. We soon separated, and each of us went by himself to a different part. I passed by a number of natives in their way to the beach; but they all stepped out of the path to make room for me, though I was without any companion, and not one of them attempted with a look or gesture to offend me. I strolled alone several miles in the back of the flat hill, or in the valley along its south-side, to a part where I had never been before. The path which I followed was hid in the thickest groves, from whence I could only now and then discern the extensive plantations which covered the whole slope of the hill. Here I frequently saw the natives employed in cutting down trees, or pruning them, or digging up the ground with a branch of a tree, instead of a spade, or planting yams, and other roots; and in one place, I heard a man singing at his work, nearly the same tune which they used to sing to us on the hill. The prospect which I beheld was so pleasing, that it did not fall much short of the beautiful scenes of Taheitee. It had this advantage besides, that all the country about me to a great distance, consisted of gentle elevations, and spacious vallies, all which were capable of culture; whereas at Taheitee the mountains rose immediately craggy, wild, and majestic from the plain, which has no where the breadth of two miles. The plantations at Tanna consist, for the greatest part of yams, bananas, eddoes,[33] and sugar-canes, all which being very low, permit the eye to take in a

32. Anders Sparrman, naturalist on the voyage.
33. Tubers, root crops.

great extent of country. Single tufted trees rise in different places, and amuse the beholder with a variety of romantic forms. The whole summit of the level hill which bounds a part of the horizon, appears shaggy with little groves, where a number of lofty palms rise over the rest of the trees.

Those who are capable of being delighted with the beauties of nature, which deck the globe for the gratification of man, may conceive the pleasure which is derived from every little object, trifling in itself, but important in the moment when the heart is expanded, and when a kind of blissful trance opens a higher and purer sphere of enjoyment. Then we behold with rapture the dark colour of lands fresh prepared for culture, the uniform verdure of meadows, the various tints upon the foliage of different trees, and the infinite varieties in the abundance, form, and size of the leaves. Here these varieties appeared in all their perfection, and the different exposure of the trees to the sun added to the magnificence of the view. Some reflected a thousand dancing beams, whilst others formed a broad mass of shadow, in contrast with the surrounding world of light. The numerous smokes which ascended from every grove on the hill, revived the pleasing impressions of domestic life; nay my thoughts naturally turned upon friendship and national felicity, when I beheld large fields of plantanes all round me, which, loaded with golden clusters of fruit, seemed to be justly chosen the emblems of peace and affluence. The cheerful voice of the labouring husbandman resounded very opportunely to complete this idea. The landscape to the westward was not less admirable than that of which I have just now spoken. The rich plain was bounded on that side by a vast number of fertile hills, covered with forests, interspersed with plantations, and beyond them rose a ridge of high mountains, not inferior to those of the Society Islands, though apparently of a much easier slope. The solitary spot from whence I beheld this rural scene was likewise favoured by nature. It was a delightful cluster of trees, which climbers and bindweeds decked with odoriferous blossoms. The richness of the soil was here extremely remarkable; for though I beheld many palms which the winds had thrown down, yet most of them bent their summits upwards from the ground, and sent forth new shoots with surprising luxuriance. Their branches were the resort of various birds, adorned with the brightest colours, which now and then struck the ear with an unexpected song not destitute of harmony. The serenity of the air, and the coolness of the breeze, contributed to make my situation still more agreeable. The mind at rest, and lulled by this train of pleasing ideas, indulged a few fallacious reflections, which encreased its happiness at that instant by representing mankind in a favourable light. We had now passed a fortnight amidst a people who received us with the strongest symptoms of distrust, and who prepared to repel every hostile act with vigour. Our cool deliberate conduct, our moderation, and the constant uniformity in all our proceedings, had conquered their jealous fears. They, who in all probability had never dealt with such a set of inoffensive, peaceable, and yet not despicable men; they who had been used to see in every stranger a base and treacherous enemy, now learnt from us to think more nobly of their fellow-creatures. Prudence, which accompanied the civilized voyagers, had no sooner fascinated the instinct of the savages, watchful for their safety, than another, no less powerful, awoke in their breast, and taught them to relish the sweets of society. They shared the abundant produce of their soil with their new acquaintance, being no longer apprehensive that they would take it by force. They permitted us to visit them in their shady recesses, and we sat down in their domestic circles with that harmony which befits the members of one great family. In a few days they began to feel a pleasure in our conversation, and a new disinterested sentiment, of more than earthly mould, even friend-ship, filled their heart. This retrospect was honourable to human nature, as it made us the benefactors of a numerous race. I fell from hence into a reverie on the pre-eminence of our civilized society, from which I was roused by the sound of approaching steps. I turned about and saw Dr. Sparrman, to whom I pointed out the prospect and communicated my ideas. We agreed in our sentiments, and set out on our return, as the hour of noon was approaching. The first native whom we met ran out of the way and hid himself in a bush. The next was a woman at the entrance of a plantation, to whom we appeared so unexpectedly, that she had no time to escape. She offered us a basket full of yamboos,[34] with a trembling hand, and with all the expressions of fear strong-ly marked in her countenance. We were surprised at this behaviour, and giv-ing her some small trifles proceeded in our way. A number of men stood be-hind the bushes in and about the plantation, and made signs to us to walk on by waving their hands towards the beach. At last, when we stepped out of the wood, we beheld two natives seated on the grass, holding one of their breth-ren dead in their arms. They pointed to a wound in his side, which had been made by a musket-ball, and with a most affecting look they told us "he is killed." We looked hastily towards the station of our people, and seeing them deserted by the natives, hurried to join them, and learn the particulars of this shocking event. A sentinel had been posted as usual to keep the natives at a distance from our party, but the sailors took the liberty of walking and trad-ing freely among them. A native, who in all likelihood had never been on the beach before, came through the croud and began to walk across the space which our people occupied. The sentry pushed him back among the rest of his brethren, who were already accustomed to this injurious treatment, and ac-quiesced in it. The new-comer, however, refused to be controuled on his own island by a stranger; he prepared once more to cross the area, perhaps with no other motive at present than that of asserting his liberty of walking where he pleased. The sentry drove him back once more, with a rude thrust sufficient to rouse a man much less irascible than a savage. He, to vindicate his right, laid an arrow on his bow, which he aimed at the aggressor; but the soldier in-stantly levelled his musket and shot him dead. Captain Cook landed in the

---

34. Not the tropical root crop (yam) but the German-speaking Forster's transliteration of *jambu:* a range of fruits from the myrtle family commonly called the rose apple, Java plum, or Malay apple.

same moment; he saw the native fall, and many of his countrymen running off to hide themselves from the cruel and treacherous people who had polluted their island. He commanded the soldier to be loaded with irons, and sent him on board the ship. He next endeavoured to appease the natives, and the natural excellence of the human heart is such, that several, especially those who came from the flat eastern hill, were persuaded to stay, and once more to trust those who had so grievously violated the laws of hospitality. Dr. Sparrman and myself were struck with the moderation of the people, who had suffered us to pass by them unmolested, when they might easily have taken a severe revenge for the murder of their countryman. We went on board with captain Cook, greatly apprehensive for the safety of my father, who still remained in the woods, accompanied by a single sailor. We had, however, the satisfaction to see him safe about a quarter of an hour after, among the party of marines who were left on the beach to protect some of our water-casks. A boat was immediately sent off, which brought him on board. He had met with the same good treatment from the natives as ourselves; they had learnt to know our disposition, and seemed to be too good tempered to confound the innocent with the guilty. Thus one dark and detestable action effaced all the hopes with which I had flattered myself. The natives, instead of looking upon us in a more favourable light than upon other strangers, had reason to detest us much more, as we came to destroy under the specious mask of friendship; and some amongst us lamented that instead of making amends at this place for the many rash acts which we had perpetrated at almost every island in our course, we had wantonly made it the scene of the greatest cruelty. Captain Cook resolved to punish the marine with the utmost rigour for having transgressed his positive orders, according to which the choleric emotions of the savage were to be repressed with gentleness, and prudently suffered to cool. But the officer who commanded on shore, declared that he had not delivered these orders to the sentry, but given him others which imported, that the least threat was to be punished with immediate death. The soldier was therefore immediately cleared, and the officer's right to dispose of the lives of the natives remained uncontroverted. We came on shore again after dinner, where our people hauled the seine, and caught a few fish. The natives on the beach were very few in number, and chiefly without arms; the murder of their countryman seemed to be forgotten, or at least they seemed to have forgiven it in their hearts. My father, with Dr. Sparrman and myself, walked about on the plain, and shot some birds. We only met a single native, who at sight of us immediately struck into a different path, and walked very swiftly to escape us. We called to him, and making all the friendly signs which we could invent, at last prevailed on him to turn back. He approached us with distrust and apprehension marked in every gesture; however, by making him some presents, his fears were removed, mutual confidence took place, and we parted very good friends. It was late in the evening when we left the shore with all our people.

THE NOBLE SAVAGE

from George Keate, *An Account of the Pelew Islands* (1788)

In 1783 the British ship the *Antelope* was wrecked off the Micronesian Pelew Islands (Palau). The islanders and their chief (Ibedul, or "Abba Thulle" as Keate called him) were outstandingly helpful, and when the *Antelope's* captain returned to England, he brought back a Palauan named Lee Boo (who like Aotourou died of smallpox) and communicated the tale to George Keate (1729–1797), an admirer of the French enlightenment *philosophes* and a correspondent with Voltaire. The resulting book became a case study of the noble savage and the inherent goodness of humanity. (See Figures 5 and 6.)

The conduct of these people towards the *English* was, from the first to the last, uniformly courteous and attentive, accompanied with a politeness that surprized those on whom it was bestowed. At all times they seemed so cautious of intruding, that on many occasions they sacrificed their natural curiosity to that respect, which natural good manners appeared to them to exact. Their liberality to the *English* at their departure, when individuals poured in all the best they had to give, and that of articles too of which they had far from plenty themselves, strongly demonstrated that these testimonies of friendship were the effusion of hearts that glowed with the flame of philanthropy; and when our countrymen, from want of stowage, were compelled to refuse the further marks of kindness which were offered them, the intreating eyes and supplicating gestures with which they solicited their acceptance of what they had brought, most forcibly expressed how much their minds were wounded to think they had not arrived early enough to have their little tributes of affection received.

Nor was this conduct of theirs an ostentatious civility exercised towards strangers.—Separated as they were from the rest of the world, the character of a stranger had never entered their imagination.—They felt our people were distressed, and in consequence wished they should share whatever they had to give. It was not that worldly munificence, that bestows and spreads its favours with a distant eye to retribution—Their bosoms had never harboured so contaminating a thought—No; it was the pure emotions of native benevolence—It was the love of man to man.—It was a scene that pictured human nature in triumphant colouring—And whilst their *liberality* gratified the sense, their *virtue* struck the heart!

Our people had also many occasions to observe, that this spirit of urbanity operated in all the intercourse the natives had among themselves. The attention and tenderness shewn to the women was remarkable, and the deportment of the men to each other mild and affable; insomuch that, in the various scenes of which they were spectators, during their stay on these islands, the *English* never saw any thing that had the appearance of contest, or passion: every one seemed to attend to his own concerns, without interfering with the business of their neighbour.—The men were occupied in their plantations, or in cutting wood, making hatchets, line, or small cords: some

FIGURE 5. Henry Kingsbury (fl. 1750–1780), "Abba Thule, King of Pellew," in George Keate, *An Account of the Pelew Islands* (1788). By permission of the National Library of Australia.

in building houses or canoes; others in making nets and fishing-tackle. The forming of darts, spears, and other warlike weapons, engrossed the attention of many more; as also the making of paddles for their boats, the fashioning of domestic utensils, and the preparing and burning the chinam.[35]—Such as had abilities to conduct any useful employment were called by the natives

35. Or *chunam:* lime for cement derived from coral or shell.

THE NOBLE SAVAGE

FIGURE 6. Henry Kingsbury (fl. 1750–1780), "Ludee, One of the Wives of Abba Thule," in George Keate, *An Account of the Pelew Islands*(1788). By permission of the National Library of Australia.

Tackelbys; of this class were reckoned the people who built, or inlaid the canoes; such also were those who manufactured the tortoise-shell, or made the pottery.

Although industry, however zealous, must be slow in producing its purpose, unaided by proper implements, and labour rendered extremely tedious from this deficiency, yet, in regions where such advantages are denied, we do not find that the ardour of attempting is abated. A steady perseverance, to a certain degree, accomplishes the end aimed at; and *Europe* hath, not without reason, been astonished at the many singular productions imported from the southern discoveries, so neatly and curiously wrought by artless hands, unassisted but by such simple tools as serve only to increase our surprize, when we see how much they have effected.—Every man, by his daily labour, gained his daily sustenance: necessity imposing this exertion, no idle or indolent people were seen, not even among those whom superior rank might have exempted; on the contrary, these excited their inferiors to toil and activity by their own examples. The King himself was the best maker of hatchets in the island, and was usually at work whenever disengaged from matters of importance.—Even the women shared in the common toil; they laboured in the plantations of yams, and it was their province to pluck out all the weeds that shot up between the stones of the paved causeways. They manufactured the mats and baskets, as well as attended to their domestic concerns. The business of tatooing was also carried on by them; those who entered on this employment were denominated *Tackelbys artheil,* or female artists.—Their manners were courteous, though they were far from being of loose, or vicious dispositions; they in general rejected connections with our people, and resented any indelicate or unbecoming freedom with a proper sense of modesty.

In such scenes of patient industry, the years of fleeting life passed on; and the cheerful disposition of the natives fully authorized our people to suppose, that there were few hours of it either irksome or oppressive. They were strangers to those passions which ambition excites—to those cares which affluence awakens.—Their existence appeared to glide along like a smooth undisturbed stream; and when the natural occurrences of life ruffled the surface, they possessed a sufficient portion of fortitude to restore to it soon its wonted calm. Their happiness seemed to be secured to them on the firmest basis; for the little which Nature and Providence spread before them, they enjoyed with a contented cheerfulness; nor were their bosoms habituated to cherish wishes which they had not the power of gratifying. And it will not surely be denied, that in civilized nations the error of a contrary conduct exhibits, among the inactive, many melancholy repining countenances; whilst it prompts more daring and uncontrouled spirits to aim at compassing their views by injustice or rapine, and to break down the sacred barrier of society.

From the general character of these people the reader, I should conceive, will be disposed to allow, that their lives do credit to human nature; and that, however untutored, however uninformed, their manners present an interesting picture to mankind.—We see a despotic government without one shade of tyranny, and power only exercised for general happiness, the subjects looking up with filial reverence to their King.—And, whilst a mild government, and an affectionate confidence, linked their little state in bonds of harmony, gentleness of manners was the natural result, and fixed a brotherly and disinterested intercourse among one another.

[. . .]

THE NOBLE SAVAGE

It should be the caution of every writer, to endeavour to disarm criticism, by meeting objections, that *may* be made.—After the good dispositions which the people of PELEW have been seen to possess, it may possibly be said, they were addicted to pilfering when opportunity offered; a censure which many, I believe, think has been too severely passed on the poor inhabitants of the southern ocean.—In the PELEW islands, it was never done but by those of the lowest class; and whenever complaint was made of any thing having been taken clandestinely away, the King, as well as his Chiefs, considered it as a breach of hospitality, nor could their indignant spirits rest till the article purloined was searched for, and if found, restored.—Should some *Eastern* Prince, magnificently decorated, accidentally, as he passed along, drop a diamond from his robe, and were a poor peasant (knowing how great an acquisition it was) to see it sparkling in the dust, where is that resistance, that self-denial, which would go on and leave it untouched?—A nail—a tool—or a bit of old iron, was to *them* the alluring diamond.—They had no penal statute against *petty larceny.* They sought only the means of rendering easier the daily toils of life, or of compassing with facility what they imperfectly accomplished by unwearied perseverance! And, I am confident, the voice of reason will unite with me in asserting, that they must have been more than men, had they acted less like men. Virtuous in the extreme would be deemed that country, where the conscience of no individual, in the cool moments of reflection, could upbraid him with a heavier transgression, than applying to his own use a bit of iron that lay before him!

In the name of humanity, then, let us judge with less rigour our fellow-creatures; and, should any one be disposed, for such trivial failings, to censure the benevolent inhabitants of PELEW, that censure, I trust, for the sake of justice, will never be passed on them by those who live in civilized and enlightened nations—for *Such* must be too well convinced of the inefficacy of the best-digested laws, and the inability of their own internal police to restrain the vices of mankind, by observing, that all which *Prudence* can revolve, *Wisdom* plan, or *Power* enforce, is frequently unable to protect their *Property* by night, or their *Persons,* at all times, even under meridian suns.—They will reflect, that every bolt and bar is a *satire* on society; and painfully recollect, that it is not the *daring plunderer* alone they have to guard against; they are assailable under the smile of *dissembled* friendship, by which the Generous and the Confiding are too often betrayed into a situation *beyond* the shelter of any *protecting* law; a wound which, perhaps, more than any other, h ʌn tortured the feelings of sensibility!

Waiting, therefore, that long-expected æra when civilization, science, and philosophy, shall bring us to a more confirmed practice of *real* virtue, it becomes us to view with charity those errors in others, which we have not as yet, been able to correct in ourselves.

If the enlightened sons of EUROPE, enjoying the full blaze of advantages unknown in less favoured regions, have hitherto made so slow an advance toward *moral perfection,* they are surely passing the severest censure on themselves if they expect to find it in a happier manner approached by the dark and unfriended children of the SOUTHERN WORLD!

from Jules Sébastian César Dumont d'Urville, *The New Zealanders: A Story of Austral Lands* (1825)

Jules Sébastian César Dumont d'Urville (1790–1842), arguably the greatest nineteenth-century navigator of the Pacific, first sailed to New Zealand as second in command on a French voyage of exploration of 1822–1825. It was on the return voyage that he wrote his epic novel—in prose but in six "cantos"—about tradition and change in Maori society. He returned to the Pacific for two further voyages in 1826–1829 and 1837–1840, but *The New Zealanders* remained unpublished until its translation into English in 1992. His depiction of New Zealand is an example of "hard" primitivism, as opposed to the "soft" variety of Commerson, Forster, and Keate. (See Figure 7.)

I am going to sing of the combats, ways and customs of a distant people,[36] whose very name has not been long known to us. On the curved surface of the globe we inhabit, in the middle of the vast expanse of the seas, the Eternal has placed an immense, untamed island which, until recently, was unknown to Europeans. Its position in the universe is diametrically opposite to that of ancient Gaul and the mortals who inhabit it are suspended precisely beneath our feet. For them, the sun is just crossing the meridian as midnight begins to chime in our country. Our twilight is their dawn and when the day-star gives colour to our countryside, they are plunged in the sombre darkness of night and Morpheus[37] is shaking his poppy seeds onto their heavy eyelids. Their seasons, too, are the opposite of ours. We languish in the stifling heat of the dog-days while they shiver in winter's icy grip and during this time, as he slows his customary pace, the sun-god seems to leave their verdant forests with regret. In our land, by contrast, his chariot deigns to give no more than fleeting warmth to our chilled plains. In these regions, Europeans are surprised to find that nothing is familiar to them. The trees which crowd the forests, the birds which twitter in their shade, even the fish which streak the seas; all is new to them. The mortals are also quite different. Europeans are prejudiced against them because of certain antisocial aspects of their character. They are scandalised above all by the determination with which the New Zealanders oppose their [the Europeans'] will, which in any case is too often arbitrary, and their judgements, which are always rash. Before long, these arrogant visitors will call the New Zealanders a ferocious and barbarous people. Yet these severe judges were ignorant of the religious dogmas and political reasons which were able to justify these cruel practices,

---

36. D'Urville adapts the first line of Virgil's Latin epic about the founding of Rome, the *Aeneid:* "I sing of arms and the man . . . ".

37. The Greek god of dreams.

THE NOBLE SAVAGE

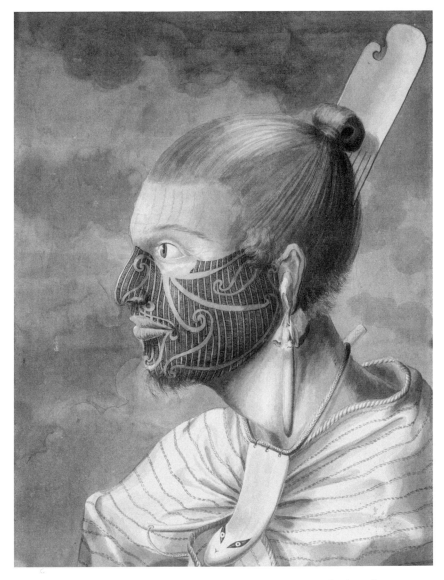

FIGURE 7. Sidney Parkinson (1745–1771), "Portrait of a New Zealand Man" (1769). By permission of the British Library.

at least to account for them and, above all, they were forgetting that throughout time, in spite of our much-vaunted civilisation, all the people of Europe, one after another, have deserved a similar reproach.

As the impartial narrator who is always faithful to the voice of truth, I will expose the facts without aversion and without flattery. If a few hideous and disgusting pictures present themselves to my pen, sometimes my brushes will also reproduce images which are cheerful and pleasant.

Along the tranquil banks of the River Kami, not far from the place where it discharges the tribute of its current into the bosom of the Pacific Ocean on the west coast of New Zealand, lived the contented and peaceful tribe of Tiami. On the ridge of quite a high hill carpeted only with ferns and creepers, were to be found its modest huts, placed in several rows according to the pre-eminence and fortunes of the families. Simple tree branches, bent in a semi-circle and tightly interlaced, formed the rustic roofs. Each hut was scarcely big enough for a couple and, as a family grew with the arrival of a baby, the parents were obliged to build a new one for the new-born child. Their fur-nishings comprised a few mats, some baskets, chests and benches worked in wood, along with stone implements, while their weapons were hung on the walls of the cabin. These were limited to axes made of serpentine, wooden spears hardened in the fire, and various kinds of clubs made from basalt or whalebone. At the very summit of the hill and near the entrance to the forti-fied settlement, one could distinguish the residence of their paramount chief, the virtuous Moudi-Pangui.[38] It was a little larger than all the others and slightly better decorated. Among these people, still living close to nature, there are no sovereigns as we have in our old kingdoms. Their most sacred, most inviolable duty is to be the first to watch over the security of all and to pay for it with their own lives. In these regions, no matter what services the sovereign has rendered to his homeland, no matter what his merits and his power, as soon as a prince finds that because of the passing years, infirmities, or even as a result of wounds gloriously received, he is incapable of marching at the head of his warriors, he must renounce his command. However, he does not wait to be informed of this. He himself makes the decision to hand over the power and places it into the hands of the relative he considers to be most worthy of it. Consequently, these people have great confidence in their chiefs and are convinced of their superiority and, although the rights attached to the throne are not at all clearly defined, they obey their rulers without ques-tion and rebellion is extremely rare.

The circumference of this village was fortified by high palisades, joined together with precision and finished off like a *chevaux de frise*.[39] In addition to this, there was a deep moat around it in the places where the terrain was naturally too accessible and a covered path, one hundred paces long, pro-vided a place from where missiles could be thrown on to the assailants. All these public works were well maintained, not that they were frequently used; the tribe of Tiami was known, on the contrary, to be one of the most cordial and peaceful of the whole island. Still, as experience had shown, there might be an ambitious sovereign, jealous neighbours and covetous strangers to re-pulse, and Moudi-Pangui, in his wisdom, had not forgotten that caution is the mother of prudence.

A glance at the land surrounding Tiami was all that was needed to see

---

38. Based on the historical Maori chief Murupaenga but also an idealized embodiment of what d'Urville took to be Maori virtues.

39. A spiky structure on a wall, intended to intimidate horsemen.

THE NOBLE SAVAGE

that the inhabitants had given themselves over to gentle and innocent occupations. There were well-cultivated fields where the starchy *kapana,* the sweet *koumara,* the nourishing *taro* and the agreeable *ti* all grew in abundance.[40] Ditches were carpeted by the briliant and useful *koradi;*[41] there were many pens specifically for pigs and huge nets covered the seashore and riverbanks. Finally, everywhere, the pretty, well-maintained paths were shaded by perfumed trees. These were all characteristics of a nation which is unaccustomed to the fury and ravages of war. Indeed, over several years it had had to withstand only two or three battles and the enemy, which was always repelled with loss of life, was unable to set foot on the land that it supposed would fall easily into its possession. It was to the brilliant qualities and considerable valour of their sovereign that these people owed their cherished advantages. More importantly, it was to him that they owed the honour of no longer being cannibals and, for that reason alone, of being as superior to their neighbours as man is to the unreasoning beast. But this pleasing metamorphosis did not come about without pain and without hindrances. It needed superior courage and talents to triumph.

SOURCES

James Cook, "Journal of the HMS *Endeavour* 1768–1771," National Library of Australia, MS 1. Reproduced by permission of the National Library of Australia.

Louis Antoine de Bougainville, *A Voyage round the World Performed by Order of His Most Christian Majesty, in the Years 1766, 1767, 1768, and 1769,* trans. Johann Reinhold Forster (London, 1772).

Philibert Commerson, "Post-Scriptum sur l'Isle de la Nouvelle-Cythère ou Tayti, par M. Commerson, Docteur en Medicin, Embarqué sur le Frégate du Roy la *Boudeuse* Commandée par M. de Bougainville" [trans. Richard Lansdown], Muséum National d'Histoire Naturelle (Paris), MS 1927. Reproduced by permission of the Muséum National d'Histoire Naturelle.

James Cook, "Account Prepared for Publication by Captain J. Cook of His Second Voyage round the World; April, 1772–July, 1774," British Library Additional MS 27888. Reproduced by permission of the British Library.

Denis Diderot, *Rameau's Nephew and Other Works,* trans. Mrs. Wilfrid Jackson (London: Chapman and Hall, 1926).

George Forster, *A Journey round the World* (London, 1777).

George Keate, *An Account of the Pelew Islands* (London, 1788).

Jules Sébastian César Dumont d'Urville, *The New Zealanders: A Story of Austral Lands,* trans. Carol Legge (Wellington: Victoria University Press, 1992). Reproduced by permission of Victoria University Press.

FURTHER READING

The Enlightenment was the most intellectually powerful movement to make serious use of the South Seas, and some knowledge of it is useful. General studies include

40. All root crops: potato, sweet potato, taro, and the root of the *dracaena* species.
41. The flax plant, source of linen material.

Dorinda Outram, *The Enlightenment* (Cambridge: Cambridge University Press, 1995); Roy Porter, *The Enlightenment* (London: Palgrave, 2001); John Yolton, *The Blackwell Companion to the Enlightenment* (Oxford: Basil Blackwell, 1992); and Roy Porter, "The Exotic as Erotic: Captain Cook at Tahiti," in G. S. Rousseau and Roy Porter, eds., *Exoticism in the Enlightenment* (Manchester: Manchester University Press, 1990). A. O. J. Lovejoy, "The Supposed Primitivism of Rousseau's *Discourse on Inequality*," in his *Essays in the History of Ideas* (Baltimore: Johns Hopkins University Press, 1948), is salutary; Walter Veit, ed., *Captain James Cook: Image and Impact; South Seas Discoveries and the World of Letters* (Melbourne: Hawthorn Press, 1972), contains useful pieces by Jack K. Dowling on Bougainville and John Dunmore on Diderot's "Supplement"; Veit's second volume of *Captain James Cook: Image and Impact,* titled *The Pacific Syndrome: Conditions and Consequences* (Melbourne: Hawthorn Press, 1979), has a good essay on the Pacific and the Enlightenment by Alan Frost.

A great deal has been written on the noble savage. See Henri Baudet, *Paradise on Earth: Some Thoughts on European Images of Non-European Man* (New Haven: Yale University Press, 1965), which is excellent and short; I. C. Campbell, "Savages Noble and Ignoble: The Preconceptions of Early European Voyagers in Polynesia," *Pacific Studies* 4:1 (Fall 1980); and A. O. Lovejoy, *Primitivism and Related Ideas in Antiquity* (Baltimore: Johns Hopkins University Press, 1935). Hoxie Neal Fairchild, *The Noble Savage: A Study in Romantic Naturalism* (New York: Columbia University Press, 1928), remains priceless for its breadth of reference; Lois Whitney, *Primitivism and the Idea of Progress in English Popular Literature in the Eighteenth Century* (Baltimore: Johns Hopkins University Press, 1934), is useful in a similar way. Ronald L. Meek, *Social Science and the the Ignoble Savage* (Cambridge: Cambridge University Press, 1976), and Anthony Pagden, *European Encounters with the New World: From Renaissance to Romanticism* (New Haven: Yale University Press, 1993), are both based on American examples but raise general issues (and Pagden discusses Rousseau and Diderot). For Rousseau, start with Patrick Riley, ed., *The Cambridge Companion to Rousseau* (Cambridge: Cambridge University Press, 2001). The greatest imaginative work of noble savagery is Tolstoy's "The Cossacks" (1862), not set in the Pacific at all; but Herman Melville's *Typee* (1846) runs Tolstoy a close second, as does Lord Byron's *The Island* (1823). Female "noble savages" had a special appeal for Western males: a phenomenon broadly surveyed in Michael Sturma, *South Sea Maidens: Western Fantasy and Sexual Politics in the South Pacific* (Westport: Greenwood Press, 2002).

Useful historical studies from each end of the telescope are David A. Chappell, "Shipboard Relations between Pacific Island Women and Euroamerican Men, 1767–1887," *Journal of Pacific History* 27:2 (Dec. 1992); and P. J. Marshall and Glyndwr Williams, *The Great Map of Mankind: British Perceptions of the World in the Age of the Enlightenment* (London: Dent, 1982), chap. 9, "Enlarging the Sphere of Contemplation." For mid- to late-eighteenth-century Pacific exploration, look not much farther than O. H. K. Spate, *The Pacific since Magellan,* vol. 3: *Paradise Found and Lost* (Canberra: Australian National University Press, 1988).

There are a great many books on Captain Cook. The monument of scholarship in the area is *The Journals of Captain James Cook,* ed. J. C. Beaglehole, 4 vols. (London: Hakluyt Society, 1955–1967), containing Cook's records but other relevant journals besides. From there, readers might go to G. M. Badger, ed., *Captain Cook: Navigator and Scientist* (Canberra: Australian National University Press, 1970), which is authoritative though elderly, or to Lynne Withey, *Voyages of Discovery: Captain Cook and the Exploration of the Pacific* (London: Hutchinson, 1987). The standard biography is J. C. Beaglehole, *The Life of Captain James Cook* (Stanford: Stanford University Press, 1974). *The Journals of Captain Cook,* ed. Philip Edwards (London: Penguin, 1999), is the most reliable selection. Recent studies include Anne Salmond, *The Trial of the Cannibal Dog: Captain Cook in the South Seas* (London: Allen Lane, 2003), and Nicholas Thomas, *Discoveries: The Voyages of Captain Cook* (London: Allen Lane, 2003), which bring modern issues and attitudes to bear. Ben Finney, "James Cook and the European Discovery of Polynesia," in Robin Fisher and Hugh Johnston, eds., *From Maps to Metaphors: The Pacific World of George Vancouver* (Vancouver: University of British Columbia Press, 1993), makes the case regarding Cook and Polynesia.

On his second voyage Cook was accompanied by an artist of genuine talent: see Geoff Quilley and John Bonehill, eds., *William Hodges, 1744–1797: The Art of Exploration* (New Haven: Yale University Press, 2004).

For Bougainville, see John Dunmore, *Storms and Dreams: Louis de Bougainville: Soldier, Explorer, Statesman* (New York: Nonsuch Publishing, 2005); for Diderot, see *"This is Not a Story" and Other Stories,* ed. P. N. Furbank (Oxford: Oxford University Press, 1993); and *Political Writings,* ed. John Hope Mason and Robert Wokler (Cambridge: Cambridge University Press, 1992).

For George Forster, see *A Journey round the World,* ed. Nicholas Thomas and Oliver Berghof (Honolulu: University of Hawai'i Press, 2000). For George Keate, see Jonathan Lamb, *Preserving the Self in the South Seas, 1680–1840* (Chicago: University of Chicago Press, 2001), chap. 8, "Starlings and Parrots; Keate and Sympathy," and the new edition of *An Account of the Pelew Islands,* ed. Karen L. Nero and Nicholas Thomas (Leicester: Leicester University Press, 2000).

3

"DARK PARTS OF THE EARTH"
The Voyage of the Duff, 1796–1798

The idea of the noble savage has never disappeared from Western thought, bound up as it is with Westerners' views not only of Pacific Islanders but of themselves. The antipodean will perhaps always be seen as bad or good, better or worse, a subject of envy or contempt: never simply the same or simply different.

But reaction to the noble savage set in quickly after the discovery of Tahiti in the late 1760s. That which had fascinated liberal gentlemen like Joseph Banks and Bougainville often shocked other readers. A key event in this development was the publication in 1773 of John Hawkesworth's *Account of the Voyages Undertaken by the Order of His Present Majesty for Making Discoveries in the Southern Hemisphere.* Hawkesworth wrote up the journals of several sea captains—in particular that of Cook—and his collection was an immense success. But that did not prevent the miscellany from attracting criticism, and here it is important to remember that late-eighteenth-century Britain was undergoing an intense religious revival: the first since the "Glorious Revolution" of 1688 had firmly reestablished a Protestant monarchy under William of Orange.

Hawkesworth's accounts of the sexual morality of the Tahitians were attractive to some, certainly; but a large number of people took a different attitude: that far from being happier then Europeans, the Islanders were heathens who urgently needed the word of the Christian god. Writing a year after Hawkesworth's account came out, the pseudonymous Peter Pindar paid standard Rousseauistic compliments to the inhabitants of Tahiti, "The Cyprus of the South, the Land of Love":

"Dark parts of the earth" in the title of this chapter is from William Ellis, *Polynesian Researches, during a Residence of Nearly Six Years in the South Sea Islands,* 2 vols. (London: Fisher, Son, and Jackson, 1829), 2:219.

No boding Presage haunts them through the Night;
No Cares revive with early Dawn of Light:
Each happy Day glides thoughtless as the last,
Unknown the future, unrecall'd the past.

But there was a thorn among the roses, as newly emerging accounts of infanticide on Tahiti suggested:

Ah! see in vain the little Suppliant plead
With silent Eloquence to check the Deed:
He smiles unconscious on th' uplifted Knife,
And courts the Hand that's arm'd against his Life.
Not his last Sighs the Mother's Bosom move;
She dooms his Death, her Sacrifice to Love:
Impatient hastes her am'rous Vows to plight,
And seals with Infant Blood the barb'rous Rite.
Reclin'd upon her Lover's panting Breast,
See in his Arms the beauteous Murd'ress prest!
No keen Remorse the wanton Trance destroys,
No thrilling Terrors damp their guilty Joys;
Nor Ties of social Life their Crimes reclaim,
Nor rigid Justice awes, nor virtuous Fame. ("PINDAR," 14, 15–16)

The life without moral sanction had its dark side despite the superficial attractions.

At first Tahiti had been presented as goodness incarnate. There was no need of Christian revelation among a people who "have a knowledge of right and wrong from the mere dictates of natural conscience" (Hawkesworth, 2:101). But such a view could not easily be reconciled with the things seen or heard of by Cook and his companions. The view began to emerge that far from representing humanity's golden age, Tahiti represented its fall into decadence. "Rousseau's savage, a being who roves the woods according to his will," the seafarer John Turnbull wrote, "exists nowhere but in his [Rousseau's] writings" (Turnbull, 201). What did exist on Tahiti was "a set of men" ("called by the natives *Mahoos*") "whose open profession is of such abomination, that the laudable delicacy of our language will not admit it to be mentioned." Turnbull went on:

Their pollution in this respect beggars all description; my hand averts from dwelling upon the subject which recals so many images of disgust and horror. Their wickedness is enough to call down the immediate judgment of heaven; and let me not be thought too presumptuous, if I assert that the hand of God is visibly amongst them. Unless their manners change, I pronounce that they will not long remain in the number of nations: the sword of disease is no less effectual than the waters of a deluge! (Turnbull, 382–383; the biblical flood, to which he refers, was believed to be in part a punishment for the unnatural sex practices of the people of Sodom.)

Once trade in alcohol and firearms was established, the end of the noble savage appeared well in sight. When the Russian explorer Thaddeus Bellingshausen visited Tahiti in 1819, he invited the Western-established king Pomare and his entourage on board for dinner:

> The King and his family partook freely of everything and even drank wine. As the water we had on board had been obtained in Port Jackson and therefore was no longer fresh, the King ordered one of the natives to serve cocoa-nut milk. The natives brought some cocoa-nuts, broke the tops very cleverly with a hammer, and ran the milk off. The King drank the wine, mixed with water, whilst continually wiping the perspiration pouring down his good-natured face. When he drank the wine neat, he proposed each time someone's health, according to the English custom, bowing and touching glasses. After dinner he asked for a cigar, smoked and drank coffee. (Bellingshausen, 264)

Bellingshausen's attitude is revealing. He expects no better; he experiences no Rousseauistic depression at the decay of an ideal when a Tahitian opens a coconut with a hammer. Indeed, he approves of (almost) all the changes made in Tahiti since the arrival of the West. "It is greatly to the credit of the missionaries," he reported,

> that they have been able to bring the islanders to such a high level of education in such a short time. A great number of the islanders read and write well; they use the Latin alphabet. In Otahiti they used to make rum from a root called Ti; probably on the suggestion of the missionaries the King prohibited the manufacture of this liquor, despite the fact that he himself is very fond of it. This prohibition was, however, of the greatest assistance in attaining the praiseworthy aim of their kindly teachers. It seems a pity that the instruction of the people has been accompanied by the suppression of all their old amusements, dances, and other games. (Bellingshausen, 286)

What Bellingshausen saw in 1819 was the outcome of a long campaign the origins of which lay not in the placidly centralist tradition of the Church of England but in that of its nonconformist and evangelizing Protestant rivals at the forefront of the English religious revival: Baptists, Episcopalians, Methodists, and in particular the Congregationalists and Independents who rejected any form of religious institutionalism. "During the last 50 years there has been a great revival of true religion among ourselves," the Reverend George Burder noted in a sermon of 1795:

> But it is astonishing and lamentable to reflect, how few and feeble the efforts of Christians . . . have been, to evangelize the Pagan part of the world. Some indeed have been valiant in preaching the Gospel at home. Others have done worthily by their excellent writings, in contending for primitive doctrine against internal enemies. But oh! where is the primitive zeal? Where are the heroes of the church—men who would willingly spend and be spent for Christ; who have the ambition not to tread a line made ready for them, but

to preach Christ, where, before, he was not named? Men who count not their lives dear, so that they might win souls for Christ. (Burder, 160)

"Modern discoveries in geography," Burder went on, "have perhaps contributed to enlarge the desires of Christians in this respect."

Captain Cook and others have traversed the globe, almost from pole to pole, and have presented to us, as it were, a new world—a world of islands in the vast Pacific Ocean, some of them as promising in the disposition of the people, as in the appearance of the country. May we not reasonably hope that a well-planned and well-conducted mission to one or more of these, seconded with the earnest prayers of thousands of British Christians, will be attended with the blessing of God, and issue in the conversion of many souls? (Burder, 163)

Burder was not the only nonconformist divine who had been reading about James Cook. Thomas Haweis had done the same, as he recorded in his autobiography:

The voyages of the great and adventurous Cook to the Southern Ocean, and his discoveries . . . could not but engage the most universal attention. Among others I read them with delight and wonder, and . . . I could not but feel a deep regret that so beautiful a part of the Creation, and the inhabitants of those innumerable Islands of the Southern Ocean should be regions of the shadow of Death, the Dens of every unclean Beast, and Habitation of Cruelty devouring literally one another. (Haweis n.d.: n.p.)

Haweis was supported by his patroness, the "pious, though rather eccentric person, Selina, countess of Huntingdon" (Russell, 100), who had led a Calvinist group known as "Lady Huntingdon's Connection" away from membership of the Church of England in 1781. Thereafter Haweis became the leading light of a group, regularly published in the *Evangelical Magazine,* that formed the backbone of the Missionary Society. The society was nondenominational, but its Calvinist emphasis on predestination and the innate sinfulness of humanity remained strong.

An inaugural meeting was held in London in September 1795, and both Haweis and Burder addressed the faithful. Burder spelled out the philanthropist's duties among the heathen. "Some of their customs are far too indelicate to be rehearsed in a Christian audience," he said. "On the coast of Tierra del Fuego, they are elevated but a small degree above the very brutes. Ought we not to pity fellow-men so degraded in the scale of society; and knowing the vast advantages of a civilized state, endeavour to civilize, may I not say, to *humanize* them?" (London Missionary Society 1795: 35). When Burder used the expression "scale of society," he had dropped into the idiom of Enlightenment rationalism. (Society has a scale, and humanity may move up and down it from brutality to civilization: the different peoples are not cemented into position by God.) This was one of the intellectual tensions working within the Missionary Society. Its confidence that people could be hauled up the ladder of society by educative means was quintessentially the product of

Enlightenment thought, yet it also rejected the cosmopolitan rationalism of men like Banks and Bougainville. As often as not the dissenters were from the provinces (Burder from Coventry, Haweis from Cornwall, and Thomas Pentycross from Berkshire), and they fought most earnestly for what Burder called "primitive zeal" and the Church of England called "enthusiasm"—the value of direct, irrational, transcendent revelation, as opposed to both reason and establishment religious mediation: "Spirit of *Hume,* the subtil; spirit of *Rousseau,* the fanciful; spirit of *Voltaire,* the cowardly tho' daring . . . tell us, what can you suggest for the happiness of the World equivalent to the Gospel? What book like the New Testament can you put into the hands of poor pagans in the *South Seas?*" (London Missionary Society 1796b: 61).

So Pentycross taunted the *philosophes* at the second general meeting of the society in 1796, by which time the faithful had dug deep and Haweis had worked hard; a ship, the *Duff,* had been found, and also a captain: a hero of war in India named James Wilson. More important still, the missionary had been found—only it was not *a* missionary at all but nearly forty, including five women and two children. Seven carpenters went aboard the *Duff:* three weavers, two tailors, two shoemakers, two bricklayers, a hatter, a smith, a gardener, a shopkeeper, a cooper, and a "gentleman's servant" (Wilson, 5–6). Only four were ordained ministers.

Sending groups of missionaries to the South Seas was not unprecedented. Priests had accompanied the Spanish voyages through the Pacific in the sixteenth century and had been involved with Mendaña's and Quirós' shortlived colonies in the Solomon Islands and Vanuatu. And in 1774 the Spaniards landed two monks, a marine, and a soldier on Tahiti itself, but they stayed less than a year and did effectively nothing. The London Missionary Society (LMS) proposed something infinitely more daring. The plan was that Wilson would transport this small community to Tahiti (and, as it transpired, a smaller one of nine males to Tonga and a yet tinier one of William Pascoe Crook all alone to the Marquesas) and leave them there. There is no modern equivalent for such a scheme; an analogy might be sending the inhabitants of a suburban street to live on Pluto. When the *Duff* might be able to return to them; how often they would be visited by Western shipping, if at all; the likely attitude of Islanders and European beachcombers to their arrival and settlement: none of these things were known. An exchange of mail would take two years.

So much for the daring aspect of the enterprise. The imaginative aspect was no less remarkable. The society envisaged nothing less than a miniature "Christian Society" (London Missionary Society 1796b: 68) transplanted to Oceania—a tiny English village without its squire below Point Venus that by the very life it lived would do more to convert the Islanders than arguments or promises of whatever kind:

> The Missionaries may avail themselves of the good opinion which they find entertained by the Heathen of those Europeans, particularly from this island, who have formerly visited them. They will also watch the first opportunities

to impress the people of the islands with the simplicity and unfeigned benevolence of their own hearts towards them, in the first instance, with respect to temporal objects and concerns; insinuating to them, without ostentation, the superior improvements in the arts of life which they have had opportunity to acquire, and expressing a cordial readiness to impart to them every instruction and assistance of that kind. At the same time, it will be becoming the character of Spiritual Missionaries, to convince the natives, as soon as it is practicable, that they set no great value on these things, or on any thing whatever belonging merely to this world; but that the chief treasure they convey is entirely of a religious and heavenly nature. (London Missionary Society 1796b: 63–64)

So, "during the time . . . that our several handicraftsmen are at work, at their several trades, the natives will crowd with curiosity around them: all readiness to instruct and inform them should be shewn" (London Missionary Society 1796b: 67). Conversion would come as the result of a kind of technical and social diffusion: seeing what the missionaries could do and how they lived would inspire the Islanders to absorb their "arts of life"—including, ultimately, their religion. (See Figure 8.)

FIGURE 8. Francesco Bartolozzi (1727–1815), "The Cession of the District of Matavai in the Island of Otaheite to Captain Wilson for the Use of the Missionaries" (179?). By permission of the National Library of Australia.

But here another important problem asserts itself in the society's program. Has a model village of any kind, whether dreamed up by despots, industrialists, social reformers, or educationalists, ever worked? Could an English community flung together at random from all parts of Britain and transplanted to Matavai Bay sustain itself? The society clearly had concerns about this. They are reflected in the "Farewel Letter from the Directors of the Missionary Society," reprinted in the *Evangelical Magazine*: "In a band of Missionaries . . . a cold negative union is not sufficient; there should be that powerful melting of love, which the apostolic exhortation demands" (London Missionary Society 1796a: 358).

The differing attitudes of the directors and the missionaries to the task immediately at hand reflect differing Western attitudes to the South Seas generally speaking. That is why the episode of the *Duff* is revealing about Western attitudes to the Pacific in ways no other historical missionary enterprise is. For the directors, the South Seas were so far away that nothing could go wrong: the Islanders were sure to be fascinated by a fretsaw or an embroidery frame and would want to comprehend the settlers' spiritual beliefs in just the same way they would want to absorb their technological advances. For the missionaries, the South Seas were so far away that *everything* might go wrong: above all, the responsibility of sustaining a model community might be too much for them. Never mind the responsibility of providing a model back home as well as overseas "when they consider the expectations, anxieties and hopes of so many Ministers of Christ, and of such multitudes of serious Christians; when they think of the observing eye of adversaries; above all when they survey the hundreds of millions of souls lying in the darkness of heathenism, who may ultimately be affected by the good or ill management, by the failure or success of this Mission" (London Missionary Society 1796b: 52). Some regarded this responsibility as positively world-historical. "We live in a period of great events, and amidst the hostile collisions of powerful nations," the secretary of the directors wrote, with the French Revolutionary wars in mind: "If the vengeance of the Almighty shall awake to meet us for our distinguished ingratitude as a people, and our marked opposition to the spirit of the religion we profess, then the disasters feared and felt at home, may surpass the trials of faithful missionaries" (Love, 263–264).

So it was that the tiny community given up to the waves must be held together, the missionaries felt, with something stronger than "melting love." The society at home took an ecumenical point of view concerning doctrinal matters. In a circular letter printed among the sermons preached at the inaugural meeting of the society, they not only did not repudiate the religious examples of Moravians, Arminians, and other (arguably) heretical Protestant sects, they wrote that "we appreciate their truly primitive example" (London Missionary Society 1795: xix). Yet they told the missionaries, as we shall see, "You must be a little Church and Community." As it turned out, the missionaries interpreted that instruction more vigorously than its formulators probably ever imagined: "The missionaries on the Duff, who during the voyage formed themselves into a little church, were hardly as liberal in this respect as the general meeting. In the very full journal of their voyage . . . under the date January 18, 1797, an entry covering many folio pages exhibits the almost total inability of the great majority either to perceive or to recognize that truth may have more than one side and be capable of more than one presentation" (Lovett, 48). To understand why they acted as they did, we need to consider what it was they thought they were confronting. In gaining that understanding, we shall gain a broader one of late-eighteenth-century European views of the South Seas.

The *Duff* experiment was a failure and was never repeated. "By 1800 . . . twenty of the thirty [male missionaries on the *Duff*] had proved either unequal or unfaithful to the work, while three had been killed in the mission service" (Lovett, 64). As such, therefore, the London Missionary Society and every other missionary organization working in the Pacific came to opt for the David Livingstone type of missionary: a highly motivated single male, seeking by power of influence to make a small number of socially powerful converts who would essentially instruct their peoples to take up Christianity. That is what finally happened in Tahiti with "King" Pomare and his ever-present missionary minder, the Reverend Henry Nott. A similar pattern emerged throughout the Pacific as the nineteenth century wore on, augmented by the recruitment of Islander missionaries from Polynesia who penetrated the Melanesian islands and New Guinea. Hawaiian recruits played a similar role in Micronesia. Thus John Williams, born the year the *Duff* set sail, who was also of the LMS and of strikingly similar social origin to many who went on the original voyage (apprentice ironmonger), benefited from a far longer training than the *Duff* recruits had received. After good success in Samoa and elsewhere, Williams was clubbed to death on a beach at Eromanga, in the New Hebrides, in 1839.

George Baxter's picture of Williams' death (1843) became something of a mid-nineteenth-century icon: the religious equivalent of similar images of Cook's murder on the shores of Kealakekua Bay, Hawai'i. But Baxter's picture was in fact one of a pair (see Figures 9 and 10). The first showed Williams on arrival rather than departure, this time at Tanna (another of the New Hebrides). On the shore are a horde of natives (some up in the trees), two chiefly types who greet Williams' longboat, and a half-Westernized Islander who presumably interprets. The boat is held steady in the water by the quintessential English sailor, and behind Williams is unmistakably the figure of a trader, who holds up beads, cloth, and a mirror. (Behind him is a box containing more beads and some suspicious-looking bottles.) At the back of the boat are two gentleman of learning, debating the scene before them. Baxter's two pictures make an uneasy combination, and in nineteenth- and twentieth-century literature, missionaries continued to be alternately applauded and reviled as the thin end to the Westernizing wedge. "They are opening up new fields for commerce; they are teaching the natives to *want*—and when they want they will work to supply their wants" (Campbell 1873: 192–193). The men of the cloth did enough damage, according to some; but in their wake came others still more rapacious: traders, freebooters, "blackbirders," and other riff-raff

FIGURE 9. George Baxter (1804–1867), "The Reception of the Rev. J. Williams, at Tanna, in the South Seas, the Day Before He Was Massacred" (1841). By permission of the National Library of Australia.

from beyond the pale. Another Russian voyager, Otto von Kotzebue, was an early critic of the effect the missionary enterprise had on traditional Islander life, and his attack was considered worthy of a rebuttal by the great Tahitian missionary William Ellis (see Kotzebue 1830 and Ellis 1831). An antimissionary stance was taken up thereafter by countless Western writers on the Pacific. "Among the islands of Polynesia," as Herman Melville put it in *Typee* (first published in 1846), "no sooner are the images overturned, the temples demolished, and the idolaters converted into *nominal* Christians, than disease, vice, and premature death make their appearance" (Melville, 233). Following Melville to the Marquesas in 1919, Frederick O'Brien was equally to the point: "The efforts of missionaries have killed the joy of living as they have crushed out the old barbarities, uprooting together everything, good and bad, that religion meant to the native. They have given him instead rites that mystify him, dogmas he can only dimly understand, and a little comfort in the miseries brought upon him by trade" (O'Brien, 83).

There can be little doubt that there is some truth in the views expressed by Kotzebue, Melville, and O'Brien. "It was the first duty of the missionary to save souls," Niel Gunson writes, "but wherever he went he brought havoc to the existing social systems" (Gunson, 333). Until the onset of the Second World War and the postcolonial era that followed, no foreign influence has been so powerful in the Pacific as the coming of Christianity, with massive

FIGURE 10. George Baxter (1804–1867), "The Massacre of the Lamented Missionary, the Rev. J. Williams and Mr. Harris" (1841). By permission of the National Library of Australia.

and irreversible implications for the religious, social, and moral traditions of indigenous peoples. But it is also true that writers like Melville and O'Brien cast the South Sea Islanders in certain roles just as missionaries cast them in other, less appealing ones. In doing so, the Islanders' antireligious champions caught them up in a web of preconception just as surely as did the missionaries. Though we are beginning to realize some of the most accurate ethnographic work carried out in the Pacific in the nineteenth century was done by missionaries like Ellis (1829) and Robert Codrington (1885, 1891), we must also acknowledge that men like them were the source of pernicious illusions. In the years following the abortive first mission to Tahiti, Bernard Smith observes, "the missions to the Pacific gradually substituted for the noble savage of the eighteenth century a strikingly contrasting type; an individual thoroughly treacherous and deceitful in his native state who could yet be transformed into a Christian citizen obedient to the laws of God and the laws of Europeans as a result of the intercession of the Holy Spirit in Christian conversion" (Smith 1985: 147). The origins of these contrasting types lie deep in the Western mind: so deep, indeed, that missionaries must be seen as objects acted upon by ideas as well as ideological agents in their own right.

from Thomas Haweis, "Memoir of the Most Eligible Part to Begin a Mission" (1795)

This was the second of two sermons Thomas Haweis (1734–1820) preached at the three-day foundational meeting of the London Missionary Society held in September 1795. His enthusiasm for the South Seas knew few bounds and is strikingly like that registered by Quirós in Chapter 1.

Of all the regions of the earth which are yet in heathen darkness, the South sea Islands appear to combine the greatest prospects of success, with the least difficulties to be necessarily surmounted.

THE CLIMATE is sufficiently known. I am afraid to speak, what is recorded, least some should think I were painting a fairy land, a new garden of the Hesperides. Suffice it, therefore, to say, what is universally admitted, that the cold of winter is never known; the trees, I believe, hardly ever lose their leaves, through the constant succession of vegetation, and the greatest part of the year, bear fruit; the heat, though a tropical country, is always alleviated by alternate breezes, whilst they sit under the shade of groves, odoriferous, as loaded with abundance; the sky serene, the nights beautiful, and the sea ever offering its inexhaustible source of food, an easy and pleasing conveyance, and a sight generally admired.

Diseases that ravage us are there unknown: we have indeed added fearfully to their number, yet health, and longevity mark the inhabitants in general, without the knowledge of medicines or physicians. If the frozen regions of the north, or the sultry humid soil of Africa, be compared with these Islands, the difference of danger is immense, and a missionary's life, abundantly more likely to be preserved in the one, than in the other.

Dependent on climate is THE EASINESS OF PROVISION. How readily that can be supplied in these islands, you need only read the concurring testimony of all who have written on the subject, and if they want our luxuries, the real necessaries of life, will there neither much engage a missionary's time or care. With the science he carries, and the arts he practises, there is little apprehension to be entertained, that he will not, with any prudent attention, have enough and to spare.

And this is as advantageous for *the work* as for themselves. The natives not harrassed by labour for daily bread, or as slaves, worked under the lash of the whip, are always sure to have abundant time for instruction. We have not, as our brethren the Moravians,[1] to follow them into the lonely wilds of a desert in their hunting, or over the fields of ice in winter, few at best, and dispersed. Here every man sitting under his coco, or bread-fruit tree, is at hand, and the very sound of a hammer, a saw, or a smith's bellows, will hardly ever fail to attract an audience. Two hundred thousand inhabitants are reckoned in the little island of Otaheite alone; all ranged around its beautiful shores, and ac-

---

1. An antique German Protestant sect approved of by nonconforming divines like Haweis because of their evangelical leanings and adherence to the Bible.

cessible by a thousand canoes in every part, with a facility that no other road, ever can afford. I need not say *the multitude of the isles will be glad thereof.* Their amount hath never yet been ascertained. We have discovered many, but probably much greater numbers are still unknown, which spot the bosom of the pacific ocean, on either side the line, from New South Wales to the coasts of Peru. But I am only giving a sketch, not a history.

I hardly know how to mention the GOVERNMENT, with which we are not perhaps perfectly acquainted. It seems monarchical, but of the mildest nature, with little authority, controuled as it appears by powerful vassals, each in his own district supreme, but with no written law, nor the use of letters, and presents a sort of patriarchal state: where the disorders seem so few, that the arm of authority is but seldom exerted. Here, so far from having any thing to fear, or any danger of abiding, some have attempted at the hazard of their lives to obtain a retreat by swimming naked from our ships, and some determined to make their future home, by a conspiracy, I was assured by the worthy captain who suffered, brought on by no disgust or dislike of him, or the service, but merely by the fascinations of beauty, and the allurements of the country.[2] [. . .]

In the uncivilized state, in which the inhabitants of Otaheite and the neighbouring islands live, our superiority, in knowledge, and what they will at first be more struck with, in the mechanic arts, we bring; these, will gain us probably such respect, that without receiving a sacrifice, as to the Eatoa, such as was offered to Cook, we shall enjoy sufficient importance with the highest as well as the lowest of that people, and (in my conscience, I speak) we have more to apprehend from being caressed and exalted, than from being insulted and oppressed. It is a beautiful French proverb, the force of which will felt in this case by every reflecting mind; *Dans la pais des aveugles, les borgnes sont rois.*[3]

Respecting their RELIGIOUS PREJUDICES. No nation of the earth, I believe, will be found without some traces of traditionary revelation. Every guilty creature feels the necessity of atonement in some shape or form. They have their victims, and their Gods: we are yet but little acquainted with these; but the little that we do know, affords the strongest evidence, that their priests, if there are such, are not invested with any persecuting power, nor can the people be averse to hear us on a religious subject, whom they reverence as their superiors almost in every other. And the very slight traces, which we have obtained of the service at their Moraïs,[4] seem strongly to imply the supposition of a future existence, and the necessity of placating as well as pleasing an offended God. [. . .]

---

2. Haweis had been in communication with Captain William Bligh, commander of the *Bounty* and victim of the famous mutiny of 1789. Bligh always insisted his men had mutinied as the result of a desire to return to the fleshpots of Tahiti rather than cruelty on his part.

3. "In the regions of the blind, he who hath but one eye, will be monarch" (Haweis' translation). *Le pays* is the correct French expression.

4. Rock platforms or open spaces found in Polynesia, which Western visitors associated with religious rites in general and human sacrifice in particular. (James Cook recorded a visit to such a place in his 1773 journal, extracted in Chapter 2.)

I shall suggest but one advantage more, among a multitude, that might be produced, that we shall have here no *false* Christianity to oppose its life and spirit; and none I hope of those disputes, which among *real* Christians, tend greatly to obstruct the work of God. We have a field wholly uncultivated, but the soil is fit for seed, and the climate genial, and coming first, we have everything in our favour, and may, without dispute or opposition, inculcate the true knowledge of God our Saviour. From the king on the throne, to the infant of a year old, I should not be surprized to see our schools thronged, and our worship attended. We know that he who made the heart can only renew it. We are sure that the residue of the spirit is with him: and he hath promised to be with us always even to the end of the world. With such divine encouragements what may we not hope for?

[. . .] THE MISSIONARIES. This is generally supposed to be the great desideratum, but I had confidence, and it is confirmed by every appearance, that we shall have such a number offer, that the difficulty will be rather, whom we shall refuse, than who shall be received. They will pass the ordeal of men judged most capable of such examination, taken from a body of ministers and others, such as this century hath, I think, never seen associated, and those selected for missionaries will assuredly be the choice of the flock, and bearing the genuine stamp of God upon them.

Respecting THEIR CONDITION. Whether the single or married brethren should be preferred, is to be a matter of much consideration. We seem hitherto to have preferred bachelors, but we wish also now to join married men, and their wives, if on further enquiries, white women will be found not to endanger the mission. I think they will greatly advance it.

Respecting *their ability.* It appears desirable to have the best informed we can find. We hope to obtain some, who are not destitute of letters, and education, but the greater number we expect from the inferior classes of life. Men expert in their several professions—who shall be found endued with good, or strong natural parts—who have given evidence of their christian walk and conversation from some considerable time past—attested by their minister, or some respectable members of the congregation, with whom they have been in communion—who have diligently read their bibles—and are able to give a clear and satisfactory account of the great leading doctrines—and if they have been in the habit of exhorting—and appear apt to teach—their call will be the more evident: vital godliness is the first qualification we require—a measure of knowledge sufficient to be useful in the way of teaching follows—this we hope also to improve—a clear devotedness of heart to the work—and a temper not hasty, but mild, patient, and conciliating, both to maintain undisturbed union with their brethren, and to gain influence among the Heathen—these appear to be the desirable missionary qualities, and will be found more at large in the discourses delivered by the associated brethren.[5]

---

5. Some in the missionary society felt that "the best education for missionaries was NONE AT ALL." and that "the next best was that which consists in teaching them to make wheel-barrows and plant turnips." For Haweis, "a plain man . . . though he comes from the forge or the shop,

from William Puckey, "A Journal Constituting of a Few Remarks of a Voyage from Portsmouth to the Society Islands in the Great South Sea, 1796"

At the opposite end of the social and educational scale from Thomas Haweis was William Puckey (1776–1827), one of a pair of brothers and Congregationalist carpenters from Fowey in the West Country of England, both of whom felt called to join the mission to Tahiti.

> [*First page missing.*] A sermon being preacht by Mr Wildbore on the same account, And my Brother being present, felt the word come with great Power on his soul, He had a longing desier to see the Kingdom of Christ flourish, Therefore the love of souls constrain'd him to offer his sevice in the Mission. And on the 2nd of March 1796 he was examined at Plymouth, & accept. [. . .]
>
> And without persuasion of any one, I felt a secret desier to accompany my Brother, My desier increasing I concluding that God in his providence had called me here for the same Purpose, I immediately opend my mind to Mr Wildbore. Who, wrote to the Directors of the Missionary Society at London of my desier, some time after a letter was sent from Plymouth, For my Brother & me & John Cock a young man of Penzance,[6] Who had been working with us. To come away as soon as possible.
>
> We Immediately Prepared, and got our tools and Cloths together, and on July 18th in the morning about 6 °Clock, I left My Dear Sister and her Child with many tears on both sides, From thence we went on Board a barge bound for Plymouth, and about 3 °Clock arrived and went on shore to the Rev^d Mr Minds home where we were kindly received. From thence we were put to the post office Inn. Where we had very good lodgings. We soon got acquainted with some of the People of Mr Minds Church who behave very kind to us, On Thursday 22nd of July we were examined and set apart by several Ministers who atended for the same purpose. The Rev^d Mr Evence Preacht from Isaiah 60^c part of the first verse, Arise Shine for thy Light is come. And two or three of the Ministers prayd and last of all Mr Jefferson[7] of Fowey who had passed the examination & Excepted with us gave us an exhortation that as we might expect many difficulties and trials, To look unto him from whence we must derive all our strength. Being a very large congregation many come and took us by the hand affectionately and bid us God speed.
>
> Mr Mind Received a letter from London of the Missionary Being ready to sail by the 1 of August was very desirous for sending us away for London with the greates speed.

---

would . . . as a missionary to the heathen, be infinitely preferable to all the learning of the schools; and would possess, in the skill and labour of his hands, advantages which barren science would never compensate" (Gunson, 36–37).

6. John Cock, born in 1773, was also a Congregationalist carpenter.

7. John Jefferson was an unusual recruit in having ecclesiastical experience; he had served as pastor of Fowey Chapel as well as earning a living as an actor and a schoolteacher. We will hear more of him and John Cock later.

But as we had not taken leave or farewell of our Parents, Duty constrained us to go to them tho they were much against our leaving of them.

On Friday morning we took horses with an intent to return back to Plymouth against night, Fowey being 24 miles from thence we rode on with great Speed And we arrivd at fey [Fowey] about 12 o'Clock. I found myself very indisposed after my journey.

I found my Dear Fathr & Mother at Dinner when we came to their home, who flew into floods of tears at our appearance. But blessed by God, I found their minds different to the standing report I had heard of them, And they now were become somewhat resind and were constrain to comply with us which gave me not a little comfort.

In the evening I reposed myself to rest, But I found my mind much trobled reflecting on the time that I must leave them whom I lovd so dear But there was somthing Implanted in my soul that far exceeded and overcame all Naturl affection, The Night being gone and past time would not tarry we must proseed to return back again having brocken our promise.

About 9 °Clock our horses was brought to the Door many of my old acquaintence came to take their farewell and My Father withdrawd to the door all things being ready to part, At the tragical sceen the all fell aweeping and so we parted *never to meet again with many present.* My Father accompanid us to the passege Boat fell on our necks weeping.

[The brothers returned to Plymouth and duly traveled by coach up to London, where they arrived some days later.]

We slept at the Tabernacle House for a few nights till Ministers coming in we were put to one Mr Leggets a Carpenters who was exceeding kind to us. But we eat our meat at Mr Wilks[8] house with several of the Missionaries.

On the 28th of July we were all Solelmnly set apart for the work of the Mission at Zion Chaple.[9] Where a great multitude of People atended. Service being over we went to the Castle & Falcon[10] where we had a very good Dinner with all the Directors of our Society.

The Ship not being ready to sail we had the opportunity of seeing much of London, it is a fine Place, but it did not dazel my eyes nether was I delighted with it, but the greates comfort which I had was to see so many Chirstains, The Soldiers of Jesus Chirst in it.

On August 9th we meet with the Directors at Haberdashers Hall[11] and Mr Jefferson was ordeaned Minster. The intention of our meeting was for the

---

8. Reverend Matthew Wilks, another divine in the missionary circle, from whom we shall hear at the end of this chapter.

9. Zion is a holy hill in Jerusalem and thus a symbol of both the city of God and the Christian faith. Zion Chapel, in The Borough on the South bank of the Thames, was a center of religious nonconformism.

10. The public house in Aldersgate in the City of London, where the London Missionary Society had been founded on 21 September 1795.

11. The headquarters of one of the ancient guilds of the City of London.

"DARK PARTS OF THE EARTH"

Directors to take their Farewell of us. The Ship now being ready to sail Many of our Chirstians friends with the Directors sat down with us at the ordinance of the Lord's supper, we had a very solemn time, many addresses we had from the minster to be strong in the Lord and in the Power of His might. Who affectionately felt for our parting and many tears were shed.

Wenesday, August 10th Embarked on board the Ship Duff at Blackwall about 5 °Clock in the morning many People were assembled on the occasion, And several of our Freind and brethren with some affectionate fathers the Directors accompanied us to Gravesend,[12] Where we arrived about noon. But we where all in confusion for so many of our Dear frinds coming on Board and taking Farewell of us causd much sorrow on my mind I longd to be going that I might lose sight of them.

Thursday 11th. We were divided into 6 messes[13] in all we were 30 men, 6 women and 3 children. My messmates were Brothers Bowell, Main Nobbs, Oaks & Crook.

In ye evening we parted with all our friends but Mr Haweis Wilks and Brockbank and got under way for Portsmouth. Friday 12th Preceeded down the River many of us was sick, some friends came off from Sheerness and brought some live stock and other necessaries. Saturday 13th past the Downs.

Lorday day 14th Dr Haweis preacht in the morning Mr Brockbanks in the afternoon, and Mr Wilks in the evening, found the word, the right food for my soule.

Monday 15th Between 8 and 9 °Clock in the evening an English sloop of war hailed us and said little black french lugger was lurking about the offing, a fresh breeze springing up we sailed very swiftly and through the good of God saw nothing of her.[14] Tuesday 16th This morning early arrived at Spithead, And one of the men of war at St Helens sent their boat unboard us as we passed, When we anchored Capt Wilson and Mr Eyer of Hackney came unboard,[15] Found the East India convoy had sailed.[16]

Friday 19th the Adamant of 50 Guns being to go as convoy with some transports &c to Gibralter we put ourselves under her protection, our friends knew not how to be kind enough to us, they have sent in a great Quantity of

---

12. Blackwall and Gravesend are points along the River Thames in and beyond the dock area. In due course, the *Duff* left the Thames estuary and followed the coastline around to the naval dockyard of Portsmouth, near the Isle of Wight on the English Channel.

13. Every ship of any size in the age of sail divided its sailors up into watches (on duty at various times of the day), themselves made up of messes: groups of men, normally around half a dozen, who cooked and ate their food together.

14. As a consqunce of the revolution of 1789, Britain had been at war with France since February 1793. In 1796 France was at the height of its power and directly threatened Britain, defended only by its naval superiority. Small ships like sloops and luggers frequently patrolled in the English Channel at the time.

15. This is John Eyre, another ordained minister, who was to become a long-serving missionary in Polynesia.

16. The *Duff* had intended to hitch a ride with a major convoy of trading vessels belonging to the East India Company, heading south for the Cape of Good Hope.

live stock bread &c and other necessaries on board surely all the earth conspire to help this Great undertaking. Lords day 21st Prayr & Preaching on board by Mr Eyer. Mr Griffin of Portsmouth. Had a comfortable, many people from Portsmouth & Portsea came on board to hear the word of God.

Monday 22nd at 4 °Clock in the afternoon Mr Wilks took his leave of us in an affectionate adress from Heb 12^C 2^V Looking unto Jesus. I was verey much affected at his parting seeing an aged man like him sheding so many tears—O! the wonderfull love of God.

Tuesday 23rd Brother Hudden & his wife left us to the heart failing of the latter. Brother Gotton came on board he fills the station of a cook for us on the Voyage and if agreeable stays with us. Thursday 25th Brothers Covers son having been ill ever since we came on board was called to leave this world. Thus Providence calls to us to be also ready. O! that I may be continually upon my watch tower to welcome the Bridegroom at his coming.

Friday 26th Br Jefferson Preacht in the evening from Psalm 113^C 1^V He exhorted us with great zeal to praise God now or we should not praise him by & by among the heathen. Saturday 27th Br Covers Child was interred at Kingston Church Yard.

Some improvements and regulations made in our Public worship. Friday Sept 2nd 1796 Rejoiced to hear from London by a letter from Lady Ann Erskin to Dr Haweis of great good being done to the Jews.[17] It gave me great encouragement in the work that I am ingagd and gave me a more earnest desier of seeing the glourious Gospell of Jesus Chirst spreading to the remotes parts of the world. Received During our stay here several letters from My Dear Parents, who seemed to be in great sorrow, I did my Indeavour to strengthen them all that I could, and my earnest Prayr was to God that they might be recociled to Him.

Lords day 4th Dr Haweis Preacht and Administered the ordinance of the Lords supper, this was a very precious time I trust I found it much to the benefit of my soule.

Tuesday 6th Blew a gale of wind from the west our anchor being foule we weighed and sailed a few miles over towards the other Bank but not finding a convenient Place returned Back to our former Station, in the course of this little cruse many of us were sick and we being unprepared the things rolling about between the decks put us in a great confusion. But thanks be to God he will not suffer us to be tempted above that we are able but will with the temptation also make a way to escape that we may be able to bear it.

Friday 9th greatly expected to sail, signal made for the morning, I prepared and got all my letters to my Friends commending them into the hands of God hoping they would not grieve or lamment for me for I am in the hands of God & and going to make known the Glories of his holy Name.

---

17. Finding himself in Portsmouth with time on his hands while the *Duff* waited to sail, Haweis set about converting the local Jewish population, to which he preached repeatedly: here was another "primitive" population the Missionary Society could bring to the light. Lady Ann Erskine was an aristocrat sharing his ambitions in this respect.

from London Missionary Society, Directors, "Counsels and Instructions for the Regulation of the Mission" (1796)

The LMS directors' instructions are as remarkable for their idealism as for their pragmatism. They envisage a small commonwealth without private property, run on democratic principles (though they expect every decision to be reached unanimously). They warn against theological nitpicking and encourage companionship. But they also address the difficult question of interracial marriage in a spirit of unusual tolerance.

from section I. Counsels for the Regulation of the
Personal Conduct and Spirit of the Missionaries

"Live together in Love and Union." Ye are brethren, but being men, are compassed about with infirmities. Bear and forbear: holding the unity of the spirit in the bond of peace. Satan's chief device will be to divide you. Form no parties, nor cabals; suppress the first movements of dispute and division; ever remember the words of the Lord: *He* is the greatest in his Kingdom; who is the *servant of all.*

We request it solemnly, we adjure you in the Great Master's name, "Love one another out of a pure heart fervently"; putting on bowels of mercy, kindness, long-suffering, forbearing one another, and forgiving one another, even though any man had a real cause of displeasure against his brother, as God for Christ's sake hath forgiven you.

Your examples must preach as powerfully as your words. But if ever bitter envyings and strife arise, you will put an effectual bar to your own usefulness, and defeat the great purpose of your Mission. Let all your zeal, therefore, be reserved for your work, and let no selfish passions mingle with it, to corrupt the simplicity which is in Christ.

You will be very differently qualified; and in some things there can be no competition between you. The talent one lacks, another possesses in a more abundant manner, and each is equally valuable and necessary for the work of God, and your mutual comfort and advantage. Remember always St. Paul's beautiful allegory of the human body:[18] every part is alike needful, for its beauty, symmetry, and preservation; and just so every member of your community should have the same care one of another.

Should evil break in upon a brother, which may the Lord preserve you from, be not hasty or harsh in your rebukes, nor too severe in your censures; a broken bone must be handled gently. You know St. Paul's direction where grievous offence had been given—"Ye that are spiritual, restore such a one in the spirit of meekness."

Watch over each other in love and fidelity; prevent, if possible, the evil; kindly conceal from your brethren lesser offences, after private admonition; the greater, if unhappily such should arise, must be censured openly: not

---

18. See, for example, Paul's First Letter to the Romans, 12:3–5.

treating him as an enemy, but admonishing him as a brother. Exclusion from your society becomes necessary, when guilt produces no humiliation; and obstinate perseverance in evil, compels the excision of the mortified limb, lest the body be infected.

Avoid as much as possible all occasions of temptation. Let no man be permitted, without leave of the community, to be absent at night from the common dormitory. In every journey, walk, occupation, let two or more brethren always be together.

Should any native women seek instruction in private, let one of our women sisters be their teachers. In public, all who please and are silent, may attend our worship and instruction.

If a brother thinks he ought to marry, let such a one take care that he be not guided by passion and fancy: *Only in the Lord* is the clear apostolic order: If therefore his desire be that he may keep himself more pure in the honourable estate of wedlock, let him communicate his wishes to his brethren, nor presume to form any secret engagements, but always act openly, with the approbation of the Mission.

Should any brother marry a native, they should build a little house near their brethren, and come under the same regulations as our own married brethren; their wives associating with our believing women, and on no account separate, but live in daily communion and worship under the same roof.

from section II. Internal Order, Administration, and Instruction

You must be a little Church and Community, and form such rules for your proceeding on the spot as may appear best suited to your circumstances: but every one is obliged to give way to the conclusions of the majority, and chearfully to acquiesce in all matters of prudential regulation, and not to follow his own opinion or will.

It is hoped that the spirit of faith, love, and humility will so pervade the whole Mission, that every individual will be ready, for the general good, to take the lowest place, and to become the servant of all. At the same time, confusion, disunion, and want of subordination, must be avoided; the Missionaries will endeavour, in humble dependance on Divine Counsel, to form and maintain such an order among themselves as is suitable to their different gifts, offices, abilities, and employments; such an order as may express solemn respect and obedience to the institutions of the New Testament; such an order as may strike the minds of the heathen with ideas of its wisdom, sweetness, utility, and dignity.

That an order so desireable, without the peculiarities of any denomination, may be secured; that the honour and purity of the ordinances of God may be maintained, and that the effects of human pride and self-sufficiency may be prevented, fixed rules are necessary and must be unanimously adopted. [. . .]

Affect not subtleties and deep points of controversy, either among yourselves or with the natives. Wave as much as possible what would lead to questions, rather than godly edifying. Attempt, not by arguments or the reasonableness, or evidences of the Christian Religion, to display your own wisdom; or, suppose you can answer and silence all their objections, adhere to the simplicity which is in Christ, trusting to the power of the Holy Ghost to take the things of Christ, and shew them to their consciences with divine conviction and effectual energy. It is the evil heart of unbelief that must be subdued; an awakened conscience feels the need of a great sacrifice: an awakened mind will always resist the Holy Ghost, and must be left to him, who only remove the darkness, and quicken from a state of death to newness of life.

It must be by divine operation and not by moral persuasion alone, that any real conversions will ever be wrought among the Heathen, or indeed among any others. [. . .]

Avoid unnecessary disputes about modes and forms; in unessential matters, let every man think for himself, and do not exaggerate the importance of things which do not affect the fundamental doctrines of Christianity.

from The Missionaries, "Journal of a Voyage to the South Seas 1 Sept. 1796–15 June 1797"

The *Duff* left Portsmouth on 10 September 1796 and arrived on 18 October at Rio de Janeiro, which it left on 20 November. Thereafter it sailed out of sight of land, below both Australia and New Zealand, until it landed at Tahiti on 5 March 1797. At first all went well on board, as prayer and discussion meetings were held with earnest punctuality. In early January 1797, a set of fifteen "Articles of Faith" was drawn up by the eight-member missionary committee for the brethren (not the sisters) to read and sign. Then trouble flared.

JANUARY 18th [1797]

Hitherto what has been inserted in this Journal have been one continued detail of unspeakable mercies, conferred by a covenant GOD upon us his unworthy creatures. Favors of the value of which we are not able to form a just estimation of. Favors for which we have often lifted up our hearts to the bountiful donor of in the exercise of humble Gratitude, of prayer and praise; mercies for which our dear brethren in the bonds of the Gospel, when they become acquainted with the account of, will join with us in attributing "Glory to GOD in the Highest."

New circumstances of a very different nature, from any that have yet transpired, since we have been embarked are to be noticed; and for which we doubt not, our dear brethren in the Lord will feel similar sensations with us of sorrow and surprize.

For some time past, some of the brethren had entertained a suspicion that Br. Jefferson and Br. Cock were not quite sound in their religious principles, knowing that both of them had been members of Arminian societies, they were fearful that the old leaven, had not been thoroughly purged out. Jefferson in his preaching had always evaded speaking upon the points in dispute between the Calvinists and Arminians, any further than answering his belief of Election.[19] Yet he had sometimes made use of expressions in his discourses in public, as have created uneasy sensations in the minds of several of his brethren, and confirmed in some measure the suspicion which they entertain'd of him. Br. Cock had at different times made use of such expressions, when speaking of the atonement of XT[20] and of the final perseverance of the Saints, as gave rise to the suspicion that he was of the same sentiment with Br. Jefferson, which was further confirm'd by the close intimacy subsisting between them, and their reading Arminian authors together.

But it appears very obvious now, that all these actions and expressions of theirs, which have been productive of such disagreeable sensations in the breasts of their brethren, have been like the workings of a subterraneous Fire, which have now broke into open Guilt.

[Testimony is now introduced and recorded relating to previous conversations, in which Jefferson and Cock revealed (arguably) heretical opinions. As a consequence some of the missionaries "requested a public meeting on Wednesday morn^g in order to have these matters more fully enquired into."]

In consequence of this request Capn. Wilson called a meeting at half past 9 this morning; Bro. Cover opened the meeting with prayer. After which Capn. Wilson as president of the meeting, informed the brethren that he had requested their attendance upon an affair that might have been settled by the committee, had it not principly related to one of the members of that committee.[21] Bro. Henry then stood up and addressing himself to the chairman explained the reason why he and several others had solicited a public meeting to be called which was as follows:

"Last Sabath afternoon when we met as usual for conversation upon some part of the Word of GOD, the text proposed for consideration was Romans 8: 29 & 30 verse.[22] The Bro. whose turn it was first to speak was Bro. Clode, the next was Bro. Cock in rotation, who requested to pass it, observing it was a difficult text and not having time enough to consider it. Afterwards it went

---

19. The seventeenth-century theologian Jacobus Arminius sought to liberalize the strict teachings of Jean Calvin, especially as regarded the doctrine of predestination: the belief that the salvation or damnation of every individual has been preordained by an omniscient and omnipotent God; that the death of Christ saved only "the elect," who were chosen arbitrarily and not on the basis of either faith or works; and that such "saints" persevered at the right hand of God eternally.

20. Atonement has a technical sense in Christian theology: the reconciliation of God and sinners, brought about by the sacrifice of Christ ("XT"). It is an essential issue for Calvinists because of their belief that all human faculties have been affected by the fall from paradise.

21. Not only was Jefferson on the missionary committee, he also kept the missionary journal at this time: a job which another missionary now took over.

22. Romans 8:29–30: "For he did foreknow, he also did predestinate to be conformed to the image of his Son, that he might be the firstborn among many brethren. Moreover whom he did predestinate, them he also called: and whom he called, them he also justified: and whom he justified, he also glorified."

from one Brother to another till it came to myself. I agreed in general with what my Brethren had said who spoke pryor to me, which was much to this effect: 'That by the foreknowledge of GOD spoken of in the text, was meant his Eternal purpose, Choise, or Election—That those whom GOD had thus chosen from all Eternity, were predestinated to be conformed to the Image of his Son, in Righteousness and true Holiness: all those were in the fullness of time called.' Here I observed that there were two calls, one an external which all had that hear the Gospel, the other an internal call, which is the Holy spirit applying the Word to the Heart, and rendering it Effectual. Further they are Justified, their sins are blotted out, and they receive a full pardon on account of the active and passive obedience of the Lord Jesus Christ: lastly they are Glorified or brought to Glory." Bro. Henry then proceeded to state the Ideas advanced by Bro. Jefferson upon the text, which was to this Effect: He avowed his belief of unconditional Election or Choise, and they who were the subjects of this choise were predestinated to be conformed to the Image of his Son; that they were effectually called by his holy spirit; that they were justified by the active and passive obedience of Christ; and that they were Gloryfy'd or Honor'd by being made partakers of the Graces of the Holy Spirit, to enable them to walk acceptably in the sight of GOD in all Holy Obedience. This definition not proving satisfactory he was requested to explain himself further when he observed that he supposed we were desirous of hearing him express his Ideas upon the "Final perseverance of the saints," when upon being answered in the affirmative, he informed us that it was a subject he had examined but as he was not altogether satisfied, he hoped that that would be considered as a sufficient reason for his not speaking upon that Head. This satisfied the Brethren, and after sometime the meeting closed with prayer. After the meeting Brother Lewis carried a volume of Dr. Wills's Works on the Covenant,[23] and requested Bro. Jefferson to read it, which he promised to do. The next morning Bro. Jefferson returned the book with thanks for the use of it. Being asked by Bro. Lewis wether he had read the part he had refered him too, J. cooly answered he had read a little of it. In the evening, to the no small consternation of several of the Brethren, J. was seen disputing with some of our Number upon this very point, and labouring with all his might to overturn the doctrine of Final perseverance, and seemingly to establish the Doctrine of "Universal Redemption." Bro. Henry concluded his speech by observing that as matters were in this disagreeable situation, he had thought it his duty to request a meeting in order that they might be further enquired into. The President then addressing himself to the brethren, enquired wether all could give their assent to the certainty of the Facts Bro. Henry had stated and was answered in the affirmative.

Bro. Jefferson then objected to what had been said concerning his having established "Universal Redemption" on Monday evening, but on Bro. Henry replying that he was not positive on that Head, and only said it seemed to

---

23. Possibly a volume from Thomas Wills' collected works, *The Spiritual Register,* 3 vols. (London, 1784–95). (Wills, like Haweis, had served as chaplain to the Countess of Huntingdon.)

him as if he was endeavouring to establish that doctrine, it was immediately dropt. Bro. Jefferson then remarked that could not conceive why the spirit of GOD, who dictated the Holy scripture, should insert so many passages relating to falling finally if such a thing was impossible. [. . .] Here Bro. Jefferson was interrogated concerning the insufficience of the atonement of Christ for the sinners salvation to which he replied by expressing his firm belief that it was compleatly sufficient. Bro. Lewis enquired of Bro. J. wether the salvation of the sinner was entirely of Grace? But instead of making any direct answer to this question, J. asserted that he would lay open to conviction, and that he would look up to GOD for his direction. He then exprest his firm belief that the Church would continue till the end of the World, but acknowledged himself quite in the dark respecting the final perseverance of individuals. The president then immediately addressing himself to Bro. Jefferson said you well know that the Missionary Society was quite calvinistical; You knew likewise the great opposition and difference that subsisted between the Calvinists and the Arminians in several important points of doctrine. Were not the doubts you have mentioned upon your mind at the time you offered yourself as a Missionary to the Directors? To which J. answered in the affirmative. Here the Chairman read an excellent statement of the Calvinistical principles, which are the points in dispute between them and the Arminians, from Encyclopaedia Britannica, under the article of Predestination.[24] To the former part of what had been read, J. express't his concurence, and then with great warmth asserted he had the grace of GOD in his Heart (pointing at the same time to his breast) and then directing his speech at the same time to the President told him that neither he, nor any one on board, nor all the Devils in Hell could ever pluck it out. Here he was called to order by Bro. Henry, who earnestly entreated him to examine himself as many had persuaded themselves they were now partakers of Grace and had yet fell at last.

[Discussion follows between Wilson, Henry, Lewis, and Eyre (on one side), and Jefferson (on the other) about doctrinal detail; the unlucky Jefferson resorts to some definitional evasions in response to questions.]

Bro. Buchanan observed now that as Bro. Jefferson had made such an open declaration of his sentiments, we can no longer consider him as a member of our Society. Bro. Main moved that Bro. J. preach no more to us, but this motion was not attended to at this time. Several of the Brethren immediately addressed Bro. J. with the warmest emotions of Grief, that it was not his person that was the object of their aversion; but his religious Tenets which to them appeared diametrically opposite to the Truth as it is in Jesus; that they

---

24. "PREDESTINATION, in general, signifies a decree of God, whereby, from all eternity, he ordained such a concatenation of causes as must produce every event by a kind of necessity. . . , in a more limited sense, for a judgment or decree of God, whereby he has resolved, from all eternity, to save a certain number of persons, from thence called elect; so that the rest of mankind being left in a state of impenitence, are said to be reprobated" (*Encyclopaedia Britannica*, first edition, 1771).

pitied, and would bear him affectionately in their Hearts at the Throne of Grace. J. likewise discovered similar sensations and declared his affection for the Brethren was not diminished, and observed it was only since last Saturday that his mind have been so much impressed with a sense of the Importance of what he had Delivered.

Bro. John Cock being now called upon to make an open declaration of his sentiments, concured exactly in opinion with Bro. Jefferson. He observed that he had lately been under great distress of Mind. He had frequently trembled to a very great degree; but that he was quite at a loss what cause to attribute it too: that when he offered himself as a Missionary to the Directors he was not examined concerning his principles, but only what related to his Conversion. Upon being interrogated concerning the doctrine of final perseverance; he asserted that a man may be in a state of Grace and favour with GOD, and Yet bring himself again under the Curse of the Law. Bro. Lewis, addressing the President, spoke of the importance of being of one heart and of one mind in the great work in which we were engaged, in such a manner as did him credit, at the same time lamenting in the tenderest manner over the breach that was now unhappily made among us by two of our number openly avowing and defending Arminian principles: and concluded by observing that it was necessary to form some plan, how we should proceed respecting them; [. . .] but as it was the general opinion of the Brethren that the greatest circumspection and tenderness was necessary in proceedings of this Nature, the meeting was adjourned till the morrow half past 9 o'clock.

JANUARY 19th

At ½ past 9 the brethren met between decks pursuant to adjournment, before the meeting was opened the president requested Bro. Jefferson and Cock to withdraw, which they did immediately. Bro. Lewis in a short, but expressive prayer supplicated the assistance of the Great Head of the Church, to direct and guide us at this critical and important juncture. The president then inform'd the meeting that should they think it necessary to exclude Bro. Jefferson and Bro. Cock from communion with them they must then elect another member in lieu of Bro. Jefferson. It was then moved that Brethren Jefferson and Cock be excluded from fellowship with us as members of the same church. Unanimously agreed. [. . .]

SATURDAY JANY. 21st

PM At 2 o'Clock the society met between decks pursuant to adjournment, for exercise when Bren. Shelly Puckey Smith Vason & Wilkinson, spoke from Romans 5th and 12th. After each of these brethren had spoken Bro. Lewis the Moderator proposed three important questions as inferences from the fundamental doctrines contained in that Text (at the same time requesting every Bro. Present to answer separately). 1st whether all the powers and faculties of the Soul are not contaminated with Sin? 2nd whether this contamination of Soul, does not deserve the wrath and condemnation of GOD? 3rdly whether

Man has any power of himself in order to extricate himself from this miserable state? To which questions each Br. Replied in the affirmative, the latter question in the negative. The moderator immediately summed up what had been said, and concluded with a short, but seasonable exortation and earnest prayer to GOD, that we might deeply be impressed with a scense of the Fall of Man, and that our Knowledge of this important Doctrine might be clear and extensive. [. . .]

[Jefferson and Cock were informed of their excommunication by letter, "united and engaged as we are, in one great and important Cause, that of conveying the glad tidings of salvation by Jesus Christ, for poor sinners, amongst the dark and unenlightened heathen; and deeply sensible of the importance of being of one heart, and of one mind, in the Great Fundamental Doctrines of the Gospel." But "public recantation of your erroneous principles," the missionaries suggested, would suffice for reacceptance in the group.]

JANY. 23d

P.M. At 2. The Society met, when the Secretary read the following Letter, which he had received in the morning from Mr. Jefferson, directed to the Society:

On board the Duff at Sea, Jany. 23. 97.
To the Church of Christ on board the Duff; Grace mercy and peace be multiplied upon all and every one of you.

Dear Brethren
First, asking pardon of Almighty GOD thro' Jesus Christ, the only mediator for my sin, committed against his divine Majesty; and the Glory of the covenant of his Grace; I next intreat your forgiveness of my wickedness, in openly throwing before you principles derogatory to *all* the Offices to the great Head of the Church, and thereby wounding your peace of mind, opening the door for the entrance of a flood of errors, and drawing upon myself your Just censure.

I humbly appeal to the awful searcher of Hearts, that the mists of darkness wherewith my mind was surrounded are dispersed and those Truths which I once saw, believed, and preached, but I so lately opposed, hath again shine resplendantly upon my mind; whereby my Sin appeared great, my heart was grieved and the goodness of GOD towards me I felt.

Humbled by my *Fall,* I can hardly expect to be admitted into Church fellowship and Communion with you again, much less to minister unto you in Holy things: yet I beseech you to remember what Man *is,* even in his best estate *vanity,* and let that love be felt for a Brother in distress a similar situation would lead you to desire.

I remain
Dear Brethren
Your sorrowful Brother
John Jefferson.

Upon hearing the contents of the above Letter, every Bro. exprest the greatest satisfaction, and we lifted up our hearts to GOD, with earnest desires that the writer of it might see more and more of the Glory of GOD in the Face of Jesus XT.

[A similar letter from Jefferson had been received by Captain Wilson, and the missionary committee immediately resolved to readmit him. In the afternoon a full meeting agreed "unanimously."]

JANY. 24th

[. . .] the Secretary submitted the following Letter to the consideration of the meeting, and which being unanimously approved of, it was ordered to be transmitted to Bro. J. without Delay.

> On board the Duff at Sea
> January 24. 1797
>
> The Church of Christ on board the Duff have received your penitential Letter bearing Date 23d. Inst. with pleasure and satisfaction and with earnest supplication to our Glorious redeemer, the Great head of the Church, for that wisdom which is profitable to direct, we have considered the contents of it; we rejoice in the assurance that your Letter gives us that GOD has indeed granted you repentance to the Acknowledgement of the Truth as it is in Jesus Christ. The Forgiveness which you intreat at our hands, what is past we give you with a distinguished pleasure. We realize the time when we hope to recieve you again into our Number, with the most lively emotions of Joy and Gratitude to GOD that the Breach which has so unhappily been made amongst us, may in his infinite mercy be soon healed. Mean time we take this method of signifying to you our request, that in Order to remove all uneasy sensations from the mind of every one concerned, you will [preach] to us Wednesday eveng. Jany. 25th, Friday eveng. Jany. 27, Lords day Jany 29th. The texts which you preach from, we shall leave to your own discretion.
>
> Done at a meeting of the whole body of Missionaries; On board the Duff at Sea. Jany. 22nd. 97. D. Bowell. Secety.

[On 25 January a conciliatory note was sent to Cock, who had written in contrite terms the day before. In the days following, Jefferson preached to the missionaries, and his public recantation was accepted on Monday 30 January. On the same day Cock was brought before the meeting, questioned, and his recantation accepted.]

MONDAY, 30th JANY.

Brethn J. and C. being called Bro. Lewis as senior minister gave them the right hand of fellowship, after which each Brother rose and shook hands with each of them in such a manner as plainly indicated that the pleasure and satisfaction which each one experience was not small. Br. Jefferson being requested to conclude the meeting with prayer, gave out the hymn of Mr Burders Coll[ection] which was sung by all present in such a manners as plainly showed, how much every ones heart was engaged in the delightful service, after which the meeting was closed by Bro. J. with a short but expressive prayer.

from Rowland Hassall, "Tahiti 1796–1799"

Rowland Hassall (1768–1820) was a Congregationalist weaver from the midlands city of Coventry, married to Elizabeth. After abandoning the mission, he became government storekeeper and later supervisor of government stock at Parramatta, New South Wales—where a local school and street still carry his name—and he died a wealthy landowner.

JANUARY THE 20th 1798. Somtime since it was determined that a New house was requisite for the reception of our property the defence of our lives and to make our watching more moderate it was thought proper that all other imployments should cease till the House is erected, accordingly we devided ourselves into different tribes, Viz some to get timber others to saw plank &c &c. Br Cover & the writer was appointed to clear the ground. About 7 oClock this morning when at labor there came an old man up to me and I inquired where he was going he told me for the priest, I asked why he was going to the P——. He answered that his Master's grandaughter was now in labor, and that he was going for him to offer the Child to his god. I requested the Old Man to call for me when the P—— was come, accordingly in about half an hour he came, and we went together towards the house. When we came within 100 yards of the house I saw the woman under a large Breadfruit tree in the midst of the long grass in greate pains without help and in the open air, you must needs think, that I was much affected at the sight, I requested that she might be taken into the house, to which they replied that their customs would not admit it, the house being sacred and if the woman was to go in before the expiration of ten days the house must be burnt down. After the child was born I went towards her and found the child lieing in the grass, with a cut all across the cheek, but a fine boy. I asked them to take him into the house and wash him &c. but they answered, the child is unclean and will be till it be given to the god twice, after which it might go into the house and not till them, upon which they brought the child to the P——. I then addressed myself to the P—— telling him that I was sorry they had such customs among them for it was enough to kill both Mother and Child, I further added, that I wished it was in my power to teach them better for we never did so in England, to which the P—— replied as soon as the English can learn our language and teach us better we will put them away, and he told me some customs which they had put away through our persuasions, Viz. there are now no human sacrifices (said he) nor so many children kil'd &c &c. I told him I was very happy to hear of it after which he was going to take the child into the Morai or burying place, which caused us to enter into further conversation, after we had been talking about 15 minutes he told me that he would not take the child but go and tell the god that he had put away that custom through my persuasion, accordingly he went to the Morai and gathered a bunch of fern and a bunch of Candle Nutt branches and tied them up in different bundles with white cloth, after which he took and set them in the ground on each side of a stone which stood upright about 2 feet out of the ground, before which he kneeled. Being now set in a praying posture, he began to pray to his god, he told him the substance of what we had been talking about and prayed him not to be angry at him for putting away that custom. Just as he had don repeating the above, there came a bird much like the Swoolow at home and churp a cheerful Note, upon which he smiled and said that god had sent that bird to inform him that he was not angry at him for putting away that custom. I asked him were his god dwelt, he told me that his god liv'd in darkness, but he always sent that bird to inform him when he was pleased.[25] I told him that birds were very common and that his god, worship, & bird, were mere vanity, &c &c. But all that I could say to him could not shake his faith in his bird, and god. After spending half an hour in the Morai we returned to the mans house, but the child was not admitted into the house till the expiration of 5 days nor the woman till 10. Note, I have every reason to belive that this child would have been kill only for the interposition of our sisters.

JANUARY THE 31st 1798. This day the Chiefs & pepal came from all quarters of the Island to hear our Message to them, when we improved the opertunity by informing them first, the intent of our Mission 2nd the desperate state they are in and proving it from their bad conduct, thirdly held forth the Blessings of Salvation to them as far as the Gospel of the Blessed God allows, to which they paid great attention and promised to perform all we reqested and acknowledged that it was all very good and we parted in peace. About 7 oClock this morning Mrs H was delivered of another Son, I have reason to call on all my friends, & powers, to praise and adore the God of our Salvation, for altho I had a thousand fears through the Dr leaving and returning home,[26] yet the Lord so kind as to spare both Root and Branch and caused her to have as good a time as ever before, My thanks are due to Bro Broomhall for he spared no paines to obtain a knowledge in surgery that he might be usefull, & the Lord blessed his labor. This day the woman that was in labor 3 days ago, came across the River naked, being as deep as her arm pitts and seemd as well as ever altho she is as delicate a woman as any among them. This week Br Cock made application to be receved again among us which caused us to have a public Meeting, the subject was attend to, and after all was said, as could be

---

25. Hassall's attitude to this incident is strange in that it never occurs to him that *his* god, and not the Tahitian's, may have sent the bird to encourage the Islander to change his ways. Apparently he does not remember the occasions in the Bible on which God sent birds as messengers: at the end of the Flood, for example, or at the baptism of Christ ("This is my beloved son, in whom I am well pleased").

26. The mission's only medically trained member, the surgeon John Gillham, had abandoned the mission altogether and gone home on the *Duff.*

said both for and against it, it was resolved that he should injoy every bennifit as a civil Member, but through some improper Acts in his life he was not to be admitted to Lords table till a further concideration took place.[27] [. . .]

MARCH THE 6th 1798. Twelve months this day sence we cast anchor in Mattavie Bay, I have to confess that we have don but little good comparatively speaking, but I hope our visit hath not been altogether in vain. These natives tho in a faint degree have had Life & Death set before them they have been told of their deplorable state and the end of their way, they have also been informed of the way of escape through the blood of the Lamb, and that in a way they have understood, and though I have no hope as to the Eternal salvation of any one, yet they have concented to the truth, by acknowledging that it was very Good. This morning we seen the sail of a ship which provd to be the Bark Nauttalus from Bengall commanded by Capt Boshop bount to the North West coast of America, but driven off by bad weather into High North Latitudes, and not being able to fetch their port, they came to O'why'ee, and from thence to Otaheite,[28] After casting anchor in the bay we found [the] ship to be very bear of stors so that they had neither Bread, nor spirits, and but very little water on board, and nothing to purches any with, but Muskets and gunpowder on which account we had a Meeting of the Body to know weather we should find them supplies or the Natives. At length it was resolved that we should find them supplies and that, on the following account, first, that if the Natives found them supplies the Capt would supplie the Natives with Muskets Powder & Balls. 2d if they did, we should be all ways in fear, for they had about four times the Number, more of these articles than we, and 3rdly, in order to keep these dreadful implements from them we thought it our duty to find them supplies accordingly we did, for which the Captain and officers were very thankfull, and in return they made us a present of a few Muskets, with Powder, and Ball, which we excepted. The Natives at this line of conduct was not pleased, for they thirsted very much for those Articles, Nay I may ad, for all we had. The Capt had the misfortune to lose 5 of his men which he brought from O'why'ee, by the act of Desertion, and they joined the Natives. After stopping a few days the Capt hove anchor, and made way for Masifuroo in order to get a frate of seal skins, and then return to Bengall.

MARCH THE 19. Sence the ship left the Bay the Natives have been in one continual broil against us, through which we have been force to keep a strong watch, Night & Day, always four upon the watch and some times more, so that our spirits are nearly exhausted for want of reinforcement. The 5 men that run away from the Nauttalus seem to spend all their time, to stir up the rage of the Natives against us. We hear of them meeting in great parties to come and take

---

27. John Cock was in trouble again, this time for cohabiting with Islander women.

28. The *Nautilus*, commanded by Captain Bishop, had encountered bad weather on a trip between Macao and America and turned into Hawai'i as a result, then headed south with a shorthanded crew. From Tahiti they intended sailing to Más Afuera, one of the Juan Fernández islands off the coast of Chile, for seal skins to take back to India. But a storm at sea forced them back to Tahiti and then on to Port Jackson (Sydney).

"DARK PARTS OF THE EARTH"

us,—therefore we cannot attend to any Business, for my own part I thought the envy of the Natives arose from our covenanting with the Capt not to let them have any firearms &c &c. as you may see above.

MARCH THE 25. Our watchings troubles & fears continue and seem to increase from all quarters. This day to our great supprize the Bark Nauttalus came into the Bay and cast anchor, being force back from her intended voyage by a strong gail of wind and much hurt in so much that was not able to put to sea till sundre repairs took place. Some of our Bretheren looking on this even as a very Singular providence they had thought of leaving this Island and going to one adjacent, but no public decision took place. To add to the Capt losses he had 3 more of his men run away from the Ship, and joind themselves to the Natives. The Natives now have a strong partie, having the men from the Nauttalus, and the Tweed, already on the Island, they have power to take us when they please, & I dout not but they would, if it was not the restraining grace of God.

MARCH THE 26th. Yesterday altho the Sabbath we had little or no Devotion, tho we had our usual round of Dutties, our Minds being pregnent with fears and troubles. This morning it was reported that the Capt was determined to have those 7 men if it cost him 20 muskets, he not having men to work the ship, on hearing the report we had a Meeting of the Body, the result of which was, that we would go to the Capt and intrest him not to let the Natives have any Muskets &c, and we would use our indeaveour to bring them on board, to which the Capt kindly agreed, in order to get the men there was four of the Bretheren appointed to go to O'pare' to see the King, Pomarra, Te'ma'ree', & Manamana; Viz. Brs Broomhall, Jefferson, Main & Wm Puckey, to try if, by any maines, they could get the Men, to take to the Ship. The first house they came to was King O'too's, the Breth attempted to deliver their message to him but all in vain, for the king was wrath and intoxecated, from thence they went towards the house of Pommarra, in their way to his house, they was overtaken by a large Mob of the King's Philistians,[29] who took and separated the Breth from each other, and ill treated them all. W.P. they took and striped nakid draging him to the water and most cruelly beat him, After which they held his head under the water till the Blood gushed out of his Nose, After they had gon this length, they let him go being nakid and almost dead and he went to Pomarra's house, Bros Jefferson & Main, they beat stript and brused but not so bad as Br Puckey. Bro J., being over generious, after they had taken part of his clothes, he freely gave them all the rest, and went to Pomarra's house nakid. Bro Broomhall being a favorite of the Native and of a very winning disposition, he came off better than the rest, but they drove him up the Mountain and took away all that he had save his trowsers, shirt and watch, after their rage was abated, the Breth all met at the house of Pomarra, and was kindly received by him. They likewise delivered their message, and he promised to send the

---

29. Inhabitants of the biblical land of Philistia, also known as Philistines: uncouth, uneducated people.

men to the ship, but he did not. Pomarra being more human than his subjects he expostulated with them about their improper behaviour towards the Breth, he also gave them food to eate, and rament to put on, and conducted them to a canoe and said that he was sorrow for it. About 8 oClock in the evening the Breth returned and we received them with joy praising God for sparing their lives in so many perils. During the time the Breth was being beat, they heard the Natives say, now is the time to go to Mattavie, we have four of them here, they cannot help them. Three of their best warers [warriors?] are here &c &c. These expressions made our Breth fear that we should be all plundered and destroyed. This evening the Natives gathered together in different parts of this District and O'pare, through which we was force to get ourselves in readiness for war we fully expected them before the rising of the sun, therefore we all stood watch through the Night, save those 4 Breth that was ill treated. But that God, who says to the Billows of the sea be still they obey his Voice, caused these Natives, not to hurt, nor come near us.

MARCH THE 27. This morning it was proposed by som of the Breth. that there should be a public Meeting of the Body to know what steps to take in our perilous situation, accordingly we all meet and Bro Jefferson was voted to the Chair, after sollomn prayer to God, for his spirit to direct, in what lay before us, there was a question put forth to know weather it was our Duty, in our present curcumstances to leave the Island, or no. Due order was attended to, and every Br. interrogated in rotation, and each spoke very freely, som of the Breth, thought it their duty to leave the Island, let the consequence be what it would. Others though hearing the above said if part of the Body went, it would be in vain, for the remainder to watch, seeing the Natives for want of strength, might do as they pleased with us, even now. There was som that thought it their duty, to leave the Island because all hopes of usefullness was cut off for the present, while others said through grace thay intended to stop and see the issue. Br Cover very judiciously observed with some others of the Breth that he thought the ship that now lay in the Bay was very Providentially brought in for our deliverence and that he thought it was our Duty as all hopes of useful-lness was cut off & we in such a confused state to imbrace the opertunity to go in the ship for Port Jackson and try what we can do there for at this time there is no other way of escape. When the writer was interrogated he observed that as an individual husband or father he had no cause to leave the Island for he never received the least insult whatever. But as a Member of this Society he had been ill treated yesterday in the vile conduct of the Natives towards the Breth. But he expect the bad before he left home, therefore it could be no ground to leave the Island. Again he observed that before long our labor and watchings would be more moderate for the house which we was so forward with would soon be complete and that with one Man on the watch we should be more safe than now with four. Further he observed that if half the Breth thought it their Duty to stop on the Island he should think so too. But he could not see his way clear, to leave the Island at present. At length we came to a vote when there was ten for going & eight for stoping yet on the Islands, but all thought it the Duty of the Married Breth, with their wives to leave some time. [. . .] This night we were force to keep a strong watch there being many Natives around our house. This day E'do', a friend or Ty'o of mine, having som property in my apartment, came in with all hast and took all he had away telling us that the Natives was coming to take all we had away.

MARCH THE 28. Those Breth that intended to go for Port Jackson was very busy in packing up for the Voyage and those who intended to remain on the Island consulting what Measures to take, having no means to defend them, and all exposed to the rage of Natives, about noon 2 of the men that deserted from the Nauttalus came to our house nakid and informed us, that there was about 700 of the Natives come to them, with Clubs, Spears, Staves &c &c. and wanted them to join their Mob, and come against us, but they refused and left them. No sooner had these men denied their help, but the Natives all in a rage took and stript them of all they had, and drove them from O'pare. Seeing these men in this condition some of the Breth gave them a few articles to cover their nakidness with, these men wanted to go on board again but the Capt refused. Having no desire to leave the Island, and my friends saying it was my duty to go, I knew not what to do, I made it my earnest prayer to God that he would direct me, but I thought all in vain, I went to bed, but found no rest through the night.

MARCH THE 29. I was telling one of my dear friends the perplexities of my minde, to which he made answer, that he could not think why I should attempt to stop, soon after Manamana came into my apartment, and intreated me not to leave the Island, and told me that Pomarra was crying at O'pitea's house, on account of me leaving them [. . .]. In about half an hour after I thought well to inform those Breth that intended to remain on the Island what had took place, and if they thought, I could be of any service at all I was very willing to stop, and Mrs H. was of the same mind, but it was not approved. Therefore, I began to prepare for the Voyage, and went on board the Nautilus, commanded by Capt Boshop, bound for Port Jackson, New Holland, about five oClock in the evening.

MARCH THE 30th 1798. Through a rumour that was through the ship, Viz. that we should have bad luck if we set sail on a Friday, the Capt thought proper not to sail till Saterday or Sunday, this morning I went on shore in company with some of the Breth, and found that they had given all the public property to Pomarra, and E'deea, and tendered to them anything of their own they desired; about Noon we took our leave of the Breth on shore, and went on board the Nautilus, which was our last visit to Otaheite. Mrs Eyre was afraid to venture in the Bark Nautilus. But she being aged there is no fear of her being hurt, for I verily belive the Natives never lust after old women but to the reverse, looking upon them as the offscouring of all.[30]

---

30. Elizabeth Eyre was sixty-four when the mission left England.

SATERDAY MARCH THE 31 1798. This morning we were informed of a war in O'pare, the contending parties were Pomarra and those persons who beat and stript the Breth. The report was that Pomarra was very angry, and determined to kill them accordingly he ordered four to be sacrificed and four more was kill in the war, about Noon the Capt hove Anchor short when unfortunately the cable broke by means of the Anchore holding in a rock which caused us to put to Sea directly, thus we left Otaheite, and made way for Port Jackson, New South Wales, after stopping 12 months & 24 days. I only sad that I left Otaheity more sorrowful than I left my own Native Country; but I indulge a hope, that I shall spend a longer space, yet, in that Island before this Mortal shall moulder to dust. But not my will, but the Lords be don.

John Harris, Letter to the Missionary Society, 29 March 1798

John Harris (1757–1819) was a Calvinist cooper from Reading, Berkshire. Whereas Rowland Hassall decided to take his family off the island, the unmarried Harris elected to stay. He continued to serve on Tahiti until 1800.

My Dearly beloved Brother

The letter dated March 12th I wrote when the ship was under sail and I expected to see her no more 'till her return in five months on her way to India. But to our great surprise she came to our harbour again in about 10 days, having been driven hither in a violent gale which lasted 80 hours. She sustained a fresh damage and the loss of much water in her hold which rendered it necessary to come to anchor again in our Bay. Her return has caused to take place the greatest transaction of our lives. It was occasioned by our entreating the Capt not to barter his muskets and powder with the Natives for the supplies he stood in need of and we ourselves undertook to victual and water his ship for him, which we did on his first arrival and at which the Natives were greatly offended, and when she arrived this last time two of his men ran on shore and the chiefs refused to deliver them up. Four of our Brethren were appointed to go to the next district to entreat the chiefs in the Captain's behalf. The District is called Opare about 8 miles from Matavie. They were met by a large company, and stripped of their clothes and Mr Puckey one of the 4 was very much beat. They sent them home naked but somebody on the way after their escape gave them some Otaheitean clothes. We were much alarmed at their treatment and gathered therefore an attack was meditated against us. Report came on the back of reports that they would come in the night and put us to death. A meeting was therefore called to take our circumstances into consideration. Bros. Maine, Cover, Puckey and others viewed our situation quite perilous and judged it eligible to entreat Captain Bishop to remove us to an adjacent Island, but none we conceived would be favourable except Uletea [Raiatea] and that we were informed was involved in War, and no alternative was conceived as suitable but that of going down to Port Jackson with the ship, and this caused great altercation and great searchings of heart, and in two days the minds of all that refused to stay in Otaheite were fully known and preparations were accordingly made for departing. Our company was 18 Men 5 Women and 4 Children. Mr Jefferson, Eyre, Bicknell, Nott, Lewis and myself agreed to continue. Mrs Eyre being far advanced in years and suffering so much in the Duff would not venture to embark again, let the consequences be what they may. But we hope the Lord will be with us and enable us to make him our refuge and strength in every distress. What awaits us we know not. Our property has exposed us to much danger from the Natives, but what our Brethren has left behind we mean to distribute among the Chiefs, and wear Otaheitean dress, for it is not safe to go far with European clothes. 'Tis a comfort to us that they do not steal our Books, pens or ink. The firing of a gun the signal of departure now sounds in my ears and I am obliged to cut short. This week is the most remarkable of my life. Our family of 27 Men, Women and Children is broken up and reduced to seven, the boxes packed and embarked on board. In 3 Days and I cannot help remarking two days before this took place my Soul was struck with much solemn reflections. It was my turn to preach the last Lord's day and I left my work on the Saturday afternoon and could fix my thoughts on no subject 'till Sunday morning the words of Peter 2 Epis: 4, 3 last verses presented themselves to me and made great impression on my spirits.[31] The next day the tryal began and on Thursday afternoon our Brothers and Sisters were all embarked on board. [. . .] The Natives are all surrounding our house and, when the ship is out of the our harbour, I expect things very remarkable will take place. We have hitherto kept guard and with our Muskets because of fear in the night, but our small number that remain are wholly defenceless but having put ourselves under the protection of almighty love we trust we shall find him our shield to defend us from all sins and all enemies and be enabled to sing the 46th Psalm come on as what may.[32] Our situations as to outward things from this hour are entirely new and truly critical. We are surrounded with abundance of enemies and many professed friends but we find there is a spirit of Treachery and false heartedness runs thro them all. Thus far I wrote on Thursday Evening 6 and a voice sounded hastily in my ears the ship was immediately a going off and I was much vexed and despaired of finishing the sheet in time but at 10 oClock a message came on shore for something left behind and informed us the ship would lye off a few hours longer. I therefore proceed to give you a little detail of the proceedings of the past hour or two, such a scene as was never beheld in the Southern Hemisphere before, that I am sure of. A great number of chests and goods guarded and protected by muskets and two small cannon or swivel mounted on the beach. Many hundreds of Natives surrounding the House like eagles

---

31. 1 Peter 4:17–19 seems appropriate to this time of "tryal": "For the time is come that judgment must begin at the house of God: and if it first begin at us, what shall the end be of them that obey not the gospel of God?"

32. Psalms 46:1: "God is our refuge and strength, a very present help in trouble," and so on.

in pursuit of their prey, and directly as the last goods were in the canoe and the last four or five Brethren ready to start, the guns were discharged and the muskets taken off on board and six of us left defenceless and the Natives crowding into the house and searching the different apartments scrambling for what was left behind in the great hurry of removal. We were struck with solemnity at the singular, unexpected and sudden scene, and our little number convened into a little room for a meeting of Prayer. Mr Eyre began with singing "Lord make us faithful to thy call," read 13 Heb.[33] I followed him with singing a hymn suitable to the occasion and read 4 ch: 2 Ep. of Peter—little thinking when I spoke upon 17 verse four days before I was so soon to see it realized in such an awful way. Mr Jefferson concluded with singing "Come holy Spirit, come let thy bright beams arise," read 9 Isaiah.[34] Fearing lest in hurrying I should lose the conveyance can therefore only glance at things. 'Tis now past 2 oClock in the morning——not having more than half an hour I am necessitated to break off, entreating my Brother to remember me to Dr Haweis, Mr Eyre and they will be pleased to make my loving respects to Mr Wilks, Hill, Platt, Love, Waugh and many other Gentlemen—entreat Dr Haweis to send me a treatise on the Name of the eternal Spirit by Mr Serle. I have his Horae Solalare – should be exceeding glad to see any posthumous works of Mr Romaine[35]—I have as far as the numbers that commence the letters—other treatises &c. that the Society shall think suitable will be received with the utmost pleasure—would entreat also two nautical almanacks for the succeeding years—I have as far as 1798. I send this by the Nautilus bound to Botany Bay, Captain Bishop—by this conveyance I cannot expect it will reach you in less than two years or more from this time except some South Sea whaler was commissioned to call on us by the Gentlemen of the Missionary Society. I would just add that notwithstanding this solemn providence I hope the Lord will bring much good out of it. I am going on board with my letter and shall take my final leave of them with the warmest desire of my heart that the Lord may be with them and carry them to their desired Port in safety. It is an unspeakable consolation to me the Lord enables me to cast a mantle of love over all failings and differences that have taken place among us. I find bowels of compassion moving in my heart towards them. I hope I shall never go to the Throne of Grace without remembering them in their least Interests.

33. See Hebrews 13:5–6: "Let your conversation be without covetousness; and be content with such things as ye have: for he hath said, I will never leave thee, nor forsake thee. So that ye may boldly say, The Lord is my helper, and I will not fear what man shall do unto me."

34. Isaiah 9 contrasts the passing, violent struggles of empires with the eternal reign of Christ: "Of the increase of his government and peace there shall be no end, upon the throne of David and upon his kingdom," and so on.

35. Ambrose Serle and William Romaine were voluminous late-eighteenth-century divines. Serle published *Horae Solitariae* [Solitary hours] in 1776.

Thomas Haweis, Letter to Joseph Banks, 12 September 1798

The pressures on the island were intolerable, but the Missionary Society was also coming under attack at home. In that context we find Haweis currying favor with and seeking endorsement from Cook's "scientific gentleman," now an authority on all things Tahitian. The remarks Haweis makes about the society's ecumenicalism and the value of "private judgment" sit oddly with the missionaries' experiences aboard the *Duff*.

Dear Sir

Your obliging favour calls for my acknowledgments, sorry to hear the painful indisposition under which you have laboured.

To a man of your candor & above vulgar prejudices, I may venture to speak freely. Can any man who has acquainted himself with our avowed sentiments, suppose we have ever taught, or countenanced any thing *contrary to the doctrinal articles of the Church of England*?[36] Sir, be assured of the contrary. But I wave theological opinions wherein we may differ; in the interests of humanity, I flatter myself we are united, & wish the greatest possible happiness, and the fullest relief from misery, to all Mankind. These were the principles, that actuated our past endeavours, & if you, Sir, & every man of reflection, read & consider the state of mental and moral depravity we are devising to correct I am persuaded we shall stand approved to every ingenuous mind, as freinds to our fellow men whatever may be our diversity of sentiments, & exclusive of all considerations of a world to come.

I wish you really knew more of our Society, the persons who compose it, & the objects they have in view. We desire to be neither exclusively Church men or dissenters, we contain a considerable number of both, and on either side of the Tweed.[37] We form no parties in religion or politics; our design rises from a broader basis. It is the inviolable rule with us, that politics never enter into our conferences, and that no exclusive mode of worship shall be prescribed to our Missionary brethren, but every man left to his private judgment, acknowledging only the doctrinal articles of the Church of England as containing the substance of our religious sentiments; supposing His Majesty as much king of North Britain, as of the South: and admitting men from both into our Work and Service alike.

You, Sir, will be above the false representations of those who know us not, as if we secretly entertained ill designs. But the present afforded a happy opportunity of offering our respectful homage to his Majesty, & exposing to the World the real sentiments of our Society, who compose no inconsiderable body of his subjects.

---

36. In 1552 the protestant archbishop Thomas Cranmer had written forty-two articles, or statements of doctrinal belief, describing the basis of the recently formed Church of England. In 1571 a revised version was produced, the "Thirty-Nine Articles," to which thereafter every clergyman in the church had to subscribe.

37. That is, on either side of the traditional border between England and Scotland ("North Britain").

I may venture to suggest to you, Sir, that nothing hath ever happened in this land, which had a happier tendency to direct the minds of men from the dangerous field of political contention[38] to the peaceable objects of general Philanthropy, than the Missionary Society. The most attached freind to Government could never have wished for effects more conducive to peace & union than have been produced, and it is obvious, that our efforts if ultimately successful must be of the most beneficial consequences to the kingdom at large.[39] I wish you, Sir, & every Bishop on the Bench,[40] would be at the pains cordially to examine and liberally to decide according to evidence. Objects seen through a false medium may appear distorted. Beauty itself thus becomes a Medusa's head.[41]

Suppose not, respected Sir, we wished to court favour in high places, or solicit patronage, these I may confidently say are beneath our views. We judged the present a fair opportunity, to refute the misrepresentations whether ignorantly or maliciously made of us, & to offer our Homage where due, a tribute in the present instance of peculiar propriety, & would have been submitted to your approbation.

I have now only to ask, if you will permit me to add your name to the list of subscribers who will be entitled to the first plates, charts & impression of the Quarto Volume, the proposals for which I take the liberty to enclose, and hope you will find it among the most interesting publications, which on this subject has engaged the public interest.[42] You will be pleased, Sir, to hear that you are remembered by these distant islanders.

But I beg pardon for having taken up so much of your time
and remain
your obliged and obedt sert

T. Haweis

Sept 12 1798

---

38. The 1790s, in the aftermath of the French Revolution, was Britain's most radical decade for over a hundred years. Habeas corpus was frequently suspended, meetings banned, and radical tracts by Tom Paine, Joseph Godwin, Mary Wollstonecraft, and others caused anxiety in government circles.

39. To Banks, Haweis writes of philanthropy replacing political contention; to the Home Secretary, Lord Dundas, he argued that the Tahitian mission was "an English incipient Colony, and every Benefit resulting from the Civilization we hope to introduce must ultimately terminate in Britain" (Gunson, 141).

40. All bishops had the right to sit in the House of Lords at Parliament, and comprised a "bench" in the chamber.

41. Medusa was a female character from Greek myth whose hair was formed of snakes and whose glance turned men to stone. She was ultimately vanquished by the hero Perseus.

42. This publication was James Wilson's *A Missionary Voyage to the Southern Pacific Ocean, Performed in the Years 1796, 1797, 1798, in the Ship Duff*, published in 1799.

"DARK PARTS OF THE EARTH"

Reverend Matthew Wilks, Letter to Mary Cover, 3 September 1799

We last met Reverend Matthew Wilks in William Puckey's account of his calling, offering hospitality to the new missionaries at home in London and moral support on board the *Duff* at Portsmouth. Puckey also recorded that Brother Cover and his wife lost a child on the ship before it set sail. Rowland Hassall wrote that Cover considered the *Nautilus* to be "very Providentially brought in for our deliverance" on its reappearance in the bay. Now the unlucky Covers are given an epistolary dressing-down by Wilks.

My dear Madam,

Notwithstanding you will receive a letter from the M^y Society by this conveyance I cannot forbear in a private capacity dropping you a line and by the same means forward you for common use the magazines, by which you will learn what we have been doing since you left England. Before this reaches you the Hilsborough, who carried Dr Vander Kemp & brethren to the Cape, will have informed you of the re equipment of the Duff under captain Robson and of her having sailed in company almost to Madeira—but on just entering the harbour of Rio Janeiro she was captured by the French. . . . [43] When the news of this disaster reached England it is not easy to conceive the afflictive impulse it gave to the religious friends; who flew to repair the loss amounting to £10000. £4000 was raised in a fortnight, and had not this intelligence been succeeded by information more afflictive still the whole would have been raised in a few weeks more. The news of yr departure from Otaheite, has inflicted such a wound, that will not easily be healed. We are not able to express our astonishment—*the enemy triumphs* and an enemy he must be to God who does triumph at the troubles of Zion. Offences will come—but woe to him by [whom] they come. A thousand thoughts revolve in my mind upon this subject, & tho' we forbear to press a public judgment upon it as it respects yourselves until we hear from you; yet I can hardly tell how to pronounce you blameless from the information received. Scores of times have I thought with pain of what you said to me on board the Duff, "That if you had not more sugar you would not go." The saying made me tremble when ever I thought of it. What must your reflexions be when you realise all the evils attendant upon this transaction—you will wish you had never been born or had died the day you proposed yourself, especially if you have not maintained the character in which you set out. The Society rejoiced on ye return of the Duff and immediately undertook to visit you and strengthen your hearts and hands—the Duff

---

43. The *Duff* was indeed refitted soon after its return to England in 1798 but captured by a French privateer as Wilks describes, leaving the missionaries on board to make their own way back to England from Rio. So it was that the missionaries in Tahiti were reinforced by the *Royal Admiral* only in July 1800, bringing nine further missionaries and much-needed stores three years after the arrival of the *Duff*.

was enlarged—and stored with everything you could want. Vast numbers of packages were sent to yᵉ Missionaries from friends, and none so many as to Mr Cover, beside what went as [illegible] stock from the Society. Among others your old friend Gregory went out and his family. Nay every thing was done that our imagination could paint as conducing to yr gratification; but—but—but—I forbear. Nevertheless I advise you not to return to England—Rather stay at Port Jackson or in the neighbourhood—you may there preserve the Christian character, and do good. May God bless you—make you there unblameable Christians & render you very useful in your life and labours, & while you are earning the meal that [illegible] on honest industry, I hope you will be willing to do all the good you can to the miserable objects around you. . . . [44] My love to all the faithful among you, & I cannot persuade myself that there are not any of this description. Remember me to yr husband from whom I expected much. We shall send to Otaheite again.

Yrs

M Wilks

SOURCES

Thomas Haweis, "A Memoir of the Most Eligible Part to Begin a Mission," in London Missionary Society, *Sermons, Preached in London, at the formation of the Missionary Society, Sept. 22. 23. 24, 1795* (London, 1795).

William Puckey, "A Journal Constituting of a Few Remarks of a Voyage from Portsmouth to the Society Islands in the Great South Sea, 1796," Council for World Missions archive, School of Oriental and African Studies, University of London, South Sea Journals, box 1: South Seas 1796–1803. Reproduced from London Missionary Society / Council for World Mission Archives.

The Directors, London Missionary Society, "Counsels and Instructions for the Regulation of the Mission," in London Missionary Society, *Four Sermons Preached . . . at the Second General Meeting of the Missionary Society. . . . To which are prefixed, the proceedings of the Meeting, and the report of the Directors, etc.* (London, 1796).

The Missionaries, "Journal of a Voyage to the South Seas 1 Sept. 1796–15 June 1797," in Thomas Haweis, "Collection of Papers re Early South Sea Missions, 1795–1802," Mitchell Library (Sydney, NSW) MSS 4190X. Reproduced by permission of the Library Council of New South Wales.

Rowland Hassall, "Tahiti 1796–1799," Council for World Missions archive, School of Oriental and African Studies, University of London, South Sea Journals, box 1: South Seas 1796–1803. Reproduced from London Missionary Society / Council for World Mission Archives.

John Harris, Letter to the Missionary Society, 29 March 1798, Council for World Missions archive, School of Oriental and African Studies, University of London, South Seas Personal, box 4. Reproduced from London Missionary Society / Council for World Mission Archives.

---

44. That is, the English convicts of the penal colony.

Thomas Haweis to Joseph Banks, 12 September 1798, Sutro Collection, California State Library (MS. LMS 1: 33). Reproduced by permssion of the California State Library.

Revd. M. Wilks to Mary Cover, 3 September 1799, in Rowland Hassall, "Correspondence," 2 vols., 1:1797–1810, Mitchell Library (Sydney) MSS A859. Reproduced by permission of the Library Council of New South Wales.

FURTHER READING

For histories of the London Missionary Society and other Pacific missionary groups, see Michael Cathcart et al., *Mission to the South Seas: The Voyage of the* Duff, *1796–1799* (Melbourne: University of Melbourne History Department, 1990); James Clifford, *Person and Myth: Maurice Leenhardt in the Melanesian World* (Berkeley: University of California Press, 1982); Bolton Glanville Corney, *The Quest and Occupation of Tahiti by Emissaries of Spain during the Years 1772–1776* (London: Hakluyt Society, 1913); John Davies, *The History of the Tahitian Mission* (London: Hakluyt Society, 1961); Rod Edmond, *Representing the South Pacific: Colonial Discourse from Cook to Gauguin* (Cambridge: Cambridge University Press, 1997); John Garrett, *To Live among the Stars: Christian Origins in Oceania* and *Footsteps in the Sea: Christianity in Oceania to World War II* (Geneva: World Council of Churches 1982 and 1992); Niel Gunson, *Messengers of Grace: Evangelical Missionaries in the South Seas, 1797–1860* (Oxford: Oxford University Press); Tom Hiney, *On the Missionary Trail: The Classic Georgian Adventure of Two Englishmen Sent on a Journey around the World, 1821–1829* (London: Chatto and Windus, 2000), concerning early-nineteenth-century activities of the LMS; Anna Johnston, *Missionary Writing and Empire, 1800–1860* (Cambridge: Cambridge University Press, 2003), part 3: "The London Missionary Society in Polynesia"; Graeme Kent, *Company of Heaven: Early Missionaries in the South Seas* (Wellington: Reed, 1972), a good introductory account up to the 1830s; Diane Langmore, *Missionary Lives: Papua, 1874–1914* (Honolulu: University of Hawai'i Press, 1989); Hugh Laracy, ed., *Marists and Melanesians: A History of Catholic Missions in the Solomon Islands* (Canberra: Australian National University Press, 1976); and Doug Munro and Andrew Thornley, eds., *The Covenant Makers: Islander Missionaries in the Pacific* (Suva: Institute of Pacific Studies, 1996). Treat Louis B. Wright and Mary Isabel Fry's glib and slapdash *Puritans in the South Seas* (New York: Henry Holt, 1936) with caution.

Missionary writing about the South Seas is voluminous: more interesting works include Hiram Bingham, *A Residence of Twenty-One Years in the Sandwich Islands,* 3rd edn. (1847); William Bromilow, *Twenty Years among Primitive Papuans* (1929); Alexander James Campbell, "An Account of the Early History of the New Hebrides Missions," in Frederick Alexander Campbell, *A Year in the New Hebrides, Loyalty Islands, and New Caledonia* (1873); M. Whitecross Paton, *Letters and Sketches from the New Hebrides* (1896), written by a dedicated missionary wife on Tanna; and M. Russell, *Polynesia: A History of the South Sea Islands* (1849), an account of the arrival of Christianity and civilization among the islands, group by group. For John Williams, see his *A Narrative of Missionary Enterprises in the South Sea Islands* (1837) and Gavan Daws, *A Dream of Islands: Voyages of Discovery in the South Seas* (New York: Norton, 1980), chap. 2. In fiction, see Charles Kingsley, *Alton Locke* (1850), chap. 1; Sylvia Townsend Warner, *Mr Fortune's Maggot* (1927); and Ruth Eleanor McKee, *The Lord's Anointed: A Novel of Hawaii* (1934).

4
THE ISLAND AS CRUCIBLE
From The Great Chain of Being to Evolution

"In the century preceding the publication of *The Origin of Species* (1859)," Bernard Smith suggests,

> The so-called "non-descript" flora and fauna collected from the Pacific . . .
> provided an unbearable number of anomalies for the Creation theory and
> the Linnean paradigm. The tension that thus developed between a wealth of
> anomaly and a poverty of theory is revealed in . . . the successive shifts at this
> time in taxonomic schemata [i.e., classificatory categorizations]. The situation
> was not resolved until the publication of a scientifically credible theory of evo-
> lution in terms of natural selection. The anomalies of the old paradigm then
> became substantive evidence for the new. (Smith 1985: viii)

Evolutionary theory could have developed on the basis of data from elsewhere
in the world. The fact remains, however, that the Pacific played a larger role in
the development of European zoological thought than its apparent emptiness
would lead us to expect.

The theory of evolution has its intellectual roots in ideas—at least as old
as Creationism—about the strangeness of life on earth. The Antipodes were
often regarded by medieval and Renaissance writers as the natural home of
unfamiliar creatures, and so the relationship of "evolutionary" thinking to the
Pacific goes far back. Many mid-eighteenth-century intellectuals believed that
the scientific voyages of James Cook, for example, "would gradually complete
the picture of the universe as a vast ordered chain of being which had been
partially known to man from earliest times. But this ancient preconception
came into conflict gradually with another preconception possessing anteced-
ents quite as venerable as the chain of being. The ancients had claimed that
things in the Antipodes were different from things in the northern hemi-

sphere; monsters dwelt there; the normal laws of nature did not hold, in fact, they were reversed" (Smith 1985: 51). The arrival of evolution required that the "normal laws of nature" should be significantly adjusted, and for that to happen a genuine "wealth of anomaly" had to encounter a "poverty of theory."

"Although the last great ocean to be explored by Europeans," the Pacific was "the first large region beyond Europe that modern scientific method came fully to grips with" (Smith 1985: 2); indeed, "the Pacific became, by the late eighteenth century, the scene of some of the most important work in European science" (MacLeod and Rehbock, xii). (See Figure 11.) This work revealed a cornucopia of hitherto unknown species, some of which really did seem to be antipodean monsters. Cook was at Botany Bay in 1770 for only a few days, but "over 70 [botanical] genera were gathered and Parkinson [the expedition artist] would sketch nearly 100 species. Here were genera completely unknown to science" (Duyker, 181). Tolaga Bay, New Zealand, was even more fruitful, offering 158 species in 126 genera, many specimens being previously unknown (Duyker, 164). The Baudin expedition to Australia of 1800–1804 involved the description of 600 species of unknown plants, and the return to Europe of 18,500 zoological specimens "representing nearly four thousand different species of which two and a half thousand were new" (Cornell, 54). The Flinders circumnavigation of Australia (1801–1803) brought back 3,900 plants, all unknown: "A small number certainly for a country nearly equal in size to the whole of Europe," the expedition botanist, Robert Brown, drily remarked, "but not inconsiderable for the detached portions of its shores hitherto examined" (Flinders, 2:536–537). Other parts of the world—South America and Africa, for example—had rich floras and faunas, but it was the speed and intensity with which the material from this "seeming endless profusion of habitable spots of land" (Cook and King, vi) was gathered and disseminated that made the Pacific unique.

The sea, we must remember, was much easier to traverse than the land, especially with the floating laboratories commanded by Bougainville, Cook, Flinders, and Baudin. "The South Pacific, Polynesia, the southern Atlantic and the Indian Ocean therefore became fields of extensive exploration long before the Amazon, Central Africa, Siberia or even some parts of Europe and North America" (Stafleu, 229). "From the abundant diversity of the Pacific," Roy MacLeod and Philip Rehbock argue,

> early explorers . . . amassed an incalculable legacy: from their travels and collections, their descriptions and narrations, came discoveries that transformed European ideas of evolution and change. The Pacific . . . challenged European views of man's place in nature, presenting evidence that ultimately broke the great "chain of being," unravelled the neoclassical fabric of the fixity of species, undermined the argument from design, and expanded European conceptions of geological time. (MacLeod and Rehbock, 1)

Australia presented the greatest such challenge, requiring European science and theology either to compel the forms of life discovered there to fit the

FIGURE 11. Daniel Beyel (1760–1823), "Johann Reinhold Forster and George Forster, Father and Son" (1781). By permission of the National Library of Australia.

great chain of being or to acknowledge that the island continent might present an antipodean otherworld—a dry run on God's part, perhaps, or some sort of infernal alter-Creation. When Barron Field referred to the kangaroo as a creature "join'd by some divine mistake" (quoted in Smith 1985: 228), he was perhaps only half joking. For Thomas Watling, the place was "a country of enchantments" and Australian fauna "such an inversion in nature as is hitherto unknown" (Watling, 15). John Hunter discussed what he called "a promiscuous intercourse between the the different sexes of . . . different animals" in the waters of Sydney Harbour: "It was wonderful to see what a vast variety of fish

THE ISLAND AS CRUCIBLE

FIGURE 12. T. Powell, "*Ornithorhyncus paradoxus*. An Amphibious Animal of the Mole Kind" (1802). Rare Printed Collections, State Library of Victoria.

were caught, which, in some part or other, partake of the shark: it is no un-common thing to see a skait's head and shoulders to the hind part of a shark, or a shark's head to the body of a large mullet, and sometimes to the flat body of a sting-ray" (Hunter, 68–69). Even Charles Darwin, whose intellectual ten-dency was to downplay difference, could not deny the anomalous nature of Australian wildlife. "If we divide the land into two divisions, according to the amount of difference," he noted, "we shall have first Australia including New Guinea; and secondly the rest of the world" (Darwin 1909: 152). Darwin's great predecessor Georges Cuvier was similarly radical: "The species of the kan-garoo, *phascoloma, dasyurus, peramela, phalanger,* or flying oppossum, with the hairy and spinous duck-billed animals denominated *ornithorinchus* and *echidna,* have astonished zoologists by presenting new and strange conforma-tions, contrary to all former rules, and incapable of being reduced under any of the former systems," he remarked (Cuvier, 63). (See Figure 12.)

The most important such former system has already been mentioned: the "great chain of being." However unfamiliar the expression is to us now, it "was the sacred phrase of the eighteenth century, playing a part somewhat analo-gous to that of the blessed word 'evolution' in the late nineteenth" (Lovejoy, 184). The idea goes back to Plato, for whom "the universe is a *plenum form-arum* [Latin: plenitude of forms] in which the range of conceivable diversity of *kinds* of living beings is exhaustively exemplified" so that "no genuine po-tentiality of being can remain unfulfilled," and "the extent and abundance of the creation must be as great as the possibility of existence and commensurate with the productive capacity of a 'perfect' and inexhaustible source" (Lovejoy,

52). In a nutshell: nature abhors a vacuum. To Plato, Aristotle added "the idea of arranging (at least) all animals in a single graded *scala naturae* [Latin: natural scale] according to their degree of 'perfection' ":

> The result was the conception of the plan and structure of the world which, through the Middle Ages and down to the late eighteenth century, many philosophers, most men of science, and, indeed, most educated men, were to accept without question—the conception of the universe as a "Great Chain of Being," composed of an immense . . . number of links ranging in hierarchical order from the meagerest kind of existents . . . through "every possible" grade up to the *ens perfectissimum* [Latin: most perfect being]. (Lovejoy, 58–59)

This conception reached its climax in Alexander Pope's *Essay on Man*, published in 1733:

> See, thro' this air, this ocean, and this earth,
> All matter quick, and bursting into birth.
> Above, how high, progressive life may go!
> Around, how wide! how deep extend below!
> Vast chain of Being, which from God began,
> Natures æthereal, human, angel, man,
> Beast, bird, fish, insect! what no eye can see,
> No glass can reach! from Infinite to thee,
> From thee to Nothing!—On superior pow'rs
> Were we to press, inferior might on ours:
> Or in the full creation leave a void,
> Where, one step broken, the great scale's destroy'd:
> From Nature's chain whatever link you strike,
> Tenth or ten thousandth, breaks the chain alike.   (POPE 1966: 248)

How could it be that an idea as old as this was not only tolerated but reached its zenith in the age of reason? The answer is that one desire of eighteenth-century intellectuals outranked any other: the desire to know where human beings stood in the world, biblical accounts notwithstanding. In Pope's day there was no better answer than this, at least in biological terms. Moreover, one early-eighteenth-century scientist had made it make sense not in intellectual terms but in practical ones. The Swedish naturalist Linnaeus had in effect begun to name the links in the chain—or in the plant kingdom section at any rate. Linnaeus did not arrange plants in any hierarchial order, but his work was still a massive advance in Adam's old task of naming the beasts. Under his auspices, "nature began to be described and given structure by a curiosity-driven, systematic empiricism . . . which replaced the emblematic and allegorical treatment of the Renaissance and earlier times" (Howe 2000: 31). Like many scientific master strokes, Linnaeus' was a deceptively simple one: "the section on plants [in his *Systema Naturae* of 1735] introduced a simple new classification called the 'sexual system' because it was based on the number of stamens (male organs) and pistils (female organs) in the flower. Admittedly artificial, it held the fort against chaos for some eighty years" (Stearn, iv). And he did not stop there: "by 1758 Linnaeus had built up a system of classification covering the whole living world as then known and had named and defined its classes, genera and species. This work was based on the general principles of classification laid down in Aristotle's *Logic*" (Stearn, v).

But there was a problem in Aristotle's view of nature: two "opposite modes of thought," as Arthur Lovejoy calls them. "The first made for sharp divisions, clear-cut differentiations, among natural objects, and especially among living beings"; "the other tended to make the whole notion of species appear a convenient but artificial setting-up of divisions having no counterpart in nature" (Lovejoy, 227). Nature must fill every gap: but how could the plenitude of forms Aristotle inherited from Plato be made consistent with well-defined distinctions *between* species? Linnaeus had elected one variable among the flowers by which to categorize them. As such, his work tended "to encourage the habit of thinking of organisms, and of other natural objects, as falling into well-differentiated classes, rather than as members of a qualitative continuum" (Lovejoy, 228). On the basis of a rigorous taxonomic schemata like this, he believed that "the earth is then nothing else but a museum of the all-wise Creator's masterpieces" (quoted in Koerner, 153).

In time the limitations of the Linnaean program began to betray themselves: "classification is not yet systematics. . . . What about the multiple affinities, what about the major task of systematics to present a picture of the structure and possible origin of the diversity of the animal and vegetable world?" (Stafleu, 291–292). What Linnaeans like Joseph Banks and Daniel Solander (a disciple of Linnaeus who accompanied Banks on Cook's first voyage) did was seek the "missing links" that would make up gaps in the chain without reducing it to an apparently orderless "qualitative continuum." As it happened, the South Seas offered two persuasive missing links. Coral grows in sunlight and is colorful, yet it can be hard: it is a link between plants and rock. The people of the Pacific, too, from Australian Aborigines, Fuegians, and Melanesians "up to" Tahitians and Marquesans (via the Maoris), constituted for eighteenth-century science a far more detailed and convincing set of "missing link" possibilities between Western humans and the apes than did the Hottentots, the pygmies, and the orangutans. The links were all there, only Western science had not found them yet.

Those not satisfied with the Linnaean museum tended to imagine a qualitative continuum rather than linked (but differentiated) isolates. For Buffon, for example, opening his *Histoire naturelle* in 1749, the error of species systematizers

> consists in a failure to understand nature's processes, which always take place by gradations. . . . It is possible to descend by almost insensible degrees from the most perfect creature to the most formless matter. . . . These imperceptible shadings are the great works of nature; they are to be found not only in the sizes and the forms, but also in the movements, the generations and the sucessions of every species. . . . [Thus] nature, proceeding by unknown gradations, cannot wholly lend herself to these divisions. (quoted in Lovejoy, 230)

Buffon's emphasis on "unknown gradations" and on the "successions" of species is very different from the ideas of Linnaeus. "The birth of biology," as Frans Stafleu puts it, "consists in the realization . . . that life must be described in terms of processes as well as status quo; that living beings have an existence in time, and not in space alone" (Stafleu, 303).

The Pacific played a major role in "the momentous finding . . . that the individual components of matter are eloquent of their own history" (Stafford, 284) and that nature constituted "a self-regulating and cyclic system" (Roger, 279). This did not amount to a wholly destructive repudiation of the great chain paradigm. That paradigm remained—and remains: modern science knows what happens to "food chains" when links are struck from them—but was re-envisaged. Before, it had been a fixed and hierarchical structure from the stones to God, many links in which were invisible to human eyes. Now, it was still a structure, still ultimately hierarchical in the sense that *Homo sapiens* is more "highly evolved" than coral, still "fixed" in the theoretical sense that nature still abhorred a vacuum and species must adapt to their environment or perish; but it was unfixed in that whereas some given number of creatures had to fill the gap between the zoophytes and human beings, what those creatures were at any given moment was constantly in flux. The chain came to look more like a spiral of DNA: a necessary arrangement in terms of the integrity of a system—but only for now. Thus "the *Origin [of Species]* tore away man's image of himself as a creature of divine fiat, set by God's deliberate choice on a rung of the ladder of organic being—a little lower than the angels, to be sure, but many rungs above the beasts" (Morton, 7).

Before this could happen, however, the Linnaean system had to give way to one taking account of "multiple affinities." Linnaeus' "sexual system" for plant taxonomy at length gave way to the "natural system" devised by Frenchman Laurent Jussieu—whose *Genera Plantarum* (1789) was largely based on the plant collection gathered by Philibert Commerson on the Bougainville voyage. Jussieu's innovation was carried further in England by Robert Brown—whose *Prodromus Florae Novae Hollandiae* (1810) was based on his work on Flinders' circumnavigation of Australia.

If it is true that "the several Cook voyages and their successors to the time of Darwin's famous voyage on the *Beagle* helped to lay the basis for the theory of biological evolution," then the conclusion seems self-evident: "only the arduous physical exploration of large areas of the earth's surface and the intensive study of the evidence of life in the different parts of the globe could provide the necessary support for such a theory" (Washburn, 330–331). Yet the second part of the statement conceals an important truth. Darwin's theory was stimulated in crucial ways by the geological and zoological work he and others had done in Britain and continental Europe. Continental South America, too, was an irreplaceable revelation, as any reader of *The Voyage of the "Beagle"* will discover. But if Darwin (and Alfred Russel Wallace, who hit on the idea of natural selection at the same time) had been confined to continental geological and biological data, the theory might not have come as soon as it did. For both men the experience of islands was critical: Wallace in the Malay Archipelago, which provided the title for his most famous book; Darwin among the islands of the Pacific and Indian oceans.

The world contains two kinds of islands: continental islands, which are fragments of similar age and geological construction to the landmasses they lie beside, and oceanic islands, produced independently from the continents. The Pacific contains many more of the latter than the rest of the world, and its oceanic islands themselves form two groups: volcanic and coralline. In fact these are the same islands at different ages: the volcanic ones are new, caused as the tectonic plates beneath the Pacific slowly move across hot spots on the earth's crust which erupt, building great mountains on the seafloor, which sometimes break the surface; coral atolls are volcanic mountains that have emerged above the surface of the sea and then subsided. If we know how much coral grows under average circumstances and we drill through an atoll till we hit volcanic rock, we should know how old an atoll is: and this is exactly what a series of late-nineteenth-century British scientific expeditions to Funafuti in present-day Tuvalu attempted to measure. As these old volcanoes have subsided, the coral reefs growing around them have kept growing toward the surface, eventually leaving a ring of coral around a lagoon where a high island used to be. As he traveled among them and came to these conclusions, these two insular varieties gave Darwin an indication of the earth's great age (for how many aeons must have passed for mountains so vast entirely to disappear?) and of its still being in its youth (for if atolls are so old, then high islands are very young). This was vital, since evolution requires much longer than the Creationists' six thousand years to account for the diversity of the biosphere. Darwin could not put an age on the earth; we now believe it to be approximately 4.5 billion years old.

But the use of islands does not end with providing extended possibilities regarding the age of the earth. When oceanic islands first emerge, they have no life on them. For millions of years they erode, accrue dust, seaweed, and other organic flotsam, sufficient eventually to make a topsoil; then seeds may float or blow there, or be carried by birds—whose ability to travel over vast stretches of empty ocean is sometimes prodigious. Small animals and insects with good exposure tolerance may come on rafts of vegetation from neighboring islands or coastlines: the oceanic islands of the Pacific possess no native mammals, no amphibians, and only a small number of reptiles; stretches of open sea act as "filters" in this respect so that we can see genera from Asia "tailing off" eastward as certain species fail to cross the gaps. But if an animal does cross the gap from mainland South America, say, to the Galapagos, it finds an environment that may be sparsely populated by other species, almost empty of predators, and with food supplies different from those to which it has been accustomed. If it survives at all, it may do unprecedentedly well, finding a host of opportunities unavailable in its native land to which it can adapt. South American iguanas once arrived on the Galapagos and took up

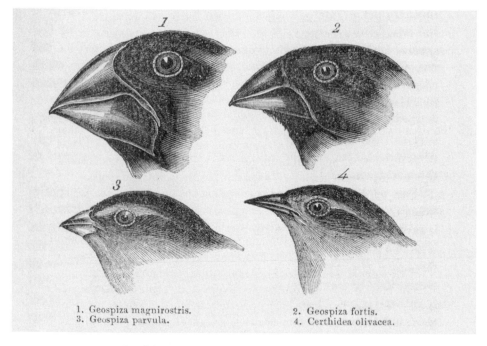

1. Geospiza magnirostris.
3. Geospiza parvula.
2. Geospiza fortis.
4. Certhidea olivacea.

FIGURE 13. Beaks of the Galapagos Finch, in Charles Darwin, *Voyage of the Beagle,* 2nd edition (1845). By permission of the National Library of Australia.

a marine habit, feeding on seaweed; finches arrived and split into different species, adapted to different food sources (see Figure 13); tortoises arrived and are—much more slowly, because their breeding cycle is so much longer—beginning to split in the same way, though at present they boast only "races" or "subspecies" spread about the islands rather than different species. (For Darwinism, there is ultimately no such thing as a species: we're all evolving.) "In the Galápagos," as Sherwin Carlquist puts it, "the ferment of recent genesis is still apparent. The Galápagos is rich not in missing links, but in 'non-missing links'" (Carlquist, 378).

So islands have a special place in the theory of evolution: "they have a restricted area and definite boundaries," as Wallace remarked in his biogeographical classic *Island Life;* the "number of species and of genera they contain is always much smaller than in the case of continents, and their peculiar species and groups are usually well defined and strictly limited in range"; "their relations with other lands are often direct and simple, and even when more complex are far easier to comprehend than those of continents." In sum:

> In islands we have the facts of distribution often presented to us in their simplest forms, along with others which become gradually more and more complex; and we are therefore able to proceed step by step in the solution of the

THE ISLAND AS CRUCIBLE

problems they present. But as in studying these problems we have necessarily to take into account the relations of the insular and continental faunas, we also get some knowledge of the latter, and acquire besides so much command over the general principles which underlie all problems of distribution that it is not too much to say that when we have mastered the difficulties presented by the peculiarities of island life we shall find it comparatively easy to deal with the more complex and less clearly defined problems of continental distribution. (Wallace, 229–230)

Islands also illustrate a cardinal principle of evolution, isolation: "a species will always stay just a . . . species unless by means of some process, the part of the population which has been pushed into a new environment becomes cut off from individuals which remain in the old environment. Isolation is thus all-important, and biologists believe that evolution of a new species without isolation is virtually impossible" (Carlquist, 111). Oliver Sacks is interested in clusters of neurological conditions rather than flora and fauna, but for him, too, islands and isolation go hand in hand. "Just as Darwin and Wallace found islands to be unique laboratories, hot-houses of nature which might show evolutionary processes in an intensified and dramatic form," he writes, "so isolates of disease excite the epidemiological mind with the promise of understandings to be obtained no other way" (Sacks, 119). An exaggerated, incurable, and inexplicable neurological disorder present only on the Micronesian island of Guam, for example, might be "the Rosetta Stone of neurodegenerative disease" (Sacks, 117), just as Darwin's finches were the Rosetta Stone of evolution.

Geographic expansion in the second half of the eighteenth century helped bring to an end "an essentially static, heirarchic, neoplatonic view of nature and society," Frans A. Stafleu notes. "The new emphasis was on enterprise, novelty and diversity. The picture of the world was no longer one of immutable, self-contained perfection, antithetic to change, but a dynamic one of creativity, of an open end to knowledge, and of the discovery of instrinsic values of diversity. . . . The open horizons of the great Pacific South revealed the existence not of perfect primitive societies but of imperfect ones of infinitely diverse novelty" (Stafleu, 218). Stafleu's comment also links this chapter to the one that follows on "the varieties of man."

from Joseph Banks, *The Endeavour Journal* (1770)

Cook's first voyage was designed to record the transit of Venus, and Charles Green from the Greenwich Observatory supervised that process. But it also carried with it an independently wealthy young botanist, Joseph Banks (1744–1820), who brought his own team of seven assistants. Banks hardly rates as a scientist as such, but the collection he made on the *Endeavour* and those he gathered together in his London headquarters made him a vitally influential European scientific figure, serving as president of the Royal Society for over forty years.

Tho these people [the Maoris] when at home defend themselves so well from the inclemencies of the Weather, yet when abroad upon their excursions which they often make in search of fern roots fish &c. they seem totaly indifferent of shelter: sometimes they make a small shade to wind ward of them but oftener omit that precaution. During our stay at *Opoorage* or Mercury bay [November 1769] such a party of Indians were there consisting of 40 or 50, who during all that time never erected the least covering tho it twice raind almost without ceasing for 24 hours together.

Their food, in the use of which they seem to be moderate, consists of Dogs, Birds, especialy sea fowl as penguins albatrosses &c, fish, sweet potatoes, Yams, Coccos, some few wild plants as sow thistles, Palm Cabbage &c. but Above all and which seems to be to them what bread is to us, the roots of a species of Fern very common upon the hills and which very nearly resembles that which grows on our hilly commons in England and is calld indifferently Fern, Bracken, or Brakes. As for the flesh of men, although they certainly do eat it I cannot in my own opinion Debase human nature so much as to imagine that they relish as a dainty or even look upon it as a part of common food. Tho Thirst of Revenge may Drive men to great lengths when the Passions are allowd to take their full swing Yet nature through all the superior part of the creation shews how much she recoils at the thought of any species preying upon itself: Dogs and cats shew visible signs of disgust at the very sight of a dead carcass of their species, even Wolves or Bears were never sayd to eat one another except in cases of absolute nescessity, when the stings of hunger have overcome the precepts of nature, in which case the same has been done by the inhabitants of the most civilizd nations.

Among fish and insects indeed there are many instances which prove that those who live by prey regard little whither what they take is of their own or any other species; but any one who considers the admirable chain of nature in which Man, alone endowd with reason, justly claims the highest rank and next to him are placd the half reasoning Elephant, the sagacious dog, the architect Beaver, &c. in Whoom instinct so nearly resembles reason as to have been mistaken for it by men of no mean capacitys, from these descending through the less informd Quadrupeds and birds to the fish and insects, which seem besides the instinct of Fear which is given them for self preservation to be movd only by the stings of hunger to eat and those of lust to propagate their species, which when born are left intirely to their own care, and at last by the medium of the Oyster, &c. &c. which not being able to move but as tost about by the waves must in themselves be furnishd with both sexes that the species may be continued, shading itself away into the vegetable kingdom for the preservation of whoom neither sensation nor instinct is wanting—whoever considers this I say will easily see that no Conclusion in favour of such a practise can be drawn from the actions of a race of beings placd so infinitely below us in the order of Nature.[1]

from James Edward Smith, *A Specimen of the Botany of New Holland* (1793)

James Edward Smith (1759–1828) was a friend of Banks and the founder of the Linnaean society of London—in fact he purchased Linnaeus' collection and library after his death in 1778. Within a short time of the founding of the English penal colony at Port Jackson, English botanists and horticulturalists became fascinated by the samples coming home from the antipodes, and botanists like Smith worked hard to fit these previously unknown species into the Linnaean sexual system, as opposed to "natural" systems like those described by Jussieu. Only the short first volume of Smith's work was ever published.

When a botanist first enters on the investigation of so remote a country as New Holland, he finds himself as it were in a new world. He can scarcely meet with any certain fixed points from whence to draw his analogies; and even those that appear most promising, are frequently in danger of misleading, instead of informing him. Whole tribes of plants, which at first sight seem familiar to his acquaintance, as occupying links in Nature's chain, on which he has been accustomed to depend, prove, on a nearer examination, total strangers, with other configurations, other œconomy, and other qualities; not only all the species that present themselves are new, but most of the genera, and even natural orders.[2]

The plant before us [Ceratopetalum gummiferum; the Red Gum tree] justifies the above remarks. Its botanical characters are so new, we can scarcely tell to what tribes it is allied; and although, from the peculiar felicity of the Linnæan sexual system, founded on parts which every plant *must* have, we are at no loss to find its class and order in that which is an artificial system, we still scarcely know what genera are its natural allies. It, however, seems most nearly related to *Dictamnus* and *Ruta,* of all the Decandria Monogynia, and may be safely, inserted near them. We dare not positively say it belongs to M. De Jussieu's natural order of *Rutaceæ,* but for the present it may be so considered, till future discoveries shall authorise us to constitute a new one. The generic char-

---

1. See Banks on Tierra del Fuego, 20 January 1769, with the botanist Daniel Solander: "Probably No botanist has ever enjoyd more pleasure in the contemplation of his Favourite pursuit than Dr Solander and myself among these plants; we have not yet examind many of them, but what we have turnd out in general so intirely different from any before described that we are never tird with wondering at the infinite variety of Creation, and admiring the infinite care with which providence has multiplied his productions suiting them no doubt to the various climates for which they were designd" (Banks, 1:226).

2. Elsewhere in the *Specimen,* Smith had spoken of "the peculiar privilege of reasoning man . . . to walk with God through the garden of creation, and be initiated into the different plans of his providence in the construction and œconomy of all these various beings: to study their dependencies upon one another in an infinitely complex chain, every link of which is essential."

acter above given certainly distinguishes it from all other genera, and the name applies to the very unusual horn-like divisions of the petals, like those in the leaves of the *Ceratophyllum* of Linnæus. One species only is already known.

from Jean Baptiste Lamarck, *Zoological Philosophy* (1809)

A key figure in pre-Darwinist thought, Jean Baptiste Lamarck (1744–1829) signals an important break from the Linnaean system and the great chain of being. In the 1770s he argued that there were two chains, for plants and animals, and in *Philosophie zoologique* he outlined a theory of transformation whereby more complex forms of life developed out of simpler ones in response to environmental changes. Moreover, such developments, he argued, could be handed on as "acquired characteristics."

> We now pass to the birds; but I must first note that there is no gradation between mammals and birds. There exists a gap to be filled, and no doubt nature has produced animals which practically fill this gap, and which must form a special class if they cannot be comprised either among the animals or among the birds.
>
> This fact has just been realised, by the recent discovery in Australia of two genera of animals, viz.:
>
> Ornithorhyncus) Monotremes (Geoff.)[3]
> Echidna)
>
> These animals are quadrupeds with no mammae, with no teeth inserted and no lips; and they have only one orifice for the genital organs, the excrements and the urine (a cloaca). Their body is covered with hair or bristles.
>
> They are not mammals, for they have no mammae and are most likely oviparous.
>
> They are not birds; for their lungs are not pierced through and they have no limbs shaped as wings.
>
> Finally, they are not reptiles; for their heart with only two ventricles removes them from that category.
>
> They belong then to a special class.

from James Montgomery, *The Pelican Island* (1828)

The son of Moravian missionaries, an abolitionist and a hymn writer, James Montgomery (1771–1854) was briefly imprisoned for his radical views in the 1790s. His work is marked by an unusual combination of piety and intellectual boldness. (A poem from 1813 is called "The World before the Flood.") *Pelican Island* is based on a passage from Matthew Flinders' *Voyage to Terra Australis* (1814) where Flinders—first circumnavigator of Australia—describes an

---

3. The duck-billed platypus.

enormous pelican rookery on Nepean Bay, Kangaroo Island, off south Australia (see Introduction). On his coral island the narrator is given and communicates a vision of a natural theodicy.

Canto Second

Life's intermitting pulse again went on:
I woke amidst the beauty of a morn,
That shone as bright within me as around.
The presence-chamber of the soul was full
Of flitting images and rapturous thoughts;
For eye and mind were open'd to explore
The secrets of the abyss erewhile conceal'd.
The floor of ocean, never trod by man,
Was visible to me as heaven's round roof;
Which man hath never touch'd; the multitude
Of living things, in that new hemisphere,
Gleam'd out of darkness, like the stars at midnight,
When moon nor clouds, with light or shade, obscure them.
For, as in hollows of the tide-worn reef,
Left at low water glistening in the sun,
Pellucid pools and rocks in miniature,
With their small fry of fishes, crusted shells,
Rich mosses, tree-like sea-weed, sparkling pebbles,
Enchant the eye, and tempt the eager hand
To violate the fairy paradise,
—So to my view the deep disclosed its wonders.
In the free element beneath me swam,
Flounder'd, and dived, in play, in chase, in battle,
Fishes of every colour, form, and kind,
(Strange forms, resplendent colours, kinds unnumber'd,)
Which language cannot paint, and mariner
Hath never seen; from dread Leviathan
To insect-millions peopling every wave;
And nameless tribes, half-plant, half-animal,
Rooted and slumbering through a dream of life.[4]
The livelier inmates to the surface sprang,
To taste the freshness of heaven's breath, and feel
That light is pleasant, and the sunbeam warm.
Most in the middle region sought their prey,
Safety, or pastime; solitary some,
And some in pairs affectionately join'd;
Others in shoals immense, like floating islands,
Led by mysterious instinct through that waste
And trackless region, though on every side

---

4. That is, corals and sponges.

Assaulted by voracious enemies,
—Whales, sharks, and monsters, arm'd in front or jaw,
With swords, saws, spiral horns, or hooked fangs.
While ravening Death of slaughter ne'er grew weary,
Life multiplied the immortal meal as fast.
War, reckless, universal war, prevail'd;
All were devourers, all in turn devour'd;
Yet every unit in the uncounted sum
Of victims had its share of bliss; its pang,
And but a pang, of dissolution; each
Was happy till its moment came, and then
Its first, last suffering, unforeseen, unfear'd,
Closed, with one struggle, life and pain for ever.
So He ordain'd, whose way is in the sea,
His path amidst great waters, and his steps
Unknown;—whose judgments are a mighty deep,
Where plummet of Archangel's intellect
Could never yet find soundings, but from age
To age let down, drawn up, then thrown again,
With lengthen'd line and added weight, still fails;
And still the cry in Heaven is, "O the depth!"

Thus, while bewilder'd with delight I gazed
On life in every shape it here assumed,
Congenial feeling made me follow it,
And try to be whatever I beheld:
By mental transmigration thus I pass'd
Through many a body, and in each assay'd
New instincts, powers, enjoyments, death itself;
Till, weary with the fanciful pursuit,
I started from that idle reverie.
Then grew my heart more desolate than ever;
Here had I found the beings which I sought,
—Beings for whom the universe was made,
Yet none of kindred with myself. In vain
I strove to waken sympathy in breasts
Cold as the element in which they moved
And inaccessible to fellowship
With me, as sun and stars, as winds and vapours:
Sense had they, but no more; mind was not there.
They roam'd, they fed, they slept, they died, and left
Race after race, to roam, feed, sleep, then die,
And leave their like through endless generations;
—Incessant change of actors, none of scene,
Through all that boundless theatre of strife!

Shrinking into myself again, I cried,
In bitter disappointment,—"Is this all?"

I sent a glance at random from the cloud,
In which I then lay floating through mid-heaven,
To ocean's innermost recess;—when lo!
Another seal of Nature's book was open'd,
Which held transported thought so deep entranced,
That Time, though borne through mightiest revolutions,
Seem'd, like the earth in motion, to stand still.
The works of ages grew beneath mine eye;
As rapid intellect calls up events,
Combines, compresses, moulds them, with such power,
That, in a little page of memory,
An empire's annals lie,—a nation's fortunes
Pass in review, as motes through sunbeams pass,
Glistening and vanishing in quick succession,
Yet each distinct as though there were but one;
—So thrice a thousand years, with all their issues,
Hurried before me, through a gleam of Time,
Between the clouds of two eternities,—
That thence they came, and that to which they tended.[5]

Immeasurable continents beneath
The expanse of animated waters lay,
Not strown,—as I have *since* discern'd the tracks
Of voyagers,—with shipwrecks and their spoils,
The wealth of merchants, the artillery
Of war, the chains of captives, and the gems,
That glow'd upon the brow of beauty; crowns
Of monarchs, swords of heroes, anchors lost,
That never had let go their hold in storms;
Helms, sunk in port, that steer'd adventurous barks
Round the wide world; bones of dead men, that made
A hidden Golgotha[6] where they had fallen,

---

5. Montgomery's eagerness to reconcile the "survival of the fittest" in the ocean world to divine providence might be compared with the missionary John Williams' discussion of coral science in chapter 2 of *A Narrative of Missionary Enterprises in the South Sea Islands* (1837): "In every age the evidences of revealed religion have advanced with the progress of sound knowledge. Indeed, it cannot be otherwise; for the God of nature, whose operations it is the providence of science to explore, is the God of the Bible; and as the God of truth, he cannot set forth in his word principles at variance with those which, as the God of nature, he has established in the material world. Both systems of knowledge, thus emanating from the same source, *must* harmonize with each other: for the Bible is something like a new edition of the book of nature. . . . If there is any apparent discrepancy in these two editions of this same great work, it arises from our inability rightly to decipher the characters employed."

6. "The Hill of the Skull," on which Christ was crucified at Jerusalem.

Unseen, unsepulchred, but not unwept
By lover, friend, relation, far away,
Long waiting their return to home and country,
And going down into their fathers' graves
With their grey hairs or youthful locks in sorrow,
To meet no more till seas give up their dead:
Some too—ay thousands—whom none living mourn'd,
None miss'd,—waifs in the universe, the last
Lorn links of kindred chains for ever sunder'd.

Not such the spectacle I now survey'd:
No broken hearts lay here; no aching heads,
For whose vast schemes the world was once too small,
And life too short, in Death's dark lap found rest
Beneath the unresting wave;—but skeletons
Of Whales and Krakens here and there were scatter'd,
The prey when dead of tribes, their prey when living:
And, seen by glimpses, but awakening thoughts
Too sad for utterance,—relics huge and strange
Of the old world that perish'd by the flood,
Kept under chains of darkness till the judgment.
—Save these, lay ocean's bed, as from the hand
Of its Creator, hollow'd and prepared
For his unfathomable counsels there,
To work slow miracles of power divine,
From century to century,—nor less
Incomprehensible than heaven and earth
Form'd in six days by His commanding word.
With God a thousand years are as one day;
He in one day can sum a thousand years:
All acts with Him are equal; for no more
It costs Omnipotence to build a world,
And set a sun amidst the firmament,
Than mould a dew-drop, and light up its gem.

This was the landscape stretch'd beneath the flood:
—Rocks, branching out like chains of Alpine mountains;
Gulfs intervening, sandy wildernesses,
Forests of growth enormous, caverns, shoals;
Fountains upspringing, hot and cold, and fresh
And bitter, as on land; volcanic fires
Fiercely out-flashing from earth's central heart,
Nor soon extinguish'd by the rush of waters
Down the rent crater to the unknown abyss
Of Nature's laboratory, where she hides
Her deeds from every eye except her Maker's:

—Such were the scenes which ocean open'd to me;
Mysterious regions, the recluse abode
Of unapproachable inhabitants,
That dwelt in everlasting darkness there.
Unheard by them the roaring of the wind,
The elastic motion of the wave unfelt;
Still life was theirs, well pleasing to themselves,
Nor yet unmuseful, as my song shall show.

Here, on a stony eminence, that stood,
Girt with inferior ridges, at the point,
Where light and darkness meet in spectral gloom,
Midway between the height and depth of ocean,
I mark'd a whirlpool in perpetual play,
As though the mountain were itself alive,
And catching prey on every side, with feelers
Ere long transformed, slight as gossamer:
Ere long transfigured, each fine film became
An independent creature, self-employ'd,
Yet but an agent in one common work,
The sum of all their individual labours.
Shapeless they seem'd, but endless shapes assume
Elongated like worms, they writhed and shrunk
Their tortuous bodies to grotesque dimensions;
Compress'd like wedges, radiated like stars,
Branching like sea-weed, whirl'd in dazzling rings;
Subtle and variable as flickering flames,
Sight could not trace their evanescent changes,
Nor comprehend their motions, till minute
And curious observation caught the clew
To this live labyrinth,—where every one,
By instinct taught, perform'd its little task;
—To build its dwelling and its sepulchre,
From its own essence exquisitely modell'd;
There breed, and die, and leave a progeny,
Still multiplied beyond the reach of numbers,
To frame new cells and tombs; then breed and die
As all their ancestors had done,—and rest,
Hermetically seal'd, each in its shrine,
A statue in this temple of oblivion!
Millions of millions thus, from age to age,
With simplest skill, and toil unweariable,
No moment and no movement unimproved,
Laid line on line, on terrace terrace spread,
To swell the heightening, brightening gradual mound,

By marvellous structure climbing tow'rds the day.
Each wrought alone, yet all together wrought,
Unconscious, not unworthy, instruments,
By which a hand invisible was rearing
A new creation in the secret deep.
Omnipotence wrought in them, with them, by them;
Hence what Omnipotence alone could do
Worms did. I saw the living pile ascend,
The mausoleum of its architects,
Still dying upwards as their labours closed:
Slime the material, but the slime was turn'd
To adamant, by their petrific touch;
Frail were their frames, ephemeral their lives,
Their masonry imperishable. All
Life's needful functions, food, exertion, rest,
By nice economy of Providence
Were overruled to carry on the process,
Which out of water brought forth solid rock.

Atom by atom thus the burthen grew,
Even like an infant in the womb, till Time
Deliver'd ocean of that monstrous birth,
—A coral island, stretching east and west,
In God's own language to its parent saying,
"Thus far, nor farther, shalt thou go; and here
Shall thy proud waves be stay'd:"—A point at first
It peer'd above those waves; a point so small,
I just perceived it, fix'd where all was floating;
And when a bubble cross'd it, the blue film
Expanded like a sky above the speck;
That speck became a hand-breadth; day and night
It spread, accumulated, and ere long
Presented to my view a dazzling plain,
White as the moon amid the sapphire sea;
Bare at low water, and as still as death,
But when the tide came gurgling o'er the surface,
'Twas like a resurrection of the dead:
From graves innumerable, punctures fine
In the close coral, capillary swarms
Of reptiles, horrent as Medusa's snakes,
Cover'd the bald-pate reef; then all was life,
And indefatigable industry;
The artizans were twisting to and fro,
In idle-seeming convolutions; yet
They never vanish'd with the ebbing surge,
Till pellicle on pellicle, and layer

On layer, was added to the growing mass.
Ere long the reef o'ertopt the spring-flood's height,
And mock'd the billows when they leapt upon it,
Unable to maintain their slippery hold,
And falling down in foam-wreaths round its verge.
Steep were the the flanks, with precipices sharp,
Descending to their base in ocean-gloom.
Chasms few, and narrow, and irregular,
Form'd harbours, safe at once and perilous,—
Safe for defence, but perilous to enter.
A sea-lake shone amidst the fossil isle,
Reflecting in a ring its cliffs and caverns,
With heaven itself seen like a lake below.[7]

Compared with this amazing edifice,
Raised by the weakest creatures in existence,
What are the works of intellectual man?
Towers, temples, palaces, and sepulchres;
Ideal images in sculptured forms,
Thoughts hewn in columns, or in domes expanded,
Fancies through every maze of beauty shown;
Pride, gratitude, affection turn'd to marble,
In honour of the living or the dead;
What are they?—fine-wrought miniatures of art,
Too exquisite to bear the weight of dew,
Which every morn lets fall in pearls upon them,
Till all their pomp sinks down in mouldering relics,
Yet in their ruin lovelier than their prime!
—Dust in the balance, atoms in the gale,
Compared with these achievement in the deep,
Were all the monuments of olden time,
In days when there were giants on the earth:
—Babel's stupendous folly, though it aim'd
To scale heaven's battlements, was but a toy,
The plaything of the world in infancy:—
The ramparts, towers, and gates of Babylon,
Built for eternity,—though, where they stood,
Ruin itself stands still for lack of work,

---

7. John Williams summarized current knowledge of coral islands in chapter 2 of his *Narrative:* "These insects first select a suitable spot, which is the summit of a volcano, or the top of a sub-marine mountain; for it is stated, that this species of coral insect do not exist in deep water. Having thus selected the spot, innumerable myriads of these wonderful little animals work with incredible diligence, until they reach the surface of the water, above which they cannot build. Drift wood and other substances, which are conveyed by currents and winds, there find a lodgement; sand &c., is washed up by the waves of the sea, and thus an island is formed. Birds visit the spot, seeds are by this means conveyed; and a soil is subsequently created by decayed vegetable matter."

And Desolation keeps unbroken sabbath:—
Great Babylon, in its full moon of empire,
Even when its "head of gold" was smitten off,
And from a monarch changed into a brute;[8]—
Great Babylon was like a wreath of sand,
Left by one tide, and cancell'd by the next:—
Egypt's dread wonders, still defying Time,
Where cities have been crumbled into sand,
Scatter'd by winds beyond the Libyan desert,
Or melted down into the mud of Nile,
And cast in tillage o'er the corn-sown fields,
Where Memphis flourish'd, and the Pharaohs reign'd;—
Egypt's gray piles of hieroglyphic grandeur,
That have survived the language which they speak,
Preserving its dead emblems to the eye,
Yet hiding from the mind what these reveal;
—Her pyramids would be mere pinnacles,
Her giant statues, wrought from rocks of granite,
But puny ornaments for such a pile
As this stupendous mound of catacombs,
Fill'd with dry mummies of the builder-worms.

Thus far, with undiverted thought, and eye
Intensely fix'd on ocean's concave mirror,
I watch'd the process to its finishing stroke:
Then starting suddenly, as from a trance,
Once more to look upon the blessed sun,
And breathe the gladdening influence of the wind,
Darkness fell on me; giddily my brain
Whirl'd like a torch of fire that seems a circle,
And soon to me the universe was nothing.

from Charles Darwin, "Galapagos Archipelago" (1839)

Charles Darwin's inclusion in the scientific expedition commanded by Captain Robert Fitzroy was almost purely accidental. Fitzroy himself had someone else in mind, and Darwin initially turned down the offer as his father
intended the young Cambridge graduate to become a clergyman. But the professor of botany at Cambridge and Darwin's own uncle overcame the son's
vacillations and the father's reservations, and Darwin (1809–1882) sailed on
board the *Beagle* in December 1831, returning five years later with a head full
of the ideas that would—after years of patient labor—make him perhaps the
world's greatest scientist. Of all the things he saw, none were more important

8. Nebuchadnezzar, legendary kind of Babylon; his humiliation is described in Daniel 4.

than the apparently paradoxical life forms of the Galapagos chain, which he visited in 1835.

SEPTEMBER 15th—The *Beagle* arrived at the southernmost of the Galapagos Islands.[9] This archipelago consists of ten principal islands, of which five much exceed the others in size. They are situated under the equatorial line, and between 500 and 600 miles to the westward of the coast of America. The constitution of the whole is volcanic. With the exception of some ejected fragments of granite, which have been most curiously glazed and altered by the heat, every part consists of lava, or of sandstone resulting from the attrition of such materials. The higher islands, (which attain an elevation of 3,000, and even 4,000 feet) generally have one or more principal craters towards their centre, and on their flanks smaller orifices. I have no exact data from which to calculate, but I do not hesitate to affirm, that there must be, in all the islands of the archipelago, at least 2,000 craters. These are of two kinds; one, as in ordinary cases, consisting of scori and lava, the other of finely stratified volcanic sandstone. The latter in most instances have a form beautifully symmetrical: their origin is due to the ejection of mud—that is, fine volcanic ashes and water—without any lava.

Considering that these islands are placed directly under the equator, the climate is far from being excessively hot; a circumstance which, perhaps, is chiefly owing to the singularly low temperature of the surrounding sea. Excepting during one short season, very little rain falls, and even then it is not regular: but the clouds generally hang low. From these circumstances the lower parts of the islands are extremely arid, whilst the summits, at an elevation of 1,000 feet or more, possess a tolerably luxuriant vegetation. This is especially the case on the windward side, which first receives and condenses the moisture from the atmosphere.

In the morning (17th) we landed on Chatham Island, which, like the others, rises with a tame and rounded outline, interrupted only here and there by scattered hillocks—the remains of former craters. Nothing could be less inviting than the first appearance. A broken field of black basaltic lava is every where covered by a stunted brushwood, which shows little signs of life. The dry and parched surface, having been heated by the noonday sun, gave the air a close and sultry feeling, like that from a stove: we fancied even the bushes smelt unpleasantly. Although I diligently tried to collect as many plants as possible, I succeeded in getting only ten kinds; and such wretched-looking little weeds would have better become an arctic, than an equatorial Flora.

The thin woods, which cover the lower parts of all the islands, excepting where the lava has recently flowed, appear from a short distance quite leafless,

---

9. The chapter reproduced is from the first edition of the *Voyage of the "Beagle"* (most of Darwin's footnotes have been removed, however). Important passages from the second edition of 1845 are added in footnotes below. (Readers should note that this is the title the book is always given nowadays; in its own time its title was *Journal of Researches into the Geology and Natural History of the Various Countries Visited by HMS Beagle.*)

like the deciduous trees of the northern hemisphere in winter. It was some time before I discovered, that not only almost every plant was in full leaf, but that the greater number were now in flower. After the period of heavy rains, the islands are said to appear for a short time partially green. The only other country, in which I have seen a vegetation with a character at all approaching to this, is at the volcanic island of Fernando Noronha, placed in many respects under similar conditions.

The natural history of this archipelago is very remarkable: it seems to be a little world within itself;[10] the greater number of its inhabitants, both vegetable and animal, being found nowhere else. As I shall refer to this subject again, I will only here remark, as forming a striking character on first landing, that the birds are strangers to man. So tame and unsuspecting were they, that they did not even understand what was meant by stones being thrown at them; and quite regardless of us, they approached so close that any number might have been killed with a stick.

The *Beagle* sailed round Chatham Island, and anchored in several bays. One night I slept on shore, on a part of the island where some black cones— the former chimneys of the subterranean heated fluids—were extraordinarily numerous. From one small eminence, I counted sixty of these truncated hillocks, which were all surmounted by a more or less perfect crater. The greater number consisted merely of a ring of red scori or slags, cemented together: and their height above the plain of lava, was not more than from 50 to 100 feet. From their regular form, they gave the country a *workshop* appearance, which strongly reminded me of those parts of Staffordshire where the great iron-foundries are most numerous.

The age of the various beds of lava was distinctly marked by the comparative growth, or entire absence, of vegetation. Nothing can be imagined more rough and horrid than the surface of the more modern streams. These have been aptly compared to the sea petrified in its most boisterous moments: no sea, however, would present such irregular undulations, or would be traversed by such deep chasms. All the craters are in an extinct condition; and although the age of the different streams of lava could be so clearly distinguished, it is probable they have remained so for many centuries. There is no account in any

---

10. From the second edition: "The natural history of these islands is eminently curious, and well deserves attention. Most of the organic productions are aboriginal creations, found nowhere else; there is even a difference between the inhabitants of the different islands; yet all show a marked relationship with those of America, though separated from that continent by an open space of ocean, between 500 and 600 miles in width. The archipelago is a little world within itself, or rather a satellite attached to America, whence it has derived a few stray colonists, and has received the general character of its indigenous productions. Considering the small size of these islands, we feel the more astonished at the number of their aboriginal beings, and at their confined range. Seeing every height crowned with its crater, and the boundaries of most of the lava-streams still distinct, we are led to believe that within a period, geologically recent, the unbroken ocean was here spread out. Hence, both in space and time, we seem to be brought somewhat near to that great fact—that mystery of mysteries—the first appearance of new beings on this earth" (Darwin 1960: 363).

THE ISLAND AS CRUCIBLE

of the old voyagers of any volcano on this island having been seen in activity; yet since the time of Dampier (1684), there must have been some increase in the quantity of vegetation, otherwise so accurate a person would not have expressed himself thus: "Four or five of the easternmost islands are rocky, barren, and hilly, producing neither tree, herb, nor grass, but a few dildoe (cactus) trees, except by the sea-side." This description is at present applicable only to the western islands, where the volcanic forces are in frequent activity.

The day, on which I visited the little craters, was glowing hot, and the scrambling over the rough surface, and through the intricate thickets, was very fatiguing; but I was well repaid by the Cyclopian scene. In my walk I met two large tortoises, each of which must have weighed at least 200 pounds. One was eating a piece of cactus, and when I approached, it looked at me, and then quietly walked away: the other gave a deep hiss and drew in its head. These huge reptiles, surrounded by the black lava, the leafless shrubs, and large cacti, appeared to my fancy like some antediluvian animals. [. . .]

I will now offer a few general observations on the natural history of these islands. I endeavoured to make as nearly a perfect collection in every branch as time permitted. The plants have not yet been examined, but Professor Henslow, who has kindly undertaken the description of them, informs me that there are probably many new species, and perhaps even some new genera. They all have an extremely weedy character, and it would scarcely have been supposed, that they had grown at an inconsiderable elevation directly under the equator. [. . .] From the presence of the Opuntias and some other plants, the vegetation partakes more of the character of that of America than of any other country.

Of mammalia a large kind of mouse forms a well-marked species. From its large thin ears, and other characters, it approaches in form a section of the genus, which is confined to the sterile regions of South America. There is also a rat which Mr Waterhouse believes is probably distinct from the English kind; but I cannot help suspecting that it is only the same altered by the peculiar conditions of its new country.

In my collections from these islands, Mr Gould considers that there are twenty-six different species of land birds. With the exception of one, all probably are undescribed kinds, which inhabit this archipelago, and no other part of the world. Among the waders and waterfowl it is more difficult, without detailed comparison, to say what are new. But a water-rail which lives near the summits of the mountains, is undescribed, as perhaps is a Totanus and a heron. The only kind of gull which is found among these islands, is also new; when the wandering habits of this genus are considered, this is a very remarkable circumstance. The species most closely allied to it, comes from the Strait of Magellan. Of the other aquatic birds, the species appear the same with well-known American birds.

The general character of the plumage of these birds is extremely plain, and like the Flora possesses little beauty. Although the species are thus peculiar to the archipelago, yet nearly all in their general structure, habits, colour of feathers, and even tone of voice, are strictly American. [. . .] A group of finches, of which Mr Gould considers there are thirteen species; and these he has distributed into four new sub-genera. These birds are the most singular of any in the archipelago. They all agree in many points; namely, in a peculiar structure of their bill, short tails, general form, and in their plumage. The females are gray or brown, but the old cocks jet-black. All the species, excepting two, feed in flocks on the ground, and have very similar habits. It is very remarkable that a nearly perfect gradation of structure in this one group can be traced in the form of the beak, from one exceeding in dimensions that of the largest gros-beak, to another differing but little from that of a warbler.[11] Of the aquatic birds I have already remarked that some are peculiar to these islands, and some common to North and South America.

We will now turn to the order of reptiles, which forms, perhaps, the most striking feature in the zoology of these islands. The species are not numerous, but the number of individuals of each kind, is extraordinarily great. There is one kind both of the turtle and tortoise; of lizards four; and of snakes about the same number.

[Darwin now provides a description of the giant tortoise, Testudo indicus, *before turning to the iguanas of the Galapagos.]*

Of lizards there are four or five species; two probably belong to the South American genus Leiocephalus, and two to Amblyrhyncus. This remarkable genus was characterized by Mr Bell, from a stuffed specimen sent from Mexico, but which I conceive there can be little doubt originally came through some whaling ship from these islands. The two species agree pretty closely in general appearance; but one is aquatic and the other terrestrial in its habits. Mr Bell thus concludes his description of *Amb. cristatus:* "On a comparison of this animal with the true Iguanas, the most striking and important discrepancy is in the form of the head. Instead of the long, pointed, narrow muzzle of those species, we have here a short, obtusely truncated head, not so long as it is broad, the mouth consequently only capable of being opened to a very short space. These circumstances, with the shortness and equality of the toes, and the strength and curvature of the claws, evidently indicate some striking peculiarity in its food and general habits, on which, however, in the absence of all certain information, I shall abstain from offering any conjecture." The following account of these two lizards, will, I think, show with what judgment Mr Bell foresaw a variation in habit, accompanying change in structure.

First for the aquatic kind *(Amb. cristatus).* This lizard is extremely common on all the islands throughout the Archipelago. It lives exclusively on the rocky sea-beaches, and is never found, at least I never saw one, even 10 yards inshore. It is a hideous-looking creature, of a dirty black colour, stupid and

---

11. "Seeing this gradation and diversity of structure in one small, intimately related group of birds, one might really fancy that from an original paucity of birds in this archipelago, one species had been taken and modified for different ends" (Darwin 1960: 365).

sluggish in its movements. The usual length of a full-grown one is about a yard, but there are some even 4 feet long: I have seen a large one which weighed 20 pounds. On the island of Albemarle they seem to grow to a greater size than on any other. These lizards were occasionally seen some 100 yards from the shore swimming about; and Captain Collnett, in his *Voyage,* says, "they go out to sea in shoals to fish." With respect to the object, I believe he is mistaken; but the fact stated on such good authority cannot be doubted. When in the water the animal swims with perfect ease and quickness, by a serpentine movement of its body and flattened tail—the legs, during this time, being motionless and closely collapsed on its sides. A seaman on board sank one, with a heavy weight attached to it, thinking thus to kill it directly; but when an hour afterwards he drew up the line, the lizard was quite active. Their limbs and strong claws are admirably adapted for crawling over the rugged and fissured masses of lava, which every where form the coast. In such situations, a group of six or seven of these hideous reptiles may oftentimes be seen on the black rocks, a few feet above the surf, basking in the sun with outstretched legs.

I opened the stomach of several, and in each case found it largely distended with minced sea-weed, of that kind which grows in thin foliaceous expansions of a bright green or dull red colour. I do not recollect having observed this sea-weed in any quantity on the tidal rocks; and I have reason to believe it grows at the bottom of the sea, at some little distance from the coast. If such is the case, the object of these animals occasionally going out to sea is explained. The stomach contained nothing but the seaweed. Mr Bynoe, however, found a piece of a crab in one; but this might have got in accidentally, in the same manner as I have seen a caterpillar, in the midst of some lichen, in the paunch of a tortoise. The intestines were large, as in other herbivorous animals.

The nature of this lizard's food, as well as the structure of its tail, and the certain fact of its having been seen voluntarily swimming out at sea, absolutely prove its aquatic habits; yet there is in this respect one strange anomaly; namely, that when frightened it will not enter the water. From this cause, it is easy to drive these lizards down to any little point overhanging the sea, where they will sooner allow a person to catch hold of their tail than jump into the water. They do not seem to have any notion of biting; but when much frightened they squirt a drop of fluid from each nostril. One day I carried one to a deep pool left by the retiring tide, and threw it in several times as far as I was able. It invariably returned in a direct line to the spot where I stood. It swam near the bottom, with a very graceful and rapid movement, and occasionally aided itself over the uneven ground with its feet. As soon as it arrived near the margin, but still being under water, it either tried to conceal itself in the tufts of sea-weed, or it entered some crevice. As soon as it thought the danger was past, it crawled out on the dry rocks, and shuffled away as quickly as it could. I several times caught this same lizard, by driving it down to a point, and though possessed of such perfect powers of diving and swimming, nothing would induce it to enter the water; and so often as I threw it in, it returned in the manner above described. Perhaps this singular piece of apparent stupidity may be accounted for by the circumstance, that this reptile has no enemy whatever on shore, whereas at sea it must often fall a prey to the numerous sharks. Hence, probably urged by a fixed and hereditary instinct that the shore is its place of safety, whatever the emergency may be, it there takes refuge.

During our visit (in October) I saw extremely few small individuals of this species, and none I should think under a year old. From this circumstance it seems probable that the breeding season had not commenced. I asked several of the inhabitants if they knew where it laid its eggs: they said, that although well acquainted with the eggs of the other kind, they had not the least knowledge of the manner in which this species is propagated; a fact, considering how common an animal this lizard is, not a little extraordinary.

We will now turn to the terrestrial species (*Amb. subcristatus* of Gray). This species, differently from the last, is confined to the central islands of the Archipelago, namely to Albemarle, James, Barrington, and Indefatigable. To the southward, in Charles, Hood, and Chatham islands, and to the northward, in Towers, Bindloes, and Abington, I neither saw nor heard of any. It would appear as if this species had been created in the centre of the Archipelago, and thence had been dispersed only to a certain distance.

In the central islands they inhabit both the higher and damp, as well as the lower and sterile parts; but in the latter they are much the most numerous. I cannot give a more forcible proof of their numbers, than by stating, that when we were left at James Island, we could not for some time find a spot free from their burrows, on which to pitch our tent. These lizards, like their brothers the sea-kind, are ugly animals; and from their low facial angle have a singularly stupid appearance. In size perhaps they are a little inferior to the latter, but several of them weighed between 10 and 15 pounds each. The colour of their belly, front legs, and head (excepting the crown which is nearly white), is a dirty yellowish orange: the back is a brownish-red, which in the younger specimens is darker. In their movements they are lazy and half torpid. When not frightened, they slowly crawl along with their tails and bellies dragging on the ground. They often stop, and doze for a minute with closed eyes, and hind legs spread out on the parched soil.

They inhabit burrows; which they sometimes excavate between fragments of lava, but more generally on level patches of the soft volcanic sandstone. The holes do not appear to be very deep, and they enter the ground at a small angle; so that when walking over these lizard *warrens,* the soil is constantly giving way, much to the annoyance of the tired walker. This animal when excavating its burrow, alternately works the opposite sides of its body. One front leg for a short time scratches up the soil, and throws it towards the hind foot, which is well placed so as to heave it beyond the mouth of the hole. This side of the body being tired, the other takes up the task, and so on alternately. I watched one for a long time, till half its body was buried; I then walked up and pulled it by the tail; at this it was greatly astonished, and soon shuffled up to see what was the matter; and then stared me in the face, as much as to say, "What made you pull my tail?"

THE ISLAND AS CRUCIBLE

They feed by day, and do not wander far from their burrows; and if frightened they rush to them with a most awkward gait. Except when running down hill, they cannot move very fast; which appears chiefly owing to the lateral position of their legs.

They are not at all timorous: when attentively watching any one, they curl their tails, and raising themselves on their front legs, nod their heads vertically, with a quick movement, and try to look very fierce: but in reality they are not at all so; if one just stamps the ground, down go their tails, and off they shuffle as quickly as they can. I have frequently observed small muscivorous lizards, when watching any thing, nod their heads in precisely the same manner; but I do not at all know for what purpose. If this Amblyrhyncus is held, and plagued with a stick, it will bite it very severely; but I caught many by the tail, and they never tried to bite me. If two are placed on the ground and held together, they will fight and bite each other till blood is drawn.

The individuals (and they are the greater number) which inhabit the lower country, can scarcely taste a drop of water throughout the year; but they consume much of the succulent cactus, the branches of which are occasionally broken off by the wind. I have sometimes thrown a piece to two or three when together; and it was amusing enough to see each trying to seize and carry it away in its mouth, like so many hungry dogs with a bone. They eat very deliberately, but do not chew their food. The little birds are aware how harmless these creatures are: I have seen one of the thick-billed finches picking at one end of a piece of cactus (which is in request among all the animals of the lower region), whilst a lizard was eating at the other; and afterwards the little bird with the utmost indifference hopped on the back of the reptile.

I opened the stomachs of several, and found them full of vegetable fibres, and leaves of different trees, especially of a species of acacia. In the upper region they live chiefly on the acid and astringent berries of the guayavita, under which trees I have seen these lizards and the huge tortoises feeding together. To obtain the acacia-leaves, they crawl up the low stunted trees; and it is not uncommon to see one or a pair quietly browsing, whilst seated on a branch several feet above the ground.

The meat of these animals when cooked is white, and by those whose stomachs rise above all prejudices, it is relished as very good food. Humboldt has remarked that in inter-tropical South America, all lizards which inhabit *dry* regions are esteemed delicacies for the table. The inhabitants say, that those inhabiting the damp region drink water, but that the others do not travel up for it from the sterile country like the tortoises. At the time of our visit, the females had within their bodies numerous large elongated eggs. These they lay in their burrows, and the inhabitants seek them for food.

These two species of Amblyrhyncus agree, as I have already stated, in general structure, and in many of their habits. Neither have that rapid movement, so characteristic of true Lacerta and Iguana. They are both herbivorous, although the kind of vegetation consumed in each case is so very different. Mr Bell has given the name to the genus from the shortness of the snout: indeed, the form of the mouth may almost be compared to that of the tortoise. One is tempted to suppose this is an adaptation to their herbivorous appetites. It is very interesting thus to find a well-characterized genus, having its aquatic and terrestrial species, belonging to so confined a portion of the world. The former species is by far the most remarkable, because it is the only existing Saurian, which can properly be said to be a maritime animal.[12] I should perhaps have mentioned earlier, that in the whole archipelago, there is only one rill of fresh water that reaches the coast; yet these reptiles frequent the sea-beaches, and no other parts in all the islands. Moreover, there is no existing lizard, as far as I am aware, excepting this Amblyrhyncus, that feeds exclusively on aquatic productions. If, however, we refer to epochs long past, we shall find such habits common to several gigantic animals of the Saurian race. [. . .]

I will not here attempt to come to any definite conclusions, as the species have not been accurately examined; but we may infer, that, with the exception of a few wanderers, the organic beings found on this archipelago are peculiar to it; and yet that their general form strongly partakes of an American character. It would be impossible for any one accustomed to the birds of Chile and La Plata to be placed on these islands, and not to feel convinced that he was, as far as the organic world was concerned, on American ground.[13] This similarity in type, between distant islands and continents, while the species are distinct, has scarcely been sufficiently noticed. The circumstance would be explained, according to the views of some authors, by saying that the creative power had acted according to the same law over a wide area.

It has been mentioned, that the inhabitants can distinguish the tortoises, according to the islands whence they are brought. I was also informed that many of the islands possess trees and plants which do not occur on the others. For instance the berry-bearing tree, called Guayavita, which is common on James Island, certainly is not found on Charles Island, though appearing equally well fitted for it. Unfortunately, I was not aware of these facts till my collection was nearly completed: it never occurred to me, that the productions of islands only a few miles apart, and placed under the same physical

---

12. Saurians: an obsolete zoological category including the lizards and the crocodiles.

13. "If this character were owing merely to immigrants from America, there would be little remarkable in it; but we see that a vast majority of all the land animals, and that more than half of the flowering plants, are aboriginal productions. It was most striking to be surrounded by new birds, new reptiles, new shells, new insects, new plants, and yet by innumerable trifling details of structure, and even by the tones of voice and plumage of the birds, to have the temperate plains of Patagonia, or the hot dry deserts of Northern Chile, vividly brought before my eyes. Why, on these small points of land, which within a late geological period must have been covered by the ocean, which are formed of basaltic lava, and therefore differ in geological character from the American continent, and which are placed under a peculiar climate,—why were their aboriginal inhabitants associated, I may add, in different proportions both in kind and number from those on the continent, and therefore acting on each other in a different manner—why were they created on American types of organization? It is probable that the islands of the Cape de Verd group resemble, in all their physical conditions, far more closely the Galapagos Islands than these latter physically resemble the coast of America; yet the aboriginal inhabitants of the two groups are totally unlike; those of the Cape de Verd Islands bearing the impress of Africa, as the inhabitants of the Galapagos Archipelago are stamped with that of America" (Darwin 1960: 378).

conditions, would be dissimilar. I therefore did not attempt to make a series of specimens from the separate islands.[14] It is the fate of every voyager, when he has just discovered what object in any place is more particularly worthy of his attention, to be hurried from it. In the case of the mocking-bird, I ascertained (and have brought home the specimens) that one species (*Orpheus trifasciatus*, Gould) is exclusively found in Charles Island; a second *(O. parvulus)* on Albemarle Island; and a third *(O. melanotus)* common to James and Chatham Islands. The two last species are closely allied, but the first would be considered by every naturalist as quite distinct. I examined many specimens in the different islands, and in each the respective kind was alone present. These birds agree in general plumage, structure, and habits; so that the different species replace each other in the economy of the different islands. These species are not characterized by the markings on the plumage alone, but likewise by the size and form of the bill, and other differences. I have stated, that in the thirteen species of ground-finches, a nearly perfect gradation may be traced, from a beak extraordinarily thick, to one so fine, that it may be compared to that of a warbler. I very much suspect, that certain members of the series are confined to different islands; therefore, if the collection had been made on any one island, it would not have presented so perfect a gradation. It is clear, that if several islands have each their peculiar species of the same genera, when these are placed together, they will have a wide range of character. But there is not space in this work, to enter on this curious subject.[15]

---

14. "I have not as yet noticed by far the most remarkable feature in the natural history of this archipelago; it is, that the different islands to a considerable extent are inhabited by a different set of beings. My attention was first called to this fact by the Vice-Governor, Mr. Lawson, declaring that the tortoises differed from the different islands, and that he could with certainty tell from which island any one was brought. I did not for some time pay sufficient attention to this statement, and I had already partially mingled together the collections from two of the islands. I never dreamed that islands, about fifty or sixty miles apart, and most of them in sight of each other, formed of precisely the same rocks, placed under a quite similar climate, rising to a nearly equal height, would have been differently tenanted; but we shall soon see that this is the case" (Darwin 1960: 379).

15. "The distribution of the tenants of this archipelago would not be nearly so wonderful, if, for instance, one island had a mocking-thrush, and a second island some other quite distinct genus;—if one island had its genus of lizard, and a second island another distinct genus, or none whatever;—or if the different islands were inhabited, not by representative species of the same genera of plants, but by totally different genera. [. . .] But it is the circumstance, that several of the islands possess their own species of the tortoise, mocking-thrush, finches, and numerous plants, these species having the same general habits, occupying analogous situations, and obviously filling the same place in the natural economy of this archipelago, that strikes me with wonder. It may be suspected that some of these representative species, at least in the case of the tortoise and of some of the birds, may hereafter prove to be only well-marked races; but this would be of equally great interest to the philosophical naturalist. [. . .] Reviewing the facts here given, one is astonished at the amount of creative force, if such an expression may be used, displayed on these small, barren, and rocky islands; and still more so, at its diverse yet analogous action on points so near each other. I have said that the Galapagos Archipelago might be called a satellite attached to America, but it should rather be called a group of satellites, physically similar, organically distinct, yet intimately related to each another, and all related in a marked, though much lesser degree, to the great American continent" (Darwin 1960: 382–383).

Before concluding my account of the zoology of these islands, I must describe more in detail the tameness of the birds. This disposition is common to all the terrestrial species; namely, to the mocking-birds, the finches, sylvicolæ, tyrant-flycatchers, doves, and hawks. There is not one which will not approach sufficiently near to be killed with a switch, and sometimes, as I have myself tried, with a cap or hat. A gun is here almost superfluous; for with the muzzle of one I pushed a hawk off the branch of a tree. One day a mocking-bird alighted on the edge of a pitcher (made of the shell of a tortoise), which I held in my hand whilst lying down. It began very quietly to sip the water, and allowed me to lift it with the vessel from the ground. I often tried, and very nearly succeeded, in catching these birds by their legs. Formerly the birds appear to have been even tamer than at present. Cowley (in the year 1684) says that the "Turtle-doves were so tame that they would often alight upon our hats and arms, so as that we could take them alive: they not fearing man, until such time as some of our company did fire at them, whereby they were rendered more shy." Dampier (in the same year) also says that a man in a morning's walk might kill six or seven dozen of these birds. At present, although certainly very tame, they do not alight on people's arms; nor do they suffer themselves to be killed in such numbers. It is surprising that the change has not been greater; for these islands during the last 150 years, have been frequently visited by bucaniers and whalers; and the sailors, wandering through the woods in search of tortoises, always take delight in knocking down the little birds.

These birds, although much persecuted, do not become wild in a short time: in Charles Island, which had then been colonized about six years, I saw a boy sitting by a well with a switch in his hand, with which he killed the doves and finches as they came to drink. He had already procured a little heap of them for his dinner; and he said he had constantly been in the habit of waiting there for the same purpose. We must conclude that the birds, not having as yet learnt that man is a more dangerous animal than the tortoise, or the amblyrhyncus, disregard us, in the same manner as magpies in England do the cows and horses grazing in the fields. [. . .]

I have not met with any account of the land birds being so tame, in any other quarter of the world, as at the Galapagos and Falkland Islands. And it may be observed that of the few archipelagoes of any size, which when discovered were uninhabited by man, these two are among the most important. From the foregoing statements we may, I think, conclude; first, that the wildness of birds with regard to man, is a particular instinct directed against him, and not dependent on any general degree of caution arising from other sources of danger; secondly, that it is not acquired by them in a short time, even when much persecuted; but that in the course of successive generations it becomes hereditary. With domesticated animals we are accustomed to see instincts becoming hereditary; but with those in a state of nature, it is more rare to discover instances of such acquired knowledge. In regard to the wildness of birds towards men, there is no other way of accounting for it. Few young birds in England have been injured by man, yet all are afraid of him: many individuals, on the other hand, both at the Galapagos and at the Falklands, have been injured, but yet have not learned that salutary dread. We may infer from these facts, what havoc the introduction of any new beast of prey must cause in a country, before the instincts of the aborigines become adapted to the stranger's craft or power.

from Charles Darwin, "Essay on Species" (1844)

After his return to England, Darwin worked on coral reefs and other geological subjects, while his ideas on evolution gradually took shape. In 1842 he wrote a thirty-five-page sketch of his theory of the origin of species by natural selection, though he was as yet unwilling to publish it. In 1844 he expanded this to an essay of 230 pages. Again he put off publishing until his case was fully supported. (Such support would gradually emerge not only from his *Beagle* materials but from countless other sources, including dog and pigeon breeding, plant hybridization, barnacles, and earthworms.) So the situation stood until Alfred Russel Wallace's remarkably similar work began to emerge in 1856 and Darwin was compelled to draft *The Origin of Species*, published in 1859.

from section Third. An attempt to explain the foregoing laws of geographical distribution, on the theory of allied species having a common descent

First let us recall the circumstances most favourable for variation under domestication, as given in the first chapter—viz. 1st, a change, or repeated changes, in the conditions to which the organism has been exposed, continued through several seminal (i.e. not by buds or divisions) generations: 2nd, steady selection of the slight varieties thus generated with a fixed end in view: 3rd, isolation as perfect as possible of such selected varieties; that is, the preventing their crossing with other forms; this latter condition applies to all terrestrial animals, to most if not all plants and perhaps even to most (or all) aquatic organisms. It will be convenient here to show the advantage of isolation in the formation of a new breed, by comparing the progress of two persons (to neither of whom let time be of any consequence) endeavouring to select and form some very peculiar new breed. Let one of these persons work on the vast herds of cattle in the plains of La Plata, and the other on a small stock of 20 or 30 animals in an island. The latter might have to wait centuries (by the hypothesis of no importance) before he obtained a "sport" approaching to what he wanted;[16] but when he did and saved the greater number of its offspring and their offspring again, he might hope that his whole little stock would be in some degree affected, so that by continued selection he might gain his end. But on the Pampas, though the man might get his first approach

16. "Sport" here meaning an animal or plant that varies from the normal type.

to his desired form sooner, how hopeless would it be to attempt, by saving its offspring amongst so many of the common kind, to affect the whole herd: the effect of this one peculiar "sport" would be quite lost before he could obtain a second original sport of the same kind. If, however, he could separate a small number of cattle, including the offspring of the desirable "sport," he might hope, like the man on the island, to effect his end. [. . .]

Let us now take the simplest natural case of an islet upheaved by the volcanic or subterranean forces in a deep sea, at such a distance from other land that only a few organic beings at rare intervals were transported to it, whether borne by the sea (like the seeds of plants to coral-reefs), or by hurricanes, or by floods, or on rafts, or in roots of large trees, or the germs of one plant or animal attached to or in the stomach of some other animal, or by the intervention (in most cases the most probable means) of other islands since sunk or destroyed. It may be remarked that when one part of the earth's crust is raised it is probably the general rule that another part sinks. Let this island go on slowly, century after century, rising foot by foot; and in the course of time we shall have instead [of] a small mass of rock, lowland and high land, moist woods and dry sandy spots, various soils, marshes, streams and pools: under water on the sea shore, instead of a rocky steeply shelving coast we shall have in some parts bays with mud, sandy beaches and rocky shoals. The formation of the island by itself must often slightly affect the surrounding climate. It is impossible that the first few transported organisms could be perfectly adapted to all these stations; and it will be a chance if those successively transported will be so adapted. The greater number would probably come from the low lands of the nearest country; and not even all these would be perfectly adapted to the new islet whilst it continued low and exposed to coast influences. Moreover, as it is certain that all organisms are nearly as much adapted in their structure to the other inhabitants of their country as they are to its physical conditions, so the mere fact that a *few* beings (and these taken in great degree by chance) were in the first case transported to the islet, would in itself greatly modify their conditions. As the island continued rising we might also expect an occasional new visitant; and I repeat that even one new being must often affect beyond our calculation by occupying the room and taking part of the subsistence of another (and this again from another and so on), several or many other organisms. Now as the first transported and any occasional successive visitants spread or tended to spread over the growing island, they would undoubtedly be exposed through several generations to new and varying conditions: it might also easily happen that some of the species *on an average* might obtain an increase of food, or food of a more nourishing quality. According then to every analogy with what we have seen takes place in every country, with nearly every organic being under domestication, we might expect that some of the inhabitants of the island would "sport," or have their organization rendered in some degree plastic. As the number of the inhabitants are supposed to be few and as all these cannot be so well adapted to their new and varying conditions as they were in their native country and habitat, we cannot believe that every place or office in the economy of the island would be as well filled as on a continent where the number of aboriginal species is far greater and where they consequently hold a more strictly limited place. We might therefore expect on our island that although very many slight variations were of no use to the plastic individuals, yet that occasionally in the course of a century an individual might be born of which the structure or constitution in some slight degree would allow it better to fill up some office in the insular economy and to struggle against other species. If such were the case the individual and its offspring would have a better *chance* of surviving and of beating out its parent form; and if (as is probable) it and its offspring crossed with the unvaried parent form, yet the number of the individuals being not very great, there would be a chance of the new and more serviceable form being nevertheless in some slight degree preserved. The struggle for existence would go on annually selecting such individuals until a new race or species was formed. Either few or all the first visitants to the island might become modified, according as the physical conditions of the island and those resulting from the kind and number of other transported species were different from those of the parent country—according to the difficulties offered to fresh immigration—and according to the length of time since the first inhabitants were introduced. It is obvious that whatever was the country, generally the nearest from which the first tenants were transported, they would show an affinity, even if all had become modified, to the natives of that country and even if the inhabitants of the same source [?] had been modified. On this view we can at once understand the cause and meaning of the affinity of the fauna and flora of the Galapagos Islands with the coast of S. America; and consequently why the inhabitants of these islands show not the smallest affinity with those inhabiting other volcanic islands, with a very similar climate and soil, near the coast of Africa.

To return once again to our island, if by the continued action of the subterranean forces other neighbouring islands were formed, these would generally be stocked by the inhabitants of the first island, or by a few immigrants from the neighbouring mainland; but if considerable obstacles were interposed to any communication between the terrestrial productions of these islands, and their conditions were different (perhaps only by the number of different species on each island), a form transported from one island to another might become altered in the same manner as one from the continent; and we should have several of the islands tenanted by representative races or species, as is so wonderfully the case with the different islands of the Galapagos Archipelago. As the islands become mountainous, if mountain-species were not introduced, as could rarely happen, a greater amount of variation and selection would be requisite to adapt the species, which originally came from the lowlands of the nearest continent, to the mountain-summits than to the lower districts of our islands. For the lowland species from the continent would have first to struggle against other species and other conditions on the coast-land of the island, and so probably become modified by the selection of its best fitted varieties, then to undergo the same process when the land had attained a moderate elevation; and then lastly when it had become Alpine. Hence we can understand why the faunas of insular mountain-summits are, as in the case of Teneriffe, eminently peculiar. Putting on one side the case of a widely extended flora being driven up the mountain-summits, during a change of climate from cold to temperate, we can see why in other cases the floras of mountain-summits (or as I have called them islands in a sea of land) should be tenanted by peculiar species, but related to those of the surrounding lowlands, as are the inhabitants of a real island in the sea to those of the nearest continent.

Let us now consider the effect of a change of climate or of other conditions on the inhabitants of a continent and of an isolated island without any great change of level. On a continent the chief effects would be changes in the numerical proportion of the individuals of the different species; for whether the climate became warmer or colder, drier or damper, more uniform or extreme, some species are at present adapted to its diversified districts; if for instance it became cooler, species would migrate from its more temperate parts and from its higher land; if damper, from its damper regions, &c. On a small and isolated island, however, with few species, and these not adapted to much diversified conditions, such changes instead of merely increasing the number of certain species already adapted to such conditions, and decreasing the number of other species, would be apt to affect the constitutions of some of the insular species: thus if the island became damper it might well happen that there were no species living in any part of it adapted to the consequences resulting from more moisture. In this case therefore, and still more (as we have seen) during the production of new stations from the elevation of the land, an island would be a far more fertile source, as far as we can judge, of new specific forms than a continent. The new forms thus generated on an island, we might expect, would occasionally be transported by accident, or through long-continued geographical changes be enabled to emigrate and thus become slowly diffused.

But if we look to the origin of a continent; almost every geologist will admit that in most cases it will have first existed as separate islands which gradually increased in size; and therefore all that which has been said concerning the probable changes of the forms tenanting a small archipelago is applicable to a continent in its early state. Furthermore, a geologist who reflects on the geological history of Europe (the only region well known) will admit that it has been many times depressed, raised and left stationary. During the sinking of a continent and the probable generally accompanying changes of climate the effect would be little, *except* on the numerical proportions and in the extinction (from the lessening of rivers, the drying of marshes and the conversion of high-lands into low &c.) of some or of many of the species. As soon however as the continent became divided into many isolated portions or islands, preventing free immigration from one part to another, the effect of climatic and other changes on the species would be greater. But let the now

THE ISLAND AS CRUCIBLE

broken continent, forming isolated islands, begin to rise and new stations thus to be formed, exactly as in the first case of the upheaved volcanic islet, and we shall have equally favourable conditions for the modification of old forms, that is the formation of new races or species. Let the islands become reunited into a continent; and then the new and old forms would all spread, as far as barriers, the means of transportal, and the pre-occupation of the land by other species, would permit. Some of the new species or races would probably become extinct, and some perhaps would cross and blend together. We should thus have a multitude of forms, adapted to all kinds of slightly different stations, and to diverse groups of either antagonist or food-serving species. The oftener these oscillations of level had taken place (and therefore generally the older the land) the greater the number of species [which] would tend to be formed. The inhabitants of a continent being thus derived in the first stage from the same original parents, and subsequently from the inhabitants of one wide area, since often broken up and reunited, all would be obviously related together and the inhabitants of the most *dissimilar* stations on the same continent would be more closely allied than the inhabitants of two very *similar* stations on two of the main divisions of the world.

I need hardly point out that we now can obviously see why the number of species in two districts, independently of the number of stations in such districts, should be in some cases as widely different as in New Zealand and the Cape of Good Hope. We can see, knowing the difficulty in the transport of terrestrial mammals, why islands far from main-lands do not possess them; we see the general reason, namely accidental transport (though not the precise reason), why certain islands should, and others should not, possess members of the class of reptiles. We can see why an ancient channel of communication between two distant points, as the Cordillera probably was between southern Chile and the United States during the former cold periods; and icebergs between the Falkland Islands and Tierra del Fuego; and gales, at a former or present time, between the Asiatic shores of the Pacific and eastern islands in this ocean; is connected with (or we may now say causes) an affinity between the species, though distinct, in two such districts. We can see how the better chance of diffusion, from several of the species of any genus having wide ranges in their own countries, explains the presence of other species of the same genus in other countries and on the other hand, of species of restricted powers of ranging, forming genera with restricted ranges.

As every one would be surprised if two exactly similar but peculiar varieties of any species were raised by man by long continued selection, in two different countries, or at two very different periods, so we ought not to expect that an exactly similar form would be produced from the modification of an old one in two distinct countries or at two distinct periods. For in such places and times they would probably be exposed to somewhat different climates and almost certainly to different associates. Hence we can see why each species appears to have been produced singly, in space and in time. I need hardly remark that, according to this theory of descent, there is no necessity of modification in a species, when it reaches a new and isolated country. If it be able to survive and if slight variations better adapted to the new conditions are not selected, it might retain (as far as we can see) its old form for an indefinite time. As we see that some sub-varieties produced under domestication are more variable than others, so in nature, perhaps, some species and genera are more variable than others. The same precise form, however, would probably be seldom preserved through successive geological periods, or in widely and differently conditioned countries.

Finally, during the long periods of time and probably of oscillations of level, necessary for the formation of a continent, we may conclude (as above explained) that many forms would become extinct. These extinct forms, and those surviving (whether or not modified and changed in structure), will all be related in each continent in the same manner and degree, as are the inhabitants of any two different sub-regions in that same continent. I do not mean to say that, for instance, the present Marsupials of Australia or Edentata and rodents of S. America have descended from any one of the few fossils of the same orders which have been discovered in these countries. It is possible that, in a very few instances, this may be the case; but generally they must be considered as merely codescendants of common stocks. I believe in this, from the improbability, considering the vast number of species, which (as explained in the last chapter) must by our theory have existed, that the *comparatively* few fossils which have been found should chance to be the immediate and linear progenitors of those now existing. Recent as the yet discovered fossil mammifers of S. America are, who will pretend to say that very many intermediate forms may not have existed? Moreover, we shall see in the ensuing chapter that the very existence of genera and species can be explained only by a few species of each epoch leaving modified successors or new species to a future period; and the more distant that future period, the fewer will be the *linear* heirs of the former epoch. As by our theory, all mammifers must have descended from the same parent stock, so is it necessary that each land now possessing terrestrial mammifers shall at some time have been so far united to other land as to permit the passage of mammifers and it accords with this necessity, that in looking far back into the earth's history we find, first changes in the geographical distribution, and secondly a period when the mammiferous forms most distinctive of two of the present main divisions of the world were living together.

I think then I am justified in asserting that most of the above enumerated and often trivial points in the geographical distribution of past and present organisms (which points must be viewed by the creationists as so many ultimate facts) follow as a simple consequence of specific forms being mutable and of their being adapted by natural selection to diverse ends, conjoined with their powers of dispersal, and the geologico-geographical changes now in slow progress and which undoubtedly have taken place. This large class of facts being thus explained, far more than counterbalances many separate difficulties and apparent objections in convincing my mind of the truth of this theory of common descent.

from Herman Melville, "The Encentadas, or Enchanted Isles" (1854)

The great American novelist Herman Melville (1819–1891) cruised the Pacific from 1841 to 1844: initially on the whaler, the *Acushnet* (when he visited the Galapagos), from which he jumped ship at the Marquesas (which adventure formed the basis of his 1846 book *Typee*); then whaling once again and spending some time on shore at Tahiti (source of his 1847 book *Omoo*) and Hawai'i; then as an ordinary seaman aboard the naval frigate *United States* (source of his 1850 book *White-Jacket*). His whaling experiences, needless to say, laid the foundations for the greatest Pacific novel: *Moby Dick* (1851). "The Encentadas" is a set of ten extraordinary metaphysical fantasies in which the Galapagos and those who have visited or lived on them offer a set of perspectives on the human condition.

Sketch Second: Two Sides to a Tortoise

In view of the description given, may one be gay upon the Encentadas? Yes: that is, find one the gaiety, and he will be gay. And indeed, sackcloth and ashes as they are, the isles are not perhaps unmitigated gloom. For while no spectator can deny their claims to a most solemn and superstitious consideration, no more than my firmest resolutions can decline to behold the spectre-tortoise when emerging from its shadowy recess; yet even the tortoise, dark and melancholy as it us upon the back, still possesses a bright side; its calapee or breast-plate being sometimes of a faint yellowish or golden tinge. Moreover, everyone knows that tortoises as well as turtle are of such a make, that if you but put them on their backs you thereby expose their bright sides without the possibility of their recovering themselves, and turning into view the other. But after you have done this, and because you have done this, you should not swear that the tortoise has no dark side. Enjoy the bright, keep it turned up perpetually if you can, but be honest, and don't deny the black. Neither should he, who cannot turn the tortoise from its natural position so as to hide the darker and expose his livelier aspect, like a great October pumpkin in the sun, for that cause declare the creature to be one total inky blot. The tortoise is both black and bright. But let us to particulars.

Some months before my first stepping ashore upon the group, my ship was cruising in its close vicinity. One noon we found ourselves off the South Head of Albemarle, and not very far from the land. Partly by way of a freak, and partly by way of spying out so strange a country, a boat's crew was sent ashore, with orders to see all they could, and besides, bring back whatever tortoises they could conveniently transport.

It was after sunset when the adventurers returned. I looked down over the ship's high side as if looking down over the curb of a well, and dimly saw the damp boat deep in the sea with some unwonted weight. Ropes were dropped over, and presently three huge antediluvian-looking tortoises, after much straining, were landed on deck. They seemed hardly of the seed of earth. We had been broad upon the waters for five long months, a period amply sufficient to make all things of the land wear a fabulous hue to the dreamy mind. Had three Spanish custom-house officers boarded us then, it is not unlikely that I should have curiously stared at them, felt of them, and stroked them much as savages serve civilized guests. But instead of three custom-house officers, behold these really wondrous tortoises—none of your schoolboy mud-turtles—but black as widower's weeds, heavy as chests of plate, with vast shells medallioned and orbed like shields, and dented and blistered like shields that have breasted a battle, shaggy, too, here and there, with dark green moss, and slimy with the spray of the sea. These mystic creatures, suddenly translated by night from unutterable solitudes to our peopled deck, affected me in a manner not easy to unfold. They seemed newly crawled forth from beneath the foundations of the world. Yea, they seemed the identical tortoises whereon the Hindu plants this total sphere.[17] With a lantern I inspected them more closely. Such worshipful venerableness of aspect! Such furry greenness mantling the rude peelings and healing the fissures of their shattered shells. I no more saw three tortoises. They expanded—became transfigured. I seemed to see three Roman Coliseums in magnificent decay.

Ye oldest inhabitants of this, or any other isle, said I, pray give me the freedom of your three walled towns.

The great feeling inspired by these creatures was that of age:—dateless, indefinite endurance. And, in fact, that any other creature can live and breathe as long as the tortoise of the Encentadas, I will not readily believe. Not to hint of their known capacity of sustaining life, while going without food for an entire year, consider that impregnable armor of their living mail. What other bodily being possesses such a citadel wherein to resist the assaults of Time?

As, lantern in hand, I scraped among the moss and beheld the ancient scars of bruises received in many a sullen fall among the marly mountains of the isle—scars strangely widened, swollen, half obliterate, and yet distorted like those sometimes found in the bark of very hoary trees, I seemed an antiquary of a geologist, studying the bird-tracks and ciphers upon the exhumed slates trod by incredible creatures whose very ghosts are now defunct.

As I lay in my hammock that night, overhead I heard the slow, weary draggings of the three ponderous strangers along the encumbered deck. Their stupidity or their resolution was so great, that they never went aside for any impediment. One ceased his movements altogether just before the mid-watch.[18] At sunrise I found him butted like a battering-ram against the immovable foot of the foremast, and still striving, tooth and nail, to force the impossible passage. That these tortoises are the victims of a penal, or malignant, or perhaps a downright diabolical enchanter, seems in nothing more likely than in that strange infatuation of hopeless toil which so often possesses them. I have known them in their journeyings ram themselves heroically against rocks, and long abide there, nudging, wriggling, wedging, in order to displace them,

---

17. In Hindu belief the world is supported on the back of a tortoise.
18. Between midnight and four a.m. on board ship.

THE ISLAND AS CRUCIBLE

and so hold on their inflexible path. Their crowning curse is their drudging impulse to straightforwardness in a belittered world.

Meeting with no such hindrance as their companion did, the other tortoises merely fell foul of small stumbling-blocks—buckets, blocks, and coils of rigging—and at times in the act of crawling over them would slip with an astounding rattle to the deck. Listening to these draggings and concussions, I thought me of the haunt from which they came; an isle full of metallic ravines and gulches, sunk bottomlessly into the hearts of splintered mountains, and covered for many miles with inextricable thickets. I then pictured these three straightforward monsters, century after century, writhing through the shades, grim as blacksmiths; crawling so slowly and ponderously, that not only toad-stools and all fungous things grow beneath their feet, but a sooty moss sprouted upon their backs. With them I lost myself in volcanic mazes; brushed away endless boughs of rotting thickets; till finally in a dream I found myself sitting crosslegged upon the foremost, a Brahmin similarly mounted upon either side,[19] forming a tripod of foreheads which upheld the universal cope.

Such was the wild nightmare begot by my first impression of the Encentadas tortoise. But next evening, strange to say, I sat down with my shipmates, and made a merry repast from tortoise steaks and tortoise stews; and supper over, out knife, and helped convert the three mighty concave shells into three fanciful soup-tureens, and polished the three flat yellowish calapees into three gorgeous salvers.

SOURCES

Joseph Banks, *The Endeavour Journal,* ed. J. C. Beaglehole, 2 vols. (Sydney: Angus and Robertson, 1962). Reproduced by permission of HarperCollins Publishers, Pty Ltd.

James Edward Smith, *A Specimen of the Botany of New Holland* (London, 1793).

Jean Baptiste Lamarck, *Zoological Philosophy,* trans. Hugh Elliott (London: Macmillan, 1914).

James Montgomery, *The Pelican Island, and Other Poems* (London: Longman, 1828).

Charles Darwin, "Galapagos Archipelago," in *Voyage of the* Beagle, 1st edn. (London: Henry Colburn, 1839); and (for footnotes) *Voyage of the* Beagle, 2nd edn. (1845; London: J. M. Dent, 1960).

Charles Darwin, "Essay on Species," in Francis Darwin, ed., *The Foundations of the "Origin of Species": Two Essays Written in 1842 and 1844 by Charles Darwin* (Cambridge: Cambridge University Press, 1909).

Herman Melville, *The Piazza Tales,* vol. 10 of *The Works of Herman Melville* (London: Constable, 1923).

19. That is, a member of the highest Indian religious caste: a priest.

General studies of the scientific work carried out in the Pacific are still thin on the ground: Roy MacLeod and Philip F. Rehbock's *Nature in Its Greatest Extent: Western Science in the Pacific* (Honolulu: University of Hawaiʻi Press, 1988) and Margarette Lincoln's *Science and Exploration in the Pacific: European Voyages to the Southern Oceans in the Eighteenth Century* (Woodbridge: Boydell and Brewer, 1998) are a start and not much more. Some promising-looking studies on the Cook era—like David Mackay, *In the Wake of Cook: Exploration, Science and Empire, 1780–1801* (Wellington: Victoria University Press, 1985), and David Philip Miller and Peter Hans Reill, eds., *Visions of Empire: Voyages, Botany, and Representations of Nature* (Cambridge: Cambridge University Press, 1996)—have less to do with the science than with the ideology behind it. By contrast, see Harry Woolf, *The Transit of Venus: A Study of Eighteenth-Century Science* (Princeton: Princeton University Press, 1959); Edward Duyker's *Nature's Argonaut: Daniel Solander, 1733–1782* (Melbourne: Miegunyah Press, 1998) and *Citizen Labillardière: A Naturalist's Life in Revolution and Exploration, 1755–1834* (Melbourne: Miegunyah Press, 2003); and William Stearn, "The Botanical Results of Captain Cook's Three Voyages and Their Later Significance," *Pacific Studies* 1:2 (Spring 1978). Despite the book's title, chapter 3 of Urs Bitterli, *Cultures in Conflict: Encounters between European and Non-European Cultures, 1492–1800* (Cambridge: Cambridge University Press, 1989), is good on European science in the Pacific. Roy MacLeod and Philip F. Rehbock, eds., *Darwin's Laboratory: Evolutionary Theory and Natural History in the Pacific* (Honolulu: University of Hawaiʻi Press, 1994), is an excellent and wide-ranging survey of the nineteenth-century scientific interest in the region. One scientific area to which the Pacific has made a significant contribution, not suprisingly, is oceanography: see Ian Jones and Joyce Jones, *Oceanography in the Age of Sail* (Sydney: Hale and Iremonger, 1992).

On Linnaeus, see Philip C. Ritterbush, *Overtures to Biology: The Speculations of Eighteenth-Century Naturalists* (New Haven: Yale University Press, 1964); Mary Louise Pratt, *Imperial Eyes: Travel Writing and Transculturation* (London: Routledge, 1992), chap. 2; and two highly recommended studies: Frans A. Stafleu, *Linnaeus and the Linnaeans: The Spreading of their Ideas in Systematic Botany, 1735–1789* (Utrecht: Oosthoek, 1971), and William T. Stearn, *Three Prefaces to Linnaeus and Robert Brown* (Weinheim: J. Cramer, 1962). For Banks, see Brian Adams, *The Flowering of the Pacific: Being an Account of Joseph Banks' Travels in the South Seas and the Story of His Florilegium* (London: Collins, 1986), and Patrick O'Brian, *Joseph Banks: A Life* (London: Collins, 1987). For Darwin, see Janet Browne's excellent *Charles Darwin: A Biography: Voyaging* (London: Pimlico, 1996) and *Charles Darwin: A Biography: Power of Place* (London: Pimlico, 2003), and Richard Lansdown, " 'An Instinct for Truth': Darwin on Galapagos," *Critical Review* 40 (2000). For Melville, see Gavan Daws, *A Dream of Islands: Voyages of Self-Discovery in the South Seas* (New York: Norton, 1980), chap. 3; Wilson Heflin, *Herman Melville's Whaling Years* (Nashville: Vanderbilt University Press, 2004); and Melville's lecture "The South Seas" in Harrison Hayford et al., eds., *The Piazza Tales and Other Prose Pieces, 1839–1860* (Evanston: Northwestern University Press, 1987).

Highly readable general accounts of island geology and biology are supplied by Sherwin Carlquist, *Island Life: A Natural History of the Islands of the World* (New York: Natural History Press, 1965); H. W. Menard, *Islands* (New York: Scientific American, 1986); and David Quammen, *The Song of the Dodo: Island Biogeography in an Age of*

Extinction (New York: Scribner, 1996). Robert H. MacArthur and Edward O. Wilson, *The Theory of Island Biogeography* (Princeton: Princeton University Press, 1967), may be mathematically too complex for general readers but is foundational in its area.

Broader historical issues are discussed in Richard H. Grove, *Green Imperialism: Colonial Expansion, Tropical Island Edens and the Origins of Environmentalism, 1600–1800* (a crucial study, though its focus lies mainly outside the Pacific); N. Jardine, J. A. Secord, and E. C. Spary, eds., *Cultures of Natural History* (Cambridge: Cambridge University Press, 1996); G. S. Rousseau and Roy Porter, eds., *The Ferment of Knowledge: Studies in the Historiography of Eighteenth-Century Science* (Cambridge: Cambridge University Press, 1980); and Barbara Maria Stafford's monumental and opulent *Voyage into Substance: Art, Science, Nature, and the Illustrated Travel Account, 1760–1840* (Cambridge, MA: MIT Press, 1984).

Popular accounts of scientific—and "scientific"—travels include L. D. Brongersma and G. F. Venema, *To the Mountains of the Stars* (1963), on a Dutch expedition to central New Guinea; L. M. D'Albertis, *New Guinea: What I Did and What I Saw* (1881); Mrs. Edgeworth David, *Funafuti; or Three Months on a Coral Island: An Unscientific Account of a Scientific Expedition* (1899); A. J. A. Douglas and P. H. Johnson, *The South Seas of To-day: Being an Account of the Cruise of the Yacht "St. George" to the South Pacific* (1926); F. H. H. Guillemard, *The Cruise of the "Marchesa" to Kamschatka and New Guinea* (1889); A. J. Marshall, *The Black Musketeers: The Work and Adventures of a Scientist on a South Sea Island at War and in Peace* (1937); Oliver Sacks, *The Island of the Colour-Blind* (1996); Octavius C. Stone, *A Few Months in New Guinea* (1880); and Charles Morris Woodford, *A Naturalist among the Head-Hunters* (1890).

5
"How Many Adams Must We Admit?"
The Varieties of Man

When Quirós approached the New Hebrides in April 1606, he responded to the welcoming signs made by the Islanders and sent a boat upriver to meet them. "Our people saw on the banks a number of hogs resembling those of *Spain*," he recorded, "and many inhabitants, which, to our great surprize, were of three different colours. Some of them were altogether black, others very white, with red beards and hair, and a third sort were mulattoes which seemed to indicate that this country must be vastly extensive." His eighteenth-century English editor added a footnote to explain Quirós' deduction: "It appears impossible to account for this diversity of colour, on the common principles assigned for it; for here are three different colours in one and the same climate, and two (the white and black) totally unmixed" (Callander, 2:157–158).

We saw in Chapter 2 that the "Noble Savage" was in part a response to late-seventeenth- and early-eighteenth-century perplexity about the new varieties of humanity Europeans encountered through explorations like Quirós'. Europeans were sure they were superior, by virtue of their religion, but no attempt was made to account systematically for the differences between themselves and the savages beyond the pale. Sixteenth- and seventeenth-century ideas of savagery "were not yet racist in the nineteenth-century sense of the term because they were not based on an explicit doctrine of genetic or biological inequality" (Fredrickson, 7). Indeed a central religious belief held Westerners of the time back from any such doctrine. "If they are human," St. Augustine had said, "they descend from Adam" (quoted in Stepan, 1), and few individuals dared to challenge the authority of the church on this issue:

"How many Adams must we admit?" in the title of this chapter is from William Lawrence, *Lectures on Physiology, Zoology, and the Natural History of Man,* 9th edn. (London: Henry G. Bohn, 1848), 166.

"Orthodox teaching was that all men were biologically distinct from animals and descended from a common stock, differences of colour being merely the result of physical environment—climate, food, soil, or, on some interpretations, excessive body-painting. Polygenism, the concept of different human species, was heretical and 'atheistic'; it was embraced only by the most isolated and heterodox thinkers" (Thomas 1983: 135).

But whereas the Bible laid down the law of monogenism (descent from one stock originating in Adam), it also left other things open for interpretation. Two events in particular had muddied the waters of the descent of man. First, one of Adam's sons (Cain) had murdered the other (Abel) and been sent wandering for his pains with a curse on his head—"a fugitive and a vagabond shalt thou be in the earth" (Genesis 4:12). Then Noah's flood had wiped out all humanity except Noah and his children, including his sons Shem, Ham, and Japheth. In due course Ham's line, too, had been found wanting and had been sentenced to be "servant of servants" to his brethren (Genesis 9:25). The possibility existed, therefore, that other races had been out there for millennia. "Johan Boemus, a German Hebraic scholar, argued as early as 1521 that all barbarous peoples descended from Ham, while all civilized men were the issue of Shem and Japheth" (Fredrickson, 10). Others were even more ingenious. The seventeenth-century scholar Isaac de la Peyrère argued on grounds of internal inconsistency in the biblical account that there had been several creations and that only the Jewish people had been destroyed in the Flood. In his *Theory of the Earth* (1611) Thomas Burnett proposed that America had been populated by an entirely nonbiblical race, right outside God's creation.

This discussion set the scene for scientific or quasi-scientific consideration of the sources of racial difference in that Boemus' position is still monogenist and historical, whereas Peyrère's and Burnett's was polygenist and absolute. For Boemus all men had been created equal and had since diverged; for the polygenists the races of humanity had been separate species since their inception. Some found examples of racial diversity from travelers' accounts and adduced polygenism as the only possible explanation (Thomas 1983: 136). Still, "any effort to distinguish among the 'races' of mankind on either anatomical, physiological, or cultural grounds was relatively negligible" (Hodgen, 213). It was the eighteenth century, therefore, that was to become "the cradle of modern racism" (Mosse, 1). "The scientific revolution of the sixteenth and seventeenth centuries," Nancy Stepan writes,

> had been primarily a revolution of physics and astronomy. Not until the late eighteenth and early nineteenth centuries did the biological and human sciences begin to undergo a comparable revolution. A science of human races could develop only when the entire globe had been explored, some knowledge of the entire range of human types gathered, and this knowledge evaluated for its accuracy. . . . Only with the development of comparative anatomy could the variation found within the human species be compared in detail with the variation found within and between other animal species. (Stepan, ix, xiii)

Until such a time, the ground was held by a mass of the orthodox, on the one hand, and a small but vocal band of free-thinking intellectuals—like the Scotsman James Monboddo, Lord Kames, and the Frenchman Voltaire—on the other.

In the middle of the eighteenth century respectable science was still dominated by monogenists like Linnaeus; what was new was the sophistication of the classificatory schemes such scientists were beginning to devise. Linnaeus arranged modern humans into four groups:

> AMERICAN: copper-coloured, choleric, erect. Paints self. Regulated by custom.
> EUROPEAN: fair, sanguine, brawny. Covered with close vestments. Governed by laws.
> ASIATIC: sooty, melancholy, rigid. Covered with loose garments. Governed by opinions.
> AFRICAN: black, phlegmatic, relaxed. Anoints himself with grease. Governed by caprice. (quoted in Hodgen, 425)

Linnaeus' scheme was nothing if not systematic. To each variety is accorded its color, psychological characteristic (or "humor"), stature, mode of clothing or decoration, and system of governance (or lack of it). The central issue was whether such characteristics were permanent or contingent. Monogenists typically argued that humanity was one species diversifed by the conditions in which it found itself and that, furthermore, the varieties merged into one another to form a continuous spectrum. The philosopher Montesquieu may not have been the originator of ethnic environmentalism, but *The Spirit of the Laws* (1748) provided massive intellectual support for it. For Montesquieu, temperature explained almost all the differences between the nervous and energetic European and the lackadaisical African: human beings were simply "more vigorous in cold climates" (Montesquieu, 231). Montesquieu's contemporary Buffon made the case with maximum emphasis. "Upon the whole," he wrote,

> every circumstance concurs in proving, that mankind are not composed of species essentially different from each other; that, on the contrary, there was originally but one species, who, after multiplying and spreading over the whole surface of the earth, have undergone various changes by influence of climate, food, mode of living, epidemic diseases, and the mixture of dissimilar individuals; that, at first, these changes were not so conspicuous, and produced only individual varieties; that these varieties become . . . more general, more strongly marked, and more permanent by the continual action of the same causes; that they are transmitted from generation to generation . . . ; and that, lastly, as they were originally produced by a train of external and accidental causes, and have only been perpetuated by time and the constant operation of these causes, it is probable that they will gradually disappear, or at least that they will differ from what they are at present, if the causes which

produced them should cease, or if their operation should be varied by other circumstances and combinations. (Buffon, 1:286)

For Buffon, white was "the primitive [i.e., originary] colour of nature, which may be varied by climate, by food and by manners to yellow, brown, and black" (Buffon, 1:280). Thus the tripartite racial scheme of the sixteenth century (European, Chinese, "Ethiopian") gave way to a four-leaved arrangement: European, Asian, American, and African.

Linnaeus and Buffon between them prepared the way for the first "explicit doctrine of genetic or biological inequality," set out by Johann Friedrich Blumenbach in a series of publications between 1775 and 1795. Blumenbach may have felt "that the Negro, like everyone else, was created in the image of God and therefore should not be treated brutally" (Mosse, 14); he may have believed that "when the matter is thoroughly considered, you see that all do run into one another, and that one variety of mankind does so sensibly pass into the other, that you cannot mark out the limits between them" (Blumenbach, 98–99); but what he brought to the science of race was comparative anatomy. It was at a crude stage—and Blumenbach complained unceasingly about the shortcomings of the anatomical specimens available for him to study—but it effectively inaugurated the science of physical anthropology.

It is no coincidence that material from the South Seas furthered Blumenbach's break with the past. The 1775 edition of his treatise "On the Natural Variety of Mankind" listed four varieties of man as Linnaeus had done. The 1795 edition contained an introduction taking the form of a letter to Joseph Banks:

> After your three years' voyage round the world, illustrious Sir, when a more accurate knowledge of the nations who are dispersed far and wide over the islands of the Pacific Ocean had been obtained by the cultivators of natural history and anthropology, it became very clear that the Linnaean division of mankind could no longer be adhered to; for which reason I . . . ceased like others to follow that illustrious man, and had no hesitation in arranging the varieties of man according to the truth of nature, the knowledge of which we owe principally to your industry and most careful observation. (Blumenbach, 150)

Blumenbach accordingly outlined a fivefold scheme: Caucasian, Mongolian, Ethiopian, American, and Malay.

So we find history repeating itself: the "wealth of anomaly" thrown up by the Southern Ocean in general and Cook's voyages in particular revealed a "poverty of theory" of just the kind examined in the previous chapter, and students of humankind struggled to make endless amounts of shading-off consistent with separate species. Did the new discoveries support either side of the argument about Creation, and if so, which? "There are but two ways of accounting for this great diversity in the human frame and constitution," Charles White wrote: "1. To suppose that the diversity, great as it is, might be produced from one pair, by the slow operation of natural causes. 2. Or to suppose that different species were originally created with those distinctive marks which they still retain" (White, 131). Both options had problems. The second was theologically heterodox, but it also failed to explain certain things. If the species were separate, how could they interbreed? Polygenists went to great pains to prove that "mulattoes" and others were, if not sterile, then at least reproductively weak or that "domesticated breeds" like humankind acted differently in this regard to wild ones. Monogenists also confronted intellectual dilemmas. If peoples responded to their surroundings as Buffon argued, why was it that the Dutchmen of the Cape of Good Hope were still as fair as Dutchmen back home, and blacks living in Europe showed no signs in themselves or their offspring of growing pale? Why was it that pictures from earliest recorded human time—the Egyptian era, for example—showed white, brown, and black people in existence way back then, already completely distinct?

In due course Blumenbach's studies on skulls would produce Camper's infamous "facial angle," from brow to chin, which put ancient Greek sculptures at the top of the racial tree and black Africans at the bottom. Camper would be followed by Anders Retzius, who "devised a simple formula to express the ratio of the length to the width of the head (the cephalic index)": "long and narrow heads were thought to be especially beautiful and a mark of the superior European" (Mosse, 28). Such scientific developments were used to enforce a racial preconception; but men like Blumenbach were still children of the Enlightenment. They firmly believed white Europeans to have a head start in the race to civilization, but that did not mean other groups were condemned to utter darkness. Humankind was in a historical process of development, and Enlightenment optimism welcomed the fact. "Belief in progress and its premise of the unity of mankind, drawn from Christianity," Robert Nisbet suggests, "made it possible to convert perceived heterogeneity into a conceptualized homogeneity: the homogeneity of a singly, temporally ordered progression of all peoples in the world from the simplest to the most advanced" (Nisbet, 149). Every newly encountered group could be shown its place in the scale of human progress, and all groups were moving up the scale toward civilization.

A reaction to Enlightenment beliefs was not slow in coming, in this field as in practically all others. "By 1850," as Nancy Stepan puts it, "racial science was far less universalistic, egalitarian and humanistic in its outlook than it had been in 1800. A fundamental re-orientation had in fact taken place" (Stepan, 1). As early as 1813 the monogenist English historian of race James Cowles Prichard had had to come to terms with this reaction. "Prichard turned to his *Researches into the Physical History of Man*," George Stocking writes in his introduction to that work, "at a historical moment which coincided with the end of a major phase in the European discovery of the rest of the world."

> In the context of this explosion of data, zoological taxonomy was undergoing revolutionary changes, which involved among other things the frequent dis-

crimination of species that had previously been regarded as one. At the same time, data on the physical, linguistic, and cultural varieties of man were also rapidly accumulating, and the physical organization of man himself had begun to be studied from a comparative point of view. A number of the scholars who engaged in the latter study were arguing that blacks were markedly dissimilar and inferior to Europeans, either in terms of the traditional notion of the Great Chain of Being, or in terms of the heterodox idea that all mankind was not descended from the same pair. In the context of all the foregoing, the possibility that there was more than one species of mankind demanded serious scientific consideration. (Prichard, xlvii)

The abandonment of Enlightenment attitudes is made painfully clear in passing from Blumenbach to his successor in comparative anatomy and palaeontology, Georges Cuvier, for whom blacks were "the most degraded race among men, whose forms approach nearest to those of the inferior animals, and whose intellect has not yet arrived at the establishment of any regular form of government, nor at anything which has the least appearance of systematic knowledge" (Cuvier, 164). Two years after Cuvier's *Essay on the Theory of the Earth* appeared in English, the surgeon William Lawrence, in his lectures on the natural history of humans, assured his audience that the superiority of whites was "the offspring of natural differences" as opposed to those "external causes" argued for by Buffon (Lawrence, 330–331).

Lawrence was a monogenist; but one could certainly be a monogenist and a racist, as his own example shows: "if it be allowed that all men are of the same *species*," Lawrence said, "it does not follow that they all descend from the same *family*" (Lawrence, 352; italics added). Robert Knox was also a monogenist, but he reminisced, "Whilst still young I readily perceived that the philosophic formula of Blumenbach led to no results: explained nothing: investigated no causes" (Knox, 19). Investigated no *consequences* might have been a more intellectually honest expression, since for Knox the "dark races of men" were simply doomed. Cuvier, according to Knox, "neither admitted nor denied the unity of man; to me the unity of man appears evident; but if so, whence come the dark races? and why is it that destiny seems to have marked them for destruction?" (Knox, 146–147). Crocodile tears barely under control, Knox was forced to watch "the old tragedy again, the fair races of man against the dark races; the strong against the feeble; the united against those who knew not how to place even a sentinel; the progressists against those who stand still—who could not or would not progress. Look all over the globe, it is always the same; the dark races stand still, the fair progress" (Knox, 149). In the mid-nineteenth century, intellectual simpletons like Victoria's consort Prince Albert could still talk of "that great end to which indeed all history points, the realisation of the unity of mankind" when opening the Great Exhibition of 1851 (quoted in Buckley, 35). And the Aborigines Protection Society, founded in London in 1863, did choose as its motto "Ab uno sanguine" (Latin: "from one blood"). But the pace was being made by men like Joseph Arthur de Gobineau, whose *Essay on the Inequality of Human Races* appeared in 1853 and mourned the inevitable loss of racial purity by dilution, or by Robert Chambers, a Buffonesque believer in environmental factors, whose sensational *Vestiges of the Natural History of Creation* (1844) took a more optimistic though equally chilling view: "The inorganic has one final comprehensive law, Gravitation. The organic, the other great department of mundane things, rests in like manner on one law, and that is,—Development" (Chambers, 360). In Gobineau's hands the dark races were a threat; in Chambers' they were an irrelevance.

The key addition here was Darwinism. Darwin's "non-biblical monogenism" (Mosse, 33) made polygenism an intellectual cul-de-sac by providing its opponents with vast amounts of evolutionary time over which humankind had diversified. But what Darwin took away with one hand, he gave with the other, for his idea of the survival of the fittest gave massive amounts of ammunition to the race science of his day. As George Fredrickson puts it: "If Darwinism undermined the theory that blacks were at a competitive disadvantage because they were created a few thousand years ago as a permanently inferior species, it did not foreclose the possibility that they had evolved through a process of natural selection . . . into a variety of the genus homo which stood . . . far below the whites in capacities necessary for survival and progress" (Fredrickson, 232). Darwin would not commit himself to race science in so many words, but he knew his ideas helped sustain it. Traveling in New Zealand, he noted, "The varieties of man seem to act upon each other in the same way as the different species of animals; the stronger always extirpates the weaker" (quoted in Merivale, 541).

The Pacific islands contributed in a number of ways to the race debate. At first, the region gave support to liberal monogenism. Polygenism thrived on the three-race model of human variety (European, Asian, and African), though it could cope with four- or five-race models at a pinch. But the South Seas threw up more varieties than had previously been dreamed of. The Melanesians were different from the Micronesians, who were different from the Polynesians, who were different from the Australians and the Tasmanians. How many separate creations would be needed to account for all these? Moreover, men like Johann Reinhold Forster testified in detail to an infinite gradation *between* these groups, which made a species-based explanation hard to confirm. This gradation also gave support to "natural," "environmental," or "evolutionary" diversity, as opposed to specific distinction. But the South Seas in time also supported racial Darwinism. The *species* might be the same, but the *races* were in competition, and nowhere else on earth did native races appear to disappear as quickly as they did in the Pacific, "unable to withstand contact with Europeans, shrivelling up and drying like a forest flower when exposed to the glare of the sun" (Johnston et al., 1:66.)

The South Seas were caught up in the detail of racial arguments as well as the broad brushwork. For early-nineteenth-century missionaries, for example, "the more 'advanced' savages, including Polynesians, were descendants of Shem, and the allegedly more 'primitive,' such as the Papuans and the Australian Aborigines, were the sons and daughters of Ham" (Howe 1993: 249). The drama of Noah could play itself out regionally as well as globally. Blumenbachian controversies of classification could also illustrate themselves in miniature in the Pacific. "The people of New Zealand," according to one mid-nineteenth-century traveler,

> belong to one of the two great and distinct races of the human family inhabiting the vast ocean of the Pacific. The dark-coloured variety, termed the Austral negroes, have a skin approaching in colour to that of the African races, with hair occasionally curly, and in some cases woolly; their skulls are of bad proportions, exhibiting a preponderating development of the occipital region; their language consists of a variety of different tongues and dialects; their social relations are in an inferior condition, and they occupy a very low grade in the human family.

By contrast to luckless Melanesians like these, the Polynesian Maori "have superior faculties, both moral and physical; and with some of them a form of government, and domestic and social regulations have attained a very advanced state" (Angas 1847: 303–304). For another writer the Polynesians could be seen as the Caucasians of the Pacific, the Micronesians as its Mongolians, and the Melanesians as its "Ethiopians"—as if the southern hemisphere truly was a replication of the north (Guppy, 99). So racial divisions laid down (as we shall see) by Forster and Dumont d'Urville persisted wholly unrevised for decades, as had the stereotypes of the medieval and Renaissance eras. The Earl of Pembroke was joking when he said, "The pleasantest forms of the human fossil we have ever met with have been in the South Seas" (Pembroke and Kingsley, 202), though a missionary ethnographer like William Ellis could see that the Pacific and the mystery of its coming to be populated were of more than strictly paleontological interest: "The vast extent of the geographical surface covered by the race of which they form an integral portion, the analogy of character, the identity of language, &c., the remote spots and solitary clusters which they occupy in the vast expanse of surrounding water, render the source whence they were derived, one of the mysteries connected with the history of our species" (Ellis 1829, 2:37).

For writers not directly caught up in the science of race, however, the Pacific could provide analogies and examples that undermined that science directly—in particular Western complacencies about the European's place at the top of the cultural and evolutionary trees. "When Britain was first visited by the Phoenicians," the editors of Cook's voyages suggested, "the inhabitants were painted savages, much less civilized than those of Tongataboo, or Otaheite; and it is not impossible, but that our late voyages may, in process of time, spread the blessings of civilization amongst the numerous islanders of the Pacific Ocean, and be the means of abolishing their abominable repasts, and almost equally abominable sacrifices" (Cook and King, 1:vii). An enlightened note of qualified superiority is struck here: the blessings of civilization are blessings, but they are not confined to a particular group in perpetuity—for where are the Phoenicians now? (We might recall Bougainville in

Chapter 2 noting that, when Julius Caesar first invaded Britain, the islanders there were as savage as any Tahitian.) A Victorian historian celebrating the longevity of the Catholic church could be even more speculative: "She was great and respected before the Saxon had set foot in Britain, before the Frank had passed the Rhine, when Grecian eloquence still flourished in Antioch, when idols were still worshipped in the temple of Mecca. And she may still exist in undiminished vigour when some traveller from New Zealand shall, in the midst of a vast solitude, take his stand on a broken arch of London Bridge to sketch the ruins of St. Pauls" (Macaulay, 535–536).

But it was an eighteenth-century Frenchman who rediscovered, albeit reluctantly, the voice and attitude of a racial relativist like Montaigne. "If we pass . . . from one part of the earth to another," Charles Fleurieu wrote:

> we shall discover, at every step, that the moral man offers to the meditation of the philosopher differences more striking than those which he observes in the physical man: in the latter, the difference most characterised is that of the *white* from the *black,* of the inhabitant of Scandinavia from the negro of Senegal; but this transition in the species is not sudden: and if we travel over the known countries of the globe, we shall pass from one colour to another by imperceptible shades: it is otherwise with the moral man: can there, for instance, be found intermediate shades between the conjugal fidelity imposed by our manners, and the prostitution honoured among the tribes disseminated over the Great Ocean? There are then virtues and vices, as there is a beauty and a deformity, of locality and opinion: change latitude, deformity changes into beauty; vice is changed into virtue.

"I do not say that it is right that this is so," Fleurieu pointed out in a footnote, "but I say that facts seem to prove that this is: I have not undertaken to paint men as they ought to be, but as they are" (Fleurieu 1801, 1:152).

from Johann Reinhold Forster, *Observations Made during a Voyage round the World* (1778)

Joseph Banks is often regarded as the leading scientist to have sailed with James Cook. In fact Johann Reinhold Forster (1729–1798)—who sailed on Cook's second voyage of 1772–1775—has a greater claim to the title, and the *Observations* is a classic to set alongside Cook's journals themselves. Bougainville, Forster, and others thought they saw two races of men living on Tahiti: one handsome, civilized, and akin to the Europeans themselves (the "Arees"); the other darker and more primitive (the "Towtows"). This distinction was in fact the result only of normal human diversity and social difference (servants spending more time in the sun, for example), but it set Forster thinking in ways that were influential throughout the century to come.

from Chapter Six, section III On the Causes of the Difference in the
Races of Men in the South Seas, their Origin and Migrations

If all mankind be of one species, and sprung from the same original stem, how then does it happen that the negroe of Senegal is so different from the inhabitant of the North of Europe? What occasions the inhabitants of O-Taheitee to be so much distinguished from the Mallicolese? We have hinted before, that these two varieties of men in the South-Seas, are descended from two distinct races. This is not decisive, and only leads us further into the same discussions, and requires us to shew what causes have produced these two distinct races or varieties of men?

The question cannot be discussed unless we consider the subject under various heads. The differences are either observed in the organic part of man, or they respect his mental and moral faculties: of the last we shall treat at large in subsequent sections; at present we intend to confine ourselves to the corporeal varieties, consisting in, 1st, colour; 2d, size; 3d, form and habit; and 4th, peculiar defects or excesses, or modifications in certain parts of the human body.

First, The colour of the human body depends no doubt upon these three great causes: 1st, exposure to the air; 2d, the influence of the sun; and 3d, some particular circumstances in the mode of living. From the best enquiries set on foot by anatomists, it appears, that all the difference of colour lies in the human skin, and especially in the outer-integument called the *cuticle,* which again is considered by them under the two denominations of *Epidermis* and *Malpighi's reticular membrane.* In white people, the *Epidermis* is a very thin, pellucid, indurated lamella, transmitting the colour of the reticular membrane immediately lying under it, which is a white or colourless, viscous or slimy substance. [. . .] And in negroes, the late ingenious Mr. *Meckel* discovered the reticulum of Malpighi to be black; but the medullar substance of the brain, the pineal gland, and the spinal marrow, together with the *plexus nervi optici,* he found grey and blackish. Others have found the blood of negroes to be deeper coloured than that of white people. The ancients knew that the spermatic liquor of negroes is of a dark hue, and this curious observation is confirmed by moderns. In a word, we find, that many of the fluids in negroes are tinged darker, and such of their solids as are of a tender and delicate texture, are likewise coloured blackish. *Meckel* suspects, that the blueish liquor which colours the medullary substance of the brain, and so easily evaporates in negroes, contributes towards the dark complexion of the mucous membrane of the cuticle, being secreted by the cutaneous nerves into the viscous reticular substance.

But let us now investigate the causes of this phaenomenon in negroes; we have already indicated the three most striking causes; the *exposure to the air,* is undoubtedly one of the most powerful: for do we not see this daily proved in our own climate; our ladies, and other people who are little exposed to the action of the air, have a fair complexion; whereas the common labourers are brown and tawny; nay our bodies furnish us with sufficient proofs; those parts which are constantly covered, are fair and delicate, but the hands being constantly exposed to the action of the air, acquire a darker hue. The negroes live in a climate which permits them to wear little or no covering at all; accordingly, we really find all the negroes naked, or very slightly covered, which undoubtedly must increase the black colour of their skin. The Taheiteans, the fairest of all the islanders in the South Sea, go almost constantly dressed and covered. The inhabitants of Tanna, New Caledonia, and Mallicollo, on the contrary are always naked, and exposed to the air, and therefore infinitely blacker than the first.

The *operation of the Sun* is undoubtedly another great cause of the dark hue in negroes; we find that nations in the same proportion, as they approach the equator, likewise become darker coloured; however, this observation is not quite universal, and ought to be modified under many circumstances. Inhabitants of islands are seldom so black as those of great continents; in Africa, between the tropics, the Easterly winds prevail the most; and as in Abyssinia these winds come over a large ocean, where they are mitigated and cooled in their passage, the inhabitants of that country are not so black as those about Senegal, which is situated in the broadest part of Africa, and where the Easterly wind having passed over the burning sands of the immense continent, is become infinitely more fiery and parching than in any other part. A higher exposure above the surface of the sea, makes a great difference in the temperature of the air; the inhabitants of Quito in Peru, though living under the line, are by no means black or swarthy. The vicinity of the sea, and its refreshing and gently fanning breezes, contribute greatly to mitigate the power of a tropical Sun. This cause cannot be applied to the difference of colour in the Taheiteans and the Mallicolese, as both nations enjoy the same advantage.

But the *peculiar modes of living* likewise, strongly co-operate with the above causes, in producing the many changes of colour in the human species. The Taheiteans are constantly cleanly, and practise frequent ablutions, encreasing by this simple elegance the fairness of their complexions, though they live within the tropics. The New Zeelanders living in the temperate zone from 34° to 47° South latitude, are more tawny, which may be in part ascribed to their uncleanliness, abhorrence of bathing, and sitting exposed to smoak and nastiness in their dirty cottages.

Secondly, The *size* of the natives of Taheitee, and all the isles peopled by the same race, certainly distinguishes them from the tribes in Mallicollo; however this difference is not so general in these nations, as to extend even to Tanna and New Caledonia, where we found many very tall and athletic persons. But the chiefs in the Society Isles, again distinguish themselves from the rest of the inhabitants, by their tall stature and corpulence. According to the doctrines of those who are skilled in philosophy, growth and size depend chiefly upon climate, food, and exercise.

The *climate* is either warm or cold. Heat adds to the action of the heart a stimulus, and accelerates its pulsation; and since in a warm climate, the solids

"HOW MANY ADAMS MUST WE ADMIT?"

are more relaxed, than in a cold one, the impulse of the blood in the arteries finds less resistance, and therefore more powerfully expands the whole frame of the body; because, every function of the parts and secretion of the liquids, is promoted with greater vigour. This we find conformable to experience, for in hot climates mankind grows more powerfully, and attains earlier maturity and puberty. On the other hand, cold assuages the stimulus, and constricts the fibres, which naturally throws the whole system into a torpor or languid state. The heart does not act powerfully enough to carry on the functions with that vigour which is required, not only to accelerate growth, but likewise to overcome the greater resistance caused by the rigid state of all the solid parts. We find in consequence of these principles, the poor inhabitants of Tierra del Fuego, a small race of people, though descended from tribes, who, on the continent of South America, in a milder climate, and more happy circumstances, are very tall and athletic.

Food another great article, both as to *quantity* and *quality,* exerts its powerful influence upon size and growth. [. . .]

Exercise in a moderate degree, is absolutely necessary to give the various part of the human frame, strength and due consistence. [. . .] The inhabitants of the South Sea isles, are by their lively temper in their early age prevented from being inactive. The happiness of their climate, the fertility of their soil, the luxuriance of vegetation, and the fewness of their wants, also make too great an exertion unnecessary: it is therefore *moderate exercise* which, among many other happy circumstances, contribute to form these tall and beautiful figures, which are so common among them.

Thirdly, Form and *habit,* are likewise subject to the same influence of climate, food, and exercise; this spares us the trouble of repeating the above mentioned arguments: for it is evident that heat dries the limbs and whole frame of body in the Mallicolese, the inhabitants of Easter-Island, the Marquesas, the Low Islands, the Towtows and lower ranks of people in the Society and Friendly Isles, who all go naked, and are much exposed to air and sun: hence, they become thin and slender; for even their bones are not strong, but solid and hard. On the other hand, cold climates give a more soft, spungy and succulent habit of body; which is easily observable in the people of Tierra del Fuego, who are a thick, squat, bony race of men. The New-Zeelanders are likewise in a milder climate, fleshy, boney, and succulent, and the Arees and better sort of people, in the Society and Friendly Isles, who carefully study, and endeavour to keep themselves cool, and avoid as much as possible, an expose to the heat of the sun, are succulent, fleshy, and fat.

Fourthly, The *peculiar defects, or excesses, or modifications of certain parts of the human body* have endemial causes, dependent upon peculiar customs, which sometimes are obvious, but at other times not easily investigated, especially when the observer has not more time to study them, than we had. [. . .]

These are the most remarkable particulars which chiefly form the variety of the two great tribes, observed by us in the South Sea isles; from whence may be inferred the powerful influence of climate, food, and peculiar customs upon the colour, size, habit, and form of body, and certain defects, excesses, or modifications of the parts; but it must be acknowledged at the same time, that the causes here enumerated are not the only ones, and particularly that climate alone does not produce such extraordinary effects; for we find that the Dutch, who have been settled at the Cape of Good Hope, during an uninterrupted course of 120 years, have constantly remained fair and similar to Europeans in every respect; notwithstanding, if we compare them with the Hottentots, the native inhabitants of that part of the world, it appears, that exclusive of the way of living and food, the climate alone cannot occasion this material and striking variety; nay, that even these causes, when united, are not sufficient to produce this effect, as some of the very remote Dutch farmers live almost in the same manner as their neighbours the Hottentots; they have wretched huts, instead of houses; lead a rambling nomadic life, attend their herds and flocks all day long, and live upon milk, the produce of the chace, and the flesh of their cattle; it is therefore evident, that if climate can work any material alteration, it must require an immense period of time to produce it; and as our lives are so short, our historical accounts so imperfect, in regard to the migrations of the human species, and our philosophical observations on the subject, all of a very modern date, it cannot be expected we can speak with precision on the subject.

It must however be observed, that when the fair Northern nations are removed into the hot tropical climates, they themselves and their progeny soon change, and gradually become somewhat more analogous in colour, and other circumstances, to the former inhabitants, whose migration is of so old a date, that no memorial of it is presented; still, however, they may be easily distinguished from these aboriginal tribes: it is likewise true, that nations removed from the vicinity of the line towards the poles, keep their native colour longer without alteration than any other people coming from colder climates, and going to live in hotter regions; but such incidents must always be compared under similar circumstances: for if two Europeans, equally fair, are removed to the same hot climate, and the one is well dressed and avoids, as much as possible, being exposed to the action of the air, and power of the sun; whilst the other finds himself obliged to work in the open air, and has hardly any rags to cover his skin; they will, of natural consequence, become widely different in colour; moreover, if this diversity in the mode of living be kept up for several generations, the character of both must of course become more strikingly different [. . .] but if negroes, and other swarthy tribes, be transplanted into temperate, or nearly cold climates, they do not immediately change, nor do they easily become fairer, but preserve their original complexion for a longer space of time. When they only intermarry in their own race, the change, if any, is imperceptible in their offspring for many generations. I will here only hint, at the probable causes of this phaenomenon; the transition, from being brown in complexion to fair, is, it seems, more difficult, than that from fair to brown; the *Epidermis* admits the beams of the sun and the action of the air, in colouring the *reticulum mucosum* brown; but when once it is coloured, nothing is sufficiently powerful to extract the brown colour; and this seems to be founded in daily experience; a man being perhaps only one day exposed to a powerful sun, shall become strongly tinted with brown; when, to remove this hue, perhaps six or eight months of close confinement, are not sufficient. It seems therefore more and more probable, that the first stamen of an embryo partakes, much of the colour, size, form and habit of the parents; and that two different tribes, having gradually undergone a different round of climates, food, and customs; and coming afterwards at different periods of time, and by different ways, into the same climate, but preserving a different mode of living, and being partly supported by different food, may nevertheless preserve an evident difference in their character, colour, size, form, and habit of body.

If we apply this induction to the two different tribes, whom we found in the South-Sea, it will appear to be highly probable, that they may be descended from two different races of men; and though living in the same climate, or nearly so, might, however, preserve a difference in character, colour, size, form and habit of body; and if I could now prove, by an historical argument, that they really are descended from two different races of men, nothing will be wanting to conviction. [. . .]

If we are desirous of tracing the races of all these islanders back to any continent, or its neighbourhood, we must cast an eye on a map of the South Sea, where we find it bordered to the East by America, to the West by Asia, by the Indian Isles on its North side, and by New Holland to the South. At first sight, it might seem probable, that these tropical isles were originally settled from America, as the Easterly winds are the most prevalent in these seas, and as the small and wretched embarkations of the natives in the South Seas, can hardly be employed in plying to windward. But if we consider the argument more minutely, we find that America itself was not peopled many centuries before its discovery by the Spaniards. There were but two states or kingdoms on this immense continent, that had acquired any degree of population, and made considerable progress in civilization; and they likewise did not originate earlier, than about 300 or 400 years before the arrival of the Spaniards.[1] The rest was occupied by a few straggling families, thinly dispersed over this vast tract of land, so that sometimes not more than 30 or 40 persons, lived in an extent of 100 leagues at very great distances from each other. Again, when the Spaniards discovered some of these islands in the South Sea, a few years only after the discovery of the continent of America, they found them as populous as we have seen them in our days: from whence it appears to be highly improbable, that these isles were peopled from America. If we moreover consult the Mexican, Peruvian, and Chilese vocabularies, and those of other American languages, we find not the most distant, or even accidental similarity between any of the American languages, and those of the South Sea Isles. The colour, features, form, habit of body, and customs of the Americans, and these

---

1. That is, the Aztecs of modern-day Mexico and the Incas of modern-day Peru.

islanders, are totally different; as every one conversant with the subject, will easily discover. Nay, the distances of 600, 700, 800 or even 1000 leagues between the continent of America and the Easternmost of these isles, together with the wretchedness and small size of their vessels, prove, in my opinion, incontestably, that these islanders never came from America.

We must therefore go to the Westward; let us begin with New Holland. All the former navigators, and especially Capt. Cook, in the Endeavour, found this immense continent very thinly inhabited. The diminutive size of its inhabitants, the peculiarity of their customs and habits, their total want of coco-nuts, cultivated plantanes, and hogs, together with the most miserable condition of their huts and boats, prove beyond all doubt, that the South Sea islanders, are not descended from the natives of New Holland. But, what is still more convincing, their language is totally different, as evidently appears from the examination of a vocabulary obligingly communicated to me by Capt. Cook. We have therefore nothing left but to go further to the North, where the South Sea isles are as it were connected with the East Indian isles. Many of these latter are inhabited by two different races of men. In several of the Moluccas is a race of men, who are blacker than the rest, with woolly hair, slender and tall, speaking a peculiar language, and inhabiting the interior hilly parts of the countries; in several isles these people are called ALFOORIES. The shores of these isles are peopled by another nation, whose individuals are swarthy, of a more agreeable form, with curled and long hair, and of a different language, which is chiefly a branch or dialect of the Malayan. In all the Philippines, the interior mountainous parts, are inhabited by a black set of people, with frizzled hair, who are tall, lusty, and very warlike, and speak a peculiar language different from that of their neighbours. But the outskirts towards the sea are peopled with a race infinitely fairer, having long hair, and speaking different languages. [. . .] The former are the more antient inhabitants, and the latter are certainly related to the various tribes of Malays, who had over-run all the East India islands before the arrival of the Europeans in those seas. Their language is likewise in many instances related to that of the Malays. The isle of Formosa or Tai-ovan [Taiwan] has likewise in its interior hilly parts, a set of brown, frizzly haired, broad faced inhabitants; but the shores, especially those to the North, are occupied by the Chinese, who differ even in language from the former. The isles of New Guinea, New Britain, and Nova Hibernia[2] have certainly black complexioned inhabitants, whose manners, customs, habit, force, and character, correspond very much with the inhabitants of the South Sea islands belonging to the second race in Nova Caledonia,[3] Tanna, and Mallicollo; and these blacks in New-Guinea, are probably related to those in the Moluccas and Philippines. The Ladrones, and the new discovered Caroline Islands, contain a set of people very much related to our first race. Their

---

2. "New Ireland" (Latin), neighboring New Britain, north of New Guinea.
3. New Caledonia (Latin: "Scotland"), the great island and French colony due east of Australia.

"HOW MANY ADAMS MUST WE ADMIT?"

size, colour, habit, manners, and customs, seem strongly to indicate this affinity; and they are according to the account of some writers, nearly related in every respect to the *Tagales* in Luçon or Manilla, so that we may now trace the line of migration by a continued line of isles, the greater part of which are not above 100 leagues distant from each other.

We likewise find a very remarkable similarity between several words of the fair tribe of islanders in the South Sea, and some of the Malays. But it would be highly inconclusive from the similarity of a few words, to infer that these islanders were descended from the Malays: for as the Malay contains words found in the Persian, Malabar, Bramanic, Cingalese, Javanese, and Malegass,[4] this should likewise imply, that the nations speaking the above mentioned languages, were the offspring of the Malays, which certainly would be proving too much. I am therefore rather inclined to suppose, that all these dialects preserve several words of a more antient language, which was more universal, and was gradually divided into many languages, now remarkably different. The words therefore of the language of the South Sea isles, which are similar to others in the Malay tongue, prove clearly in my opinion, that the Eastern South Sea isles were originally peopled from the Indian, or Asiatic Northern isles; and that those lying more to the Westward, received their first inhabitants from the neighbourhood of New Guinea.

We have therefore, I apprehend, probable proofs that these islanders came originally from the Indian Asiatic isles, on which we have pointed out two races of inhabitants, such as we found them in the South Sea isles: it should seem therefore, that these two distinct races are descended from the two distinct Indian tribes. If we had good vocabularies of the various languages spoken in these isles, we should then be enabled to trace their original back to a particular tribe. But as we labour under a deficiency in this respect, I have endeavoured in the annexed table to give a general view of many languages, which of course, must confirm my former assertions. I flatter myself with having done as much as could be expected in my situation, and therefore leave the rest to better instructed, and more enlightened ages.

from Chapter Six, section V Various Progress, which the Nations we saw, have made from the Savage State towards Civilization

Previous to other positions, mankind seem not originally to have lived in the extremities of what we commonly call the temperate zones; nor to have chosen these cold, inhospitable climates for their abode. The mild happy climate in, or near the tropics, the rapid growth of animals and vegetables in these places; the facility of procuring food, and shelter against the inclemencies of the weather; the variety and succession of fine and wholesome spontaneous roots and fruit, all lead us to suppose that man was originally settled there. We ought to be confirmed in this idea, by considering that the first nakedness of

---

4. Malabar, a region of India; Brahmanic, pertaining to the priestly caste among Hindus; Sinhalese, the language of Ceylon (now Sri Lanka); Malagasy, Madagascar.

man in a savage state, is by no means calculated to bear the vicissitudes and inclemencies of the Northern and Southern extremities of the *temperate,* or the vigour of the two *frozen* zones; and that if ever men are found settled in these unhappy regions, it has been owing either to chance or cruel necessity.

The inhabitants of the islands in the South Sea, though unconnected with highly civilized nations, are more improved in every respect, as they live more and more distant from the poles. Their food is more varied, and abundant; their habitations more roomy, neat, and adapted to the exigencies of the climate; their garments more elegant, improved, and ingenious; their population is greater; their societies better regulated; their public security against foreign invaders more firmly established; their manners more courteous, elegant, and even refined; their principles of morality better understood, and generally practised; their minds capable of, and open to instruction; they have ideas of a supreme being, of a future state, of the origin of the world; and the whole contributes greatly to increase their happiness, in its natural, moral and social branches, both as individuals, and as a nation. On the contrary, the wretched mortals towards the frozen zone, are the most debased of all human beings, in every respect. Their food is scanty, loathsome, and precarious; their habitations the most miserable huts that can be imagined; their garments rough, and by no means sufficient to screen them against the rigours of the inhospitable climate; their societies thin, and without any mutual ties or affection; exposed to the insults of all invaders, they retreat to the most inhospitable rocks, and appear insensible to all that is great and ingenious; a brutish stupidity is their general characteristic; and whenever they are the strongest, they are treacherous, and act in opposition to all the principles of humanity and hospitality. May we not then infer from the above premises, that man unconnected with highly civilized nations, approaches in more happy climates, nearer to that state of civilization, and happiness, which we enjoy; that human nature is really debased in the savages, who inhabit the frozen extremities of our globe, and that their present situation is as it were, a preternatural state. I wish not to be misunderstood; the happiness which European nations enjoy, and are capable of, becomes, on account of the degeneracy of a few profligate individuals, very much debased, and mixed with the miseries, which are entailed upon our civilized societies, by luxury and vice; if therefore the felicity of several European or Asiatic nations, seem to be inferior to that of some of the nations in the South Sea, it is owing to the above-mentioned causes, since it does not seem to follow, that a high degree of civilization must necessarily lessen, or destroy natural, moral, or social happiness.

I believe the nations inhabiting the frozen extremities of our globe to be degenerated and debased from that original happiness, which the tropical nations more or less enjoy. I was first persuaded into this belief, from the state in which we found the inhabitants of Tierra del Fuego and New Zeeland, and by comparing their situation, with that of their neighbours.

The people on TIERRA DEL FUEGO, about Christmas Bay, were not numerous; and if we are to judge from the general appearance of the country, and from the numbers seen by other navigators, there cannot be a great population in these inhospitable climates. These were the Southernmost lands, wherein we found human creatures, who not only appeared to us to be wretched, but to be themselves conscious of their own misery, and forlorn situation; several boats, with natives, came to our ship, and none of them had any other garment than a piece of Sealskin, which did not reach so far as to cover half their buttocks, and came barely over the shoulders; their head and feet, and whole body, were exposed to a degree of cold in the midst of summer, which appeared to us sharp, though we were well clad, having found the temperature of the air generally from 46° to 50° of Fahrenheits thermometer; neither the men nor the women, had any thing to cover their privities; their bodies smelled highly offensive from the rancid train oil which they frequently use, and the rotten seals flesh which they eat; and I am of opinion, their whole frame of body is thoroughly penetrated with this disagreeable smell. Their habitations consist of a few sticks, tied together, so as to form a kind of shell, for a low, open, roundish hut; they join the neighbouring shrubs together, and cover the whole with some wisps of dry grass, and here and there a few pieces of seals-skin are tied over; one fifth or sixth of the whole circumference, is left open for a door, and the fire place; their utensils and furniture, which we had an opportunity of observing, consisted of a basket, a kind of mat-satchel, a bone-hook, fixed to a long stick of a light kind of wood, for disengaging the shellfish from the rocks, a rude bow and some arrows. [. . .] Their food, beside the above-mentioned seals, are shell-fish, which they broil and devour; they were shivering, and appeared much affected with the cold: they looked at the ship and all its parts with a stupidity and indolence, which we had not hitherto observed in any of the nations in the South Seas, had all an empty stare in their countenances, and expressed hardly any desires or wishes to possess any thing which we offered, and thought it might become desirable to them; they were destitute of all convenience or ease, shewed no signs of joy or happiness, and seemed to be insensible to all natural, moral, or social feelings, and enjoyments, and occupied with nothing but their wants and wretchedness. [. . .]

DUSKY BAY is the Southernmost place on New-Zeeland, we touched at; the latitude of the place where the astronomers observatory was fixed, being 45° 47' South.[5] We found this bay, which has several leagues of extent branching out into spacious inlets, stocked with many kinds of fowl, crowded with prodigious quantities of the best flavoured fish, and its rocks covered with numerous herds of seals; all which abundance would naturally invite people, who solely subsist upon fish and fowl, to settle here, and to become very numerous. But we found only three families in all this bay: their habitations consisted of a few sticks stuck into the ground, and meanly covered with flags and rushes: they had no idea of cultivating or planting; their garments were such as covered the upper part of the body, and left the legs and part of the

---

5. Cook visited Dusky Sound, on the extreme southwest of South Island, from 26 March to 11 May 1773.

thighs exposed, and they squatted down to shelter them under their clothes, which commonly were remarkably uncleanly; and the families settled here, seemed to be independent of each other. When we came to QUEEN CHARLOTTE'S SOUND,[6] we found on the shores of that equally spacious water, four or five hundred people, and some of them paid deference to several old men, as *Tringoboohee, Goobaya,* and *Teiràtoo,* who were it seems their chiefs. Fish were in this place equally abundant, but of a sort inferior in taste and goodness; wild fowl, especially of the aquatic kind, were scarcer, and we saw but one seal, though our two ships resided here at different times. The people were clad in the same manner as in the former place; their habitations, especially on their hippas or strong holds, were better, cleanlier, and lined on the inside with reeds; they had no plantations, but they knew the names of *Tarro* and *Goomalla,* which the inhabitants of the tropical isles give to the *Arum esculentum* and the *Convolvulus Batatas.*[7] This, in my opinion, evidently proves that they were descended from a tribe, who had cultivation, and who had lost or neglected this way of supporting themselves, either because they found greater plenty of fish, and animal food; or because they fled their country in so precipitate a manner, that they could not take any roots with them; or lastly, from mere Supineness and indolence; for we saw them eat fern roots, a very insipid, coarse, and wretched food. Whatever may be the real cause, the climate would certainly allow of planting *eddoes*[8] and *potatoes,* being in 41° 5' South latitude; and it is evident that the natives were degenerated and debased from a more perfect and more happy state. The inhabitants of the Northern isle, who came off to us, had better boats, and were clad in finer garments; but we could not make many observations on their situation as we saw them only in a transitory manner; however, the published accounts of the preceding voyage, and those which I was favoured with by Capt. Cook, agree in this, that they had very extensive, regular, well-cultivated plantations, inclosed in very firm and neat fences, made of reeds; that they acknowledged the authority of a chief in a district of 80 leagues at least, where our people found justice administered by inferior chiefs; and that they seemed to live in that district in greater security and more comfortably than in any other part of the isle.

The natural inferences drawn from these data, seem to prove, that mankind being more numerous in or near the tropics, and very thinly scattered towards the cold extremities of our globe, the human species was originally settled in or near the tropics, and from thence spread towards the extremities. Secondly, the instances given here, evince likewise the truth of what we advanced before, viz. that the human species, when unconnected with the highly civilized nations, is always found more debased in its physical, mental, moral and social capacity, in proportion as it is removed from the tropical regions. It seems therefore probable that savage nations in cold climates, con-

---

6. On Cook Strait, on the extreme north of South Island; visited 18 May to 7 June 1773.

7. Taro and sweet potato: both edible root crops widespread in the Pacific.

8. Or coco yam, within the same botanical family as the taro.

"HOW MANY ADAMS MUST WE ADMIT?"

tract a harshness or rigidity in their fibres and frame of body, which causes sluggishness, indolence and stupidity of mind; their hearts grow insensible to the dictates of virtue, honor and conscience, and they become incapable of any attachment, affection or endearment.

Let us now turn our eyes to O-Taheitee, the queen of tropical isles, and its happy inhabitants, and extend our view to all the Society and Friendly Isles. Though we found the population to be very great in proportion to the extent of country, yet we were led to believe that a much greater number of inhabitants might be supported on these islands, and in ages to come might be found there, if no accidents should happen, or unless such manners and regulations should be introduced as tend to check or stop the progress of population. The fertility of the soil on those extensive plains, and numerous valleys, the rapid vegetation and constant succession of coco-nuts, bread-fruit, apples, bananas, plantanes, eddoes, potatoes, yams, and many other fine fruits and roots; the regular division of lands in private property, well and neatly fenced in; the particular care shewn by the inhabitants to the dogs, hogs, and fowls, which are their only domestic animals; the convenience and neatness of their houses and boats, their ingenious contrivances for fishing; the taste and elegance shewn in many of their utensils and houshold furniture; their dresses so well adapted to the climate, so curiously varied both in their texture and dyes; their delicacy of manners, true courtesy and politeness; their chearful and open behaviour; their goodness of heart, and hospitality; their knowledge of plants, birds, fishes, shells, insects, vermes,[9] and all the branches of animated nature; their acquaintance with the stars, and their motion, with the seasons and winds; their poetry, songs, dances, and dramatic performances; their theogony and cosmogony, the various ranks and regulations of civil society; their establishments for defence, and for repelling and retaliating injuries offered to their state; all these conspire to prove that they are infinitely superior to the before mentioned tribes; and even point out the true causes of their greater happiness. The climate certainly contributes a great deal to their felicity, and might be justly deemed the main source of it. However, as we found farther to the West, new isles in the same happy climate, and in the same latitude, the inhabitants of which, were nevertheless, infinitely inferior in point of civilization, and more defective in the enjoyments of real happiness; it seems to follow, that there must be, beside the above-mentioned, some other cause of this remarkable circumstance. [. . .]

We have represented the savages living in the frozen extremities of our globe, as the most debased, degenerated, and wretched: and it is nevertheless, that though their condition appear to us forlorn, and they themselves be in our eyes the outcast of the human species; they do not think so meanly of their own situation; nay, so far from supposing themselves unhappy; they rather glory in the advantages of their way of living, and none of them would exchange his cold climate for that is more temperate, his wretched hut for a

---

9. Plural of the Latin *vermis,* a worm.

comfortable European house, nay, not even for the most magnificent palace; he thinks his piece of seals-skin a more becoming dress than the best silks and brocades; nor would he prefer a well-seasoned ragout[10] to a piece of stinking seals flesh. To be controuled by wise laws and regulations, is what the spirit of some of these rambling barbarians could never brook; and independence, licentiousness, and revenge their favourite passions, render them absolutely unfit for any well-regulated society, and cause in them a general contempt for our way of living, where order and subordination take place. They think themselves happy, nay, happier than the best regulated nation, and every individual of them is so perfectly contented with his condition, that not even a wish is left in his breast for the least alteration.

But a mind accustomed to meditation, and able to affix to every thing its true value, must certainly perceive, that this situation of the savage or barbarian, is nothing more than a state of intoxication; his happiness and contentment founded on mere sensuality is transitory and delusive; the sum of all his enjoyments is so small, so defective in its particulars, and of so little value, that a man in his senses cannot but think himself happy that he was born in a civilized nation, educated in a country where society is as much improved as is possible; that he belongs to a people who are governed by the mildest laws, and have the happiest constitution of government, being under the influence of civil and religious liberty.

If therefore the happiness of the savage is not so eligible, as some philosophers will make us believe, who never viewed mankind in this debased situation; it is certainly the wish of humanity, and of real goodness, to see all these nations brought nearer to a more improved, more civilized, and more happy state, without the addition of these evils, which abuses, luxury and vice have introduced among our societies. Human nature is capable of great improvements, if men only knew how to proceed in order to effectuate this great and noble purpose. The greater part of them are too unreasonable in their wishes, too rapid and violent in their proceedings, and too sanguine in their expectations. They wish this change should take place immediately, their methods for bringing it about are contrary to human nature, and sometimes they overlook the progress of improvement, because it is slow. If we consider the progress of man as an individual, from birth to manhood, we find it very slow and gradual, though ever so much care be taken to improve the body, as well as the intellectual and the moral faculties, and to instill early into the mind the seeds of social virtue. We can never pass over the years of childhood, and youth, and make infants men; not even by the most accomplished education. Thus likewise, the approach towards civilization, must be left to time; it is a work of ages to bring the mind of a whole nation to maturity. Nor can it be forced or accelerated by the best instructions. From *animality* nations ripen into *savages*, from this state they enter into that of *barbarism*, before they are capable of *civilization*, and how many degrees of refinement does not even this situation admit?

---

10. Stew (French).

"HOW MANY ADAMS MUST WE ADMIT?"

Infancy is in individuals, merely animal life. In the same manner the lowest degree of degeneration in collective bodies is ANIMALITY. *Childhood* is undesigning, harmless, and innocent; private property and personal security of others, are ideas which the boy is to be taught when he emerges from infancy, for he knows of no other law than that of the strongest. The SAVAGE has likewise no idea of the personal security of any other besides himself, nor thinks better in regard to private property: he kills where he is the strongest, and he robs where he cannot otherwise obtain the possession of what he covets. *Adolescence* is the age of violent passions, breaking out in outrages against all the principles of morality; carrying away like an impetuous flood whatever opposes its desires: the youth has the dawning of understanding and reason, and if the mental faculties are not improved in this stage, and the passions made subservient to reason, he degenerates into profligacy, and brings on his own ruin. The BARBARIAN is likewise fiery and violent, without controul and principles, nay, capable of the most detestable outrages; nations in this state want education and improvement more than in any other. *Manhood* and a *mature age,* are similar to the CIVILIZED STATE, and have therefore several degrees.

These remarks will give a general outline of the real condition of these nations, of the improvements which philosophers can with propriety wish for them, and of the progress they may be expected to have made from the little intercourse with Europeans. I have been frequently asked, what improvements and progress in civilization the inhabitants of the islands in the South Sea appeared to me to have made since Europeans came among them. A few years in regard to a nation, are a few moments in a man's life, a man may learn very useful things materially affecting his situation in life in a few hours; but it would be next to impossible to point out in his character, his mode of living, his conversation, and his actions a few hours after this acquisition, the advantages he can or will derive from thence; this holds likewise in regard to nations; a few years cannot bring on a material change among them. We carried hogs and fowls to New Zeeland; and dogs and pigs to New Caledonia, dogs to Tanna, Mallicollo, and the Friendly Isles, and goats to O-Taheitee; these animals will no doubt in time cause a material change in the way of living of these nations; but as we could give no more than one couple of goats and a few of the other species of animals, it will require a succession of years before they can multiply, and become so numerous, that every inhabitant may have several of them, and thus be enabled to employ them in food. The use of iron tools is another article, which would, in time, become a great improvement to their mechanical employments; but as those tools which we procured for them were by no means in sufficient number, that every man might be provided with a compleat set, the changes which they have produced, are, as yet, very inconsiderable; nay, as these isles have no productions, which might tempt any European nation to set on foot a regular and constant navigation to them; it is probable, that in a few years they will be entirely neglected; if therefore the iron tools imported, had been so numerous, that every man could have had his share, the natives would have entirely laid aside their own stone hatchets, stone chissels, and other implements, and would, perhaps, by length of time, have forgotten the manner of making them. This circumstance, must of course, have become very distressing to them; used to our tools, without possessing the art of making them, or the still greater art of procuring iron, from whence they might be manufactured, and having laid aside and forgotten the method of forming their substitutes of stone, they would, instead of being improved, have been thrown back several ages in their own improvements. We did not communicate intellectual, moral, or social improvements to the natives of the isles; nor could these be expected from the crew of a man of war; those who might be deemed capable of enlarging their minds with new ideas relative to science, arts and manufactures, of instilling the principles of true morality and virtue into their breasts, or of communicating to them notions of a well regulated government, and diffusing throughout a numerous nation, that spirit of charity, attachment, and disinterested love of the community, which ought to glow in the breast of every reasonable member of society, had neither time nor leisure for such an undertaking in the few days of our abode among them, especially as none had a thorough knowledge of the several languages, and as each had a different pursuit to attend, which had been delegated to him by his superiors, when this expedition was set on foot.

from James Cowles Prichard, *Researches into the Physical History of Man* (1813)

James Cowles Prichard (1786–1848) was a pioneer of English ethnology, and his *Researches* was for many years the standard work in the field. Here he pursues Forster's arguments about the causes of color difference in humanity. Was it the result simply of climate, as had seemed self-evident in the eighteenth century, or was the degree of civilization also involved? To test this hypothesis, Prichard needed two sample groups: a black race widely spread over various climates (as in Africa) and a population apparently possessing varied degrees of civilization (as in the Pacific).

We now proceed to inquire what effects Cultivation or Civilization may produce on the human race, and how far it may be considered as predisoposing to variations of complexion.

The difficulty in this part of our subject is to find an example of a race of people of which one tribe is savage, and the other civilized. By such instances, if many were to be found, we might ascertain what effects civilization is calculated to produce.

The natives of the South Sea islands afford us an example of a race of people scattered through a wide extent of space, in which they occupy insulated and divided points, and are thus cut off from all communication with each other. We shall enter more fully hereafter into the history of these tribes. It is sufficient to say at present that there is great reason to believe them all to be branches of one stock. Their affinity is clearly proved in many instances by identity of language and manners. Now of these nations some are absolute savages, living on the precarious sustenance which is afforded them by the spontaneous fruits of the earth, and altogether destitute of clothing, absolutely in the natural and unimproved state: others on the contrary have made considerable advancement in the arts of life, and inhabit a country which by its extraordinary fertility and abundant supply of the most nutritious food gives them all the advantages of a perfect agriculture, and they use clothing manufactured from the bark of the mulberry tree. The people are here divided into different ranks, and the higher class are very much in the same circumstances, with the better orders of society in the civilized communities of Europe.[11] The savage tribes are all of them completely Negroes, quite black, and the greater number have woolly hair, and resemble the Africans in their anatomical structure; some of them have black complexions, with hair crisp and curled but not woolly. Of this precise description are the major part of the people of New Zealand. Now the inhabitants of the latter country are incontestably a tribe of the same identical race, which furnished the population of the Society isles. These are the most civilized of the whole stock. The lower people among them nearly resemble the New Zealanders in their complexion and appearance, but the better rank have a skin which is at least as fair as that of our brunettes in Europe. But what is most directly to our purpose, some individuals in this luxurious community of the Society isles, have been born with all the characters of the sanguine temperament, with a florid white complexion, and hair of a light brown flaxen or red colour, in short with the precise characters of the German or Teutonic race. Here then we have a fair example of the greatest diversity of the human species, depending on the condition of society, and on the mode of life. The influence of climate would here have a contrary tendency, for the white people are much nearer the equator than many of the black tribes.

There is no reason to doubt, that if a whole nation were placed in the same circumstances with the better sort of people in the Society isles, their offspring would become similarly transmuted. The chief points in which they differ from the lower class in the same country, and from the cognate branches which still preserve their barbarous manners, and Negro characters in other islands, are the abundance of sustenance and cloathing, and the comparative luxury and delicacy of life, which they enjoy. In a similar manner civilized nations in general, are distinguished from savage ones.

This view of the causes of varieties in our species is confirmed by considering the analogous phaenomena in other kinds. We have seen reason to believe that cultivation and domestication are the chief causes of deviation from the primitive colour and form in the vegetable and animal tribes.

It derives confirmation also from other facts in the history of mankind. It was mentioned above, that in the hottest parts of Africa there is one nation of Negroes, the Foulahs,[12] who are not black, nor have woolly hair, but are of a tawny complexion, and have hair of a soft silky texture, approaching to the

---

11. Prichard is clearly thinking of Tahiti: "the Society isles."
12. Or Fula, a nomadic people of West Africa.

European characters. These people, it may be remembered, were observed to be more civilized than the other tribes, and the generally prevalent idea of their superiority over the more savage races makes it probable, that the moral difference between them has been of long standing.

Dr. S. S. Smith has given us an example of similar diversity produced in a short time in the Negroes settled in the southern districts of the United States of America. And although we do not consent to all the reasonings of this author, yet his observation of the fact is not the less valuable. He remarks that the field slaves live on the plantations, and retain pretty nearly the rude manners of their African progenitors. The third generation in consequence preserve much of their original structure, though their features are not so strongly marked as those of imported slaves. But the domestic servants of the same race are treated with lenity, and their condition is little different from that of the lower class of white people. The effect is that in the third generation they have the nose raised, the mouth and lips of moderate size, the eyes lively and sparkling, and often the whole composition of features extremely agreeable. The hair grows sensibly longer in each succeeding race; it extends to three, four, and sometimes to six or eight inches. [. . .]

When the disposition to variation is excited by civilization, it is probable that it may proceed more rapidly in producing its effects in some climates than in others. There are not wanting facts, which prove that local situation and moderate temperature, promote the tendency to the production of light varieties. [. . .]

It will be proper to recapitulate in this place our inferences concerning the effects of climate and of civilization on the human species.

We endeavoured in the first instance to shew that there is no foundation for the common opinion which supposes the black races of men to have acquired their colour by exposure to the heat of a tropical climate during many ages. On the contrary the fact appears to be fully established that white races of people migrating to a hot climate, do preserve their native complexion unchanged, and have so preserved it in all the examples of such migration which we know to have happened. And this fact is only an instance of the prevalence of the general law, which has ordained that the offspring shall always be constructed according to the natural and primitive constitution of the parents, and therefore shall inherit only their connate peculiarities and not any of their acquired qualities.[13] It follows that we must direct our inquiry to the connate varieties, and to the causes which influence the parent to produce an offspring deviating in some particulars of its organization from the established character of the stock. What these causes are seems to be a question which must be determined by an extensive comparison of the phaenomena of vegetable and animal propagation. It appears that in the vegetable world cultivation is the chief exciting cause of variation. In animals climate certainly lays the foundation of some varieties, but domestication or cultivation is the great principle which every where calls them forth in abundance. In the human species we endeavoured to ascertain what

---

13. "Connate": innate, congenital, as opposed to qualities "acquired" during life.

comparative effect these two principles may produce, and first to determine whether climate alone can furnish any considerable variation in tribes of men uncultivated or uncivilized. We compared the appearances of two great races of uncivilized people, each of which is scattered through a great portion of the world, and which, taken collectively, constitute nearly all the savage tenants of the globe. It resulted from this comparison, that little effect is produced by the agency of climate alone on savage tribes. Varieties indeed appear more ready to spring up in moderate than in intensely hot climates, but they are not sufficient to produce any considerable change on the race. Civilization however has more extensive powers, and we have examples of the greatest variation in the human complexion produced by it, or at least which can scarcely be referred to any other cause, viz. the appearance of the sanguine constitution in a race generally black. Lastly it appears that in races which are experiencing the effect of civilization, a temperate climate increases the tendency to the light varieties, and therefore may be the means of promoting and rendering the effect of that important principle more general and more conspicuous.

from William Lawrence, *Lectures on Comparative Anatomy, Physiology, Zoology, and the Natural History of Man* (1817)

Like Prichard, William Lawrence (1763–1867) was trained as a doctor, and he served as surgeon at St. Bartholomew's Hospital in London from 1829 to 1862. A disciple of Blumenbach, he translated his *Short System of Comparative Anatomy* in 1807, and in his lectures given at the Royal College of Surgeons, he demonstrates an ethnological interest far more focused on anatomy than Prichard's broader approach. Here he picks up Blumenbach's fivefold organization of human variety and puzzles over the "Malay" variety as an intermediary between the Caucasian and the Negro.

The fifth, or Malay variety, including the inhabitants of the numerous Asiatic islands, and those of the Great Pacific Ocean, constitutes an intermediate link between the European and Negro. The cranium is moderately narrowed and slanting at its anterior and upper part; the face large, and all its parts fully developed; the jaws more or less prominent.

It must be confessed that the numerous tribes included within the boundaries of this variety differ considerably from each other; and consequently, that the whole cannot fall within any one clearly-marked character. The Papua race are described as having all the appearance of Negroes. I have seen no skull, nor any representation of one, belonging to a native of New Guinea. The New Hollanders certainly partake of the Negro form, yet are still easily distinguishable from African Negroes. In the two heads engraved by Blumenbach the forehead rather slants above the eyes, but the head rises to a considerable height at the coronal suture. The nose is not so flat, nor the zygoma[14] so

---

14. The cheekbone, connecting the cranial and facial bones.

prominent, as in the African. The alveolar edge of the upper jaw projects in front;[15] the chin is not cut off, as in the Negro. The crania of New Hollanders which I have seen correspond with these. In some, as in a female skull in the College Museum, the superior incisors are placed as obliquely as in the Negro; but none have so low a forehead and vertex[16] as some of that race.

The Otaheitean skull does not differ in any essential points from the European formation, so far as the cranium goes. The front and lower part of the forehead may be a little contracted and slanting. The face is altogether large, and the upper jaw fully developed; its alveolar portion, too, projects slightly in front.

The head of a native of Nukahiwah, one of the group called the Marquesas Islands, presents a very beautiful and symmetrical organization corresponding to the descriptions of the great stature, fine proportions, and strength of these islanders. Except that the face is larger, its lower part especially more considerable and prominent than in the best models of the Caucasian variety, and that the jaws and teeth altogether have a marked projection, this head is not very essentially distinguished from that form. The forehead is indeed more slanting than in the intellectual European heads; but the whole structure has unequivocal marks of an organization calculated for strength.

The skull of a Buggess, from the island of Celebes,[17] has the low slanting forehead, large face, and prominent jaws of the true Negro; but it combines the lateral expansion, particularly across the cheeks, of the Mongolian variety.

The arrangement of skulls under the five general forms just described is, in a great measure, arbitrary. It must not, therefore, be taken in a strict sense; we must not expect to find all the individuals, comprised under each of these varieties, decisively distinguished by the assigned characters from all others. In the endless diversity of individual forms, many instances are met with, in each variety, of organizations approaching to those of the others: so that among many Europeans and Negroes we might select skulls in which it would be difficult to determine the predominant character. The two intermediate forms between the Caucasian middle, and the Ethiopian and Mongolian extremes, complete the series of gradations. Of the numerous tribes or nations in each division, some come nearer to one and some to the other of the two immediately joining varieties. Thus the natives of some islands in the South Sea are hardly to be distinguished in countenance and head from Europeans; while others approach as near to the Negroes. The Marquesans, the Society, Friendly, and Sandwich Islanders, might be almost arranged under the Caucasian variety; while the natives of New Guinea, New Holland, Van Diemen's Land, New Britain, &c. Louisiade, &c. have strong claims to be admitted into the Ethiopian division; and those of Solomon Islands, the New Hebrides, and New Zealand, form so many points of transition between the two. The same observation holds good of the other varieties. Hence, if we had numerous

---

15. The alveolar edge of the jaws is where the teeth are situated.
16. The crown of the head.
17. Bugis, an indigenous people and language of Sulawesi (Celebes), Indonesia.

specimens of each, we might arrange them in such a manner that the interval between the most perfect Caucasian model and the most exaggerated Negro or Mongolian specimens should be filled with forms conducting us from one to the other by almost imperceptible gradations. We must therefore conclude that the diversities of features and of skulls are not sufficient to authorize us in assigning the different races of mankind in which they occur to species originally different. This conclusion will be strengthened by the analogies of natural history. The differences between human crania are not more considerable, nor even so remarkable, as some variations which occur in animals confessedly of the same species. The head of the wild boar is widely different from that of the domestic pig. The different breeds of horses and dogs are distinguished by the most striking dissimilarities in the skull: in which view the Neapolitan and Hungarian horses may be contrasted. The very singular form of the skull in the Paduan fowl[18] is a more remarkable deviation from the natural structure than any variation which occurs in the human head.

from Jules Sébastian César Dumont d'Urville, "The Islands of the Pacific" (1832)

The extent of Dumont d'Urville's voyages in the Pacific (1822–1825 and 1826–1828) lent unique authority to his analysis of the races of the region. (He would conduct a further expedition in 1837–1840.) The word "Polynesia" had been coined by the French geographer Charles de Brosses, in 1756, to cover all the islands of the Pacific. Johann Reinhold Forster had begun to divide the region up into human varieties. But it was Dumont d'Urville who, in his presentation to the Geographical Society of Paris, formulated a clear geographic distinction between "four principal and fundamental divisions" of Oceania: Polynesia, Micronesia, Malaysia (the Philippines and the eastern islands of Indonesia), and Melanesia. (See Figure 14.) These divisions having been set out, he turns to the human qualities of their inhabitants.

Melanesia is separated from Malaysia by a line that passes to the west of the island of Waigiou from the westernmost point of New Guinea and east of the Aru islands;[19] from Micronesia by a gently oblique line in the direction of the equator bending toward the southeast; and from Polynesia by a flexible line that, leaving the eastern part of Santa Cruz,[20] travels just to the east of the islands of Fiji and goes toward the southwest between New Holland and New Zealand.

---

18. The Paduan, or Polish, chicken is the most superb of the crested breeds, with a dramatic topknot of feathers spreading from a protuberance on its skull.

19. Dumont d'Urville is describing a line west of Waigeo (at the extreme west of New Guinea) and curling sharply to the southeast between the islands of Malaku (in the Banda Sea) and the New Guinea mainland.

20. The Santa Cruz group of islands, north of Vanuatu.

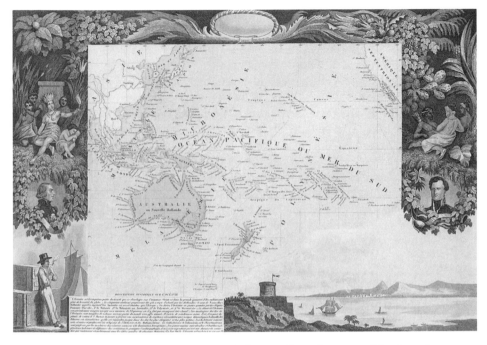

FIGURE 14. Emile Levasseur (1828–1911), "Océanie," in *Atlas universel de géographe physique* (1847). By permission of the National Library of Australia.

Van Diemen's Land (or Tasmania) will be the southernmost extremity of Melanesia; the immense island of New Holland (which, following English usage, we more usually refer to as Australia) is the most important part since it alone can constitute a continent. New Guinea and the islands attached to it also make up a large portion of it; and finally the Louisiade Archipelago,[21] New Britain, New Ireland, the Solomon Islands, Santa Cruz, Espirito Santo, the Loyalty Islands,[22] New Caledonia, and Fiji must be included.

All the peoples occupying this great division of Oceania are men of a blackish color more or less dark, with hair frizzy or tightly curled (or sometimes almost woolly), with a broad nose, a large mouth, disagreeable features, and limbs that are often very thin and rarely well formed. The women are still more hideous than the men, in particular those who have breast-fed, since their breasts directly become saggy and drooping, and they lose on the spot the bit of charm they had in their youth. Their restricted languages vary infinitely, often enough on the same island. These blacks nearly always gather in enfeebled groups in which the chief enjoys the role of arbitrary authority, exercised often in a style as tyrannical as the typical little African despot. As they

---

21. Off the eastern end of New Guinea.
22. Northeast of New Caledonia.

are much further withdrawn into a state of barbarism than the Polynesians and Micronesians, we find among them neither forms of governmnent, nor laws, nor regularly established religious ceremonies. Their social institutions seem all to be still in their infancy; and their state of mind and intelligence are normally far inferior to those of the copper-colored race.

It is true that many of these people are still hardly known. The natural enemies of the white man, they have always demonstrated an obstinate defiance of and a pronounced antipathy to Europeans, and the latter have generally had cause to repent their contact with their treacherous hosts. Neither Cook, nor Bougainville, nor any of the navigators who succeeded them have had with the Melanesians those relations of good friendship that they enjoyed maintaining and increasing with the hospitable peoples of Polynesia. [. . .]

Among the many varieties of the Melanesian race it seems to me that the most advanced is that of Fiji. Despite their ferocity and their appetite for cannibalism, these natives have laws, have arts, and form something like the body of a nation. Genuinely handsome men can be found among them; their language is richer, more resonant, and more regular than those of the western islands; and their navigational skills yield nothing to those of the other race. Among them I have found individuals gifted with an intelligence and a capacity for judgment remarkable among savages. But it is obvious that they owe these advantages to their proximity to the Tongans and to the frequent exchanges they have had with the Polynesian race.

The same must be said of the peoples of Santa Cruz, the New Hebrides, and the Solomon Islands: they have had relations more or less intimate and frequent with the Polynesians, because it can be seen that the latter have spread to the islands of Rotuma, Anuta, Tikopia, and Taumako, lying close to islands occupied by the Melanesians.[23] At Vanikoro I myself have been convinced of frequent contacts taking place between the two races and of the more intimate connections that often follow in their wake. This is the origin of those many shades of difference observed by various navigators in these islands, normally gathered under the headings of black, mulatto, or white—the first being the Melanesians, the last the Polynesians, and the mulattoes those hybrid products of interbreeding between the black and copper-colored races. This melting pot was observed in New Ireland and its neighboring islands; probably it is still to be found farther toward the west along the coasts of New Guinea.

It is important to note that the less communication they have with Polynesians, the more impoverished the Melanesians appear as regards their social institutions. Thus the inhabitants of New Ireland, New Britain, the Louisiade Archipelago, and the southern coasts of New Guinea are quite inferior to the groups living on islands farther to the east. All the Melanesians, however

---

23. These are "Polynesian outlier" islands, where Polynesian cultures are found within the Melanesian zone: Rotuma (north of Fiji), Anuta, Tikopia, Taumako, and Vanikoro (in the Santa Cruz group).

(with the exception of the Australians and the New Caledonians), are familiar with the bow and arrow; some even know how to make earthenware pots. Presumably they owe these innovations to their neighbors in the west.[24]

Those who occupy the lowest rung in this race are evidently the inhabitants of Australia and Tasmania. Puny and miserable beings, gathered into feeble tribes, peculiarly disgraced by nature, and reduced as much by the poverty of their soil as by their own indolence and stupidity to a desperately precarious existence, they speak pitifully limited languages, varying from group to group and offering no analogies whatever with those the rules of which are better established. All their industry is reduced to making nets, spears, wretched bark canoes, and capes from skins of the possum or the kangaroo. Some know how to construct bark huts that are reasonably well finished, others simple shelters out of branches covered with brushwood; but there are those who, living and wandering constantly in the open, are content during their hours of rest to protect their shoulders under a scrap of bark pulled off a neighboring tree. The only traces of religious ideas these men have concern the existence of evil spirits always ready to torment them and a confused belief in a new life awaiting them after death.

We should point out that a fair number of Australians seem to approach the Polynesians in terms of their color, verging on the deeply tanned; but the briefest examination of their features and their build is sufficient to place them in the black race to which they belong. The Australians are to the Melanesians as the Hottentots are to the Ethiopian race—and it should be understood that there are important similarities between the Hottentots and the Australians.

However degraded and however miserable the human species appears to us in this condition, we believe it to be the primitive and natural state of the Melanesians, leaving aside the physical deformities brought about by the dietary deficiencies of a soil as unproductive as that of Australia. The condition of these beings is a little improved on the more fertile coasts of New Guinea and its neighboring islands; their appearance is less unprepossessing and their intelligence somewhat developed. It is only by settling on the islands, however, that the Melanesians have been able to have those contacts with the Polynesians that have seen their race little by little abandon their primitive type and receive a host of varying shades. It seems that at New Caledonia, where the condition of the soil is similar to that of Australia, the Melanesian character has undergone less perceptible modifications, despite the proximity of that territory to those of Tanna and Erromango: so Labillardière[25] quite naturally compared the New Caledonians to the Tasmanians.

I should add that in my opinion the Melanesian race could, in theory, have occupied the majority of the islands of Oceania. There are still to be seen among the lower classes in Tahiti individuals who, in color, build, and facial characteristics, approach the Melanesian type. Cook also found in Tahiti a

---

24. That is, in "Malaysia."

25. Jacques Julian de Labillardière (1755–1834), scientist aboard the French Pacific expedition of 1791–1794, commanded by Bruni d'Entrecasteaux.

tradition that suggested that a whole tribe of ferocious blacks still lived among the mountains of the island only a short while before his arrival. This was probably the sad remains of the early possessors of the ground, and the men I mentioned are the halfbreed issues of a mixture of the conquerors with the conquered. [. . .]

Finally, it is today almost a certain fact that the *Alfourous* of Timor, Seram, and Buru,[26] the Mountain Negritos or *Aetas* of Mindanao,[27] the *Indios* of the Philippines, the *Ygolotes* of Luzon, the Negrillos of Borneo, the blacks of Formosa,[28] the Andaman Islands, Sumatra, Malacca, and those of Cochin[29] called *Moys* or *Kemoys* all belong to that same primitive race of Melanesians who must have been the first settlers of Oceania. They lived there in little tribes, and in an almost natural state until the time when these islands are invaded by new peoples arriving from the west and belonging to the yellow or copper-colored race. The first invasion, which was traumatic no doubt, gave way to Polynesian colonies extending throughout the islands receding toward the east. Later emigrations—probably partial ones—successively populated the islands of Micronesia.

I have no hesitation in believing that the Polynesians arrived from the west, meaning from Asia; but I am not at all sure that they are descended from the Hindus. They probably had an origin common with theirs; but the two peoples had already been separated for a long time before one of them came to populate Oceania.

The story is the same when it comes to the conclusions various travelers have arrived at about the similarities observed between the Polynesians and the Malays. There is no doubt that in days of old the two peoples had relations with each other. Protracted study has revealed about sixty words that are evidently common to both languages, and that is sufficient to prove an ancient connection. But there are too many physical differences for us to suppose that the Polynesians amount only to a Malay colony.

The people of Malaysia who seem to me to have most similarity with the Polynesian race are the inhabitants of the interior of the Celebes, known as the Alfourous. That name instantly suggested to me the idea of black-colored men, with fuzzy hair and broad noses: that is, true Melanesians. Judge my amazement, then, when I saw individuals whose color, build, and facial characteristics involuntarily reminded me of the features I had seen in Tahiti, Tonga, and New Zealand. The similarities appeared so striking and so complete that I enthusiastically urged Governor Merkus[30] (who was accompanying me at the time) to make a study of their customs, religious ideas, and their language, since they employed an idiom quite different from the Malays. If the Celebes Alfourous' language presents more similarities with Polynesian than

---

26. At the eastern end of the Indonesian archipelago, to the west of New Guinea.
27. Southernmost large island of the Philippines.
28. Now Taiwan.
29. Coastal province of southern Vietnam.
30. Hendrik Merkus de Kock, lieutenant governor-general of Dutch Indonesia, 1822–1830.

with Malay itself, then I would not hesitate to believe that the Celebes have been one of the cradles of the Polynesian race or at least one of the principal staging posts in their march toward the east.

In this relation, a careful study of the *Dayaks* or *Eïdehans* of Borneo and the *Battas* of Sumatra will be no less important. The explorer Nicholas[31] has already outlined numerous similarities between the customs of the Battas and those of the New Zealanders.

There is room to believe that the Micronesians owe their origin chiefly to the islands of Luzon and Mindanao; Chinese and Japanese colonies might have arrived accidently on one of the Micronesian islands and their descendants might have become mixed with those of the Tagalogs.[32]

As for the Papuans, though they are not perhaps the most attractive variety of the Melanesian race, there are grounds for the suspicion that they have come more recently from the western regions, perhaps the Andaman Islands, Ceylon, or possibly Madagascar. One of the strongest reasons for believing them to be strangers to the regions they presently occupy is that they are always found on the shores of those areas, and that with the Papuans, or at least close alongside them, are found the authentic Melanesians called *Arfakis, Alfourous,* or *Endamènes.* From this mixture of Papuans, Alfourous, and Malays come a host of shades of diversity that constantly disrupt the calculations of the observer. But it can be pointed out that the Papuans properly so called occupy only a tiny part of the coast of New Guinea, and I believe they extend to the east hardly any farther than Geelwinck Bay.[33] Farther on it is genuine Melanesians like them who inhabit New Britain, New Ireland, etc.

After this account it is easy to see that I have no time whatsoever for that multiplication of races argued for by various modern authors. Returning to Forster's simple and lucid scheme, extended by Chamisso,[34] I recognize only two truly distinct races in known Oceania: the Melanesian race, which is itself only a branch of the black race of Africa, and the tanned or copper-colored Polynesian race, which is only an offshoot of the original yellow race of Asia.

May I be permitted to say, in passing, that in all the human species on the surface of the globe there seem to me only three sections or divisions meriting the name of truly distinct races. The first is the white, more or less colored at birth, supposedly originating in the Caucasus, and which occupies practically the whole of Europe, from where it has spread to every corner of the earth. The second is the yellow, capable of taking many copper or bronze shades, apparently coming from the central plateau of Asia and spreading little by little throughout that continent and its neighboring islands, onto the islands of Oceania, and ultimately into America by way of the Bering Strait.

The third is the black race, assumed to originate in Africa, of which it

---

31. See John Nicholas, *Narrative of a Voyage to New Zealand* (London, 1817).

32. Indigenous people of Luzon.

33. Now Geelvink or Cenderawasih Bay in northwest Irian Jaya.

34. Adalbert von Chamisso (1781–1838), naturalist on the 1815–1818 Pacific voyage commanded by Otto von Kotzebue (1787–1846).

occupies the largest part, which has also spread into the southern coasts of Asia, the islands of the Indian Ocean, those of Malaysia, and those of Oceania, too.

I can hardly debate here the issue of whether these three races are of equal antiquity or whether they in fact belong to three different and successive creations or developments, but I will point out that nature has hardly gifted them equally where intellectual qualities are concerned. It must be said that in each of these races she sought to limit the intellectual faculties of man in strikingly different ways.

From these organic differences it naturally follows that wherever the two latter races find themselves alongside each other, the black must obey the yellow or disappear; but when the white race enters the lists with the other two, it must dominate, even when it finds itself numerically inferior. The history of every people and the accounts of every traveler bring us every time to the carrying out of this law of nature. A people of the yellow race is hardly ever seen complying with the law of a tribe of blacks; neither are white people seen to submit to the yoke of the other races, except under unusual circumstances or unless sheer force of numbers defeat intellectual superiority.

from Anonymous, "On Aboriginal Savage Races of Man" (1866)

This extract is from a review of *The Aborigines of Australia,* by Gideon Lang, published in Melbourne in 1865. Lang starts from the premise that "the existence of the Australian aboriginal is morally as well as physically remarkable for nothing so much as its unmitigated wretchedness" and never deviates from this line of argument, insisting that Aboriginal people govern themselves "by a code of rules and a set of customs which form one of the most cruel tyrannies that has ever, perhaps, existed on the face of the earth." This was not grounds for extermination, and Lang regretted the black massacres he reported; but he was pessimistic about the Aborigines' chances of survival.

Modern colonisation has developed a new feature in human affairs, the immediate juxtaposition of the most highly civilised with the most savage races. Antiquity knew nothing of this. The Greeks and Romans never saw anything lower than barbarians. They were never face to face with men of "the stone period." It needed the progress of another two thousand years to bring the musket and the tomahawk, the rifle and the boomerang, into direct conflict. Only by faint tradition, and at many removes through travellers' tales, were ichthyophagi and anthropophagi known,[35] even remotely, to the writers of classic antiquity. The successive grades of culture were then geographically shaded off, the two extremes never coming into direct contact. It needed such an improvement in navigation as would permit the circumnavigation of the

---

35. Fish-eaters and man-eaters, respectively.

globe, ere the latter result could be produced. And the fact that it has been achieved, indicates that humanity has arrived at another and a higher stage of development than was ever before attained. By it the past is superannuated, and the future opens a new field of ethnic experience to mankind.

"The extinction of races" is, no doubt, a recurrent fact, of which archæology affords ample demonstration. In "the struggle for existence," the weak go down.[36] It always was so. It is, perhaps, best that it should be so. At all events, it is a stern necessity that must be accepted, and against which it is in vain to protest. The refinement of an advancing civilisation, reinforced even by the mild precepts of Christianity, seems utterly inoperative for its prevention. Never was the advent of the civilised man more destructive to the unfortunate savage than in this nineteenth century. The arrival of the former is simply the death-warrant of the latter, who perishes as by a law of nature. All this is, no doubt, very melancholy, especially in the process; although its result, as in the case of all natural laws, will, beyond question, be beneficial.

Such phenomena should make the advocates of the *unity,* and especially of the EQUALITY of all races, pause in the course of their fluent argument. Here is the world-wide fact, that the savage hunter is irreclaimable by the civilised man; that he perishes in the process of improvement, and dies out in the act of transition. It is, of course, comparatively easy to go into the details of this miserable process, and with weak but well-meaning philanthropy object now to the shooting down, and then to the rum bottle, and anon to the terrible diseases which we introduce among primitive peoples; but after all, the sombre fact remains, that they disappear, and after a few generations of occupation by the superior type, are nowhere to be found.

Such melancholy facts are suggestive of grave reflections to the anthropologist. Are there savage races, that is, types of mankind, who from structure, temperament, and their accompanying mortal qualities, are fitted only for the savage state of existence, with its wild impulses, its unrestrained passions, its imperfectly developed moral sentiments, and its almost utterly neglected intellectual faculties? Are not such human beings akin so far to certain species of animals, that practically defy domestication? They are formed for the wilderness, and die when *it* is reclaimed. Their habitat is in the prairie and the forest, not the field and the city. They are constituted for a certain environment, and expire when removed from its bracing and healthful influences.

We do not yet know what civilisation really implies in relation to the physique of mankind. There is no question that the cranial, and with it the cerebral type of civilised men, is different from that of savages. But is this the sum total of the elements of differentialism? Are there not also diversities in the volume and power of the viscera, in the disposition of the bones and muscles, and in the character and action of the skin; and as a necessary accompaniment of all

---

36. The expression is Darwin's, from chapter 3 of *The Origin of Species* (1859). Darwin's follower and interpreter Herbert Spencer coined a similar phrase when he spoke of "the survival of the fittest" in his *Principles of Biology* (1866).

this, is there not considerable difference between the corporeal functions of the hunter, the nomad, and, the agriculturist, more especially when the latter is of high Caucasian type? These are important questions, of which we are only in the early process of obtaining, a satisfactory solution. We want a comparative anatomy of man. We want men of the highest medical and surgical attainments, who, like Dr Pruner Bey,[37] have enjoyed the enviable privilege of residing among alien races, to give us the results of their experience. Hitherto this has been done very imperfectly; and, in the case of many races, has not even been attempted, so that as yet we have received but the first instalment of such knowledge. Enough, however, has been accomplished to show us that racial diversity is not confined to the externals of sort, and colour, but extends also to internal structure, and of course to function, whether in health or disease. Now if this be so, then by civilising the savage we place him in an unnatural condition, one unsuited to his organisation, and for which he is not constituted either in body or mind. Can we, then, wonder at the result? Is not his ultimate disappearance unavoidable, whatever may be the processes employed for its accomplishment, and however virtuous and well-disposed may be the colonists with whom he comes in contact?

We are aware that these are doctrines not likely to commend themselves very readily to the favourable consideration of "aborigines protection societies" and other philanthropic bodies, whose anthropology is much too sentimental for the admission of such stern facts or such unpleasant conclusions. Neither will our various missionary societies readily tolerate statements and opinions so opposed to their favourite processes of conversion and Bible civilisation. They have accepted, as a matter of faith, that "the heathen" are a part of the inheritance of Christ; and without more ado, they proceed to gather them in. But, alas! to sheep of this character, even the best managed fold is little better than a polite slaughterhouse. They are baptised unto death. They are numbered with the elect, to their temporal destruction. That Christianity is a Caucasian faith, seems never even to have been suspected by the members of either our Catholic or Protestant propaganda, who accordingly will doubtless regard even our allusion to such a fact, as an instance of glaring and shameless impiety. Well, we can only say missionary enterprise is an experiment upon a grand scale to test the possibility of diffusing the ideas of one race of men among those of another; and while within certain limits this is no doubt possible, there are, we have no hesitation in asserting, ethnic demarcations so wide, that to overstep them is practically impossible. [. . .]

Both the Flora and Fauna of Australia point it out as a peculiarly characterised area. In a sense, it is older than America, as America is older than Europe, Asia, and Africa. Its living types are elsewhere archaic, that is, fossilised. Its quadrupeds are still marsupial. What, then, are its men? Socially, they are still in the stone period. They have the spear, but not the bow. They

---

37. Franz Pruner-Bey (1808–1882), French physical anthropologist, most noted for his categorization of human hair.

have the hut of interwoven boughs, but not the tented wigwam, which can be struck and carried from place to place. There are gradations even among savages. The Indian of North America would regard an Australian with a degree of pity bordering on contempt. And, perhaps, justly so. His canoe and his mocassins proclaim that he is the pupil of a more advanced school. We know nothing of the chronology of savage progress, except that it seems to have been inconceivably slow. From the Australian boomerang to the American bow, may imply a gulf of ten thousand years, nay, for aught we know to the contrary, may, perhaps, imply not simply historic, but geologic time, like the corresponding transition from marsupial to placental organisation in the quadrupedal sphere.[38]

Australia is the great *southern* continent. Do we yet know what this means? Are the telluric[39] influences alike on both sides of the equator? Is not the northern hemisphere preponderantly positive, and the southern as predominantly negative? And, as a result of this, do not animate types in the former tend to cerebral and thoracic development, while in the latter they as persistently tend to the lumbar and abdominal?[40] And is not this equivalent to saying, that the first are essentially masculine, and the second feminine in their organic proclivities and profounder characteristics? And here, again, by going south, do we not find that we are going back to the archaic types of our own hemisphere, and of our own continent? What, functionally regarded, is the advance of organisation from the zoophyte to man, but the gradual development of cerebration and respiration, accompanied by a corresponding and proportionate diminution of alimentation and reproduction? The line of advance is so obvious, that its direction cannot be doubted. As anthropologists, have we yet given these matters due consideration? Is it to be supposed that influences productive of such results in the animal are without effect in the human sphere?[41]

---

38. The marsupials are an order of mammals in which young are born in an undeveloped state by comparison with placental mammals, among which the fetus develops for longer in the womb.

39. Of or from the earth; from Tellus, a Roman earth goddess.

40. "Thoracic," from the thorax, or chest; "lumbar" the section of the spine between the rib cage and the pelvis.

41. See, for example, Alfred Russel Wallace's influential paper "The Origin of Human Races and the Antiquity of Man Deduced from the Theory of 'Natural Selection'" (1864). There Wallace discusses "the harsh discipline of a sterile soil and inclement seasons" in the north: "Under their influence, a hardier, a more provident, and a more social race would be developed, than in those regions where the earth produces a perennial supply of vegetable food and where neither foresight nor ingenuity are required to prepare for the rigours of winter. And is it not the fact that in all ages, and in every quarter of the globe, the inhabitants of temperate have been superior to those of tropical countries? All the great invasions and displacements of races have been from North to South, rather than the reverse; and we have no record of there ever having existed, any more than there exists to-day, a solitary instance of an indigenous inter-tropical civilization" (Smith 1991: 14–26).

Johann Reinhold Forster, *Observations Made During a Voyage Round the World* (London, 1778).

James Cowles Prichard, *Researches into the Physical History of Man* (London: John and Arthur Arch, 1813).

William Lawrence, *Lectures on Comparative Anatomy, Physiology, Zoology, and the Natural History of Man* (1817; London: Henry G. Bohn, 1848).

Jules Sébastian César Dumont d'Urville, "Sur les Iles du Grand Ocean" [trans. Richard Lansdown], *Bulletin de la Société de Géographie* 105 (Jan. 1832).

Anon., "On Aboriginal Savage Races of Man," *Popular Magazine of Anthropology* 2 (April 1866).

FURTHER READING

The most important contributions to a history of racial thinking about the Pacific have been made by K. R. Howe, in "The Intellectual Discovery and Exploration of Polynesia," in Robin Fisher and Hugh Johnston, eds., *From Maps to Metaphors* (Vancouver: University of British Columbia Press, 1993); in *Nature, Culture and History: The "Knowing" of Oceania* (Honolulu: University of Hawai'i Press, 2000); and in *The Quest for Origins: Who First Discovered and Settled New Zealand and the Pacific Islands?* (Auckland: Penguin, 2003). Several studies provide intellectual contextualization: Michael Banton, *Racial Theories* (Cambridge: Cambridge University Press, 1998); George M. Fredrickson, *The Black Image in the White Mind: The Debate on Afro-American Character and Destiny, 1817–1914* (New York: Harper and Row, 1971); Margaret Hodgen, *Early Anthropology in the Sixteenth and Seventeenth Centuries* (Philadelphia: University of Pennsylvania Press, 1964); Winthrop D. Jordan, *White over Black: American Attitudes to the Negro, 1550–1812* (Williamsburg: Institute of Early American History, 1968); Annemarie de Waal Malefijt, *Images of Man: A History of Anthropological Thought* (New York: Knopf, 1974); George L. Mosse, *Towards the Final Solution: A History of European Racism* (London: J. M. Dent, 1978); D. J. Mulvaney, "The Darwinian Perspective," in Ian Donaldson and Tamsin Donaldson, eds., *Seeing the First Australians* (Sydney: Allen and Unwin, 1985); and Anthony Pagden, *The Fall of Natural Man: The American Indian and the Origins of Comparative Ethnology* (Cambridge: Cambridge University Press, 1982). Nancy Stepan's *The Idea of Race in Science: Great Britain, 1800–1960* (London: Macmillan, 1982) is a first-rate study.

Andrew Sinclair's *The Savage: A History of Misunderstanding* (London: Weidenfeld and Nicolson, 1977) is accessible and strong on imaginative writers, as is Brian V. Street's *The Savage in Literature: Representations of "Primitive" Society in English Fiction, 1858–1920* (London: Routledge and Kegan Paul, 1975).

On Forster see Michael Hoare, ed., *The Resolution Journal of Johann Reinhold Forster, 1772–1775* (London: Hakluyt Society, 1982), and Michael Hoare, *The Tactless Philosopher* (Melbourne: Hawthorn, 1976); on Prichard see George W. Stocking Jr.'s introduction to his edition of *Researches into the Physical History of Mankind* (Chicago: University of Chicago Press, 1973); on Dumont d'Urville see Helen Rosenman, ed., *Two Voyages to the South Seas by Jules S-C Dumont d'Urville*, 2 vols. (Melbourne: Melbourne University Press, 1987); Susan Hunt et al., *The Lure of the Southern Seas: The Voyages of Dumont d'Urville, 1826–1840* (Sydney: Historic Houses Trust, 2002); and Bronwen Douglas, "Art as Ethno-historical Text: Science, Representation and Indigenous Presence in Eighteenth and Nineteenth Century Voyage Literature," in Nicholas Thomas and Diane Losche, eds., *Double Vision: Art Histories and Colonial Histories in the Pacific* (Cambridge: Cambridge University Press, 1999). A complete translation of "Sur les îles du Grand Ocean" by Isabelle Ollivier, Antoine de Biran, and Geoffrey Clark is to be found in *Journal of Pacific History* 38:2 (2003), 163–174.

Evidence for the influence of the Forster/Dumont d'Urville theory in the nineteenth century is to be found in J. B. Jukes, *Narrative of the Surveying Voyage of HMS "Fly"* (1847); Robert Gordon Latham, *The Natural History of the Varieties of Man* (1850); Charles Pickering, *The Races of Man and Their Geographical Distribution* (1850); John Elphinstone Erskine, *Journal of a Cruise among the Islands of the Western Pacific* (1853); W. L. Ranken, "South Sea Islanders," *Journal of the Anthropological Institute of Great Britain and Ireland* 6 (1877); and the sections on the Pacific in Harry Johnston et al., *The Living Races of Mankind* (1902). Representative of other, more fanciful theories is Abraham Fornander, *An Account of the Polynesian Race, Its Origin and Migrations* (1878–1885).

6

THE ISLAND AS COLONY
From Backwater to "Ocean of the Future"

Terms like "colonialism" or "imperialism" evoke certain images: individuals using any means available to paint more of the world pink, or light blue, or whatever is the color of national choice; strategic visions-cum-imperatives of men like Cecil Rhodes eventually running into the sand; the "scramble for Africa"; nineteenth-century heads of state like Bismarck and Disraeli making treaties in European capitals and watering places, where swathes of Central Africa or outposts in the Mediterranean or the Far East were swapped about as the fortunes of war dictated; or the Congo of Joseph Conrad's *Heart of Darkness,* despoiled by Leopold II, king of the Belgians.

In fact colonialist expansion in the South Seas was intermittent, negligent, and reluctant, however profound its effects were to be. "The British were early adventurers in the Pacific Ocean, but tardy settlers. The Empire which to-day has three of its nations [Australia, New Zealand, and Canada] chiefly concerned in the destiny of that ocean . . . went there most reluctantly as a colonist" (Fox 1928: 138). Such reluctance was understandable. Britain's experience with its American colonies in the eighteenth century, for example, suggested that once such colonies had the wherewithal to be useful they demanded independence: so why become involved in a no-win situation? Besides, Victorian laissez-faire policies hardly encouraged a vigorous colonialism. Between 1874 and 1906, accordingly, Britain acquired 112,000 square miles of Pacific territory and several hundred thousand Pacific Islanders in "a state of absent-mindedness" rather than by any grand acquisitive plan of the kind hatched by Spanish explorers of the sixteenth century (Oliver, 137). Alone among the great powers of the late nineteenth century, Germany did purposefully seek a Pacific empire and came into conflict with other states accordingly. However, though the German government was more self-assertive in backing the claims of its citizens in the

Pacific and in stretching its imperial muscles, it still did so through German firms in the region rather than directly. The South Seas had almost none of the commercial importance of Africa, with its stores of ivory, gold, and diamonds, and of the Suez Canal, jugular route to and from the vast population of British India. It was as a "sphere of influence" that the Pacific appeared to require the attention of the West: to keep other powers in check; ensure that national interest was served; maintain a free trading medium around and between China, Australia, the western seaboards of North and South America, and the Panama Canal (both before and after its construction); and extend a degree of protection to those individuals who chose to make their careers so far from home.

It was in imperial terms, then, rather than colonial ones, that the South Seas came to be of sufficient importance to be completely parceled out among the Western powers by the end of the nineteenth century: "In fact the Pacific islands did not become incorporated in the European empires as part of any grand design to partition the world, nor simply to give expression to an irrational European fantasy of racial superiority. There was a multiplicity of motives and a diversity of circumstances ... and the process extended fitfully not over two decades, but over six" (Campbell 1990: 136). Thus, Ian Campbell goes on, "France, which acquired part of its empire in indifference, governed it the same way; Germany, which was frankly concerned with exploiting and developing resources, got on with the job expeditiously; Britain, having lacked a positive policy previously, continued to be guided by ad hoc principles; the United States of America created an environment for business; and Dutch neglect of western New Guinea was almost total" (1990: 156). In fact, most islands were gathered under the Western wing out of a sense of benevolent altruism, however misplaced. In many cases the great powers genuinely thought they were providing law instead of anarchy, peace instead of violence, and decent administration instead of corruption.

And so the picture stood on the eve of the First World War: Hawai'i, as Frank Fox described the situation,

> is a United States possession. The same power is represented in the South Pacific by its control of a portion of the Samoan group [American Samoa]. The British Empire holds the Fiji group, some of the Solomon Islands, a portion of New Guinea, and various small islets, such as the Gilbert group [Kiribati], the Ellice group [Tuvalu], Norfolk Island, the Tonga or Friendly Islands, and Fanning Island [Tabuaeran in Kiribati]; and, of course, the self-governing Dominions of Australia and New Zealand. France holds, conjointly with Great Britain, the New Hebrides [Vanuatu], and has exclusive control of New Caledonia, the Society Isles [Tahiti], the Austral Isles, the Marquesas Isles, and the Low Archipelago [Tuamotu]. Germany has a portion of Papua, a portion of the Solomons, and a portion of the Samoan group [Samoa]. The Dutch hold a portion of New Guinea [Irian Jaya]. The possessions of the British Empire are in part under the direct control of Australia or of New Zealand, and in part are administered as Crown Colonies by the High Commissioner for the Pacific, who has his headquarters at Fiji. (Fox 1913: 16)

(In his survey Fox overlooks Micronesia, which in 1913 was under German control except for Guam, which belonged to America.) Players on this complicated and far-flung board might come and go as events dictated—after their defeat in the First World War, the Germans, for example, were sent packing and their place taken by the British in New Guinea and the Japanese in Micronesia—but the game remained relatively stable until the Second World War reduced Britain and France to second-rate powers, removed the Japanese, made the United States the dominant Pacific influence, and began the process of decolonization: a process almost entirely complete today.

As imperial points on the map securing trading links, spheres of influence, and naval hegemony, the Pacific islands had real and lasting importance in the West's view of the world. "Situated as they are," a veteran whaler opined regarding the Hawaiian islands, "they are in the central point of the vast Pacific, and communicating with the continent of America on the east, and with Asia on the west, and to the south west, with the numberless islands of Polynesia, they seem to be destined to be the seat of a flourishing empire" (Olmsted, 263). As colonies, in the strict sense of the term, such islands bulked much less large in writers' imaginations. But what exactly is a colony "in the strict sense of the term"? Classically, a colony is what Francis Bacon had in mind in his essay "Of Plantations": "the children of former kingdoms," where a settler society comes out from, say, Britain to Virginia, and makes a new and permanent home abroad. These were the kind of settlements Bismarck described as "establishments freely founded by German subjects—branches of the German nation, so to speak" (quoted in Roberts, 51). "The aim of this Company," Edward Gibbon Wakefield wrote of his New Zealand Company of settlers, "is not confined to mere emigration, but is directed to colonization in its ancient and systematic form. Its object is to transplant English society with its various gradations in due proportions, carrying out our laws, customs, associations, habits, manners, feelings—everything of England, in short but the soil" (quoted in Fox 1928: 152). By this definition the number of colonies in the South Seas could almost be counted on the fingers of one hand: Australia (colony, 1788) and New Zealand (colony, 1840) preeminently, Hawai'i (annexed, 1898), Fiji (annexed, 1874), New Caledonia (protectorate, 1853), and perhaps Tahiti (protectorate, 1842)—though the French element settled in Tahiti was and remains more a bureaucratic and administrative cadre than the fundamentally agricultural community Bacon envisaged in 1625.

In his *Lectures on Colonization and Colonies* Herman Merivale made a distinction between two varieties of colonial settlement: "subsistence" and "trading." (Merivale, 3: lecture 10.) The former might be exemplified by the northern American states of New England or colonial New South Wales before the wool boom of the 1820s: small farmers spreading out slowly from an initial landfall and growing crops to support the local population. "Trading" colonies might be exemplified by the southern states of the United States or the colonies in the Caribbean and South America: rapid exploitation of land to harvest single crops (wool, tobacco, cotton, sugar, cocoa, coffee) for export back to Europe. This latter form required large amounts of freely available land and cheap labor to service it: thus the slave trade to the Caribbean and North and South America, and the use of convict labor in New South Wales.

The insular Pacific was something of a mixture in this respect but a major player in neither category. There is precious little land in the Pacific, and what is there is often either precipitous (on the volcanic islands) or of limited fertility (on the coralline ones). Those of reasonable landmass did, accordingly, develop agriculture on what Merivale would call "systematic" terms: cattle in New Caledonia, cotton but ultimately sugar in Fiji, sugar and fruit in Hawai'i. Labor also presented a problem, at least according to white settlers. The Australian Aboriginal and the Polynesian could not be trained to work, it seemed; and thus Melanesian Islanders were introduced on Queensland sugar farms, Indians came to Fiji, Vietnamese to the New Hebrides (British and French condominium, 1906), and Chinese and Japanese to Hawai'i. So it was that Australia, New Zealand, Hawai'i, Fiji, and New Caledonia (in that order of importance) became the only "trading" colonies of the South Seas in the sense of sustaining a permanent settler society living off the income provided by agricultural exports.

Wool, lamb, beef, sugar, and fruit were not the only trading commodities coming from the region, however. Other products figured largely, but only for limited periods of time and in limited markets. A key market, for example, was the Chinese one. At first, Westerners had traded silver from South America for Chinese products like silk, porcelain, tea, and opium; later they traded furs from Canada for the same products; later still they discovered that certain items from the Pacific islands could contribute to this process of exchange. The Chinese had a taste for dried sea slugs; they also used sandalwood for incense and items of furniture, and large stands of this tree were dotted about the islands. (An easy way to find it was simply to set fire to some forest and wait for the sandalwood to betray itself by its scent.) Pearls had currency throughout the world, as did seashell for buttons and marquetry. Cotton was successful in Fiji during the intermission provided by America's Civil War; then it faded away as quickly as it had come. It was whale oil, however, that was the Pacific's first and only supercrop, and far and away the most important commercial influence in the Westernization of the Pacific in the nineteenth century.

But all these resources dried up long before the century was over. Sandalwood was exhausted in a generation; pearls and sea slug lasted hardly any longer; and whaling in the Pacific, which had started as early as the 1790s, was already past its heyday when Melville's *Moby Dick* was published in 1851—though it lingered on until other sources of oil destroyed it almost completely by the end of the century. One other crop—another source of oil, as it happens—did linger on in commercial quantities right up until the Second World War, and perhaps it could be called the only "systematic" indigenous crop of the South Seas: copra, the semidried flesh of the coconut, once the product of large German plantations in Samoa and elsewhere as well as countless smaller operations throughout the islands. In the modern era sugar and fruit survived in Fiji and Hawai'i, but otherwise attention turned almost exclusively to mineral resources: for example, the vast amounts of petrified seabird dung (guano) to be found on Nauru and Ocean Island (Banaba), fertilizers made from which raised crops throughout the British empire; and previously inaccessible reserves of gold, nickel, copper, and other metals to be found in New Guinea, Bougainville, and New Caledonia. None of these temporary El Dorados went on to sustain settler communities. When the pearls were ripped out of one lagoon, the pearler and his divers moved on; when the last sandalwood had fallen, the logger disappeared; when Ocean Island had been reduced to pock-marked rubble, the phosphate miner went away; and when Moby Dick decamped, so did Captain Ahab, leaving no trace except some dilapidated tryworks on deserted coastlines and some Yankee connections in the whaling ports-of-call.

Not much of this was foreseen by the powers in 1800. The United States was a fledgling nation then and Germany not a state at all; the French and the British were at each other's throats until Waterloo and had problems of their own in the years immediately following it. After James Cook's voyages, Stephen Roberts argued, "the actual exploitation of the Pacific lingered. There was something like a state of retarded animation." The period 1797–1840 was "pre-eminently a time in which the humanitarianism of 'the philosophical navigators' of the eighteenth century was carried on" (Roberts, 33–34). Traders and resource hunters were feeling their way out into the wide blue yonder during that period—particularly from Sydney—and missionaries were going about their business, too: but neither group welcomed colonial interference. The traders feared overregulation (or just regulation), and the missionaries felt colonization to be itself a corrupting force. As the century wore on, however, the religious revival began to die down, and French and British ships began to return to the islands, representing centralized interests (often liberal ones, it should be noted, to do with protecting Islanders from unregulated or unsupervised development) and strategic thinking from home. Moreover, New Zealand, the only truly planned colony in the South Seas—the only one built up by large numbers of free settlers exporting themselves to preselected sites of settlement—had at the settlers' own request become a British dominion in 1840. (There were several planned acts of settlement in various regions of New Zealand, including Scottish emigrants in the Otago area. New Zealand–related selections below focus on the Anglican "Canterbury Settlement," also in the South Island.) The Australasian British colonies thereafter began to explore their Pacific surroundings and to demand security from the perceived threat of foreign interference. In such an environment, the lack of interest expressed by the centralized authorities in London, Paris, or Washington had quite the reverse effect out on the colonial fringe: "The reluctance of the governing Power of the British race in the Home Country to establish an empire in the South Pacific found a curious response in the stubborn resoluteness of the colonists who settled in Australia and New Zealand to be more English than the English themselves, to be as aggressively Imperialistic almost as the men of the Elizabethan era" (Fox 1912: 95). So the British navy became involved, willy-nilly, in patrolling the region as more of its nationals washed up there. (As the hero of Rolf Boldrewood's blithely imperialistic novel concerning "the Maori wars" in New Zealand put it: "We can't afford to lose such a brace of islands as these, the nearest approach, in climate, soil, and adaptation to the British race, of any land yet occupied. Not to be thought of" [Boldrewood, 272].)

What was true for the British became so for the French, the Americans, and ultimately the Germans. Even as such infant colonies and trading arrangements grew, so the importance of the region began to assert itself, if only in its own eyes. So further ships were sent and stations established; and consulates were set up in colonial backwaters; and squabbles erupted between consular officials; and native rulers were selected, feted, and fought over by the representatives of the great powers whose interest was reluctant, to say the least. Samoa was the victim of the worst of these cockfights when the British, German, and American consuls went head to head on the shores of Apia harbor, each backing different chiefs for dominance and calling in battleships accordingly, until a cyclone in March 1889 sank the American and German vessels. Ten years later Samoa was divided between Germany and the United States. In Tahiti, the Marquesas (annexed, 1842), Fiji, Samoa, and Hawai'i, well-intentioned or just plain meddlesome individuals, self-appointed representatives, sea captains, or missionaries involved their home governments in acts of colonial acquisition that they would never have initiated if left to their own devices. Often enough, too—and here the pattern is strikingly different from that observable in Africa or India, and related to the comparative poverty of the South Seas in resource terms—such acts of interference were the reverse of exploitive or tyrannical. Many individuals sought quite positively to protect the Islanders and their ways of life: from missionaries, from traders, from "blackbirders," from Westerners of different nationalities, even from the Islanders themselves. Often they went to considerable lengths to prop up Islander "kings" or "queens," even when such monarchs were Western inventions in themselves or proved quite unsustainable for other reasons.

Thus the pattern of Pacific colonialism is a complex one. At one extreme it was possible for a Victorian imperialist like James Anthony Froude—in *Oceana: Or England and Her Colonies* (1886)—to envisage a global commonwealth of English-speaking colonies in which the words of "Rule Britannia" would come true. At the other, it is possible to come across an expression from an American naval officer sent to Micronesia after the Second World War and recognize that it rings true of the entire colonial effort and not merely of the mid-1950s: "It was a time of limited resources and benign expedients" (Meredith, 181). It was possible to be a colonialist without being an imperialist, like the Canterbury settler Robert John Godley, who was as Anglophile as he was independent. It was possible to behave as the trader Eduard Hernsheim did in New Ireland and still believe yourself to be an influence for civilization:

The tobacco habit first had to be artificially inculcated in the natives in order to create a constant demand for a quickly consumed commodity, in place of goods made of iron which remained serviceable over a long period. The natives who had been in Matupi brought back pipes and tobacco, and soon schools for smoking were set up with the traders as instructors, in which the new pastime was propagated, so that in a few years' time tobacco was the most coveted and indispensable commodity among the natives. (Sack and Clark, 60)

Hernsheim could record such innovations in New Ireland but still write of New Britain, the island next door:

True, the natives there were still savage cannibals who had no idea of European culture, or of property and law. But in those great land masses, lying there silent and mysterious under a burning sun, my imagination could visualize how everything could one day be brought to life: how the virgin forest would be replaced by plantations which, like those in Java and India, could produce immense quantities of produce for the European market. It took several decades before this dream was realised, but it was in fact realised: the coasts of these regions have been charted, settlements established, hundreds of plantations started, the natives pacified and the islands now linked by large comfortable steamers to every continent. (Sack and Clark, 77)

So the dreams of an eighteenth-century colonialist like Edward Callander apparently came true, at the cost of a great deal of rainforest: "Who can doubt," Callander wrote of the Pacific,

that this vast tract must furnish objects innumerable, both of commercial advantage and curiosity, equal to any that were found in America by the first discoverers? Numbers of people, entirely different from us, and from each other, in their figure, customs, manners and religion: Their animals, insects, fishes, plants, medicinal herbs, fruits, metals and fossils entirely of another species. Thus this world must present with many things intirely new, as hitherto we have had little more knowledge of it, than if it had lain in another planet. . . . We must also remember how much they [the Islanders] would profit, by adopting our ideas of a regular and well-ordered society; their minds would be opened, and formed, their savage manners softened: In short, those nations would become men, who have just now nothing human but their figure. (Callander, 1:10–11)

A hundred years later George French Angas could complacently record that "British and American commerce have opened up a trade with numerous islands that must ultimately lead to their civilization" (Angas 1866: x). The reality, of course, was very different. In fact a great deal of the grief of colonialism had been foreseen (in symbolic and dramatic terms at least) in Shakespeare's *The Tempest* (1611), where the indigenous Islander Caliban is converted into a slave by two exiles from the court of Milan, the wizard Prospero and his daughter Miranda. "This island's mine," Caliban protests,

by Sycorax my mother,
Which thou tak'st from me. When thou cam'st first,
Thou strok'st me, and made much of me, wouldst give me
Water with berries in't, and teach me how
To name the bigger light, and how the less,
That burn by day and night. And then I loved thee,
And showed thee all the qualities o'th'isle,
The fresh springs, brine-pits, barren place and fertile.
Cursed be I that did so! All the charms
Of Sycorax—toads, beetles, bats fight on you!
For I am all the subjects that you have,
Which first was mine own king; and here you sty me
In this hard rock, whiles you do keep from me
The rest o'th'island.   (SHAKESPEARE, 76)

Another Victorian crystal ball gazer like George French Angas, Charles Wentworth Dilke, argued that "no possible series of events can prevent the English race itself in 1970 numbering 300 millions of beings—of one national character and one tongue. Italy, Spain, France, Russia become pigmies by the side of such a people" (Dilke, 573). The Pacific being the shared backyard of the Americans, Canadians, Australians, and New Zealanders, he opined, "the fortune of the Pacific shores is inevitably brilliant" (Dilke, 287). Some flew even higher, declaring the Pacific "the ocean of the ultimately unified earth" before the Second World War tore apart and repatched it (Brown, 2:160). These fantasies or aspirations underlay a good deal of colonial thinking in general; they even underlay a good deal of the liberalism and benevolence that are an unexpected feature of colonial thinking about the South Seas in particular. "To the Anglo-Saxon race is given the sceptre of the globe," wrote an apologist for missionary-induced civilization in 1849, "but there is not given either the lash of the slave-driver or the rack of the executioner. . . , humanizing, not destroying, as they advance; uniting with, not enslaving, the inhabitants with whom they dwell, the British race may be improved with vigour and capacity in the Eastern Hemisphere, and the emigrants whom we see around us may become the progenitors of a people destined to exceed the glories of European civilisation, as much as they have outstripped the wonders of ancient enterprise" (Russell, 429).

from "The Canterbury Association: Farewell to the New Zealand Emigrants," *Illustrated London News* (1850)

The *Illustrated London News,* founded in 1842, was a weekly magazine that pioneered the use of engraving and, later, photography in print media. Enormously successful, this precursor of the modern news magazine continued until the

FIGURE 15. "The Canterbury Colonists: Scene at Gravesend," from *Illustrated London News* (7 September 1850). By permission of the National Library of Australia.

1970s, and though its anonymous articles originally covered national stories, it quickly took an interest in international events. (See Figure 15.).

A few weeks ago we recorded the proceedings at a *déjeuner*[1] given in the East India Import Dock to the higher class of emigrants as a kind of farewell on leaving their native land; and on Monday we had the pleasure of being present at a dinner given to the labouring emigrants, in booths erected for the purpose in the fields adjoining Wate's Hotel, Gravesend, the hotel itself not being able to accommodate so large a party. About 600 persons sat down to an excellent dinner of good old English fare, while many friends of the emigrants were within the tents, and appeared to take great interest in the proceedings. Nor were parties outside at all inactive, a regular fair appearing to have sprung up on the spur of the moment, to meet the wishes and the wants of the multitude assembled in the vicinity of the refreshment booths. [. . .]

The scene seemed to carry us back to bygone years, when the Pilgrim Fathers went forth over perilous seas (linked together by one faith) to establish colonies in far-off lands, and build cities in wild wooded wastes which had before borne no imprint but that of beasts of the chase, or the footmark the Indian hunter left behind when pursuing them. Stern men, such as Cromwell selected his Ironsides from, and staid matrons who, during the civil war, laid aside their psalters to load arquebusses, were the unflinching elements out of

---

1. Lunch (French). Until modern times lunch was a meal associated with the upper classes, who had the leisure to eat it; working people ate before and after the working day, not in the middle of it.

which our colonies were formed in those stormy old times.[2] Neither gaols nor workhouses were emptied to people those early settlements,[3] but firm high-souled men and women went out, accompanied by their ministers and grave elders, such as in more ancient days assembled in our Saxon witanagemotes,[4] full of moral resolves, and gave them laws, and established another England, in which they could worship God according to the dictates of their own consciences. They weeded not the garden to transplant its sickly and seedy roots, but (so to speak) took out the very seed, and the purest mould, and formed for themselves strong and healthy beds, that produced such fruit as tempted and attracted others to sally forth and cultivate their newly-discovered fields.

Of similar materials to these is the Canterbury Settlement, in New Zealand, to be formed, and more than a million acres to be peopled, by those who are of one faith—members of the English Church—and who are to begin by building schools and erecting places of worship, and thus providing for the intellectual and spiritual wants of the community. Food and raiment and shelter are not all they undertake to supply, but ample provision is made for much higher and holier purposes.

None who are really poor and wretched accompany them; such as go out as servants and labourers are men and women of good character, and members of the English Church. The Archbishop of Canterbury is at the head of the Association, which numbers among its members noblemen and gentlemen, and those connected with the Church—in short, we shall not err by calling it a religious community. Hunger, and crime, and sin, and sorrow, and nakedness, and wretchedness they leave behind. Except the working emigrants who accompany them, we believe nearly the whole of the settlers are large purchasers of land—some few of those who have speculated remaining here. They are also at liberty to establish their own form of government—to be, in fact, free and independent of England. It will be seen that they set out with such wealth, respectability, and numbers as surpass all that our former colonists ever possessed, but that they take away none of our unemployed or needy poor.

What we witnessed last Monday, awakened no painful feelings, for they were not people actually compelled to leave their country because they were unable to obtain a living in it, like the many thousands who covet but the common necessaries of life, and cannot obtain them. We turned from the well-spread tables then before us, and thought of the poverty and wretchedness of those who drag out a miserable existence in our over-crowded cities; the thousands who stand

---

2. The author is thinking of the Pilgrims who set sail from Plymouth for New England in 1620. He identifies them with the Parliamentary forces led by Oliver Cromwell in the English Civil War of 1642–1649, who defeated the Royalists supporting King Charles I. (An "arquebuss" is an antique variety of musket.)

3. Whereas the colonies in Australia at the time of writing were and had been settled by convicts.

4. A supreme council of England in Anglo-Saxon times.

> Houseless near a thousand homes,
> And near a thousand tables pine for want of food;[5]

who bring no old memories into the crowded city, in which many of them were born. Home, with its green boughs rustling above the rippling stream—the murmur of the bee—the shout of the cuckoo, and the mellow song of the golden-billed blackbird were never to them old, familiar sounds; they have nothing to sigh over, to look back upon and regret. The word "Home" to many of them has no charm, has never been surrounded with comfort; it is but a shifting from attic to attic, or from cellar to cellar; it but conjures up unhealthy back-rooms, and high, dead walls, and breathless courts, which when the wind reaches, it only stirs the sleeping poison, and scatters wider the stench of a thousand stagnant sewers. There they sit and hear of holidays and merry seasons, in which they have no share; the Christmas bells but ring out to them telling that nights are long and coals dear; and they are compelled to sit and listen to those sounds in the darkness, or by the glimmering of a handful of fire, for they are too poor to purchase even a candle. Spring processions and Whitsun[6] holidays but tell them there are pleasant places somewhere, which people are rushing out of town to see, though for them the flowers grow not, nor have they ever rested under the cooling shadow of a green tree. All they know of time is by feeling hungry, and struggling against sleep, while "stitch, stitching," keeping no other record of the hours but by the number of stitches they take,[7] or how long it will be before they can afford to eat again, while hunger is gnawing within, though the insufficient meal is but just concluded. Their homes were places from which they were many a time turned out, because they could not pay the rent, then left to stand shivering and starving in the street, until some one, who numbered as many miseries as they, all but the want of a wretched roof for a covering, invited them in—and they sat crouching beside the fireless grate, thankful that, in addition to hunger, they had not to endure

> The pitiless pelting of the outer storm.[8]

They have nothing to offer one another but sympathy—nothing to give but sigh for sigh, as they mingle tears with tears. What have they to throw a charm over home? Where is the comfortable bed on which to repose when their labour is ended? Behold that heap of rags and straw in the dark corner of the room! Where are their pictures to enliven the walls? their flowers, to tell that

---

5. Slightly misquoted from William Wordsworth's poem of 1798, "The Female Vagrant" (later published as "Guilt and Sorrow").

6. Whitsun is the seventh Sunday after Easter, so it falls in late spring or early summer.

7. Many of the English poor were economically trapped in piecework, as in modern-day sweatshops in the garment trade.

8. Adapted from King Lear's lines during his mad scene on the heath (act 3, scene 4): "Poor naked wretches, wheresoe'er you are, / That bide the pelting of the pitiless storm. . . ."

spring or summer has come? The imagination must form a landscape where the mortar has broken away—the only white patch in that dirty dwelling; their flowers of summer are dying in that broken jug where the halfpenny nosegay is placed, purchased when hunger needed appeasing, because memory was pining for nourishment, and the heart and eye were weary of those black roofs and tall chimneys, and they wanted to look on something which God had made, for,

> Though man has power to build a town,
> He cannot make the thistledown,
> Which every wind doth shake.[9]

Mighty England, with all her glory, has but left them heirs to misery. When such as these are borne away to another country, we can almost picture the guardian angels that would accompany them hiding their faces with their hands as they speed along with their white wings expanded above the vessel, as if weeping for these poor outcast daughters. But Hope, with her "golden hair" streaming out, would herald the way, pointing to other stars beyond the rim of the horizon, far over the sea, and bidding them remember that God is also there; that there are no crowded courts and starving populace in those lands, where Health would stand with roses in her hands to plant in their pale cheeks, while honest Labour waved his sickle to welcome them to the thatched hut, which, stored with plenty, would send its blue smoke under the green trees, and then in coiling shadows over the golden harvest-field. Alas! these go not out with the Canterbury Colonists. We should consider the present emigrants as going before to prepare the way for their feebler or poorer brethren. Their intelligence, capital, and enterprise will, we trust, create such a demand for labour, that they will invite the misery and poverty left at home to join them in the happy land of Canterbury, where we hope plenty will be found for all. May their turn soon come, and may they speedily join those who are now on their way; and, when it does, may the sea on which they will sleep flow around them with a gentle murmur—may the breeze visit them as softly as a mother's breath when she bends over her slumbering infant, and so dream during their long voyage over the ocean. May they at last anchor in a foreign land, where they will find a home such as they have never known.

Here, where there is not even room for their dead, but where the last silent tenant is removed to make room for the next comer, what have they to weep over? Nothing! No one, perhaps, would be by to close their dying eyes, or, when they turned their faces to the cold wall, to bid "God bless them!" No friendly hand to lift them down those stairs up which they had so often gone with aching hearts, but be borne by pauper arms, in a pauper's coffin, to a nameless grave, the very hillock of which would be levelled within a month after they had been thrust beneath it, as if there was neither room for them

---

9. Quotation unidentified, but quasi-biblical sentiments like these are common in early-nineteenth-century British religious literature.

living nor dead. Who would not pray to heaven to send them a prosperous voyage (as those were prayed for on Tuesday) as they fly from a shore which brings to memory only misery, where the only hours of happiness they knew were those which went winged over their unconscious childhood, when hunger was scarcely felt while they played, and sorrow forgotten when they slumbered—when the Angel of Sleep came and carried away the very memory of wretchedness until they awoke again. May the peaceful daisies soon blow about their home in a land where there is plenty, and to spare, and human life is not made up of labour, hunger-pangs, and short, fitful, moaning snatches of slumber, which is not sleep. May they, like those who are now preceding them, find a home around which to twine their affections, with a few trees and flowers that they can love and call their own, where the sun has room to get near them at morning, and can give them a parting smile before he sets at night, and no tax is laid on the window through which he shines,[10] but where he comes streaming free as when, first launched from God's almighty hand, he went thundering with a golden trail of glory behind, until the voice of the Omnipotent bade him stop in the immensity of space. May they find verdant valleys over which no board ever looked, threatening the wanderer with imprisonment for trespassing,[11] but where the land is as free as it is to the foot of the bird, and where, in time, the tall church-spire may rise and the Sabbath-bell ring, and the hum of childish voices be heard coming from beneath the blossoming trees in the orchard where they are at play. When we turn to such a picture as this, and look at the haunts of wretchedness they now inhabit, we are compelled to acknowledge Emigration as a blessing.

from Charles St. Julian, *Notes on the Latent Resources of Polynesia* (1851)

Charles St. Julian (1819–1874) was a journalist and newspaper editor in Sydney. His pronounced interest in the future of the Pacific led him eventually to a variety of advisory and consular positions with the then independent kingdom of Hawai'i. In 1862 he was declared bankrupt, and he spent the rest of his career as a local councillor and magistrate in New South Wales.

The advancement of the islanders in civilisation has hitherto been seriously retarded by the existence of a strong antagonistic feeling between the missionaries and the traders.

Facts enough have been quoted to show that the missionaries, in watching over the interests of the people they are sent to instruct, could scarcely

---

10. The British government levied a tax on windows during the eighteenth and nineteenth centuries. It was abolished in 1851, a year after this piece was published.

11. The much-hated Poor Law of early-nineteenth-century Britain was administered by local boards, who often treated vagrants and beggars cruelly.

fail to come into collision with the irregular and unprincipled class of traders before referred to. These people have been accustomed, in their dealings with the islanders, to indulge so freely in brutality and fraud, that these vices have become a distinguishing characteristic of all their proceedings. To inculcate humanity and honesty, therefore, is to denounce the whole of this class.

We find, consequently, that it is this description of trader who is most strongly opposed to missionary enterprises. In fact, his feelings towards all missions and missionaries have more the character of a fixed and determined hatred than of a mere feeling of opposition. But this feeling of antagonism is not confined to the semi-piratical class in question. In a milder form it is very generally diffused even among the merchants and traders whose proceedings are fair and open, and whose reputation is unquestionably good. Mere prejudice is the chief cause of this. But when such feelings are found to exist among a respectable and intelligent class of men, there is usually some real grounds for them. It is so in this instance. The missionaries have earned this opposition by their strenuous efforts to impede the progress of commerce by every channel not under their own immediate direction, and by their efforts, successful in most instances, to obtain and exercise an exclusive political and social influence among the races they are sent to Christianize.

The merchant and the missionary ought to act in concert, and with perfect friendliness of feeling; for, guided by such a spirit, each could aid most materially the exertions of the other. The labours of the missionary pave the way for the enterprise of the merchant, and the former completes what the latter has begun. Civilization is best commenced by the communication of Christian knowledge. Under the humanising influence of this knowledge trade and settlement are rendered secure in places where before the commencement of missionary exertions the latter would have been impossible, and the former very hazardous. Commerce completes the work. Whatever of civilization the islanders possess has had its origin in missionary enterprise and missionary zeal; but where there has been any material advance, as at the Sandwich Islands and Tahiti, it is to commerce that this advance must be attributed. [. . .]

While some of the missionaries have done much to retard the progress of commercial enterprise, others have used every effort to promote the material as well as the spiritual advancement of the islanders. The martyred Williams[12] underwent a long series of hardships and misfortunes, without suffering himself to be turned aside from his career of usefulness, or without even allowing his energies to be materially damped. And all his efforts and measures appear to have been judicious. His labours were for the most part crowned with success, and his name will long abide in the grateful recollection of the people to whom he imparted the truths of Christianity, and the advantages of civiliza-

---

12. The missionary John Williams, murdered at Eromanga in the New Hebrides in 1839.

13. Jean-Baptiste Épalle was appointed Catholic vicar apostolic for Melanesia in 1844 and took a ship with thirteen clerics from Sydney to the Solomon Islands in 1845, where he was killed in intertribal fighting.

THE ISLAND AS COLONY

tion. Of the results which have attended the labours of the Catholic missionaries, but little is known. That little, however, is good. No danger or difficulty has sufficed to deter these devoted men. And the blood of Bishop Epalle[13] and his fellow-martyrs has not been shed in vain, for except in some of the more northern islands, where the Catholic missionaries have adventured among the most savage races, and have braved the most unhealthy climates, their efforts appear to have been crowned with peculiar success.

And while the missionary paves the way for commerce, so commerce may be said to pave the way for the missionary. The desultory trade first carried on among the islanders, even with all its disadvantages, is usually the means of awakening these people to a sense of the gain to be derived from a more intimate connexion with the white man. They are predisposed therefore to receive and protect the missionary, in the hope of acquiring, by his aid and instruction, the knowledge and the wealth of his race.

So long as the missionary and the merchant confine themselves each to their own proper limits, the former to the communication of instruction, and the latter to fair, honest, straightforward trading, or to the establishment of well organised settlements; their efforts must be mutually beneficial. If persons of either class depart from this course, then those of the other become a check upon their proceedings, and animosities cannot fail to arise. By the creation and encouragement of these ill-feelings, both parties suffer. But it is the unfortunate islander who sustains the greatest amount of injury. By observing the difference between the two classes of white men, his confidence in both is greatly weakened, if not wholly destroyed. Deprived thus of his guide, he is too apt to relapse into his original barbarism.

The true interests of the missionary and of the merchant, in the pursuit of their respective avocations, are, therefore, identical. And the resources of the Polynesian Islands can only be fully and profitably developed by the formation of permanent establishments upon them. By such establishments the profits of the merchant would be increased; British influence and interests, and more especially the influence of this city,[14] political as well as commercial, would be maintained and expanded; and the advancement of the Polynesian in the path of civilization would be accelerated. The only persons who would suffer would be the unprincipled men who prey upon the simplicity and upon the weakness of these races, and with this class few will have any sympathy.

from Henry T. Cheever, *The Island World of the Pacific* (1851)

Henry Cheever (1814–1897) was an American Congregationalist missionary who worked in Hawai'i in the late 1840s. His book combines a social and natural history of Hawai'i with an earnest plea for its responsible development as a Christian but not Westernized independent nation.

---

14. St. Julian was writing for the *Sydney Morning Herald,* still a leading newspaper in Australia.

God's providences have been too marked and many towards this rising nation and its band of missionaries to allow a doubt that His banner will still be held over it, and that the Gospel shall be allowed to try its efficacy to elevate and preserve this so recently idolatrous and miserable race. Is it too much to hope that the causes of national extinction and decay may yet be arrested, and that the people of Hawaii nei may yet become the joy and pride of the earth? a glorious example to all the world of a regenerated race of heathen: forming an illustrious exception to that melancholy rule of destiny by which all the races of savages seem melting away before the arts, and vices, and enterprise of the white man. Whether or not it be true, as some assert, that "commerce is digging the grave of this nation," we do not pretend to decide. It is quite certain that most of those who go there *to deal in commerce* little care, provided only that a race of intelligent, enterprising Anglo-Saxons supplant them, and occupy the soil in which the Hawaiians are quietly entombed.

If such shall ever be the melancholy fact, let those remember whose contact with the race has been demoralizing and deadly, "Be sure your sin will find you out." The injured shades of Hawaiians will meet their destroyers in another world with stern and terrible recrimination. Your ships and your men, will they say, brought the vice and disease that have been our ruin. You *foreigners lent your whole influence to make the Hawaiian Islands one great brothel!* You opposed and slandered our teachers, and did all you could to nullify the force of their instructions. If "Christian merchants" came among us, what did they more than others but make us hewers of wood and drawers of water to themselves? When and how were they known to help our teachers? or to consecrate the gains made among us to the Christian work of saving our souls? Whether, intent only upon gain, it was in your heart to do so or not, ye did but help the process of our extermination and decay. "The Christian's God that paid the debt," whom many of us rejoiced to find, now taketh vengeance, and pays in eternity the wrongs of time.

In the history of the world since the Christian era, the settlement of foreigners for the mere purposes of gain among nations of savages, so far from being beneficial, has been found detrimental to *their* growth and prosperity. The new-comers have gradually over-run and dispossessed the native races, or they have become the mere serfs and menials of those that were first received on bare sufferance.

It remains to be seen whether the Hawaiians will form an exception to this rule. What is eminently needed is, that devoted laymen of the different professions and trades go and settle there on purpose to do good, not with the selfish design of merely enriching themselves, but with the disinterested intention of benefiting the nation by teaching the useful arts, industrious habits, and ways of developing the physical resources of civilized life. Such men, with the virtues of economy, prudence, and thrift, could any where get a livelihood, and they could everywhere do great good.

from John Robert Godley, "Inaugural Address to the Lyttleton Colonists' Society at Its First Meeting" (1852)

Lyttleton is the province of New Zealand around Christchurch in the South Island, named in honor of Lord Lyttleton (mentioned in the *Illustrated London News* article above). John Robert Godley (1814–1862) served as director of Edward Gibbon Wakefield's New Zealand Company, managing director of the Canterbury Association, and effective governor of Lyttleton between 1851 and 1852, before ill health sent him back to England.

To begin with: I hold, paradoxical as it may appear, that the besetting sin of all society in a new country is, not idleness, but industry; or rather (to put this proposal in a less startling form), that society suffers as much by men working too much as by their working too little. You know what the old proverb says "all work and no play" makes people,[15] and I am always afraid of our exemplifying its truth. I am always afraid of our becoming very "dull boys." Of course, you understand me, when I talk of too much work, I do not mean work in its widest and highest sense, as embracing and operating upon the whole domain of nature and art, and as signifying the exercise of every faculty of man—his imagination, his intellect and his heart, his soul and his body. Of work, so understood, there can never be too much; for, in this sense, the secret of civilization, the key to progress, the primary law of God's universe, is work.[16] My idea of the state of perfection towards which man ought to be tending and striving is that of a state where all should be workers and none should be drones; a state where every one in his sphere, and according to his ability, should be ever contributing to the consummation of the universal work for which man was created and made. Do not for a moment suppose then that I advocate indolence, or that I undervalue the nobleness of work. All I mean to say is, that there may be too much of merely mechanical work, of work devoted to the sole purpose of making money, and providing the body with creature comforts; that there may be too much wool growing, too much store keeping, too much wood cutting, too much digging, to the neglect and exclusion of pursuits which cultivate the intellect and purify the heart. That Divine saying, "Man doth not live by bread alone, but by every word that proceedeth out of the mouth of God," is (if I may say so without presumption) of a far wider application than at first sight appears. What, I ask you, are the glories of nature and the treasures of art, what are the gifts of genius and the wonders of science, but words proceeding out of the mouth of God—words to which we are bound to listen—words which it is our duty to interpret and to obey—words which it is a sin against God to disregard and to forget in the pursuit of "bread alone"? I know how invidious it is to hold such language

15. "All work and no play makes Jack a dull boy."
16. A quintessentially Victorian belief. See Thomas Carlyle's *Past and Present* (1843), book 3, chapter 1: "Blessed is he who has found his work; let him ask no other blessedness."

to hard-working, hard-faring men. I know how easy it is for them to turn upon me if so disposed, and to reply, "It is all very well for you to talk, but how are working men to find time for such things?" The retort is plausible but unsound. I must repeat, that no man anywhere, least of all any man here, is justified in saying that he can afford no time for improving his mind and cultivating his taste. There are unlimited degrees, of course, in the amount of improvement and cultivation which men can find time for; but all men can afford some time: men in a new country can afford plenty of time for objects of the character I speak of. Depend upon it your happiness will be greater, your conscience lighter, your cares fewer, if you determine to spend some portion of your time and faculties and means in communing with the spiritual world; if you will occasionally forget for a while the present, and enter into relations with the past and the future; if you will recollect at times that what we see and hear and touch constitutes but a small part of the realities among which we live, and which shall endure when time shall be no more.

Knowing, I say, how adverse the prevailing current of tone and presentiment in a colonial community is to the view which I am advocating, I rejoice exceedingly whenever any incident occurs to interrupt the ordinary course of that current, and to force us as it were to keep a sabbath or a jubilee. For example, I appeal to those among you who were present the other day on the solemn occasion of laying the corner-stone of our first church, when there was a general suspension of business in our little town, and almost every one seemed more or less to keep a religious holiday. Did you not feel that the time was well spent, and that it was good for you to be there? While you watched the performance of the Church's rites, while you listened to the words of her services, while you observed the earnest attention of the surrounding crowd, and thought of the holy work that was in hand, did you not feel for the moment carried away and elevated, as it were, beyond and above yourselves? Were you not transported in imagination to the scenes of your childhood and your home, with all the tender and sacred recollections attached to them? Did you not hear the chime of the bells? Did you not see the spire among the trees? Did you not wander through the green churchyards where those whom you have loved and lost are sleeping? And as the illusion passed away, and the reality came back to you, could you fail to turn in thankfulness of soul to the God of your fathers, who had brought you from the ends of the earth to found a new branch of the ancient Church to His glory and honour here? I am sure the impression produced by such scenes is real, though it may be but too fleeting: I am sure it leaves, on many a heart, an elevating and sanctifying influence behind it. There is nothing of course in the enterprise in which we are just now engaged that is calculated to excite the imagination or to touch the heart, like the religious ceremony to which I have just referred; but it may so far be classed under the same category for the purposes of my argument, that the primary object of its promoters has been to interest the people by its means in subjects of a nature removed in some respects from the sphere of their ordinary business; such subjects as philosophy, history, politics, science, and art. Our object is to impart useful information, and to educate public opinion, on subjects of general interest; and we propose that this should be done by every legitimate and available method; by means of books, of lectures, and of discussions. We wish to lay the first stone of a great educational institution, which shall grow with our growth and strengthen with our strength; and we more especially wish to base it on sound, comprehensive, and durable principles, because we feel that the founders of a new nation have a vast burden of responsibility laid upon them. In fact, they can do nothing of a public nature for themselves alone; nothing, therefore, of which it can be said that is of trifling importance. As the twig is bent, the tree will grow. Incalculable results lie hid in every step we take, and nations yet unborn may rue through ages the consequences of our errors and our sins. This thought should be perpetually present with us, not to daunt, but to encourage. As is the responsibility to be borne, so is the honour to be won. It is but at rare intervals in the world's history that so great opportunities are offered to such as we are. Let us show ourselves not unworthy of, not unequal to, our high vocation.

from "A Ramble through the New Zealand Court," *Illustrated London News* (1886)

Thirty-six years after reporting on the Canterbury emigration, the *Illustrated London News* visited the Colonial and India Exhibition, held at the Albert Hall in London. Then, the magazine had discussed what England was sending out to New Zealand; now, it turned its attention to what the colony was sending back. (See Figures 16 and 17.)

The Exhibition Rambler has a store of pleasant surprises in "Col.-India." None more delightful than that which is afforded by a stroll northward from the quaint Old London street of Dick Whittington's period, past the south-west basin, and into the charming Fernery of New Zealand. A Fairlight Glen in beauty is this semi-realisation of a New Zealand fern gully, inspection of one conspicuous object in which, however, recalls the melancholy saying of the Maoris—"As foreign clover is killing our ferns, so the Maori will disappear before the white man."

Fortunate enough to have as guide an accomplished Past Master in Great Exhibitions, the erudite and active Mr. Peter Lund Simmonds, F.L.S., invaluable Secretary to the New Zealand Commission, we pause on the summit of the Fernery opposite the Maori Tomb of the Arawa Chief, Waata Taranui, one of the interesting native curiosities brought over by Dr. Walter L. Buller, C.M.G., F.R.S. This wooden tomb is painted brown and black, is surmounted by grotesque wooden figures, and embellished with the iridescent "ear-shells" and tufts of white feathers so freely used in ornamentation by the New Zealanders. Quitting this wealth of ferns somewhat reluctantly, and following our nimble cicerone[17] into the bright and varied court itself, we soon have ample

---

17. Guide (Italian).

FIGURE 16. "Section of Kauri Pine," "Kauri Pine—from a Photograph," and "The 'Vegetable Sheep,'" from *Illustrated London News* (2 October 1886). By permission of the National Library of Australia.

proof that the Executive Commissioners, Sir Francis Dillon Bell, K.C.M.G., Agent-General for the colony, and Sir Julius Von Haast, K.C.M.G., F.R.S., one of the most famous and eminent Naturalists of our time, have secured an admirable representation of the products and manufactures and natural history of New Zealand.[18]

The Maoris (supposed to have settled in New Zealand some six hundred years ago from the "Hawaiki" Islands, in the Pacific) have the southern section of the court entirely devoted to them. Dr. W. L. Buller is a prominent exhibitor here. He has, in the first place, adorned the walls with M. G. Lindauer's vivid paintings of well-tattoed chiefs, among which we recognise an excellent portrait of our old friend, Tawhiao, the Maori King, whose recent visit to London will not be forgotten. Tawhiao does not lack humour. Chancing to drop into the Savage Club[19] during his stay here, the Maori King happened to occupy a seat next the late Dr. Pope, one of the most corpulent men in London. With a twinkle in his eyes, possibly stimulated by the cannibalistic tastes of an ancestor, the Maori King cast an admiring glance at the rotund form beside him and, turning to the present writer, exclaimed, "Kahpi!" which I understood to be Maori for "Very good!" At any rate, poor Dr. Pope (unwishful to serve as a Maori meal) speedily sank into a chair at the other end of the smoking-room. "In this connection," one examines with particular attention Mr. Lindauer's likeness of "Matene Te Matuku, a former Man-Eater." Fortune-hunters, for their part, may prefer to gaze at the same artist's portrait of the comely "Ru-

---

18. Messrs. Simmonds, Buller, Bell, and Von Haast come labeled as members of the British establishment. F.L.S. is Fellow of the Linnaean Society; F.R.S. is Fellow of the Royal Society; C.M.G. is commander of the feudal order of St. Michael and St. George; K.C.M.G. is knight commander of the same order.

19. Named after the early-eighteenth-century poet Richard Savage and founded in 1857, this exclusive London dining club is still in existence in Whitehall Place.

THE ISLAND AS COLONY

FIGURE 17. "Maori Store-House, in the Native Section," from *Illustrated London News* (2 October 1886). By permission of the National Library of Australia.

ruhira Karena, a Maori Heiress." The carved Pataka, or Maori store-house, for which the public is also indebted to Dr. Buller, is delineated among our Illustrations. Wearing the usual mat in shawl-fashion, a native woman is modelled in the act of gathering provisions from this storehouse, which is brightened here and there with the familar "ear-shell." The ethnological collection is altogether very valuable. Here are to be seen in cases Maori war trumpets, greenstone weapons and greenstone native ornaments, a sheaf of beautifully-carved war weapons, the model of a war canoe, a goodly array of hand-made and dyed flaxen mats, used by natives as garments; precious relics of the feathers of the moa; beautifully-carved wooden boxes for preserving provisions; handsome feather mats; and a rich variety of old stone implements used by the Maoris. [. . .]

In the instructive geological section, Mr. Simmonds first calls attention to the raised models of the North and South Islands and Stewart's Island, which form the fruitful and temperate Britain of the South, to which the Dutch name of New Zealand has been given. The large and serviceable geological and statistical maps are next pointed out, and well merit the passing praise bestowed upon them. There are about a score of cases of New Zealand minerals and stones. But the rambler who inclines to skim the cream of the Exhibition without too great an expenditure of time may elect to gather his information from the commanding trophies, which are indicated in the general view of the New Zealand court. Eyes involuntarily glisten at sight of the huge gilded monoliths which stand for the total export of New Zealand gold up to 1885—value £42,327,907—and sparkle yet more in face of the safeguarded case of golden quartz, nuggets, and fine alluvial gold. One is informed by the communicative living encyclopaedia who courteously acts as pilot that gold was discovered in the colony in 1812; but that it was not until 1852 that the gold-mines of Coromandel first attracted attention to the district of Cape Colville Peninsula,[20] which forms the chief centre of true lode-mining operations in New Zealand. But the yield of gold therefrom has been small compared with the alluvial gold obtained from the auriferous sand since 1861 in Otago.[21] With a keen eye for the natural riches of the soil, Mr. Simmonds is not a whit less enthusiastic in dilating on the stands of antimony, copper ore, and smelted copper; on the prevalence of iron ores in the colony, on the exhibits of silver ore ("270 oz. to the ton," he whispers, in a tone of rapt admiration), and on the large and fine blocks of coal in the Fernery from the Wallsend Colliery, Greymouth, and from the Granite Greek Colliery ("Seam of fifty-three feet!" he exclaims). And it may be mentioned, à propos, that the output of the New Zealand coal-mines up to the end of 1884 was 3,005,120 tons.

Re-entering the court, we come to a full stop in front of the section of the trunk of the colossal Kauri pine; and Mr. Simmonds shows a piece of timber containing the gum it yields prolifically, and then indicates the photograph, which affords some notion of the great height attained by this monarch of the forest. There are giants in these days. Finest tree in New Zealand, the Kauri grows to an altitude of 120 ft. to 160 ft., has a diameter at the base of 10 ft. to 20 ft., the massive trunk sometimes attaining a height of 80 ft. to 100 ft. before branching. Kauri is most useful. Its timber is in great request for spars and masts, the planking of ships, and for house-furnishing; and at the Thames gold-field Kauri serves for mine-props.[22] The Kauri pine grows north of Mercury Bay in the North Island. Its gum is usually found in fossils at the base of the trees. How admirably the Kauri gum is utilised for ornaments may be judged from an inspection of the cases of Mr. H. P. Barber and of Mr. E. B. Reynolds, of Auckland. Opposite, we find the large greenstone sent by Mr. John Hislop, Dunedin, and note a brisk sale going on in greenstone jewellery, the attendant in a fez (why fez?) holding up, with loyal pride, the fine greenstone watch-pendant, mounted in gold, and made for the Prince of Wales; while Mr. Simmonds whispers audibly that the Queen ordered a New Zealand greenstone paper-knife and scent-bottle. Close handy now to the towering Timber Trophy, the varieties of woods of the colony are enumer-

20. The Coromandel Peninsula, with Cape Colville at its head, is due east of Auckland, in the North Island of New Zealand.

21. Gold was discovered in the Otago region of the South Island in 1861, and the region's capital, Dunedin, experienced a decade of wealth and expansion as a result.

22. Thames is the chief town of the Coromandel Peninsula.

ated, among the most high-prized being the aforesaid kauri, manuka, totara, black birch, kowhai, and matai; and Mr. Simmonds might be a Blundell Maple himself, so eloquent does he wax over the certainly exquisitely-finished pieces of furniture exhibited, masterpieces of deft cabinet-making and turning. As he says, the adaptability of New Zealand woods to the finest kind of work, and the skill of the colonial artisans, are alike proved to demonstration here by an elegant table beautifully inlaid with an infinite number of different woods, and a variety of desks and admirable furniture generally, and notably by the handsome cabinet presented to Sir Joseph Hooker, the work of Mr. Anton Seuffert. Leaving this department, the indomitable Simmonds scuds to the other end of the court in order to expatiate on the rare quality of the wool produced by the New Zealand long-wooled sheep ("Export in '84 amounting to £3,267,527!"); and to dwell upon the increasing export of the frozen carcasses of sheep and lambs to England, cheap joints of which frozen meat are in great demand in the Colonial Market, held in the South Promenade of the Exhibition. As for the similarly fine grain exhibits, and especially the luxuriant specimens of native grasses, they are pegs on which to hang the fact that the exports of agricultural and farm produce rose from £262,930 in 1875 to £1,891,887 in 1884.

Were any venturesome Oliver Twist of to-day to intrude into the New Zealand Court, he would indubitably vary the Dickensian formula, and ask Mr. Simmonds for "Moa."[23] And "Moa" would be readily supplied. For the "Moa" is the "lion" of Sir Julius Von Haast's superb Natural History Collection of New Zealand. Of course, Sir Julius Von Haast's skeletons of the Moa, the extinct ostrich-like bird of the colony, reminds our chatty guide of Sir Richard Owen's great achievement, that of building up a Moa, not exactly from his inner consciousness, but from a single bone sent home from New Zealand.[24] In fine, we take our dessert off the Moa, and learn that this race of gigantic birds must have died out at an earlier date than the first Maori occupation of New Zealand, as the bones were found by Sir Julius Von Haast "deeply embedded in the gravels and swamps, while the evidences of human occupation are confined to the surface-soil, shelter-caves, and sand-dunes." Strolling round to admire Sir Julius Von Haast's valuable specimens of the Natural History of New Zealand, one finds something of interest at each step. Here, for instance, is the very peculiar mountain plant, aptly nicknamed "vegetable sheep" by the New Zealand shepherds,[25] inasmuch as it unquestionably most closely resembles the wool of a sheep. [. . .]

---

23. In Charles Dickens' *Oliver Twist* (1837) the charity boy hero approaches the master of the workhouse at dinner time to say: "Please, sir, I want some more."

24. Richard Owen was a leading Victorian anatomist, paleontologist, and intellectual opponent of Darwin.

25. A plant of the genus *Raoulia*: "This mound-like 'shrub' is formed of hundreds of stems, crowded densely and growing at the same rate, so that the surface of the mound appears very smooth. On each of these stems there is a dense clothing of minute, scaly-like woolly leaves, so closely oppressed to each other and the stems that each individual leaf is almost imperceptible" (Carlquist, 211).

I think I have now referred to all the objects of general interest save the food exhibits (which speak for themselves) and the numerous pictures of New Zealand scenery, which will amply repay a visit to the Albert Hall. Finally, I have to return my warm thanks to Mr. Simmonds for the information he readily and courteously supplied respecting the New Zealand Court.

from Julian Thomas ("The Vagabond"), *Cannibals and Convicts* (1887)

John Stanley James (1853–1896), aka Julian Thomas, was an English-born journalist with a shady past who published a successful series of investigative sketches in Australian newspapers in the mid-1870s under the pen name "The Vagabond." In 1878 the *Sydney Morning Herald* sent him to report on an indigenous uprising in the French colony of New Caledonia.

It was high noon under a blazing sun. We had just finished the brilliant attack on the native village near Tia, in which we proudly distinguished ourselves by destroying acres of bananas and yams. Under the shade of a cocoanut tree we reposed after our toil, and breakfasted heartily, recking little of the skulls of massacred convicts which lay around.[26] My companions, Captain Rathouis and Lieutenant Maréchal, who had charge of the expedition, were hardy warriors, who jested at the signs of mortality. After all, it was not our fault that we did not meet the enemy. We meant fighting, and if the foe disappointed us, and we had to revenge ourselves upon the innocent vegetation, I suppose I was the only one who felt mean about it. *À la guerre, comme la guerre!*[27] After breakfast I was asked if I would like to ride to La Foa, and see the spot where the first massacre took place. I was very willing, and we started off accompanied by a corporal's guard. There were four miles of lonely road. Every now and then we passed the burnt dwelling houses of some *concessionnaire*,[28] but the fertile crops were still standing. The Canaque[29] was more civilised than we were, in that he never destroyed what was meant for food. Carelessly and gaily

---

26. New Caledonia had been annexed by the French in 1853. Ten years later it was designated a penal colony, and between 1863 and 1896 (when the system was abolished) 20,000 convicts were sent from France. As the indigenes were not protected under law and had no property rights, their land was constantly under threat from settlers. This led to a series of uprisings, the most serious of which was the Kanak Rebellion of 1878–1879 (centered on the village of La Foa), in which two hundred settlers and at least one thousand indigenes died. In 1887 the Melanesian population was brought under colonial government and required to stay on reserves.

27. An idiomatic expression along the lines of "When the going gets tough, the tough get going" (French).

28. A convict who has served his time and has been granted a piece of land to farm in the colony.

29. French version of Melanesian word "Kanaka," meaning "man," used indiscriminately by whites to refer to Islanders of any hue and origin but since reappropriated by some Melanesians. (Thus modern-day campaigners for the independence of New Caledonia refer to the colony as "Kanaky.")

we cantered along till we came to the site of the telegraph office. Everything was in ruins. Crossing the river by the ford we rode to the spot where Colonel Galli Passeboc was killed. The dense jungle on each side of the track might have concealed a hundred foes. It was not considered safe to go farther. In the ruins of the old gendarmerie,[30] skulls and bones were lying about. They belonged to bodies which had been destroyed by fire, after having been unburied for days, and having been partially devoured by pigs. I never wanted to eat pork in New Caledonia. At this point we had a surprise. A beautiful little filly trotted into the yard, and was immediately seized by us. For many a long day she had been haunting the neighbourhood of her burnt stable, missing, no doubt, the companionship of her kind, and the tender care of her master. He was dead. His skull she spurned with her hoof as she pranced around; but she would be happier with her new owners than running wild in the bush. I fancied that regular daily meals, and corn and water in plenty, would make up for the loss of a freedom which might imply a considerable amount of hunger and thirst. In the gardens of the dead gendarmes some excellent salad was still growing, and our soldiers loaded themselves with this. As we returned, we halted in a cocoanut grove, and a tree was cut down to obtain milk of the young fruit. I did not approve of this wasteful destruction, especially as the liquor was to me sickly and nauseous; but I am glad to say that here the wholesale destruction of cocoanut-trees was not carried on as by the troops of Colonel Wendling. [. . .]

Le père Rivière,[31] as his officers lovingly called him—"For, see you," said they, "he commands in all, but of the rest is *bon camarade*"[32]—was, as ever, kind to me at night; and he and M. Rathouis conferred as to what they would show me. On the morrow there was to be an ordinary expedition to make a circuit of the neighbourhood. In a day or two a blockhouse at La Foa was to be built, of which Captain Lafont would be the commander. "Will you go to Moindou, and see the chief Baptiste?" I was asked. I had great pleasure in assenting. "Afterwards you had better ride to Taremba, and assist at the court-martial on the Canaques in prison there," I was told. Again I thanked the Commandant Rivière, and felt that I was a lucky journalist in meeting with such courtesy and consideration.

In the early morning, Captain Rathouis and myself took horse for Moindou. We had a guard of four soldiers, although my companion said it was not necessary, as everything on that side of La Foa was quiet. Baptiste, I was told, was a man of very great intelligence, a very good French scholar, and a rival of Ataï's.[33] The country through which we passed was dreary and desolate,

---

30. Police station (French).

31. "Father" Rivière, as if he had the unmilitary bearing of a priest. This is Henri Rivière, a French military hero, who died in 1886 leading 250 troops to conquer Hanoi in north Vietnam, then a French colony.

32. In this context, "one of us"; "doesn't stand on rank" (French).

33. Ataï was the Kanak chief responsible for the attack on the La Foa police station in June 1878, betrayed and killed by rival leaders later in the same year.

with no vegetation but the niaouli.[34] Moindou was the first real settlement I had seen in New Caledonia. There were stores, and a church, and the Hôtel Beaumont, and numbers of thatched cottages. The surroundings were all tropical; but the domestic life was entirely French. The barefooted children in the streets, the women chatting at the store, the men in blouses smoking and gesticulating fiercely—all reminded one of France. This was entirely a civil settlement. There were no "soldiers" here; and M. de Laubarede, the supreme authority, took the title of mayor of the commune. It was quite a peaceful village, and, looking at the calm quiet of everything, one was inclined to hope that these ex-convicts and communists,[35] who had their "concessions" of land here, were becoming healthier, wealthier, and wiser by their return to first principles—the tilling of the soil. M. de Laubarede was, in real truth, the civil *directeur* and magistrate of this "agricultural centre." He had only a gendarme to assist him in enforcing authority; but since the outbreak of these troubles he had drilled most of the inhabitants of the village, forming a *garde nationale*,[36] at which the officers of the camp joked very much. A rough, but strong, stockade had also been formed round the director's house, to act as a refuge in case of attack.

When we arrived, some very seedy individuals turned out of the guardhouse, and received us with military honours. "Don't laugh," said Captain Rathouis, and I remained grave as the sphinx. We found the *maire*[37] in a state of great excitement, as an ex-convict had been murdered, *le nommé Brière*,[38] employed by a settler some three miles from the village. Whilst M. Rathouis obtained all the particulars of the case, I listened patiently, and at last asked: "But do you know that the Canaques did this?" "It must be they; for both legs were cut off—taken to eat, no doubt." I was not so sure of this. I remembered that this was a settlement of ex-criminals, and it seemed to me that private revenge could at that time easily satisfy itself, while the odium would be thrown on the natives. But shortly I heard something which changed my views. The day before, it appeared that a pig belonging to M. Boyer had been speared. In return, his men (ex-convicts) had fired into a party of natives, and killed a man and a woman. *Le nommé Brière*'s death was evidently in revenge for this. No doubt he had rendered himself personally obnoxious to the natives. But M. Rathouis and myself said we would go and see Baptiste and inquire into these things. My companion had confidence in this chief's fidelity to the

---

34. A ubiquitous evergreen "paperbark" of the Myrtle family and national symbol of New Caledonia.

35. A significant group among the convicts was of "communards," political prisoners associated with the Paris Commune, a socialist uprising of 1870–1871 cruelly put down by the authorities. Twenty thousand communards were killed, and seven thousand were deported, most to New Caledonia. Among them was the anarchist and humanitarian Louise Michel, who was given amnesty and returned to France in 1880, publishing her *Mémoires* in 1886.

36. National guard (French): reservists.

37. Mayor (French).

38. The said Brière (French).

French, knowing him well—as he thought. I much wished to get the intelligent Canaque's view of the question. However, we waited for the return of a party composed of a gendarme and some of the *garde nationale,* who had been sent out to reconnoitre; and shortly they came back. The village of Baptiste was deserted! He and all his men must have joined the rebels! That is the conclusion we came to; although, in my mind, there was an idea that if this chief had meant to commence hostilities, he would have done so by killing a few more libérés,[39] if not by indulging in a general massacre.

Captain Rathouis made the round of the village, and harangued the crowd at the *magasin.*[40] The women drew near and listened, and seemed deeply impressed when their husbands were exhorted to fight for them and their children. My friend soared into the poetic regions, in depicting the happy homes and hearths which they must defend, and in telling them that it was necessary to keep good watch by night and day, and in all things to obey M. de Laubarede. That gentleman threw in a word every now and then. Some of the women wept, and although I fancied a few of the men were sulky, the oration was a success, and we left with a promise from all to follow the instructions given them. At the end of the village, by the river, which here ran deep and strong, we found another guard-house. There was another parade and another oration. But this time the ex-communists did not want any military work. There were murmurs in the ranks. In vain M. Rathouis appealed to them. "You have your families and your concessions to defend!" One young man pointed out that, after keeping watch all night, he could not work his ground. He did not want to be sentry at the stockade. It was all very well for soldiers; for they had their wine and tafia,[41] and coffee and sugar. If the *garde nationale* of Moindou had the same, it would be different. The citizen soldiers were evidently on strike, and Captain Rathouis sadly came to the conclusion that it would be necessary to have a military post there.

After breakfast we drove to Teremba, and there we met the officers who had just returned from burning the mutilated body of *le nommé Brière.* I was told that it was a horrid sight. I again feasted the gubernatorial fleas in the gubernatorial bed at night, waiting for the court martial on the morrow. There did not appear to be much, if any, evidence against the prisoners. It was alleged that they knew of the outbreak and did not warn the authorities. I asked Captain Rathouis what would be done with them. He said, "They will be deported to the Isle of Pines till the trouble is over."[42] In the morning, when some of the officers from Fouwharii were to have come over to assist at the court martial, we were disturbed by a messenger from Moindou. He reported that he had been attacked by the Canaques on the road. He said he fired twice and

---

39. Freed men (French): former convicts.

40. Shop, store (French).

41. A kind of rum.

42. In the reprisals following the Kanak Rebellion, hundreds of Melanesians were deported to the Isle of Pines, at the extreme south of New Caledonia.

repulsed the natives; but the information was very vague. It caused consternation amongst us, however, and did not tend to make the judges at the *conseil de guerre*[43] merciful. But I, who closely examined and questioned the man, believe he was lying, or grossly exaggerating through fear. He might have seen a few natives; but that was all. However, this attack on the *courier* was gravely recorded by M. Varnauld in the archives of the *arrondissement*.[44] Mounted couriers were galloping between Teremba and La Foa all the morning, and at noon there came an order from the Commandant Rivière which distressed me. It ordained an act illogical, unjust, and useless in its results. The killing of Boyer's pigs was a bad thing for *le nommé Brière, libéré*, but it was equally bad for five Canaque prisoners in the calaboose. They were to be taken to the spot where the ex-convict was killed, to be there shot, and their bodies burnt as a warning to their friends. It was really hard on these poor wretches that, after being locked up for a month, they should be punished like this without even a form of trial. Reprisals are sometimes justifiable; but in this instance I think not. Besides, what were we going to do when the next *libéré* was killed? The supply of Canaque prisoners would run short after these had been executed. "Will you assist at the execution?" M. Varnauld courteously asked me. "Certainly!" I answered. "I came here to learn all I could, and I wish to see how the heathen Canaque dies."

At three o'clock there was a commotion in the settlement of Teremba. Around the calaboose the convicts and inhabitants gathered. In all countries and amongst all people the *morituri*[45] are objects of curiosity. The pleasurable excitement of viewing the doomed ones compensated for the loss of the siesta. In front of the post fifty men were paraded—thirty soldiers and sailors armed with chassepots, ten *franc tireurs*[46] with old rifles, and ten convicts with axes only. The prison doors were opened, and five natives were brought forth. Four were handcuffed in pairs; and they were all joined by a stout rope. The last was a boy of only thirteen; the others of ages ranging from twenty-five to forty. All were quite naked except one, who had still the striped jersey worn by the boatmen of the port. Round his neck the boy had a small key suspended by a piece of string. I wondered whether he had ever possessed a box, or only wore it as an ornament. Another wore a garter adorned with shells; another had a string of beads round his neck. Their woolly hair had been dyed red by lime; some rude combs were stuck therein. They were splendid specimens of humanity; not large men, but with beautifully formed limbs. Two had broad noses and thick lips, but two had almost European features, one being very handsome, with fine eyes, which fixed themselves on mine inquiringly. He seemed to seek a friend, and it might be that he saw the sympathy which was in my soul.

---

43. Court-martial (French).

44. French administrative entity: a subdivision of a *département*.

45. Those about to die (Latin): an expression used of the gladiators who performed in the Roman circuses.

46. A *franc tireur* (literally "free shooter") is an irregular soldier; the *chassepot* was a rifle employed by the French army after 1866, named after its inventor.

THE ISLAND AS COLONY

In colour, these men were light brown; in each the brain was well developed. They were of a race far superior to the Australian savage. They all looked curiously at the preparations, and listened to the orders of M. Varnauld. Now, *le chef d'arrondissement* was not a general favourite. Evil things were said of his conduct during the first days of the outbreak. He was accused of being harsh, and over-cautious. I can only speak of M. Varnauld as I knew him. To me he always proved a kind host and courteous gentleman. I considered him the model of a French *préfet*.[47] He was punctilious and exact, a man of great method and neatness in everything. Of his person, attire, and surroundings he was very particular, a point alone which would prejudice one of Anglo-Saxon descent in his favour. This was the only occasion I had of judging of M. Varnauld as a commander; and I am bound to say that he gave his orders clearly, and carried out everything in the most perfect manner.

Such men to the front, those to the rear, some specially to guard the prisoners; and, if they attempted to escape, or, if any attack *en route*[48] was made, to shoot them down; these were the orders. I marched at the head with M. Varnauld, who, in his white gloves and small brass gorget,[49] signifying that he was on service, looked quite a captain. A surgeon was with us. I asked if the prisoners knew their fate, and was told not. For six miles we toiled through the blazing sun. It was hard work; and it seemed to me cruel to drag those poor wretches out thus far to kill them. I watched them curiously as we marched along. The boy alone had a timid, curious look. I wished that the young savage with the handsome face and the fine eyes would not look at me with those glances of intelligence. To my dying day they will haunt me. When we entered the *niaouli* scrub, our two mounted guides scoured along our flanks with revolvers in hand ready to fire if a grasshopper stirred. But nothing was to be seen. At last we emerged on cultivated land. Some houses were seen around; these, however, were all deserted, the inhabitants having taken refuge in Moindou. Then we came to some stables and farm buildings, and the thatched hut of *le nommé Brière*. That these had not been destroyed was another proof, to my mind, that the murder of this man was an act of individual vengeance. His bones were visible in the ashes of the fire where the body was burnt.

A halt was called here for a time, whilst the convicts pulled down some palings and made a funeral pyre. Our prisoners were told to sit down. Did they know what they were brought hither for? The boy had broken off a small branch of the niaouli tree, and was beating off the mosquitoes from himself and his next neighbour. The rest talked in low tones. What were we waiting for? In a few minutes there was a call to attention. Down the path from the other side a body of men marched. It was a column of the *garde national* of

---

47. Prefect (French): regional administrator.

48. On the way (French).

49. A military badge of rank, taking the form of a half-moon-shaped piece of ceremonial armor worn on the chest just under the neck.

Moindou, headed by M. de Laubarede. We saluted; the new comers wheeled round, and then M. Varnauld addressed the prisoners. "Because your chief and those of your tribe have killed and pillaged," he said, "and because they have gone into revolt, and because *le nommé Brière* was killed on this spot, therefore you, *maudits* and *misérables,*[50] are condemned *passer par les armes.*" This was the substance of M. Varnauld's address. He accused the men of all the crimes of Atai and Baptiste. The logic was bad, I thought, and the fury into which he tried to lash himself was thrown away. Nobody interested, but the men about to die, heard it; and they would soon be past all knowledge. And they? Did they understand this idiom, "to pass by arms"? One would hardly think so. The boy carelessly brushed away the mosquitoes, one smiled, the others were impassible as before. "Have you anything to say?" asks M. Varnauld. They shook their heads, and replied *"rien."*[51] For a few minutes they were allowed to talk to each other, and then they were marched a few yards farther on into the camp of niaouli trees.

The orders were given clearly and quietly. There were five trees in line; to these they were bound. The boy was first uncoupled and taken to the tree, his hands tied behind him, and a bandage placed round his eyes. Then the others must have known the fate in store for them! But they did not wince or take any notice. One by one the process was repeated, the *surveillant*[52] and a convict, who appeared to take brutal delight in the work, "officiating." There was not the slightest resistance or murmur from the prisoners. The last was my handsome friend. Released from his fellow, he remained for a couple of minutes perfectly free and unshackled, and again looked at me with those wistful eyes. Why did he not make one effort for life and freedom? If he had started, I would have bet that in the bush none of our rifles could hit him. I almost felt mad with the man, and my lips found words which he would not understand. *"Par ici,"*[53] cried the *surveillant*—the Canaque was looking at me. *"Sacré nomme de Dieu!"*[54] said the man, rushing forward, seizing the prisoner's wrist, and giving him a torrent of abuse for not being in a hurry to go to be killed. I felt indignant at this, and then the comical side of the question struck me. None of the men made the slightest resistance, although each one could have knocked the *surveillant* down with ease. As they stood bound to the trees, I could not think what familiar scene I was reminded of. Then I remembered my youthful readings about Uncas and Chingachgook in "The Last of the Mohicans."[55] M. Varnauld gave the order, twenty men were told off, six to each prisoner. At five paces these took aim, and at the words "make ready," the chassepots and minies[56] were levelled, the *libérés* who were in the firing

<hr />

50. "Lost" and "miserable" beings (French), sentenced to be shot.
51. Nothing (French).
52. Supervisor (French).
53. Over here (French).
54. Idiomatic oath: literally "Holy name of God" (French).
55. Characters from the novel of high-minded Native American noble savages by James Fenimore Cooper (1826).

THE ISLAND AS COLONY

party being quite eager for the signal. And the victims against the trees?—four stood up erect, with chests inflated, and every nerve and muscle strung, ready to die like warriors. The boy alone had his head sunk on his breast. The word was given—a discharge—and three bodies slid softly to the ground. "The doctor to the ground," shouted M. Varnauld. I accompanied him. The other two bodies sank down. There was not a word nor a groan. The *coup de grace*[57] was given to three who yet lived by the revolver of the *surveillant. Le nommé Brière* and the pigs of Boyer were avenged. "Blood for blood!"

I had seen thousands of corpses in my life, but never immediately after death a naked one. It was a new and not a pleasant sensation to see these bodies dragged along the ground. *Rigor mortis*[58] not having set in, the flesh presented a horrible flabby, quivery appearance. A convict with glee took a red handkerchief from the head of one of the deceased, and another tried to remove the jersey, but was ordered to desist. Dragged to the pile of wood, the bodies were thrown on, and some straw having been lighted, and other fuel heaped up, a fierce blaze went up to heaven. The smell of burning flesh is not nice, and I retreated to a distance, to smoke and moralise.

Shortly we formed column and marched back to dinner with what appetite we might. At table M. Varnauld said, "They died bravely enough." One of the mess retorted, "Oh! they are only brutes; they don't believe in a future, and so have no fear!" Then I—"Monsieur, we are taught in the classics that the highest virtue known to the ancients was to die as these men died. Again, in the glorious revolution of '89, when your *'noblesse'*[59] went to the scaffold" (he was a Breton Catholic and a Legitimist to whom I spoke), "their chief pride was that they died with *sang froid.*[60] They had not more courage than these poor Canaques. Let us be just. They perished like heroes, and I drink to the dead."

from William Churchward, *My Consulate in Samoa* (1887)

In 1879 the British had set up the "Municipality of Apia" in Samoa, under which the local chief Malietoa was installed and supervised by the consuls of Britain, Germany, and the United States. The Berlin Treaty of 1889 confirmed these arrangements, under which an indigenous king had effectively no influence on events. Unsurprisingly, Malietoa's authority was constantly challenged by other Samoan groups. In 1899 western Samoa was handed over to the Germans,

---

56. Anglicization of the French Minié rifle, again named after its inventor.

57. Finishing stroke; quietus (French).

58. Stiffness of death (Latin).

59. Nobility (French): many French aristocrats were executed in the aftermath of the French Revolution of 1789. A Catholic from provincial France who believed in the order of royal succession by primogeniture (a legitimist) would have been particularly proud of aristocratic stoicism displayed at that time.

60. Literally "cold blood": coolly (French).

American Samoa to the Americans, and the British pulled out altogether. William Churchward (1844–1920) oversaw the early part of this process as British consul on the island.

In the beginning of December [1884] the Samoans had for some time been in active and continuous argument over the value of the wording of their latest peace agreement, in which it was stated that Malietoa was to resign at the end of seven years, and that then a general election should be held by the whole nation to select whom they wished to reign.

The opposition insisted that this meant that at the end of the prescribed period the present King was to stand on one side, and that their man, the Vice-King, was entitled to succeed. They had been wasting their entire time in these jealous squabbles instead of legislating for the good of their country before it struck either side that they were drifting dangerously near to a split up again, and, indeed, a single indiscreet word from the King would have produced a war; but he bore all these vexatious proceedings with wonderful patience, and at last asked the Consuls to come and give him the benefit of their support and views on the matter in question.

There is no general Parliament-house for a Samoan session. Each political division has a house told off for its particular use, and discussion is carried on from house to house; the speaking member, standing out a few paces in front, and leaning on his long orator's staff, with fly-flap over his shoulder, holds forth to all within earshot in his most eloquent manner; whilst generally the previous speaker, motionless as a bronze statue, will remain in listening attitude in his place, to receive all that may be said in contradiction or in support of his just delivered opinion.

There never is any vote-taking as we at home understand the matter; all the real business in that way is done by delegates from the originators of schemes circulated amongst the various district houses and assemblies. In differences upon serious subjects, the whole thing turns upon whether the proposers or dissentients are strong enough in party to fight out their opinion. If the opposition consider that they are, they will leave the Government, go home and prepare for eventualities, defying openly all efforts to reduce them to obedience; and if not, they will remain until an opportunity occurs to try again.

On arrival we were seated in the same house with the King, which fact was immediately taken advantage of by the opposition to hint in the politest manner in the world that he was trying to intimidate them; but at the same time they said they were very glad to see the foreign representatives amongst them, and to hear anything they in their wisdom would wish to say.

Having given them a few words of advice in turn, to the effect that it would be a good thing for them if they were to drop all such disturbing arguments until they had established their system of government on a solid basis, such as would command the respect of all their well-wishers, we left them to their own devices, after they had thanked us for our good wishes, and requested us to visit them again when they had seriously discussed what we had told them.

The adjourned meeting came off two days later, when we were invited to hear the decision that had been arrived at. When we appeared, the leader of the opposition, after making a review of the whole discussion, and thanking us for our presence, informed us that they, the opposition, being there at all was a sign that they had taken our advice, and would shelve the disturbing question until Samoa had a strong Government, or, at all events, until the seven years had expired. In the interval, they would occupy their whole time with public legislation.

The Samoan nation is, without doubt, quite incapable of forming or carrying on for any length of time anything like a stable Government by themselves, and the natives are well aware that such is the case. Their political history for the past thirty or forty years fully establishes that fact. Within that period they have seen themselves making fresh departures, one after the other, each new one hopefully tending towards a final settlement of the country, but only to meet with continual failure, either through their own native jealousies or through some foreign interference in their affairs.

Their treaty relations with foreign Powers, the real meaning of which the few who signed did not rightfully understand, whilst the great majority of the nation knew nothing at all of their existence until called to account for some breach of a clause in the treaties of which they were ignorant, only served to involve them in many more complications than ever they were in before.

One treaty has a clause whereby the Samoan Government agrees to ratify all land transactions previous to its existence, an admirable arrangement, considering the multitude of shady ways in which land was formerly acquired. These treaties have never proved of the smallest benefit to the natives; but, on the contrary, have from the time they were made supplied the foundation for many an act of oppression.

Samoa never will be settled until some Power takes her in hand. The natives know it, and openly say so themselves; but for choosing the country they would wish to be annexed to, they have had to suffer many persecutions, which, however, have not in the smallest degree shaken their resolution. They are painfully aware of their hopeless weakness, and heartily sick of the shuttlecock, no-child-of-mine sort of existence that they have to endure, tossed about between three nationalities, each jealous of the other, and who will neither let them alone nor take them up.

Their choice for annexation is most decidedly British, for which they have petitioned over and over again since very old times. American protection they sought once, but to Germany they never have appealed, though several times ordered to do so.

The following is the text of the last Samoan petition to Great Britain, sent to the Governor of New Zealand to be telegraphed to her Majesty the Queen:

"*To her Majesty Queen Victoria, Queen of Great Britain and Ireland.*

"Mulinuu, Samoa, 5th *November,* 1884

"Your Majesty,

"We, the King and Chiefs of Samoa, now write to your Majesty, that you will grant this our humble request.

"Our King wrote nearly a year ago begging your Majesty to take possession of Samoa, and we have waited anxiously for a reply, but have received none.

"Your Majesty, great is our respect for your Government, and we know that you will protect our people, and that they will be contented under your rule; and we therefore earnestly pray your Majesty to relieve us from our great anxiety and trouble by extending your Government over Samoa, and either making it a British colony, or allowing us to be governed by New Zealand.

"Your Majesty, our minds are full of trouble, and we are much afraid that other nations desire to take our country against the wish of our people, and we therefore implore your Majesty to save us by granting our petition.

"We wish to make this clear to your Majesty, that we the King and Chiefs will give over our country to the government of Great Britain, and we rely upon your Majesty to protect our people.

"We pray to God that He will bless your Majesty and Government.

(Signed) "Malietoa, *King of Samoa,*
Tupua, *Vice-King*"

Here follow the signatures of fifty-two in number, representing the whole Samoan Government and nation.

Whilst walking down the beach, I turned in at the Court House where a case was in course of trial. It was that of a native who had attempted to steal a pair of trousers, of which attempt the evidence of the woman in charge of the store was quite sufficient to convict him; in fact, he never denied the charge. He received his award without a murmur, and requesting to ask a few questions of the magistrate, began:

"You white men always tell us it is wrong to fight."

"Yes," said the magistrate.

"And whether right or wrong, to fight is against the law and punishable by the magistrate?"

"Yes."

"If one fights and the other does not, the one who fights is convicted of assault and punished?"

"Yes, if so proved."

"Then," exultingly burst out this injured man, "punish that woman, for when I was running off with the trousers she punched me in the back two or three times, and I did not hit her."

He went off to be locked up, bewailing the inconsistency of "papalagi" law.

FIGURE 18. Paula David, "Street in Apia, Western Samoa" (c. 1890). By permission of the Mitchell Library, State Library of New South Wales.

from Robert Louis Stevenson, *A Footnote to History* (1892)

Robert Louis Stevenson (1850–1894), the feted author of *Treasure Island,* cruised the Pacific extensively in 1888–1889 before purchasing land in Samoa, where he hoped to recoup his health. (See Figures 18 and 19.) He settled outside Apia in 1890 and surprised his public by devoting his attention to the colonial politics of his new home. *A Footnote to History* is his account of the Western powers' role in exacerbating chiefly disputes on Samoa in the 1880s. This extract is from chapter 2, "The Elements of Discord: Foreign."

> The huge majority of Samoans, like other god-fearing folk in other countries, are perfectly content with their own manners. And upon one condition, it is plain they might enjoy themselves far beyond the average of man. Seated in islands very rich in food, the idleness of the many idle would scarce matter; and the provinces might continue to bestow their names among rival pretenders, and fall into war and enjoy that awhile, and drop into peace and enjoy that, in a manner highly to be envied. But the condition—that they should be let alone—is now no longer possible. More than a hundred years ago, and following closely on the heels of Cook, an irregular invasion of adventurers began to swarm about the isles of the Pacific. The seven sleepers of Polynesia stand, still

FIGURE 19. Paula David, "Soldiers from an English Warship and Natives on the Verandah of Robert Louis Stevenson's House in Apia, Western Samoa" (c. 1890). By permission of the Mitchell Library, State Library of New South Wales.

but half aroused, in the midst of the century of competition.[61] And the island races, comparable to a shopful of crockery launched upon the stream of time, now fall to make their desperate voyage among pots of brass and adamant.

Apia, the port and mart, is the seat of the political sickness of Samoa. At the foot of a peaked, woody mountain, the coast makes a deep indent, roughly semicircular. In front the barrier reef is broken by the fresh water of the streams; if the swell be from the north, it enters almost without diminution; and the war-ships roll dizzily at their moorings, and along the fringing coral which follows the configuration of the beach, the surf breaks with a continuous uproar. In wild weather, as the world knows, the roads are untenable.[62] Along the whole shore, which is everywhere green and level and overlooked by inland mountain-tops, the town lies drawn out in strings and clusters. The western horn is Mulinuu, the eastern, Matautu; and from one

61. According to Christian legend, seven young men walled up in a cave at Ephesus by Roman persecutors fell asleep for two hundred years before waking and returning to life.

62. Here "roads" refers to approaches to a port by sea. The world knew how dangerous Samoan waters could be from a cyclone that hit Apia in March 1889 and destroyed Western shipping gathered there.

to the other of these extremes, I ask the reader to walk. He will find more of the history of Samoa spread before his eyes in that excursion, than has yet been collected in the blue-books or the white-books of the world.[63] Mutinuu (where the walk is to begin) is a flat, wind-swept promontory, planted with palms, backed against a swamp of mangroves, and occupied by a rather miserable village. The reader is informed that this is the proper residence of the Samoan kings; he will be the more surprised to observe a board set up, and to read that this historic village is the property of the German firm.[64] But these boards, which are among the commonest features of the landscape, may be rather taken to imply that the claim has been disputed. A little further east he skirts the stores, offices, and barracks of the firm itself. Thence he will pass through Matafele, the one really town-like portion of this long string of villages, by German bars and stores and the German consulate; and reach the Catholic mission and cathedral standing by the mouth of a small river. The bridge which crosses here (bridge of Mulivai) is a frontier; behind is Matafele; beyond, Apia proper; behind, Germans are supreme; beyond, with but few exceptions, all is Anglo-Saxon. Here the reader will go forward past the stores of Mr. Moors (American) and Messrs. MacArthur (English); past the English mission, the office of the English newspaper, the English church, and the old American consulate, till he reaches the mouth of a larger river, the Vaisingano. Beyond, in Matautu, his way takes him in the shade of many trees and by scattered dwellings, and presently brings him beside a great range of offices, the place and the monument of a German who fought the German firm during his life. His house (now he is dead) remains pointed like a discharged cannon at the citadel of his old enemies. Fitly enough, it is at present leased and occupied by Englishmen. A little further, and the reader gains the eastern flanking angle of the bay, where stands the pilot-house and signal post, and whence he can see, on the line of the main coast of the island, the British and the new American consulates.

The course of his walk will have been enlivened by a considerable to and fro of pleasure and business. He will have encountered many varieties of whites,—sailors, merchants, clerks, priests, Protestant missionaries in their pith helmets, and the nondescript hangers-on of any island beach. And the sailors are sometimes in considerable force; but not the residents. He will think at times there are more sign-boards than men to own them. It may chance it is a full day in the harbour; he will then have seen all manner of ships, from men-of-war and deep-sea packets to the labour-vessels of the German firm and the cockboat island schooner; and if he be of an arithmetical turn, he may calculate that there are more whites afloat in Apia Bay than whites ashore in the whole Archipelago. On the other hand, he will have en-

---

63. Varieties of reports commissioned by the British Parliament into matters of all kinds, social and political.

64. That is, Deutsche Handels-und-Plantagen-Gesellschaft (German Trading and Plantation Company), formed in 1879 after the original German firm of Goddefroys was declared bankrupt. Its main business was copra from coconut plantations.

countered all ranks of natives, chiefs and pastors in their scrupulous white clothes; perhaps the king himself, attended by guards in uniform; smiling policemen with their pewter stars; girls, women, crowds of cheerful children. And he will have asked himself with some surprise where these reside. Here and there, in the back yards of European establishments, he may have had a glimpse of a native house elbowed in a corner; but since he left Mulinuu, none on the beach where islanders prefer to live, scarce one on the line of street. The handful of whites have everything; the natives walk in a foreign town. A year ago, on a knoll behind a barroom, he might have observed a native house guarded by sentries and flown over by the standard of Samoa. He would then have been told it was the seat of government, driven (as I have to relate) over the Mulivai and from beyond the German town into the Anglo-Saxon. To-day, he will learn it has been carted back again to its old quarters. And he will think it significant that the king of the islands should be thus shuttled to and fro in his chief city at the nod of aliens. And then he will observe a feature more significant still: a house with some concourse of affairs, policemen and idlers hanging by, a man at a bank-counter overhauling manifests, perhaps a trial proceeding in the front verandah, or perhaps the council breaking up in knots after a stormy sitting. And he will remember that he is in the *Eleele Sa,* the "Forbidden Soil" or Neutral Territory of the treaties; that the magistrate whom he has just seen trying native criminals is no officer of the native king's; and that this, the only port and place of business in the kingdom, collects and administers its own revenue for its own behoof by the hands of white councillors and under the supervision of white consuls. Let him go farther afield. He will find the roads almost everywhere to cease or to be made impassable by native pig-fences, bridges to be quite unknown, and houses of the whites to become at once a rare exception. Set aside the German plantations, and the frontier is sharp. At the boundary of the *Eleele Sa,* Europe ends, Samoa begins. Here, then, is a singular state of affairs: all the money, luxury, and business of the kingdom centred in one place; that place excepted from the native government and administered by whites for whites; and the whites themselves holding it not in common but in hostile camps, so that it lies between them like a bone between two dogs, each growling, each clutching his own end.

Should Apia ever choose a coat of arms, I have a motto ready: "Enter Rumour painted full of tongues."[65] The majority of the natives do extremely little; the majority of the whites are merchants with some four mails in the month, shopkeepers with some ten or twenty customers a day, and gossip is the common resource of all. The town hums to the day's news, and the bars are crowded with amateur politicians. Some are office-seekers, and earwig[66] king and consul, and compass the fall of officials, with an eye to salary. Some are humourists, delighted with the pleasure of faction for itself. "I never saw so good a place as this Apia," said one of these; "you can be in a new conspiracy every day!" Many, on the other hand, are sincerely concerned for the future of the country. The quarters are so close and the scale is so small, that perhaps not any one can be trusted always to preserve his temper. Every one tells everything he knows; that is our country sickness. Nearly every one has been betrayed at times, and told a trifle more; the way our sickness takes the predisposed. And the news flies, and the tongues wag, and fists are shaken. Pot boil and cauldron bubble![67]

Within the memory of man, the white people of Apia lay in the worst squalor of degradation. They are now unspeakably improved, both men and women. To-day they must be called a more than fairly respectable population, and a much more than fairly intelligent. The whole would probably not fill the ranks of even an English half-battalion,[68] yet there are a surprising number above the average in sense, knowledge, and manners. The trouble (for Samoa) is that they are all here after a livelihood. Some are sharp practitioners, some are famous (justly or not) for foul play in business. Tales fly. One merchant warns you against his neighbour; the neighbour on the first occasion is found to return the compliment: each with a good circumstantial story to the proof. There is so much copra in the islands, and no more; a man's share of it is his share of bread; and commerce, like politics, is here narrowed to a focus, shows its ugly side, and becomes as personal as fisticuffs. Close at their elbows, in all this contention, stands the native looking on. Like a child, his true analogue, he observes, apprehends, misapprehends, and is usually silent. As in a child, a considerable intemperance of speech is accompanied by some power of secrecy. News he publishes; his thoughts have often to be dug for. He looks on at the rude career of the dollar hunt, and wonders. He sees these men rolling in a luxury beyond the ambition of native kings; he hears them accused by each other of the meanest trickery; he knows some of them to be guilty; and what is he to think? He is strongly conscious of his own position as the common milk cow; and what is he to do? "Surely these white men on the beach are not great chiefs?" is a common question, perhaps asked with some design of flattering the person questioned. And one, stung by the last incident into an unusual flow of English, remarked to me: "I begin to be weary of white men on the beach."

from Frank Fox, *Problems of the Pacific* (1912)

Australian-born journalist and imperialist Frank Fox (1874–1960) was news editor at the *London Morning Post* when he wrote *Problems of the Pacific*. He returned to the same issue in *The Mastery of the Pacific: Can the British and the United States Agree?* in 1928. He served with distinction in World War I and was a prolific author on Australian themes.

The Pacific is the ocean of the future. As civilisation grows and distances dwindle, man demands a larger and yet larger stage for the fighting-out of the ambitions of races. The Mediterranean sufficed for the settlement of the is-

---

65. See Shakespeare's *Henry IV* (2), "Induction."
66. Gain the attention of.
67. See Shakespeare's *Macbeth,* act 4, scene 1, lines 10–11.
68. The number of soldiers in a battalion varies, but eight hundred is a fair approximation.

sues between the Turks and the Christians, between the Romans and the Carthaginians, between the Greeks and the Persians, and who knows what other remote and unrecorded struggles of the older peoples of its littoral. Then the world became too great to be kept in by the Pillars of Hercules, and Fleets—in the service alike of peace and war—ranged over the Atlantic. The Mediterranean lost its paramount importance, and dominance of the Atlantic became the test of world supremacy.

Now greater issues and greater peoples demand an even greater stage. On the bosom of the Pacific will be decided, in peace or in war, the next great struggle of civilisation, which will give as its prize the supremacy of the world. Shall it go to the White Race or the Yellow Race? If to the White Race, will it be under the British Flag, or the flag of the United States, or of some other nation? That is the problem of the Pacific. [. . .]

To-day the west coast of the Pacific is held by the European Power of Russia; by the aspiring Asiatic Power of Japan, which within half a century has forgotten the use of the bow and the fan in warfare and hammered its way with modern weapons into the circle of the world's great Powers; by China, stirring uneasily and grasping at the same weapons which won greatness for Japan; by a far-flung advance guard of the great Power of the United States in the Philippines, won accidentally, held grimly; by England's lonely outposts, Australia and New Zealand, where less than five millions of the British race hold a territory almost as large as Europe.

Sprinkled over the surface of the ocean, between East and West, are various fortresses or trading stations, defending intererests or arousing cupidities. German and France are represented. The United States holds Hawaii, the key to the Pacific coast of North America, either for offence or defence. Great Britain has Fiji and various islets. The Japanese Power stretches down towards the Philippines with the recent acquisition of Formosa.

Here are seen all the great actors in European rivalry. Added to them are the new actors in world-politics, who represent the antagonism of the Yellow Race to the White Race. Before all is dangled the greatest temptation to ambition and cupidity. Who is master of the Pacific, who has the control of its trade, the industrial leadership of its peoples, the disposal of its warrior forces, will be master of the world. [. . .]

Japan has everything but money to equip her for a bold bid for the mastery of the Pacific before the completion of the Panama Canal. Europe has taught to Japan, in addition to the material arts of warfare, a cynical faith in the moral value, indeed the necessity, of war to national welfare. She considers that respect is only to be gained by war: that war with a European nation is an enterprise of small risk: that in short her experience with the Russian Fleet was fairly typical of war with any European Power. She believes that she has the most thoroughly efficient army and navy, considering their size, in the world and has much to justify the belief. [. . .]

The British Empire—holding Australia and New Zealand with an audacious but thin garrison; having in India a powerful rear base for supplies; holding a great part of the North-West Coast of America with a population as yet scanty but beginning to develop on the same lines as the Australasian people—is clearly well situated to win and to hold the mastery of the Pacific. Such mastery would have to be inspired with peaceful ideals; it could not survive as an aggressive force. It is indeed the main strength of the British position in the Pacific that it is naturally anxious, not for a disturbance but for a preservation of the present state of things, which gives to the British Empire all that a reasonable ambition could require. It is wise and easy to be peaceable when one has all the best of the spoils. [. . .]

Supposing [. . .] the United States to continue her present industrial and commercial progress; supposing her to gradually tighten her hold on the rest of the American continent; supposing her to overcome certain centrifugal forces now at work, the problem of the Pacific, should the United States decide to play a "lone hand," will be solved. It will become an American lake, probably after a terrible struggle in which the pretensions of the Yellow Races will be shattered, possibly after another fratricidal struggle in which the British possessions in the Pacific, Australia, and New Zealand, equally with Canada, will be forced to obedience.

But is there any necessity to consider the United States and the British Empire as playing mutually hostile parts in the Pacific? They have been the best of friends there in the past. They have many good reasons to remain friends in the future. A discussion as to whether the Pacific Ocean is destined to be controlled by the American or by the British Power could be reasonably ended with the query: Why not by an Anglo-Celtic union representing both?

SOURCES

"The Canterbury Association: Farewell to the New Zealand Emigrants," *Illustrated London News*, 7 October 1850.

Charles St. Julian, *Notes on the Latent Resources of Polynesia* (Sydney: Sydney Morning Herald, 1851).

Henry T. Cheever, *The Island World of the Pacific* (New York: Harper and Brothers, 1851).

John Robert Godley, "Inaugural Address to the Lyttleton Colonists' Society at Its First Meeting," in Godley, *Writings and Speeches*, ed. James Edward Fitzgerald (Christchurch: Press Office, 1863).

"A Ramble through the New Zealand Court," *Illustrated London News*, 2 October 1886.

Julian Thomas, *Cannibals and Convicts: Notes of Personal Experiences in the Western Pacific* (London: Cassell, 1887).

William Churchward, *My Consulate in Samoa: A Record of Four Years' Sojourn in the Navigators Islands, with Personal Experiences of King Malietoa Laupepa, His Country, and His Men* (London: Bentley, 1887).

Robert Louis Stevenson, *A Footnote to History: Eight Years of Trouble in Samoa* (London: Cassell, 1892).

Frank Fox, *Problems of the Pacific* (London: Williams and Norgate, 1912).

Readers might start with A. Grenfell Price, *The Western Invasions of the Pacific and Its Continents: A Study of Moving Frontiers and Changing Landscapes, 1513–1858* (Oxford: Oxford University Press, 1953), or Jean Ingram Brookes, *International Rivalry in the Pacific Islands, 1800–1875* (Berkeley: University of California Press, 1941). For Britain, see John Bach, *The Australia Station: A History of the Royal Navy in the South West Pacific, 1821–1913* (Sydney: University of New South Wales Press, 1986); W. P. Morrell, *Britain in the Pacific Islands* (Oxford: Oxford University Press, 1960); Jane Samson, *Imperial Benevolence: Making British Authority in the Pacific Islands* (Honolulu: University of Hawai'i Press, 1998); Deryck Scarr, *Fragments of Empire: A History of the Western Pacific High Commission, 1877–1914* (Canberra: Australian National University Press, 1967); and Margaret Steven, *Trade, Tactics and Territory: Britain in the Pacific, 1783–1823* (Melbourne: Melbourne University Press, 1983). For France, John Dunmore, *Visions and Realities: France in the Pacific, 1695–1995* (New York: Heritage Press, 1997); Stephen Henningham, *France and the South Pacific: A Contemporary History* (Sydney: Allen and Unwin, 1992); and C. W. Newbury, *Tahiti Nui: Change and Survival in French Polynesia, 1767–1945* (Honolulu: University of Hawai'i Press, 1980). For Germany, Peter Hempenstall, *Pacific Islanders under German Rule: A Study in the Meaning of Colonial Resistance* (Canberra: Australian National University Press, 1976). For the United States, C. Hartley Grattan, *The United States and the South West Pacific* (Melbourne: Oxford University Press, 1961); W. Patrick Strauss, *Americans in Polynesia, 1783–1842* (East Lansing: Michigan State University Press, 1962); and Grant K. Goodman and Felix Moos, eds., *The United States and Japan in the Western Pacific: Micronesia and Papua New Guinea* (Boulder: Westview Press, 1981).

Island-centered accounts include Peter Hempenstall and Noel Rutherford, *Protest and Dissent in the Colonial Pacific* (Suva: Institute of Pacific Studies, 1984); Max Quanchi and Ron Adams, eds., *Culture Contact in the Pacific: Essays on Contact, Encounter and Response* (Cambridge: Cambridge University Press, 1993); and two important monographs: Caroline Ralston, *Grass Huts and Warehouses: Pacific Beach Communities of the Nineteenth Century* (Canberra: Australian National University Press, 1977), and Dorothy Shineberg, *They Came for Sandalwood: A Study of the Sandalwood Trade in the South-West Pacific, 1830–1865* (Melbourne: Melbourne University Press, 1967).

For colonial New Zealand see James Belich, *Making Peoples: A History of New Zealand: From Polynesian Settlement to the End of the Nineteenth Century* (London: Allen Lane, 1996); for Samoa see Paul Kennedy, *The Samoan Tangle: A Study in Anglo-German-American Relations* (St. Lucia: University of Queensland Press, 1974); for penal New Caledonia, see Alice Bullard, *Exile to Paradise: Savagery and Civilization in Paris and the South Seas, 1790–1900* (Stanford: Stanford University Press, 2000), and John Connell, *New Caledonia or Kanaky? The Political History of a French Colony* (Canberra: Australian National University Press, 1987).

On trade, settlement, and resources, see H. C. Brookfield, *Colonialism, Development and Independence: The Case of the Melanesian Islands in the South Pacific* (Cambridge: Cambridge University Press, 1972); Donald Denoon, *Settler Capitalism: The Dynamics of Dependent Development in the Southern Hemisphere* (Oxford: Oxford University Press, 1983); and Marion Diamond, *Creative Meddler: The Life and Fantasies of Charles St Julian* (Melbourne: Melbourne University Press, 1990). For the German companies, see A. E. Bolland, "The Financial Adventures of J. C. Goddefroy and Son in the Pacific," *Journal of Pacific History* 16:1 (Jan. 1981), and Stewart Firth, "German Firms in the Pacific Islands," in J. A. Moses and P. M. Kennedy, eds., *Germany in the*

Pacific and the Far East (St. Lucia: University of Queensland Press, 1977). Traders' experiences are recorded in Edward Lucett, *Rovings in the Pacific, from 1837 to 1849* (London: Longman, 1851); Dorothy Shineberg, ed., *The Trading Voyages of Andrew Cheyne, 1841–1844* (Canberra: Australian National University Press, 1971); Litton Forbes, *Two Years in Fiji* (London: Longman, 1875); Peter Sack and Dymphna Clark, eds., *Eduard Hernsheim: South Seas Merchant* (Boroko, PNG: Institute of Papua New Guinea Studies, 1983); Everard Im Thurn and Leonard C. Wharton, eds., *The Journal of William Lockerby, Sandalwood Trader, in the Fijian Islands during the Years 1808–1809* (London: Hakluyt Society, 1925); Alfred Tetens, *Among the Savages of the South Seas: Memoirs of Micronesia, 1862–1868* (Stanford: Stanford University Press, 1958); and E. H. Lamont, *Wild Life among the Pacific Islanders* (London: Hurst and Blackett, 1867).

On the literature of Pacific colonialism, see Rod Edmond, *Representing the South Pacific: Colonial Discourse from Cook to Gauguin* (Cambridge: Cambridge University Press, 1997); Diana Loxley, *Problematic Shores: The Literature of Islands* (London: Macmillan, 1990); Bill Pearson, *Rifled Sanctuaries: Some Views of the Pacific Islands in Western Literature to 1900* (Auckland: University of Auckland Press, 1984); and Vanessa Smith, *Literary Culture and the Pacific: Nineteenth-Century Textual Encounters* (Cambridge: Cambridge University Press, 1998).

Classic literature from the Pacific colonial period includes Herman Melville's *Omoo* and *Moby Dick,* and Robert Louis Stevenson's "The Beach of Falesá" and *The Ebb-Tide,* collected in Stevenson, *South Sea Tales,* ed. Roslyn Jolly (Oxford: Oxford University Press, 1996). Other "colonial" novels with a Pacific setting include R. M. Ballantyne, *The Coral Island* (1858); James Fenimore Cooper, *Mark's Reef; or The Crater* (1847); Rider Haggard, *When the World Shook* (1919); Harriet Martineau, *Dawn Island* (1845); Felix Maynard and Alexandre Dumas, *The Whalers* (1858); and Jules Verne, *The Mysterious Island* (1874). The Australian short story writer Louis Becke is well regarded by some; his most important collections are *By Reef and Palm* (1894) and *The Ebbing of the Tide* (1896). For Stevenson see his *In the South Seas,* ed. Neil Rennie (London: Penguin, 1998), and *Vailima Papers* (London: Heinemann, 1924); Gavan Daws, *A Dream of Islands: Voyages of Self-Discovery in the South Seas* (New York: Norton, 1980), chap. 5; Kenneth MacKenzie, "The Last Opportunity: Robert Louis Stevenson and Samoa, 1889–1894," in Deryck Scarr, ed., *More Pacific Islands Portraits* (Canberra: Australian National University Press, 1979); and Barry Menikoff, " 'These Problematic Shores': Robert Louis Stevenson in the South Seas," in Simon Gatrell, ed., *To the Ends of the Earth* (London: Ashfield Press, 1992).

For contemporary writing about "the colonies" as resource or political issue, see William Brown, *New Zealand and Its Aborigines* (1845); Frederick Alexander Campbell, *A Year in the New Hebrides, Loyalty Islands, and New Caledonia* (1873); H. Stonehewer Cooper, *The Islands of the Pacific* (1888); Walter Coote, *The Western Pacific* (1883); William Fox, *The War in New Zealand* (1866); J. G. Goodenough, *Journal of Commodore Goodenough . . . during His Last Command as Senior Officer on the Australian Station, 1873–1875* (1876); Herbert Meade, *A Ride through the Disturbed Districts of New Zealand* (1871); and J. H. de Ricci, *Fiji: Our New Province in the South Seas* (1875). Guy H. Scholefield, *The Pacific: Its Past and Its Future and the Policy of the Great Powers from the Eighteenth Century* (1919), gives a British retrospective in the immediate aftermath of World War I.

A representative sample of colonial travel literature might include George French Angas, *Savage Life and Scenes in Australia and New Zealand* (1847), and *Polynesia* (1866); Théodore-Adophe Barrot, *Unless Haste Is Made: A French Skeptic's Account of the Sandwich Islands in 1836,* trans. Daniel Dole (1978); Theodore F. Bevan, *Toil, Travel, and Discoveries in British New Guinea* (1890); Mary Stuart Boyd, *Our Stolen Summer* (1890); Annie Brassey, *A Voyage in the "Sunbeam"* (1879); John Gaggin, *Among the Man-Eaters* (1900); C. F. Gordon-Cumming, *A Lady's Cruise in a French Man-of-War* (1882); Henry Byam Martin, *The Polynesian Journal,* ed. Edward Dodd (1981); Edward T. Perkins, *Na Motu: or, Reef-Rovings in the South Seas* (1854); and W. D. Pitcairn, *Two Years among the Savages of New Guinea* (1891).

7

ANTHROPOMETRY, ETHNOLOGY, RELATIVISM
The Island for Anthropologists

Chapter 5 sought to illustrate how the South Seas contributed to a particular intellectual issue that was debated in the late eighteenth and early nineteenth centuries: the question of whether humankind had its origins in one race (monogenism) or in many (polygenism). That issue was intellectually resituated by Darwin, whose work suggested that one species might incorporate different varieties, or "races," themselves in competition with one another. This chapter picks up that debate, but in particular it charts the development of the more objective and more holistic study we call anthropology.

This consitutes one caveat with regard to this chapter: it is related to Chapter 5 but seeks to illustrate a Western intellectual development separate from racialism. There is a second warning to be issued. This chapter constitutes neither a survey nor an anthology of Pacific anthropology: its emphasis is on the contribution made to the science of anthropology by the South Seas and not vice versa. This explains why foundational pieces of missionary ethnography (by William Ellis, say, or Robert Codrington) and equally important late-twentieth-century publications are neither discussed nor excerpted in these pages.

In 1904 the American anthropologist Franz Boas addressed the International Congress of Arts and Sciences in St. Louis. As founding father of this new academic specialism, Boas placed it among its peers with care: "The speculative anthropology of the 18th and of the early part of the 19th century," he said, "is distinct in its scope and method from the science which is called anthropology at the present time" (Boas, 260). A theoretical distinction between anthropology's "speculative" and "scientific" eras could be made, no doubt. A practical distinction is not so easily come by. Anthropology in some form or another goes back to Hippocrates, whose essay "Airs, Waters, Places" (500 BC) is an analysis of cultural variety as a product of the environment, or to Herodotus, who contrasted the lucky and lackadaisical Egyptians with the work-toughened Greeks. In the nineteenth century anthropological manuals were regularly issued to travelers by institutions like the British Association for the Advancement of Science; Albert Meier's *Certain Brief and Special Instructions for Gentlemen, Merchants, Students, Soldiers, Mariners, etc.,* published in English in 1589, requested similar studies of "the disposition and spirit of the people" his readers might encounter. Bernard Varen, similarly, published a *Geographia Generalis* in 1650, which listed categories of observations to be made among strange races: "Stature, shape, skin colour, food habits; Occupation and arts; Virtues, vices, learning, wit; Marriage, birth, burial, name giving; Speech and language; State and government; Religion," and so on (Malefijt, 44). In the late Renaissance "it became axiomatic that contemporary savage cultures, possessed of the properties of oldness and persistence, also possessed historical intimations. They could be used as a form of documentation" (Hodgen, 333). The myth of the noble savage itself, as Anthony Pagden points out, "came . . . to occupy a crucial position in a gradually evolving conjectural history of human origins" (Pagden, 14). In intellectual projects such as these, where does speculation end and science begin?

In the eighteenth century conjecture and speculation began to grow tighter in focus. The philosopher Immanuel Kant delivered a series of lectures on "Anthropology from a Pragmatic Point of View" in 1772–1773 and again in 1796–1797 (see Kant). These lectures may not be what we would call "pragmatic" or even practical, but Kant devoted sections to "The Characters of Nations" and "The Characters of Races." His compatriot Johann Gottfried von Herder, in his *Outlines of a Philosophy of the History of Man,* expressed what he called "an anthropological wish" for a gallery of illustrations of humankind and welcomed the "laudable spirit of observation" in travelers like Cook's second-voyage *savant,* Johann Reinhold Forster (Herder, 162). "The mind of a speculative reader," the English *philosophe* George Keate remarked, "in the dispersed families of the world, traces the hand of Providence guiding all things with unerring wisdom.—He marks it balancing with equal scale its blessings to the children of men; and considers human nature, however unadorned, when dignified by virtuous simplicity, as one of the noblest objects of our contemplation" (Keate, 97).

Similar currents were flowing in France. Charles Fleurieu accompanied Captain Étienne Marchand on his circumnavigation of the globe between 1790 and 1792, and he, too, saw the peoples that he met as important "objects of our contemplation":

> The moment when Europeans communicate, for the first time, with newly-discovered people is that for studying them: at a later period, the intercourse of strangers produces changes in the natural habits of these people; presently the primitive features confounded with the new, and adulterated by this mixture, become imperceptible, and end by escaping them. It is by partial studies, it is by contemplating the man of every country under his first cover, and, as

it were, in his original dress, that we shall be able to succeed in graduating the scale of human intelligence. (Fleurieu, 1:258)

Like Keate, Fleurieu knew something needed to be done, intellectually, with "newly discovered people": but what kind of "partial studies" did he have in mind? As F. C. T. Moore points out: "There have been observant travellers from the first. But not anthropologists," who undertake "the *systematic* study of social phenomena" (Degérando, 1; italics added). Contemplaters of the human condition like Keate and Fleurieu, no less than empiricists like James Cook, needed a systematic substructure if their observations were to become genuinely anthropological in character. It was in France at the turn of the eighteenth century that this requirement would be addressed for the first time.

Though the word "anthropology" goes back to the late sixteenth century, "anthropologist" was first used at the end of the eighteenth. The second usage recorded was in the *Edinburgh Review* of 1805, referring to a voyage of Pacific exploration recently returned to French shores: the expedition of 1800–1804 commanded by Nicholas Baudin. The Baudin voyage to Australia was intended by the Napoleonic administration to mark a return by France to southern waters, which had come to be regarded since Cook's voyages and the establishment of a penal colony at Port Jackson as intellectually and politically a dominion of England. As was often the case with French voyages of discovery, great care and large sums were expended by the government. Postrevolutionary France was intensely proud of its scientific institutions, and scientists were called in en masse to advise Baudin and his contingent. The Académie des Sciences and the Société de Medicine had both given instructions to the lost Lapérouse expedition of 1785–1788, particularly on anatomical and physiological issues. By the time Baudin set sail, there was a new national scientific body to consult, one with intellectual ambitions themselves of a revolutionary order: the Société des Observateurs de l'Homme, founded in 1799. The Society of Observers of Mankind had among its aims the formation of a *muséum special* devoted to the history of humanity, and its members hoped Baudin would gather exhibits for it. Their hopes must have been high, as Baudin, his second-in-command, and the expedition's botanist and zoologist were all in the society. Accordingly:

> Assistance was sought from the Observateurs to formulate instructions on ethnographic observations. The result was two memoirs written in 1800 which marked a milestone in the development of the nascent discipline of anthropology. In their areas of concern they represented two tides of ideas, one that of the *philosophes* of the "Classe des sciences morales et politiques" of the Institut, the fading fine light of the end of the eighteenth century; the other a precursor to the tradition of French medical anthropology and of the racial and typological preoccupations of the nineteenth century. (Jones, 37)

These were a remarkable pair of papers. The treatise by Joseph-Marie Degérando basically sets out the principles of cultural anthropology; that by

Georges Cuvier sets out those of physical anthropology. As Rhys Jones suggests, the first looked back to Enlightenment racial liberalism and the prospect of a rationally unified humanity; the second looked forward to the racial determinism of the nineteenth century. By the time these instructions were delivered, however, there was no one to put them into effect. The scientific staff for the Baudin expedition had been chosen, and no anthropologist was on it.

There then appeared from the French provinces a medical student named François Péron, who managed to give a paper on anthropology to the Institut. "It seemed necessary," Péron announced, "to prove that it is impossible to arrive at a proper study of the natural history of humanity while limiting oneself to the study of degenerate and degraded man of civilized society. Is it not from the people most distant from our civilization and as a result closest to nature that we will have to draw the elements of that history? Is it not in the savage man alone that traces of the robust majesty of natural man can be found?" (Copans and Jamin, 116). The minister for the marine was as a result imposed upon to make Péron a late appointment to the voyage, albeit as "anatomiste des animaux" (Degérando, 21). "The most novel and significant aspect" of the Baudin expedition, therefore, "was the inclusion of anthropology among its scientific objectives" (Hughes, 65). "The 'prehistoric age of anthropology' was nearing its end, and the first intimations of field research were becoming visible" (Bitterli, 173).

Regrettably, Péron's contribution to this development proved a false dawn. Part of the reason for his obscurity in the history of anthropology was that when he came to practice as the world's first field researcher, in Tasmania in 1802, he tended to favor Cuvier's "zoological" project rather than Degérando's "cultural" one. "Our observer of mankind"—as Baudin ironically referred to him (Baudin, 490)—carried with him the "dynamometer," a spring-loaded contraption designed to measure the strength of the subject's arms. He measured Frenchmen, Mauritians, English soldiers and convicts at Port Jackson, Australian Aborigines, and Tasmanians, and on the basis of his findings asserted that "the physical degeneration of man is in proportion to his state of civilization" (Péron, 314)—meaning that the less civilized you were, the *weaker* you proved to be. Péron poured scorn on Rousseauist fancies of the noble savage and the natural man accordingly. It was this kind of physical determinism that dominated nineteenth-century anthropology and became attached to the racialist theories of that era.

But Péron was doubly unlucky. To modern eyes he appears a Cuvierist racial determinist. But while the Baudin expedition was at sea, the Degérandoist program of cultural investigation was discredited, too. "Between leaving and returning to France, great changes had occurred in the intellectual climate. . . . The Class of Moral and Political Science at the Institut National had been suppressed in 1803. . . . The École Polytechnique, with its 'pure' scientists and engineers, gained a decisive ascendancy over the École de Medicine, with which most of the Observateurs had been associated. The term *idéologue* itself was to become a term of abuse" (Jones, 63).

Napoleon had come back in 1799 from an abortive campaign in Egypt having learned one lesson at least: "L'homme sauvage," he remarked, "est un chien" (the wild man is a dog: quoted in Samson, 9). Priorities changed markedly in the years after Baudin set sail, "the view now being adopted that French interests were more important than the rights of natives, and that the only true knowledge was useful knowledge in its relationship to those interests" (Plomley, 12). So the first anthropologist, who cut his teeth in the South Seas before dying of tuberculosis at the age of thirty-five, has been passed over by ancients and moderns alike. A hundred years later anthropologists would return to the field, however, and again their destination would be the South Seas.

"During the nineteenth century," as Boas put it in 1904, "the classificatory aspect was combined with the historical one and the leading discussion related to the discovery of mental differences between the zoological varieties or races of men, and to the question of monogenism and polygenism." Thus we find, he went on, "about the middle of the nineteenth century the beginnings of anthropology laid from three distinct points of view: the historical, the classificatory and the geographical. About this time the historical aspect of the phenomena of nature took hold of the minds of investigators in the whole domain of science" (Boas, 262). By "historical" here Boas means "evolutionary," and physically determinist ("classificatory") evolutionism was the staple diet of nineteenth-century anthropology. A founding father of British anthropology, Edward B. Tylor, analyzed "savage" races in terms of their being "survivals": silent indicators of white humankind's remote past. "History points the great lesson," he wrote, "that some races have marched on in civilization while others have stood still or fallen back" (Tylor, 74). To the anatomist H. Klaatsch, Australian Aborigines were "a stationary remnant of primitive humanity," and to C. S. Wake they represented "the childhood of humanity itself, revealing to us the condition of mankind . . . not . . . long after man's first appearance on the earth" (quoted in Mulvaney, 69, 70). The island of St. Matthias (northwest of New Ireland) was a place, the pioneering anthropologist Richard Parkinson wrote, "where we are set down suddenly in the middle of a slice of human antiquity" (Parkinson, 141).

One of the few ways in which Western anthropologists were able to think about remote peoples without employing a Darwinian perspective was in terms of "capsule descriptions of virtues and vices" (Hodgen, 191). "Long before psychological anthropology became systematized," Annemarie Malefijt writes, "it was generally recognized that human groups could be characterized by overall personality traits. Often enough, this resulted in the formulation of unanalyzed stereotypes, depicting whole nations as brave, proud, cruel, sentimental, aggressive, or meek" (Malefijt, 293). Large amounts of Victorian ethnography were written in this spirit. Late in the nineteenth century, however, there emerged an idea that called both Darwinian and "capsule description" approaches into question. The principle of the "psychic unity of mankind" bypassed physical and evolutionary determinism in favor of "specific histori-cal, social, and human factors" (Malefijt, 134) that influenced a fundamen-tal and universal set of human potentialities. In doing so, it denied both the physically determined outcomes of evolution and the apparently permanent stereotypes associated with "capsule description."

By stressing historical, social, and human factors, "psychic unity" re-turned anthropology to the cultural or social perspective of Degérando. Franz Boas' work "on the relative merit of length-breadth, length-height indices of the skull and the effects of environmental influences upon growth pro-cesses in general," for example, concluded by substantially discrediting the racial determinism of physical anthropology: "if environmental conditions affect these measurements," after all, "they can hardly be used as a criterion for long-term racial identity" (Weltfish, 127). When anthropology abandons such views, Boas felt, "it impresses us with the relative value of all forms of culture, and thus serves as a check to an exaggerated valuation of the standpoint of our own period, which we are only too liable to consider the ultimate goal of human evolution" (Boas, 273). As Margaret Mead (one of Boas' students) put it: "We went into the field not to look for *earlier* forms of human life, but for forms that were *different* from those known to us" (Mead 1973: 141; italics added). So it was that, as the nineteenth century came to an end, physical an-thropology gave way to the anthropology of culture, defined by Tylor as "that complex whole which includes knowledge, belief, art, law, morals, custom and any other capabilities and habits acquired by man as a member of society" (quoted in Peacock, 3).

Such a shift is plainly visible in the work of the British anthropological pioneer W. H. R. Rivers, whose *History of Melanesian Society* is an object les-son in evolutionism giving way to culture. "My own standpoint altered very profoundly while I was writing the theoretical discussion contained in this volume," Rivers confessed:

> I began as a firm adherent of the current English school, being almost exclu-sively interested in the evolution of belief, custom and institution, paying little attention to the complexity of individual cultures. . . . At a definite point in my argument I was led to see that Melanesian society is complex. (Rivers, 2:1)

In Rivers' view

> the study of primitive psychological processes "leads us into no mystical dawn of the human mind, but introduces us to concepts and beliefs of the same order as those which direct our own activities." The difference between the savage and the civilized, then, was no longer considered one of evolutionary distance, but merely one of different social and physical environments. (Howe 2000: 47)

It followed that these "different social and physical environments" were now worthy of study in their own right. "What is most needed at the present day," Rivers' disciple A. C. Haddon wrote, "is intensive study of limited areas. . . . Although we know a good deal about many forms of social organisation, we find in very few cases is the knowledge sufficiently precise to explain them" (Haddon 1910: 154). Indeed, "on the spot and from the people themselves" had been Haddon's watchword as early as 1898, when "armchair" anthropologists like Tylor and J. G. Frazer—who depended for books like *Primitive Culture* and *The Golden Bough* on reports from correspondents out in the savage world—were still in the intellectual vanguard (Haddon 1898: xxii). "What oceans of error we should have been spared," Tom Harrisson wrote in the next anthropological generation, "if those who write about the 'savage,' primitive mentality, etc., had done more primitive living!" (Harrisson, 113). "The shift in method towards fieldwork," as Nicholas Thomas puts it, "parallelled a break from evolutionary and diffusionist speculation in favour of a scientific, law-seeking functionalism" (Thomas, 1989: 19).

Without question the most important—though not unprecedented—applicator of law-seeking functionalism to "the kaleidoscope of tribal life" (Malinowski 1922: 4) was the Polish anthropologist Bronislaw Malinowski, whose work was carried out in the Trobriand Islands, east of New Guinea during the First World War. But a formulation like Thomas' makes the enterprise sound less bewildering, less innovative, and more blandly "scientific" than it evidently was. "The goal is," Malinowski said,

> to grasp the native's point of view, his relation to life, to realise *his* vision of *his* world. We have to study man, and we must study what concerns him most intimately, that is the hold which life has on him. In each culture, the values are slightly different; people aspire after different aims, follow different impulses, yearn after a different form of happiness. In each culture, we find different institutions in which man pursues his life-interest, different customs by which he satisfies his aspirations, different codes of law and morality which reward his virtues or punish his defections. To study the institutions, customs, and codes or to study the behaviour and mentality without the subjective desire of feeling by what these people live, of realising the substance of their happiness—is, in my opinion, to miss the greatest reward which we can hope to obtain from the study of man. (Malinowski 1922: 25)

Two elements stand out in this remarkable passage: First, its emphasis on the tactile and the sensuous (grasping, realizing, finding, feeling), itself so powerfully evoked in "the hold which life has" on the anthropological subject—never mind the "participant observer." Second, its cultural relativism: for in each culture values, aims, impulses, and forms of happiness are different, and each culture produces different institutions, customs, and codes, with an integrity as real as the observer's own. Then there is a third element, crowning the other two: that the observer should experience the "*subjective desire*"—not the scientific one—to discover for himself or herself "the substance of their happiness" and "through realising human nature in a shape very distant and foreign to us" to "have some light shed on our own" (Malinowski 1922: 25). It is this combination of elements that so often finds a voice when later anthropologists reflect on their vocation. "I am more convinced than ever," Margaret Mead wrote from Arapesh Alitoa in 1932, "that the way to do field work is never to come up for air until it is all over" (Mead 1977: 128). "Although a cliché," Hortense Powdermaker recalled, "the saying is true that insight into one's self inevitably deepens understanding of others. As I suffered on the tortuous paths along which the second analysis led me, I remembered Malinowski's frequent quotation of the Greek, 'Know thyself,' to his students" (Powdermaker, 39).

Adam Kuper describes "the rules" of British social anthropology fieldwork, but it is clear they had a good deal in common with the concurrent American "cultural" tradition: "One had to spend at least a year, preferably two, in the field, working as soon as possible entirely in the vernacular, living apart from other Europeans and to some extent as a member of the community one was studying; and above all, the anthropologists had to make a psychological transference—'they' had to become 'we' " (Kuper, 296). This transference is at heart insular. Anthropological narratives and those of island discovery both typically involve leaving home, crossing a boundary, and attempting to understand the natives. Malinowski's "enactment of Rivers' program," George Stocking writes, "involved a shift in the primary locus of investigation, from the deck of the mission ship or the verandah of the mission station to the teeming center of the village, and a corresponding shift in the conception of the ethnographer's role, from that of inquirer to that of participant 'in a way' in village life" (Stocking, 93). "One of the ways in which men are led to make most vividly manifest the values and habits of thought which underlie their own social attitudes," J. W. Burow remarked, "is by contact with ways of life and thought which are alien to them" (quoted in Marshall and Williams, 2). The deeper the contact, the more vivid the manifestation. Many years after Margaret Mead's trip to the Mundugumor people of New Guinea, Nancy McDowell revisited both the people and Mead's original fieldnotes. "Ethos is more difficult than other topics to discern from notes," she concluded, "partly because it is an abstraction and partly because . . . it is heavily dependent on individual interpretation and potentially ethnocentric contrast with Western ideology, categories, and assumptions" (McDowell, 294). The deeper the contact, the more complete the self-exposure, precisely because it is ultimately dependent on "individual interpretation"—what Malinowski called "subjective desire."

So it was "that culture gradually came to replace nature as an explanatory paradigm for human behavior and organization . . . from about the beginning of this [the twentieth] century, and that the experiences of and in the Pacific islands played a significant part in this process" (Howe 2000: 54–55). The South Seas gave anthropology a false start with François Péron's Tasmanian shenanigans, but Haddon's expectation of "intensive study of limited areas" came true with huge dividends among the islands of Oceania, and in particular in mainland and island Melanesia. This is true for one reason in particular. Polynesia has been settled comparatively recently and is comparatively homogeneous, culturally speaking, as a result. Melanesia, by contrast, is the most ethnically and linguistically diverse region on earth. "Although anthropology is concerned generally with society, it has a special interest in one kind of society, the small community" (Peacock, 38), and nowhere else has more small and distinct communities than Melanesia. In the formative days of institutionalized anthropology, therefore (in the first forty years of the twentieth century, from Rivers to Mead), Melanesia became the focus for an amount of anthropological research wholly disproportionate to its geographical significance, at almost the rate of one doctoral monograph per village, providing an apparently inexhaustible amount of data for studies of primary cultural elements like totemism, cosmology, kinship, ritual, and child-rearing. So the Pacific made good the promise it had held out to Degérando in the dusk of the Enlightenment.

In the years leading up to the Second World War, however, there came a shift. "By the beginning of World War II, anthropological interest in Polynesia . . . had waned noticeably," writes one historian (Ferdon, 96), and Melanesia followed suit. "Oceania, with its small, bounded, apparently simple cultures was displaced as the main area for field work by Africa, with its large, sprawling, and often highly differentiated societies" (Kuper, 324). Evans-Pritchard's African studies began to outpace those based in Oceania. After Africa, anthropology would turn its attention to larger and more sprawling societies yet, in Asia and ultimately in the West itself, but modern anthropology's "home" might well be said to have been Melanesia in the first third of the twentieth century.

In fact the asset of Melanesian anthropology turned out to be a liability. "Many American cultural anthropologists of Mead's time were prone to what [Roger] Keesing labels a 'mosaic' view of human culture—each culture was a separate little piece, a unique creation adapted to its environment yet unconnected to the cultures around it" (McDowell, 29). Just as the theory of evolution had its birth in an insular view of nature provided by the Galapagos, so anthropology had its institutional birth in an insular view of culture: in Tahiti, Tasmania, the Trobriand Islands, and the isolated settlements of New Guinea. Insular, but also antipodean: "Rigidity of status," as J. C. Furnas wittily puts it, "delights him [the average anthropologist] in Samoa and disgusts him in Boston" (Furnas, 481). But in the end anthropology was brought to bear on the Western societies where it had been invented: "Anthropology was an aspect of the intellectual history of western civilization—at its worst the mortician of that civilization—laying out and presenting victimized cultures to public scrutiny after the explorer, trader, soldier, missionary and administrator had done their work. But at its most authentic it was the discipline reflecting the self-consciousness of our society in crisis" (Diamond, 2).

from Joseph-Marie Degérando, *The Observation of Savage Peoples* (1799)

After his work for the Society of Observers of Mankind, Joseph-Marie De-gérando (1772–1842) lectured in moral philosophy at the Lyçée de Paris and published *A Comparative History of Systems of Philosophy* in 1804. Later he helped found French societies for the promotion of national industry and for the improvement of elementary education, and continued to publish widely on the latter topic.

It seems astonishing that, in an age of egoism, it is so difficult to persuade man that of all studies, the most important is that of himself. This is because egoism, like all passions, is blind. The attention of the egoist is directed to the immediate needs of which his senses give notice, and cannot be raised to those reflective needs that reason discloses to us; his aim is satisfaction, not perfection. He considers only his individual self; his species is nothing to him. Perhaps he fears that in penetrating the mysteries of his being he will ensure his own abasement, blush at his discoveries, and meet his conscience.

True philosophy, always at one with moral science, tells a different tale. The source of useful illumination, we are told, like that of lasting content, is in ourselves. Our insight depends above all on the state of our faculties; but how can we bring our faculties to perfection if we do not know their nature and their laws? The elements of happiness are the moral sentiments; but how can we develop these sentiments without considering the principle of our af-fections, and the means of directing them? We become better by studying ourselves; the man who thoroughly knows himself is the wise man. Such re-flection on the nature of his being brings a man to a better awareness of all the bonds that unite us to our fellows, to the re-discovery at the inner root of his existence of that identity of common life actuating us all, to feeling the full force of that fine maxim of the ancients: "I am a man, and nothing human is alien to me."[1]

But what are the means of the proper study of man? Here the history of philosophy, and the common voice of learned men give reply. The time for systems is past. Weary of its centuries of vain agitation in vain theories, the pursuit of learning has settled at last on the way of observation. It has recog-nized nature as its true master. All its art is applied in listening carefully to that voice, and sometimes in asking it questions. The Science of Man too is a natural science, a science of observation, the most noble of all. What science does not aspire to be a natural science? Even art, which men sometimes con-trast with nature, aims only to imitate her.

The method of observation has a sure procedure; it gathers facts to com-pare them, and compares them to know them better. The natural sciences are in a way no more than a series of comparisons. As each particular phe-

---

1. A remark of the Roman playwright Terence.

nomenon is ordinarily the result of the combined action of several causes, it would be only a deep mystery for us if we considered it on its own: but if it is compared with analogous phenomena, they throw light each on the other. The particular action of each cause we see as distinct and independent, and general laws are the result. Good observation requires analysis; now, one carries out analysis in philosophy by comparisons, as in chemistry by the play of chemical affinities.

Man, as he appears to us in the individuals around us, is modified at the same time by a multitude of varying circumstances, by education, climate, political institutions, customs, established opinions, by the effects of imitation, by the influence of the factitious needs that he has created. Among so many diverse causes that unite to produce that great and interesting effect, we can never disentangle the precise action that belongs to each, without finding terms of comparison to isolate man from the particular circumstances in which he is presented to us, and to lift from him those adventitious forms under which, as it were, art has hidden from our eyes the work of nature.

Now, of all the terms of comparison that we can choose, there is none more fascinating, more fruitful in useful trains of thought than that offered by savage peoples. Here we can remove first the variations pertaining to the climate, the organism, the habits of physical life, and we shall notice that among nations much less developed by the effect of moral institutions, these natural variations are bound to emerge much more prominently: being less distinguished by secondary circumstances, they must chiefly be so by the first and fundamental circumstances belonging to the very principle of existence. Here we shall be able to find the material needed to construct an exact scale of the various degrees of civilization, and to assign to each its characteristic properties; we shall come to know what needs, what ideas, what habits are produced in each era of human society. Here, since the development of passions and of intellectual faculties is much more limited, it will be much easier for us to penetrate their nature, and determine their fundamental laws. Here, since different generations have exercised only the slightest influence on each other, we shall in a way be taken back to the first periods of our own history; we shall be able to set up secure experiments on the origin and generation of ideas, on the formation and development of language, and on the relations between these two processes. The philosophical traveller, sailing to the ends of the earth, is in fact travelling in time; he is exploring the past; every step he makes is the passage of an age. Those unknown islands that he reaches are for him the cradle of human society. Those peoples whom our ignorant vanity scorns are displayed to him as ancient and majestic monuments of the origin of ages: monuments infinitely more worthy of our admiration and respect than those famous pyramids vaunted by the banks of the Nile. They witness only the frivolous ambition and the passing power of some individuals whose names have scarcely come down to us; but the others recreate for us the state of our own ancestors, and the earliest history of the world.

And even should we not see in savage peoples a useful object of instruction for ourselves, would there not be enough high feelings of philanthropy to make us give a high importance to the contact that we can make with them? What more moving plan than that of re-establishing in such a way the august ties of universal society, of finding once more those former kinsmen separated by long exile from the rest of the common family, of offering a hand to them to raise them to a happier state! You who, led by a generous devotion on those far shores, will soon come near their lonely huts, go before them as the representatives of all humanity! Give them in that name the vow of brotherly alliance! Wipe from their minds the memory of cruel adventurers who sought to stay with them only to rob or bring them into slavery; go to them only to offer benefits. Bring them our arts, and not our corruption, the standard of our morality, and not the example of our vices, our sciences, and not our scepticism, the advantages of civilization, and not its abuses; conceal from them that in these countries too, though more enlightened, men destroy each other in combat, and degrade each other by their passions. Sitting near them, amid their lonely forests and on their unknown shores, speak to them only of peace, of unity, of useful work; tell them that, in those empires unknown to them, that you have left to visit them, there are men who pray for their happiness, who greet them as brothers, and who join with all their hearts in the generous intentions which lead you among them.

Georges Cuvier, "Research Instructions into the Anatomical Differences of the Races of Man" (1799)

Georges Cuvier (1769–1832) succeeded the great zoologist Lamarck as professor of comparative anatomy at the Jardin de Plantes, Paris, at the young age of thirty-six. Unlike Lamarck, Cuvier had no time for principles of change or evolution in animal species, but his classifications of animals by reference to their skeletal structures put comparative anatomy on a firm footing, systematically speaking. Accordingly, he published widely on the organization of the animal kingdom and the history of life on earth.

> In a field of study where the first steps have hardly been taken, instructions must be kept to a minimum. Not until the basic principles have been established will it be possible to ask travelers for more detailed observations. [. . .]
>
> The observations made by travelers and entrusted to their journals can be relied on in vain. Experience proves that where natural history is concerned description however precise is vague, and comparisons made between objects present and absent are worthless. The greatest naturalists have confounded or mistakenly distinguished easily identifiable beings because they did not have them under their eyes at the same time. What will happen when it comes to objects where the differences are so fine and so easily misread even when such objects are seen side by side? Everybody knows that even the greatest painters often poorly grasp the characteristics of the Negro and only depict a white man smeared with soot.

The drawings to be found in modern books of voyages, although done on the spot, basically follow the rules and the proportions that the draughtsman learned in the European schools, and there is perhaps not one of them on whom the naturalist can depend to lay the foundation of later studies.

It is absolutely necessary, therefore, to gather anatomical samples from the same location and to compare them in all their relations within that locality. That is the foundation from which observations on the external appearance and mental qualities of each race can be assembled. Men themselves, collected alive, would no doubt be the best materials for an exact comparison of the varieties of the human species, but even if we overlook the excruciating difficulties of a task of this nature, we should not (even if we could) sacrifice the happiness or violate the wishes of our fellow creatures to satisfy simple scientific curiosity. The best we can hope from travelers, therefore, are numerous and accurate likenesses and anatomical samples. If such objects are accompanied by observations made on the spot with intelligence and with care, they will be adequate for our studies.

Special study is necessary for the kind of likenesses we require; we must combine the merits of conventional portraits with a geometrical precision that can be obtained only in certain poses of the subject's head but that must be adhered to rigorously nevertheless. Therefore, a clear profile must always be supplied alongside a portrait full-face. Nor is the choice of individuals a matter of indifference, where choice is available at all. Different ages, the different sexes, and the different conditions of each people should be illustrated. The costumes and the various markings with which most savage races disfigure themselves (and which common travelers have described to us with such care) only serve to disguise the true character of the physiognomy. It is vital that the artist represent all the heads with the same arrangement of the hair, as simply as possible, above all in the way least likely to conceal the forehead or distort the form of the skull. Adornments, headbands, earrings, and tattoos should be entirely ignored. The draughtsman should have made himself familiar with Camper's important dissertation on the ways of rendering the features of the various races; however imperfect it may be, it will furnish him with productive ideas if he has the temperament of a true artist.[2]

As regards anatomical samples, the first and the most important to obtain is the skull. Some we have already, but it is vital our collection be complete. Besides which we have hardly any illustrating the differences of age and sex among the various races. These objects will not be as easy to come by as portraits, therefore travelers must neglect no opportunity to visit places where the dead are laid out, or where they will be witness to any form of fighting or take part in it. Whenever they have, in any way whatever, a body at their disposal, they should carefully note everything that relates to the individual who became the corpse, in so far as that is possible. Whole skeletons would be infinitely desirable. Can anyone believe that nowhere, in any published work,

---

2. See Figures 20 and 21, derived from Dumont d'Urville's Pacific expedition of 1837–1840 but essentially conforming to Cuvier's requirements on this point.

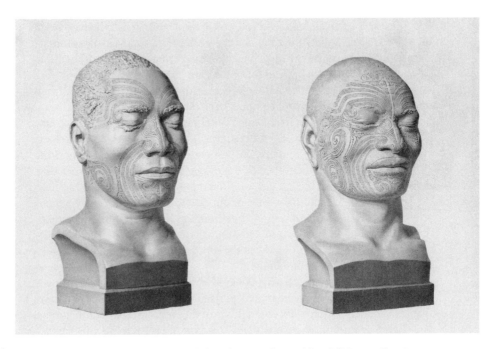

FIGURE 20. J. B. Léveillé, "Poukalem (Native of Otago)" and "Matoua-Tawai (Native of Korora-Reka)," in J. S. C. Dumont d'Urville, *Voyage au pole sud: Anthropologie: Atlas,* plate 14 (1842). By permission of the National Library of Australia.

does there exist a detailed comparison even of the skeletons of white men and Negroes?

The preparation of such samples will probably not be difficult. Boiling bones in a solution of soda and caustic potash, and disencumbering them of their flesh parts, takes just a few hours. Sailors may object to those activities, which strike them as barbaric, being carried out on board their ships; but on an expedition the aim of which is the advancement of science, the leaders must be governed by reason alone and should be able to inculcate such an attitude in their crews.

The flayed bones of each skeleton should be wrapped in a linen bag, without any attempt at order; they can be reassembled at home. Each separate head should be wrapped similarly, to prevent pieces becoming detached. Each parcel should be labeled. At present it should be convenient to bring back heads still fleshed, which would be immensely useful for correcting and perfecting any drawings. All that needs to be done is to place them in a solution of mercury bichlorate. Having been immersed for a while, they should be pulled out and allowed to dry. They will then become as hard as wood, while retaining their original form, and are immune to the attentions of insects.

Though the collection of the objects described above would be of inter-

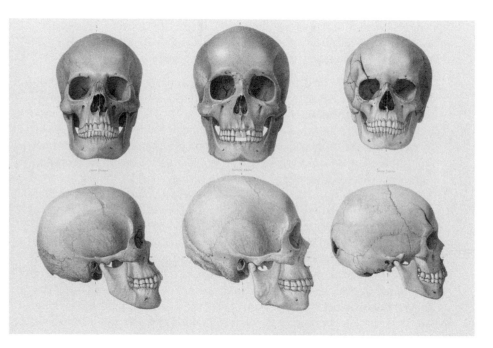

FIGURE 21. Hermann Raunheim, Skulls of New Zealand and Hawaiʻi, in J. S. C. Dumont d'Urville, *Voyage au pole sud: Anthropologie: Atlas,* plate 32 (1842). By permission of the National Library of Australia.

est wherever it were carried out, it should be done with maximum care, if possible, in places where the inhabitants are still insufficiently understood. So the Papuans, or inhabitants of New Guinea (who have long been regarded as similar to the Negroes), the inhabitants of all parts of New Holland, those of the islands of the South Seas, the inhabitants of the Straits of Magellan (or Patagonians), and the Madagascans should attract the special attention of travelers.

from François Péron, "Maria Island: Anthropological Observations" (1803)

François Péron (1775–1810) was a classic product of Napoleonic France: a young military veteran and medical student, he was also a passionate polymath, who became scientist-in-chief on the Baudin expedition as his colleagues left the voyage or succumbed to disease. (He was as much interested in zoology and climate as he was in anthropology.) Baudin died before the voyage ended, and the task of publishing its work fell to Péron, who hated his captain: his account of the voyage therefore brought the entire voyage into disrepute. Some of his qualities are evident in this account of the Aborigines of Maria Island, northeast of modern-day Hobart, Tasmania.

The study of man as he is around us deserves an equal hold upon our attention and our thoughts in twenty different ways. Almost a stranger still to all principles of social organisation, without arts, without laws, without chiefs properly speaking, without clothing, without culture, without fixed habitation, he presents himself to us with that valuable combination of characters which constitute Natural Man. Never perhaps has so immense a quarry been opened up for philosophy. Everything is curious in such a being, everything interesting: his antiquity, his origin, the changes in his affairs and his traditions in this regard, his customs, his language, his feelings, his ideas, his physical constitution, his increase in numbers, his infirmities, his longevity, his relationship to the climate, etc., etc. One must consider everything in order to study, analyse and meditate deeply upon each of these different questions. This is the story of Nature and of all mankind. Faithful trustee for the fundamental rights of the human species, he preserves them intact in their basic completeness. It is among these people, then, that we are able to rediscover those precious rights which we have lost following the upheavals among peoples and the progress of civilisation. We see it here, and also in the virtues of savage man and his vices. We will look into here both the resources he receives from Nature and the obligations to which Nature necessarily subjects him. From the careful comparison of these resources and needs, we know we cannot fail to obtain precious information as to the extent of his pleasures and enjoyments, as well as his privations and sufferings.

The connection between means and resources should therefore show us the connection between the benefits and disabilities attached to this state of man, who is close to the zero point of civilisation. We can then try to find out what useful modifications and what harmful changes the progress of civilisation has been able to bring successively to this primitive state, and by a long succession of accurate observations and a scrupulous grouping of their results, we can perhaps reach the correct solution of this enquiry, one which is so difficult and so subtle that again today it divides all the moralists and philosophers. We can decide, perhaps, if, when man is entirely left on his own, brought up not to fear the promptings of his senses and the fire of his natural passions, he is truly as good and as perfect as he is happy, particularly in the way several philosophers have recently suggested him to be. Again, we can decide if this state of nature, so celebrated today, is truly one of innocence, virtue and happiness. We can then analyse more certainly the effects of civilisation on man, determining them more exactly, as well as the benefits and the drawbacks. [. . .]

In the reconnaissance around Maria Island I have just completed with my friend Boullanger, we were not able to make any contact with the natives. However, wishing to have an opportunity of studying them, the day after my return I set out again at five o'clock in the morning accompanied by Citizen Petit the artist.

It was not long before I saw a fire on the shore which led me to hope I would meet the natives there. We landed at this place and our hopes were not disappointed, fourteen natives gathered around a large fire welcoming us joyfully, their delight a mingling of surprise, wonder and pleasure. *Médî, médî* (sit down, sit down) were the first words they addressed us. We did so and they gathered around us. [. . .]

After having thus disposed of our arms here and there, both parties took stock of one another for a little time. We were so novel to one another! The natives wanted to examine the calves of our legs and our chests, and so far as these were concerned we allowed them to do everything they wished, oft repeated cries expressing the surprise which the whiteness of our skin seemed to arouse in them. But soon they wished to carry their researches further. Perhaps they had doubts whether we were the same sort of beings as themselves, perhaps they suspected we were of a different sex. However it may be, they showed an extreme desire to examine our genital organs, but as this examination was equally displeasing to us all, they insisted on it only in the case of Citizen Michel, one of our sailors, who by his slight build and lack of beard seemed he must be more likely to set their minds at rest. But Citizen Michel, whom I begged to submit to their entreaties, suddenly exhibited such striking proof of his virility that they all uttered loud cries of surprise mingled with loud roars of laughter which were repeated again and again. This condition of strength and vigour in the one among us who seemed the least likely surprised them extremely. They had the air of applauding the condition as if they were men in whom it was not very common. Several of them showed with a sort of scorn their soft and flaccid organs and shook them briskly with an expression of regret and desire which seemed to indicate that they did not experience it as often as we did.

Undoubtedly, it would be imprudent to state clearly and in simple terms the reality of such an important observation, but I think I have a duty to point out here that I firmly intend not to neglect later on to go more deeply into the question. Henceforth I must even add that, among the quite large number of natives I have seen up to the present, I have not yet found anyone in this state as often as among civilised men who are at the same time young, healthy and vigorous. Like most animals, do they only experience the need for love at fixed and intermittent periods? Will the continuity of desire and consequently that of sensual enjoyment therefore be also one of the benefits of civilisation? Undoubtedly it is not necessary to make up one's mind about this without due consideration, because it is a question which is both too important and too delicate. However, if we pay attention to the all important influence of physical conditions on the origin of desire, on its aggravation and its continuity, I believe it will be very difficult not to agree with me, if not about the periodicity of desire and the demands of love in the people with whom we are concerned, then at least upon their rarity, in view of the long intervals between them. Indeed, if we take everything into consideration and remember that the temperature at which we live is always quite high, if we take account of the abundance of our food and its quality, the tranquillisers and strong liquors we make use of, the idleness we so often experience, and if we take into account the influence of the heart, which is so strong, and of our education, our reading, our finery, our ornaments, our training, our social gatherings, etc., etc., we can soon understand that everything in civilised man predisposes him to give birth to desire in order to sustain him and rekindle his passions unceasingly at all periods of the year and on almost all the occasions of life.

On the other hand, wandering amid the woods and forests, without clothing, without asylum, exposed perpetually to the inclemency of a damp and cold climate, often lacking the sustenance necessary for life, strangers to all kinds of tranquillisers and spirituous liquors, scarcely knowing sleep and far from being given up like the idle rich to the languor of idleness, does not natural man find he is placed in a situation where everything combines to reduce the keenness of his desires, to deaden them, and to quench them promptly in the midst of the rigours of winter, and sometimes also the anxieties of lean times. Must this vigour, which we know can be invigorated in a hundred ways foreign to our nature, be preserved by overcoming all the physical conditions which must destroy it in the men of whom we are speaking? [. . .]

I must certainly not pass over in silence one very interesting observation which I made then. It is that *they do not appear to have any idea of the act of kissing*. In vain did I apply successively to several among them in order to make them understand what it was I wished to know, but their comprehension was at fault. When, in order to leave no doubt as to what I was asking, I wanted to bring my face close to theirs to kiss them, they all had that look of surprise and uneasiness which an unknown act always arouses in us; and when on kissing them I said: *gouanarana* (what do you call that?), *nidegô* (I do not know, I do not understand) was their unanimous response. The idea of caressing does not seem to be any less strange to them. In vain did I make all the appropriate gestures peculiar to this action, but their surprise indicated their ignorance, and *nidegô* served to show me that they had no conception of it. Consequently, these two actions, kissing and caressing, which are so full of charm and which seem to us so natural, appear equally unknown to savage natural man. This double source of the most lively enjoyment, of the most exquisite sensations of love and sensual delight do not exist for them. Indeed I will not forget in my future reports concerning the natives of these countries to follow up this interesting observation, which is all the more curious because physical structure seems to play the most important role here, one which alone seems to suffice to explain this marvellous ignorance. Indeed, a kiss, whatever may be the part on which one sets it, always arouses a feeling of pleasure which seems to be special to this act and which makes it so precious and so dear to us, especially when it exerts its influence upon a young person, fresh and good to look upon. But the sensual feeling which is produced in us by a kiss, is clearly due to the close application of one or several

ANTHROPOMETRY, ETHNOLOGY, RELATIVISM

parts of our body at one and the same time and to a surface which is more or less delicate; and always the acuteness of the pleasure produced by this action depends upon the sensitivity of the part which experiences it and on the delicacy with which it is practised. It is for that reason that of all kisses perhaps the least stimulating is the one which is effected by the simple application of two cheeks one to another; the kiss on the mouth is much more tender and much more delicate; and that which a happy lover savours rapturously on the palpitating bosom of his mistress is undeniably one of the most profound sensations and the most voluptuous which one can experience. Caresses are not essentially different from kissing, and what I have said of this last activity and what I have yet to say about it, is equally applicable to them. Now, I wish to prove that the pleasure produced by a kiss, everything being equal in other respects, is found to be all the more keen as the sensitivity of the organs is more perfect, and as this itself depends on their delicacy and on their greater excitability, it follows that the cutaneous organ being the principal site of the sensation, everything that can in any way modify its excitability must also exercise a powerful influence on the acuteness of the sentiment produced by the kiss. Hardened by its constant exposure to the inclemency of the weather and the vicissitudes of so rigorous a climate, it becomes almost entirely insensitive through the cruel necessity of sleeping naked on the ground, and above all by the custom of lacerating the flesh, as they do when grieving. The cutaneous organ of these men could not still possess that delicacy of structure and excitability, the direct cause of this exquisite sentiment of which I have spoken. *Kisses* and *caresses* then become acts which are equally indifferent to those who receive them as to those who make them. This character of indifference is enough to proscribe them, for under this hypothesis, what object would they have? And why would one practise them? For us civilised men, both sentiments exhibit very different characters. Easily protected by our clothing and furs, we brave the rigours of the climate, and our habitations shelter us from the heats of summer. We ignore those slights and painful lacerations which everything around can inflict upon us, and which the *child of nature,* forced to wander absolutely naked in the midst of dense forests and precipitous mountains, must endure at every moment. Accordingly, we experience on our *sense organ* neither continuity of sensation which is alone sufficient to deaden sensibility, nor that *intensity of feeling* which destroys it. As a result, this organ must retain in us so much the more animation as we exercise it the less; and in the caress and the kiss it must provide us with those delightful and voluptuous sensations which, indeed, they produce in us, which are so natural to us and which it yet seems must be thought of as one of the *benefits of civilisation.* This proposition becomes still more likely when I come to deal with the organs of generation and observe nature by these means. Instinct and experience conserve for these essential parts that delicacy of feeling and excitability which are absolutely indispensable for the accomplishment of the grand design of nature.

from Horatio Hale, *United States Exploring Expedition,*
1838–1842, vol. 6: *Ethnology and Philology* (1846)

After serving as ethnologist aboard the United States Exploring Expedition commanded by Charles Wilkes, Horatio Hale (1817–1896) worked as a lawyer in Ontario. He continued to publish widely on anthropological themes, however, particularly the languages of native North Americans. These publications constituted an important influence on Franz Boas, the father of modern American anthropology.

It is not a little remarkable that though the Feejeeans are an ingenious, shrewd, quick-witted people, surpassing the Polynesians in their knowledge of various arts, and have a more regular and artificial system of government, they are yet spoken of by all voyagers as savages, and uniformly treated as such, while the Polynesians are regarded rather as a semi-civilized race. Nor can there be any doubt that this distinction, so universally and involuntarily made, is a just one. Yet it is difficult to perceive, at the first view, the grounds on which it rests. We shall be told that civilization belongs to the character more than to the intellect; but granting this to be correct, we may still be at a loss to discover in what respect the Feejeeans are inferior to the Polynesians. The portrait which we have had to draw of the latter is by no means prepossessing. If the Feejeeans are ferocious in war, without natural affection, parricides and cannibals, there are few of the Polynesian tribes to whom the same description will not apply. That proneness to sensuality, moreover, which is common among the latter is wanting in the former, and the domestic ties are more sacred among them.

The truth perhaps is, that the differences in the character, as in the physiognomy of the two races, lies not so much in any particular trait, as in a general debasement of the whole,—a lower grade of moral feeling, and a greater activity of the evil passions. The Polynesians seem to be cruel, dishonest, and selfish, rather because they have always been so, and no better path has ever been opened to them, than from any violent propensity to those vices. The proof of this is found in the fact that a very brief intercourse with foreigners has, in most cases, been sufficient to induce them to lay aside their worst practices, and adopt many of the improvements of civilization. But the Feejeeans are by nature and inclination a bloodthirsty, treacherous, and rapacious people. Their evil qualities do not lie merely on the surface of the character, but have their roots deep in their moral organization. In forty years of intercourse with the same class of civilized men to whom the Polynesians were indebted for their earliest instructions in many valuable arts, they have learned from them nothing but the use of firearms,—and though no visitor can have failed to express his horror at the customs of cannibalism, infanticide, and human sacrifice, not the slightest effect has been produced upon the natives. The Feejeean may be said to differ from the Polynesian as the wolf from the dog; both, when wild, are perhaps equally fierce, but the ferocity of the one may be easily subdued, while that of the other is deep-seated and untameable.

One quality, however, for which the Feejeeans are eminently distinguished, and in which they differ widely from the Polynesians, is their disposition to treachery, and, connected with it, their capacity for dissimulation. During our intercourse with them, we had continually occasion to observe this trait in their dealings with us and with one another. They live a life of constant suspicion, no one daring to trust even the members of his own family. A native never leaves his own home unarmed, and the people in every town are constantly on the watch against a sudden invasion from the neighbouring tribes, however apparently peaceful. Their internal history, as related by themselves, is full of instances of perfidy and treason. The group is divided into a number of independent states, connected among themselves by peculiar relations, somewhat as in the little republics of ancient Greece. Among these states constant intrigues and machinations are carried on, and that with a degree of shrewdness and craft that frequently excited our astonishment. All the arts of that baser species of state policy which we are accustomed to look upon as the growth of a corrupt civilization, are thoroughly understood and continually practised by this extraordinary race of savages. To weaken a rival state by secretly exciting its dependencies to revolt,—to stir up one class of society against another, in order to take advantage of their dissensions,—to make an advantageous treaty with a powerful foe, by sacrificing a weak ally,—to corrupt the fidelity of adherents, by bribing them with the anticipated spoil of their own master,—to gain a battle before it is fought, by tampering with the leaders of the opposing force,—all these, and many other tricks of the Machiavelian school,[3] are perfectly familiar to the subtle chieftans of Viti. In treating of the system of government which prevails in the group, we shall have occasion to show more distinctly the influence which this trait in the native character has upon their political relations.

from Edward B. Tylor, "On the Tasmanians as Representatives of Palæolithic Man" (1893)

The founding father of cultural anthropology in Britain, Edward Burnett Tylor (1832–1917) was professor of anthropology at Oxford from 1896 to 1909. Perhaps his most important contribution was the massively influential *Primitive Culture* (1871), which applied the principles of Darwinian evolution to human societies, sketching a progress from primitive communities to advanced civilizations and finding the roots of the latter in the former. Here he discusses the Tasmanian Aborigines as in effect living fossils, representing stone-age varieties of technology.

> From the foregoing evidence it appears that the Tasmanians, up to the time of the British colonization in the present century, habitually used stone implements shaped and edged by chipping, not ground or polished. These belong,

---

3. The greatest political work of the Renaissance, Niccolo Machiavelli's *The Prince* (1513), is a defense of administrative pragmatism—some would say, cynicism.

notwithstanding their modern date, to the order of the very ancient "palæo-lithic" implements of the Drift and Cave Periods, from which the later imple-ments of the "neolithic" order are distinguished by greater variety of form and skill of finish, and especially by the presence of grinding or polishing.[4] The comparison of the Tasmanian stone implements with those of the an-cient world impresses on us the fact that the rude modern savage was con-tent to use a few forms of implement for all purposes of cutting, chopping, &c., these being flakes as struck off the stone, and such flakes or even chance fragments trimmed and brought to a cutting edge by striking off chips along the edge of one surface only, whether completely or partly round. Such tools are known to the Stone Age of the Old World. Mere chips of flint, &c., no doubt always served for much of the cutting and scraping which they were at least as well adapted to as more artificially made flakes would have been. The special though simple "scraper" edged by chipping from one surface, more or less closely corresponding both in shape and mode of making with the Tasmanian, belongs to the palæolithic period, where it is especially character-istic of the cave deposits of Le Moustier in Dordogne,[5] while similar though usually neater examples continue to be found in the neolithic period. The Tasmanian, though using types of implement not unfamiliar to palæolithic man, is not known to have attained to making any implement approaching the characteristic palæolithic pick chipped into symmetrical form, and edged and pointed by chips taken in order from both surfaces. If it may be taken that the information from Tasmania is conclusive in this respect, it will appear that the savages there, within this century so miserably erased from the catalogue of the human race, were representatives of stone age development, a stage lower than that of the Quaternary period.[6] Even should specimens of higher order be found in Tasmania, they will leave untouched the conclusion now established by abundant evidence, that during the present century the natives habitually made and used for the ordinary purposes of life stone implements of a low palæolithic kind.

The apparent ignorance of the Tasmanians of the art of fixing a stone implement in a handle, unless where natives of Australia had introduced among them their own mode of fitting, raises an interesting question as to hafting among the palæolithic men of Europe. Of the stone implements of the Drift and Caves, many are evidently made from stone chosen to fit the hand, or shaped with a view to grasping, while no certain evidence proves them to have been ever fixed in the wooden handles so certainly familiar in neolithic times. It is apt to be assumed that the Drift flint picks were stuck into clubs,

---

4. The paleolithic and the neolithic are the "old" and the "new" Stone Ages, the neolithic being marked by the introduction of agriculture, the domestication of animals, and the polishing of stone implements (as opposed to mere chipping).

5. This region of France has often provided examples of Stone Age life, most famously in 1940 when the painted caves of Lascaux were discovered.

6. The Quaternary succeeded the Tertiary geological epoch and is associated with Pleisto-cene and Recent strata of the last two million years.

bound in withes,[7] or otherwise halted, but this opinion seems generally due to an unwillingness to conceive even of most ancient savages as wanting the ingenuity to realize the advantage of an axe-handle. The force of this assumption is, however, lessened by the descriptions of the modern Tasmanians as not conscious of this want, but being content to grasp their rudely chipped cutting stones in their hands. It being indubitable that hand-grasped stone implements were used by these rude modern people for purposes for which, had they known of handles, they could easily and would certainly have had recourse to them, it results that we have no right to assume the wooden haft to have belonged to the earliest Stone Age, but are obliged to allow that it may have been invented at a later period of industrial development.

Of degeneration in culture as accounting for the low state of implement-making in Tasmania, there is at present no evidence, nor is it easy to imagine their rude tools as the successors of higher ancestral forms. Had they had even the hatchet of their Australian neighbours, sharpened by rubbing its edge on a grit-stone, and bound into a withe or cemented to a stick, it is hardly conceivable that they should have abandoned such a tool for a rudely-sharpened cutting stone gripped in the hand; they would have lost more time and pains in the first day than would have sufficed to replace the better implement. Such carelessness would not indeed agree with the careful and patient skill which they, like other savages, gave to finishing their rude implements to the most serviceable point, in which they would spend hours and even days, regardless of trouble. The well-known readiness with which they took to European tools, shows an appreciation of labour-saving which contrasts strongly with the idea that at any time, possessing ground stone hatchets with handles, they abandoned them for chipped stones grasped in the hand. It seems more likely to consider that in their remote corner of the globe they may have gone on little changed from early ages, so as to have remained to our day living representatives of the early Stone Age, left behind in industrial development even by the ancient tribes of the Somme and the Ouse.[8]

Such being the position of the Tasmanians as modern tribes in the lowest Stone Age, the study of their culture in other respects affords valuable though imperfect guidance to formation of opinion as to the earliest distinctly recognizable period of human civilization.

from A. C. Haddon, "A Plea for an Expedition to Melanesia" (1906)

A. C. Haddon (1855–1940) served as reader in ethnology at Cambridge from 1904 to 1925 and published widely during that time. Perhaps his most crucial contribution to the science was his leadership of the Cambridge University

---

7. Flexible twigs.

8. River regions of northern France and eastern England, respectively, where ancient human remains have frequently been found.

Torres Strait Expedition of 1898–1899, where the basic principles of anthropological fieldwork were formed, involving a team of experts in fields such as psychology and linguistics. Here we find him arguing for a similar expedition to Melanesia at large.

The islands of Melanesia have yet to be studied from a geomorphological point of view, and their geology is extremely little known. Botanists would welcome a more ample knowledge of the flora of the district as a whole and of particular portions of it, and many problems of plant structure, distribution, and ecology require detailed investigation on the spot. The same remarks apply to zoologists. Botanists and zoologists alike would welcome an opportunity for extensive or intensive study of the systematic distributional or biological problems of plants and animals in Melanesia.

There are also many anthropological problems in Melanesia that require investigation in the immediate future, since the dying out or modification of arts, crafts, customs, and beliefs that is now taking place, and the shifting and mixing of populations, will soon render their solution difficult and even impossible. On the other hand, there are many districts never yet visited by a white man, and many islands of which science has no knowledge.

There is a certain amount of variation in the physical character of the people of these archipelagoes that requires local study for its explanation. A good deal is known in a general way about the arts and crafts of the Melanesians, but an investigation of the kind proposed would verify existing data, add an immense number of trustworthy facts, and localities could be ascertained of unlocated specimens in our museums, and the uses of doubtful objects could in many cases be discovered. By a combination of these two lines of enquiry, the physical and the cultural, the nature, origin, and distribution of the races and peoples of the West Pacific could be elucidated. Melanesia is peculiarly suitable for studying the stages of the transition from mother-right to father-right,[9] and it would be important to discover the causes that have led to this transformation, and the steps that mark its progress. With this is associated the evolution of the family and the distribution and inheritance of property. Melanesia is also a favourable area for tracing the emergence of government. What are required at the present day are intensive studies of restricted areas, since it is only by careful regional study that the real meaning of institutions and their metamorphoses can be understood. The same applies equally to all the manifold beliefs and usages that are grouped under the term religion. The psychology of backward peoples has been greatly neglected, and the opportunity of a well-equipped expedition would do much to encourage students to undertake this research.

---

9. Early theorists of the family (such as Friedrich Engels) argued that societies evolved from the anarchy of matrilineal descent (established by the self-evident fact of giving birth) to the higher form of patrilineal descent based in monogamy: a key institution in the development of civilization, according to such writers.

It is superfluous to extend this plea, as all ethnologists will agree that this work requires to be done, and that without delay. The presence of Government officials, missionaries, traders, and of returned indentured labourers tends rapidly to modify or destroy the old customs. Much has already disappeared in many places; we are yet in time in many others if we do not delay.

Dr. Haddon is convinced that the best means of accomplishing the end in view is to organise a prolonged expedition to the Pacific with the absolute control of a comfortable and steady steamer. The permanent staff on board should consist at least of the director, doctor, photographer, two stenographers, who should also be typists, and, if possible, an artist. Accommodation should be provided for a number of investigators, but these would not necessarily form part of the permanent staff. They would be conveyed to the district which they were to study and be removed therefrom when it was time to leave. The director would arrange with each investigator when the vessel would return, and the investigator would be left with all the apparatus, food, and trade that he required.

The general routine should be as follows:—an anthropological investigator would be expected to work on the general lines laid down by the director. When the vessel returned, all those on board would be required to help the investigator according to their several abilities; the expedition photographer would be placed at his disposal, and dances and ceremonies would also be kinematographed. The investigator would orally amplify his rough notes and dictate them to the stenographers, and, so far as possible, all notes should be typed in duplicate before the departure of the investigator, and a revision made of them before finally leaving the spot.

from Bronislaw Malinowski, *A Diary in the Strict Sense of the Term* (1917–1918)

Having worked at the London School of Economics since 1910, Bronislaw Malinowski (1884–1942) received funding for six months' fieldwork on Mailu Island, New Guinea, in 1914–1915. After a brief sojourn in Australia, he went to the Trobriand Islands for a year, returning to Australia in 1916. In October 1917 he departed for a second year's work in the Trobriands (see Figure 22): work which would form the basis for his pathbreaking work on the *kula* system of interisland ritual barter as well as other profoundly influential studies of myth, magic, and sexuality. We join him in the village of Oburaku on the island of Kiriwina.

THURSDAY, 12.20 [1917]. I got up at 6 (awoke at 5:30). I didn't feel very buoyant. Made the *rounds* of the village. Tomakapu gave me explanations concerning the sacred grove near his house. It had been raining all night; mud. Everybody was in the village. The *policeman* joined me at 9, I set to work with him. [. . .] I

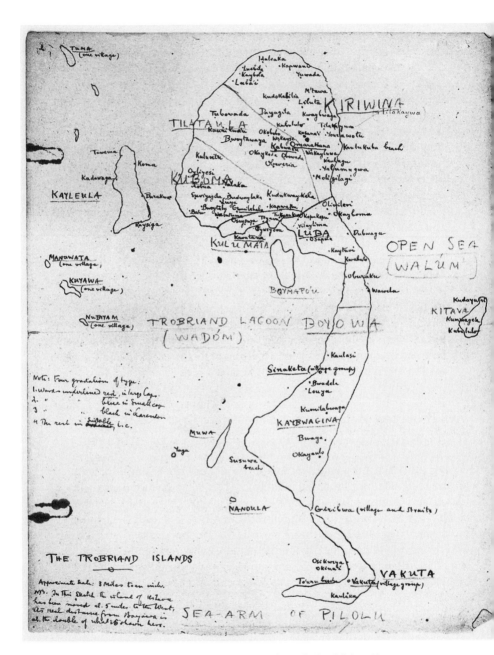

FIGURE 22. Bronislaw Malinowksi, "The Trobriand Islands" (1918?).
By permission of the Library, London School of Economics.

felt again the joy of being with real *Naturmenschen.*[10] Rode in a boat. Many observations. I learn a great deal. General *Stimmung* [atmosphere], style, in which I observe tabu. Technology of the hunt, which would have required weeks of research. Opened-up horizons filled me with joy. We made a *cruise around this part of the lagoon*—as far as Kiribi, and then to Boymapo'u. Extraordinary sight of fishes darting through the air, jumping into nets. I rowed with them. I removed my shirt and had a kind of sun bath. The water attracted me, I wanted to bathe, but somehow I did not—why? Because of my lack of energy and initiative, which had done me so much harm. Then, this began to weary me; hunger. The charm of open expanses gave way to feeling of absolute emptiness. [. . .] Then, around 5, I went to Tudaga where I took a census. I came back; the sunset was a blazing brick color. Some *natives* observed a *Tumadawa* fish and 12 or 13 boats set out in pursuit of it. I tried to catch up with them, but I felt a bit tired. I put down my oars, and I thought of N.S., and of South Australia.[11] S.A. is to me one of the most charming parts of the world. The intense feelings I had going back there last time. N.S. and my love affair with her is the soul of this paradise. Now, with N.S. lost, the paradise too is lost. I don't want to go back there, ever. I thought about all this and composed a letter to her in my mind. I don't want to lose her friendship.—Beyond doubt, my love for her was one of the purest, most romantic things in my life. Friendship for her? If she were healthy, strong? *No*—her way of taking life would be impossible for me. Entirely impossible. We would have talked to each other as though shouting from different rooms. And yet I feel regrets. If I could cancel it all out, and never possess her soul? This fatal urge to get to the bottom, to achieve absolute spiritual mastery. I certainly sinned against her, I heartlessly sacrificed her to a more secure relationship.—I felt poorly when I returned. Drank tea only. I chatted a bit, but without any specific aim. Enema. . . . Slept well.

FRIDAY, 12.21. Awoke late, at 7. [. . .] Rain; violent shit near the graves. I resolved never again to take cathartics compound!—Laziness: I'd like to break the monotony, to *"take a day off."* This is one of my worst tendencies! But I shall do the opposite: finish some routine tasks, "the ethnographic diary,"[12] rewrite my census notes and yesterday's impressions. This morning I felt poorly; my hands were numb (= tired heart); fogginess; general weakness, "touching bottom in the stream of vitality."—I thought of E.R.M., about a letter to her. [. . .] Then I

---

10. "Nature-men" (German). All words in italic are in languages other than Malinowski's native Polish.

11. When Malinowski left Australia for the Trobriand Islands in October 1917, he was romantically torn between Nina Stirling (N.S.) and Elsie Rosaline Masson (E.R.M.): daughters of professors at the universities of Adelaide and Melbourne, respectively. Malinowski and Masson married in 1919.

12. "I am keeping now an Ethnographic diary, recording all the events that happen, but it is not minute enough and does not record the *normal* so much as the *abnormal* and it is the first that really matters" (Wayne, 1:80).

wrote down my impressions of yesterday's expedition. Then to Walasi, where I took a census. . . . I was very tired; after lunch (fish and taro) went to bed. Woke up around 4 very tired. I thought of a passage from Stevenson's letters in which he speaks of a heroic struggle against illness and exhaustion.[13]—Then in a boat to Kwabulo. I asked questions concerning the names of the trees and the lagoon and decided to study the language systematically, compiling a *vocabulary. Waya* [inlet] Kwabulo—a shaded narrow streamlet between groups of mangroves. In Kwabulo—afternoon atmosphere—the cool dusk on the black earth and golden-green gleams. . . . Inspected Inuvayla'u's *kwila* [penis].[14] Bought bananas, *momyapus* [papayas], one stone. Return. Intense glow in the west—golden red, surrounded by the monotonous liquid blue of sky and sea. I planned to make a drawing of the clouds for E.R.M., and other drawings for her—in addition to the silhouette of the mountains I sketched aboard the "Itaka."[15] I was again alone—emptiness of moonlit night on the lagoon. I rowed vigorously and thought about—? Came back very tired. Drank tea and went to bed, without eating anything, after a talk with Morovato Kariwabu, about fishing, the names of trees, etc.—All that day longing for civilization. I thought about friends in Melbourne. At night in the *dinghy,* pleasantly ambitious thought: I'll surely be "an eminent Polish scholar." This will be my last ethnological escapade. After that, I'll devote myself to constructive sociology: methodology, political economy, etc., and in Poland I can realize my ambitions better than anywhere else.—Strong contrast between my dreams of a civilized life and my life with the savages. I resolve to eliminate the elements (components) of laziness and sloth from my present life. Don't read novels unless this is necessary. Try not to forget creative ideas.

SATURDAY, 12.22. Woke up very late (slept badly, 3 gr. of calomel the night before). Under the mosquito net I thought about relation between the historical *point of view* (causality as in respect of *extraordinary,* singular things) and the sociological point of view (in respect of normal course of things, the sociological *law* in the sense of the laws of physics, chemistry). "Historicists" à la Rivers = investigate geology and geological "history," ignoring the laws of physics and chemistry. The physics and chemistry of history and ethnography = social psychology. Sociological mechanics and chemistry = the individual soul in relation to collective creations.[16]—In the morning I walked to *sopi* [water hole] and thought about language as a product of collective psychology. As

---

13. Malinowski had with him *Vailima Letters* (1895), a collection of Robert Louis Stevenson's correspondence with his friend Sidney Colvin from 1890 to his death in 1894. The passage Malinowski is thinking of is probably one in the last letter of the collection (6 October 1894).

14. Inuvayla'u was a local legendary chieftan, whose penis and testicles were thought to be represented by stone landmarks. See Malinowski's *Sexual Life of Savages* (1929), chapter 12, section 4.

15. The vessel that carried Malinowski from Samarai, at the extreme eastern tip of New Guinea, to the Trobriands.

16. This is a highly significant passage, in which Malinowski begins to open up a distinction between fundamentally historical anthropology of the kind practiced by W. H. R. Rivers and his own "structural" concerns.

a *"system of social ideas."* Language is an objective creation, and as such it corresponds to the *institution* in the equation: social imagination = institution + individual ideas. On the other hand, language is an instrument, a vehicle for individual ideas, and as such it must be considered first when I study the other component of the equation. Then I worked on fishing terms [. . .]. I *overhauled* the sketch I had written spontaneously. Results satisfactory. Slept after lunch. [. . .] Sunset in a gamut of scarlets and ochers. We came back by moonlight. Discussed the geography of the lagoon with Morovato. I rowed vigorously. Gorged myself with bananas and rice. I am quite drowsy, get under the mosquito net. *"Subversive"* thoughts—I resolved to control them. But [gone] too far. Slept very badly. Weak heart, numb hands.

SUNDAY, 12.23. Day set aside for writing Christmas letters. In the morning diarrhea. Then straight back to the *tent.*[17] Read Stevenson a little. Under the mosquito net wrote the easiest and the most trivial letters. [. . .] At about 12 watched making of *Saipwana* in the village. Then came back, slept, wrote more letters. Very tired, I lay down and dozed, woke up still tired but stronger. *Crab* with cucumbers. Then a short rest. The *niggers* were noisy[18]—everybody idle because it was Sunday. [. . .] At about 6, on the lagoon. Marvelously translucent evening. Children sail in a boat and sing. I am full of yearnings and think about Melbourne (?). Some worries about E.R.M.—when I realize what threatens her I am drenched in cold sweat. I think of how much she has suffered, waiting for news of C.E.M.[19]—At moments I lose sight of her. Sensually, she has not succeeded in subjugating me. I rowed as far as Kaytuvi, returned by moonlight; lost in reverie, clouds, water. General aversion for *niggers,* for the monotony—feel imprisoned. [. . .] Fell asleep quickly around 10.

MONDAY 24. Got up at 7, walked around the village. *Kumaidona tomuota biousi wapoulo* [everyone has gone fishing]. This annoyed me a little. [. . .] I decided to take pictures. I blundered with the camera, at about 10—spoiled something, spoiled one roll of film. Rage and mortification. *Up against fate. After all it will probably do its work.* Photographed females. Returned in a state of irritation. Nevertheless I wrote E.R.M. Am hoping to get letter from her. Gradually she came back to me. I began to "feel her" again. Lunch (still irritated, gave my order to Ginger with tears in my voice).[20] Then I wrote

---

17. See Figure 23.

18. To modern eyes "nigger" is an extreme term of racial abuse, but Malinowksi doesn't generally use the expression with animus. (The form his racism takes, therefore, is casual rather than intense, and the expression is italicized here only because Malinowski employs a non-Polish expression.) Malinowski wrote of his return to a Kiriwina village he had visited previously: "After I came here, I went round the village and it was real fun to see the old niggers again. You know how little sentiment I put into my relations with the niggs and with regard to my whole life here. But coming here, seeing all these familiar yet slightly altered sights again, was so intensely reminiscent of my time here three years ago that it gave and gives me a thrill" (Wayne, 1:151).

19. Masson had been in love with Charles Matters, who died during the Gallipoli campaign in Turkey, 1915.

20. "Ginger" (real name Derusira) was a New Guinean manservant Malinowski had picked up in Samarai.

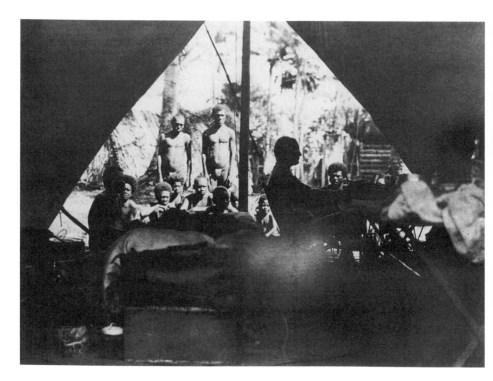

FIGURE 23. William Hancock, Malinowski in his tent, Omarakana (1918?). By permission of the Library, London School of Economics.

some more, rather an effort, but I felt there were many things I should tell her. At 4:30 Wilkes and Izod appeared on the horizon. I was decidedly displeased, they bothered me. *In fact,* they spoiled my afternoon walk. I showed them Inuvayla'u's *kwila* in Kwabulo. What is terrible is that I am unable to free myself completely from the atmosphere created by *foreign bodies:* their presence takes away from the scientific value and personal pleasure of my walk. I saw and felt the utter drabness of the Kiriwina villages; I saw them through their eyes (it's fine to have this ability), but I forgot to look at them with my own.—The conversation: criticizing the government, especially Murray.[21] The poetic trip through the mangroves spoiled by the chatter. [. . .] Went to bed at 10. Intense, deeply emotional thoughts (sensuality of the most refined kind) about E.R.M. Feeling that I'd like to have her as my wife and the idea of having sensual pleasure with other women has *quelque chose de funeste.*[22] I thought about our moments together, and how I never obtained the true reward which the very fact of possessing her must give me. I missed her—I wanted to have her near me again. Visions of her with her hair down. Does

21. J. H. P. Murray, lieutenant governor of British New Guinea at the time.
22. Something dire [about it] (French).

ANTHROPOMETRY, ETHNOLOGY, RELATIVISM

intense longing always lead to extremes? Perhaps only under mosquito netting.—Woke up at night, full of lecherous thoughts about, *of all the people imaginable,* my landlord's wife! This must stop! That I am not absolutely sure that I might not seduce my best friend's wife, that after such a strong surge of longing for E.R.M., that this could happen—*c'est un peu trop!*[23] This has got to stop once and for all.—Yesterday I felt fine during the day. Completely forgot it was Christmas Eve. But just now, this very morning, when I couldn't sleep, Mother was thinking of me and was missing me. My God, my God, how terrible it is to live in a continuous ethical conflict. My failure to think seriously about Mother, Stás,[24] Poland—about their sufferings there and about Poland's ordeal—is disgusting! [. . .]

12.26. In the morning mad *scramble* with letters. Difficulties in writing to N.S. Official letters concerning extension of leave. After lunch, talk with Wilkes, who turns out to be an amateur of colored women and says that some districts in Nigeria are *"very bad."* His admiration for Conrad mortified me.[25] After they were gone I looked at *war pictures* for half an hour, and then began to look over my own things. Unpacked *foodstuffs* and got it all sorted out with Ginger's help. This will enable me to figure out what and how I should eat, etc. Then in a *dinghy* on the *creek* with E.R.M.'s spirit. I was very energetic, and felt in good shape (I had relaxed—my ethnographic work is hard). [. . .]

12.27. Got up fairly late. Planned to go over my papers and begin work. But the packing took a long time. After lunch I again rummaged in my things. At about 4 went with Bill[26] to Mission Station. [. . .] I shudder at the thought of how life looks from their point of view [. . .] stupid, unpleasant jokes about my *Austrian nationality* and the effect is depressing. These fellows have such fabulous *opportunities*—the sea, ships, the *jungle,* power over the natives—and don't do a thing! Supper with Bill. Bootlicking letter to Symons. At 8:30 went to Oburaku. At first I felt *out of sorts,* and if I hadn't been convinced that a walk would do me good, my nervous state would probably have resulted in total exhaustion. Between Olivilevi and Vilaylima I was very energetic; then somewhat tired, but not too much. A shallow lagoon; an amusing fellow from Osaysaya carried me, the dark bare earth with mangrove roots like a section

---

23. It's a bit much! (French).

24. Stanislaw Witkiewicz, who had traveled to Australia with Malinowski but returned to Europe to fight in the First World War. Like many expatriate Poles of his era—most notoriously Joseph Conrad—Malinowski was assailed by feelings of guilt at pursuing a life elsewhere at a time when his homeland was threatened by Germany and Russia alternately.

25. One of the novels Malinowski read while in the field was Conrad's *Heart of Darkness.* In his Mailu Island diary of 1915, he associated himself directly with Conrad's Mr. Kurtz: "On the whole my feelings toward the natives are decidedly tending to 'Exterminate the brutes'" (Malinowski 1967: 69).

26. This is William Hancock, a local planter and trader who extended a good deal of help and hospitality to Malinowski on his second trip to the Trobriands and who took the photograph that appears as Figure 23 above.

of vegetation. Fish leaping all around. Thoughts, feeling, and moods: no interest in ethnology. In the morning when I had packed up and was wandering around Gusaweta, constant longing for E.R.M. (The previous evening, violent surge of longing when I looked at her photos.) Strong feeling of her personality; she is my wife *de facto* and I should think of her as my wife. As for ethnology: I see the life of the natives as utterly devoid of interest or importance, something as remote from me as the life of a dog. During the walk, I made it a point of honor to think about what I am here to do. About the need to collect many documents. I have a general idea about their life and some acquaintance with their language, and if I can only somehow "document" all this, I'll have valuable material.—Must concentrate on my ambitions and work to some purpose. Must organize the linguistic material and collect documents, find better ways of studying the life of women, *gugu'a* [household items], and system of "social representations." Strong spiritual impulse. I looked through my books and took Rivers, German books, poems; outside of my work, I must lead an intellectual life, with E.R.M. for my *companion*. I visualize the happiness of possessing her so intensely that I am seized with polycratic fear lest something so perfect actually came true.—Nonetheless, knowing that she loves me, is thinking of me, that everything I feel for her is reciprocated, I am happy.

[. . .]

THURSDAY 21 [March 1918]. Slept a long time—"catching up on my sleep"—I feel I needed it. I feel a little knocked out; but not unwell. [. . .] The view from my tent, just a few steps from the sea—bounded on the left by the green wall of the bay and a rock, and the prow of a wrecked *waga* [canoe] at the right—is fabulous.—Wrote diary, neglected since departure from Sanaroa.[27] I must draw up a system of investigation on the Amphletts. In the morning I wrote a long time, started ethnogr[aphy] fairly late. Worked at first with Anaibutuna and Tovasana, who are not bad, but not *first-class informants*. After lunch Kipela and an old man; I got annoyed with the latter and chased him away. For a moment I was afraid that this would spoil my business, then Kipela successfully resolved the difficulties. At 6, in the *dinghy* with Ginger to *lalang* [long grass] peninsula. Once again joy when I am on the deep green waters, and the island covered with dense green vegetation gradually reveals itself. The lower arm of the bay runs toward a few little red and black rocks *(just a bunch of warm blood-stained red in the dark brown)*, wrapped in verdant plumes. The luxuriance surrounding the crevices, suspended over bare rocks, climbing up the bare walls, gives the landscape a specific tropical character. There emerges the rounded top of the island, covered with *lalang*.—I feel strong and healthy and crave a long walk. [. . .] We tried unsuccessfully to make our way through

---

27. On 13 March Malinowski had temporarily left the Trobriands. Bad weather carried him past his destination—Gumasila, in the the Amphlett group of islands, described lyrically below—and forced him to land at Sanaroa, in the D'Entrecasteaux group nearby. On the nineteenth he arrived at Gumasila, and on 4 April he returned to the Trobriands.

the little rock and the trees coming down to the water; we took the dinghy back to the promontory, and along the sandy beach to the bushes. There, surrounded with *taboo palms*. Then again view of the beach through fallen tree trunks. I rowed coming back. Such pleasure to explore, to make contact with the tropics. Thought about E.R.M., about telling her all this. [. . .]

Main themes of life: joyous relief at living peacefully, without being persecuted by rascals, incomparably easier relationship with the natives. [. . .] Happiness, fullness of life (yesterday, because I felt healthier) as a result of the new surroundings, new work, new type of work. My tent, a few steps from the water, always has the sound of gentle plashing, and the noise of torrents up above in the lofty green wall.—Emotionally: calm attachment to E.R.M.; thoughts about Mother; last night sensual-emotional throwback to N.S. [. . .] Intellectually: comparative ideas (Melanesian histories) concerning the situation of these fellows. Yesterday I understood the charm of *"survey study"* à la Rivers, the encompassing of broad areas as a single whole. But this projection of space onto time (two-dimensional or rather multi dimensional entity) is very dangerous.

FRIDAY 22. Main currents of life: Ethnogr. work which goes very well, *thanks to* Tobawona. [. . .] In the morning wrote diary carefully, then to the village; all the *Sine-sine* in their huts. Tobaw. came. Worked on death and belief in *Tuma* [after-world]; it went very well. In the afternoon (violent downpour opened *creek* to the sea) again Tobaw. *et Co.* This kind of work—superficial, without going into details—is much lighter and more amusing than the work in Kiriwina. At 6 we set out for Gumawana.[28] Black cloud on the northern horizon. In the dinghy I sketched a plan of the village. Tob. unwilling to land. The fellows sat dully on stones, *independent, sulky, unfriendly—true islanders!* Then I got ashore, walked among the houses. Again spellbound by the picturesque village. A black shadow slowly strangling the yellowish light blended with the silvery glow of the moon behind clouds. Domdom: a big *tilted pyramid,* 2 replicas to the left, 1 to the right—*a chain of almost geometrical uniformity, yet impressive and rhythmic.* Returned fairly late; threatening clouds approach. Rocks all around. To the left, the dark, complicated, richly decked wall of Gumasila; to the right Omea (Domdom), *the top overbridged by the dark cloud.* Koyatabu visible, blue, cut only on top by a line of little white clouds. We sailed around a stone. Distant view of Nabwageta and clear outlines of smaller islands. Behind the promontory, a rain cloud. I felt a curious desire to be caught in a real rain once without any protection. I began to roar out a Wagner melody.[29] The cloud—or rather rain—moved closer and covered us like a white sheet. Exactly like a cold *shower bath;* wind. The dinghy filled with water. My watch, fear of *tabekusi* [capsizing]. Back home; I dried myself off.—Work on the dictionary. Could not fall asleep for a long time;

---

28. The main village of Gumasila; Malinowski had been staying nearby, at Nu'agasi.

29. Richard Wagner (1813–1883), German composer of romantic and mythological operas.

thoughts offensive to E.R.M., struggled against them—most dangerous those about N.S. But when I got to the point of imagining giving up E.R.M., I realized this would be impossible. Fearing I had caught cold, I took *Dover powder,* quinine, and aspirin. Slept well.

SATURDAY 23. Equinox. Woke up at 9, a bit uncertain as to how I'd feel. Epsom salts, tea. Worked with Tobawona, who is going stale on me, and who left in the middle to go fishing; Kipela stayed on, and he was not too bad.—After lunch (read a weak story by Kipling)[30] set out for Gumawana. [. . .] As usual, joy; I planned photographs, looked at the sea bottom. Right before Gumaw. I realized that "I had forgotten the keys"—dismayed, but controlled myself. *Census.* Continued happiness at the surroundings: delighted in the view of Koyatabu; sketched Domdom. I was given sago.—We went to Sarakeikeine. Looked at Gumawana—immensely beautiful silhouette. Two rocks rise up out of the vegetation, *like two truncated pillars out of a heap of overgrown ruins.* The sea striving, advancing in orderly rows of long smooth waves. I rowed. At moments I didn't know which way to look—at the exquisite silhouette of Gumasila or the vigorous harmonies of Domdom, or the symphony of pastel colors on the distant mountains of the big island.—Sarakeikeine. Flights of birds against the clouds dotting them like buckshot. We startled flocks of *dawata* and pigeons *(bunebune).* The cliff—a red conglomerate on the southeast, and northwest hollowed out into a deep vault—grottoes; on the other sides, steep.—We went back. I recalled night with Gilmour[31] when we dropped anchor here. *"Mere rocks"* he said, and with dark, sharp profiles. I had imagined them as sheer black volcanic cliffs—and the villages had seemed pasted on to the steep side, near the water. This accounts partly for my longing for these islands.—I thought about this *in terms of a letter to* E.R.M. (The previous day, returning with Tobaw. before the rain, when the light was simply magical, to E.R.M.: *This is quite like a symphony.*) [. . .] We turned back. The big island vanished in the dark. Mixed light of dusk and moon rising between the islands. I rowed. Echo. Again planned ethnogr. work.—Supper, dictionary. I walked around gazing at the stars. Mars glowed red through a break in the clouds. The moon overhead.

SUNDAY, 3.24. First clear morning. Koyatabu clearly visible. I could see the top covered with *lalang.* The wind from the west rising up to the very top and cutting across it with shadows. A steep green slope plunging down a slanting wall that is plowed by deep, narrow furrows (dark narrow ribbons) along a single deep hollow on the left: a waterfall. Yesterday, when the whole sky was covered by thick dark stratus clouds, Koyatabu was in the sun against the clear sky on the horizon. For the first time I understood the effect of phosphorescence: the same as the effect of moonlight: light more concentrated <u>in</u> a small area than <u>around</u> it. (Thought about how to formulate this for E.R.M.) Today got up at 8, took a walk, delighted in the view extending as far as the pointed

---

30. Rudyard Kipling (1865–1936), English novelist and short-story writer.
31. A Methodist missionary who had begun to investigate the *kula* practice.

peak (replica of Koyatabu) and mountains of Goodenough.[32] I was afraid that everybody might go out on *poulo* [fishing], for the water was calm and there was no wind or rain.—Still happy with the surroundings. I want no change, nor news, I am not bored. The smells (yesterday moss, seaweed, and flowers, the wind was from the island; today the fragrance of tuberoses on the beach), the rustling stream, the jungle, the shady wall with its sumptuous covering of tropical trees. [. . .] *Evening (from 10 to 11) Tobawona etc. Explanation of kula, stars, some myths.—Night full of dreams, Cracow. Thoughts, tender and passionate, of E.R.M.*

MONDAY, 3.25. That day Gumasila and Nu'agasi men left for *kula* at Boyowa. Whether because of *secretiveness* or superstition, they always conceal their departures from me (Mailu, Omarakana,[33] here).—Got up at 9, as usual. Did not notice anything (the day before, Kipela had been washing and cleaning himself up—was this for a last visit to his fiancée or part of the *kula* program?). Went to Gumawana (peeved but not discouraged). The women hidden, as usual. I saw a few from a distance. Not too much confusion. I went to the *bwayamas* [storehouses] and observed packing of pottery! Only pots, sago and *nuya* [coconut]. I couldn't persuade them to get out *bogana sago* [sago from the boga palm]. Took a few pictures. Saw Gumawana in the morning for the first time. No trace of magic ceremonies or farewells. Boys go, including even 2- and 3-year-old children. The boats are punted to the promontory where the sails are unfurled (I didn't see this). Came back at 12:30—the Nu'agasi were just leaving—I could not even photograph them. Fatigue. Lay down—closed my mind, and at this moment revelations: spiritual purity. *"Heed kindly other people's souls, but don't bury yourself in them. If they are pure, then they reflect the world's everlasting Beauty, and then why look at the mirrored picture if you can see the thing itself face to face? Or else they are full of the tangled woof of petty intrigue and of that it is better to know nothing."* I had revelations (very familiar) of the endless sordid petty threads running from man to man of hatred, intrigue, inquisitiveness. After lunch, still tired; read Kipling; rested. At 4 began to work with Mataora—garden. They lied, concealed, and irritated me. I am always in a world of lies here.—At 6 I learned that the fellows had come back. Boats and Anaibutuna. Marvelous evening. Boats at the promontory. In my boat I enjoyed the view of Gumasila from this side, of Koyatabu and other mountains. Then I rowed around the promontory, the moon hidden behind lacy clouds. I felt I was on the sea 8° lat. and 149° longit. (or something like it) Greenwich. Distinct feeling that next to this actual ocean, different every day, covered with clouds, rain, wind, *like a changing soul is covered with moods—*that beyond it there is an Absolute Ocean, which is more or less correctly marked on the map but which exists outside all maps and outside the reality accessible to observation.—*Emotional origin of Platonic Ideas.*—Came back,

---

32. One of the D'Entrecasteaux islands.
33. Village where Malinowski had worked on his first visit to the Trobriands.

sat on the beach. Moonlit night. White sand, over it dark shapes squat, in the distance the expanse of sea and outline of the hills. In the distance, the sea and the profiles of mountains. Combination of moods: Baia di Napoli[34] and Gumawana "from inside." Thought about how to describe all this for E.R.M. The moon, the sea, the mood. The moon induces a specific, clearly defined mood, I hum "Laraisebrue, and then there was Suzanna, pretty, pale, and virtuous." Expression of feelings, complementary social milieu, imaginary. Suddenly *I tumble back* into the real milieu with which I am also in contact. Then again suddenly they stop existing *in their inner reality,* I see them as an *incongruous yet artistic and savage, exotic = unreal, intangible, floating on the surface of reality, like a multicolored picture on the face of a solid but drab wall.* I came back, Anaibutuna raced with the boys. Delightful feeling that now I alone am the master of this village with my *"boys."*[35]—The moon above the hill makes pale reflections on the glistening leaves. Supper; I ate slowly, lazily, being tired. Thought?—Took out the *dinghy* after supper. Gazed at the stars: Southern Cross—E.R.M. Stás. Atwood *(Semolina Pudding);* Sirius, Canopus—the two largest stars a *"poor show"!* Came back, and to bed.

TUESDAY 26. Planned excursion to Domdom. Awakened by Tobawona with a fish. Got up, in a hurry to set out for Domdom.—Then found out that they had no intention of going. Tobawona in a bad humor, but polite—an excellent informant. Worked until lunch. Then unnecessarily read R&B, and finished a story by Kipling. Fatigue. In the afternoon *poulo,* but work went very slowly. Finished at 6; rowed in the dinghy around the island. Very tired. [. . .] We go around the promontory and turn eastward. No need for compass because rising moon and setting sun determine direction. All attention focused on the island. Mood of "the other side." The shore runs east-west from promontory to promontory, with indentations (bays). The slopes considerably less steep, meadows of *lalang* cover the hills down to the sea, especially in the 2nd bay. Here and there dense jungle in tiers. Two peninsulas like two arms stretched into the sea, covered with *lalang.* Charming, amusing little clusters of dense vegetation nestling in gaps near the shore, at the foot of the *lalang*-covered hills. Joyful feeling of recognition. This island, though not "discovered" by me, is for the first time experienced artistically and mastered intellectually. The moon struggles with the gray light of the misty sunset, when we round the 2nd promontory and glimpse Domdom. Then big waves, and my thoughts bog down in sluggishness and nausea. I notice that the stretch between Gumawana and my village is by far the loveliest. Evening; after supper I sit on a chair by the sea, humming waltzes. A moment of fear: have I lost taste for good music? Think of E.R.M. and that I must tell her solemnly that I look upon her as my wife. "The sacramental sacredness of the marriage bed."

34. The Bay of Naples, on the western coast of central Italy: a famous scenic spot.
35. By "boys" here Malinowski means Islander men, whom Westerners frequently referred to in this way.

from Margaret Mead, *Sex and Temperament in Three Primitive Societies* (1935)

In popular terms, Margaret Mead (1901–1978) was the most influential anthropologist of the twentieth century. Studies like *Coming of Age in Samoa* (1928) reached a genuinely mass readership, in large part because Mead insisted on applying lessons learned in remote communities to the Western world in which she was read. *Sex and Temperament* considers three New Guinea communities—the mountain-dwelling Arapesh, the river-dwelling Mundugumor, and the lake-dwelling Tchambuli—among whom she worked between 1931 and 1933. Here again, her discussion of "primitive" child-rearing had implications for society at large.

from chapter 4. Early Influences That Mould the Arapesh Personality

During its first months the child is never far from someone's arms. When the mother walks about she carries the baby suspended from her forehead in its special small net bag, or suspended under one breast in a bark-cloth sling. This latter method is the beach custom, the net-bag carrier belongs to the Plains, and the mountain women use both, depending in great part upon the health of the child. If the child is fretful and irritable, it is carried in the sling, where it can be given the comforting breast as swiftly as possible. A child's crying is a tragedy to be avoided at any cost, and this attitude is carried over into later life. The most trying period for the mother is when her child of three or so is too old to be comforted by the breast and too young and inarticulate to state clearly the reasons for its weeping. Children are held a great deal, often in a standing position so that they can push with their feet against the arms or legs of the person who holds them. As a result infants can stand, steadied by their two hands, before they can sit alone. Suckled whenever they cry, never left far distant from some woman who can give them the breast if necessary, sleeping usually in close contact with the mother's body, either hung in a thin net bag against her back, crooked in her arm, or curled on her lap as she sits cooking or plaiting, the child has a continuous warm sensation of security. It is only subjected to two shocks, and both of these have their reverberations in later personality development. After the first few weeks, during which it is bathed in a gingerly fashion with warmed water, the child is bathed under a jetting spout of cold water that is catapulted out upon it from a tipped bamboo water-carrier, a harsh, abrupt cold shock. Babies uniformly resent this treatment, and continue to hate the cold and the rain throughout their lives. Also when an infant urinates or defecates, the person holding it will jerk it quickly to one side to prevent soiling his or her own person. This jerk interrupts the normal course of excretion and angers the child. In later life, the Arapesh have notably low sphincter-control, and regard its loss as the normal concomitant of any highly charged situation.

For the rest the little baby's life is a very warm and happy one. It is never left alone; comforting human skin and comforting human voices are always beside it. Both little boys and little girls are enthusiastic about babies—there is always someone to hold the child. When the mother goes to the garden to work, she takes a small boy or girl along to hold the baby, instead of laying the baby down on a piece of bark or hanging it up for the morning in its little net bag. If the little nurse is a boy, he will hold the child in his arms, if a girl, she will wear the baby-bag on her back.

When the child begins to walk the quiet continuous rhythm of its life changes somewhat. It is now becoming a little heavy for the mother to carry about with her on long trips to the garden, and furthermore it can be expected to live without suckling for an hour or so. The mother leaves the child in the village with the father, or with some other relative, while she goes to the garden or for firewood. She returns often enough to a crying and disgruntled baby. Repentant, desirous of making restitution, she sits down and suckles the child for an hour. This rhythm, which begins as an hour's absence and an hour's compensatory suckling, develops into longer and longer periods, until by the time the child is three or so it is often being given a day's abstinence—supplemented, of course, by other food—followed by a day's nursing, in which the mother sits all day, holding the child on her lap, letting it suckle as it wishes, play about, suckle again, play with her breasts, gradually regain its sense of security. This is an experience that the mother enjoys as much as the child. From the time the little child is old enough to play with her breasts, the mother takes an active part in the suckling process. She holds her breast in her hand and gently vibrates the nipple inside the child's lips. She blows in the child's ear, or tickles its ears, or playfully slaps its genitals, or tickles its toes. The child in turn plays little tattoos on its mother's body and its own, plays with one breast while suckling the other, teases the breast with its hands, plays with its own genitals, laughs and coos and makes a long, easy game of the suckling. Thus the whole matter of nourishment is made into an occasion of high affectivity and becomes a means by which the child develops and maintains a sensitivity to caresses in every part of its body. It is no question of a completely clothed infant being given a cool hard bottle and firmly persuaded to drink its milk and get to sleep at once so that the mother's aching arms can stop holding the bottle. Instead, nursing is, for mother and child, one long delightful and highly charged game, in which the easy warm affectivity of a lifetime is set up.

Meanwhile, as the child grows older it learns to substitute new delights for its mother's breasts during her ever lengthening absences. It learns to play with its lips. This play it sees all about it among the older children, and the older children also play with the baby's lips and so set the first part of the pattern that fits in so well with the child's temporary loneliness and hunger. Interestingly enough, no Arapesh child ever sucks its thumb or sucks one finger continuously.[36] But it engages in every other conceivable type of lip-play.

---

36. "It is probable that thumb-sucking, absent among most primitive people, is a habit built up in the first few months of life, a period during which primitive children are almost always suckled when they cry" [Mead's note].

It flicks its upper lip with its thumb, with its first finger, with its second finger; it blows out its cheeks and pounds them; it bubbles its lips with the palm of its hand, with the back of its hand; it tickles the inside of its lower lip with its tongue; it licks its arms and its knees. A hundred different stylized ways of playing with the mouth are present in the play of the older children and gradually transmitted to the developing child.

This lip-play is the thread of behaviour which binds together the child's emotional life, which ties the happy security it felt in its yielding mother's arms to placid enjoyment of the long evenings by the fireside among its elders, and finally to a contented, unspecific sexual life. The Arapesh themselves regard playing with the lips as the symbol of childhood. Young boys and girls who tell legends that properly should only be told by grown-up people are warned to bubble their lips afterwards so that their hair will not become prematurely grey. And boys who have been initiated are told by the older men to cease playing with their lips; are they still children that they should do so? At the same time they are permitted to substitute betel-chewing and smoking, so that the lips, so long accustomed to constant stimulation, shall not be lonely. But the girls are permitted to bubble their lips until they have borne children, and we shall see how this fits in with the way in which the women's development is accounted slower than the men's.

from chapter 11. The Development of the Individual Mundugumor

The Mundugumor man-child is born into a hostile world, a world in which most of the members of his own sex will be his enemies, in which his major equipment for success must be a capacity for violence, for seeing and avenging insult, for holding his own safety very lightly and the lives of others even more lightly. From his birth, the stage is set to produce in him this kind of behaviour. When a Mundugumor woman tells her husband that she is pregnant, he is not pleased. It makes him a marked man. When he goes among a group of men who are carving a slit gong, they will officiously and with broad grins brush up the chips lest he tread upon any of them, which would be bad for the child, whom he does not want, and for the slit gong, from the manufacture of which he is thus publicly excluded. If he fences a garden, someone else will insert the posts; if he gathers ratan in the bush, some impudent small boy will warn him to pluck only the green ratan or the child will stick fast in his wife's womb. These taboos, which might unite him to his wife in care for the child if having a child were something to look forward to among the Mundugumor, are used by his associates to aggravate his annoyance with his wife. He abuses her for having become pregnant so quickly, and curses his anti-pregnancy magic that he had set in motion in vain. If he has intercourse with her after she is known to be pregnant, he runs a further risk; she may have twins, the second child being the result of more male stimulation, which is all that a male is believed to contribute, semen that, by continual stimulation of a blood-clot, causes it to develop into a child. The father's interest, therefore, instead of being enlisted on the side of the child is already enlisted against it. And the pregnant woman associates her pregnancy with sexual deprivation, her husband's anger and repudiation, and the continual risk that he will take another wife and temporarily desert her altogether. This latter he is particularly likely to do if the new woman who attracts his attention has to be fought for—as is usually the case. Whether she is the wife or the daughter of another man, the new husband first has to elope with her, then defend her against the party of enraged men who will come to fight over her, and finally compensate them for her either with a woman from his kindred or with a valuable sacred flute. During the course of such proceedings he naturally does not confide in his pregnant wife, and she often finds herself stranded with someone of her own relatives while her husband is careening off after a rival. So to the mother, even more than to the father, the coming child is unwelcome. The first highly charged days of marriage in which an active interest in sex held them both together have given place to anger, hostility, and very often to charges of infidelity, as the husband refuses to believe that he is responsible for this unwelcome event.

This attitude towards children is congruent with the ruthless individualism, the aggressive specific sexuality, the intra-sex hostility, of the Mundugumor. A system that made a son valuable to a man as an heir, as an extension of his own personality, might combine the Mundugumor personality type with an interest in parenthood, but under the Mundugumor rope and marriage system, a man has no heirs, only sons who are hostile rivals by definition, and daughters who, defend them as he will, will eventually be torn from him. A man's only hope of power and prestige lies in the number of his wives, who will work for him and give him the means to buy power, and in the accident of the occurrence of some mild characters among his brothers. The phrase "a man who has brothers" occurs every now and again in their remarks, and this means a man who, by a stroke of luck, has some weak-willed, docile brothers who will follow his lead, and instead of disputing his progress will form a more or less permanent constellation about him in his middle age. Allies whom he can coerce and bully in the days of his strength, not sons who will come after him and by their strength mock his old age, these are his desire. A wife who becomes pregnant has therefore hurt a man at his most vulnerable spot; she has taken the first step towards his downfall by possibly conceiving a son. And for herself, she has shifted her husband's active sexual interest into angry frustrated resentment—for what? Possibly to bear a daughter, who will be her husband's, not hers.

Before the child is born there is much discussion as to whether it shall be saved or not, the argument being partly based upon the sex of the child, the father preferring to keep a girl, the mother a boy. The argument is weighted against the mother, however, because her father and brothers also prefer a girl. Boys in the kin-group lead to trouble if there are not enough girls to purchase wives for them; and, even if they have a sufficient number of sisters, aggressive boys are apt to carry off additional women who will have to be fought over. The chance of survival of a Mundugumor child increases with order of birth, the first child having the poorest chance. Both father and mother are less intensely upset by the advent of later children, and also once a son is born it is absolutely necessary that he should have a sister to exchange for his wife. This feeling that one's very social existence depends upon having a sister was vividly illustrated when a Mundugumor woman offered to adopt one of our Arapesh boys. The earnest of the offer was that she promised him—with her husband's approval, of course—one of her daughters as a sister, thus assuring him a proper position in Mundugumor society. A girl-child, therefore, has a better chance of survival than a boy; she is an advantage to her father, to her brothers, and also to the entire kin-group on both sides, who, if she is not requisitioned at home, may use her to compensate for one of her cousin's wives.

There is also some feeling that once one son is kept, he might as well have brothers. If a child survives long enough to be washed instead of being bundled up in the palm-spathe upon which the delivery took place and thrown into the river, it will not be killed afterwards, although it may be treated most summarily and exposed to many risks to which young children are not subjected among most primitive peoples. Also if a man deserts his wife during her pregnancy, his chances of having a son survive are much higher, for he will not be there to command her to kill it. In a polygynous household, furthermore, each rival wife insists upon having a son, and the husband is enmeshed in a net of cause and effect from which he seldom entirely extricates himself. [. . .]

It is into such a highly charged world, a world constantly disposed to hostility and conflict, that the Mundugumor infant is born. And almost from birth, unless it is an adopted child and the constant stimulating of its suckling is needed for the first few months to produce milk, the child's preparation for an unloved life is begun. Very little babies are kept in a carrying-basket, a closely woven, rough-plaited basket, semi circular in profile, which the women wear suspended from their foreheads as the Arapesh women wear their net bags. (And as the Arapesh call the womb by the word for net bag, so the Mundugumor call the womb by the word for carrying basket.) But whereas the Arapesh net bag is flexible, adapting itself to the child's body and exerting pressure to curl the body in upon itself in a pre-natal position, and is furthermore so slight that it interposes no barrier between the child and its mother's warm body, the Mundugumor basket is harsh and stiff and opaque. The child's body must accommodate itself to the rigid lines of the basket, lying almost prone with its arms practically pinioned to its sides. The basket is too thick to permit any warmth from the mother's body to permeate it; the child sees nothing but the narrow slits of light at both ends. Women wear the babies only when they are walking from one place to another, and as most of their expeditions are short, to their own fishing *barads* and sago-bush, they usually leave them at home, hung up in the house. When a baby cries it is not fed at once; instead some bystander resorts to the standard method of soothing restless infants. Without looking at the child, without touching its body, the mother or other woman or girl who is caring for it begins to scratch with her finger-nails on the outside of the basket, making a harsh grating sound.

Children are trained to respond to this sound; it seems as if their cries, originally motivated by a desire for warmth, water, or food, were conditioned to accepting often this meagre remote response in their stead. If the crying does not stop, the child is eventually suckled.

Mundugumor women suckle their children standing up, supporting the child with one hand in a position that strains the mother's arm and pinions the arms of the child. There is none of the mother's dallying, sensuous pleasure in feeding her child that occurs among the Arapesh. Nor is the child permitted to prolong his meal by any playful fondling of his own or his mother's body. He is kept firmly to his major task of absorbing enough food so that he will stop crying and consent to be put back in his basket. The minute he stops suckling for a moment he is returned to his prison. Children therefore develop a very definite purposive fighting attitude, holding on firmly to the nipple and sucking milk as rapidly and vigorously as possible. They frequently choke from swallowing too fast; the choking angers the mother and infuriates the child, thus further turning the suckling situation into one characterized by anger and struggle rather than by affection and reassurance.

SOURCES

Joseph-Marie Degérando, *The Observation of Savage Peoples,* trans. and ed. F. C. T. Moore (London: Routledge and Kegan Paul, 1969). Reproduced by permission of Taylor and Francis Books, Ltd.

Georges Cuvier, "Note instructive sur les recherches à faire relativement aux différences anatomiques des diverses races d'Hommes" [trans. Richard Lansdown], in Georges Hervé, "À la recherche d'un manuscrit: Les instructions anthropologiques de G. Cuvier pour le voyage du *Géographe* et du *Naturaliste* aux Terres Australes," *Revue de l'École d'Anthropologie de Paris* 10 (1910).

François Péron, "Maria Island: Anthropological Observations," trans. N. J. B. Plomley, in Plomley, *The Baudin Expedition and the Tasmanian Aborigines 1802* (Hobart: Blubber Head Press, 1983). Reproduced by permission of the Blubber Head Press.

Horatio Hale, *United States Exploring Expedition during the Years 1838, 1839, 1840, 1842, under the Command of Charles Wilkes, U.S.N.,* vol. 6: *Ethnology and Philology* (1846).

Edward Burnett Tylor, "On the Tasmanians as Representatives of Palaeolithic Man," *Journal of the Anthropological Institute of Britain and Ireland* 23 (1894).

A. C. Haddon, "A Plea for an Expedition to Melanesia," *Nature* 74 (1906).

Bronislaw Malinowski, *A Diary in the Strict Sense of the Term,* trans. Norbert Guterman (New York: Harcourt Brace / London: Routledge and Kegan Paul, 1967). Reproduced by permission of Taylor and Francis Books, Ltd.

Margaret Mead, *Sex and Temperament in Three Primitive Societies* (New York: William Morrow / London: Routledge and Kegan Paul, 1935). © 1935, 1950, 1963 by Margaret Mead. Reproduced by permission of HarperCollins Publishers, Inc.

Readers wholly new to anthropology will learn a lot in a short time from Paul A. Erickson, *A History of Anthropological Theory* (Peterborough, Ontario: Broadview Press, 1998); James L. Peacock, *The Anthropological Lens: Harsh Light, Soft Focus* (Cambridge: Cambridge University Press, 2001); and Hortense Powdermaker, *Stranger and Friend: The Way of an Anthropologist* (London: Secker and Warburg, 1967). For other histories of anthropology, see: Stanley Diamond, ed., *Anthropology: Ancestors and Heirs* (The Hague: Mouton, 1980); Merwyn S. Garbarino, *Sociocultural Theory in Anthropology: A Short History* (Prospect Heights: Waveland Press, 1983); Stephen Jay Gould, *The Mismeasure of Man* (London: Penguin: 1996), based on American material but with chapters on physical anthropology, craniology, craniometry, and so forth; Elman R. Service, *A Century of Controversy: Ethnological Issues from 1860 to 1960* (Orlando: Academic Press, 1985); Sydel Silverman, ed., *Totems and Teachers: Perspectives on the History of Anthropology* (New York: Columbia University Press, 1981), which has good chapters on Boas and Malinowski; Fred W. Voget, *A History of Ethnology* (New York: Holt, Rinehart and Winston, 1975); and by the doyen of the field, George W. Stocking Jr.: *Bones, Bodies, Behavior: Essays on Biological Anthropology* (Madison: University of Wisconsin Press, 1988), the introduction to which is excellent on physical anthropology, and the superb *Victorian Anthropology* (New York: Free Press, 1987), which despite its title restricts itself to neither England nor the Victorian era.

Studies including a varying degree of Pacific focus include James Clifford, *The Predicament of Culture: Twentieth-Century Ethnography, Literature and Art* (Cambridge, MA: Harvard University Press, 1988); Christopher Herbert, *Culture and Anomie: Ethnographic Imagination in the Nineteenth Century* (Chicago: University of Chicago Press, 1991); Michael C. Howard, "A Preliminary Survey of Anthropology and Sociology in the South Pacific," *Journal of Pacific Studies* 9 (1983); Felix M. Keesing, *Social Anthropology in Polynesia: A Review of Research* (London: Oxford University Press, 1953); and Nicholas Thomas, *Out of Time: History and Evolution in Anthropological Discourse* (Cambridge: Cambridge University Press, 1989).

On Péron, start with George Stocking's essay "French Anthropology in 1802," in his *Race, Culture, and Evolution: Essays in the History of Anthropology* (New York: Free Press, 1968), and Péron's own *A Voyage of Discovery to the Southern Hemisphere* (London, 1809). See also Jacqueline Bonnemains, Elliott Forsyth, and Bernard Smith, eds., *Baudin in Australian Waters* (Melbourne: Oxford University Press, 1988); and Frank Horner, *The French Reconaissance: Baudin in Australia, 1801–1803* (Melbourne: Melbourne University Press, 1987). Degérando, Cuvier, and Péron are collected in Jean Copans and Jean Jamin, eds., *Aux origines de l'anthropologie française* (Paris: Jean Michel Place, 1994).

On the 1899 Torres Strait expedition, see A. C. Haddon, *Head-Hunters: Black, White, and Brown* (London: Methuen, 1901), *The Races of Man and Their Distribution* (Cambridge: Cambridge University Press, 1924), and *Reports of the Cambridge Anthropological Expedition to the Torres Strait* (Cambridge: Cambridge University Press, 1901–1935), vol. 1: *General Ethnography;* and W. H. R. Rivers, *The History of Melanesian Society* (Cambridge: Cambridge University Press, 1914).

On Malinowski see George Stocking, "Empathy and Antipathy in the Heart of Darkness," in Regna Darnell, ed., *Readings in the History of Anthropology* (New York: Harper and Row, 1974); "The Ethnographer's Magic: Fieldwork in British Anthropology from Tylor to Malinowski," in Stocking, ed., *Observers Observed: Essays in Ethnographic Fieldwork* (Madison: University of Wisconsin Press, 1983); and "Maclay, Kubary, Malinowski: Archetypes from the Dreamtime of Anthropology," in Stocking, ed., *Colonial Situations: Essays on the Contextualization of Ethnographic Knowledge* (Madison: University of Wisconsin Press, 1991). See also Christina A. Thompson, "Anthropology's Conrad: Malinowski in the Tropics and What He Read," *Journal of Pacific History* 30:1 (June 1995); and Michael Young, *Malinowski: Odyssey of an Anthropologist, 1884–1920* (New Haven: Yale University Press, 2004). Jutta Malnic, *Kula: Myth and Magic in the Trobriand Islands* (Sydney: Cowrie Books, 1998), is intensely evocative and full of exquisite photographs; and Helena Wayne, ed., *The Story of a Marriage: The Letters of Bronislaw Malinowski and Elsie Masson,* 2 vols. (London: Routledge, 1995), provides the emotional background to the *Diary*. (See also chapters in James Clifford and Christopher Herbert, above.)

On Margaret Mead see Nancy McDowell, *The Mundugumor: From the Field Notes of Margaret Mead and Reo Fortune* (Washington, D.C.: Smithsonian Institution Press, 1991); and Margaret Mead, *Blackberry Winter: My Earlier Years* (New York: William Morrow, 1972), and *Letters from the Field, 1925–1975* (New York: Harper and Row, 1977). Controversy has arisen about the degree to which Mead was imposed upon by her Pacific informers: see Derek Freeman, *Margaret Mead and Samoa: The Making and Unmaking of a Anthropological Myth* (Canberra: Australian National University Press, 1992); and Lenora Foerster and Angela Gillam, *Confronting the Margaret Mead Legacy: Scholarship, Empire, and Myth in the South Pacific* (Philadelphia: Temple University Press, 1992).

Representative nineteenth-century works of Pacific ethnography include Robert Codrington, *The Melanesians* (1891); John Crawfurd, "The Malayan and Polynesian Languages and Races," *Journal of the Ethnological Society of London* (1848); William Ellis, *Polynesian Researches* (1829); James Gordon Frazer, *The Native Races of Australasia* (notebooks, published in 1939); Henry Brougham Guppy, *The Solomon Islands and Their Natives* (1887); Richard Parkinson, *Thirty Years in the South Seas* (translated 1999); George Turner, *Samoa* (1884); and Thomas Williams, *Fiji and the Fijians* (1859).

Accessible works of Pacific anthropology from its mid-twentieth-century heyday include Gregory Bateson, *Naven* (1934); Ruth Benedict, *Patterns of Culture* (1934); Raymond Firth, *We, the Tikopia* (1936); Bronislaw Malinowski, *Argonauts of the Western Pacific* (1922), and *Magic, Science and Religion and Other Essays* (1948); Margaret Mead, *Coming of Age in Samoa* (1929); Tom Harrisson, *Savage Civilization* (1937); Roy Rappaport, *Pigs for the Ancestors* (1967); and Peter Worsley, *And the Trumpets Shall Sound: A Study of "Cargo" Cults in Melanesia* (1957). Also see Joel Bonnemaison, *The Tree and the Canoe* (1986).

8

THE COLONIAL INTERREGNUM
AND THE SECOND WORLD WAR

The Offices of Humanity

The South Seas had by 1900 been almost entirely parceled out among the great powers, though these acts of territorial acquisition were more the outcome of imperial agendas than colonial ones. "How can a little State, hemmed in by powerful and growing neighbours, maintain her independence?" the colonial administrator Basil Thomson asked in 1894. "We do not want Tonga, and yet we cannot allow any other great power to take our place there. If Tonga must be taken, it is we who must take her; but though I am not 'Little Englander,' I have seen enough of our small possessions to know that the increased incentive to British trade that may result from the hoisting of a flag does not compensate for the weakness that a host of half bankrupt islands throws upon the Empire" (Thomson 1894a: 287).

After the First World War had reorientated the imperial world order and other economic developments had finally revealed the slender resources of Pacific islands, individuals increasingly began to follow Thomson in questioning the nature and even the value of Western rule in such far-flung places. As early as 1889, a New Zealand politician had drawn a distinction between what he called the "Romaic" system of colonial rule (associated with France and Spain), "with its spirit of centralization," and the "Teutonic" system (associated with Germany and England), with its "inherent tendency to decentralization and reliance upon individual action" (Moss, 53). This distinction is a direct antecedent of one made forty years later by Stephen Roberts, between "Native Independence" (associated with British liberalism) and "Direct Rule" (involving "a few European officials trampling on native customs"). For Roberts, "the British theory of native independence and the French system of direct rule" were both failures, because it was "evident that the natives were clearly incapable either of maintaining kingdoms of their own, or of developing along the lines of Western constitutionalism" (Roberts, 151–152). In short, colonialism was not working, whereas real independence was as yet unimaginable. Roberts' solution to this dilemma was what he—borrowing the expression from the nineteenth-century administrator of colonial Africa Lord Lugard—called Indirect Rule, taking a variety of different possible models and combining local agency and custom (which Roberts valued highly) with adequate political standards.

There were three important elements lying behind the notion of Indirect Rule: the conclusion that places like Pacific islands were more trouble than they were worth, the admission that indigenous custom had to be granted some integrity, and a benevolent (though deeply paternalistic) liberalism in Western attitudes to Pacific Islanders that went back to Captain Cook himself:

> When the recesses of the globe are investigated, in order to promote general knowledge, and not with a prospect of enlarging private dominion; when we traverse the globe to visit new tribes of our fellow-creatures, as friends, wishing to learn their existence, for the express purpose of bringing them within the pale of the offices of humanity, and to relieve their wants, by communicating to them our superior attainments; the voyages projected by his gracious Majesty George the Third, and carried into execution by Captain Cook have not, it is presumed, been entirely useless. Some rays of light must have been darted on the Friendly, Society, and Sandwich islands, by our repeated intercourse with them. Their stock of ideas must naturally be enlarged, and new materials must have been furnished them for the exercise of their reason, by the uncommon objects we exhibited to them. (Cook and King, 1:vii)

This threefold combination of factors produced—approximately between the last third of the nineteenth century and the Second World War, though it lives on in certain forms to this day—what I call the literature of the "colonial interregnum." It is a sentimental and moral era rather than a strictly historical one, falling between imperialism and the postcolonial period ushered in by the Second World War. As such it exists alongside the system of Indirect Rule proposed by Stephen Roberts, and one of the reasons the ethos it embodies has never passed away is that something like Indirect Rule continues to govern the lives of Pacific Islanders at the present time. The agencies providing tutelary supervision nowadays may be "the international community," the World Bank, the World Trade Organization, or the bewildering array of organizational bodies Pacific states have themselves evolved, but Indirect Rule is still what it feels like to many or looks like from the outside.

"Paternalism as an administrative imperative" may have "reached new heights particularly during and after World War II" (Howe 2000: 86), but earlier texts suggest that what the editors of Cook's account call "the offices of humanity" went back well into the nineteenth century. I have in mind a subgroup of the literature of colonialism—the memoir of colonial service—

and the particular pattern to which that subgroup tends to conform. *From the Middle Temple to the South Seas*, by a former chief police magistrate in Fiji (Alexander); *In Savage Islands and Settled Lands*, by the former aide-de-camp to the governor of Queensland (Baden-Powell); *My Consulate in Samoa* (Churchward); *Polynesian Reminiscences*, by a former consul in Samoa and Fiji (Pritchard); *My Adventures among South Sea Cannibals*, by the former government agent in Queensland, Australia (Rannie); *From My Verandah in New Guinea*, by the former deputy commissioner for the Western Pacific and acting special commissioner for New Guinea (Romilly); *South Sea Reminiscences*, by the former colonial secretary of the Leeward Islands and district commissioner in Fiji (St.-Johnston); *South Sea Yarns*, by the former resident commissioner in Fiji (Thomson 1894b): this is only a sampling of the large number of British productions in this vein.

Such books described a situation in which the colonial power had no reason to stay, but its sense of responsibility and marginal strategic interest forbad it to leave. Islanders could no longer be seen as doomed to die out in the face of progress. Indigenous populations had in fact generally recovered from the onslaught of contagious disease. But Islander life had been massively disturbed, particularly where diet and health were concerned. Rousseau's noble savage had become overweight and diabetic, with rotten teeth, tuberculosis, and mosquito-borne diseases; traditional food sources had been eradicated or polluted, and many Pacific people now lived on tinned meat and bagged flour. A need was felt to make amends and to address "the repayment of the debt which the white man owes to the brown man in the Pacific," as the former high commissioner for the Western Pacific put it (Luke, 67). Islanders had to learn to look after themselves—with friendly white assistance.

This ethos was expressed in two ways in particular. Writers might retreat to remote, "historical," "political," or "administrative" attitudes. "Fortunately there is much room for constructive planning," one such commentator wrote, "between colonialism of the old exclusive type and international supervision in the full sense." "Helping such groups to cross the gap from the Stone Age to modern conditions, and gain a worthwhile place in the world that is now in the making offers one of the greatest challenges to the spirit of democracy and humanity" (Keesing, xxii, xxiv). "It is time," another such postcolonial strategist believed,

> for the chapter of aggressive Imperialism in the world's history to close. In the past many countries have played their part in the events which that chapter records.... They have all won great territories by conquest or colonization; and in some cases have kept, in other cases failed to keep, what they have gained. The Mandate system of the League of Nations is an avowal, to which the majority of the governments of the world have agreed, that, for the future, territories should not be taken from backward peoples but should, if protectorate is necessary, be safeguarded and developed in the interests of their present inhabitants. (Fox 1928: 245)

But there was another voice of the colonial interregnum, as an American doctor's memoir of public health work in the 1920s and 1930s suggests: "I was beginning to see that one old bad theory was losing ground—the belief that the native . . . is an economic unit to be exploited till he dies. Governments once blind and cruel were beginning to see light. The British High Commission, controlling five island groups, was struggling toward better things. So was progressive New Zealand with her mandates and possessions over wide stretches of Polynesia" (Lambert, 110–111). S. M. Lambert's language is different from the tone of Frank Fox or Felix Keesing: it is subjective, emotive, and judgmental—"personal," in short. This is a new South Sea note: a moral rejection of imperialist attitudes on the part of individuals sent out to deliver administrative axle grease to populations being prepared for future independence. In treating, teaching, or training Islanders, or in administering justice to them, such individuals came to see themselves more as neutral parties than as government representatives, and came to see the Islanders as individuals like themselves rather than undifferentiated "natives."

Time after time, books of this kind open with a naive but wholesomely well-intentioned young person summoned to some metropolitan office of humanity, undergoing an interview, then being shown a spot on the map where he or she is to conquer disease, teach English, remedy poor diet, hold court, or round up felons. Time after time, too, the ill-prepared but idealistic young person then becomes immersed in a community made up of lovable eccentrics, some of whom will be white like himself but most of whom will be Islanders—now given names, family histories, and psychological characteristics for the first time in Western literature. Moreover, the administrative work such individuals carry out is no longer an arm of nineteenth-century centralized government seeking to protect its citizens abroad but a distinctly island-oriented, proactive, reformist, twentieth-century institution: still intrusive—much more so—but intruding to do good.

But bureaucracy has its drawbacks, and literature of this kind proposes that bureaucracy is profoundly alien to the South Seas. So the massive organizations these individuals represented—the Foreign and Commonwealth Office, the League of Nations, the Rockefeller Foundation, the South Pacific Commission, and so on—must be humanized, and this the authors concerned achieve in countless ways: by self-deprecation, by asserting their modesty, by admitting to inoffensive human weaknesses, by presenting their soft side (a love of nature, poetry, innocent things, children, pretty views), and above all by dwelling on their own eccentricity or idiosyncrasy. The tasks they have been sent to do are carried out, but it is the *way* the job is done that is emphasized, with particular stress on interpersonal qualities of empathy and affection. Individuals represent themselves as unworldly, innocent, dreamy, enthusiastic, yet it is also clear they are resourceful, pragmatic, uncomplaining, and indefatigible.

The recipients of this benign paternalism, the victims of these do-gooders, are characterized in three ways accordingly: they may become in effect white themselves and start organizing village self-help groups, clinics, schools, and so forth (thus reflecting the author's practical utility); they may remain passive recipients but are then seen as representatives of peoples themselves wholly lovable, however childlike and irresponsible (thus reflecting the writer's parental virtues); or they may join the privileged dramatis personae of named whites for some reason: they are *particularly* helpful, pathetic, obstinate, hopeless, refined, giving, loving (thus reflecting the author as a whole). This refined sentimentalism suggests weakness or surrender on the part of Western authors themselves. A pattern of islands or pieces of paradise are glimpsed only momentarily before the writer departs, leaving the islands to their original tenants: Islanders, wind, and sea. Repeated across hundreds of books, the pattern is very strong, though its aim is to leave the impression that there is no pattern, only an effortless but poignant departure, in which the colonial official imagines himself or herself as a migrating bird who can leave no trace and do no harm to an island whose immemorial natural balance the author is only helping to restore or preserve. So it is that the apparently sophisticated modern Westerner is more addicted to a fantasy of the South Seas than any of his or her eighteenth- and nineteenth-century predecessors.

Empty Spaces to Fight For

The attitude of the United States to the Pacific was unresolved for many years. In part this is readily understandable. The nation did not exist when the South Sea Islands were rediscovered in the 1760s and 1770s, and though America now possesses thousands of miles of Pacific coastline, this was not always so: the United States began in the east, and the principle of "manifest destiny," according to which it had the right "to overspread and possess the whole of the continent which Providence has given us for the development of the great experiment of liberty and federated self-government entrusted to us" (quoted in Dulles, 3), was first stated as late as 1845. "The western coast of the continent was separated from the Atlantic by so vast an expanse of desert and mountain that it was for long believed absolutely impossible that any settlement Americans might make on the Pacific could have political connections with the United States" (Dulles, 2). To these politicohistorical considerations should be added a geographic one: to look west from continental America toward Hawai'i means looking over a void of 2,500 miles; looking east from Australia to, say, New Caledonia, involves a distance of 750 miles—and New Caledonia is reasonably close to the New Hebrides, which are reasonably close to Fiji, which is reasonably close to Samoa and Tonga, which are reasonably close to Tahiti, and so on. The eastern Pacific is almost empty; the western Pacific is at least speckled with human settlement.

So America's involvement with the Pacific is an ambivalent one. On the one hand, writers with their feet in the nineteenth century stress America's young and aggressive temper as a new global power, whose destiny came to involve Oregon, California, Alaska, Samoa, Hawai'i, and the Philippines in turn. On the other, there is the admission that America has not been as active in the Pacific as it might have been. On the one hand: "an ambition to win the mastery of the Pacific and control its rich commerce runs persistently through the entire history of the United States" (Dulles, 1). ("The Pacific should be ours, and it must be"; "The Pacific is our natural property. Our great coast borders it for a quarter of the world" [Lafarge, 278, 153].) On the other hand: "American interest in insular geography waxes and wanes with the economic tides. The distant South Pacific islands, almost forgotten since the days of the whaler and the guano ships, have again suddenly been brought into sharp focus" (Krieger, 1).

What brought these distant islands into sharp focus and resolved this ambivalence for good and all was America's entry into the Second World War, brought about by a devastatingly successful air raid on Pearl Harbor, Hawai'i, by the Japanese in December 1941. "Before 1941 Americans could afford to ignore an ocean which to them had an unknown meaning," James Michener suggested. "Our nineteenth-century inland pioneers had established the cry, 'On to the Pacific!' But when they reached the mighty ocean, like frightened children they turned their backs upon it and left it for others to develop" (Stroven and Day, vii). In the war's immediate aftermath, however, the lesson was clear: "the South Seas are Uncle Sam's baby" (Furnas, 4). The British, the French, and the Japanese had been decisively replaced as Pacific powers, and a new manifest destiny, one hundred years younger than the first, made itself apparent.

The Japanese offensive for which Pearl Harbor served as a prelude was as dramatic as any in military history: by February 1942 the Japanese had evicted the British garrison from Singapore; in May Japanese submarines were discovered in Sydney Harbour. By August Japanese forces reached their furthest extent, holding Indonesia, the Philippines, the northern half of New Guinea, Micronesia in its entirety, and the Solomon Islands south to Guadalcanal. Port Moresby was saved only by heroic Australian resistance, and Darwin was bombed repeatedly. But if the Japanese assault was prodigious, so in time was the American response. In May and June of 1942—within six months of Pearl Harbor—the Japanese navy was arrested in the battles of the Coral Sea and Midway. In August Marines landed at Guadalcanal and began the murderous process by which American troops (assisted by Australians and eventually by the British Navy) worked their way back to the west and the north in a pincer movement. One thrust went up the island chains of Micronesia under Admiral Nimitz: Tarawa (November 1943), Kwajelein (January 1944), Guam (July 1944), Peleliu (September 1944), and ultimately the Japanese island of Iwo Jima (February 1945). The other went up the northern shores of New Guinea and hence to the Philippines under General MacArthur. The two met at the Japanese island of Okinawa in June 1945; in August atomic bombs were dropped on the Japanese cities of Hiroshima and Nagasaki, and the war ended.

The loss of life among Allied forces in this campaign was frightful and increased in intensity as the Allies came nearer to the Japanese mainland. "It is . . . a military maxim," William Manchester writes,

> that casualties of 30 percent are usually the most a fighting unit can endure without losing combative spirit. Tarawa, where over 40 per cent fell, proved that wasn't true of the Marine Corps. And as we approached Japan, the casualty rates of our rifle regiments rose higher and higher. On Peleliu the First Marines lost 76 per cent; on Okinawa the Twenty-ninth Marines lost 81 per cent. Thus they seized islands whose defenders would have flung other invaders back into the surf. (Manchester, 255)

"During the six-month struggle for the island [of Guadalcanal], 4,123 Americans had fallen," Manchester remarks; "on Iwo Jima 25,851 Marines would be lost in less than four weeks, and the price of the eighty-two day fight for Okinawa, the greatest bloodletting of all, would be 49,151 Americans" (Manchester, 193). These appalling rates of attrition caused the U.S. administration to decide to employ the atomic bomb, for no one could foresee the loss of life were Allied troops to fight a prolonged campaign on the Japanese mainland.

The fighting on the islands was also of an unparalleled nature. Japanese troops were heroic, too; but they also engaged in acts of barbarism Allied troops could scarcely comprehend. Normal rules of war regarding surrender or the treatment of prisoners and civilians simply went by the board—on both sides. "Why," Manchester asks, "does the mere mention of the southwest Pacific cause the men who fought there to shudder? Why does so genteel an author as Herman Wouk, whipped into a white-lipped rage at the mere thought of Guadalcanal, write that it 'was and remains "that fucking island" '? Why was combat there considered—correctly—worse than Stalingrad?" (Manchester, 93).

Manchester's answer—that the immediate interior of such islands was completely disorientating—is surely only part of the explanation he seeks. First you had to *reach* that interior. What made the island landings of the early 1940s comparable with the bloodiest and most degrading battles of any war was the utter exposure of the invading troops. There could be no element of surprise, since increased naval and airborne activity made the target self-evident, and Japanese forces had spent months digging themselves into redoubts with perfect coverage of the shore. Typically, landing craft unloaded troops directly onto reefs at some distance from the beach-head, and Marines walked across sharp coral in water up to the hips, in the direct path of enemy gunfire (Figure 24). Beach-heads once captured were waterless coral shelves, with all vegetation and shelter eradicated. In a landscape like this, the piers of an old jetty were sufficient to shelter hundreds of men, but one stubbornly held Japanese gun emplacement could jeopardize even more. No environment could be more different from the *Islands of Enchantment* (Coombe) the *Scented Isles and Coral Gardens* (Mackellar), or the *Pastels from the Pacific* (Lenwood) celebrated by late-colonial writers (Figure 25).

FIGURE 24. Troops of the First Marine Division head toward beaches of Peleliu Island (1944). © Australian Picture Library / Corbis.

The island war in the Pacific was uniquely distressing because of the terrain—whether that was the coral of Tarawa or the jungle of Bougainville—certainly, and the nature of Japanese resistance, too. But there were additional things to cope with. Another veteran of the conflict has this to offer about "the battles fought out there": "what was different about them, compared to the battles and campaigns in Europe and North Africa, was their utter remoteness from the continents, the history, the civilizations that men from Western nations knew" (Hynes 1998: 159). A pilot in the Battle of Britain was defending the land over which he flew; a British Tommy in the trenches of the First World War knew that the channel and his home were directly behind him; an American soldier fighting across Normandy or up the boot of Italy at least had legendary cities like Paris, Rome, and Berlin as his destinations. But marines fighting in Guadalcanal were thousands of miles from Hawai'i, let alone Denver, Dallas, or New York—and they were heading *west*, yet farther from home, across islands that bore no relation to anything in their experience and no self-evident relation to the security of their homeland. "Out there," Hynes continues, "the war life was all there was: no history was visible, no monu-

FIGURE 25. Destruction on Peleliu, September 1944. © Australian Picture
Library / Corbis.

ments of the past, no cities remembered from books. There was nothing to
remind a soldier of his other life: no towns, no bars, nowhere to go, nowhere
even to desert to" (Hynes 1998: 159). Micronesian islands often appeared
empty of physical culture, as villages and villagers alike disappeared before
the soldiers' advance. How would sailors feel, then, who so rarely saw land?
"There ought to be," Hynes suggests, "a psychological name for this sense of
self astray in vastness" (Hynes 1998: 167).

So combatants conceived of the islands in ways it seems no Westerner
had imagined before: "simply as enemy positions that needed to be seized
or neutralized" (Meredith, xi). "The valley was on Guadalcanal Island, but
it might have been anywhere" (Hersey, 5). When Samuel Hynes arrived at
Saipan (near Guam) in 1944, he was struck to find it had a sugar industry:

> It felt wrong to me, that the war should have passed through this place where
> something useful had been done. The other islands I had seen that had been
> fought over had been nothing to begin with—a few palm trees, a few natives,
> maybe, and a Japanese garrison—ideal empty spaces to fight for. But this is-

Introduction   327

land had a real community, with roads and factories, little towns, docks. What I was feeling, I suppose, was that it was like home, or a possible home, a place that my imagination could populate and live in, and that the ruined buildings were wounds in a real landscape. (Hynes 1988: 189)

Combatants from the Pacific theater hardly ever describe the islands at all. To find this kind of suppression of the physical environment, we have to go back to Daniel Defoe's classic, *Robinson Crusoe* (1719), of whose eponymous hero it has been said: "He sees no beauty in the sea or in flowers or birds; indeed, he scarcely troubles to see his island at all, save as an officer might reconnoitre the terrain where the enemy lurks" (Lewis, 31). "Napoleon said that his soldiers' only view of Russia was the pack of the man in front" (Manchester, 11), and what was true of the Frenchmen invading Russia in 1812 was true of Robinson Crusoe and the marines in the Pacific theater: they were too consumed by anxiety to take stock of their surroundings or to wonder where the Islanders were. It is hardly surprising that a historical ethnocentrism bordering on nihilism surfaces occasionally in military memoirs of the Pacific: "Nothing is happening here now," William Manchester said on revisiting the Solomon Islands in the 1970s (Manchester, 211). "The islands haven't changed since a million men altered the course of the war in countless local engagements."

Other old beliefs would not lie down either, even under these conditions. Reporting the first landing at Guadalcanal, Foster Hailey sounds every inch like Quirós, Cook, or Stevenson in one of their more meditative moments: "the morning," he wrote "was one of those beautiful, cool sunrises when everything seems to be in tune except the men who inhabit the earth" (Hailey, 195). The islet of Mogmog in Ulithi atoll (north of Yap, in the Caroline Islands of Micronesia) was depopulated by the Americans (the original inhabitants being moved to nearby Fasserai) to create an "elaborate recreation centre" with the promising invitation "Welcome to Mogmog—Paradise of the Pacific" (Meredith, 104–105). But like every other island paradise in Western history, Mogmog was something other and something less than the sign foretold:

Shiny aluminium cans in hand you went up over a little rise and saw the swamp, where by now all the foliage had been stripped and most of the trees and bushes pulled down and stamped into a greasy mash of mud covered with sailors in blue dungarees arguing and drinking their two cans of beer. Here and there a pipe had been driven into the soaked ground and a funnel inserted into the end to make a crude urinal. These were in constant use. Fights broke out now and again between crews of different ships, and there were even a few drunks who had managed to buy their beer from some of the nondrinkers. Mostly, however, even hardened sailors, wild for liberty and drink, blanched at the sight of Mog Mog, and there was—an unheard of thing—a long line of men back at the landings waiting to return to their ships. (Kernan, 142–143)

THE COLONIAL INTERREGNUM

from C. A. W. Monckton, *Some Experiences of a New Guinea Resident Magistrate* (1921)

Charles Arthur Whitmore Monckton (1872–1936) arrived at Samarai, at the extreme eastern tip of the mainland of New Guinea, in 1895, with a friend and a letter of introduction to the governor, Sir William MacGregor. His later period as resident magistrate was marked by a series of exploratory and punitive expeditions into the interior, and he was retired in 1907.

The day following our arrival in Samarai loud yells of "Sail Ho!" from every native on the island announced that the *Merrie England*[1] was returning from the Mambare River, where the Lieut.-Governor had been occupied in punishing the native murderers of a man named Clarke, the leader of a prospecting party in search of gold; and in establishing at that point, for the protection of future prospectors, a police post under the gallant but ill-fated John Green. Clarke's murder was destined, though no one realized it at the time, to be the beginning of a long period of bloodshed and anarchy in the Northern Division—then still a portion of the Eastern Division. These events, however, belong to a later date and chapter.

On her voyage south from the Mambare, the *Merrie England* had waited at the mouth of the Musa River, while Sir William MacGregor traversed and mapped that stream. Whilst so engaged, accompanied by but one officer and a single boat's crew of native police, His Excellency discovered a war party of north-east coast natives returning from a cannibal feast, with their canoes loaded with dismembered human bodies. Descending the river, Sir William collected his native police and, attacking the raiders, dealt out condign and summary justice, which resulted in the tribes of the lower Musa dwelling for many a year in a security to which several generations had been strangers.

Some little time after the ship had cast anchor, my friend and myself received a message that Sir William was disengaged; whereupon we went on board to meet, for the first time, the strongest man it has ever been my fate to look upon. Short, square, slightly bald, speaking with a strong Scotch accent, showing signs of over-work and the ravages of malaria, there was nothing in the first appearance of the man to stamp him as being out of the ordinary, but I had not been three minutes in his cabin before I realized that I was in the presence of a master of men—a Cromwell, a Drake, a Cæsar or Napoleon—his keen grey eyes looking clean through me, and knew that I was being summed and weighed. Once, and only once in my life, have I felt that a man was my master in every way, a person to be blindly obeyed and one who must be right and infallible, and that was when I met Sir William MacGregor.

Years afterwards, in conversation with a man who had held high command, who had distinguished himself and been much decorated for services in Britain's little wars, I described the impression that MacGregor had made

---

1. The long-serving gubernatorial yacht in New Guinea's eastern British province.

upon me, the sort of overwhelming sense of inferiority he, unconsciously to himself, made one feel, and was told that my friend had experienced a like impression when meeting Cecil Rhodes.[2]

The story of how Sir William MacGregor came to be appointed to New Guinea was to me rather an interesting one, showing the result, in the history of a country, of a fortunate accident. It was related to me by Bishop Stone-Wig, to whom it had been told by the man responsible for the appointment, either Sir Samuel Griffiths, Sir Hugh Nelson, or Sir Thomas McIlwraith, which of the three I have now forgotten. Sir William, at the time Doctor MacGregor, was attending, as the representative of Fiji, one of the earlier conferences regarding the proposed Federation of Australasia;[3] he had already made his mark by work performed in connection with the suppression of the revolt among the hill tribes of that Crown Colony. At the conference, amongst other questions, New Guinea came up for discussion, whereupon MacGregor remarked: "There is the last country remaining, in which the Englishman can show what can be done by just native policy." The remark struck the attention of one of the delegates, by whom the mental note was made, "If Queensland ever has a say in the affairs of New Guinea, and I have a say in the affairs of Queensland, you shall be the man for New Guinea." When later, New Guinea was declared a British Possession, Queensland had a very large say in the matter, and the man who had made the mental note happening to be Premier, he caused the appointment of Administrator to be offered to MacGregor, by whom it was accepted.

Of Sir William, a story told me by himself will illustrate his determination of character, even at an early age, though not related with that intention.

MacGregor, when completing his training at a Scotch University, found his money becoming exhausted; no time could he spare from his studies in which to earn any, even were the opportunity there. Something had to be done, so MacGregor called his old Scotch landlady into consultation as to ways and means. "Well, Mr MacGregor, how much a week can you find?" "Half a crown." "Well, I can do it for that." And this is how she did it. MacGregor had a bowl of porridge for breakfast, nothing else; two fresh herrings or one red one, the cost of the fresh ones being identical with the cured one, for dinner, and a bowl of porridge again for supper. Thus he completed his course and took the gold medal of his year.

This thoroughness and grim determination MacGregor still carried into his work; for instance, it was necessary for him, unless he was prepared to have a trained surveyor always with him on his expeditions, to have a knowledge of astronomy and surveying. This he took up with his usual vigour, and I once witnessed a little incident which showed, not only how perfect Sir Wil-

---

2. Colonial statesman (1853–1902) and prime minister of the Cape Colony of South Africa, with grandiose dreams regarding British imperial Africa.

3. The federation of the separate Australian colonial states to form a nation (including, at one stage, New Zealand) was discussed frequently during the late nineteenth century. Federation came in 1901; New Guinea was annexed at Queensland's insistence in 1884.

liam had made himself in the subject, but also his unbounded confidence in himself. We were lying off a small island about which a doubt existed as to whether it was within the waters of Queensland or New Guinea. The commander of the *Merrie England*, together with the navigation officer, took a set of stellar observations; the chief Government surveyor, together with an assistant surveyor, took a second set; and Sir William took a third. The ship's party and the surveyors arrived at one result, Sir William at a slightly different one; an ordinary man would have decided that four highly competent professional men must be right and he wrong; not so, however, MacGregor. "Ye are both wrong," was his remark, when their results were handed to him by the commander and surveyor. They demurred, pointing out that their observations tallied. "Do it again, ye don't agree with mine"; and sure enough Sir William proved right and they wrong.

My part in this had been to hold a bull's-eye lantern for Sir William to the arc of his theodolite, and to endeavour to attain the immobility of a bronze statue while being devoured by gnats and mosquitoes. Therefore later I sought Stuart Russell, the chief surveyor, with the intention of working off a little of the irritation of the bites by japing at him. "What sort of surveyors do you and Commander Curtis think yourselves? Got to have a bally amateur to help you, eh?" "Shut up, Monckton," said Stuart Russell, "we are surveyors of ordinary ability, Sir William is of more than that." [. . .]

Sir William told my friend and myself, that for two reasons he could not offer either of us employment in his service. Firstly, that the amount of money at his disposal, £12,000 per annum, did not permit of fresh appointments until vacancies occurred; secondly, that his officers must be conversant with native customs and ways of thought, which experience we were entirely lacking. His Excellency, however, told us that he had just received word of the discovery of gold upon Woodlark Island,[4] to which place the ship would at once proceed, and that we might go in her; an offer we gladly accepted.

Then for the first time I met Mr. F. P. Winter, afterwards Sir Francis Winter, Chief Magistrate of the Possession; the Hon. M. H. Moreton, Resident Magistrate of the Eastern Division; Cameron, Chief Government Surveyor; Mervyn Jones, Commander of the *Merrie England;* and Meredith, head gaoler.

Winter had been a law officer in the service of Fiji, and upon the appointment of Sir William MacGregor to New Guinea, had been chosen by him as his Chief Justice and general right-hand man; the wisdom of which choice later years amply showed. Widely read, a profound thinker, possessed of a singular charm of manner, simple and unaffected to a degree, Winter was a man that fascinated every one with whom he came in contact. I don't think he said an unkind word or did a mean action in his life. Every officer in the Service, then and later, took his troubles to him, and every unfortunate out of the Service appealed to his purse.

Moreton, a younger brother of the present Earl of Ducie, had begun life in

---

4. In the eastern Trobriand Islands, north of Samarai.

the Seaforth Highlanders;[5] plucky, hard working, and the best of good fellows, he was fated to work on in New Guinea till, with his constitution shattered, an Australian Government chucked him out to make room for a younger man; shortly after which he died.

Cameron, the surveyor, was another good man, and wholly wrapped up in his work. Of Cameron it was said, that he imagined that surveyors were not for the purpose of surveying the earth but that the earth was created solely for them to survey. He, good chap, was luckier than Moreton, for his fate was to die in harness; he being found sitting dead in his chair, pen in hand, with a half-written dispatch in front of him.

Mervyn Jones was a particularly smart seaman and navigator; educated at Eton for other things, the sea had, however, exercised an irresistible fascination for him; being too old for the Navy, he had worked up into the Naval Reserve through the Merchant Service, and thus had come out to command the *Merrie England*. The charts of the Coral Sea owe much to his labour, and to that also of his two officers, Rothwell and Taylor. All these officers were destined later to share a more or less common fate: Jones died of a combination of lungs and malaria, Taylor of malaria at sea, whilst Rothwell was invalided out of the service. Meredith was taking a gang of native convicts down to Sudest Island;[6] they had been lent by the New Guinea Government to assist in making a road to a gold reef discovered there which was now being opened by an Australian company. It was here that he and many of his charges left their bones. [. . .]

From Sudest the *Merrie England* went on to Woodlark Island, from whence the discovery of gold had been reported by a couple of traders, Lobb and Ede. These two men were a very good example of the old gold-field's practice of "dividing mates." Lobb was a professional gold or other mineral prospector, who had sought for gold in any land where it was likely to occur; when successful, his gains, however great, soon slipped away; when unsuccessful, he depended on a "mate" to finance and feed him, in diggers' language, "grub stake" him, until such time as his unerring instinct should again locate a fresh find. Ede was a New Guinea trader owning a cocoanut plantation on the Laughlan Isles,[7] together with a small vessel. Ede landed Lobb on Woodlark with a number of reliable natives, and, keeping him going with tools, provisions, etc., at last had his reward by word from Lobb of the discovery of payable gold. Thereupon they had reported their discovery and applied for a reward claim to the Administration, together with the request that the island should be proclaimed a gold-field; and at the same time had informed their trader friends, some twenty in all, of what was to be gained at the island.

---

5. A famous Scottish regiment of the British army.

6. Now Tagula, in the Louisiade Archipelago, stretching out into the Coral Sea from Samarai.

7. A group of islands in the Milne Bay region of eastern New Guinea.

Lobb and Ede, with their twenty friends, formed the European population of the island when the *Merrie England* arrived there; with the exception of Lobb, there was not an experienced miner in the lot. The twenty were a curious collection of men: an ex-Captain in Les Chasseurs D'Afrique,[8] whom later on I got to know very well, but who, poor chap, was always most unjustly suspected by the diggers of being an escapee from the French convict establishment at New Caledonia, merely because he was a Frenchman; an unfrocked priest, who by the way was a most plausible and finished scoundrel; and the son of the Premier of one of the Australian colonies; these now, with Ede and myself, constitute the sole survivors of the men who heard Sir William declare the island a gold-field. Here it was that an ex-British resident, and the son of a famous Irish Churchman, jostled shoulders with men whose real names were only known to the police in the various countries from which they hailed. "Jimmy from Heaven," an angelic person, who was once sentenced to be hanged for murder and, the rope breaking, gained a reprieve and pardon, hence his sobriquet; "Greasy Bill"; "Bill the Boozer"; "French Pete"; and "The Dove," a most truculent scoundrel; the names they answered to sufficiently explain the men.

All nationalities and all shades of character, from good to damned bad, they however held two virtues in common: a dauntless courage and a large charity to the unfortunate; traits which will perhaps stand them in better stead in the bourne to which they have gone than they did in New Guinea.

from Arthur Grimble, *A Pattern of Islands* (1952)

As he says, Arthur Grimble (1888–1956) was initially appointed to colonial service in the Gilbert and Ellice Islands (now Kiribati and Tuvalu) in 1913. He served there as district officer from 1916 to 1926 and as resident commissioner from 1926 to 1932, when he was relocated to the West Indies. As an undergraduate at Cambridge University, he had met the English anthropologist W. H. R. Rivers, and Grimble continued to be a keen gatherer of ethnographic information in the Gilberts: an interest that surfaces frequently in his colonial reminiscences.

I was nominated to a cadetship in the Gilbert and Ellice Islands Protectorate at the end of 1913. The cult of the great god Jingo was as yet far from dead.[9] Most English households of the day took it for granted that nobody could be always right, or ever quite right, except an Englishman. The Almighty was be-

---

8. A light cavalry version of the famous French Foreign Legion, the chasseurs fought in North Africa and in European wars until its disbandment in 1962.

9. "Jingoism" was a manifestation of British patriotic imperialism at the end of the nineteenth century; the phrase comes from a popular song of 1878 about Russian threats to Britain's ally, Turkey: "We don't want to fight, but, by jingo, if we do, / We've got the ships, we've got the men, we've got the money too." And so forth.

yond doubt Anglo-Saxon, and the popular conception of Empire resultantly simple. Dominion over palm and pine (or whatever else happened to be noticeably far-flung) was the heaven-conferred privilege of the Bulldog Breed. Kipling had said so.[10] The colonial possessions, as everyone so frankly called them, were properties to be administered, first and last, for the prestige of the little lazy isle where the trumpet-orchids blew.[11] Kindly administered, naturally—nobody but the most frightful bounder could possibly question our sincerity about that—but firmly too, my boy, firmly too, lest the school-children of Empire forget who were the prefects and who the fags.[12] Your uncles—meaning every man Jack of your father's generation, uncle or not, who cared to take you by the ear—all said you'd never be a leader if you weakened on that point. It was terrifying, the way they put it, for Stalky represented their ideal of dauntless youth, and you loathed Stalky with his Company as much as you feared him;[13] but you were a docile young man, and, as his devotees talked, you felt the seeds of your unworthiness sprouting into shameful view through every crack in your character.

The Colonial Office spoke more guardedly than your uncles. It began by saying that, as a cadet officer, you were going to be on probation for three years. To win confirmation as a member of the permanent administrative staff, you would have to pass within that time certain field-examinations in law and native language. This seemed plain and fair enough, but then came the rider. I forget how it was conveyed, whether in print or by word of mouth; but the gist of it was that you could hardly hope to be taken on as a permanent officer unless, over and above getting through your examinations, you could manage to convince your official chiefs overseas that you possessed qualities of leadership. The abysmal question left haunting you was—did the Colonial Office mean leadership in the same sense as Kipling and your uncles? If it did, and if you were anything like me, you were scuppered.

I was a tallish, pinkish, long-nosed young man, fantastically thin-legged and dolefully mild of manner. Nobody could conceivably have looked, sounded or felt less like a leader of any sort than I did at the age of twenty-five. Apart from my dislike of the genus Stalky, I think the only positive things about me were a consuming hunger for sea-travel and a disastrous determination to write sonnets. [. . .]

The fear of being packed home from the Gilbert and Ellice Islands in disgrace, after three years of probation, for having failed to become the kind

---

10. There is an extended allusion in this piece to some lines from "Recessional" (1897) by the English poet, short story writer, and ambivalent apologist for colonialism Rudyard Kipling (1865–1936): "God of our fathers, known of old, / Lord of our far-flung battle-line, / Beneath whose awful Hand we hold / Dominion over palm and pine."

11. That is, Great Britain: an allusion to another of Kipling's patriotic poems, "The Long Trail."

12. In British public schools young pupils often become the unofficial servants ("fags") to senior boys ("prefects").

13. Another allusion to Kipling, this time to his novel for boys *Stalky and Co.* (1899), the eponymous hero of which is an idealized stereotype of the English public schoolboy.

of leader my uncles wanted me to be, began to give me nightmares. A moment came when I felt that the instant sack for some honest admission of my own ineptitude would be easier to bear than that long-drawn-out ignominy. In any case, I decided, someone at the top ought to be warned of my desperate resolve never to become like Stalky. It sounded rather fine, and lonely, and stubborn, put like that; but I fear I didn't live up to the height of it. I did, indeed, secure an interview at the Colonial Office, but my nearest approach to stubbornness with the quiet old gentleman who received me there was to confess, with a gulp in my throat, that the imaginary picture of myself in the act of meting out imperial kindness-but-firmness to anybody, anywhere in the world, made me sweat with shame.

The quiet old gentleman was Mr. Johnson, a Chief Clerk in the department which handled the affairs of Fiji and the Western Pacific High Commission. That discreet title of his (abandoned today in favour of Principal and Secretary) gave no hint of the enormous penetrating power of his official word. In the Western and Central Pacific alone, his modest whisper from behind the throne of authority had power to affect the destinies of scores of races in hundreds of islands scattered over millions of square miles of ocean. I was led to him on a bleak afternoon of February, 1914, high up in the gloomy Downing Street warren that housed the whole Colonial Office staff of those days. The air of his cavernous room enfolded me with the chill of a mortuary as I entered. He was a spare little man with a tenuous sandy beard and heavily tufted eyebrows of the same colour. He stood before the fire, slightly bent in the middle like a monkey-nut, combing his beard with one fragile hand and elevating the tails of his cut-away coat with the other, as he listened to my story. I can see him still, considering me over his glasses with the owlish yet not unkindly stare of an undertaker considering a corpse. (Senior officials in the Colonial Office don't wear beards today, but they still cultivate that way of looking at you.) When I was done, he went on staring a bit; then he heaved a quiet sigh, ambled over to a bookcase, pottered there breathing hard for a long while (I think now he must have been laughing), and eventually hauled out a big atlas, which he carried to his desk.

"Let us see, now," he murmured, settling into his chair, "let us see . . . yes . . . let us go on a voyage of discovery together. Where . . . precisely . . . are the Gilbert and Ellice Islands? If you will believe me, I have often been curious to know."

He started whipping over the pages of the atlas; I could do nothing but goggle at him while he pursued his humiliating research.

"Ah!" he chirruped at last, "here we have them: five hundred miles of islands lost in the wide Pacific. Remote . . . I forbear, in tenderness for your feelings from saying anything so Kiplingesque as far-flung. Do we agree to say remote and *not* far-flung?" He cocked his wicked little eye at me.

I made sounds in my throat, and he went on at once, "Remote . . . yes . . . and romantic . . . romantic! Eastwards as far as ship can Sail . . . up against the gateways of the dawn . . . coconut-palms, but of course *not* pines, ha-

ha! . . . the lagoon islands, the Line Islands, Stevenson's islands! Do we accept palms, *not* pines? Do we stake our lives on Stevenson, not Kipling? Do we insist upon the dominion of romance, *not* the romance of dominion? I should appreciate your answer."

I joyfully accepted Stevenson and ruled Kipling out (except, of course, for *Puck of Pook's Hill* and *Kim,* and the *Long Trail,* and others too numerous to mention); but my callowness squirmed shamefully at romance. He became suddenly acid at that: "Come, come! You owe perhaps more to your romanticism than you imagine—your appointment as a cadet, for example." The truth was, according to him, that I had been the only candidate to ask for the job in the Gilbert and Ellice Islands. But for that . . . if, in fact, I had been up against the least competition . . . well . . . who could say? As I, for one, could not, he leaned back in his chair and fired a final question at me: "I may take it, may I not, that, despite certain doubts which you entertain about the imperialism of Mr. Kipling and . . . hm . . . a great many of your betters, you still nurse your laudable wish to go to the Central Pacific?"

I replied yes, sir, certainly, sir, but how was I going to tackle this thing about leadership, sir.

He peered at me incredulously, rose at once, and lifted his coat-tails again at the fire, as if I had chilled whatever it was. "I had imagined," he confided in a thin voice to the ceiling, "that I had already—and with considerable finesse— managed to put all that in its right perspective for this queer young man."

"However," he continued, after a long and, to me, frightful silence, "let us dot our i's and cross our t's. The deplorable thing about your romanticism is that you display it as a halo around your own head. You seem to think that, when you arrive in the Gilbert and Ellice Islands, the entire population will forthwith stop work to stand with bated breath awaiting your apotheosis as a leader among them."

The blend of venomous truth and ghastly unfairness in this bit deep into my young soul; I opened my mouth to protest, but he overrode me: "You permit me to proceed? Thank you. Now, believe me, your egocentric surmise is grotesquely incorrect. You will encounter out there a number of busy men interested primarily in only one thing about you, namely, your ability to learn and obey orders. These will severely deplore any premature motion of your own to order them—or, in fact, anybody else—about. They will expect you to do as you are told—neither more nor less—and to do it intelligently. In the process of learning how to obey orders with intelligence and good cheer, you may, we hope, succeed in picking up some first, crude notions about the true nature of leadership. I say 'we hope' because that is the gamble we, in the Colonial Office, have taken on you. Kindly do your best to justify it."

Though his tone had been as cutting as his words, the flicker of a smile had escaped once or twice, as if by permission, through his beard. I got the notion that the smiles meant, "You incredible young ass! Can't you see *this* is the way round to put it to your uncles?" But when I gave him back a timid grin, he asked me sharply why. I answered sheepishly that he had eased my mind, because truly, truly I didn't want to go ordering anybody round any more than he wanted me to.

At that, his manner changed again to one of sprightly good humour. He began to tell me a whole lot of things about a cadet's training in the field (or, at least, the training he thought I was destined to get in the Central Pacific) that nobody else had ever hinted at. As I understood the burden of it, it was that I would serve my first year or so of probation on Ocean Island,[14] the administrative capital of the Protectorate, where I would be passed from department to department of the public service to learn in successive order, from a series of rugged but benevolent Heads (all of whom quite possibly harboured a hidden passion for the writings of R.L.S.), the basic functions of the Secretariat, the Treasury, the Magistrate's Court, the Customs, the Works Department, the Police, the Post Office, and the Prisons organization. I don't know what magic he used—he certainly never spoke above a chirp; but he managed to make that arid list of departmental names roll from his lips like the shouting of golden trumpets upon my ear. I had a vision as he spoke: the halo he had mentioned burst into sudden glory around my head. . . .

. . . It was dawn. I was hurrying, loaded with papers of the utmost import, through the corridors of a vast white office building set on an eminence above a sapphire ocean. I had been toiling all night with the Chief Secretary, the Treasurer, the Magistrate, the Collector of Customs, the Commissioner of Works, the Chief of Police, the Postmaster General, and the Keeper of the Prisons. The job was done! I had pulled them all through. Just in time! There in the bay below lay a ship with steam up, waiting for final orders. I opened a door. A man with a face like a sword—my beloved Chief, the Resident Commissioner himself—sat tense and stern-eyed at his desk. His features softened swiftly as he saw me: "Ah . . . you, Grimble . . . at last!" He eagerly scanned my papers: "Good man . . . good man! It's all there. I knew I could trust you. Where shall I sign? . . . God, how tired I am!" "Sign here, sir . . . I'll see to everything else . . . leave it *all* to me." My voice was very quiet, quiet but firm . . .

". . . and remember this," broke in the voice of Mr. Johnson, "a cadet is a nonentity." The vision fled. The reedy voice persisted: "A cadet washes bottles for those who are themselves merely junior bottle-washers. Or so he should assess his own importance, pending his confirmation as a permanent officer."

He must have seen something die in my face, for he added at once, "Not that this should unduly discourage you. All Civil Servants, of whatever seniority, are bottle-washers of one degree or another. They have to learn humility. Omar Khayyam doubtless had some over-ambitious official of his own epoch chiefly in mind when he wrote 'and think that, while thou art, thou art but *what thou shalt be,* NOTHING: thou shalt not be less.'[15] Sane advice, especially for cadets! Nevertheless, you would do well to behave, in the presence of your

---

14. Now Banaba, part of Kiribati, a "phosphate island" near Nauru.

15. Mr. Johnson is quoting from Edward FitzGerald's translation of a traditional Persian text, *The Rubáiyát of Omar Khayyám,* first published in 1859, which had an immense vogue in the Victorian and Edwardian eras.

seniors, with considerably less contempt for high office than Omar seems to have felt. Your approach to your Resident Commissioner, for example, should preferably suggest the attitude of one who humbly aspires to 'pluck down, proud clod, the neck of God.' "[16]

Who was I, to question the rightness of this advice? I certainly felt no disposition to do so then (I don't remember having felt any since) and, as he showed no further wish to pursue the topic, I passed to another that had been on my mind. A marriage had been arranged. My pay as a cadet would be £300 a year, plus free furnished quarters. Did he think a young married couple could live passably well on that at Ocean Island? I pulled out a written list of questions about the local cost of living. At the word "marriage" he started forward with a charming smile, light-stepping as a faun, whisked the paper from my hand, laid it on the mantelpiece, and turned back to face me: "Ah . . . romance . . . romance again," he breathed, "a young couple . . . hull-down on the trail of rapture . . . the islands of desire . . . but there is method, too . . . let us look before we leap . . . the cost of living! A businesslike approach. Very proper. Well . . . now . . . hmm . . . yes . . . my personal conjecture is that you should find the emoluments adequate for your needs, provided always, of course, that you neither jointly nor severally acquire the habit of consuming vast daily quantities of champagne and caviare. Remember, for the rest . . . in your wilderness . . . how the ravens fed Elijah . . . or was it Elisha?"[17]

And that was that about the cost of living. I was too timid to recover my list from the mantelpiece.

Thus finally primed in the Colonial Office for exploding as a bottle-washer upon the Gilbert and Ellice Islands, I sailed with Olivia from England on March 6th, 1914.

from Norman Mailer, *The Naked and the Dead* (1948)

America's greatest living writer, Norman Mailer (1923–) served with the 112th Cavalry in the Philippines during the Second World War and shot to fame with his first novel: a Dostoevskian analysis of the will to power in general and his homeland in particular as registered in the lives of an infantry platoon sent on a hapless mission behind enemy lines on the fictional island of Anopopei.

They were all quiet again. The tension between them had collapsed like a piece of moist paper shredding of its own weight. All of them except Croft were secretly relieved. But the patrol to come draped them in a shroud of gloom. Each retreated into silence and his private fears. Like an augury, the night was coming closer.

---

16. Grimble adapts the last stanza of "Any Saint" by the English Catholic poet Francis Thompson (1859–1907): "Rise; for heaven hath no frown / When thou to thee pluck'st down / Strong clod! / The neck of God."

17. It was Elijah who was fed by ravens when sent into exile by God; see 1 Kings, 17.

Far in the distance they could see Mount Anaka rising above the island. It arched coldly and remotely from the jungle beneath it, lofting itself massively into the low-hanging clouds of the sky. In the early drab twilight it looked like an immense old gray elephant erecting himself somberly on his front legs, his haunches lost in the green bedding of his lair. The mountain seemed wise and powerful, and terrifying in its size. Gallagher stared at it in absorption, caught by a sense of beauty he could not express. The idea, the vision he always held of something finer and neater and more beautiful than the moil in which he lived trembled now, pitched almost to a climax of words. There was an instant in which he might have said a little of what he was feeling, but it passed and he was left with a troubled joy, an echo of rapture. He licked his lips, mourning his wife again.

Croft was moved as deeply, as fundamentally as caissons re-settling in the river mud. The mountain attracted him, taunted and inflamed him with its size. He had never seen it so clearly before. Mired in the jungle, the cliffs of Watamai Range had obscured the mountain. He stared at it now, examined its ridges, feeling an instinctive desire to climb the mountain and stand on its peak, to know that all its mighty weight was beneath his feet. His emotions were intense; he knew awe and hunger and the peculiar unique ecstasy he had felt after Hennessey was dead, or when he had killed the Japanese prisoner. He gazed at it, almost hating the mountain, unconscious at first of the men about him. "That mountain's mighty old," he said at last.

And Red felt only gloom, and a vague harassment. Croft's words bothered him subtly. He examined the mountain with little emotion, almost indifference. But when he looked away he was bothered by the fear all of the men in the platoon had felt at one time or another that day. Like the others, Red was wondering if this patrol would be the one where his luck ran out.

Goldstein and Martinez were talking about America. By chance they had chosen cots next to each other, and they spent the afternoon lying on them, their ponchos drawn over their bodies. Goldstein was feeling rather happy. He had never been particularly close to Martinez before, but they had been chatting for several hours and their confidences were becoming intimate. Goldstein was always satisfied if he could be friendly with someone; his ingenuous nature was always trusting. One of the main reasons for this wretchedness in the platoon was that his friendships never seemed to last. Men with whom he would have long amiable conversations would wound him or disregard him the next day, and he never understood it. To Goldstein men were friends or they weren't friends; he could not comprehend any variations or disloyalties. He was unhappy because he felt continually betrayed. [. . .]

Goldstein went on talking. He had some constraint, for Gallagher was the man he had hated most in the platoon. The warmth and friendliness he felt toward him now were perplexing. Goldstein was self-conscious when he saw himself as a Jew talking to a Gentile; then every action, every word, was dictated to a great extent by his desire to make a good impression. Although he was gratified when people liked him, part of his satisfaction came from the idea that they were liking a Jew. And so he tried to say only the things that would please Gallagher.

Yet in talking about his family, Goldstein experienced once more an automatic sense of loss and longing. Wistful images of the beatitudes of married life drifted in his head. He remembered a night when he and his wife had giggled together in the darkness and listened to the quaint pompous snoring of their baby. "Children are what makes life worth while," he said sincerely.

Martinez realized with a start that he was a father too. He remembered Rosalie's pregnancy for the first time in years. He shrugged. Seven years now? Eight years? He had lost count. Goddam, he said to himself. Once he had been free of the girl he had remembered her only as a source of trouble and worry.

The fact that he had begotten a child made him vain. Goddam, I'm okay, he said to himself. He felt like laughing. Martinez make a kid and run away. It gave him a malicious glee, as though he were a child tormenting a dog. What the hell she do with it? Knock her up. Goddam! His vanity swelled like a bloated belly. He mused with naive delight about his potency, his attraction for women. That the child was illegitimate increased his self-esteem; somehow it made his role more extravagant, of greater magnitude.

He felt a tolerant, almost condescending affection for Goldstein. Before this afternoon he had been a little afraid of him and quite uneasy. They had had an argument one day and Goldstein had disagreed with him. Whenever that happened, Martinez would react inevitably like a frightened schoolboy reprimanded by his teacher. There had never been a time when he was comfortable as a sergeant. But now he had been bathed in Goldstein's affection; he no longer felt Goldstein had despised him that day. Goldstein, he is okay, Martinez said to himself.

He became conscious of the vibration of the boat, its slow pitching advance through the swells. It was almost dark now, and he yawned and curled his body down farther beneath the poncho. He was slightly hungry. Lazily, he debated whether to open a ration or merely to lie still. He thought of the patrol, and the quick fear it roused made him alert again. Oh. He expelled his breath. No think about it, no think about it, he repeated to himself.

He became conscious abruptly that Gallagher and Goldstein were no longer talking. He looked up, and saw nearly all the men in the boat standing on their cots or chinning themselves on the starboard bulkhead. "What're they lookin' at?" Gallagher asked.

"It's the sunset, I think," Goldstein said.

"Sunset?" Martinez gazed at the sky above him. It was almost black, clotted with ugly leaden rain clouds. "Where the sunset?" He stood up on his cot, straddling his feet on the side poles, and stared into the west.

The sunset was magnificent with the intensity and brilliance that can be found only in the tropics. The entire sky was black with the impending rain except for a narrow ribbon along the horizon. The sun had already disappeared, but its reflection was compressed, channeled into a band of color where the sky met the water. The sunset made an arc along the water like the cove of a harbor, but a strange and illusory harbor, washed in a vivid spectrum of crimson and golden yellows and canary greens. There was a string of tiny clouds shaped like miniature plump sausages and they had become a royal stippled purple. After a time, the men had the impression they were staring at a fabulous island which could have existed only in their imagination. Each detail glowed, became quiveringly real. There was a beach whose sands were polished and golden, and on the false shore a grove of trees had turned a magnificent lavender-blue in the dusk. The beach was separate from everything they had ever known; it possessed every outcropping of rock, every curve of sand dune on a barren and gelid shore, but this beach was alive and quivering with warmth. Above the purple foliage the land rose in pink and violet dales, shading finally into the overcast above the harbor. The water before them illumined by the sunset had become the deep clear blue of the sky on a summer evening.

It was a sensual isle, a Biblical land of ruby wines and golden sands and indigo trees. The men stared and stared. The island hovered before them like an Oriental monarch's conception of heaven, and they responded to it with an acute and terrible longing. It was a vision of all the beauty for which they had ever yearned, all the ecstasy they had ever sought. For a few minutes it dissolved the long dreary passage of the mute months in the jungle, without hope, without pride. If they had been alone they might have stretched out their arms to it.

It could not last. Slowly, inevitably, the beach began to dissolve in the encompassing night. The golden sands grew faint, became gray-green, and darkened. The island sank into the water, and the tide of night washed over the rose and lavender hills. After a little while, there was only the gray-black ocean, the darkened sky, and the evil churning of the gray-white wake. Bits of phosphorescence swirled in the foam. The black dead ocean looked like a mirror of the night; it was cold, implicit with dread and death. The men felt it absorb them in a silent persuasive terror. They turned back to their cots, settled down for the night, and shuddered for a long time in their blankets.

It began to rain. The boat churned and pushed through the darkness, wallowing only a hundred yards offshore. Over them all hung the quick fearful anticipation of the patrol ahead. The water washed mournfully against the sides of the boat.

from Richard Tregaskis, *Guadalcanal Diary* (1943)

Richard Tregaskis (1916–1973) started his career as a journalist in Boston. He later followed the Pacific theater as correspondent for the International News Service, being one of only two war correspondents attached to the Guadalcanal campaign of August–December 1942: the first American counterattack on land after Pearl Harbor. He later covered both the Korean and Vietnam wars, the latter for ten years.

My taking off my clothes last night, with a view to sleeping more comfortably, turned out to be a great mistake. Just after midnight this morning, my sleep was shattered by explosions coming very close. The instant reflex action took me out of bed and on to the ground, flat. I knew that the others were leaving our tent, dashing for the dugout. I fumbled for my helmet and couldn't find it.

I could hear heavy gunfire, in a sequence that I knew instantly was ominous: the metallic, loud brroom-brroom of the guns going off, then the whistle of the approaching shells, then the crash of the explosions, so near that one felt a blast of air from the concussion.

I ran for the dugout, not stopping even for slippers, but hit the deck and stopped dead still just inside the tent flap when I heard more shells on the way. The crash of the explosions dented in my eardrums, and I could hear the confused sounds of debris falling.

Colonel Hunt and I arrived at the dugout at the same moment. We bumped into each other at the entrance and then backed away and I said, "You go first, Colonel." He said politely with a slight bow, "No, after you." And we stood there for a few moments, arguing the matter, while the shells continued to fall. The colonel too had decided to sleep comfortably last night and now wore only his "scivvie" drawers and shirt. We must have made a comical couple, for I took a riding for the rest of the day about the Alphonse-and-Gaston act performed in underwear and under fire.

But the humour of that moment was soon gone. When the barrage halted, we could hear a blubbering, sobbing cry that was more animal than human. A marine came running to the dugout entrance to say that several men had been badly wounded and needed a corpsman.[18] And the crying man kept on, his gurgling rising and falling in regular waves like the sound of some strange machine.

I edged around a smashed tent toward the sound and found myself amidst a scene of frightfulness. One grey-green body lay on its back. There was a small, irregular red hole in the middle of the chest.

Near by lay the wounded man who had been crying in the night. A big, muscular fellow, he lay on his right side, while a doctor bandaged the shredded remains of one leg, and a corpsman worked on the twisted, gaping mouth of a wound which bared the other leg to the bone.

His face and shoulders lay in the centre of a sheet of gore. Face wounds rained blood on the ground. A deep excavation through layers of tissue had been made in one shoulder. The other shoulder, too, was ripped by shrapnel. I could see now how he made the terrible noise. He was crying, sobbing, into a pool of blood. The blood distorted the sound of his wailing, as water would have done, into a bubbling sound. The sound still came in cycles, rising to peaks of loudness. One of the wounded man's hands moved in mechanical circles on the ground, keeping time with his cries.

---

18. A stretcher bearer.

There were others wounded. Two dim lights, set in a square dark shape, marked an ambulance, standing by. Corpsmen were loading it. The squeak of the stretchers sliding into place, a sound much like that of a fingernail scratched across a blackboard, I shall never forget.

Next to the smashed tent stood the splintered trunk of a palm tree. The top of the tree had fallen on to another tent, squashing one side of it. The tent walls which still stood had been torn by flying shell fragments.

Back at Colonel Hunt's headquarters shack, I found Captain Hodgess, the Australian guide, telling how the tree-top had fallen on to his bunk. He found humour in the matter. "First time I ever had a tree in bed with me," he said. He was uninjured.

When the wounded had been carted off, we went tentatively back to bed. And we were glad to hear our planes taking off, obviously in an attempt to attack the Jap ships which had been bombarding us.

In the calm morning light, we found that our damage and casualties in the shelling had been amazingly slight when one considered the possibilities. Only the one shell, which had come so close to my tent, had caused any injuries. That missile had exploded when it struck the top of the palm tree. The downward blast of the explosion had killed the one marine who had died instantly. The marine, whom we had heard crying in the night, had also been hit by that shell. He died of his injuries before morning. Two others had been seriously wounded but would not die. About ten had suffered slight wounds from the flying fragments. The damage had been confined to the two tents, a few holes in surrounding structures, and the broken palm tree. We made up for the tree to some degree by serving the hearts-of-palm, a choice part of the branch, for lunch to-day.

In general, it seemed amazing that the enemy could throw so many rounds of ammunition into our camp and do so little damage.

from Peter Medcalf, *War in the Shadows* (1986)

The Americans had nominally defeated Japanese forces in Bougainville, at the top of the Solomon Islands chain, in late 1943, and Australian troops were sent in to "mop up." But the Japanese proved a resilient enemy in frightful conditions, and the campaign lingered on until the end of the war. Born in 1925, the young Medcalf served throughout the campaign and was discharged in 1946 suffering the effects of malaria and blast-damaged hearing. After gaining a degree in chemistry, he went on to a career in the cosmetics industry.

Thick clouds gathered, and thunder muttered in the foothills; short, sharp storms swept the swamps, and rain gradually set in. The water level in the surrounding marshes rose and slowly invaded our home. We improved our tattered shelters with large banana fronds and jacked our bush bunks higher out of the mud. Food was short again, and several men were sent back suffering from skin diseases and unknown fevers. A patrol tried to find a short cut to the coast, and became lost for two days in the swampy wastes of the Tavera estuary.

An urgent radio message: Japs reported in Sisiruai, a village about six miles inland; so Perce decided to take our platoon and find the place, and clean it out.

Early morning, overcast, and the scouts led us through the wire; ten yards into the heavy growth the water was knee-deep. Slowly the line splashed ahead. We sank to the waist in clammy brown slush as the ground fell away. Bert backed up suddenly and prodded a lump of floating bark with his rifle. A foot-long centipede, bright orange in the dim light, rode on the debris, its wide head waving gently as it bobbed by.

We were heavily loaded with spare ammunition; the weight around our necks dragged us off balance as we tripped and stumbled on tangled snags below the surface. I clambered over a half-submerged log and a grenade slipped from my belt to be lost in the mire. An hour passed and we halted for a smoke. Sad Sack floundered up and took the Bren[19] from Bomber; and word filtered back, a big creek, too deep to cross. The lead section changed and turned inland to see if the creek narrowed or grew shallow. It showed as a twenty-yard gap in the undergrowth, with the water moving sluggishly coastwards.

Hours passed, and we found a tall tree fallen across the stream. Gingerly we inched over, straddling the slippery trunk until we could swing down into the shallows on the far bank. Midday, but too cloudy and dim to see the sun. We leant against tree trunks, up to our knees in the black mire, and munched dry biscuits and bully from the tin. Joey from 6 Section was shivering and running a temperature; he could not eat, but would not let us carry his pack. We swigged dank chlorinated water from our bottles and moved on.

Ahead thunder rumbled, light faded, and lightning flickered through the trees. No sign of dry land, black tree boles anchored in a black, liquid desolation. We floundered on in increasing darkness. Lightning flared closer; sharp thunderclaps, and a dull roaring through the undergrowth. Rain started, sharp, stinging drops, intensifying, bitterly cold. An ear-splitting crack and a blue-white glare, the air sharp with ozone, and the rain lanced down. The line stopped. We turned our backs to the deluge; it hammered down upon us, harder, harder, deafening! The surface of the swamp was smashed upwards in flying spray—we were blind, disoriented, staggering in the flailing dark chaos. A faint, thin shout, lost in the din. I staggered, bumped into a sapling and clung frantically; someone clutched my belt, and hung on.

Slowly the uproar died away. The downpour slackened and we lifted our heads, mouths gaping, gasping for breath. Men stood waist-deep, shivering as if beaten. The light dull, glaucous, thick with moisture—leaves and branches littered the surface of the swamp.

---

19. A heavy machine gun so named from its places of manufacture: Brno, Czechoslovakia, and Enfield, England.

THE COLONIAL INTERREGNUM

"Jesus!" a shaky voice said, "wonder what it's like when the bloody drought breaks!"

We slowly re-formed, and the line moved ahead. My equipment weighed me down, boots sinking in the soft viscous slime, my body forcing a slow, turbid wave before me as I lurched forward. The day dragged to a close, the light died, and the patrol weaved to a halt in a tangle of trees looped with trailing vines.

Slow drops of moisture formed silent rings on the dark surface of the water. I felt totally done, standing legs apart, hip-deep, drooping, completely and absolutely miserable. I looked at the rest of the section—they seemed no better.

Perce floundered by. "Eat something, and make yourselves comfortable for the night. We won't need pickets in this place." We looked at him in thorough disgust; he had a large, fat leech clinging to the back of his neck. He deserved it!

Slowly we gathered ourselves and looked for somewhere to sleep. The ground was impossible—if there was any, it was under three feet of dark, muddy water. Fergie climbed a tree, hung his equipment on a branch, and draped his long frame along a thick limb. Others followed suit, wedging themselves in tree forks or making rough nests of branches and vines.

It grew dark, and I was too tired to look for a decent tree. An inch-thick vine looped from the tree-tops; I cut a long length, threw it over a branch and passed it under my armpits. I relaxed, hanging in the loop, leaning back against the tree trunk. A firefly drifted by—blink, blink—his cold green light softly reflected on the black water. Quiet rustlings, a cough, a muttered curse, as the platoon tried to settle. The water round my hips slowly grew chill. Rotting tree limbs and vegetation shone around us in a soft, eerie phosphorescent glow.

Half asleep, I heard a scrabbling noise, and a loud splash. Someone had fallen out of bed.

The night grew pitch-black, mosquitoes whined and stung. Too tired to care, I hung in the vine. The long night dragged on. I didn't give the crocodiles a thought!

I woke gasping, choking—I was almost under water. The bloody vine had broken! Stagger up, clutch the tree trunk, stand shivering, hugging it in the darkness. Incredibly, somebody snored.

Slowly the night passed. Dim morning light: we choked down a few mouthfuls of cold rations, slung our loads and pushed on following a compass bearing, looking for Sisiruai.

We never found it. For two nights and three days we struggled through a waste of rotting swamp. At dusk one night we heard dogs barking, but we could not find Sisiruai. We saw no living thing, other than an army of leeches and mosquitoes. Always the mosquitoes! They even stung through our shirts; our faces swelled, and the backs of our hands and our faces became lumpy and stiff.

On the third day we staggered back to the perimeter. Some were sick, all completely beaten down; we resembled pale, yellow-skinned corpses as we splashed out of the swamp and lurched tiredly to our shelters.

After a time I sat up and awkwardly unlaced my boots and gaiters. I slowly peeled off my rotting socks.

The soles of my feet came off with my socks.

There were letters from home. Things were not too good, my girl wrote. People were complaining about the brown-out:[20] with the war retreating from the mainland they didn't think it was needed any more. Meat rationing was a nuisance, and her mate Sally had had a lot of trouble getting enough clothes ration coupons for her bridesmaid's dress. She had been to the races last Saturday after work with some of the girls from the bank; they were talking of going to the pictures one night with Sally's fiancé who was an American pilot, but it was hard to get tickets, particularly for the shows in town. Did I think the war would be over soon?—and don't do anything too dangerous.

Jesus Christ!

I looked at my cotton-wool-wrapped feet. That sadist, Harpo the Herbalist, our first-aid corporal, had doused them in liquid mycozol and assured me I was fit for action. Only the wounded were evacuated, "or," said Harpo, "if you've got a temperature of 105."

from E. B. Sledge, *With the Old Breed at Peleliu and Okinawa* (1980)

Eugene Bondurant Sledge (1923–2001) served with the Fifth Marines throughout the bloody and perhaps strategically unnecessary campaign on Peleliu, on the southern tip of what is now known as Palau (the old "Pellew Islands"), in September–October 1944. After the war he worked as a biology professor in his native Alabama. *With the Old Breed* (i.e., the marines) is one of the most highly valued memoirs of 1939–1945, having an immediacy reminiscent of Tolstoy's *Sebastopol Sketches* from the Crimean War.

We left the craters and approached the pillbox cautiously. Burgin ordered some of the men to cover it while the rest of us looked over the fallen Japanese to be sure none was still alive; wounded Japanese invariably exploded grenades when approached, if possible, killing their enemies along with themselves. All of them were dead. The pillbox was out of action thanks to the flamethrower and the amtrac.[21] There were seven enemy dead inside and ten outside. Our packs and mortars were only slightly damaged by the fire from the amtrac's 75mm gun.

Of the twelve Marine mortarmen, our only casualties were Redifer and

---

20. A "brownout" is a reduction in electricity use for power conservation rather than security (a "blackout").

21. An armed *am*phibian vehicle with *tract*or treads.

Leslie Porter, who had taken some grenade fragments. They weren't hurt seriously. Our luck in the whole affair had been incredible. If the enemy had surprised us and rushed us, we might have been in a bad fix.

During this lull the men stripped the packs and pockets of the enemy dead for souvenirs. This was a gruesome business, but Marines executed it in a most methodical manner. Helmet headbands were checked for flags, packs and pockets were emptied, and gold teeth were extracted. Sabers, pistols, and *hari-kiri* knives[22] were highly prized and carefully cared for until they could be sent to the folks back home or sold to some pilot or sailor for a fat price. Rifles and other larger weapons usually were rendered useless and thrown aside. They were too heavy to carry in addition to our own equipment. They would be picked up later as fine souvenirs by the rear-echelon troops. The men in the rifle companies had a lot of fun joking about the hair-raising stories these people, who had never seen a live Japanese or been shot at, would probably tell after the war.

The men gloated over, compared, and often swapped their prizes. It was a brutal, ghastly ritual the likes of which have occurred since ancient times on battlefields where the antagonists have possessed a profound mutual hatred. It was uncivilized, as is all war, and was carried out with that particular savagery that characterized the struggle between the Marines and the Japanese. It wasn't simply souvenir hunting or looting the enemy dead; it was more like Indian warriors taking scalps.

While I was removing a bayonet and scabbard from a dead Japanese, I noticed a Marine near me. He wasn't in our mortar section but had happened by and wanted to get in on the spoils. He came up to me dragging what I assumed to be a corpse. But the Japanese wasn't dead. He had been wounded severely in the back and couldn't move his arms; otherwise he would have resisted to his last breath.

The Japanese's mouth glowed with huge gold-crowned teeth, and his captor wanted them. He put the point of his kabar[23] on the base of a tooth and hit the handle with the palm of his hand. Because the Japanese was kicking his feet and thrashing about, the knife point glanced off the tooth and sank deeply into the victim's mouth. The Marine cursed him and with a slash cut his cheeks open to each ear. He put his foot on the sufferer's lower jaw and tried again. Blood poured out of the soldier's mouth. He made a gurgling noise and thrashed wildly. I shouted, "Put the man out of his misery." All I got for an answer was a cussing out. Another Marine ran up, put a bullet in the enemy soldier's brain, and ended his agony. The scavenger grumbled and continued extracting his prizes undisturbed.

Such was the incredible cruelty that decent men could commit when reduced to a brutish existence in their fight for survival amid the violent death,

---

22. Japanese: *harakiri*, literally "stomach-cutting." A knife used for suicide by disembowelment.

23. Marine-issue combat knife.

terror, tension, fatigue, and filth that was the infantryman's war. Our code of conduct toward the enemy differed drastically from that prevailing back at the division C[ommand] P[ost].

The struggle for survival went on day after weary day, night after terrifying night. One remembers vividly the landings and the beachheads and the details of the first two or three days and nights of a campaign; after that, time lost all meaning. A lull of hours or days seemed but a fleeting instant of heaven-sent tranquility. Lying in a foxhole sweating out an enemy artillery or mortar barrage or waiting to dash across open ground under machine-gun or artillery fire defied any concept of time.

To the noncombatants and those on the periphery of action, the war meant only boredom or occasional excitement; but to those who entered the meat grinder itself, the war was a nether world of horror from which escape seemed less and less likely as casualties mounted and the fighting dragged on and on. Time had no meaning; life had no meaning. The fierce struggle for survival in the abyss of Peleliu eroded the veneer of civilization and made savages of us all. We existed in an environment totally incomprehensible to men behind the lines—service troops and civilians.

[...]

The wind blew hard. A drizzling rain fell out of a leaden sky that seemed to hang just above the ridge crest. Shattered trees and jagged rocks along the crest looked like stubble on a dirty chin. Most green trees and bushes had long since been shattered and pulverized by shell fire. Only the grotesque stumps and branches remained. A film of fine coral dust covered everything. It had been dust before the rain, but afterward it was a grimy coating of thin plaster.

The overwhelming grayness of everything in sight caused sky, ridge, rocks, stumps, men, and equipment to blend into a grimy oneness. Weird, jagged contours of Peleliu's ridges and canyons gave the area an unearthly alien appearance. The shattered vegetation and the dirty-white splotches peppering the rocks where countless bullets and shell fragments had struck off the weathered gray surfaces contributed to the unreality of the harsh landscape.

Rain added the final touch. On a battlefield rain made the living more miserable and forlorn and the dead more pathetic. To my left lay a couple of bloated Japanese corpses teeming with maggots and inactive flies who seemed to object to the rain as much as I did. Each dead man still wore the two leather cartridge boxes, one on either side of his belt buckle, neat wrap leggings, labi shoes,[24] helmets, and packs. Beside each corpse lay a shattered and rusting Arisaka rifle, smashed against a rock by some Marine to be certain it wasn't used again.

Cans of C rations and K ration boxes, opened and unopened, lay around

---

24. Standard issue for Japanese troops, these shoes had a separate "toe" section for the big toe, leaving a characteristic track.

our gun pit along with discarded grenade and mortar shell canisters. Scattered about the area were discarded U.S. helmets, packs, ponchos, dungaree jackets, web cartridge belts, leggings, boondockers,[25] ammo boxes of every type, and crates. The discarded articles of clothing and the inevitable bottle of blood plasma bore mute testimony that a Marine had been hit there.

Many tree stumps had a machine-gun ammo belt draped over them. Some of these belts were partially filled with live cartridges. Amid all this evidence of violent combat, past and continuing, I was interested in the fact that spent, or partially so, machine-gun ammo belts so often seemed to be draped across a shattered stump or bush rather than lying on the ground. In combat, I often experienced fascination over such trivia, particularly when exhausted physically and strained emotionally. Many combat veterans told me they also were affected the same way.

All around us lay the destruction and waste of violent combat. Later, on the muddy clay fields and ridges of Okinawa, I would witness similar scenes on an even vaster scale. There the battlefield would bear some resemblance to others described in World War II. During the muddy stalemate before Shuri,[26] the area would resemble descriptions I had read of the ghastly corpse-strewn morass of Flanders during World War I.

These, though, were typical modern battlefields. They were nothing like the crazy-contoured coral ridges and rubble-filled canyons of the Umurbrogol Pocket on Peleliu. Particularly at night by the light of flares or on a cloudy day, it was like no other battlefield described on earth. It was an alien, unearthly, surrealistic nightmare like the surface of another planet.

I have already mentioned several times the exhaustion of the Marines as the campaign wore on. Our extreme fatigue was no secret to the Japanese either. As early as 6 October, nine days before we were relieved, a captured document reported that we appeared worn out and were fighting less aggressively.

The grinding stress of prolonged heavy combat, the loss of sleep because of nightly infiltration and raids, the vigorous physical demands forced on us by the rugged terrain, and the unrelenting, suffocating heat were enough to make us drop in our tracks. How we kept going and continued fighting I'll never know. I was so indescribably weary physically and emotionally that I became fatalistic, praying only for my fate to be painless. The million-dollar wound[27] seemed more of a blessing with every weary hour that dragged by. It seemed the only escape other than death or maiming.

In addition to the terror and hardships of combat, each day brought some new dimension of dread for me: I witnessed some new, ghastly, macabre facet in the kaleidoscope of the unreal, as though designed by some fiendish ghoul

---

25. Marine-issue boots.

26. Town in southern Okinawa, in the Ryukyu archipelago between Japan and Taiwan, scene of a climactic campaign in April–June 1945, after which the Americans bombed Hiroshima and Nagasaki in August.

27. That is, one serious enough to have you repatriated without leaving you maimed for life.

to cause even the most hardened and calloused observer among us to recoil in horror and disbelief.

Late one afternoon a buddy and I returned to the gun pit in the fading light. We passed a shallow defilade we hadn't noticed previously. In it were three Marine dead. They were lying on stretchers where they had died before their comrades had been forced to withdraw sometime earlier. (I usually avoided confronting such pitiful remains. I never could bear the sight of American dead neglected on the battlefield. In contrast, the sight of Japanese corpses bothered me little aside from the stench and the flies they nourished.)

As we moved past the defilade, my buddy groaned, "Jesus!" I took a quick glance into the depression and recoiled in revulsion and pity at what I saw. The bodies were badly decomposed and nearly blackened by exposure. This was to be expected of the dead in the tropics, but these Marines had been mutilated hideously by the enemy. One man had been decapitated. His head lay on his chest; his hands had been severed from his wrists and also lay on his chest near his chin. In disbelief I stared at the face as I realized that the Japanese had cut off the dead Marine's penis and stuffed it into his mouth. The corpse next to him had been treated similarly. The third had been butchered, chopped up like a carcass torn by some predatory animal.

My emotions solidified into rage and a hatred for the Japanese beyond anything I ever had experienced. From that moment on I never felt the least pity or compassion for them no matter what the circumstances. My comrades would field strip their packs and pockets for souvenirs and take gold teeth, but I never saw a Marine commit the kind of barbaric mutilation the Japanese committed if they had access to our dead.

When we got back to the gun pit, my buddy said, "Sledgehammer, did you see what the Nips did to them bodies? Did you see what them poor guys had in their mouths?" I nodded as he continued, "Christ, I hate them slant-eyed bastards!"

"Me too. They're mean as hell," was all I could say.

from Vern Haugland, *Letter from New Guinea* (1943)

Vern Haugland (1908–1994) was a war correspondent whose light plane crashed in thick jungle in New Guinea in 1942. After wandering alone for five weeks in the bush on the verge of starvation, he was found by tribespeople and brought to a missionary station, thence to a hospital in Port Moresby. He awoke to find himself the first noncombatant to have been awarded the Silver Star, given to him by General MacArthur himself; but before coming around, he experienced a prolonged period of quasi-comatose breakdown in which dreams of all kinds came to him. Haugland went on to publish, many years later, a history of downed American fighter pilots in the Second World War.

This was a period of complete delirium, during all of which I was very close to death. It lasted three weeks, from the time darkness shuttered my brain, in the missionaries' house at Sirimidi, until I awoke in a hospital in Port Moresby. Of what actually had been happening I knew nothing; but of what went on in that interminable dream I remembered a jumble of things.

The dream from beginning to end was of the struggle between good and evil. It was a tale of the past and the future of Man, as I watched it unreel like a motion picture in my inflamed mind.

Before describing this fantasy that went on and on in a hodgepodge of scenes and actions which seemed wholly unrelated but which dovetailed toward the end, let me reiterate that I had never been of a notably religious frame of mind. [. . .]

In my delirium Father Newman became, at various times, my father, my brother and my own self as I had been in past worlds and also as I might be in worlds to come. Jack Salzman became St. John, then St. John the Second, St. John the Third, and finally St. John the Divine. In my conscious mind I hadn't the remotest idea who St. John had been (if there was a St. John), nor did I remember ever hearing or reading about several St. Johns or a St. John the Divine.[28]

In my dream some great force was writing a new Book of Revelation on the wall of the missionaries' hut—writing it by burning out the letters in brown outline on the whitish wood. From my bed on the floor, I was having difficulty in reading it.

(Not until I was reading the Bible, in the hospital while I was recovering, did I discover that it ends with the Book of Revelation—the Revelation of St. John the Divine. But perhaps subconsciously I remembered it from my youthful confirmation studies; or perhaps in semidelirium at the hut, while I lay reading the prayer book and Bible the missionaries had lent me, portions of what I had read clung to my mind and reappeared in distorted form in my delirium.)

From this new Book, it seemed in my delirium, I was slowly learning the secret of the universe, solving the mystery of life itself. And it was all so simple, so ridiculously easy that a child could understand it. We human beings on earth should have been able to figure it out by studying the Bible and by using common sense.

There was no such thing as death; there was only life everlasting. And there was that long, long battle between good and evil—between God and the devil—which good, or God, would win in the end.

Scientists have phrased it this way: There can be no destruction of matter. Matter changes its form but is not destroyed.

Stated in other terms, man does not die. He passes from one form to another, and slowly—ever so slowly—he progresses upward. Slowly he advances through what might be called a great smelter of souls. During this infinitely slow process the evil in every man, the evil in the universe, is compressed into

---

28. According to legend St. John ("the Divine"), one of Christ's four apostles, saw the Revelation, which constitutes the final book of the Bible, on the island of Patmos in the Aegean. It is a vision of apocalypse, much like Haugland's dream.

an ever smaller and smaller space. It gets blacker and more concentrated as the refinement process continues. It is ridiculously small in comparison with the vast amount of good; but if the refinement process halts for an instant, evil has the faculty of clouding up the universe quickly, of discoloring good works and soiling good souls.

This was the line of logic that ran through my delirium. I reasoned, too, that each man had a capacity for good and evil, and that slowly through the ages Man was becoming better, and making of his earthly environment a better world.

Since extremes attract, I dreamed, the greatest evil always would be countered—and defeated—by the greatest good. Today, my fancy told me, mankind faced the greatest force for evil that had been assembled in many centuries: the destructive force as represented by Hitler and his henchmen. But God had seen to it that the world had the ability to muster up against this dark force the greatest power for good that had ever made itself known and felt.

My dreams carried me through a series of better and better worlds— through worlds in the Dark Ages when people were so cruel to each other that the earth was a hell of its own, through parts of the world where there had been superstition and witch-hunting and worship of strange idols, and on into worlds of the future where life was more exciting and thrilling than it had ever been before, yet where evil had less and less space and finally no space at all.

It seemed that, just as there were concentric rings of the world, steadily improving and approaching the heaven to which all men openly or secretly aspired, there were concentric rings of hell, each more terrible and darker than the one before. And I was amazed to find myself in New Guinea after having toured several of these strange worlds, and to discover that in this little-known island, far back in the mountains, were caves that linked the lowest world with the topmost hell. Thus I had come to the fact that hell literally was underground, that it was an unending spiraling tunnel into darkness, a mine into the very heart of evil.

Surprisingly I found myself in the clutches of evil beings and slipping into consecutive hells. There I learned that I had been in the deepest hell of all, because ages before I had been one of the first to lie and first to sin. Somehow I had worked my way into the world again, only to slip back. But now, as I observed with new eyes the wretched creatures in the upper hells, I saw that all of them still had good in their souls but were too weak to fight against the dark. In the upper hells they eked out an existence on pallid, tasteless foods growing beside a black-flowing river. In the lower regions, the river cut too deeply between sharp rocks to be reached, and the poor creatures lived on soot, the essence of blackness itself.

"All these hells need for a fresh start for everybody," I said to myself, "is light and sun—goodness and truth." I witnessed the introduction, in some manner the details of which I no longer recall, of light into one of the upper hells. The results were astonishing. Heavy green vegetation sprang up alongside the river, and brilliant fruits and vegetables appeared. The sinners ate heartily, washed off their sooty bodies and flocked out into the sunlight. Before my astonished eyes they turned from ghastly, skeletal folk into attractive human beings. Their attitude changed, too. Instead of hating and distrusting each other, they all became friends with complete faith in each other. This action, amazingly, cast strong new light back into other hells. The layers of hells receded and the layers of better and better worlds increased. [. . .]

In my journeys through delirium, I discovered that just as there were many in hell who could work their way back into good grace if given a little assistance, so there were many in the upper planes who did not deserve to be there. I was to learn that these persons—the fakes, the phonies, the falsifiers, those who sought to hide and deny their inner wickedness instead of expelling it—eventually would be discovered and sent back to their proper levels, to start the weary way over again.

Thus, slipping and climbing, stumbling and rising, man in his slow, tortured journeying would work his way someday into the perfect world. This part of my delirium was, I thought, a look into the future. How distant the future was, I was not informed.

It seemed to me that I was lying on my back, being borne gently along in a swinging hammock, and that scenes from the perfect world were playing upon the clouds above me.

I saw the perfect breakfast, and was set aback a bit upon discovering that it consisted of hot buttered crumpets. The perfect dessert was papaya. Personally, I preferred fresh pineapple to papaya, and many a breakfast dish to crumpets.

Away back in my delirium it had been shown to me that Hollywood was the wickedest city on earth. This was a painful surprise to me, as I had greatly enjoyed that city and had admired many of its people—persons in the motion-picture industry and out of it. Now I was gratified to find, in this perfect world, a new Hollywood, the perfect city. It sprawled, as before, over and around the blue Hollywood hills, but it was much more beautiful than of old.

Gradually I began to understand that what I saw in this wonderful future world were ideal meals and cities and people. Thus perfection did not mean merely one perfect article of each kind, but an endless number and variety, each giving perfect joy and satisfaction. This is why perfection will never get monotonous or tiresome, I told myself.

The show went on. I saw perfect children—rather, "ideal" children—and they were not greatly different from many beautiful and well-behaved youngsters I had known in the world of 1942. There were perfect men and women, attractive in appearance and charming in manner, understanding each other completely, rich with peace and perfect fellowship.

There was the ideal home in the country, housing the ideal married couple. Leading from their front door was the ideal ski run, skiing being an ideal sport. It wound for miles through beautiful scenery and circled back at last to the ideal home. It had such a variety of slopes, all perfect, that one run over the course was sufficient to enable a novice to ski as swiftly and gracefully as Dick Durrance, Alf Engen and Friedl Pfeiffer combined.[29]

This future world was run by an ideal government. In the world I had known in 1942, money had been one of the greatest sources of trouble because, to such a great extent, it represented power. Money, with its ability to purchase power, often fell into greedy, unscrupulous hands. Even churches, at times, almost forgot their religion in the struggle for more money, more power—for supremacy over other churches.

In this fine future world, science had eliminated drudgery and left only pleasant tasks. No longer needing servants—since there were no menial duties to be performed—mankind had become truly democratic. Money had disappeared when the need for it expired. Co-operation had succeeded competition as a driving economic force, each individual doing his own work conscientiously and well, then turning to the aid of others. As dietary and sunlight deficiencies disappeared throughout the world, through new inventions that were in fact new miracles, racial differences and extremes in skin pigmentation largely vanished, leaving a true brotherhood of man with racial differences sufficient only to make for interesting variety without social discrimination.

In such a manner I dreamed on and on, endlessly. Each man, to enter this perfect world, must introduce into it something new in the ideal. My assignment seemed to be the "perfect newspaper." I had no idea how to invent an ideal newspaper, but I was sure God would come through with an idea.

In this endless touring of new and old worlds and ancient hells, I found myself equipped with a motion-picture camera and making a pictorial record of my travels instead of taking notes as a reporter normally would. One of my most difficult tasks was to edit these mixed-up scenes and to correlate the films into a smooth-running whole. [. . .]

Much of my delirium concerned the immediate future of mankind, the world of tomorrow that would follow this most terrible of wars. In my delirium I recorded the final victory of the United Nations, then went on into the overwhelming task of rebuilding the world.

Great men and women directed the rebuilding, in my dream, and a greatly improved world resulted. President and Mrs. Roosevelt, Hoover, and Willkie, the king and queen of England, Stalin, Chiang Kai-shek, Queen Wilhelmina—a long list of persons vitally interested in the welfare of all peoples,[30] today and in generations to come.

---

29. All champion skiers of the 1930s.

30. Franklin D. Roosevelt (1882–1945), American president, and his wife Eleanor (1884–1962), humanitarian; Herbert Hoover (1874–1964), American president defeated by Roosevelt in 1932; Wendell Willkie (1892–1944), Republican rival to Roosevelt, campaigner for world peace and author of *One World* (1943); George VI (1895–1952) and Queen Elizabeth, the Queen Mother (1900–2002); Joseph Stalin (1879–1953), Russian communist dictator; Chiang Kai-shek, or Jiang Jieshi (1887–1975), Chinese nationalist leader; Queen Wilhelmina of the Netherlands (1890–1962), heroic symbol of Dutch wartime resistance while exiled in London.

THE COLONIAL INTERREGNUM

The shattering blows of this war had taught man that it was stupid to be evil, intelligent to be on the side of the good. If all men became evil they could only set upon each other and destroy, as the Nazis had done. If they all worked for the good of man, they could only help each other unselfishly and could only make a better, easier world. So much in this world was perfection already—sunshine and moonlight, flowers and trees and grass, the taste of foods, the smile of a friend, the grand manner in which the days unfold into the seasons—that man came to understand that his principal task was to improve himself. Himself, and his works.

There came a great day in my long career of delirium. Was it the Day of Judgment, the second coming of Christ, or what? I couldn't tell. But I seemed to be lying in bed, under a mosquito netting. I went away, and while I watched the bed from a distance it became a shroud of white over a coffin or tomb, yellowed by the flickering light of candles. Before my eyes the light brightened into a great glow, and the shrouded coffin began to take on the brilliance of a golden throne. An indistinct figure arose on the throne, so bright I had to shield my eyes. For a moment I feared I would miss the climax of my story for inability to see.

But no; the figure pointed skyward, and I raised my eyes toward the clouds. There, in glorious depth and color, started unwinding the motion-picture story of mankind.

"The perfect movie," I told myself. "The ideal entertainment, just as a bad film is the worst form of amusement.

"No; I get it now. It's the story of Man, screened on the sky so that all may read it at once. It's brand-new journalism! It's the perfect newspaper!

"It shows how mankind, aspiring to perfect the world, built a pathway to heaven. It's a movie being screened in heaven—heaven on earth!"

The newsreel in the sky provided a climax for my siege of delirium. Thereafter I suffered through a series of dreams in which dimly outlined persons, most of them looking like Japanese, kept yelling at me, and trying to lay hands on me and take me away when I wasn't looking. Weary from constant efforts to outwit them, I called frequently for help, and time again searched their ranks for a familiar and friendly face.

from Nancy Phelan, *Pieces of Heaven* (1996)

Born in Australia in 1913, Nancy Phelan spent some years in England before returning in 1946. In 1951 she joined the South Pacific Commission Literature Bureau, based in Sydney, where she worked for five years developing visual material—posters and short films, in particular—for various Pacific Island communities, particularly in the area of health. This involved much travel in the region. We join her on a visit to Arthur Grimble's Gilbert Islands (now Kiribati).

The launch moved slowly, towing its loaded barge. After the travelling, the anticipation, the excitement we were slightly confused, not sure what to expect; but as we became aware of our surroundings tension relaxed, calmness descended. The afternoon faded. Colour drained from the lagoon, the line of land ahead grew dark. In the west the sky flamed and flared. Pallor came into the gold, the red died out; the white-hot furnace sank to a rich smouldering glow but the light still lingered. Shadows, a little breeze, crept across the lagoon. Passengers grew quiet; Gilbertese and government officials sat gazing dreamily at the west.

For a long time, we seemed to make no progress, the far-off line of Bairiki came no nearer; then someone said, "We're there!" and it was the wonderful moment of arrival which in the atolls is unlike arrival anywhere else; for as you approach the dark-green blur comes into focus and there is a chalk-white beach and slender coconuts leaning forward, reaching out to the sea. Subtleties of colour and chiaroscuro are revealed, the pure sand, the strange pandanus, the gleaming shallows and gentle clatter of water. All is brilliant, clear, uncluttered, perfect. Stillness, tranquillity come out to meet you as the boat nears shore.

After the blue volcanic peaks of the high islands, stepping ashore on an atoll is like seeing the Parthenon after a lifetime of Renaissance painting. It is like regaining a lost world, being transported back in time. Everything is different when we grow up, bigger or smaller, better or worse, but these little islands remain as we pictured them in childhood. They are the islands where the treasure was buried, where the parrot screeched, where the ribs of the hulk rotted in the sandy cove. They are so innocent, clean and beautiful they could only be imagined by children. There is nothing the same in our adult lives, nothing quite like them in the world.

The boat slid into the jetty and we climbed ashore. It was the moment I had been waiting for since the day I first looked down from the air on a coral island lagoon. [. . .]

People had come to meet us, the Resident Commissioner and Mrs Bernacchi, government officers and their wives. We were led to a beautiful building a few yards from the beach, set among coconut trees and green grass. The walls were waist-high, made of *te ba,* the mid-rib of the coconut leaf, and the roof was of silver-grey thatch. There were friendly voices, drinks, invitations, offers of help, but we were impatient to see our new surroundings, and as soon as the party was over we went back to the beach.

It was a different world out there; after the talking and laughter the silence was almost tangible. While we had been inside the moon had risen; now, eclipsed by the trees, it gave a luminous twilight that muted all colour and contrast. Out on the reef and on the curved beach of the next islet the bright lamps of fishermen caught the surface of the lagoon. A few faint sighs and rustles of water . . . distant voices singing. . . . In a strange way the sounds did not break the silence, they lay on the surface, leaving the depths undisturbed.

A family came along the beach with their lantern, their catch of fish strung in a dangling bunch . . . red *pareu*, green *pareu*, yellow *pareu*, dark wet hair and brown limbs lit by the swinging lamp. On the sand, almost invisible in the shadow of the trees, we watched as they padded past. Like the distant sounds they did not disturb the silence, they were part of it.

Slowly the moon came round and over the coconut trees, blanching and silvering their leaves. It shone down white on the sand and the black lagoon. Far out a pale mist moved across the sea. All else was suspended. There was a strangeness, a sense of being excluded, not a threat but a cosmic indifference; not waiting, which implies expectation, rather a non-being. We had ceased to exist, become nothing and everything.

During the night I woke, puzzled by the absence of the ship's vibration and movement; then in the silence came an unmistakable sound, the dull heavy thud of a coconut falling to the ground. Reassured, I went back to sleep.

At the Transit Quarters we were looked after by a plausible Ellice Islander named Nelson Man o'War. He was a spare, darkish little man with big spaced-out teeth, an expectant manner and a large, pretty Ellice wife. Smiling and speechless, crowned with flowers, she waddled about placidly pushing a broom, followed by a timid procession of little Ellice Islanders. Nelson was the driving force, hounding her through the housework, giving directions and or-ders, prancing round like a terrier manoeuvring an elephant. We never knew her name. She spoke no English and no Gilbertese and collapsed into giggles when we tried to communicate with my smattering of Samoan.

We had been warned to be firm with Nelson, that he was a rogue and would take advantage of our ignorance. We didn't mind if he did, we were under the spell of his glib tongue and fertile imagination. We had brought crates of tinned goods which he was supposed to cook for us, to supplement whatever fresh food was available, but he cooked very little. The reason, he ex-plained, was because he couldn't get eggs "and if you don't have eggs, Madam, you suffer." He couldn't get eggs because he was an Ellice Islander and had no land or coconut trees on Tarawa. We told him we didn't want eggs and would rather have pawpaw for breakfast than baked beans and tinned beet-root, but though he listened attentively, looking devout, he continued to dish out beetroot and beans every morning. When we gave him money to buy chickens and pawpaw they rarely appeared, and when, diffidently, we asked why, he gave the same reply—Ellice Islanders had no land, no coconut trees on Tarawa.[31]

We gave up, fascinated by Nelson's faith in his own blatant lies. He was far too busy with plans of his own to do much cooking for us. He was making sweets, probably with our sugar (he called them Fond Ants), and sickly drinks which he sold to the gullible Gilbertese. He had great schemes for bringing

---

31. Perhaps being an Ellice Islander did cause difficulties for Nelson in the Gilbert Islands, but Tarawa had been the site of another tremendous and horrifying American landing and cam-paign against the Japanese in November 1943. Coconut trees were at a premium, even twelve years later.

prosperity to the Gilberts and helping Ellice people on Tarawa by preserving eggs and bananas, both almost unobtainable on the island, as well as buying hand-looms for weaving woollen scarves, a novel industry for tropical islands.

Nelson and his fellow Ellice Islanders were Polynesians, closer to Samoans than to the Gilbertese, who are Micronesians and physically shorter and rather darker. We had heard that the Gilbertese were difficult, surly, even violent at times; ships' captains complained they were troublemakers, took offence too easily and were given to fighting with knives, but we had also been conditioned by Maude,[32] who, after nearly a lifetime with them described them as among "the gentlest and most lovable people on earth." We had come ready to love, which is not a bad way to start in any country.

We knew already that these people were extremely sensitive and would kill or commit suicide over shame or loss of face; that they venerated their ancestors and traditions, that family loyalty dominated their lives, but they felt no obligation to outsiders—as in Maude's story of the man who let a mother and baby drown because they were not his family.

We knew also that the Gilbertese have a curious custom called *bubuti* which morally obliges those who have to hand out to relatives who have not (but who must reciprocate when they can), a system that can be exploited. People who receive a windfall may find everything *bubuti'd* away from them by their relations. It all sounded faintly alarming.

At first glance the Gilbertese looked very reserved, even surly, but we quickly found this could give way easily to the merriest, most irresistible smile, and that these tough, dignified atoll people were also friendly, courteous, honest, rather blunt and humorous in a down-to-earth, bawdy way. It was not at all hard to become fond of them. [. . .]

Since Bairiki was a government station it was not entirely Gilbertese. Local life went on in the villages but there were fibro[33] offices here and there among the pretty native houses. A few buildings, including the Residency, had solid walls with thatched roofs; there were government offices of *te ba* and thatch, a fibro post office, a Land Rover and a couple of Public Works trucks that carried thatch up and down the atoll. Some government departments were on different islets—Cooperatives Officer on Betio, Education on Bikenibeu, Health on Aboakoro.

The British Raj as represented on Tarawa was a group of pleasant, youngish, rather harassed men from the UK, Australia and New Zealand, all bedevilled by paperwork. The officials and their wives were very hospitable and

---

32. H. E. Maude, executive officer of the Literature Bureau. Previously, Maude had served under Arthur Grimble as resident commissioner of the Gilbert and Ellice Islands; in later life he would be a distinguished academic specializing in Pacific history, based at the Australian National University.

33. An abbreviation of "fibrocement," a compressed blend of asbestos and cement commonly used (in sheet form) as a building material in Australia.

friendly to us personally, but suspicious and critical, even hostile to the South Pacific Commission. Though we were on leave, we felt that since we would not have got to the Gilberts without our Commission background we had better do some public relations. By the time we left the colony people were starting to write in for Social Development services and I had taken the pictures for a series of cooperatives filmstrips.

The lagoon was the centre of life; launches ran across it like buses, carrying passengers and mail; cargo was moved by boat, patients went to hospital by boat, the doctor made his rounds by boat. The Gilbertese were not cowed by officialdom; they would board any government launch they fancied and make themselves at home on the roof, singing, playing guitars, feeding babies, so that official services often looked like a picnic party.

In principle the mail launch ran at set hours, but you never knew when it would actually go; though it was usually late, sometimes it left early. The boats had splendid names: *Nunua*—Tiger Shark; *Nei Teanti*—the Woman Ghost; *Nei Niinanoa*—the Navigatress (the launch that got lost) and best of all, *Half-Tide Rock,* a tug named after an accident. It towed barges about, loaded with thatch, timber and Gilbertese.

Across the lagoon, joined to Bairiki by a sand strip on which you could walk at low tide, was Betio, Tarawa's seaport and commercial centre. Twelve years after the Battle of Tarawa it was a strange South Sea island with its ruined Japanese guns and fortifications, its search lights, tank-traps and pillboxes all in decay, its short, squat coconut trees, not tall enough to give shade. This made Betio very hot, there was a feeling of being exposed; instinctively you looked overhead for the green feathery ceiling of leaves. The sparseness meant you could see for yards ahead yet the island was full of elaborate baked-enamel traffic signs, bought cheaply by some bargain-minded official.

Rather tough, slightly cocky, with its absurd traffic signs, Betio had a definite personality. Despite its ruins, its piles of rusting metal and the fact that its soil had been soaked with blood, the atmosphere was not morbid. During the Second World War, in three days nearly five thousand men had been slaughtered there. Before invading Tarawa the United States military had consulted all available sea-captains and former residents of the Gilberts who knew the islands intimately. Despite this expert information the American Command had ordered the landing on Betio at dawn, at low tide, when landing craft could not get close to the beach. The Marines, clearly visible, had to disembark and wade across the reef while the Japanese poured fire into their ranks. Hundreds never reached the shore; as one wave of men fell another advanced over their bodies, to fall in their turn. By the time the island was taken it had been swept bare of everything but the stinking corpses of Japanese and Americans piled up in their thousands.

As our friends had predicted, there was Nothing To Do in the Gilberts, yet our days were not long enough. Very early, we swam from the immaculate beach where the shallows were clear and motionless. We lay under the trees watching white herons stroll on green grass and faraway sails passing on the lagoon. After lunch there was siesta and when the heat had gone from the day we walked to the ocean side of the islet where the wind blew in steadily, constantly. We explored the reef at low tide but came back to the western beach in time for the sunset. The end of the day is beautiful in these islands, slow, rich, serene. Sometimes we saw the green flash as the sun sank into the sea, quick and brilliant as though the water had quenched the fire and turned it to emerald.

But it was at night that Bairiki was loveliest; with darkness, in some miraculous way the islet regained its true essence. The seat of government disappeared with its buildings, its files and papers and colonial red tape; there were only black trees in silhouette, ashen sand, surf breaking out on the reef, and above the lagoon a platinum disc staring down. Sometimes torches flared on the reef and voices came through the darkness, quiet, flat, drained of warmth and resonance . . . evocative, like voices heard across a valley, from the long train halted in the night. More often there was no sound. On this little islet, so insignificant, so alone in the ocean, one came close to another dimension, to forces that ignored human existence.

SOURCES

C. A. W. Monckton, *Some Experiences of a New Guinea Resident Magistrate* (London: John Lane, 1921).

Arthur Grimble, *A Pattern of Islands* (London: John Murray, 1952). Reproduced by permission of John Murray Publishers.

Norman Mailer, *The Naked and the Dead* (New York: Harold Holt, 1948). © Norman Mailer 1948. Reproduced by permission of The Wylie Literary Agency (UK) Ltd.

Richard Tregaskis, *Guadalcanal Diary* (New York: Random House, 1943). © 1943 by Random House, Inc. Reprinted by permission of Modern Library, a division of Random House, Inc.

Peter Medcalf, *War in the Shadows* (St. Lucia: University of Queensland Press, 2000). Reproduced by permission of the University of Queensland Press.

E. B. Sledge, *With the Old Breed at Peleliu and Okinawa* (New York: Ballantine Books, 1980). © 1980 by E. B. Sledge. Reproduced by permission of Presidio Press, an imprint of The Ballantine Publishing Group, a division of Random House, Inc.

Vern Haugland, *Letter from New Guinea* (New York: Farrar and Rinehart, 1943).

Nancy Phelan, *Pieces of Heaven: In the South Seas* (St. Lucia: University of Queensland Press, 1996). Reproduced by permission of the University of Queensland Press.

FURTHER READING

For the twentieth-century Pacific see K. R. Howe, Robert C. Kiste, and Brij Lal, *Tides of History: The Pacific Islands in the Twentieth Century* (Honolulu: University of Hawai'i Press, 1994).

Travel books and recollections of the "colonial interregnum" period include Guy

Batham, *Drifting around the South Seas* (1959); R. Reynall Bellamy, *Mixed Bliss in Melanesia* (1934); Frank Burnett, *Summer Isles of Eden* (1923); Francis E. Clark, *Our Journey around the World* (1895), including the author's wife's "Glimpses of Life in Far Off Lands, as Seen through a Woman's Eyes"; John Cromar, *Jock of the Islands* (1935); Errol Flynn, *Beam Ends* (1937), concerning the Hollywood actor's early adventures in New Guinea; Clifford Gessler, *Road My Body Goes* (1937); Agnes Gardner King, *Islands Far Away* (1920); John Lafarge, *Reminiscences of the South Seas* (1901), a painterly book by an eminent American artist; Eric Muspratt, *My South Sea Island* (1931); three titles by Frederick O'Brien—*Atolls of the Sun* (1922), *Mystic Isles of the South Seas* (1921), and *White Shadows in the South Seas* (1919)—of which the earliest is by far the best; Lilian Overell, *A Woman's Impressions of German New Guinea* (1923); George Robert Charles Herbert, Earl of Pembroke, and George Henry Kingsley ["The Earl and the Doctor"], *South Sea Bubbles* (1911); Winifred Ponder, *An Idler in the Islands* (1924); W. Lavallin Puxley, *Green Islands in Glittering Seas* (1925); and John Vandercook, *Dark Islands* (1937). Most such books are unreadable now; exceptions are Wilfred Fowler's *This Island's Mine* (1959), a memoir of colonial service possessing an unusual degree of candour and antisentimentalism, and Margery Perham's *Pacific Prelude: A Journey to Samoa and Australasia, 1929* (1988), a shrewd, objective, and intelligent book by a diplomat and eminent biographer.

On Arthur Grimble see Barrie Macdonald, "Grimble of the Gilbert Islands: Myth and Man," in Deryck Scarr, ed., *More Pacific Islands Portraits* (Canberra: Australian National University Press, 1979).

For the Second World War see Stewart Firth, "The War in the Pacific," in Donald Denoon, ed., *The Cambridge History of the Pacific Islanders* (Cambridge: Cambridge University Press, 1997); William Manchester, *Goodbye, Darkness: A Memoir of the Pacific War* (Boston: Little, Brown, 1979); Lin Poyer, Suzann Falgout, and Laurence Marshall Carucci, *The Typhoon of War: Micronesian Experiences of the Pacific War* (Honolulu: University of Hawai'i Press, 2001); David Smurthwaite, *The Pacific War Atlas, 1941–1945* (Melbourne: CIS Cardigan Street Publishers, 1995); and Geoffrey M. White and Lamont Lindstrom, eds., *The Pacific Theater: Island Representations of World War II* (Melbourne: Melbourne University Press, 1990). Bruce Adams, *Rust in Peace: South Pacific Battlegrounds Revisited* (Sydney: Antipodean Publishers, 1975), has excellent photographs; Bruce Bahrenburg, *The Pacific: Then and Now* (New York: Putnam's, 1971), is similar: a journalistic but evocative trip to Pacific war sites.

John Barrett's *We Were There: Australian Soldiers of World War II* (Ringwood, Vic.: Viking, 1987) relates the recollections of Australians; Samuel Hynes, *The Soldiers' Tale: Bearing Witness to Modern War* (London: Pimlico, 1998), does the same for American troops. For the Pacific theater in particular, see Patrick K. O'Donnell, *Into the Rising Sun* (New York: Free Press, 2002); Richard B. Frank, *Guadalcanal: The Definitive Account of the Landmark Battle* (New York: Penguin, 1992); Merill B. Twining, *No Bended Knee: The Battle for Guadalcanal* (Novato, CA: Presidio Press, 1998); Eric M. Hammel and John E. Lane, *Bloody Tarawa* (Pacifica, CA: Pacifica Press, 1999); and the well-illustrated series Pan/Ballantine Illustrated History of World War II: *Pearl Harbor* (A. J. Barker), *New Guinea* (John Vader), *Guadalcanal* (Graeme Kent), and *Tarawa* (Henry Shaw).

For individual soldiers' and journalists' recollections of the Pacific, see Henry Gullett, *Not as a Duty Only: An Infantryman's War* (Melbourne: Melbourne University Press, 1976); Foster Hailey, *Pacific Battle Line* (New York: Macmillan, 1944); John Hersey, *Into the Valley: A Skirmish of the Marines* (London: Hodder and Stoughton, 1943); George P. Hunt, *Coral Comes High* (New York: Harper Brothers, 1946); Samuel Hynes, *Flights of Passage* (New York: Pocket Books, 1988); George Johnston, *New Guinea Diary* (Sydney: Angus and Robertson, 1944); Alvin Kernan, *Crossing the Line: A Bluejacket's World War II* (Annapolis: Naval Institute Press, 1994); John Lardner, *Southwest Passage: The Yanks in the Pacific* (Philadelphia: Lippincott, 1943); Peter Ryan, *Fear Drive My Feet* (Melbourne: Melbourne University Press, 1959); and Gordon Saville, *King of Kiriwina: The Adventures of Sergeant Saville in the South Seas* (London: Leo Cooper, 1974). Willard Price's *Rip Tide in the South Seas* (London: Heinemann, 1936) reflects on prewar Micronesia and the author's concerns about Japanese ambitions there.

Apart from *The Naked and the Dead,* distinguished fiction having its origin in the Pacific theater includes James Jones, *From Here to Eternity* (1951), and *The Thin Red Line* (1962); James Michener, *Tales of the South Pacific* (1947); and Herman Wouk, *The Caine Mutiny* (1951).

9
DISILLUSION
From Noa Noa *to the H-Bomb*

The late nineteenth and early twentieth centuries were periods of intellectual disillusionment in the Western world. On the basis of their respective findings in biology, philosophy, economics, and psychology, Darwin, Nietzsche, Marx, and Freud had effectively suggested that mankind was the sport of circumstance rather than circumstance being the sport of man. Anthropologists had once believed that a study of "primitive" humanity would shed light on the early phases of a rational historical development common to all humanity. Now the old seemed no longer to stand in rational connection with the modern—though it obviously could not be separated from it. In fact, what twentieth-century travelers found most disturbing in the South Seas was neither the old nor the modern, but the collision between them.

Many writers were themselves the carrier of the condition they detested. For Weston Martyr, writing in 1941: "South Sea islands are all the same, except that some are high and some low. The low islands are coral atolls, very pretty to look at—from a distance. They can always be counted on to provide bad water, bad food, bad mosquitoes, bad smells, dangerous navigation, boredom, and coconuts. On high islands there is better water, more to eat, and more disease" (Martyr, 103). For Elinor Mordaunt, writing in 1927, Samarai (at the eastern end of New Guinea) was "an island like a blended jewel"— until you got ashore, when it proved itself "a place, for the greater bulk of white people anyhow, at once of overcrowding and maddening loneliness: of longings and despairs; of struggles and dangers; of evil-speaking, lying and slandering; a place like an enamelled-jewelled box, made to hold marionettes and packed with real flesh and blood human beings" (Mordaunt, 23–24).

Anxiety about modernity breaking in on Islander cultures was as old as contact itself. James Cook and others had long since been concerned about communicable diseases, alchohol, and guns, and the effect these would have on those they visited. But such things were seen to be bad in and of themselves; in the twentieth century the feeling began to grow that even the good parts of Western culture and technology went bad among the islands: the agents of destruction this time were anodyne, widespread, habitual, and everyday—and more dangerous as a result. "Primitives did not change," John Vandercook suggested in 1937:

> Essentially, their customs, tools, beliefs and methods were fixed, altering through gradual evolutionary processes such as follow defeats in war, the exhaustion of land, migrations, and the like, but rarely through invention, rarely through the stimuli which individual creation so continually exerts upon the Western way of life. Then, abruptly, primitive man was confronted by mechanical and social variety as completely strange as if it had dropped upon him from the moon. (Vandercook, 121–122)

What were stimuli in the West became inharmonious intrusions elsewhere. "Only sixty years ago," as Mark Twain economically remarked of the Fijians, "they were sunk in darkness; now they have the bicycle" (Twain, 94). The apparent delicacy and vulnerability of island environments made "the modern" more absurd and more grotesque:

> We spent two days at Raratonga. I spent half an hour ashore. The first thing I saw ashore was an "automobile" marked R73. . . . Even scenically, viewed from the steamer, Raratonga is not within a million miles of the New Hebrides. In fact it is ugly. The inhabitants are cheeky niggers who talk a mixture of American and Australian, keep motor cars, have Trade Unions and look like Jack Johnson. Aitutaki [like Raratonga, in the present-day Cook Islands] was very much better. I wandered about there quite a lot, dreaming old dreams. But I'm afraid it can't be very long before the Kerlonial blight attacks it. Thence to Raietea (Society Ids.). Not too bad, but spoiled by swarms of Chows with their filthiness. ("Asterisk," 286)

"Asterisk" didn't hate Pacific islands; he hated modernity and his inability to escape it. What modernity brought with it, authors like "Asterisk" imply, are materialism (with its attendant commercialism) and racial impurity ("niggers" and "Chows"). (Jack Johnson, between 1908 and 1915 the first black American heavyweight boxing champion, was himself therefore a kind of racial upstart, as far as some white Americans were concerned.) The Second World War accelerated this process in an unprecedented way. According to Felix Keesing, the American reconstruction of the Pacific in the mid-1940s was more catastrophic than the original Japanese invasion: "Such an occupation," he said, "hit the placid island life as a kind of cultural hurricane" (Keesing, xviii). It is not surprising, then, that a note of distaste similar to that of "Asterisk" is struck by Paul Theroux, seventy years after the former's visit in 1923:

> Fiji is like the world you thought you left behind—full of political perversity, racial fear, economic woes, and Australian tourists looking for inexpensive

salad bowls. . . . Fully half the population is ethnic Indian—Muslims, Parsees, Buddhists—wearing turbans and skull-caps, and Hindus with big staring red dots on their foreheads. They run shops that sell over-priced "duty-free" merchandise and native curios, spears, napkin rings, the salad bowls, and other nameless-looking bits of hacked wood. (Theroux, 290)

The world you thought you left behind arises to meet you in all its grisly detail. "Journeys, those magic caskets full of dreamlike promises, will never again yield up their treasures untarnished," as Claude Lévi-Strauss put it in an orgy of self-pity dating from 1955. "A proliferating and overexcited civilization has broken the silence of the seas once and for all."

Now that the Polynesian islands have been smothered in concrete and turned into aircraft carriers solidly anchored in southern seas, when the whole of Asia is beginning to look like a dingy suburb, when shanty towns are spreading across Africa, when civil and military aircraft blight the primeval innocence of the American or Melanesian forests even before destroying their virginity, what else can the so-called escapism of travelling do than confront us with the more unfortunate aspects of our history? . . . The first thing we see as we travel round the world is our own filth, thrown into the face of mankind.

"Mankind has opted for monoculture" (Lévi-Strauss, 43–44), and the very primitiveness of places like the Pacific makes the accleration into modernity more depressing. "The last relic of the great Melanesian race rots away" in Malekula and "nobody cares. . . . Nothing is done to help the most interesting, in many ways the most admirable, people left in the Pacific. These men and women have all their old zest and vigour, all the will to live, their old enthusiasm and dogmatic pride. It is only the material aspects of 'civilization' that have tainted them" (Harrisson, 122–123).

Tom Harrisson and Claude Lévi-Strauss were anthropologists, "Asterisk" (real name, Robert Fletcher) a plantation manager, but all three responded to "the so-called escapism of traveling." With writers like Mark Twain and Paul Theroux, we encounter people seeking escape in a much more direct fashion: people we would nowadays call tourists. The figure of the tourist is an eighteenth-century invention (already anatomized in Laurence Sterne's *A Sentimental Journey* of 1768) but a twentieth-century phenomenon and a key part of the literature of disillusion. "Discovery has largely disappeared; sightseeing has taken its place" (Batten, 143). In fact, whereas we could be forgiven for regarding the tourist as a more or less indifferent product of modern capitalism, he or she is nothing of the kind. The tourist is a symptom of capitalism in its fullest development, unanticipated even by an analyst of the system like Karl Marx.

A brief summary of part of Marx's theory may make the connection between tourism and the modern condition clear (and here I depend on Dean MacCannell's study, *The Tourist: A New Theory of the Leisure Class*).

For Marx, capitalism depended on an economic gap between the labor value of an object or a service (its worth as arrived at by the amount of human labor that has gone into its design or discovery, manufacture, distribution, and so forth) and its exchange value (the price it can achieve in the market). Put bluntly, that is the source of profit. There may be many reasons why a consumer is prepared to pay more than an object or service is worth in labor terms or to pay for things that serve no real material need at all; important among them is what Marx called "commodity fetishism." Each commodity, Marx argued, takes on an identity (itself abstract and arbitrary) in a quasi-linguistic code of symbolic meanings, simply by virtue of having an exchange value. The object is no longer simply an object of utility but an embodiment of social, industrial, and economic relations. By taking on this identity, too, the commodity becomes an object of desire and possession, and above all of essence. A purely social quality or desideratum can appear to be "natural": innate to the commodity concerned. MacCannell quotes a typical piece of advertiser's copywriting to illustrate his theme: "Don't talk sports action, experience it with positive vehicle control! Enjoy the safety and comfort of taut, flat, balanced cornering. Stop plowing on turns, under or oversteer, wheel hop and spin, boatlike handling. Eliminate dangerous body roll and rear end steering effect. Feel the thrill of a perfectly balanced car" (quoted in MacCannell, 21). On offer here is clearly not just a set of wheels but an experience (or "feel") the consumer may never have wished for until it was presented in these terms.

It has turned out that objects cannot be stripped of commodity fetishism through the comparatively simple intellectual process of demythologizing that Marx himself anticipated, and that "culture" is to a very large extent built on the principle of the fetishization of essence. The zone of object valorization appears to be where we live, breathe, and have our being. Under the conditions of communism, Marx expected, the entire economic process would become a transparent one, and fetishism would wither away. Thus leaders like Mao and Pol Pot sought to "deculturate" or "disenculture" the societies over which they ruled by exterminating the people and objects most valued by people at large: teachers, doctors, schools, books, and so on.

Another link in the Marxist argument brings us back to tourists. The gap between labor value and exchange value does more than provide profit: it alienates modern industrial humankind from its labor, since the worker is no longer laboring to feed and clothe himself or herself but in order to enter the hall of mirrors of the modern economy. One symptom of this alienation is the distinction that arises between work (now rendered meaningless) and leisure (now invested with a significance it never possessed in the conditions of precapitalist production). The vacation, then, is both the ultimate symptom of the alienation that capitalism produces and the most fetishized commodity of them all. The vacation is *all* essence, all "feel," all exchange, and no utility. Furthermore, the more exotic the vacation, the greater the degree of fetishization: the greater the "feel" of strangeness and defamiliarization, the greater the sense of leisure or release from alienation. (A technical innovation of capitalist production is the "division of labor"; an attraction perennially held out to vacationers is to "become one with yourself.") Inexorably, humankind—Western humankind, that is to say—has pursued this phenomenon across the globe: in the history of British tourism, Blackpool, the Norfolk Broads, and the Isle of Wight gave way to the Costa del Sol and Marbella, which gave way to the islands of the Aegean, which gave way to Thailand, Malaysia, Bali, and Australia. The antipodes are the islands of leisure and release for the populations of the West now as they were for classical heroes in Hesiod's *Works and Days* and Lucian's *The True History*—only in a sadder spirit, summed up by Max Weber in *The Protestant Ethic and the Spirit of Capitalism* (1904):

> No one knows yet who will inherit this shell [of industrial capitalism] in the future: whether at the end of its prodigious development there will be new prophets or a vigorous renaissance of all thoughts and ideals or whether finally, if none of this occurs, mechanism will produce only petrification hidden under a kind of anxious importance. According to this hypothesis, the prediction will become a reality for the last men of this particular development of culture. Specialists without spirit, libertines without heart, this nothingness imagines itself to be elevated to a level of humanity never before attained. (quoted in MacCannell, 33)

The author of *Rambles in Polynesia* was an early supporter of Pacific tourism, concluding as he did that "the salubrious, congenial climate of the islands, their picturesque scenery, and their noble and interesting people, will render them favourite resorts of the holiday-seeker" ("Sundowner," viii). By 1906 the attractions of the region seemed even more self-evident—but so did the anxiety:

> Now then, colonials, and you with the tired brain, whoever you may be, come along! Perhaps you belong to the Civil Service, and are worried to death in the "Mill of Red Tape." Follow, oh, follow to where there is peace. There's time for the trip in your annual holiday; then cull from the savings and take a ticket. . . . And if you are a lady, bored by the vagaries of artificial "society," longing for the beautiful and the freedom of Nature, you come too, and bring your relations. Go to the Union or the Oceanic Company and book for Tahiti. The fares are cheap enough; and, after all, what's the good of money unless rationally used? You cannot take it with you across the Styx, and it may happen that you'll get notions from your dusky sisters—only, for God's sake, be *yourself*. (Wragge, 118–119)

Be *yourself*: the offer held out by leisure to heal the scars of industrial alienation could hardly be clearer, and leisure amidst the conditions of preindustrial primitivism offers double value in this respect.

"Why did I think I could change things in my life without changing myself?" the heroine of a modern novel of Pacific disillusion asks herself (McWilliam, 12). "Changing yourself" and "being yourself" can be thought of as parts of one process, which demands the capacity to discover authenticity in your surroundings: the yearning tourists bring with them from the rest of their alienated lives. MacCannell analyzes "the attraction" in terms of three elements: the tourist, the sight, and the marker (MacCannell, 41). The marker must point to the essence of the sight and enter the language of commodity fetishism but also transcend it. "A place, a gesture, a use of language are understood not as given bits of the real but as suffused with ideality, giving on to the *type* of the beautiful, the extraordinary, or the culturally authentic" (Frow, 125). The feel will be real because the sight is outside the hall of mirrors: something solid that has not melted into the air, to borrow a phrase from Marx. "The Other of modernity," as John Frow puts it, "is defined by the absence of *design*—of calculation or of interested self-awareness. It must therefore exist outside the circuit of commodity relations and exchange values (although it is only accessible through this circuit, one form of the basic contradicition of the tourist experience)" (Frow, 129). Something from the antipodes will have authenticity conferred upon it precisely because it is found on the other side of the world from "petrification hidden under a kind of anxious importance."

But twentieth-century travel writers, as often as not, are remorselessly skeptical about such "Others of modernity." "I'd give you three weeks to be sick to death of the most lovely island that ever had sea around it," "Asterisk" wrote in 1916:

> solitude without health or wealth or books or cooks is not compensated for by the marvellous beauty of a palm tree hanging over a coral reef. Wait till you've cursed the sun for sinking to an empty horizon minutes on end; till you've felt excited at the approach of a canoe with two or three dirty natives from somewhere else—a glimpse of the outside world. It is the knowledge that one is "right up against it" that is so appalling; that one is bound to go on living this rat's existence for months if not years to come. ("Asterisk," 148–149)

Every authenticity, in other words, is a staged authenticity: the marker points not to some realm of value outside of, or preexisting, Western commerce but to something fake—and the biggest fake of all is the tourist himself or herself: the contemporary equivalent of the "libertine without heart" Max Weber imagined. (Anything reminding the traveler of this fact is peculiarly hateful; so it is that what tourists loathe more than anything else is other tourists.) "At the Polynesian Cultural Center [in Hawai'i]," Kerry Howe reports, "Pacific island students from the Brigham Young University act as 'natives,' climbing coconut trees and rubbing sticks to make fire while being stared at by tourists in canoes paddled along canals that surround the cluster of 'islands.' It is a Polynesian Disneyland" (Howe 2000: 27). "I am feeling so disappointed," "Asterisk" recorded:

> I had looked forward to such a lot. I cannot quite explain to you what I expected to find in the South Seas . . . but I am sure I have not found it. I tell myself over and over again that these are not the South Sea Islands at all, that

I must wait until I have seen Tahiti and Aitutaki and the Marquesas. I repeat to myself ad nauseam that when I see those islands I must be free from sordid cares, free to do nothing or anything that pleases my fancy. I say that the near presence of even one Cornstalk [his expression for some Australians living nearby] is enough to spoil anything, however intrinsically beautiful it is. For these people are vulgar and horrid and petty-minded and ignorant. And then the natives here are loathsome. They are simply hideous, mis-shapen, lice-stricken savages. And the scenery is only very mediocre. There are times when I wax enthusiastic, but to be absolutely honest I have seen infinitely more lovely scenery in England and without the unpleasant accompaniments of fevers and mosquitoes and cockroaches and rats. No, I am not there yet. I must be thankful that I am on the way, and that I am within reasonable distance of realising my dreams. Remember that I am passing no judgment on the South Seas. I merely suspend it, which is, after all, a fairly reasonable thing to do. ("Asterisk," 42)

And when in due course "Asterisk" got off his island near New Caledonia and traveled to Raratonga, what awaited him? An automobile, license plate R73.

Dean MacCannell writes:

In our society, intimacy and closeness are accorded much importance: they are seen as the core of social solidarity and they are also thought by some to be morally superior to rationality and distance in social relationships, and more "real." Being "one of them," or at one with "them," means, in part, being permitted to share back regions with "them." The variety of understanding held out before tourists as an ideal is an *authentic* and *demystified* experience of an aspect of some society or other person. (MacCannell, 94)

Paul Theroux traveled the Pacific for months, looking for perfect paddling conditions for his canoe. (He found them in the end, predictably enough, in the fiftieth state of his home country: Hawai'i.) On the Fijian coast,

all the land was spoken for. This was fine in theory but it made camping on this Nandi to Suva stretch impossible. And anyway I did not want to camp within hailing distance of the Golden Sands Motel or the Coral Coast Christian Camp. There was either a house or a village or a hotel on every mile of the southern coast, which was both densely populated with locals and also tourist-ridden—Aussies and New Zealanders, mostly, with sunburned noses, seeming somewhat disappointed by the tameness of this part of Fiji and wearing T-shirts that said *My Job is So Secret Even I Don't Know What I'm Doing* and *It's Not Beer, Mate, This Is Just a Fat Shirt*. (Theroux, 303)

Theroux fails to see that the targets of his disgust are (mildly) disgusted, too. What disappoints the Australians and the New Zealanders is what disappoints the author himself: "the tameness of this part of Fiji." Whether the reporter knows it or not, he is "one of them": one of the Australasians with their embarrassing T-shirts. At the beginning of the twenty-first century, in

FIGURE 26. Mushroom cloud over the Bikini Atoll, 25 July 1946. © Australian
Picture Library / Bettmann.

fact, Islander locals may come to see people like Theroux as an entirely new
kind of threat: where Western tourists collect, terrorists aim to strike. So
much for the "tameness" of remote destinations.

The literature of disillusion from the Pacific is full of signs that point in con-
tradictory directions. Some of them are unambiguously real signs, out there
for all to see in postmodern Oceania. The coral atolls at Bikini and Muru-
roa, for example, are among the most fragile ecosystems on earth; now they
are irradiated for centuries as a result of nuclear tests (see Figure 26). The
nuclear Pacific is itself one vast staged inauthenticity. Julian Evans discusses
the American nuclear base at Kwajalein in the Marshall Islands in an extract
below, but he is not the first to have done so:

> Yet there, in the centre of Kwajalein is Macy's Department Store with state-
> side housewives in resort shorts carrying out their parcels and chattering
> about bargains and the last shipment of monkey-pod bowls. And just be-
> yond is Suburbia itself; neat houses for scientists and technicians, with lawns
> primly squared off and manicured, and full of children and children's toys.
> There are tennis courts, bowling alleys, a marina, six movies, a hospital, a
> beauty shop, buses, club houses, showers of flowers in all the hedges, and a
> soft salt sea breeze.

"It is," William Peck concludes, in a striking reversal, "like a display of 20th
Century culture . . . to be preserved in a cornerstone for the future (after the
holocaust) unbelieving generations to admire . . . or denounce. It is like the
disordered sequences of a dream" (Peck, 137). Here the relation of materialism to essence—the relation of the shops and the shoppers to "Suburbia
itself" and the American dream this tiny and remote edifice is devoted to

FIGURE 27. Two Spartan missiles launched controlled by a single missile site radar (MSR), part of continuing safeguard system tests at the Kwajalein range (1971). © Australian Picture Library / Bettmann / Corbis.

defending—is as poignant as it is shocking, passing as it does right down to lawns, which are "squared off" like troops or draughtsman's right angles but also "manicured" like the housewives' hands. The same colossal irony invades the fact that, come the final conflagration, this tiny island, the receiver of hundreds of warheads, might itself survive to record a way of life devastated at its point of origin (see Figure 27).

South Sea Island politics, too, are riddled with contradictions of these

Introduction   371 kinds: the Council of Chiefs in Fiji, which so many of its citizens cheerfully yet ruefully call the Council of Thieves, for example, or modernity in the form of democracy there, which is stretched like a band-aid over the political and ethnic divisions the country cannot heal and cannot name. Fiji operates no fewer than three electoral rolls, all along ethnic lines (Fijians, Indians, "other groups"), in a constitution with the implicit and sometimes explicit aim of preventing "Fijians" from ever being outvoted by "foreigners." A tourist like Julian Evans finds it hard to cope with staged authenticities so obviously bogus: "The surface of life was as bland as a commercial, and if you were happy when the sun shone, and when there was a grog bowl or a drinks waiter nearby, then Fiji was the place for you. I hated it. The world was full of torture for fun, conspiracies of silence, cruelty much worse than this dullness. But people—tourists and Fijians—wandered around in teeshirts that said 'Don't worry—Be happy' and I wanted to shoot them" (Evans, 113).

Once more, it may be, the South Seas acts as a distant mirror in this regard. First, the political mechanisms chosen by Pacific nations in the post-colonial era have been without exception Western mechanisms (whether Franco-American presidential, "Westminster" parliamentary, or some blend of the two). Second, the deterioration of democracy in the Pacific into a sight plus a marker laid on for foreign, aid-providing inspection is a warning to democracies young and old throughout the world, a warning more profound than the slogans people choose to wear on teeshirts. "The logic of tourism," John Frow concludes, "is that of a relentless extension of commodity relations and the consequent inequalities of power between center and periphery, First and Third Worlds, developed and underdeveloped regions, metropolis and countryside" (Frow, 151).

from Paul Gauguin, *Noa Noa* (1893)

Alongside Paul Cezanne and Vincent van Gogh, Paul Gauguin (1848–1903) was a member of the profoundly influential "post-Impressionist" group of painters responsible, it has been argued, for cubism, expressionism, and primitivism, respectively, in modern art. Of profoundly bourgeois background, he abandoned both his career as a stockbroker and, in time, his family to pursue his vocation in a number of travels and artistic communities, coming to a climax with two sojourns in Tahiti (1891–1893 and 1895–1901) and one in the Marquesas Islands from September 1901 until his death in May 1903 (see Figures 28, 29, and 30). *Noa Noa* was drafted at the end of 1893 and entrusted to his proposed collaborator the poet Charles Morice, who went on to supplement and cannibalize Gauguin's work in the years following his death. What follows is extracted from the artist's original manuscript.

FIGURE 28. Paul Gauguin (1848–1903), "Soyez amoureuses, vous serez heureuses" [Be loving, and you will be happy] (1902). The Saint Louis Art Museum.

FIGURE 29. Paul Gauguin (1848–1903), "Women, Animals, and Foliage" ["Paradis perdu"] (1902). The Saint Louis Art Museum.

FIGURE 30. Paul Gauguin (1848–1903), "Eve" (1898–1899). Frank B. Hubachek Collection, 1951.5. © The Art Institute of Chicago.

I

For 63 days I have been on my way, and I burn to reach the longed-for land. On June 8th we saw strange fires moving about in zig-zags—fishermen. Against a dark sky a jagged black cone stood out. We were rounding Moorea and coming in sight of Tahiti. A few hours later the dawn twilight became visible, and slowly we approached the reefs of Tahiti, then entered the fairway and anchored without mishap in the roads. To a man who has travelled a good deal this small island is not, like the bay of Rio Janeiro, a magic sight. A few peaks of sub[merged] mountain [were left] after the Deluge; a family climbed up there, took root, the corals also climbed, they ringed round the new island.

At ten in the morning I called on Governor Lacascade, who received me as a man of consequence entrusted by the Government with a mission—ostensibly artistic but mainly consisting in political spying. I did all I could to undeceive the political people, it was no good. They thought I was paid, I assured them I was not.

At that time the king was fatally ill, and every day an end was expected.[1] The town had a strange look: on the one hand the Europeans—traders, officials, officers and soldiers—continued to laugh [and] sing in the streets, while the natives assumed grave expressions [and] gossiped in low voices around the palace.

And in the roadstead an unusual stir of boats with orange sails, upon the blue sea frequently crossed by the silvered ripples from the line of the reefs. The inhabitants of the neighbouring islands were coming in, each day, to be present at their king's last moment, at the final taking-over of their islands by the French. For their voices from on high brought them warning— (every time a king is dying, their mountains, they say, have sombre patches on some of their slopes at sunset).

The king died and lay in state in his palace, in the full-dress uniform of an admiral.

There I saw the queen—Marau was her name—decorating the royal room with flowers and draperies. When the director of public works asked my advice about arranging the apartment artistically, I signed to him to look at the queen as, with the fine instinct of the Maoris,[2] she gracefully adorned and turned everything she touched into a work of art.

"Leave it to them," I replied.

Having only just arrived, rather disappointed as I was by things being so far from what I had longed for and (this was the point) imagined, disgusted as I was by all this European triviality, I was in some ways blind. And so I

---

1. Tahiti had become a French protectorate in 1847 and a French colony on the abdication of King Pomare V in 1880. Pomare was allowed to call himself "king" and fly the old Tahitian flag but only for the rest of his life. His death on 12 June 1891 therefore brought Tahitian hopes for independence to an end.

2. By "Maori" Gauguin means "Polynesian."

saw in the already aging queen a stout ordinary woman with some remnants of beauty. That day the Jewish element in her blood had absorbed all else. I was strangely wrong. When I saw her again later, I understood her Maori charm; the Tahitian blood began to get the upper hand once more, the remembrance of her ancestor the great chieftain Tati conferred on her, on her brother, on the whole of that family in general, a real impressiveness. In her eyes, a sort of vague presentiment of those passions which shoot up in an instant—an island rising from the Ocean and the plants beginning to burgeon in the first sunshine.

For two days the singing of *hyménées*—choruses. Everyone in black. Dirges. I thought I heard Beethoven's *Sonate pathétique*.

Funeral of Pomaré.—6 o'clock, the cortege leaves the palace. The troops . . . the authorities . . . black clothes white helmets. All the districts marched in order, and each with its chief bearing the French flag. Great mass of black —So [they went] till [they reached] the part called Arne. A monument there, indescribable in its contrast with the beautiful scenery. A formless heap of coral lumps bound together with cement. Speech by Lacascade—usual cliché—translated afterwards by the interpreter. Speech by the Protestant Pastor, then a reply by Tati, the queen's brother.

That was all—Carriages into which the officials piled, as though returning from the races —

Along the road, confusion. The indifference of the French set the example, and all this people, so grave during the last few days, began laughing again; *vahines* once more took their *tanes* by the arm, wagging their buttocks, while their broad bare feet ponderously trampled the dust of the roadway. Arrived near the Fatana river, a general scattering. In some places women, hiding among the stones, crouched in the water with their skirts raised to the girdle, cleansing their thighs of the soiling dust from the road, [and] cooling their knees which the march and the heat had chafed. Thus restored they again took the road for Papeete, their breasts leading and the conical shells which tipped their nipples drawing the muslin of their dresses to a point, with all the suppleness and grace of a healthy animal, and spreading round about them that mixture of animal scent and of sandalwood and gardenias. "*Teine merahi Noa Noa* (now very fragrant)," they said.

That was all—everything went back to normal. There was one king less, and with him were vanishing the last vestiges of Maori customs. It was all over—nothing but civilized people left.

I was sad, coming so far to . . . [3] Shall I manage to recover any trace of that past, so remote and so mysterious? and the present had nothing worth-

---

3. Gauguin left here two rows of dotted lines, but a later manuscript fills in the idea: "I was seized by a profound sadness. To have travelled so far only to find the very thing from which I had fled! The dream which led me to Tahiti was cruelly contradicted by the present; It was the Tahiti of times past that I loved. And I could not resign myself to the belief that it was totally destroyed, that this beautiful race was no more, that nothing had survived of its ancient splendour. How should I manage to recover the traces of that past . . . " (Wadley, 69).

while to say to me. To get back to the ancient hearth, revive the fire in the midst of all these ashes. And, for that, quite alone, without any support.

Cast down though I am, I am not in the habit of giving up without having tried everything, the impossible as well as the possible. My mind was soon made up. To leave Papeete as quickly as I could, to get away from the European centre. I had a sort of vague presentiment that, by living wholly in the bush with natives of Tahiti, I would manage with patience to overcome these people's mistrust, and that I would Know.

An officer of the *gendarmerie*[4] graciously offered me his carriage and his horse. I left, one morning, in search of my hut.

My *vahine* went with me (Titi was her name)—almost an English girl but she spoke a little French. That day she had put on her best dress, a flower behind her ear,—and her sugarcane hat, which she had plaited, was adorned, above its ribbon of straw flowers, with a trimming of orange-coloured shells. Her black hair hung loose over her shoulders; like this she looked really pretty —. She was proud of being in a carriage, she was proud of being well-dressed, she was proud of being the *vahine* of a man she believed to be important and highly paid. All this pride had nothing absurd about it, so well adapted is their cast of features for wearing dignity. Ancient memories of great chieftains (a race that has had such a feudal past)—

I well knew that all her mercenary love was composed merely of things that, in our European eyes, make a *whore,* but to one observer there was more than this. Such eyes and such a mouth could not lie.

There is, in all of them, a love so innate that, whether mercenary or not mercenary, it is still Love.

Besides I w——[5]

In short, the journey passed pretty quickly—a little insignificant conversation, and scenery that was rich all the time but not very varied. Always to the right the sea, the coral reefs, and expanses of water which sometimes rose in smoke when the encounter with the rocks was too violent.

At noon we reached the 45th kilometre—the Mataiea district.

I visited the district and in the end found rather a fine hut, which the owner consented to let to me; he would build another next door, to live in.

On our way back, next day in the evening, Titi asked me if I would agree to take her with me. "Later, in a few days, when I've moved in."

I realized that this half-white girl, glossy from contact with all those Europeans, would not fulfil the aim I had set before me. "I shall find them by the dozen," I said to myself. But the country is not the town.

And besides, is it necessary to *take them* in the Maori fashion *(Mau Saisis)?*[6]

---

4. Police station (French).
5. In the manuscript, "Puis je v.": perhaps *Puis je voulais,* "Besides I wanted."
6. *Mau* is the Tahitian equivalent of the French verb *saisir,* "to seize."

And I did not know their languages.

The few young girls of Mataiea who do not live with a *tane* (man) look at you with such frankness, [such] utterly fearless dignity, that I was really intimidated. Also, it was said that many of them were sick. Of that sickness which the civilized Europeans have brought them in return for their generous hospitality. After a little while I let Titi know that I would be happy if she would return. And yet in Papeete she had a terrible reputation. She had buried several lovers in succession.

II

Description [of] landscape—Shore side—Picture of the woodcutter—. Inland. The mango seen against the mountain, over the entrance to the impressive cave—

I went, that evening, to smoke a cigarette on the sands by the sea-shore. The sun was rapidly approaching the horizon, was beginning to hide behind the Isle of Moorea, which I had on my right. Against its light the mountains stood out in strong black upon the blazing sky, all those crests like ancient battlemented castles. While all those lands crumble in the deluge, there still remains, respected by these waves (rumour of some immense crowd)—there still remains, of a whole feudal society that has vanished for ever, the protecting Crest—that one nearest the sky, looking down at the deep waters, and majestically (though its cleft has an ironical look) pitying, maybe, the multitude [that has been] engulfed for having touched the tree of knowledge that attacks the head. Sphinx.

Night came quickly. This time again, Moorea was asleep. I fell asleep, later, in my bed. Silence of a Tahitian night.

Only the beating of my heart could be heard. The reeds of my hut in their spaced rows were visible from my bed with the moonlight filtering through them like an instrument of music. Pipo our ancestors called it, Vivo is their name for it. But silent (it speaks at night through memories). I fell asleep to that music. Above me, the great high roof of screw-pine leaves,—the lizards dwell there. In my sleep I could imagine space above my head, the vault of heaven, not a prison in which one stifles. My hut was Space, Freedom.

Near my hut there was another hut (*Fare amu,* house to eat in). Nearby, a pirogue—while the diseased coconut-palm looked like a huge parrot, with its golden tail drooping and a huge bunch of coconuts grasped in its claws —

The nearly naked man was wielding with both hands a heavy axe that left, at the top of the stroke, its blue imprint on the silvery sky and, as it came down, its incision on the dead tree, which would instantly live once more a moment of flames—age-old heat, treasured up each day. On the ground purple with long serpentine copper-coloured leaves, [there lay] a whole Oriental vocabulary—letters (it seemed to me) of an unknown, mysterious language. I seemed to see that word, of Oceanic origin: *Atua,* God. As *Taäta* or *Takata* it reached India and is to be found everywhere or in everything. [. . .]

A woman was stowing some nets in the pirogue, and the horizon of the blue sea was often broken by the green of the waves' crests against the coral breakers —

I was truly alone there, we observed one another. After two days I had exhausted my provisions, I had imagined that with money I would find all that is necessary for nourishment. The food is there, certainly, on the trees, on the mountain-slopes, in the sea, but one has to be able to climb a high tree, to go up the mountain and come back laden with heavy burdens; to be able to catch fish [or] dive and tear from the sea-bottom the shells firmly attached to the rocks. So there I was, a civilized man, for the time being definitely inferior to the savage, and as, on an empty stomach, I was pondering sadly on my situation, a native made signs to me and shouted, in his language, "come and eat." I understood. But I was ashamed and, shaking my head, refused. A few minutes later a child silently laid at the side of my door some food cleanly done up in freshly picked leaves, then withdrew. I was hungry, so silently I accepted. A little later the man went by and with a kindly expression, without stopping, said to me a single word: "*Paia.*" I understood vaguely. "Are you satisfied?"

On the ground under some clusters of broad pumpkin leaves I caught sight of a small dark head with quiet eyes.

A little child was examining me, then made off timorously when its eyes met mine. . . . These black people, these cannibal teeth, brought the word "savages" into my mouth.

For them, too, I was the savage. Rightly perhaps.

I began to work—notes, sketches of all kinds. Everything in the landscape blinded me, dazzled me. Coming from Europe I was constantly uncertain of some colour [and kept] beating about the bush: and yet it was so simple to put naturally on to my canvas a red and a blue. In the brooks, forms of gold enchanted me—Why did I hesitate to pour that gold and all that rejoicing of the sunshine on to my canvas? Old habits from Europe, probably,— all this timidity of expression [characteristic] of our bastardized races —

To initiate myself properly into the character of a Tahitian face, into all the charm of a Maori smile, I had long wanted to make a portrait of a woman who lived close by, who was of true Tahitian descent.

I asked her permission one day when she had plucked up the courage to come into my hut and look at some photographs of paintings. While she was examining with a great deal of interest some religious pictures by the Italian primitives, I tried to sketch some of her features, especially that enigmatic smile of hers. She made a nasty grimace, went away,—then she came back. Was it an inner struggle, or caprice (a very Maori trait), or even an impulse of coquetry that will surrender only after resistance? I realized that in my painter's scrutiny there was a sort of tacit demand for surrender, surrender for ever without any chance to withdraw, a perspicacious probing of what was within. [She was,] in fact, not pretty by European standards: Beautiful all the same—all her features had a raphaelesque harmony in their meeting curves,[7] while her mouth, modelled by a sculptor, spoke all the tongues of speech and of the kiss, of joy and of suffering; that melancholy of the bitterness that mingles with pleasure, of passivity dwelling within domination. An entire fear of the unknown.

I worked fast, with passion. It was a portrait resembling what my eyes *veiled by my heart* perceived. I believe it was chiefly faithful to what was within. That sturdy fire from a contained strength. She had a flower behind her ear, which was listening for her fragrance. And her forehead in its majesty recalled, with its raised lines, that phrase of Poe's: "There is no perfect beauty without a cer——"[8]

She looked with particular interest at a photograph of Manet's Olympia.[9] With the words I had already learned in that language (for two months I had not spoken a word of French) I questioned her. She told me this Olympia was truly beautiful: I smiled at that opinion and was moved by it. She had the sense of the beautiful (and the Ecole des Beaux Arts considers that [picture] horrible!). She added, all of a sudden, breaking the silence that presides over a thought: "It's your wife."

"Yes," I lied. Me, the *tane* of Olympia!

I asked if I might paint her portrait. "*Aita* (no)," she said in a tone almost of rage, and went away.

This refusal really depressed me.

An hour later she came back in a beautiful dress—Caprice, desire for the forbidden fruit—She smelled good she was all adorned and I worked with haste—I suspected that this decision of hers was not firm—Portrait of a woman *Vahine no te tiare [Woman with a Flower]—*

A period of work—Alone. I saw plenty of calm-eyed young women, I wanted them to be willing to be taken without a word: taken brutally. In a way a longing to rape. The old men said to me, speaking of one of them: "*Mau tera* (take this one)." I was timid and dared not resign myself to the effort—

I let Titi know that I wanted her to come. She came. But being already civilized, used to an official's luxury, she did not suit me for long. I parted from her.

[. . .]

7. That is, a linear purity of the kind associated with the Italian Renaissance artist Raphael (1483–1520).

8. Gauguin quotes from American writer Edgar Allan Poe's tale "Ligeia" (1838), where the narrator himself, describing his lost love, misquotes a remark by the seventeenth-century philosopher Francis Bacon from his essay "Of Beauty": "There is no excellent beauty that hath not some strangeness in the proportion."

9. A scandalous picture by the French impressionist Edouard Manet (1832–1883), depicting a well-known Parisian prostitute, whose knowing stare at the viewer is more unsettling than her nudity. A traditional art institution like the School of Fine Arts in Paris would certainly have found the picture disturbing at the time (1865).

DISILLUSION

IV

Every day gets better for me, in the end I understand the language quite well, my neighbours (three close by, the others at various distances) regard me almost as one of themselves; my naked feet, from daily contact with the rock, have got used to the ground; my body, almost always naked, no longer fears the sun; civilization leaves me bit by bit and I begin to think simply, to have only a little hatred for my neighbour, and I function in an animal way, freely—with the certainty of the morrow [being] like today; every morning the sun rises serene for me as for everyone, I become carefree and calm and loving. I have a natural friend, who has come to see me every day naturally, without any interested motive. My paintings in colour [and] my wood-carvings astonished him and my answers to his questions taught him something. Not a day when I work but he comes to watch me. One day when, handing him my tools, I asked him to try a sculpture, he gazed at me in amazement and said to me simply, with sincerity, that I was not like other men; and he was perhaps the first of my fellows to tell me that I was useful to others. A child. . . . One has to be, to think that an artist is something useful.

The young man was faultlessly handsome and we were great friends. Sometimes in the evening, when I was resting from my day's work, he would ask me the questions of a young savage who wants to know a lot of things about love in Europe, questions which often embarrassed me.

One day I wished to have for sculpture a tree of rosewood, a piece of considerable size and not hollow. "For that," he told me, "you must go up the mountain to a certain place where I know several fine trees that might satisfy you. If you like, I'll take you there and we'll carry it back, the two of us."

We left in the early morning.

The Indian paths in Tahiti are quite difficult for a European: between two unscalable mountains there is a cleft where the water purifies itself by twisting between detached boulders, rolled down, left at rest, then caught up again on a torrent day to be rolled down further, and so on to the sea. On either side of the stream there cascades a semblance of a path: trees pell-mell, monster ferns, all sorts of vegetation growing wilder, more and more impenetrable as you climb towards the centre of the island.

We went naked, both of us, except for the loincloth, and axe in hand, crossing the river many a time to take advantage of a bit of track which my companion seemed to smell out, so little visible [it was], so deeply shaded.— Complete silence,—only the noise of water crying against rock, monotonous as the silence. And two we certainly were, two friends, he a quite young man and I almost an old man in body and soul, in civilized vices: in lost illusions. His lithe animal body had graceful contours, he walked in front of me sexless . . .

From all this youth, from this perfect harmony with the nature which surrounded us, there emanated a beauty, a fragrance *(noa noa)* that enchanted my artist soul. From this friendship so well cemented by the mutual attraction between simple and composite, love took power to blossom in me.

And we were only . . . the two of us—

I had a sort of presentiment of crime, the desire for the unknown, the awakening of evil—Then weariness of the male role, having always to be strong, protective; shoulders that are a heavy load. To be for a minute the weak being who loves and obeys.

I drew close, without fear of laws, my temples throbbing.

The path had come to an end . . . we had to cross the river; my companion turned at that moment, so that his chest was towards me. The hermaphrodite had vanished; it was a young man, after all; his innocent eyes resembled the limpidity of the water. Calm suddenly came back into my soul, and this time I enjoyed the coolness of the stream deliciously, plunging into it with delight—"*Toe toe,*" he said to me ("it's cold"). "Oh no," I answered, and this denial, answering my previous desire, drove in among the cliffs like an echo. Fiercely I thrust my way with energy into the thicket, [which had] become more and more wild; the boy went on his way, still limpid-eyed. He had not understood. I alone carried the burden of an evil thought, a whole civilization had been before me in evil and had educated me.

We were reaching our destination.—At that point the crags of the mountain drew apart, and behind a curtain of tangled trees a semblance of a plateau [lay] hidden but not unknown. There several trees (rose-wood) extended their huge branches. Savages both of us, we attacked with the axe a magnificent tree which had to be destroyed to get a branch suitable to my desires. I struck furiously and, my hands covered with blood, hacked away with the pleasure of sating one's brutality and of destroying something. In time with the noise of the axe I sang:

"Cut down by the foot the whole forest (of desires)
Cut down in yourself the love of yourself, as a man
would cut down with his hand in autumn the Lotus."

Well and truly destroyed indeed, all the old remnant of civilized man in me. I returned at peace, feeling myself thenceforward a different man, a Maori. The two of us carried our heavy load cheerfully, and I could again admire, in front of me, the graceful curves of my young friend—and calmly: curves robust like the tree we were carrying. The tree smelt of roses, *Noa Noa.* We got back in the afternoon, tired. He said to me: "Are you pleased?" "Yes"—and inside myself I repeated: "Yes."

I was definitely at peace from then on.

I gave not a single blow of the chisel to that piece of wood without having memories of a sweet quietude, a fragrance, a victory and a rejuvenation.

Jack London, "The Red One" (1918)

Having shot to fame in 1900 with *The Son of a Wolf* (1900), a collection of stories based on his adventures as a prospector in the Klondike, Jack London (1876–1916) wrote prolifically and often journalistically from his wide experiences as oyster pirate, miner, slum dweller, war correspondent, ardent socialist, and alcoholic. These also included an intrepid set of cruises across the Pacific in his yacht, the *Snark* (1906–1908). These trips went some way to undermining his health, which was not restored by prolonged visits to Hawai'i in his later years.

There it was! The abrupt liberation of sound, as he timed it with his watch, Bassett likened to the trump of an archangel. Walls of cities, he meditated, might well fall down before so vast and compelling a summons. For the thousandth time vainly he tried to analyze the tone-quality of that enormous peal that dominated the land far into the strongholds of the surrounding tribes. The mountain gorge which was its source rang to the rising tide of it until it brimmed over and flooded earth and sky and air. With the wantonness of a sick man's fancy, he likened it to the mighty cry of some Titan of the Elder World vexed with misery or wrath. Higher and higher it arose, challenging and demanding in such profounds of volume that it seemed intended for ears beyond the narrow confines of the solar system. There was in it, too, the clamor of protest in that there were no ears to hear and comprehend its utterance.

—Such the sick man's fancy. Still he strove to analyze the sound. Sonorous as thunder was it, mellow as a golden bell, thin and sweet as a thrummed taut cord of silver—no; it was none of these, nor a blend of these. There were no words nor semblances in his vocabulary and experience with which to describe the totality of that sound.

Time passed. Minutes merged into quarters of hours, and quarters of hours into half hours, and still the sound persisted, ever changing from its initial vocal impulse yet never receiving fresh impulse—fading, dimming, dying as enormously as it had sprung into being. It became a confusion of troubled mutterings and babblings and colossal whisperings. Slowly it withdrew, sobby sob, into whatever great bosom had birthed it, until it whimpered deadly whispers of wrath and as equally seductive whispers of delight, striving still to be heard, to convey some cosmic secret, some understanding of infinite import and value. It dwindled to a ghost of sound that had lost its menace and promise, and became a thing that pulsed on in the sick man's consciousness for minutes after it had ceased. When he could hear it no longer, Bassett glanced at his watch. An hour had elapsed ere that archangel's trump had subsided into tonal nothingness.

Was this, then, *his* dark tower?—Bassett pondered, remembering his Browning and gazing at his skeleton-like and fever-wasted hands. And the fancy made him smile—of Childe Roland bearing a slug-horn to his lips with an arm as feeble as his was.[10] Was it months, or years, he asked himself, since he first heard that mysterious call on the beach at Ringmanu? To save himself he could not tell. The long sickness had been most long. In conscious count

---

10. Alluding to the allegorical poem "Childe Roland to the Dark Tower Came" by Robert Browning (1812–1889), concerning the hero's nightmarish pilgrimage through a hostile wasteland. On reaching his object—a mysterious tower—the hero blows dauntlessly on his horn.

of time he knew of months, many of them; but he had no way of estimating the long intervals of delirium and stupor. And how fared Captain Bateman of the blackbirder *Nari*? he wondered; and had Captain Bateman's drunken mate died of delirium tremens[11] yet?

From which vain speculations, Bassett turned idly to review all that had occurred since that day on the beach of Ringmanu when he first heard the sound and plunged into the jungle after it. Sagawa had protested. He could see him yet, his queer little monkeyish face eloquent with fear, his back burdened with specimen cases, in his hands Bassett's butterfly net and naturalist's shot gun, as he quavered in Beche de mer English:[12] "Me fella too much fright along bush. Bad fella boy too much stop'm along bush."

Bassett smiled sadly at the recollection. The little New Hanover[13] boy had been frightened, but had proved faithful, following him without hesitancy into the bush in the quest after the source of the wonderful sound. No fire-hollowed tree-trunk, that, throbbing war through the jungle depths, had been Bassett's conclusion. Erroneous had been his next conclusion, namely, that the source or cause could not be more distant than an hour's walk and that he would easily be back by mid-afternoon to be picked up by the *Nari*'s whaleboat.

[Bassett now recalls the events of his disastrous expedition: he and Sagawa were attacked by "bushmen," and the servant lost his life. Bassett escaped with two lost fingers and a injury to his scalp and evaded capture, walking deeper and deeper into the island and becoming sicker as he walked, moving ever closer to the source of the mysterious sound. After what might be a week of wandering, he is discovered at death's door by an Islander woman.]

And then had come Balatta. In the first shade, where the savannah yielded to the dense mountain jungle, he had collapsed to die. At first she had squealed with delight at sight of his helplessness, and was for beating his brain out with a stout forest branch. Perhaps it was his very utter helplessness that had appealed to her, and perhaps it was her human curiosity that made her refrain. At any rate, she had refrained, for he opened his eyes again under the impending blow, and saw her studying him intently. What especially struck her about him were his blue eyes and white skin. Coolly she had squatted on her hams, spat on his arm, and with her finger-tips scrubbed away the dirt of days and nights of muck and jungle that sullied the pristine whiteness of his skin.

---

11. A fit of the shakes brought on by excess drinking. The *Nari* was engaged in bringing Melanesian Islanders to work on Australian sugar plantations: "blackbirding," as the business was called.

12. From the French *bêche de mer:* the sea cucumber, sea slug, or trepang gathered from tropical seas, dried, and sold as a luxury item in China. But here, by extension, pidgin, the English-based common language of the South Seas, so named by Westerners (sometimes as "Beach-la-mar").

13. An island off New Ireland, north of New Guinea.

And everything about her had struck him especially, although there was nothing conventional about her at all. He laughed weakly at the recollection, for she had been as innocent of garb as Eve before the fig-leaf adventure. Squat and lean at the same time, asymmetrically limbed, string-muscled as if with lengths of cordage, dirt-caked from infancy save for casual showers, she was as unbeautiful a prototype of woman as he, with a scientist's eye, had ever gazed upon. Her breasts advertised at the one time her maturity and youth; and, if by nothing else, her sex was advertised by the one article of finery with which she was adorned, namely a pig's tail, thrust through a hole in her left ear-lobe. So lately had the tail been severed, that its raw end still oozed blood that dried upon her shoulder like so much candle-droppings. And her face! A twisted and wizened complex of apish features, perforated by upturned, sky-open, Mongolian nostrils, by a mouth that sagged from a huge upper-lip and faded precipitately into a retreating chin, and by peering querulous eyes that blinked as blink the eyes of denizens of monkey-cages.

Not even the water she brought him in a forest leaf, and the ancient and half-putrid chunk of roast pig, could redeem in the slightest the grotesque hideousness of her. When he had eaten weakly for a space, he closed his eyes in order not to see her, although again and again she poked them open to peer at the blue of them. Then had come the sound. Nearer, much nearer, he knew it to be; and he knew equally well, despite the weary way he had come, that it was still many hours distant. The effect of it on her had been startling. She cringed under it, with averted face, moaning and chattering with fear. But after it had lived its full life of an hour, he closed his eyes and fell asleep with Balatta brushing the flies from him.

When he awoke it was night, and she was gone. But he was aware of renewed strength, and, by then too thoroughly inoculated by the mosquito poison to suffer further inflammation, he closed his eyes and slept an un-broken stretch till sun-up. A little later Balatta had returned, bringing with her a half dozen women who, unbeautiful as they were, were patently not so unbeautiful as she. She evidenced by her conduct that she considered him her find, her property, and the pride she took in showing him off would have been ludicrous had his situation not been so desperate.

Later, after what had been to him a terrible journey of miles, when he collapsed in front of the devil-devil house in the shadow of the breadfruit tree, she had shown very lively ideas on the matter of retaining possession of him. Ngurn, whom Bassett was to know afterward as the devil-devil doctor, priest, or medicine man of the village, had wanted his head. Others of the grinning and chattering monkey-men, all as stark of clothes and bestial of appearance as Balatta, had wanted his body for the roasting oven. At that time he had not understood their language, if by *language* might be digni-fied the uncouth sounds they made to represent ideas. But Bassett had thor-oughly understood the matter of debate, especially when the men pressed and prodded and felt of the flesh of him as if he were so much commodity in a butcher's stall.

Balatta had been losing the debate rapidly, when the accident happened. One of the men, curiously examining Bassett's shotgun, managed to cock and pull a trigger. The recoil of the butt into the pit of the man's stomach had not been the most sanguinary result, for the charge of shot, at a distance of a yard, had blown the head of one of the debaters into nothingness.

Even Balatta joined the others in flight, and, ere they returned, his senses already reeling from the oncoming fever-attack, Bassett had regained possession of the gun. Whereupon, although his teeth chattered with the ague and his swimming eyes could scarcely see, he held onto his fading consciousness until he could intimidate the bush men with the simple magics of compass, watch, burning glass, and matches. At the last, with due emphasis of solemnity and awfulness, he had killed a young pig with his shotgun and promptly fainted.

Bassett flexed his arm-muscles in quest of what possible strength might reside in such weakness, and dragged himself slowly and totteringly to his feet. He was shockingly emaciated; yet, during the various convalescences of the many months of his long sickness, he had never regained quite the same degree of strength as this time. What he feared was another relapse such as he had already frequently experienced. Without drugs, without even quinine, he had managed so far to live through a combination of the most pernicious and most malignant of malarial and black-water fevers. But could he continue to endure? Such was his everlasting query. For, like the genuine scientist he was, he would not be content to die until he had solved the secret of the sound.

Supported by a staff, he staggered the few steps to the devil-devil house where death and Ngurn reigned in gloom. Almost as infamously dark and evil-stinking as the jungle was the devil-devil house—in Bassett's opinion. Yet therein was usually to be found his favorite crony and gossip, Ngurn, always willing for a yarn or a discussion, the while he sat in the ashes of death and in a slow smoke shrewdly revolved curing human heads suspended from the rafters. For, through the months' interval of consciousness of his long sickness, Bassett had mastered the psychological simplicities and lingual difficulties of the language of the tribe of Ngurn and Balatta, and Gngngn— the latter the addle-headed young chief who was ruled by Ngurn, and who, whispered intrigue had it, was the son of Ngurn.

"Will the Red One speak to-day?" Bassett asked, by this time so accustomed to the old man's gruesome occupation as to take even an interest in the progress of the smoke-curing.

With the eye of an expert Ngurn examined the particular head he was at work upon.

"It will be ten days before I can say 'finish,' " he said. "Never has any man fixed heads like these."

Bassett smiled inwardly at the old fellow's reluctance to talk with him of the Red One. It had always been so. Never, by any chance, had Ngurn or any other member of the weird tribe divulged the slightest hint of any physical characteristic of the Red One. Physical the Red One must be, to emit the wonderful sound, and though it was called the Red One, Bassett could not be sure that red represented the color of it. Red enough were the deeds and powers of it, from what abstract clews he had gleaned. Not alone, had Ngurn informed him, was the Red One more bestial powerful than the neighbor tribal gods, ever a-thirst for the red blood of living human sacrifices, but the neighbor gods themselves were sacrificed and tormented before him. He was the god of a dozen allied villages similar to this one, which was the central and commanding village of the federation. By virtue of the Red One many alien villages had been devastated and even wiped out, the prisoners sacrificed to the Red One. This was true to-day, and it extended back into old history carried down by word of mouth through the generations. When he, Ngurn, had been a young man, the tribes beyond the grass lands had made a war raid. In the counter raid, Ngurn and his fighting folk had made many prisoners. Of children alone over five score living had been bled white before the Red One, and many, many more men and women.

The Thunderer was another of Ngurn's names for the mysterious deity. Also at times was he called The Loud Shouter, The God-Voiced, The Bird-Throated, The One with the Throat Sweet as the Throat of the Honey-Bird, The Sun Singer, and The Star-Born.

Why The Star-Born? In vain Bassett interrogated Ngurn. According to that old devil-devil doctor, the Red One had always been, just where he was at present, forever singing and thundering his will over men. But Ngurn's father, wrapped in decaying grass-matting and hanging even then over their heads among the smoky rafters of the devil-devil house, had held otherwise. That departed wise one had believed that the Red One came from out of the starry night, else why—so his argument had run—had the old and forgotten ones passed his name down as the Star-Born? Bassett could not but recognize something cogent in such argument. But Ngurn affirmed the long years of his long life, wherein he had gazed upon many starry nights, yet never had he found a star on grass land or in jungle depth—and he had looked for them. True, he had beheld shooting stars (this in reply to Bassett's contention); but likewise had he beheld the phosphorescence of fungoid growths and rotten meat and fireflies on dark nights, and the flames of wood-fires and of blazing candle-nuts; yet what were flame and blaze and glow when they had flamed, and blazed and glowed? Answer: memories, memories only, of things which had ceased to be, like memories of matings accomplished, of feasts forgotten, of desires that were the ghosts of desires, flaring, flaming, burning, yet unrealized in achievement of easement and satisfaction. Where was the appetite of yesterday? the roasted flesh of the wild pig the hunter's arrow failed to slay? the maid, unwed and dead, ere the young man knew her?

A memory was not a star, was Ngurn's contention. How could a memory be a star? Further, after all his long life he still observed the starry night-sky unaltered. Never had he noted the absence of a single star from its accustomed place. Besides, stars were fire, and the Red One was not fire—which last involuntary betrayal told Bassett nothing.

"Will the Red One speak to-morrow?" he queried.

Ngurn shrugged his shoulders as who should say.

"And the day after?—and the day after that?" Bassett persisted.

"I would like to have the curing of your head," Ngurn changed the subject. "It is different from any other head. No devil-devil has a head like it. Besides, I would cure it well. I would take months and months. The moons would come and the moons would go, and the smoke would be very slow, and I should myself gather the materials for the curing smoke. The skin would not wrinkle. It would be as smooth as your skin now."

He stood up, and from the dim rafters grimed with the smoking of countless heads, where day was no more than a gloom, took down a matting-wrapped parcel and began to open it.

"It is a head like yours," he said, "but it is poorly cured."

Bassett had pricked up his ears at the suggestion that it was a white man's head; for he had long since come to accept that these jungle-dwellers, in the midmost center of the great island, had never had intercourse with white men. Certainly he had found them without the almost universal Beche de mer English of the west South Pacific. Nor had they knowledge of tobacco, nor of gunpowder. Their few precious knives, made from lengths of hoop-iron, and their few and more precious tomahawks, made from cheap trade hatchets, he had surmised they had captured in war from the bushmen of the jungle beyond the grass lands, and that they, in turn, had similarly gained them from the salt water men who fringed the coral beaches of the shore and had contact with the occasional white men.

"The folk in the out beyond do not know how to cure heads," old Ngurn explained, as he drew forth from the filthy matting and placed in Bassett's hands an indubitable white man's head.

Ancient it was beyond question; white it was as the blond hair attested. He could have sworn it once belonged to an Englishman, and to an Englishman of long before by token of the heavy gold circlets still threaded in the withered ear lobes.

"Now your head . . . " the devil-devil doctor began on his favorite topic.

"I'll tell you what," Bassett interrupted, struck by a new idea. "When I die I'll let you have my head to cure, if, first, you take me to look upon the Red One."

"I will have your head anyway when you are dead," Ngurn rejected the proposition. He added, with the brutal frankness of the savage: "Besides, you have not long to live. You are almost a dead man now. You will grow less strong. In not many months I shall have you here turning and turning in the smoke. It is pleasant, through the long afternoons, to turn the head of one you have known as well as I know you. And I shall talk to you and tell you the many secrets you want to know. Which will not matter, for you will be dead."

"Ngurn," Bassett threatened in sudden anger. "You know the Baby Thunder in the Iron that is mine." (This was in reference to his all-potent and all-awful shotgun.) "I can kill you any time, and then you will not get my head."

"Just the same, will Gngngn, or some one else of my folk get it," Ngurn complacently assured him. "And just the same will it turn and turn here in the devil-devil house in the smoke. The quicker you slay me with your Baby Thunder, the quicker will your head turn in the smoke."

And Bassett knew he was beaten in the discussion.

What was the Red One?—Bassett asked himself a thousand times in the succeeding week, while he seemed to grow stronger. What was the source of the wonderful sound? What was this Sun Singer, this Star-Born One, this mysterious deity, as bestial-conducted as the black and kinky headed and monkey-like human beasts who worshiped it, and whose silver-sweet, bull-mouthed singing and commanding he had heard at the taboo distance for so long?

Ngurn had he failed to bribe with the inevitable curing of his head when he was dead. Gngngn, imbecile and chief that he was, was too imbecilic, too much under the sway of Ngurn, to be considered. Remained Balatta, who, from the time she found him and poked his blue eyes open to recrudescence of her grotesque, female hideousness, had continued his adorer. Woman she was, and he had long known that the only way to win from her treason to her tribe was through the woman's heart of her.

Bassett was a fastidious man. He had never recovered from the initial horror caused by Balatta's female awfulness. Back in England, even at best, the charm of woman, to him, had never been robust. Yet now, resolutely, as only a man can do who is capable of martyring himself for the cause of science, he proceeded to violate all the fineness and delicacy of his nature by making love to the unthinkably disgusting bushwoman.

He shuddered, but with averted face hid his grimaces and swallowed his gorge as he put his arm around her dirt-crusted shoulders and felt the contact of her rancid-oily and kinky hair with his neck and chin. But he nearly screamed when she succumbed to that caress so at the very first of the courtship and mowed and gibbered and squealed little, queer, pig-like gurgly noises of delight. It was too much. And the next he did in the singular courtship was to take her down to the stream and give her a vigorous scrubbing.

From then on he devoted himself to her like a true swain as frequently and for as long at a time as his will could override his repugnance. But marriage, which she ardently suggested, with due observance of tribal custom, he balked at. Fortunately, taboo rule was strong in the tribe. Thus, Ngurn could never touch bone, or flesh, or hide of crocodile. This had been ordained at his birth. Gngngn was denied ever the touch of woman. Such pollution, did it chance to occur, could be purged only by the death of the offending female. It had happened once, since Bassett's arrival, when a girl of nine, running in play, stumbled and fell against the sacred chief. And the girl-child was seen no more. In whispers, Balatta told Bassett that she had been three days and nights in dying before the Red One. As for Balatta, the breadfruit was taboo to her. For which Bassett was thankful. The taboo might have been water.

For himself, he fabricated a special taboo. Only could he marry, he explained, when the Southern Cross rode highest in the sky. Knowing his astronomy, he thus gained a reprieve of nearly nine months; and he was confident that within that time he would either be dead or escaped to the coast with full knowledge of the Red One and of the source of the Red One's wonderful voice. At first he had fancied the Red One to be some colossal statue, like Memnon, rendered vocal under certain temperature conditions of sunlight.[14] But when, after a war raid, a batch of prisoners was brought in and the sacrifice made at night, in the midst of rain, when the sun could play no part, the Red One had been more vocal than usual, Bassett discarded that hypothesis.

In company with Balatta, sometimes with men and parties of women, the freedom of the jungle was his for three quadrants of the compass. But the fourth quadrant, which contained the Red One's abiding place, was taboo. He made more thorough love to Balatta—also saw to it that she scrubbed herself more frequently. Eternal female she was, capable of any treason for the sake of love. And, though the sight of her was provocative of nausea and the contact of her provocative of despair, although he could not escape her awfulness in his dream-haunted nightmares of her, he nevertheless was aware of the cosmic verity of sex that animated her and that made her own life of less value than the happiness of her lover with whom she hoped to mate. Juliet or Balatta?[15] Where was the intrinsic difference? The soft and tender product of ultra-civilization, or her bestial prototype of a hundred thousand years before her?—there was no difference.

Bassett was a scientist first, a humanist afterward. In the jungle-heart of Guadalcanal he put the affair to the test, as in the laboratory he would have put to the test any chemical reaction. He increased his feigned ardor for the bushwoman, at the same time increasing the imperiousness of his will of desire over her to be led to look upon the Red One face to face. It was the old story, he recognized, that the woman must pay, and it occurred when the two of them one day, were catching the unclassified and unnamed little black fish, an inch long, half-eel and half-scaled, rotund with salmon-golden roe, that frequented the fresh water and that were esteemed, raw and whole, fresh or putrid, a perfect delicacy. Prone in the muck of the decaying jungle-floor, Balatta threw herself, clutching his ankles with her hands, kissing his feet and making slubbery noises that chilled his backbone up and down again.

14. Memnon was king of the Ethiopians in Greek myth; his name is associated with a massive ruined statue of the pharaoh Amenhotep III, which emitted a weird sound when struck by the rays of the rising sun.

15. That is, the idealized young heroine of Shakespeare's *Romeo and Juliet*.

She begged him to kill her rather than exact this ultimate love-payment. She told him of the penalty of breaking the taboo of the Red One—a week of torture, living, the details of which she yammered out from her face in the mire until he realized that he was yet a tyro in knowledge of the frightfulness the human was capable of wreaking on the human.

Yet did Bassett insist on having his man's will satisfied, at the woman's risk, that he might solve the mystery of the Red One's singing, though she should die long and horribly and screaming. And Balatta, being mere woman, yielded. She led him into the forbidden quadrant. An abrupt mountain, shouldering in from the north to meet a similar intrusion from the south, tormented the stream in which they had fished into a deep and gloomy gorge. After a mile along the gorge, the way plunged sharply upward until they crossed a saddle of raw limestone which attracted his geologist's eye. Still climbing, although he paused often from sheer physical weakness, they scaled forest-clad heights until they emerged on a naked mesa or tableland. Bassett recognized the stuff of its composition as black volcanic sand, and knew that a pocket magnet could have captured a full load of the sharply angular grains he trod upon.

And then, holding Balatta by the hand and leading her onward, he came to it—a tremendous pit, obviously artificial, in the heart of the plateau. Old history, the South Seas Sailing Directions, scores of remembered data and connotations swift and furious, surged through his brain. It was Mendana who had discovered the islands and named them Solomon's, believing that he had found that monarch's fabled mines. They had laughed at the old navigator's child-like credulity; and yet here stood himself, Bassett, on the rim of an excavation for all the world like the diamond pits of South Africa.[16]

But no diamond this that he gazed down upon. Rather was it a pearl, with the depth of iridescence of a pearl; but of a size all pearls of earth and time welded into one, could not have totaled; and of a color undreamed of any pearl, or of anything else, for that matter, for it was the color of the Red One. And the Red One himself Bassett knew it to be on the instant. A perfect sphere, fully two hundred feet in diameter, the top of it was a hundred feet below the level of the rim. He likened the color quality of it to lacquer. Indeed, he took it to be some sort of lacquer, applied by man, but a lacquer too marvelously clever to have been manufactured by the bush-folk. Brighter than bright cherry-red, its richness of color was as if it were red builded upon red. It glowed and iridesced in the sunlight as if gleaming up from underlay under underlay of red.

In vain Balatta strove to dissuade him from descending. She threw herself in the dirt; but, when he continued down the trail that spiraled the pit-wall, she followed, cringing and whimpering her terror. That the red sphere had been dug out as a precious thing, was patent. Considering the paucity of

---

16. At the time London was writing, the open-pit diamond mines of Kimberley, in South Africa, were the largest and deepest excavations in history.

members of the federated twelve villages and their primitive tools and methods, Bassett knew that the toil of a myriad generations could scarcely have made that enormous excavation.

He found the pit bottom carpeted with human bones, among which, battered and defaced, lay village gods of wood and stone. Some, covered with obscene totemic figures and designs, were carved from solid tree trunks forty or fifty feet in length. He noted the absence of the shark and turtle gods, so common among the shore villages, and was amazed at the constant recurrence of the helmet motive.[17] What did these jungle savages of the dark heart of Guadalcanal know of helmets? Had Mendana's men-at-arms worn helmets and penetrated here centuries before? And if not, then whence had the bush-folk caught the motive?

Advancing over the litter of gods and bones, Balatta whimpering at his heels, Bassett entered the shadow of the Red One and passed on under its gigantic overhang until he touched it with his finger-tips. No lacquer that. Nor was the surface smooth as it should have been in the case of lacquer. On the contrary, it was corrugated and pitted, with here and there patches that showed signs of heat and fusing. Also, the substance of it was metal, though unlike any metal or combination of metals he had ever known. As for the color itself, he decided it to be no application. It was the intrinsic color of the metal itself.

He moved his finger-tips, which up to that had merely rested, along the surface, and felt the whole gigantic sphere quicken and live and respond. It was incredible! So light a touch on so vast a mass! Yet did it quiver under the finger tip caress in rhythmic vibrations that became whisperings and rustlings and mutterings of sound—but of sound so different; so elusive thin that it was shimmeringly sibillant; so mellow that it was maddening sweet, piping like an elfin horn, which last was just what Bassett decided would be like a peal from some bell of the gods reaching earthward from across space.

He looked to Balatta with swift questioning; but the voice of the Red One he had evoked had flung her face-downward and moaning among the bones. He returned to contemplation of the prodigy. Hollow it was, and of no metal known on earth, was his conclusion. It was right-named by the ones of old-time as the Star-Born. Only from the stars could it have come, and no thing of chance was it. It was a creation of artifice and mind. Such perfection of form, such hollowness that it certainly possessed, could not be the result of mere fortuitousness. A child of intelligences, remote and unguessable, working corporally in metals, it indubitably was. He stared at it in amaze, his brain a racing wild-fire of hypotheses to account for this far-journeyer who had adventured the night of space, threaded the stars, and now rose before him and above him, exhumed by patient anthropophagi, pitted and lacquered by its fiery bath in two atmospheres.

---

17. That is, "motif," a repeated theme in a work of art, literature, or music.

But was the color a lacquer of heat upon some familiar metal? Or was it an intrinsic quality of the metal itself? He thrust in the blade-point of his pocket-knife to test the constitution of the stuff. Instantly the entire sphere burst into a mighty whispering, sharp with protest, almost twanging goldenly if a whisper could possibly be considered to twang, rising higher, sinking deeper, the two extremes of the registry of sound threatening to complete the circle and coalesce into the bull-mouthed thundering he had so often heard beyond the taboo distance.

Forgetful of safety, of his own life itself, entranced by the wonder of the unthinkable and un-guessable thing, he raised his knife to strike heavily from a long stroke, but was prevented by Balatta. She upreared on her own knees in an agony of terror, clasping his knees and supplicating him to desist. In the intensity of her desire to impress him, she put her forearm between her teeth and sank them to the bone.

He scarcely observed her act, although he yielded automatically to his gentler instincts and withheld the knife-hack. To him, human life had dwarfed to microscopic proportions before this colossal portent of higher life from within the distances of the sidereal universe. As had she been a dog, he kicked the ugly little bushwoman to her feet and compelled her to start with him on an encirclement of the base. Part way around, he encountered horrors. Even, among the others, did he recognize the sun-shriveled remnant of the nine-years girl who had accidentally broken Chief Gngngn's personality taboo. And, among what was left of these that had passed, he encountered what was left of one who had not yet passed. Truly had the bush-folk named themselves into the name of the Red One, seeing in him their own image which they strove to placate and please with such red offerings.

Farther around, always treading the bones and images of humans and gods that constituted the floor of this ancient charnel house of sacrifice, he came upon the device by which the Red One was made to send his call singing thunderingly across the jungle-belts and grass-lands to the far beach of Ringmanu. Simple and primitive was it as was the Red One's consummate artifice. A great king-post, half a hundred feet in length, seasoned by centuries of superstitious care, carven into dynasties of gods, each superimposed, each helmeted, each seated in the open mouth of a crocodile, was slung by ropes, twisted of climbing vegetable parasites, from the apex of a tripod of three great forest trunks, themselves carved into grinning and grotesque adumbrations of man's modern concepts of art and god. From the striker king-post, were suspended ropes of climbers to which men could apply their strength and direction. Like a battering ram, this king-post could be driven end-onward against the mighty, red-iridescent sphere.

Here was where Ngurn officiated and functioned religiously for himself and the twelve tribes under him. Bassett laughed aloud, almost with madness, at the thought of this wonderful messenger, winged with intelligence across space, to fall into a bushman stronghold and be worshiped by ape-like, man-eating and head-hunting savages. It was as if God's Word had fallen into the muck mire of the abyss underlying the bottom of hell; as if Jehovah's Commandments had been presented on carved stone to the monkeys of the monkey cage at the Zoo; as if the Sermon on the Mount had been preached in a roaring bedlam of lunatics.

The slow weeks passed. The nights, by election, Bassett spent on the ashen floor of the devil-devil house, beneath the ever-swinging, slow-curing heads. His reason for this was that it was taboo to the lesser sex of woman, and, therefore, a refuge for him from Balatta, who grew more persecutingly and perilously loverly as the Southern Cross rode higher in the sky and marked the imminence of her nuptials. His days Bassett spent in a hammock swung under the shade of the great breadfruit tree before the devil-devil house. There were breaks in this program, when, in the comas of his devastating fever-attacks, he lay for days and nights in the house of heads. Ever he struggled to combat the fever, to live, to continue to live, to grow strong and stronger against the day when he would be strong enough to dare the grass-lands and the belted jungle beyond, and win to the beach, and to some labor recruiting, black-birding ketch or schooner, and on to civilization and the men of civilization, to whom he could give news of the message from other worlds that lay, darkly worshiped by beast-men, in the black heart of Guadalcanal's mid-most center.

On other nights, lying late under the breadfruit tree, Bassett spent long hours watching the slow setting of the western stars beyond the black wall of jungle where it had been thrust back by the clearing for the village. Possessed of more than a cursory knowledge of astronomy, he took a sick man's pleasure in speculating as to the dwellers on the unseen worlds of those incredibly remote suns, to haunt whose houses of light, life came forth, a shy visitant, from the rayless crypts of matter. He could no more apprehend limits to time than bounds to space. No subversive radium speculations[18] had shaken his steady scientific faith in the conservation of energy and the indestructibility of matter. Always and forever must there have been stars. And surely, in that cosmic ferment, all must be comparatively alike, comparatively of the same substance, or substances, save for the freaks of the ferment. All must obey, or compose, the same laws that ran without infraction through the entire experience of man. Therefore, he argued and agreed, must worlds and life be appanages to all the suns as they were appanages to the particular sun of his own solar system.

Even as he lay here, under the breadfruit tree, an intelligence that stared across the starry gulfs, so must all the universe be exposed to the ceaseless scrutiny of innumerable eyes, like his, though grantedly different, with behind them, by the same token, intelligences that questioned and sought the meaning and the construction of the whole. So reasoning, he felt his soul go

18. At the end of the nineteenth century, the New Zealand–born physicist Ernest Rutherford discovered the ultimate instability of matter by experimenting on radium.

forth in kinship with that august company, that multitude whose gaze was forever upon the arras of infinity.

Who were they, what were they, those far distant and superior ones who had bridged the sky with their gigantic, red-iridescent, heaven-singing message? Surely, and long since, had they, too, trod the path on which man had so recently, by the calendar of the cosmos, set his feet. And to be able to send such a message across the pit of space, surely they had reached those heights to which man, in tears and travail and bloody sweat, in darkness and confusion of many counsels, was so slowly struggling. And what were they on their heights? Had they won Brotherhood? Or had they learned that the law of love imposed the penalty of weakness and decay? Was strife, life? Was the rule of all the universe the pitiless rule of natural selection? And, and most immediately and poignantly, were their far conclusions, their long-won wisdoms, shut even then in the huge, metallic heart of the Red One, waiting for the first earth-man to read? Of one thing he was certain: No drop of red dew shaken from the lion-mane of some sun in torment, was the sounding sphere. It was of design, not chance, and it contained the speech and wisdom of the stars.

What engines and elements and mastered forces, what lore and mysteries and destiny-controls, might be there! Undoubtedly, since so much could be inclosed in so little a thing as the foundation stone of public building, this enormous sphere should contain vast histories, profounds of research achieved beyond man's wildest guesses, laws and formulæ that, easily mastered, would make man's life on earth, individual and collective, spring up from its present mire to inconceivable heights of purity and power. It was Time's greatest gift to blindfold, insatiable, and sky-aspiring man. And to him, Bassett, had been vouchsafed the lordly fortune to be the first to receive this message from man's interstellar kin!

No white man, much less no outland man of the other bush-tribes, had gazed upon the Red One and lived. Such the law expounded by Ngurn to Bassett. There was such a thing as blood brotherhood, Bassett, in return, had often argued in the past. But Ngurn had stated solemnly no. Even the blood brotherhood was outside the favor of the Red One. Only a man born within the tribe could look upon the Red One and live. But now, his guilty secret known only to Balatta, whose fear of immolation before the Red One fast-sealed her lips, the situation was different. What he had to do was to recover from the abominable fevers that weakened him and gain to civilization. Then would he lead an expedition back, and, although the entire population of Guadalcanal be destroyed, extract from the heart of the Red One the message of the world from other worlds.

But Bassett's relapses grew more frequent, his brief convalescences less and less vigorous, his periods of coma longer, until he came to know, beyond the last promptings of the optimism inherent in so tremendous a constitution as his own, that he would never live to cross the grass lands, perforate the perilous coast jungle, and reach the sea. He faded as the Southern Cross rose higher in the sky, till even Balatta knew that he would be dead ere the nuptial date determined by his taboo. Ngurn made pilgrimage personally and gathered the smoke materials for the curing of Bassett's head, and to him made proud announcement and exhibition of the artistic perfectness of his intention when Bassett should be dead. As for himself, Bassett was not shocked. Too long and too deeply had life ebbed down in him to bite him with fear of its impending extinction. He continued to persist, alternating periods of unconsciousness with periods of semi-consciousness, dreamy and unreal, in which he idly wondered whether he had ever truly beheld the Red One or whether it was a nightmare fancy of delirium.

Came the day when all mists and cobwebs dissolved, when he found his brain clear as a bell, and took just appraisement of his body's weakness. Neither hand nor foot could he lift. So little control of his body did he have, that he was scarcely aware of possessing one. Lightly indeed his flesh sat upon his soul, and his soul, in its briefness of clarity, knew by its very clarity, that the black of cessation was near. He knew the end was close; knew that in all truth he had with his eyes beheld the Red One, the messenger between the worlds; knew that he would never live to carry that message to the world—that message, for aught to the contrary, which might already have waited man's hearing in the heart of Guadalcanal for ten thousand years. And Bassett stirred with resolve, calling Ngurn to him, out under the shade of the breadfruit tree, and with the old devil-devil doctor discussing the terms and arrangements of his last life effort, his final adventure in the quick of the flesh.

"I know the law, O Ngurn," he concluded the matter. "Whoso is not of the folk may not look upon the Red One and live. I shall not live anyway. Your young men shall carry me before the face of the Red One, and I shall look upon him, and hear his voice, and thereupon die, under your hand, O Ngurn. Thus will the three things be satisfied: the law, my desire, and your quicker possession of my head for which all your preparations wait."

To which Ngurn consented, adding:

"It is better so. A sick man who cannot get well is foolish to live on for so little a while. Also, is it better for the living that he should go. You have been much in the way of late. Not but what it was good for me to talk to such a wise one. But for moons of days we have held little talk. Instead, you have taken up room in the house of heads, making noises like a dying pig, or talking much and loudly in your own language which I do not understand. This has been a confusion to me, for I like to think on the great things of the light and dark as I turn the heads in the smoke. Your much noise has thus been a disturbance to the long learning and hatching of the final wisdom that will be mine before I die. As for you, upon whom the dark has already brooded, it is well that you die now. And I promise you, in the long days to come when I turn your head in the smoke, no man of the tribe shall come in to disturb us. And I will tell you many secrets, for I am an old man and very wise, and I shall be adding wisdom to wisdom as I turn your head in the smoke."

So a litter was made, and, borne on the shoulders of half a dozen of the men, Bassett departed on the last little adventure that was to cap the total adventure, for him, of living. With a body of which he was scarcely aware, for even the pain had been exhausted out of it, and with a bright clear brain that accommodated him to a quiet ecstasy of sheer lucidness of thought, he lay back on the lurching litter and watched the fading of the passing world, beholding for the last time the breadfruit tree before the devil-devil house, the dim day beneath the matted jungle roof, the gloomy gorge between the shouldering mountains, the saddle of raw limestone, and the mesa of black, volcanic sand.

Down the spiral path of the pit they bore him, encircling the sheening, glowing Red One that seemed ever imminent to iridesce from color and light into sweet singing and thunder. And over bones and logs of immolated men and gods they bore him, past the horrors of other immolated ones that yet lived, to the three-king-post tripod and the huge king-post striker.

Here Bassett, helped by Ngurn and Balatta, weakly sat up, swaying weakly from the hips, and with clear, unfaltering, all-seeing eyes gazed upon the Red One.

"Once, O Ngurn," he said, not taking his eyes from the sheening, vibrating surface whereon and wherein all the shades of cherry-red played unceasingly, ever a-quiver to change into sound, to become silken rustlings, silvery whisperings, golden thrummings of cords, velvet pipings of elfland, mellow-distances of thunderings.

"I wait," Ngurn prompted after a long pause, the long-handled tomahawk unassumingly ready in his hand.

"Once, O Ngurn," Bassett repeated, "let the Red One speak so that I may see it speak as well as hear it. Then strike, thus, when I raise my hand; for, when I raise my hand, I shall drop my head forward and make place for the stroke at the base of my neck. But, O Ngurn, I, who am about to pass out of the light of day forever, would like to pass with the wonder-voice of the Red One singing greatly in my ears."

"And I promise you that never will a head be so well cured as yours," Ngurn assured him, at the same time signaling the tribesmen to man the propelling ropes suspended from the king-post striker. "Your head shall be my greatest piece of work in the curing of heads."

Bassett smiled quietly to the old one's conceit, as the great carved log, drawn back through two-score feet of space, was released. The next moment he was lost in ecstasy at the abrupt and thunderous liberation of sound. But such thunder! Mellow it was with preciousness of all sounding metals. Archangels spoke in it; it was magnificently beautiful before all other sounds; it was invested with the intelligence of supermen of planets of other suns; it was the voice of God, seducing and commanding to be heard. And—the everlasting miracle of that interstellar metal! Bassett, with his own eyes, saw color and colors transform into sound till the whole visible surface of the vast sphere was a-crawl and titillant and vaporous with what he could not tell was color or was sound. In that moment the interstices of matter were his, and the interfusings and intermating transfusings of matter and force.

Time passed. At the last Bassett was brought back from his ecstasy by an impatient movement of Ngurn. He had quite forgotten the old devil-devil one. A quick flash of fancy brought a husky chuckle into Bassett's throat. His shotgun lay beside him in the litter. All he had to do, muzzle to head, was press the trigger and blow his head into nothingness.

But why cheat him? was Bassett's next thought. Head-hunting, cannibal beast of a human that was as much ape as human, nevertheless Old Ngurn had, according to his lights, played squarer than square. Ngurn was in himself a fore-runner of ethics and contract, of consideration, and gentleness in man. No, Bassett decided; it would be a ghastly pity and an act of dishonor to cheat the old fellow at the last. His head was Ngurn's, and Ngurn's head to cure it would be.

And Bassett, raising his hand in signal, bending forward his head as agreed so as to expose cleanly the apiculation to his taut spinal cord, forgot Balatta, who was merely a woman, a woman merely and only and undesired. He knew, without seeing, when the razor-edged hatchet rose in the air behind him. And for that instant, ere the end, there fell upon Bassett the shadow of the Unknown, a sense of impending marvel of the rending of walls before the imaginable. Almost, when he knew the blow had started and just ere the edge of steel bit the flesh and nerves, it seemed that he gazed upon the serene face of the Medusa, Truth—And, simultaneous with the bite of the steel on the onrush of the dark, in a flashing instant of fancy, he saw the vision of his head turning slowly, always turning, in the devil-devil house beside the breadfruit tree.

from Julian Evans, *Transit to Venus: Travels in the Pacific* (1992)

Julian Evans was born in 1955 and spent his early childhood in Brisbane, Australia, where his father worked in the British diplomatic service. Many years later, in England, he saw photographs of Peacekeeper missiles launched from California reentering the atmosphere above Kwajalein atoll in the Micronesian Marshall Islands: an independent republic in a compact of free association with the United States that guarantees the United States the use of the islands for missile testing. The photographs inspired a set of travels to New Caledonia, Fiji, and Samoa, then north through Tuvalu and Kiribati to Kwajalein itself.

To Venus

We came in off the ocean in a tremorless glide, the sea below decorated by a necklace of slender islands that made its way to the line of the horizon and vanished. The twelve-seater Dornier landed without a murmur on the white concrete runway. After the brutal braking I was used to on short coral airstrips, the plane seemed to be taxiing for hours to the terminal building.

Through the window on my left I took in hangars, piles of oil-drums and equipment, low-rise offices with fat white vans with fat black tyres parked outside, a hovering helicopter and two more on the ground, and against the sky there were three white radomes that looked like enormous golfballs.

Out of the right-hand window I saw coconut palms and a knot of men in shorts and baseball caps, talking as they walked between them. There wasn't a great deal of room between the runway and the ocean's surf—it really was one hell of a landing strip—but my eyes did not deceive me. On this side the men really were trailing golf carts, and what they were trailing them over really was a nine-hole golf course.

The policeman on security duty grinned and said: "You have a real nice time."

Don Michael was waiting, with itinerary in hand.

"I suggest you get some breakfast, and I'll pick you up around ten-thirty for a briefing."

He loaded my bag into one of the white Dodges and left me at the hotel.

I walked down Ocean Road to the Pacific Dining Room on Eighth Street, a clattering white and chromium hall where people sat far apart from each other in order to be alone with their breakfast. For $4.25 you loaded a tray with as much as you wanted: pawpaw, cereals, yoghurt, grilled bacon, sausages, tomatoes, eggs easy over, beans, fries, hash browns, toast, and then a little cheese or a couple of oranges to finish off with.

After twenty weeks of a diet that lately hadn't varied much between fish and breadfruit and coconut and more fish, I had no stomach for any of this, and picked up a slice of pawpaw and some toast and coffee.

It was nice to know that the capability to satisfy that kind of appetite was there if you wanted to use it. Plenty of people did. Most of the diners, in huge horrible Babygro tracksuits, beat the Polynesians for size; they could have trampled a Sumo wrestler underfoot. They walked back to the line for repeat orders of sausages and a second double shake (and later in the day I saw three of them in the cafeteria down the street, making just as swift work of two beef subs and a pizza). As they ate, they had a look of watchful, possessive concentration on their face.

Kwajalein was all about capability. The range briefing was given by Lt-Colonel Harrison, a genial man in spectacles and combat fatigues who was on crutches from a bad case of jogger's ankle. (At Kwajalein base, apart from golf, you could play almost any sport you cared to. Tennis, softball, volleyball, basketball, handball, and there was an eight-lane bowling alley. But what everyone was involved in, one way or another, was the major-league baseball of governments—more world-series than the World Series. They called the atoll, or more accurately the lagoon it enclosed, the catcher's mitt. The pitcher was in California, at Vandenberg Air Force Base. The ball reached speeds of up to 16,000 kph, and the only play they were aiming for was a strike.)

"Kwajalein became the US Army's major range in 1964," Col Harrison started. Since then, anything between 300 and 600 unarmed intercontinental ballistic missiles—he wasn't sure—had been test-fired from the west coast of America at its lagoon. When it was not using what Col Harrison proprietorially called "one of the most extensive collections of radars and computers ever assembled" to play baseball with Minuteman, Peacekeeper and Trident missiles, the range did not sleep. "It is a key component of Pacific Command's satellite defence and space surveillance network. Kwajalein is also a testbed for the space interceptor weapons of the Strategic Defense Initiative."

Pacific Command's size beggared belief.

"320,000 troops of the Army, Navy, Marine Corps and Air Force; the Seventh Fleet and Third Fleet; long-range bomber bases; early-warning systems and space tracking stations; attack submarines on permanent rotating patrol."

If you were CINCPAC (the commander-in-chief, Pacific Command), I thought, you were liable to be almost as powerful as the President.

The Pacific was America's destiny. Ever since she had won the war in the Pacific—a war she kept her allies out of—she had seen the Pacific as her great western frontier. All through the late 1980s, while we were being told that the apparatus of the Cold War was being dismantled, the US President (who played a baseball star or two in his time) and his Navy Secretary John Lehman were *increasing* the size of the Pacific Fleet from 200 to 300 ships. And naval nuclear weapons, particularly the US Navy's real hotshot armaments, the hunt-in-the-dark, hide-in-the-dark submarine-launched ballistic missiles, were being kept right off the agenda of all the arms talks, despite Soviet suggestions to include them.

This was the ocean's most interesting characteristic. You could do all of this, set up a sphere of influence over half the world's surface, and no one reported it. You could talk noisily about peace in one part of the planet, and continue quietly to arm in another, and no one said a word. Peace had been brilliantly transformed into another PR concept.

Although Kwajalein was west of the Pacific Date Line, Col Harrison explained, and thus a day ahead of mainland America, the atoll followed the same calendar as California. This was so the men at Vandenberg and the men at Kwajalein were quite clear about what day a mission was supposed to go off on.

"Kwajalein's attributes as a target are unparalleled," he said. "Its position in relation to launch points; its isolation from population centres; and its versatility as a tracking and intercepting point."

In Majuro Giff Johnson had said: "Listen. In any war, missiles will be subject to all kinds of unverifiable assumptions about their reliability and accuracy. Both sides' weapons will have to fly over the North Pole, for one thing. The joke among missile designers is that if the US ever gets itself into a nuclear war, the President can be sure of just one thing: he will be able to blast the daylights out of Kwajalein Atoll."

"Did you hear about the Peacekeeper mission last night?" Col Harrison asked.

I had. I already knew that I wasn't going to see a mission come in. I wasn't surprised or particularly disappointed. Why should I be surprised? The keepers of the range, so generous with their time in passing on all the theory and foreplay of weapons testing, preferred to keep that single intimate, split-second, climactic moment to themselves. It was natural. It was only human.

But the maintenance man at the hotel, Randy from Tennessee, had seen it.

"Boy, it was real neat," he said.

"That mission," said Col Harrison, "took twenty-seven minutes from launch to impact, a distance of 8000 kilometres. Its ten RVs splashed down in prearranged sectors of the lagoon and ocean, monitored by long-wavelength tracking radars and short-wavelength imaging radars. The phased-array Altair radar, with its dual field of vision, one of only three in the free world, can spot with a single millisecond pulse a metal object the size of a basketball 4800 kilometres away. Then, when an RV gets close enough, we have the Tradex radar, and that will give you a gnat's-ass view of it."

RV was short for re-entry vehicle, the piece that was bussed off the main body of the missile in mid-flight and re-entered the atmosphere in free fall to hit the target. Each RV, when armed, carried a 330-kiloton charge. Trident II, the "silo-buster" which would supposedly destroy Soviet missiles before they could be launched, would carry eight RVs—each with a charge of 475 kilotons.

A missile was a mission. A warhead was a re-entry vehicle. 330 kilotons was twenty-six times more powerful than the Hiroshima bomb: you called something carrying the equivalent of over 3 million tons of TNT a Peacekeeper. You changed the terminology and you avoided the real significance of things. To the personnel on the range—most of them were scientists and contractors rather than soldiers—this epistemological legerdemain was second nature. They were happy with the euphemisms. They didn't think about it. They were—they all were—real friendly and real polite. No one ever used the "n" word.

The base was clean and it was nice and neatly laid out, spacious and airy. The wind blew all day and dropped its wings at dusk; the temperature/humidity was a constant 85/85.

Off Ocean Road, to the left of Eighth Street, was the sportsfield, with the athletic spire of a Nike-Zeus missile from the Sixties mounted on one edge and the open-air movie theatre on the far corner. Between Sixth and Eighth Street you could find everything else you needed: the Pacific Dining Room, post office, Macy's department store, the library, Bank of Guam and the golf pro shop. In a trailer next to the cycle racks was the Surfside beauty parlour. There was a theatre, a club and a video library called Tape Escape that took

$14,000 a month in tape rentals at a dollar a tape. To get to the beach you went down Lagoon Road, right for the family beach, left for the bachelors'.

The brick officers' houses, shadowed with palms and frangipani trees, stood in quiet streets with children's bikes lying in the front yards. The high school was here too. On the tip of the island stood Silver City, 250 stainless steel trailers that some residents just lived in and others had lavished verandahs and patios on and the occasional Doric colonnade or conservatory.

Kwajalein was tidy, quiet, ordinary: suburban trailer-park America at its best. (No Marshallese lived here of course. The Army paid rent to the landowners and sent them to Ebeye, the next island along, from where they commuted to the base to work.) It was *better* than America. No private cars were allowed; people cycled or took the bus or even sometimes walked. And the residents felt comfortable and safe. It was so homey some of them kept renewing their contracts. In Macy's I met a jelly of a woman in a pink tracksuit who had been on Kwaj (rhymed with Dodge) for eleven years.

"It's real nice here. You know there's no drugs, no violence, no street crime, no rape. The high school is terrific. It's a great place to bring up the kids."

You heard this everywhere. *Real nice:* they became scary words. For a place at the heart of America's military future, which had probably contributed more to the arms race than anywhere else on Earth, Kwajalein's greatest triumph was its niceness. It was true. The base was calm, beautiful, friendly. In the club at lunchtime, a place where people stuck to soft drinks and ate huge salads with the taste frozen out of them, the conversation was about contracts (to renew or not to renew) and girlfriends (just renewed) and the weekend. [. . .]

And Atlantis

The next day I was supposed to go to Ebeye, but that evening I went back to the club. Outside, a fat blonde girl said:

"So you're a newspaperman? You be careful on Ebeye. Are you staying the night?"

"That's the plan."

"Are you crazy? Don't mix with those women. They are diseased."

"What do you mean?"

"They're mudhens. You go to the club there and you'll catch something."

The policeman from the airfield came past.

The blonde girl said: "This guy's going to spend the night on Ebeye."

The policeman grinned at me. "I thought I'd go tomorrow."

The blonde girl turned away. We were both crazy and sick. "Oh yeah, I forgot. He's got a mudhen."

Inside the club, with the salad bar rolled off the dance floor, you socialised in deep brown armchairs. Everyone danced with everyone: it was real nice, to begin with. The sound system had everything from Tammy

Wynette to Lisa Stansfield and Marillion.[19] The favourite cocktail was a B52—vodka, kahlua and Baileys. Trays of tumblers filled with the murky drinks went forth with impressive frequency.

As I watched from the bar, gradually a change came over the room. The air began to be filled with suppressed, bad behaviour; the dancing was terrible, as wooden as your parents' parties.

I turned back to the bar, a line of single men in baseball caps. Wendell was a hard-featured man in his fifties. He was also a policeman. "Nuthin to police." Humpbacked cowries were his obsession.

Wendell introduced me to his friend Rex. Rex asked me what I was doing. He had a thin face scored by nerves, and a moustache. He said: "Yeah, I did some writing a while ago, maybe ten years. Won a competition in World of Poetry. Bob Hope presented the prize."

Wendell guffawed. "Rex, you never said you were a poet."

Rex was injured by the scorn.

"What about your damn shells?" he said and turned his back on his friend. He was out of the Army now but he had done two tours in Vietnam, one in helicopter gunships, one in charge of a reconnaissance platoon. Bombing Cambodia was no bad thing. He didn't blame Nixon, he blamed the generals. There was a line of trucks waiting to go in and get the VC,[20] but they were never allowed to.

"Have another beer. I've learnt some fascinating things about the Marshallese. I've decided I should learn some of their language." He spent most of his free time in the library. "You've got to do something. I've been here forty days, and I tell you I'm climbing the wall."

There was no need to ask about Vietnam. It kept cropping up. Another couple of helicopter pilots, one white, one black, both vets, stepped in. I had one in each ear, on the balls of their feet, wired.

"America's pulled a lot of small countries out of a lot of tight spots. What *I* want to know is, who ever helped out America?" said one.

The other one said: "You know what nigger means, man? N-i-g-g-e-r. You hear what I'm sayin? It don't mean nuthin, because I can still keep the Commies out, black or white. And I'll tell you sumthin else. I never took no fuckin newspapermen on my missions. They said, 'You gotta.' I just grabbed their notebooks and stomped them in the mud."

Fifteen years later, after a handful of B52s, the nerves and reflexes were coiling up all over again. The war was still on, it could be won. Kwajalein was just R & R. The pilots were thinking about air sports, hover-cover, shoot

---

19. Tammy Wynette is a timeless—and ageless—star of American country music; Lisa Stansfield and Marillion were British pop stars of the time with far less longevity, in rhythm and blues and "progressive" rock, respectively.

20. Viet Cong: communist guerrilla forces in South Vietnam. Richard Nixon resigned as U.S. president a year before the Vietnam war ended in 1975; earlier he had sanctioned the bombing of Cambodia, where, it was argued, the Viet Cong had training camps.

them if they freeze, shoot them if they run. We've got to keep the Commies out.

Maybe it was the B52s. Anything that tasted that disgusting couldn't be good for you. [. . .]

I took the landing craft to Ebeye in a downpour. I half-suspected what I would find. To create Kwajalein, they had also had to invent Ebeye. Ten thousand Marshallese lived here on an islet of forty hectares. The children were as thick as flies, the plywood barracks so close you had to sidle between them to get to the shore.

The shore: the density of garbage gave it the appearance of a clumsy land reclamation project. Everywhere there were oil-drums, old trucks, earthmovers, the carcasses of cars, freight containers, transmissions, tyres, split bags of household waste, beer cans, disposable nappies. Among the bonanza of waste, the children crawled and played, grinning, their faces streaked with rust.

What had I found? Nothing that people wanted to talk about or look at or visit, unless, like the easy-going policeman, they had a mudhen here. But why shouldn't ugliness take on mythic proportions? I had stumbled on another new Pacific myth, man-made like the thunderbolts the islanders watched overhead. Almost treeless, sanitationless, overrun by children under fourteen, it was no earthly island. It was the lost slum of Atlantis.

The rain sluiced down the walls of the barracks as I stumbled to the office of the mayor, Alvin Jacklick. He was said to have achieved a lot for Ebeye, along with the Kwajalein Atoll Development Corporation. The sewers no longer backed up into the one-room houses. They had desalination and power plants. The streets and sidewalks were paved. Hepatitis was no longer endemic.

But his lugubrious optimism in the future was unjustified, as he conceded, by the facts. They had around $21 million a year in lease payments, wages and income tax. Instead of luxury, the appearance of the place was a sort of joke tribute to the unfettered application of cash. The Marshallese landlords were failing to distribute the rent income among their people. The over crowding was worse than ever. The super-slum conditions had brought about a conformist promiscuity.

"I can tell you," Jacklick said, "that *every* man is seeing, apart from his wife, at least three other women."

Who was to blame? Everyone was screwing everyone else with gusto. What else was there to do except despair? The Marshallese were passive but not browbeaten. The children laughed and scrambled over hazardous garbage, their parents (whoever they were) caught the landing craft every day to the base and got on with their lives. The Americans had not intended to create Ebeye the way it was, even though they had ignored for years the biological time-bomb it had become and maintained rigorous apartheid at Kwajalein for health and education facilities. I thought of the woman in Macy's: "Kwajalein's a great place to bring up the kids."

There was nothing to be done. The clock couldn't be turned back, Ebeye couldn't be cured. Small improvements would occur, but nothing that would be allowed to disrupt its chief purpose as a segregated labour reservoir for the base. Of course if the Americans hadn't come, wishful thinking said it would be as it was: an ordinary, undisturbed coral island. But wishful thinking was more the province of the Americans than of the Marshallese.

Nothing, not even a suppressed lust to shake off the real nice atmosphere at the base and be crazy and sick with a mudhen, could have induced me to stay the night. I ran through the pouring rain to catch the last landing craft back to the base. On the way I passed a small Marshallese girl. The rain had collected in a rusty oil-drum outside her rotting barrack. Bathing in the water sloshing in the bottom, her wet head was just visible over its rim.

You couldn't say the Americans were evil. But they were terrifying.

I walked to breakfast down Ocean Road for the last time. The Pacific Dining Room was full of people beating anxiety with the $4.25 breakfast.

Past the baseball diamond, I noticed something I hadn't seen before.

There were no coconuts on the palms. The familiar clusters of swollen ochre and green fruit were missing. When I happened upon him later, Don was surprised I should ask about them.

"Oh, we get the Marshallese to cut all the coconuts down. They truly are a hazard. Can you imagine what it would be like if one of those mothers fell on your head?"

At lunchtime I went to the club, then packed my bag. My laundry had been done and I took a scalding shower. As the jets of water smacked my shoulders, I had a bizarre pang of regret. Why should I mind leaving this spruce and beautifully organised colony of scientists? Was it the expensive bed, or the gentle shush of the high-grade air-conditioning, or the shower—this wonderful high-pressure shower—one of mankind's greatest inventions? But there was also all this security and enfolding warmth. Immobility; ordinariness; being in someone else's system and not having to think; some power bigger than you (the Bomb—a Christian creation); oh, the relief of the same comfortable life to look forward to tomorrow.

Movement saved me. Don arrived in the Dodge. At the airfield the Marshallese in transit to Majuro sat in suspended animation on wooden benches. We walked out to the picket fence and watched the plane for Majuro drop gently out of a pearl-powder sky.

Don had dug out some mementoes for me from his office at the control tower: a calendar, a brochure about the Strategic Defense Initiative, and a Kwajalein baseball cap. I thanked him, and for ten minutes we talked nostalgically about England, where he had spent four years stationed at Lakenheath.

I had found the best souvenir in the club at lunchtime. I had trousered a handful of the club's paper napkins. These showed a cartoon of the sun rising behind the silhouette of a palm tree. From the lagoon next to it, a baby black missile leapt joyously, like a spawning salmon.

from Larry McMurtry, *Paradise* (2001)

Larry McMurtry (born 1936) is a prolific novelist, author of *Lonesome Dove* and *Terms of Endearment* among other titles. As his mother drew near the end of a long life—including a forty-three-year marriage to McMurtry's father—the author quixotically took a trip as far from his hometown of Archer City, Texas, as could be imagined: to the Marquesas Islands in the remote Pacific. There he reflected on his parents' marriage and landlocked life.

I stay on deck almost all night, as the captain steers us through the Tuamotus.[21] At dawn we are anchored, well out in a broad bay. Several of the ports we deliver to have docks that only the whaleboats can approach. Supplies are off-loaded into whaleboats and likewise we tourists. This morning we visit Takapoto, a long, skinny, sandy patch of land. Watching the crew load blocks of concrete into the whaleboats is impressive, but a greater challenge comes when they have to get sixty passengers, some of them elderly and rather frail, down the rattly ladder into the bobbing boats. Time and again the crew effects this transition without anyone being hurt, sometimes lifting people bodily into the unsteady whaleboat.

Takapoto has a dock, but the tide is out and the whale-boats can't get to it, which makes it necessary for us to wade ashore—the first of many wadings. It's a rocky, slippery beach, which produces a good deal of teetering and tottering among the waders, but eventually we all straggle out of the sea and up to the copra shed—the first of many copra sheds. Copra is the one thing no community lacks.

At the copra shed a Tuamotuan band, led by a very stout singer with no front teeth, is wailing away as we wander up. The band members seem to be enthusiastic about our arrival, but most of the people assembled at the copra shed—about twenty young men and a few kids—wear listless looks. An elderly man wearing a wonderful hat of flowers seems to be a kind of headman. Besides the listless young men and the barefoot children there are many skinny dogs.

A predominance of listless youths, barefoot children, and skinny dogs makes my heart sink: I think of Haiti, or of the loungers around the grocery store on any Indian reservation. Takapoto has something of this feeling. The Tuamotuans are darker than the Tahitians—less admixed—and most places, dark is the color of poverty. This island, in some places, is barely a half mile wide; in twos and threes we wandered down the spine of it toward the craft sheds. The band followed us, traveling in tiny pickups. The headman with the nice flower hat—or perhaps he isn't a headman, just a village elder of some kind—zips past us on a bright blue motor scooter. The motor scooters and the tiny pickups were the only motor vehicles which seemed to work on Takapoto. Many cars, either parked or abandoned here and there, conspicu-

---

21. What used to be known as the "Dangerous Isles": a low-island group to the east of Tahiti famous as a hazard for shipping.

ously do not work. Their numbers, coupled with their intense state of dilapidation, reinforced the sense of being on an Indian reservation.

We walked through a coconut plantation and saw some copra drying on a platform. A fair number of pigs nosed about, their life expectancies short. They were as skinny as the dogs, and their abundant piglets were not much larger than rats.

I have survived into my sixty-fourth year by never underestimating the belligerence of swine. I keep a wary eye on the sows. Some of our group, now spread out over a mile or more of sand, would be easy prey for those sows. Fortunately the pigs hold their peace. They may know that summary justice awaits them if they injure the tourists.

Despite its down-at-the-heels appearance, Takapoto has an industry—a real industry, as opposed to a native craft. On this island black pearls are cultivated. As we approached the shed where local crafts were to be exhibited, we passed strings of oysters, hung on the line like socks. The black pearls are created by a fairly elaborate process: a tiny speck of shell from a Mississippi River mussel is inserted into each oyster and left there for five years, after which the pearls can be harvested.

Five or six tables filled with bracelets and necklaces made from these little pearls are on view. To me they seem uninteresting, as nearly identical as two peas in a pod. Nonetheless the ladies of the group, not wanting to miss their first opportunity to shop, fall on these trinkets with glad cries and purchase quite a few.

Better than the pearls, in my opinion, were the children of the islands. Several of them, quick as minnows, arranged themselves in the windows of a nearby shack, posed to be photographed. And they *were* photographed, though not exhaustively enough for one little girl, who burst into tears when the shutters ceased to click. Another little girl, immaculately dressed in a blue floral shirt, played the castanets in the little four-piece band. Now and then the old man with the flower hat played along for a song or two, thumping an instrument with only one string. He thumped along happily, about a half beat behind the band.

Despite the allure of the costly black pearls, few would argue that Takapoto is much like paradise. It is too low and too scrubby, with no dramatic mountains rising into the mists. Socially, there appeared to be even less to do on Takapoto than there would be, say, in Archer City. A place where the pigs are as skinny as the dogs is a place that's lucky to have those copra subsidies.

Still, the visit to Takapoto was redeemed, for me, by the women—numerous, large, and comfortable in their largeness, dignified but not solemn. The three children with us, Eduardo, Carolina, and Anna [. . .] clearly delighted them, as did their own children. The chubby little girl playing the castanets was very proud of herself, and her parents were just as proud. Very few men were in evidence; the women seemed to be in charge of the oyster farms. The men were mainly small fellows—they hung back, more interested in staying out of the way of the women than in mixing with the tourists.

By the time we straggled back to the little copra shed, the tide was thundering in. It was easy to see why the Tuamotus were sometimes called the Low Archipelago—Takapoto had no heights. The whaleboats came for us, but boarding them was tricky. Had my mother been with us I imagine she would have chosen life on Takapoto rather than to allow herself to be lifted by a large Polynesian male into the heaving boats.

At the craft shed one or two of the old women had been quietly sewing. It was mainly the younger women who dangled black pearls before the greedy eyes of the tourists. The old women sewed, a craft that seems to have almost disappeared from American life. In my youth all women sewed. My mother and sisters sewed constantly; they were very competent at it, and if they hadn't been would have had very few new clothes. In this age of malls it takes an effort to recall how little people in post-Depression America actually bought. For a time in my childhood we even made our own soap—it was one of the last things my grandmother turned her hand to. She was as proud of her soap as the little Tuamotuan girl was of her skill with the castanets. When my mother's sisters came to visit, which was often, what they mainly did was sew, comparing new patterns they had culled from magazines; they sewed dresses, blouses, and skirts while they visited.

I suppose the outbreak of unchecked consumerism that surged through America in the sixties was not unlike what happened in Tahiti when Captain Cook showed up in the islands and showed the natives cotton cloth. The islanders didn't need many clothes, and still don't, but they quickly came to prefer the soft cottons of Manchester to the tapa cloth they had been wearing, which was made from bark. At the sight of Western goods the islanders became crazed with desire, as crazed as the women of the *Aranui* had been when they saw those glistening pearls. So it was with my mother and her sisters. Once store-bought clothes became available, they ceased to sew; what had been a general skill became a specialized craft, one done elsewhere, not at home in the kitchen or the bedroom. In the last years of her life, if my mother needed a dress altered, she took the dress to an aged seamstress she knew, an old woman who still practiced a once universal skill. Sewing machines, once as common as coffeepots in American homes, are now mainly to be found in flea markets—they are artifacts of an earlier, more self reliant age.

from Joana McIntyre Varawa, *Changes in Latitude:
An Uncommon Anthropology* (1989)

Joana McIntyre Varawa spent her childhood in Chicago and Los Angeles before studying anthropology at a California university. After raising a family, she moved to Hawai'i, where she worked as a harbormaster. As her chosen home became increasingly overdeveloped she escaped for a six-month trip to Fiji, where she met her future husband, Malé Varawa, and joined life in his village. Hers is a record of the difficulties and the pleasures of the new life she made.

We have just boiled some water on the Primus and made Ovaltine.[22] It is the middle of the night, and we are sitting companionably by the light of a kerosene lamp at a low table next to one another. Malé is copying Fijian songs into his songbook with grave attention. I am writing and listening to the soft rain sounds on the *bola* of our newly finished *bure*.[23] We are, finally, in our own home together.

The tape is playing a sad Fijian song, a song about love and loss. "*Sa oti, sa oti* (it's finished, finished)." The song discomforts me somewhat because last week Malé and I had a crisis over a former girlfriend who was visiting in the village. I found a letter she wrote to him about an evening they had spent together while I thought he was drinking *yaqona*;[24] I remember that night for having awakened in the middle of it and having gone in search of Malé, who I assumed was still drinking grog somewhere. I prowled through the sleeping village hunting for a light or the soft murmur of voices that would tell me someone was awake, but I couldn't find Malé anywhere. My fear rose like a flood tide, and I woke Momo, who went through the village calling Malé. A few minutes later Malé stumbled out of the darkness with a barely believable story about falling asleep in a *bure* at the other side of the *koro*.[25] Then I found the letter.

There were tears, and threats from both of us, until we reached some sort of equilibrium and the promise from Malé that it was *sa oti* (finished). Now, listening to the sad words of this song, I read into his interest something ominous, and then remember that my meditation of the last two days has been on the subject of self-inflicted pain.

I am trying to understand how the mind heals itself. I believe that my body can heal itself if given the right conditions of care and cleanliness and time. I see what happens to my body when I scratch an inoffensive mosquito bite. By irritating what is already irritated, I inflame it. It then gets swollen and painful and forms a boil in the heat. The boil takes a long, long time to come to a head, a time of pain and discomfort. When it finally does come to a head, it discharges a disgusting load of blood and pus for days, slowly draining and crusting over. If I leave it alone and keep it covered so the flies can't eat on it, it will slowly heal, a process taking from three to six weeks. If I start scratching when it is healing, it will break out in an adjacent area, and I will have a new boil. If I had left the bite alone in the first place and kept my skin clean, there might never have been a boil.

Is my mind like that? Do I scratch and scratch at trouble, inflame the source? How do I control my memory so that it doesn't continually irritate me? Can my mind heal itself?

---

22. A chocolate and malt flavored hot drink, first patented in Britain in 1906.

23. *Bola:* building material made from woven palm leaves (Fijian); *bure:* traditional house (Fijian).

24. The Fijian equivalent for the narcotic root of the *Piper methysticum,* known elsewhere in the Pacific as *kava.*

25. *Koro:* village (Fijian).

Two days ago I went to Labasa by myself to shop and be alone for a few hours. I spent a night in the luxury of a hotel room, reading *Zen and the Art of Motorcycle Maintenance*,[26] trying to understand my relationship to Malé. Cut off from my own language and culture, my reactions to Malé's actions are very often touchy and emotional. Nothing around me seems to support my better sense of myself; my competence is all in another area. I have traveled around the world by myself and on Galoa I cannot find my way around in the bush; I get lost going to the garden. My independence needs telephones and cars and the materials of another culture. Here I am weak, unable, and, very often, unstable.

Reading that book reminded me of the usefulness of reason. My own language reassures me, for here I am constantly surrounded by foreign conversation that makes no sense and keeps me from having even a sensible interior monologue. Here in Fiji, much more even than at home, I need to think. And here, too often, I cannot, and do not, think.

Very often I am unhappy, and I blame my unhappiness on the conduct of others. My mind is constantly searching for flaws, for bites to scratch. If I have a lover, it is all the easier, because I can blame him for not loving me, or for not loving me enough, or for any number of possible bad things that cause my unhappiness.

In Labasa I thought about my relationship with Malé and confronted the fact that since I am often unhappy and he is most often happy, and since his happiness does not derive from me, but from his own sources, I am jealous. The only way I can get his attention is to blame him for my unhappiness and to point out his faults. This, of course, makes him unhappy, so I have succeeded in making both of us miserable. Then he rejects me, goes elsewhere to be happy, so I have proved that I was right about him—he doesn't love or understand me.

This is a classic no-win situation: I lose by winning. I see it more clearly with Malé than with any other lover, for he has little skill or interest in the complicated psychological game Americans often mistake for relationship; and instead of participating, he just gets dense and goes outside. Joking with cousins is infinitely preferable to trying to answer the elusive question—do you love me? I guess it is exactly Malé's inability to cooperate in this mental morass that makes me see it more clearly than I ever have before. It is a valuable lesson, perhaps one of the most important in my life at this time.

Maybe I instinctively understood this when I chose to come back to Fiji and try to build a life here in what sometimes seems like an incomprehensible—or worse—situation. Maybe I understood that it is necessary to take myself out of the known and perfected complications of my own culture and see myself in the stark mirror of an entirely different one.

I believe that if Malé and I can construct a love together—for it is defi-

---

26. A best-selling American novel of the mid-1970s by Robert M. Pirsig about a motorcyle-riding professor of Greek philosophy and his troubled son.

nitely a construction and not a gift—then, in fact, it will be love, and not the blind panic I have previously experienced under that name.

So here we are, at home in companionable quiet, listening to the rain continue its ministrations. Sonny, our dog, is a warm golden presence beside us, and Malé's beauty a dark shadow on the intricate brown-and-black-and-white pattern of the *tapa*.

Our *tabua*—heavy, polished, inscrutable—contains its own memories.[27] It hangs in the central place of pride and honor against the *tapa*, reminding me of my promise to marry. The crisis has passed, the tape has finished its sad song, and Malé has gone to the coolness of our bed. I turn down the lamp and follow him. It is time to sleep. "*Moce* (goodnight), Malé."

It rained for the rest of the night, and in the early morning, when I went out under the umbrella to pee, the sky and sea were the same gray mist, scarcely distinguishable. This is a rain that will last for days and days, a slow steady gray enveloping rain that says rest, be peaceful, there is nothing to do, there is no need to tear around in search, stay still and be warm and listen—for that is what is offered today.

Malé lets me sleep a long while after I come in from my early-morning peeing: a delicious, comfortable sleep. What was bad has passed between us, leaving a gentle warmth, a forgiving and closeness that did not exist before. The wheel has balanced and rolls smoothly.

Malé calls me, "Wake up, sweetie, here's your coffee," and my eyes open to his smiling happy face. The lamp is open and glowing. While I drink my coffee, Malé plays his guitar and sings. His voice is warm and rich, very beautiful.

I take a book and lie in the dim light of the *bure* door. Through the coarse woven *bola* of the makeshift shutter, I see the gray sea and sky. The bright colors of the boat, floating in the mist, remind me of the dream time. I read for a while, but the complications of thought bore me. On the ground just in front of me, growing almost inside the *bure,* is one tiny green plant brightening the rain-saturated sand. A drop falls on the plant, it trembles.

Inside the *bure* it is dark—from the gray sky, the closed doors. The typing table is a clutter of papers, dead ash of mosquito punk, cigarette butts, my notebooks and books, a silent radio, and the bright glow of the lantern. A spray of spider ginger buds that I picked a few days ago has blossomed; dead petals form a brown corolla around the bottom of the newly opened pink-white flowers. Their perfume is heavy and intoxicating. Malé's guitar leans against the *tapa;* a pile of newspaper-wrapped *yaqona* bundles waits on the new mat.

Our new *bure* is reassuringly beautiful. It is green and fresh, the logs fragrant, their bark unmarred by the intrusion of termites and spiders. I am

---

27. *Tabua:* ceremonial whale's tooth used in important ceremonies—in this case, betrothal (Fijian).

living inside a big fresh green basket, and it enchants me. The architecture of the *bure* is calming: the lean of the poles, the textures of the woven *bola* and mats, the human motion contained yet not frozen into the requirements of the straight edge. Here I am surrounded by the evident work of human hands in concert with the organic materials of this earth—coconut palm leaf, pandanus leaf tree trunks and saplings, vines. We are at home under the *baka* tree;[28] from the opening of the doorway I see its huge trunk, the hanging roots, the drifting leafy branches. I don't know where the *tëvoro*[29] goes in the rain. I suspect he, too, is gentled and resting.

Malé has gone into the bush with Toa to pick the breadfruit we will eat this afternoon. Before he left we talked about what we will have for dinner. We have not yet blessed this *bure* with a family feast, and today we shall. Malé will buy a chicken from a neighbor, kill, and clean it; and I will cook it on the Primus stove with potatoes and onions brought from Labasa. That is what today is for: to rest, to cook and eat with the family, and to be thankful for the life and for the love.   [. . .]

In the dark stifling night, Malé's *tëvoro* comes out. I wake under the mosquito net with a sharp pain in my side and ask Malé to massage it for me. He tells me that the pain is because I yell at him. His *tëvoro* is causing the pain.

"It is because when you yell I only laugh at you; I don't hit you. If I hit you, I would kill you, so I just wait. I know that something bad will happen to you."

This is better than silence. At least Malé is talking about what upsets him. I want to know more; I calm myself to listen.

"Is it like your aunty's pain?"

"Yes."

"Because of the Fijian thing, because I am not acting like a Fijian?"

Silence.

"You have had a pain in your stomach for a year or more. Is it because you are doing something wrong?"

"No, my pain is different. But your pain is from my *tëvoro*. So I just wait."

A low quiet wave comes in, cleans my spirit, a release.

"Do you really hate me?"

"Yes."

"Did you ever love me?"

No answer.

I go out and lie under the *baka* tree, the dark leaves strain the starlight, glints of distance shimmer among the leaves. This is something I can understand. Hatred is an easier emotion than love, and Malé's *tëvoro* an honest participant in our relationship. Paradoxically it brings us closer. Hatred in the air is harmless. Exposure kills it. Hatred can live only in the remote cor-

28. *Baka:* banyan tree (Fijian).
29. *Tëvoro:* bad spirit (Fijian).

ners of the soul, feeding on itself. We are finally beginning to communicate. We are bridging a gap deeper than differences in language, a deep-sea trench that lies between our cultures.

We are trying to construct a marriage. A delicate structure wrought in time. We can harmonize our cultural differences if we can appreciate them. Culture is a garment that clothes the soul. We may never be able, or even want, to exchange our cloaks, but what matters is the perception of each other's realities, even if the reality is hatred. I know the hatred will pass and come again, so will love; it is inevitable. I do not fear Male's *tëvoro*, only his remoteness. A tiny corner has been lifted, a passageway I wish to follow.

A while ago, bewildered by our failures, I asked Malé's brother-in-law Nacã to help me try to understand the Fijian man. He told me that nothing is hidden; the emotions flow freely; there is no evasion. But he also told me that the head of man is sacred, *tabu,* and that it would be years before Malé yielded his head to me. You must change, said Nacã. You have the experience, the education, the ability to change. Malé cannot change. He is of the village, of the *vanua,*[30] and if he were to change, he would be lost, neither European nor Fijian, robbed of his strength, of his way.

I know that I cannot go back; I have opened something that I must complete; I can no longer go back to my old ways, the easy superficial satisfactions of status, the fancy food and clothes that soon become boring, the repetitive relationships that I flee from as soon as they become difficult or demanding. I know that I must learn to replace my huffy pridefulness when someone criticizes me or tells me what to do with a more substantial sense of my own dignity and value.

I also know that I love Malé, that I respect and appreciate his character, the self-confidence that derives from his being secure in his culture and not questioning it. Ever since my early education in anthropology led me into questioning my own cultural values, into seeing them as one cluster of many possible responses to the problem of figuring out how to live gracefully through human life, I have been confused and unstable. Fantasy was my response, and now I have led myself to the testing ground of my fantasies. It is unlikely that I can ever believe in fantasy again.

SOURCES

Paul Gauguin, *Noa Noa,* ed. Nicholas Wadley, trans. Jonathan Griffin (London: Phaidon, 1985).
Jack London, *The Red One* (New York: Grosset and Dunlap, 1918).
Julian Evans, *Transit of Venus: Travels in the Pacific* (London: Secker and Warburg, 1992). Reproduced by permission of A. P. Watt, Ltd., on behalf of the author.

---

30. *Vanua:* as Varawa defines it, "land, region, place; a physical and mystical union of land, sea, and chief" (present in many Pacific languages).

Larry McMurtry, *Paradise* (New York: Simon and Schuster, 2001). © 2001 by Larry McMurtry. Reproduced by permission of the Simon and Schuster Adult Publishing Group.

Joana McIntyre Varawa, *Changes in Latitude: An Uncommon Anthropology* (New York: Atlantic Monthly Press, 1989). Reproduced by permission of the author.

FURTHER READING

For "decolonization" see Muriel E. Chamberlain, *The Longman Companion to European Decolonisation in the Twentieth Century* (London: Longman, 1998); Roger C. Thompson, *The Pacific Basin since 1945: A History of the Foreign Relations of the Asian, Australasian and American Rim States and the Pacific Islands* (London: Longman, 1994), chaps. 4 ("Independence for some Pacific Islands, 1945–1980") and 8 ("Conflicts and Coups in the Islands since 1980"); Stephen Henningham, *The Pacific Island States: Security and Sovereignty in the Post–Cold War World* (New York: St. Martin's, 1995); and K. R. Howe, Robert C. Kiste, and Brij Lal, *Tides of History: The Pacific Islands in the Twentieth Century* (Honolulu: University of Hawai'i Press, 1994). Issues of cultural and political authenticity left in the wake of this process are discussed in Roger Keesing, "Creating the Past: Custom and Identity in the Contemporary Pacific," *Contemporary Pacific* 1:1–2 (Spring and Fall 1989); Jocelyn Linnekin, "On the Theory and Politics of Cultural Construction in the Pacific," *Oceania* 62 (1992); and Peter Larmour, "A Foreign Flower? Democracy in the South Pacific," *Pacific Studies* 117:1 (March 1994).

Paul McGuire's *Westward the Course: The New World of Oceania* (Melbourne: Oxford University Press, 1942) is the last book to imagine a Western imperium stretching from Hawai'i to Malaysia. For writers reporting on the later stages of Pacific colonialism or decolonization, see David Bradley, *No Place to Hide, 1946–1984* (Hanover: University of New England Press, 1983); Wilfred Burchett, *Pacific Treasure Island: New Caledonia* (Melbourne: Cheshire, 1941); John Wesley Coulter, *The Pacific Dependencies of the United States* (New York: Macmillan, 1957); the excellent book by J. C. Furnas, *Anatomy of Paradise: Hawaii and the Islands of the South Seas* (New York: William Sloane, 1946); David L. Hanlon, *Remaking Micronesia: Discourses over Development in a Pacific Territory, 1944–1982* (Honolulu: University of Hawai'i Press, 1998); P. F. Kluge, *The Edge of Paradise: America in Micronesia* (New York: Random House, 1991); E. J. Kahn Jr., *A Reporter in Micronesia* (New York: Norton, 1966); Scott L. Malcolmson, *Tuturani: A Political Journey in the Pacific Islands* (London: Hamish Hamilton, 1990); Joseph C. Meredith, *A Handful of Emeralds: On Patrol with the "Hanna" in the Postwar Pacific* (Annapolis: Naval Institute Press, 1995); David Nevin, *The American Touch in Micronesia* (New York: Norton, 1977); and Robert Trumbull, *Paradise in Trust: A Report on the Americans in Micronesia, 1946–1958* (New York: William Sloane, 1959).

For the nuclear Pacific, see Stewart Firth, *Nuclear Playground* (Sydney: Allen and Unwin, 1987).

For theoretical studies of tourism, see Dennison Nash, *Anthropology of Tourism* (London: Pergamon, 1996); Valene L. Smith, ed., *Hosts and Guests: The Anthropology of Tourism* (Philadelphia: University of Pennsylvania Press, 1989), which has essays on Tonga and the Polynesian Cultural Center in Hawai'i; and John Urry, *The Tourist Gaze: Leisure and Travel in Contemporary Societies* (London: Sage, 1990). Regional studies include Ngaire Douglas, *They Came for Savages: 100 Years of Tourism in Melanesia* (Lismore, NSW: Southern Cross University Press, 1996); C. Michael Hall and Stephen J. Page, eds., *Tourism in the Pacific: Issues and Cases* (London: International Thomson Business Press, 1996); and DiAnne Reid Ross and Bryan H. Farell, *Source Materials for Pacific Tourism* (Santa Cruz: Center for Pacific Studies, University of California, 1975).

For travel writing as a literary genre, see Peter Hulme and Tim Youngs, eds., *The Cambridge Companion to Travel Writing* (Cambridge: Cambridge University Press, 2002); and Barbara Korte, *English Travel Writing from Pilgrimages to Postcolonial Expeditions* (London: Palgrave, 2000).

For the literature of Pacific disillusion, see W. F. Alder, *The Island of Vanishing Men: A Narrative of Adventure in Cannibal-Land* (1922), an early example of antagonistic skepticism; J. Macmillan Brown, *The Riddle of the Pacific* (1924), on Easter Island as the last remaining fragment of a drowned Polynesian continent; Mel Kernahan, *White Savages in the South Seas* (1995); Louis Nowra, *Abaza: A Modern Encyclopaedia* (2001), an unusual and unforgiving novel of a failed Pacific Island state; T. L. Richards, *White Man, Brown Woman* (1932); and Alec Waugh, *Hot Countries* (1930). Two twentieth-century British authors with special links to the region are Rupert Brooke (see *Collected Poems* [1918] and *Letters from America* [1916]) and Somerset Maugham (see *The Moon and Sixpence* [1919] and *The Trembling of a Leaf* [1921]). Classic travel literature is provided by Isabella Bird, *The Hawaiian Archipelago: Six Months among the Palm Groves, Coral Reefs, and Volcanoes of the Sandwich Islands* (1875); and Mark Twain, *Following the Equator* (1897). (See also A. Grove Day, ed., *Mark Twain's Letters from Hawaii* [1967].) Latter-day travel books include Gavin Bell, *Tusitala: Travels in the Pacific after Robert Louis Stevenson* (1994); John Dyson, *The South Seas Dream: An Adventure in Paradise* (1982); Miles Hordern, *Voyaging the Pacific: In Search of the South* (2002); Tony Horwitz, *Blue Latitudes: Boldly Going Where Captain Cook Has Gone Before* (2003); Michael Moran, *Beyond the Coral Sea: Travels in the Old Empires of the South-West Pacific* (2003); Ian Rankin, *Dead Man's Chest: Travels after Robert Louis Stevenson* (1987); and Gavin Young, *Slow Boats Home* (1985).

For Gauguin, see Gavan Daws, *A Dream of Islands: Voyages of Self-Discovery in the South Seas* (New York: Norton, 1980), chap. 6, "Paul Gauguin"; David Sweetman, *Paul Gauguin: A Complete Life* (London: Hodder and Stoughton, 1995); and the highly recommended Stephen Eisenman, *Gauguin's Skirt* (London: Thames and Hudson, 1997). On Jack London's South Seas see his *The Cruise of the "Snark"* (1911) and *Tales of the Pacific*, ed. Andrew Sinclair (London: Penguin, 1989); and David A. Moreland, "The Quest that Failed: Jack London's Last Tales of the South Seas," *Pacific Studies* 8:1 (Fall 1984).

WORKS CITED

Adams, Henry Brooks. 1968. *Tahiti: Memoirs of Arii Taimai*. Ridgewood: Gregg Press.

Alexander, Gilchrist. 1927. *From the Middle Temple to the South Seas*. London: John Murray.

Angas, George French. 1847. *Savage Life and Scenes in Australia and New Zealand*. London: Smith, Elder.

———. 1866. *Polynesia: A Popular Description of the Physical Features, Inhabitants, Natural History, and Productions of the Islands of the Pacific*. London: Society for the Propagation of Christian Knowledge.

Anon. 1720a. *Battle of the Bubbles, Shewing their Several Constitutions, Alliances, Policies, and Wars; from their First Suddain Rise, to their Late Speedy Decay*. London.

———. 1720b. *Exchange-Alley: or, the Stock-Jobber turn'd Gentleman . . . a Tragi-Comical Farce*. London.

"Asterisk" (pseud. Robert Fletcher). 1923. *Isles of Illusion*. London: Constable.

Baden-Powell, B. F. S. 1892. *In Savage Islands and Settled Lands: Malaysia, Australasia, and Polynesia, 1888–1891*. London: Richard Bentley.

Banks, Joseph. 1962. *The Endeavour Journal*. Ed. J. C. Beaglehole. 2 vols. Sydney: Angus and Robertson.

Batten, Charles L. 1990. "Literary Responses to the Eighteenth-Century Voyages." In Derek Howse, ed., *Background to Discovery: Pacific Exploration from Dampier to Cook*, 128–159. Berkeley: University of California Press.

Baudet, Henri. 1965. *Paradise on Earth: Some Thoughts on European Images of Non-European Man*. New Haven: Yale University Press.

Baudin, Nicolas. 1974. *The Journal of Post Captain Nicolas Baudin, Commander-in-Chief of the Corvettes* Géographe *and* Naturaliste, *Assigned by Order of the Government to a Voyage of Discovery*. Trans. Christine Cornell. Adelaide: Libraries Board of South Australia.

Bellingshausen, Thaddeus. 1945. *The Voyage of Captain Bellingshausen to the Antarctic Seas 1819–1821*. Trans. Frank Debenham. 2 vols. London: Hakluyt Society.

Bitterli, Urs. 1989. *Cultures in Conflict: Encounters between European and Non-European Cultures, 1492–1800*. Trans. Ritchie Robertson. Cambridge: Polity Press.

Blumenbach, Johann Friedrich. 1865. *Anthropological Treatises*. Trans. and ed. Thomas Bendyshe. London: Longman.

Boas, Franz. 1974. "The History of Anthropology." In Regna Darnell, ed., *Readings in the History of Anthropology*, 260–273. New York: Harper and Row.

Boldrewood, Rolf. 1899. *War to the Knife: or, Tangata Maori*. London: Macmillan.

Bougainville, Louis Antoine de. 1772. *A Voyage Round the World Performed by Order of His Most Christian Majesty, in the Years 1766, 1767, 1768, and 1769*. Trans. Johann Reinhold Forster. London.

Brown, J. Macmillan. 1927. *Peoples and Problems of the Pacific*. 2 vols. London: T. Fisher Unwin.

Buckley, Jerome Hamilton. 1966. *The Triumph of Time: A Study of Victorian Concepts of Time, History, Progress, and Decadence*. Cambridge, MA: Harvard University Press.

Buffon, George Louis Lecler, Comte de. 1834. *A Natural History, General and Particular, Containing the History and Theory of the Earth. . . .* Trans. William Smellie. 2 vols. London: Thomas Kelly.

Burder, George. 1795. "Address to the Serious and Zealous Professors of the Gospel." *Evangelical Magazine*, April, 160–163.

Burney, James. 1803. *A Chronological History of the Discoveries in the South Sea or Pacific Ocean*. 5 vols. London: Hansard.

Callander, John, ed. 1766. *Terra Australis Cognita: Or, Voyages to the Terra Australis, or Southern Hemisphere, during the Sixteenth, Seventeenth, and Eighteenth Centuries*. 3 vols. Edinburgh.

Camoëns, Luis de. 1963. *The Lusiad, or Portugals*. Trans. Richard Fanshawe. 1655. London: Centaur Press.

Campbell, Frederick Alexander. 1873. *A Year in the New Hebrides, Loyalty Islands, and New Caledonia*. Geelong, Vic.: George Mercer.

Campbell, I. C. 1990. *A History of the Pacific Islands*. St. Lucia: University of Queensland Press.

Carlquist, Sherwin. 1965. *Island Life: A Natural History of the Islands of the World*. New York: Natural History Press.

Chambers, Robert. 1844. *Vestiges of the Natural History of Creation*. London: John Churchill.

Chappell, David A. 1995. "Active Agents versus Passive Victims: Decolonized History or Problematic Paradigm?" *Contemporary Pacific* 7:2 (Fall), 303–326.

Churchill, A., and J. Churchill. 1704. *A Collection of Voyages and Travels*. 4 vols. London.

Churchward, William. 1887. *My Consulate in Samoa: A Record of Four Years' Sojourn in the Navigators Islands*. London: R. Bentley.

Codrington, Robert. 1885. *The Melanesian Languages*. Oxford: Oxford University Press.

———. 1891. *The Melanesians: Studies in their Anthropology and Folklore*. Oxford: Oxford University Press.

Cook, James. 1955–1967. *Journals*. Ed. J. C. Beaglehole. 4 vols. London: Hakluyt Society.

Cook, James, and James King. 1785. *A Voyage to the Pacific Ocean . . . in the Years 1776, 1777, 1778, 1779, and 1780*. 4 vols. London: John Fielding.

Coombe, Florence. 1911. *Islands of Enchantment: Many-Sided Melanesia.* London: Macmillan.

Coote, Walter. 1883. *The Western Pacific. Being a Description of the Goups of Islands to the North and East of the Australian Continent.* London: Sampson Low.

Copans, Jean, and Jean Jamin, eds. 1994. *Aux origines de l'anthropologie française.* Paris: Jean-Michel Place.

Cornell, Christine. 1965. *Questions Relating to Nicolas Baudin's Australian Expedition, 1800–1804.* Adelaide: Library Board of South Australia.

Cowles, Virginia. 1960. *The Great Swindle: The Story of the South Sea Bubble.* London: Collins.

Cuvier, Georges. 1817. *Essay on the Theory of the Earth.* Trans. Robert Jameson. Edinburgh: Blackwood.

Dalrymple, Alexander. 1767. *An Account of the Discoveries Made in the South Pacifick Ocean Previous to 1764.* London.

Dampier, William. 1927. *A New Voyage round the World.* Ed. Albert Gray. London: Argonaut Press.

Darwin, Charles. 1960. *Voyage of the* Beagle. 2nd edn. 1845. London: J. M. Dent.

Darwin, Francis, ed. 1909. *The Foundation of the Origin of Species: Two Essays Written in 1842 and 1844 by Charles Darwin.* Cambridge: Cambridge University Press.

Defoe, Daniel. 1979. "The Anatomy of Exchange Alley: or a System of Stock-Jobbing" (1719). In Laura Ann Curtis, ed., *The Versatile Defoe: An Anthology of Uncollected Writings by Daniel Defoe,* 263–275. London: George Prior.

Degérando, Joseph-Marie. 1969. *The Observation of Savage Peoples.* Trans. and ed. F. C. T. Moore. London: Routledge and Kegan Paul.

Denoon, Donald, with Stewart Firth, Jocelyn Linnekin, Malama Meleisa, and Karen Nero, eds. 1997. *The Cambridge History of the Pacific Islands.* Cambridge: Cambridge University Press.

Diamond, Stanley, ed. 1980. *Anthropology: Ancestors and Heirs.* The Hague: Mouton.

Dilke, Charles Wentworth. 1869. *Greater Britain.* London: Macmillan.

Douglas, Bronwen. 1998. *Across the Great Divide: Journeys in History and Anthropology.* Amsterdam: Harwood Academic Publishers.

Dulles, Foster Rhea. 1938. *America in the Pacific: A Century of Expansion.* 2nd edn. Boston: Houghton Mifflin.

Dunmore, John. 1979. "Rousseau's Noble Savage: A New Zealand Case History." In Walter Veit, ed., *Captain James Cook: Image and Impact. South Seas Discoveries and the World of Letters,* vol. 2: *The Pacific Syndrome: Conditions and Consequences,* 160–172. Melbourne: Hawthorn Press.

Duyker, Edward. 1998. *Nature's Argonaut: Daniel Solander 1733–1782.* Melbourne: Miegunyah Press.

Eisler, William. 1995. *The Furthest Shore: Images of Terra Australis from the Middle Ages to Captain Cook.* Cambridge: Cambridge University Press.

Ellis, William. 1829. *Polynesian Researches, during a Residence of Nearly Six Years in the South Sea Islands.* 2 vols. London: Fisher, Son, and Jackson.

——. 1831. *A Vindication of the South-Sea Missions from the Misrepresentations of O. von Kotzebue, Captain in the Russian Navy.* London: F. Westley and A. H. Davis.

Evans, Julian. 1992. *Transit of Venus: Travels in the Pacific.* London: Secker and Warburg.

Ferdon, Edwin N. 1968. "Polynesian Origins." In Andrew Vayda, ed., *Peoples and Cultures of the Pacific,* 95–111. New York: Natural History Press.

Finney, Ben. 1993. "James Cook and the European Discovery of Polynesia." In Robin Fisher and Hugh Johnston, eds., *From Maps to Metaphors: The Pacific World of George Vancouver*, 19–34. Vancouver: University of British Columbia Press.

Fleurieu, Charles P. C. 1801. *A Voyage Round the World 1790–1792, Performed by Étienne Marchand*. 2 vols. London: Longman.

Flinders, Matthew. 1814. *A Voyage to Terra Australis . . . in the Years 1801, 1802, and 1803*. 2 vols. London: G. and W. Nicol.

Fox, Frank. 1912. *Problems of the Pacific*. London: Williams and Norgate.

———. 1913. *Oceania*. London: Adam and Charles Black.

———. 1928. *The Mastery of the Pacific: Can the British and the United States Agree?* London: John Lane.

Fredrickson, George M. 1981. *White Supremacy: A Comparative Study in American and South African History*. New York: Oxford University Press.

Frow, John. 1991. "Tourism and the Semiotics of Nostalgia." *October* 57:123–152.

Furnas, J. C. 1946. *Anatomy of Paradise: Hawaii and the Islands of the South Seas*. New York: William Sloane.

Garagnon, Jean. 1982. "French Imaginary Voyages to the Austral Lands in the Seventeenth and Eighteenth Centuries." In Helen Wallis et al., *Australia and the European Imagination*, 87–105. Canberra: Humanities Research Centre.

Gordon, Thomas, and J. Trenchard. 1721. *A Collection of All the Political Letters in the "London Journal," to December 17, Inclusive, 1720*. London.

Gregory, Jeremy, and John Stevenson. 2000. *Longman Companion to Britain in the Eighteenth Century*. London: Longman.

Grove, Richard H. 1995. *Green Imperialism: Colonial Expansion, Tropical Island Edens and the Origins of Environmentalism*. Cambridge: Cambridge University Press.

Gunson, Niel. 1978. *Messengers of Grace: Evangelical Missionaries in the South Seas 1797–1860*. Oxford: Oxford University Press.

Guppy, Henry Brougham. 1887. *The Solomon Islands and Their Natives*. London: Swan Sonnenschein.

Haddon, A. C. 1898. *The Study of Man*. London: John Murray.

———. 1910. *History of Anthropology*. London: Watts.

Hailey, Foster. 1944. *Pacific Battle Line*. New York: Macmillan.

Harrisson, T. H. 1936. "Living with the People of Malekula." *Geographical Journal* 88:97–127.

Haweis, Thomas. n.d. "Autobiography," vol. 1, 1773–1796. Mitchell Library (Sydney) MSS B1176.

———. 1795. "The Very Probable Success of a Proper Mission to the South Sea Islands." *Evangelical Magazine*, July, 261–270.

Hawkesworth, John. 1773. *An Account of the Voyages undertaken by the order of his present Majesty for making Discoveries in the Southern Hemisphere. . . .* 3 vols. London.

Herder, Johann Gottfried von. 1800. *Outlines of a Philosophy of the History of Man*. Trans. T. Churchill. London: J. Johnson.

Hersey, John. 1943. *Into the Valley: A Skirmish of the Marines*. London: Hodder and Stoughton.

Hobbes, Thomas. 1968. *Leviathan*. Ed. C. B. MacPherson. Harmondsworth: Penguin.

Hodgen, Margaret. 1964. *Early Anthropology in the Sixteenth and Seventeenth Centuries*. Philadelphia: University of Pennsylvania Press.

Horace. 1644. *All the Odes and Epodes of Horace.* Trans. Henry Rider. London.

Howe, Kerry. 1984. *Where the Waves Fall: A New South Sea Islands History from First Settlement to Colonial Rule.* Honolulu: University of Hawaiʻi Press.

———. 1993. "The Intellectual Discovery and Exploration of Polynesia." In Robin Fisher and Hugh Johnston, eds., *From Maps to Metaphors: The Pacific World of George Vancouver,* 245–262. Vancouver: University of British Columbia Press.

———. 2000. *Nature, Culture, and History: The "Knowing" of Oceania.* Honolulu: University of Hawaiʻi Press.

Howitt, William. 1838. *Colonization and Christianity: A Popular History of the Treatment of the Natives by Europeans in All Their Colonies.* London: Longman.

Hughes, Miranda. 1988. "Tall Tales or True Stories?: Baudin, Péron, and the Tasmanians, 1802." In Roy MacLeod and Philip F. Rehbock, eds., *Nature in Its Greatest Extent: Western Science in the Pacific,* 65–86. Honolulu: University of Hawaiʻi Press.

Humboldt, Alexander von. 1849. *Cosmos: A Sketch of a Physical Description of the Universe.* Trans. E. C. Otté. 4 vols. London: Bohn.

Hunter, John. 1793. *An Historical Journal of the Transactions at Port Jackson and Norfolk Island.* London.

Hutcheson, Archibald. 1720a. "The Conclusion." In *A Collection of Calculations and Remarks Relating to the South-Sea Scheme and Stock, which Have been Already Published,* 117–119. London.

———. 1720b. "The Second Postscript." In *A Collection of Calculations and Remarks Relating to the South-Sea Scheme and Stock, which Have been Already Published,* 89–91. London.

———. 1720c. "Several Calculations and Remarks Relating to the South-Sea Scheme and the Value of that Stock." In *A Collection of Calculations and Remarks Relating to the South-Sea Scheme and Stock, which Have been Already Published,* 37–77. London.

Hynes, Samuel. 1988. *Flights of Passage.* New York: Pocket Books.

———. 1998. *The Soldiers' Tale: Bearing Witness to Modern War.* London: Pimlico.

Jack-Hinton, Colin. 1969. *The Search for the Islands of Solomon.* Oxord: Oxford University Press.

Johnson, J. W. 1982. "The Utopian Impulse and Southern Lands." In Helen Wallis et al., *Australia and the European Imagination,* 41–58. Canberra: Humanities Research Centre.

Johnston, Harry, et al. n.d. [1902]. *The Living Races of Mankind.* 2 vols. London: Hutchinson.

Jones, Rhys. 1988. "Images of Natural Man." In Jacqueline Bonnemains, Elliott Forsyth, and Bernard Smith, eds., *Baudin in Australian Waters: The Artwork of the French Voyage of Discovery to the Southern Lands 1800–1804,* 35–64. Melbourne: Oxford University Press.

Kant, Immanuel. 1974. *Anthropology from a Pragmatic Point of View.* Trans. and ed. Mary J. McGregor. The Hague: Martinus Nijhoff.

Keate, George. 1788. *An Account of the Pelew Islands.* London.

Keesing, Felix M. 1945. *The South Seas in the Modern World.* Rev. edn. New York: John Day.

Kernan, Alvin. 1994. *Crossing the Line: A Bluejacket's World War II Odyssey.* Annapolis: Naval Institute Press.

Knox, Robert. 1850. *The Races of Men: A Fragment.* Philadelphia: Lea and Blanchard.

Koerner, Lisbet. 1996. "Carl Linnaeus in his Time and Place." In N. Jardine, J. A. Secord, and E. C. Spary, eds., *Cultures of Natural History*, 145–164. Cambridge: Cambridge University Press.

Kotzebue, Otto von. 1830. *A New Voyage Round the World, in the Years 1823, 24, 25, and 26.* London: H. Colburn and R. Bentley.

Krieger, Herbert W. 1943. *Island Peoples of the Western Pacific: Micronesia and Melanesia.* Washington, D.C.: Smithsonian Institution.

Kuper, Adam. 1980. "Great Britain: Functionalism at Home. A Question of Theory." In Stanley Diamond, ed., *Anthropology: Ancestors and Heirs*, 293–315. The Hague: Mouton.

Lafarge, John. 1912. *Reminiscences of the South Seas.* New York: Doubleday.

Lambert, S. M. 1942. *A Doctor in Paradise.* London: J. M. Dent.

Latham, Robert Gordon. 1851. *The Ethnology of the British Colonies and Dependencies.* London: John van Voorst.

Lawrence, William. 1848. *Lectures on Comparative Anatomy, Physiology, Zoology, and the Natural History of Man.* 9th edn. London: Henry G. Bohn.

Lenwood, Frank. 1917. *Pastels from the Pacific.* London: Oxford University Press.

Lévi-Strauss, Claude. 1976. *Tristes Tropiques.* Trans. John and Doreen Weightman. Harmondsworth: Penguin.

Lewis, Roy. 1964. Introduction to Paul Giraudoux, *Suzanne et le Pacifique.* London: University of London Press.

London Missionary Society. 1795. *Sermons, Preached in London, at the formation of the Missionary Society, Sept. 22. 23. 24, 1795: to which are prefixed memorials respecting the establishment and first attempts of that society.* London.

———. 1796a. "A Farewel Letter from the Directors of the Missionary Society, to the Missionaries Going Forth to the Heathen in the South-Sea Islands, August 9 1796." *Evangelical Magazine*, September, 353–359.

———. 1796b. *Four Sermons Preached . . . at the Second General Meeting of the Missionary Society. . . . To which are prefixed, the proceedings of the Meeting, and the report of the Directors, etc.* London.

Love, John. 1796. *Sermons Preached on Public Occasions, with Fifteen Addresses to the People of Otaheite.* London.

Lovejoy, Arthur O. 1964. *The Great Chain of Being: A Study of the History of an Idea.* Cambridge, MA: Harvard University Press.

Lovejoy, Arthur, and George Boas. 1935. *Primitivism and Related Ideas in Antiquity.* Baltimore: Johns Hopkins University Press.

Lovett, Richard. 1899. *The History of the Missionary Society 1795–1895.* 2 vols. Henry Frowde.

Lucian. 1927. *The True Historie.* Trans. Francis Hickes. London: The Golden Cockerel Press.

Luke, Harry. 1945. *Britain and the South Seas.* London: Longman.

Macaulay, Thomas Babington. 1850. *Critical and Historical Essays Contributed to the "Edinburgh Review."* London: Longman.

MacCannell, Dean. 1976. *The Tourist: A New Theory of the Leisure Class.* New York: Schocken.

Mackellar, C. D. 1912. *Scented Isles and Coral Gardens: Torres Straits, German New Guinea, and the Dutch East Indies.* London: John Murray.

MacLeod, Roy, and Philip F. Rehbock, eds. 1988. *Nature in its Greatest Extent: Western Science in the Pacific.* Honolulu: University of Hawai'i Press.

Malefijt, Annemarie de Waal. 1974. *Images of Man: A History of Anthropological Thought*. New York: Knopf.

Malinowski, Bronislaw. 1922. *Argonauts of the Western Pacific*. London: Routledge and Kegan Paul.

———. 1967. *A Diary in the Strict Sense of the Term*. Trans. Norbert Guterman. New York: Harcourt Brace / London: Routledge and Kegan Paul.

Manchester, William. 1979. *Goodbye, Darkness: A Memoir of the Pacific*. Boston: Little, Brown.

Marshall, P. J. and Glyndwr Williams. 1982. *The Great Map of Mankind: British Perceptions of the World in the Age of the Enlightenment*. London: J. M. Dent.

Martyr, Weston. 1941. *The Wandering Years*. Edinburgh: Blackwood.

McDowell, Nancy. 1991. *The Mundugumor: From the Field Notes of Margaret Mead and Reo Fortune*. Washington, D.C.: Smithsonian Institution Press.

McWilliam, Candia. 1994. *Debateable Land*. London: Bloomsbury.

Mead, Margaret. 1973. *Blackberry Winter: My Earlier Years*. London: Angus and Robertson.

———. 1977. *Letters from the Field 1925–1975*. New York: Harper and Row.

Melville, Herman. 1996. *Typee*. Ed. Ruth Blair. Oxford: Oxford University Press.

Menard, H. W. 1968. *Islands*. New York: Scientific American.

Meredith, Joseph C. 1995. *A Handful of Emeralds: On Patrol with the "Hanna" in the Postwar Pacific*. Annapolis: Naval Institute Press.

Merivale, Herman. 1861. *Lectures on Colonization and Colonies, Delivered before the University of Oxford, 1839, 1840, and 1841*. London: Longman.

Montaigne, Michel de. 1991. *Complete Essays*. Trans. M. A. Screech. London: Penguin.

Montesquieu, Charles de Secondat, Baron de. 1989. *The Spirit of the Laws*. Trans. and ed. Anne M. Cohler et al. Cambridge: Cambridge University Press.

Moorehead, Alan. 1966. *The Fatal Impact: An Account of the Invasion of the South Pacific 1767–1840*. London: Hamish Hamilton.

Mordaunt, Elinor. 1927. *The Further Venture Book*. New York: Century.

More, Thomas. 1908. *Utopia*. Trans. Ralph Robinson. 1556. London: Macmillan.

Morton, Peter. 1984. *The Vital Science: Biology and the Literary Imagination, 1860–1900*. London: Allen and Unwin.

Moss, Frederick J. 1889. *Through Islands and Atolls in the Great South Sea*. London: Sampson, Low, Searle, and Rivingstone.

Mosse, George L. *Toward the Final Solution: A History of European Racism*. London: J. M. Dent.

Mulvaney, D. J. 1985. "The Darwinian Perspective." In Ian Donaldson and Tamsin Donaldson, eds., *Seeing the First Australians*, 68–75. Sydney: Allen and Unwin.

Nisbet, Robert. 1980. *History of the Idea of Progress*. New York: Basic Books.

Novak, Maximilian E. 2001. *Daniel Defoe: Master of Fictions*. Oxford: Oxford University Press.

O'Brien, Frederick. n.d. *White Shadows in the South Seas*. London: Hodder and Stoughton.

Oliver, Douglas. 1962. *The Pacific Islands*. Cambridge, MA: Harvard University Press.

Olmsted, Francis Allyn. 1841. *Incidents of a Whaling Voyage: to Which are Added Observations on the Scenery, Manners and Customs, and Missionary Stations of the Sandwich and Society Islands*. New York: Appleton.

Pagden, Anthony. 1993. *European Encounters with the New World: From Renaissance to Romanticism.* New Haven: Yale University Press.

Parkinson, Richard. 1999. *Thirty Years in the South Seas: Land and People, Customs and Traditions in the Bismarck Archipelago and on the German Solomon Islands.* Trans. John Dennison and J. Peter White. Bathurst, NSW: Crawford House.

Peacock, James L. 2001. *The Anthropological Lens: Harsh Light, Soft Focus.* 2nd edn. Cambridge: Cambridge University Press.

Peck, William M. 1997. *A Tidy Universe of Islands.* Honolulu: Mutual Publishing.

Pembroke, George Robert Charles Herbert, Earl of, and George Henry Kingsley ["The Earl and the Doctor"]. 1911. *South Sea Bubbles.* London: Macmillan.

Péron, François. 1809. *A Voyage of Discovery to the Southern Hemisphere, Performed by Order of the Emperor Napoleon, During the Years 1801, 1802, 1803, and 1804.* London.

Petrie, W. M. Flinders, ed. 1895. *Egyptian Tales, Translated from the Paypri: First Series, Fourth to Twelfth Dynasty.* London: Methuen.

"Pindar, Peter." 1774. *Otaheite: A Poem.* London.

Plomley, N. J. B. 1983. *The Baudin Expedition and the Tasmanian Aborigines, 1802.* Hobart: Blubber Head Press.

Pope, Alexander. 1966. *Poetical Works.* Ed. Herbert Davis. Oxford: Oxford University Press.

——. 2000. *Selected Letters.* Ed. Howard Erskine-Hill. Oxford: Oxford University Press.

Powdermaker, Hortense. 1967. *Stranger and Friend: The Way of an Anthropologist.* London: Secker and Warburg.

Prichard, James Cowles. 1973. *Researches into the Physical History of Man.* Ed. George W. Stocking Jr. Chicago: University of Chicago Press.

Pritchard, W. T. 1866. *Polynesian Reminiscences or, Life in the South Pacific Islands.* London: Chapman and Hall.

Rannie, Douglas. 1912. *My Adventures among South Sea Cannibals: An Account of the Experiences and Adventures of a Government Official among the Natives of Oceania.* London: Seeley, Service.

Rivers, W. H. R. 1914. *The History of Melanesian Society.* 2 vols. Cambridge: Cambridge University Press.

Roberts, Stephen J. 1927. *Population Problems of the Pacific.* London: George Routledge.

Roger, Jacques. 1980. "The Living World." In G. S. Rousseau and Roy Porter, eds., *The Ferment of Knowledge: Studies in the Historiography of Eighteenth-Century Science,* 255–283. Cambridge: Cambridge University Press.

Romilly, Hugh Hastings. 1885. *From My Verandah in New Guinea: Sketches and Traditions.* London: David Nutt.

Rousseau, Jean-Jacques. 1979. *Emile or On Education.* Trans. and ed. Allan Bloom. New York: Basic Books.

——. 1996. *Discourse on Inequality.* Trans. Franklin Philip. Oxford: Oxford University Press.

Russell, M. 1849. *Polynesia: A History of the South Sea Islands, Including New Zealand.* London: Thomas Nelson.

Sack, Peter, and Dymphna Clark, eds. 1983. *Eduard Hernsheim: South Sea Merchant.* Boroko, New Guinea: Institute of Papua New Guinea Studies.

Sacks, Oliver. 1996. *The Island of the Colour-Blind*. London: Picador.

St.-Johnston, T. R. 1922. *South Sea Reminiscences*. London: Fisher Unwin.

Samson, Jane. 1998. *Imperial Benevolence: Making British Authority in the Pacific Islands*. Honolulu: University of Hawai'i Press.

Scarr, Deryck. 1990. *The History of the Pacific Islands: Kingdoms of the Reefs*. London: Macmillan.

Shakespeare, William. 1996. *The Tempest*. Ed. Anne Barton. London: Penguin.

Smith, Bernard. 1985. *European Vision and the South Pacific*. 2nd edn. New Haven: Yale University Press.

———. 1992. *Imagining the Pacific: In the Wake of Captain Cook*. Melbourne: Melbourne University Press.

Smith, Charles H., ed. 1991. *Alfred Russel Wallace: An Anthology of his Shorter Writings*. Oxford: Oxford University Press.

Stafford, Barbara Maria. 1984. *Voyage into Substance: Art, Science, Nature, and the Illustrated Travel Account, 1760–1840*. Cambridge, MA: Massachussetts Institute of Technology Press.

Stafleu, Frans A. 1971. *Linnaeus and the Linnaeans: The Spreading of Their Ideas in Systematic Botany, 1735–1789*. Utrecht: Oosthoek.

Stearn, William T. 1962. *Three Prefaces on Linnaeus and Robert Brown*. Weinheim: J. Cramer.

Stepan, Nancy. 1982. *The Idea of Race in Science: Great Britain 1800–1960*. London: Macmillan.

Stocking, George W. Jr. 1983. "The Ethnographer's Magic: Fieldwork in British Anthropology from Tylor to Malinowski." In Stocking, ed., *Observers Observed: Essays in Ethnographic Fieldwork*, 70–120. Madison: University of Wisconsin Press.

Stroven, Carl, and A. Grove Day, eds. 1949. *The Spell of the Pacific: An Anthology of its Literature*. New York: Macmillan.

"Sundowner." 1887. *Rambles in Polynesia*. London: European Mail Ltd.

Theroux, Paul. 1992. *The Happy Isles of Oceania: Paddling the Pacific*. London: Penguin.

Thomas, Keith. 1983. *Man and the Natural World: Changing Attitudes in England 1500–1800*. London: Allen Lane.

Thomas, Nicholas. 1989. *Out of Time: History and Evolution in Anthropological Discourse*. Cambridge: Cambridge University Press.

Thomson, Basil. 1894a. *Diversions of a Prime Minister*. Edinburgh: William Blackwood.

———. 1894b. *South Sea Yarns*. Edinburgh: William Blackwood.

Turnbull, John. 1813. *A Voyage Round the World in the Years 1800, 1801, 1802, 1803, and 1804*. 2nd edn. London: A. Maxwell.

Twain, Mark. 1897. *Following the Equator*. New York: American Publishing Company.

Tylor, Edward B. 1894. *Anthropology: An Introduction to the Study of Man and Civilization*. New York: Appleton.

Vandercook, John W. 1937. *Dark Islands*. New York: Harper and Brothers.

Wadley, Nicholas, ed. 1985. *Noa Noa: Gauguin's Tahiti*. London: Phaidon.

Wallace, Alfred Russel. 1881. *Island Life: or, the Phenomena and Causes of Insular Faunas and Floras*. New York: Harper and Brothers.

Washburn, Wilcomb E. 1967. "The Intellectual Assumptions and Consequences of

Geographical Exploration in the Pacific." In Herman R. Friis, ed., *The Pacific Basin: A History of its Geographical Exploration,* 321–334. New York: American Geographical Society.

Watling, Thomas. 1794. *Letters from an Exile in Botany-Bay to his Aunt in Dumfries.* Penrith, NSW.

Wayne, Helena, ed. 1995. *The Story of a Marriage: The Letters of Bronislaw Malinowski and Elsie Masson.* 2 vols. London: Routledge.

Weltfish, Gene. 1980. "Franz Boas: The Academic Response." In Stanley Diamond, ed., *Anthropology: Ancestors and Heirs,* 123–147. The Hague: Mouton.

White, Charles. 1799. *An Account of the Regular Gradation in Man.* London.

Williams, Glyndwr, and Alan Frost, eds. 1988. *Terra Australis to Australia.* Melbourne: Oxford University Press.

Williams, John. 1837. *A Narrative of Missionary Enterprises in the South Sea Islands.* London: J. Snow.

Wilson, James. 1799. *A Missionary Voyage to the Southern Pacific Ocean, Performed in the Years 1796, 1797, 1798, in the Ship Duff.* London: T. Chapman.

Wragge, Clement. 1906. *The Romance of the South Seas.* London: Chatto and Windus.

INDEX

Stevenson, Robert Louis, 17, 303, 333–338
Sydney, Australia, 9

Tahiti and Tahitians, 8, 18, 66, 71, 72–92, 110–111, 136–142, 142–144, 211, 372–382
Tasman, Abel, 7
Tasmania and Tasmanians, 7, 222, 289–293, 295–297
"Terra Australis," 6, 9, 15, 35, 37, 41–47
Theft, 5, 40, 69, 73, 75, 79, 85, 87, 91, 103–104, 347, 357
Tierra del Fuego, 208–209
Tonga, 7
Torres, Luis Vaéz de, 6, 42
Tourism, 365–370, 406–408
Trobriand Islands (New Guinea), 299–310
Tuomatus Islands, 38, 406–408

Utopia and utopianism, 11–14, 16, 40, 81, 95–96, 116, 350–355, 402, 411–412

Vanuatu. *See* New Hebrides
Veiras, Denis: *L'Histoire des Séverambes*, 14
Vespucci, Amerigo: *Mundus Novus*, 15
Violence, 9, 19–20, 24, 39–40, 79, 97–98, 139–142, 254–261, 324–325, 342–343, 346–350, 400–404
Wallis, Samuel, 7–8
Williams, John, 117
Women, 12, 40, 52, 74–80, 82, 83, 95, 102, 122, 128, 136–138, 141, 220, 298, 373–381, 384–385, 389, 402; and civilization, 40, 54–57, 69, 83, 390, 407–408

ABOUT THE EDITOR

Richard Lansdown is assistant professor of English at James Cook University in Cairns, Australia. He is the author of *Byron's Historical Dramas* (1992), *The Autonomy of Literature* (2001), and a number of articles on nineteenth-century British literature. He was the editor of the *Critical Review* from 1994 to 2002, and his edition of Henry James' *The Bostonians* was published by Penguin Classics in 2000. .